Understanding
PeopleSoft 8

Understanding
PeopleSoft® 8

Lynn Anderson

Cap Gemini Ernst & Young U.S., LLC

SYBEX®

San Francisco · Paris · Düsseldorf · Soest · London

Associate Publisher: Richard Mills
PeopleSoft Press Adviser: Marcia L. Conner
Contracts and Licensing Manager: Kristine O'Callaghan
Acquisitions and Developmental Editors: Kim Goodfriend,
Christine McGeever
Editors: Jim Gabbert, Suzanne Goraj
Production Editor: Dennis Fitzgerald
Technical Editor: Tomkin Lee
Graphic Illustrator: Eric Houts, epic
Electronic Publishing Specialist: Franz Baumhackl
Proofreaders: Jennifer Campbell, Amey Garber, Nelson
Kim, Leslie E.H. Light, Nancy Riddiough
Indexer: Nancy Guenther
Book Designer: Franz Baumhackl
Cover Designer: Caryl Gorska, Gorska Design

Library of Congress Card Number: 00-111765

ISBN: 0-7821-2930-7

This book is dedicated to my dad, who always encouraged me to reach for the stars, do my best, and believe that anything is possible if you worked hard enough for it. I've learned that the same is true in business and in systems implementations!

Foreword

PeopleSoft 8 clearly establishes PeopleSoft as the dominant provider of enterprise e-business solutions. To deliver PeopleSoft 8, we increased research and development spending to 27 percent, a level greater than that of any other company in the history of high technology. Why? To redesign our entire product offering with a pure Internet architecture that will enable you to conduct your business in ways never before possible. To enable you to extend your organization's reach to encompass your customers, employees, and suppliers in a collaborative network. *To enable you to compete and win in the Internet economy.*

What's driving the shift to a pure Internet architecture? The same thing that always drives fundamental technology transformations: real and compelling ROI benefits, such as lower infrastructure and administrative costs, combined with new revenue generation in the global economy. PeopleSoft enables you to build a collaborative enterprise—a network of your customers, employees, and suppliers working together to gain competitive advantage. Simply stated, PeopleSoft 8 provides the underlying platform for e-business.

To meet, embrace, and promote this architectural shift, PeopleSoft products have undergone a radical transformation. We've redesigned 14,000 application panels into pure Internet pages to open up the heart of enterprise management information to your customers, employees, and suppliers. We've delivered 59 new collaborative e-business applications—pure Internet applications for customer management, enterprise management, and supplier management. PeopleSoft 8 delivers best-in-class integrated solutions that can be implemented quickly to speed your time to benefit.

It's my pleasure to introduce *Understanding PeopleSoft 8,* the first title in the PeopleSoft Press series from Sybex. Author Lynn Anderson and her team at Cap Gemini Ernst & Young have done an outstanding job of bringing key areas into clear focus—from a broad, insightful history of ERP systems all the way to detailed discussions of what's involved in going live on PeopleSoft 8 and managing post-production support.

Whether you're evaluating, implementing, administering, or using PeopleSoft 8 as your e-business platform, you're sure to find much value in the pages that follow.

Ram Gupta

Ram Gupta
Executive Vice President, Products & Technology
PeopleSoft, Inc.

Acknowledgments

Many people and organizations helped make this book happen, and I'm sure I'll neglect to mention some of them here. My apologies in advance.

Thanks go first to our clients and staff who worked with us to implement Enterprise Resource Planning systems over the past several years. These folks deserve much of the credit for the content and insight this book provides.

To Russell Daum, Herb Schul, and Bill Boucher, who got this project going, and to those who jumped in to help finish it—Ajay Kansal, Christine Volk, Ken Becker, Robert Wolverton, Tom Tretter, Heywood Chang, Radhika Patel, Jennifer Janeczko, Richard Miller, Rishi Bhatnagar, and Anastasia Ginzbursky—thanks for your help. Thanks also to Stephen Raff for his advice, encouragement, and assistance whenever needed.

And, finally, thanks to my family—Jeff, Jennifer, Aubrey, and Matt—for their love and support, and for putting up with me through all those missed dinners and family time because of the overriding demands of my work schedule.

Without each and every one of you, this book wouldn't have been possible.

Contents at a Glance

Contents

Chapter 3   An Overview of the PeopleSoft Architecture   55

Chapter 7   Analyzing Company Requirements   171

Chapter 20   A Closer Look at Supply Chain Management   549

Chapter 24   What's Next on the Horizon   655

Introduction

While implementing a complex and far-reaching system such as PeopleSoft, many organizations lose track of the project's original purpose and expected benefit. We hope that this book will give you the guidance you need to keep your PeopleSoft implementation on track, to ease the pain of this undertaking, and perhaps even to make it a rewarding experience.

In PeopleSoft's latest release, PeopleSoft 8, many areas within the application have changed, while many others have remained the same. The new Web applications of PeopleSoft 8 are designed to provide e-business functionality and expanded flexibility for your organization. However, the same purposeful and consistent management of your people, processes, and technology that was critical to your success in the past will also be a key to your future success. By laying out a solid foundation, measuring your progress based on that foundation, understanding the impacts of change, and keeping abreast of changes in technology and business, you'll have a much better chance of success. Whether you are implementing this application for the first time or are upgrading to this new application and technology, this book should provide some valuable insight into how to successfully handle this complex task.

About the Book

Cap Gemini Ernst & Young, a PeopleSoft Global Implementation Partner since 1991 and a global consulting organization, has conducted more than 200 successful PeopleSoft implementations and applied hundreds of thousands of hours of experience toward these initiatives. We have partnered with PeopleSoft in the development and testing of various portions of the application, starting early with the HRMS product and continuing most recently with the portal development efforts and a health care industry solution. As the original auditors of PeopleSoft, CGEY has been with the organization from the start. CGEY's strength in Europe and Australia has made it a leading PeopleSoft partner in Europe and Asia, helping to expand the product globally. CGEY's leading services in ERP systems, IT implementations, and world-class knowledge-management techniques have received recognition by the industry and IT analysts alike, including the Gartner Group, Forrester Research, and International Data Corporation.

The experience garnered from these implementations were the foundation for the development of this book. By sharing the lessons learned and experience gained, we hope that others can benefit from our experience, derive greater value from their implementations, and be in a much better position to have a successful implementation.

Lead author Lynn Anderson, Vice President of PeopleSoft Services for CGEY in the Americas, has been implementing PeopleSoft applications since 1991 and PeopleSoft version 2. She has experience in all areas of the application, from HRMS and Financials to Supply Chain Management. She has served in technical programming roles and functional configuration roles, and has also served as a project manager for several Fortune 500 companies. As leader of PeopleSoft Services for CGEY, she works closely with PeopleSoft strategists and product specialists in Pleasanton, California, keeping abreast of the latest product developments with the application.

Although no implementation is foolproof, the author hopes that through reading this book, you will better understand the complexity of PeopleSoft implementations and the foundation you'll need in order to be successful, as well as collect tips and techniques that will help along the way.

What You Need to Know

You should find this book valuable regardless of whether you have heard of the PeopleSoft ERP system. The book is designed to provide a basic understanding of the key ingredients behind implementing a complex business system such as PeopleSoft. No special prerequisites or training are needed prior to reading the book. You may find it useful even if your organization isn't planning to implement a new ERP system any time soon.

If you already have an ERP system in place, you may still find this book great reading, because it will help you with future upgrades or change initiatives around your ERP system. And you don't necessarily have to be implementing the PeopleSoft application for this book to prove valuable—although it does use specific examples and insights geared toward the PeopleSoft system. Most of the book's content can be applied to any ERP or major change initiative you may be undertaking.

Is This Book for You?

This book is geared toward individuals who want a good overall understanding of the main components of an ERP implementation, from beginning to end. It covers the people, processes, and technology issues you might face during such an implementation. The book is not meant to be a programming text or a detailed, step-by-step guide to the implementation process. Rather, it's meant to serve as a basic guide and overview of the areas you should look at to help you through an implementation. Executives, project sponsors, managers, and members of a team, as well as those affected by change, should find this guide helpful in understanding all components of any major change initiative, such as a PeopleSoft ERP implementation.

If you need additional insight into the PeopleSoft application, look at the PeopleSoft Web site (`www.peoplesoft.com`) as well as PeopleSoft's online user manuals (PeopleBooks) and training manuals, which provide more detailed package information.

Chapter Walk-Through

The first chapter of this book looks at the history and foundation of ERP systems, to help you understand how these systems evolved and why organizations are implementing them. Chapter 2 focuses on PeopleSoft, providing a functional overview of the application modules; and Chapter 3 provides a technical perspective on PeopleSoft's architecture.

To help you lay the foundation necessary to support your implementation, Chapter 4 outlines methods for developing a convincing business case for implementing the system or improving an existing implementation. Chapter 5 addresses the management of your implementation, including the process, technology, and people issues connected to it.

Chapter 6 helps you establish the appropriate infrastructure, and Chapter 7 outlines the process requirements needed to support your solution. Chapter 8 addresses the steps necessary to design the best solution for your business, and Chapter 9 helps you prepare your organization for the upcoming changes in order to ensure the success of your implementation.

The next chapters address the various implementation steps and issues, including:

- ▶ Prototyping (Chapter 10)—how to physically and more rapidly design a solution for your organization

- ▶ Converting data and developing interfaces (Chapter 11)

- ▶ Technical issues (Chapter 12)

- ▶ Security (Chapter 13)—the various internal and external components as well as requirements to consider when designing security features

- ▶ Testing (Chapter 14)—focusing on the types of testing that are recommended before your implementation goes live

- ▶ Going live (Chapter 15)—looking at global elements that contribute to a successful go-live effort

- ▶ Post-production support (Chapter 16)—covering both the structure needed to keep your implementation up and running and the transition from a project to a production environment

The next part of the book, "Configuring the Specifics," provides an in-depth technical analysis of the PeopleSoft application, including advice on configuration issues and alternatives. Chapters 17 and 18 review the HRMS application suite, Chapter 19 covers the Financials area, and Chapter 20 discusses the Supply Chain Management (manufacturing and distribution) applications.

The final chapters tackle the steps necessary to set up support for your solution and to keep your customers and end users productive and accepting of this new way of doing business as you move into the future. Chapter 21 teaches you to assess your current support network and to leverage it to support your new solution. Chapter 22 presents essential training concepts and ways to continuously keep your users up to speed on the newest solutions. Chapter 23 looks at future steps for integration, where the market is heading, and what else might be in store for you and your organization, now that you have an ERP system in place. And Chapter 24 looks at where the next generation of ERP systems, ERP II, is heading and where the vendors are focusing their strategies for the future.

How to Use This Book

Although you may prefer to read the chapters in the order in which they appear, doing so is not essential for getting the most out of this book. The book follows the basic timeline or progression of a project, and the chapters are grouped according to similarity of content. You might find that a group of chapters in the middle of the book, such as those covering the more technical and development issues (Chapters 11 through 13) or the detailed functionality of the PeopleSoft application (Chapters 17 through 20), is an appealing starting point. Conversely, if your primary concern is giving end users a smooth transition to PeopleSoft, you might prefer to begin with Chapters 21 and 22.

Whatever approach you take when reading this book, we hope you will find helpful insight that aids you in your never-ending quest for perfection and keeps you ahead of your competition. We are thrilled to be able to assist you on this journey and to help you reap the rewards. At a minimum, we hope you'll find this book of some value and that it will provide some enjoyable hours of learning.

As you are reading this book, the ERP market and the PeopleSoft application are changing. Always keep that in mind. Stay up-to-date with your readings on the trends in these important areas of your business, and keep in touch with the vendor's direction, through your account manager, special interest groups, analysts' reports, PeopleSoft's newsletters and Web site, and your consulting partners. Technology and applications are never static, and in this world of nanoseconds and rapid change, you can never do too much.

Good luck, and happy reading.

Part I

Getting Started

The first four chapters of this book are the foundation chapters—those that will help you get started on your journey toward implementing and leveraging your PeopleSoft application. They lay a foundation for the more detailed, project-oriented analysis that lies ahead. After reading these chapters, you should have a better understanding of what Enterprise Resource Planning applications are—and, more specifically, the PeopleSoft applications—and be able to create the key components to help make your implementation a success and to get you started on the right foot.

CHAPTER 1

Enterprise Resource Planning with PeopleSoft

FEATURING:

- ▶ What ERP is
- ▶ The history of ERP
- ▶ Why companies implement ERP systems
- ▶ Who the major ERP vendors are
- ▶ Why companies choose PeopleSoft
- ▶ What the major ERP trends are

This chapter will cover the basic makeup of Enterprise Resource Planning (ERP) systems, their history, and the reasons companies are implementing these systems. To understand how to effectively implement the PeopleSoft application, you must understand the history and evolution of the ERP marketplace—where these systems came from and how they were developed. You must understand the differentiators behind the major ERP vendors and why companies might choose PeopleSoft over other ERP vendors. With a basic understanding of these topics, you will be in a better position to leverage PeopleSoft's strengths and create the most value for your company.

Finally, in this chapter we'll cover some of the major trends in the ERP market space, including the areas of e-commerce and executive reporting, or decision support information. When reviewing these trends, try to determine how your organization might benefit from them, leveraging the power of the Internet and the power of your organization. These new trends look at extending your ERP application outside administrative efficiency and into growth- and operations-oriented areas, thereby taking your organization to the next level.

You must walk before you can run (as the saying goes), so before we can dive into the PeopleSoft application and understand how to drive value from an implementation, we need to understand the basics of an ERP system and what it's supposed to accomplish. What has made companies go out and seek these systems, and why did companies like PeopleSoft and SAP emerge to what they are today? Was Dave Duffield (the original CEO and founding father of People-Soft) just bored with the human resource systems marketplace, or did his customers demand more? Even though Dave is the adventurous type, we tend to believe that PeopleSoft would not have grown so rapidly if it hadn't had its ear tuned to the marketplace and its customers.

What Is ERP?

So what is an ERP system anyway, and why should your organization invest in one? And if you've already invested in one, why is it not paying off like you thought it would?

ERP stands for Enterprise Resource Planning. ERP systems support your business (or enterprise) through the optimizing, planning, maintaining, and tracking of your resources. These systems have the ability to integrate the functions that make up the backbone of most businesses, such as financials, manufacturing, and distribution. In turn, they help to balance and optimize the enterprise.

The various business processes that generally make up an ERP system can be broken down into four areas:

▶ Human resources management systems

▶ Financial systems

▶ Distribution systems

▶ Manufacturing systems

Each of these four major application areas contains various components. For example, the HRMS (human resources management systems) area includes the processes that track and pay your employees. In Chapter 2, "A PeopleSoft Overview," Chapter 17, "A Closer Look at HRMS," and Chapter 18, "HRMS Specifics," we'll address the specific HR functionality available through PeopleSoft. However, in all ERP HR systems, one can generally find these major functional components:

Human resources   Includes the processes that provide basic record-keeping features and information regarding your employee population as well as more advanced features such as career planning, succession planning, training administration, safety and health, salary planning, recruiting, and position tracking

Benefits   Generally covers the benefit offerings and tracks the elections of your employees, including programs such as your 401(k) retirement plan, health and welfare plans, insurance, disability and sick plans, vacation and leave programs, stock plans, and pension offerings

Payroll   Includes the processes that create and pay your employees, including their specific earnings and deductions

The financial systems application generally includes the processes that perform and support your financial processes, including:

General ledger   Includes and tracks each debt and credit and performs the basic tracking of your profit and loss (P&L) and balance statements

Budgeting   Includes forecasts, actuals, and trends for each organizational component of your business

Financial reporting   Includes the basic features of reporting your financial performance (profits and losses) for the major components of your business and provides analytical tools to evaluate your business

Billing and accounts receivable   Includes tracking of your outstanding receipts and collections as well as production of bills to your outstanding debtors

Accounts payables   Analyzes and tracks vendor payments, including looking at optimal payment cycles for meeting your business needs while sustaining your payment commitments

Asset management   Tracks your company's assets as well as calculates depreciation and other impacts for your financials

Projects   Includes tracking of internal work projects and their associated activities, resources, and costs

Other   Includes functions such as treasury management, performance management, and expense tracking (which in some cases is a financial systems process as well as an HRMS process)

Details on the specific PeopleSoft functionality within the financials area can be found in Chapter 2, "A PeopleSoft Overview," and Chapter 19 "A Closer Look at Financials."

There are also ERP applications that include the distribution systems functions (or as PeopleSoft refers to them, supply chain management) such as the processes of procuring supplies, tracking inventory, and ordering products, as well as functions that support the major manufacturing systems processes such as designing, creating, and producing products based on demand (both real-time and perceived). In the PeopleSoft application, system functionality and specifics can be found in Chapter 2, "A PeopleSoft Overview," and Chapter 20, "A Closer Look at Supply Chain Management."

All these application areas are considered part of the ERP model. In essence, you are looking at an integrated backbone consisting of both operational (manufacturing) and transactional (administrative and logistical) applications that will help streamline your enterprise, cut your costs, improve your revenue growth, and better serve your employees and customers. Figure 1.1 shows the major application areas and how together they create your ERP system. The power of the ERP system derives from the degree to which these components are integrated and optimized together to provide the most value to your organization.

Figure 1.1 **Major components of an ERP system**

Financials

ERP

Supply Chain Management

Human Resources Management

The History of ERP Systems

The ERP model did not develop overnight. It took years to emerge and is still evolving today as we move into a post-ERP era. One of the important lessons to learn from this history is that these systems are transformational and ever-changing. You are embarking on a never-ending program, not just a one-time implementation project. How an organization adapts and responds to these changes is the real challenge. Flexible and fast-moving companies are the ones that are really leveraging and taming these systems—it takes an openness to change and commitment from above to be successful with an ERP system.

Let's take a trip back in time and look at the evolution of these systems and how they continue to transform. ERP systems tended to follow the automation trends and business issues of their time from the early 1960s, when automation meant developing a system to fulfill a single process (such as automating the ability to pay an employee or to pay a vendor), through the 1980s, when total quality management was the business buzzword and all systems needed to incorporate this feature into their processes. In the following sections we'll look at each new business era or decade starting with the 1960s, when automated systems were emerging, and how technology trends affected business automation and eventually led to the ERP systems we have in place today.

Departmentalized Systems

Before early ERP-type systems emerged, in the prehistoric age of the 1960s and early '70s, company systems were custom-developed and created by each "department" organization such as human resources, billing, or accounts payable. This departmentalization created "islands of automation" as shown in Figure 1.2. These systems weren't integrated with each other or interactive in nature. Often data was re-entered or rekeyed into these systems one at a time, or custom interfaces were developed to get the information from one place to the other. In many cases information was duplicated and found in several places, although in some instances common "system tables" were used to share data between applications. These systems proved to be effective in helping to streamline processes within a department but failed to integrate processes that fell across departments and shared common data.

Figure 1.2   **Departmentalized systems—islands of automation**

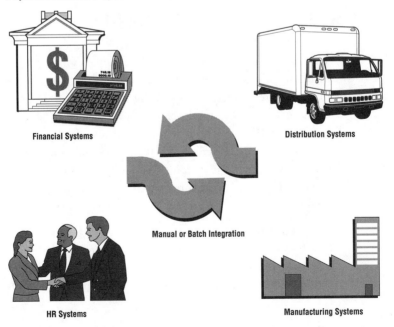

Financial Systems

Distribution Systems

Manual or Batch Integration

HR Systems

Manufacturing Systems

Once the companies saw the improvements these systems generated within their departments, which basically covered the simpler back-office administrative process areas, executives and the marketplace demanded more from a company, including operational efficiencies. They realized that if systems could improve the more basic administrative processes, why not see if they could also handle the more complex operational processes? Hence, in the 1970s, MRP (manufacturing resource planning) systems emerged.

MRP Systems

In the 1970s, dubbed the "era of efficiency," businesses began looking at improving their operations based on market demand and the prevalence of automation on the shop floor. Because the manufacturing chain was the center of their operations, it became the focus for this integration. This operational view spawned the development of MRP systems.

Not only were companies looking to automate their basic shop-floor systems, but they needed to optimize the resources needed to create their product and therefore decrease their production costs. Based on that need, various vendors such as SAP developed MRP systems to focus on this resource integration. Figure 1.3 shows the basic components that the initial MRP vendors integrated in order to obtain these efficiencies within their operations.

Figure 1.3   **1970s MRP systems**

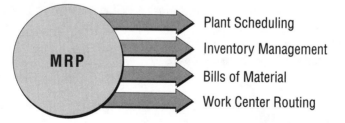

During this era, one of the leaders in automation and operational efficiencies was General Electric, which was constantly looking for ways to improve its business and produce better products. Its persistence resulted in improved systems including ones that drew on operations research methodology, which was used by the military, in mainstream corporate American factories, to produce weapons more efficiently. This efficiency-focused methodology allowed GE to be a renowned leader in the area of efficiency.

Basically, what an MRP system did was pass key information from one part of the manufacturing process to another, such that all the resources could be optimized. For instance, when an order was being produced, the integration of the order entry, manufacturing, and inventory systems allowed the organization to better purchase and plan for inventory based on the demand and production schedules; as a result, inventory costs and time to market were decreased.

Vendors began to develop solutions for this area based on market demand. MRP systems helped automate and improve the efficiency of manufacturing processes while decreasing development costs.

MRP II Systems

The second phase of ERP development occurred in the 1980s, when businesses increased the integration of their business and focused their attention on more quality measures. This focus was called total quality management (TQM). When companies responded by shifting their operational business focus to a total quality perspective, operations expanded their reach into logistical and financial processes. This broader focus led to the MRP II evolution. Applications such as financial management, sales order management, logistics management, and lot control, in addition to the manufacturing processes already encompassed, originated in this second phase of MRP. Figure 1.4 shows how the MRP system expanded to include these new areas of focus when vendors responded to the need for including quality measures into the manufacturing process.

Figure 1.4   **1980s MRP II systems**

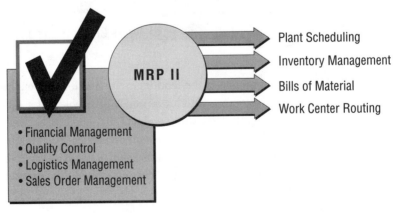

ERP Systems

Finally, in the 1990s, businesses decided that there were benefits to integrating all their core systems across their internal enterprise. This integration would result in decreased costs, increased performance, and the ability to view the entire enterprise to help make better business decisions. Vendors responded to this need with an ERP system—one that cuts across the entire enterprise to decrease costs and increase efficiencies. Figure 1.5 shows the integration of the operational systems with the administrative systems found in the human resources and financial areas.

Figure 1.5 **1990s ERP systems**

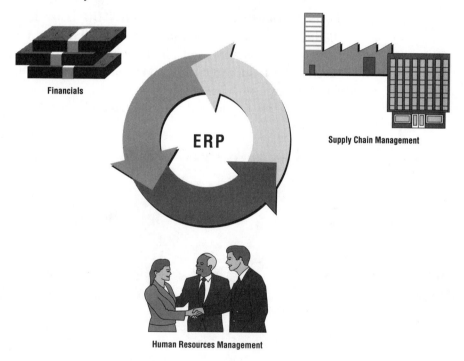

During the early stages of ERP development, the focus was on driving efficiencies through decreasing the transaction-oriented and deployment costs, rather than on the revenue-generation activities. Pressures of the year 2000 (Y2K) and European Monetary Unit (euro) changes served to accelerate the deployment of these ERP systems into organizations to support these very tactical business issues. However, in most of these implementations, because the companies were looking for tactical solutions rather than more strategically focused ones, their implementations were less than optimized and they have not leveraged all the revenue-generating potential of these systems. But due to the increased pressures of the marketplace, demands for the speed and flexibility that are necessary in the 21st century, and the need to support a "connected Internet-enabled economy" over the next few years, companies will be expecting more from their systems.

The ERP systems of the 1990s promised many things: increases in quality, better information, customer satisfaction, ability to respond, productivity, and decreases in time to market, product cost, personnel, management layers, delivery time, inventory levels, and much more.

Figure 1.6 illustrates the transition of the MRP II and ERP systems through the 1980s and '90s. As you can see from the diagram, in the mid-'90s, the ERP systems that were available surpassed the MRP II solutions with enough functionality to support all areas of the business, making them viable solutions for the enterprise. When this happened, companies jumped on the ERP bandwagon, eager to join in on the savings (and subsequent pains if they were not prepared).

Figure 1.6   **Functionality shift from MRP II to ERP systems**

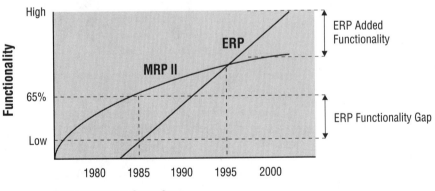

Source: Adapted from Gartner Group

Moving from an MRP solution to an ERP solution, businesses had to be focused on the enterprise and not just the individual components. They had to have a clear vision, managing expectations up front and outlining the value an ERP system would bring.

When you implement this major new business strategy and integrate processes with a customer focus in mind, remember that this is truly a major transformation program and should not be listed or sold as anything else. An ERP implementation goes across the entire enterprise and must have the executive sponsorship necessary to instill widespread changes across the organization.

Table 1.1 outlines some of the changes an organization must undergo in migrating from an MRP-centric to an ERP-centric organization.

Table 1.1   **Comparison of MRP and ERP Models**

MRP Model	ERP Model
Multiple systems	Single, integrated system
Duplicate/independent data	Shared data
Plant/location-specific	Enterprise focus
Operational focus	Focus across departments
Autonomous units	Dependencies

Note   Companies that have already implemented these systems—either partially or across the board—but are looking for increased benefits should seriously question whether the business benefits have been outlined and progress has been measured. In addition, you should ensure that your company has obtained the proper level of sponsorship and support across the enterprise. As you move forward, we recommend that you again benchmark and measure your processes, create a future-state vision, and target your plan around achieving that vision. Then track your progress against that plan continuously. Lastly, you might want to view the migration in Table 1.1 and really assess whether you have achieved a true ERP state or whether you are using an ERP system with an MRP mind-set.

Post-ERP

What's on the horizon for 2001 and beyond? Where are businesses headed in the future, and how are ERP systems transforming themselves in order to keep up with the changing pace of business and technology? What does ERP II or post-ERP hold for us?

With the Internet and e-commerce playing an increasingly broad role, package vendors are moving toward integrating businesses with other businesses or a connected enterprise made up of suppliers and vendors as well as the organization. You might have heard this referred to as an "inter-enterprise value network." Also, vendors are looking at flexible solutions with more concentration on industry-specific solutions and modules that can be plugged and played depending on what business or industry an organization or network supports. To borrow from Tom Peters (renowned writer, author of the best sellers *In Search of Excellence* and *A Passion for Excellence,* and business innovation guru): "Systems are never status quo…they are either getting better or becoming worse." It's up to your organization to drive to the better end by applying value drivers to your work.

Now that the demands of the more tactically focused issues are behind us (e.g., Y2K) and most companies have implemented an ERP solution, the next level of demand that we are seeing emerge is for businesses to differentiate themselves in the market and to help drive more focus toward revenue-generating applications. The new-era ERP solutions must be flexible, easy to customize, adaptable to a new business model of the organization, and able to differentiate the organization from the market. Organizations must be prepared to identify the core areas that will remain vanilla and concentrate on the market differentiators that they will invest in customizing. Therefore, the vendors that will remain must have flexible, easy-to-use development tools as well as the ability to upgrade those components while moving rapidly forward. In addition, organizations will be focused on decision support tools that will help their customers react to changes and make informed decisions faster.

Why Do Companies Implement ERP Systems?

Why should you care about an ERP system, and why should your company implement one? Because many organizations are currently using disparate systems that are not integrated and in essence require duplicate data entry. Also, leaders or managers in the organization have to look at numerous systems in order to get the information they need to make key business decisions.

ERP systems can help solve these issues—the benefits are plentiful. ERP systems do the following:

► Integrate key data to avoid duplicate entry, which saves you time and money in both resource and opportunity costs.

► Allow you to view key company data in one system, which in turn allows you to make informed decisions and analyze your organization more easily.

► Cut down on maintenance and support costs, including information resource or technology support, as well as reduce training, since all your major applications are on a single system.

► Streamline processes by automating and integrating the applications. The systems can even create new areas of business opportunity. For instance, on the purchasing side, an individual can submit a purchasing request. Since the procurement and financial systems are integrated and use the latest technology work flow, you can submit the request, get approvals electronically, order the supply from your preferred vendor, pay for the supply once it is received, and track the payment for financial and budgeting purposes—all in one fell swoop. An individual can go to one place to view the request, check the status of the request, and confirm that the payment has been made.

Where are ERP packages going, and why should you implement a package rather than just develop your own unique custom application? There are some key benefits in implementing a package solution rather than a custom one:

► Best practices from many organizations were used to develop the application package.

► The vendor must keep up with the latest changes in technology to stay competitive. Therefore, the latest tools and techniques are incorporated into the application. This is evident through the use of analytical tools (e.g., online analytical processing), the integration of data warehousing and reporting, work flow (automatically triggering, or "flowing," work to be done based on another activity, such as sending a message to a manager to approve a supply requisition once it's entered into the system and, once the manager approves it, sending the order to the vendor), Web enablement, and e-commerce, just to name a few. As the technology changes and focuses on the business, the vendor incorporates it into the package and the user/customer reaps the benefits—assuming that the user can upgrade to the latest release offerings.

▶ Your organization does not have to employ hordes of programmers to support a custom application for these business functions.

A package has some disadvantages over a custom application:

▶ The organization lacks control on version/release functionality. Although most vendors do seek advice on what functions and features are needed to enhance its package, the package is still not controlled by just one organization.

▶ The organization may need to train and maintain a core team that understands the package features and technical functions in order to support it, and these resources may not be leveraged easily with other systems.

▶ You don't have as much control in product support as you would have with your own system.

▶ You may not have market-differentiating processes since everyone is using a packaged system built on best practices.

As mentioned earlier, a key feature of package solutions is that they're constantly being updated with the latest and greatest technological solutions for your business. These updates allow you to leverage the emerging technologies within your business, but you must analyze these new features, implement them effectively, and induce change almost yearly to your organization. This constantly changing environment may be hard to manage. Today's greatest tools such as data warehousing, OLAP (online analytical processing), and Web applets can be replaced quickly by tomorrow's plug-and-play features. So being prepared for these changes and creating an atmosphere where change is welcome are big pluses for your organization.

Based on what we're seeing in the business world, it would be a good idea for your organization to establish what value you're trying to achieve before digging into the ERP system and determining the specific package or features to implement. We're consistently surprised by the number of organizations that let their IT group implement their ERP solution without major sponsors and players from the organization leading the effort and being highly involved. We're also surprised by the organizations that have the business supporting the implementation but have no clear vision of what the future holds and haven't identified the obstacles that might lie ahead to block the effectiveness of the solution. We encourage you to take an honest look at your current organization and functions and ask yourself, "Are we getting the most out of this service?" And if not, why not? Many organizations think backwards in choosing their ERP systems, focusing on their current solutions and state and not on where they really could be, given a new slate and a new way of doing business. They think the package itself is the panacea and will force its best practices on the business. They forget how to drive the business value, which the package only makes possible. As a result, they create an as-is solution or maybe one that's marginally better than the one they had, rather than a new, innovative solution that will push them ahead of their competition. Which group does your company fall into?

Note A good example of looking into the future is implementing key performance indicators within a system. First, you have to define what a key performance indicator is for your particular business or group. Next, you need to decide how you might use the indicator to improve your business performance and to drive results.

Who Are the Major ERP Vendors?

Once an organization has determined that it should implement an ERP solution, has benchmarked its current state, and has created a vision of its future state, it determines which packages are available on the market and why one should be chosen over the others.

When looking at proposed solutions for its business needs, a company needs to understand the history of the vendor, who their clients are, and where their strengths and weaknesses lie. Today, three major ERP vendors, SAP, Oracle, and PeopleSoft, have emerged as the market leaders, taking a large share of the market, especially the larger enterprise companies. Others, such as J.D. Edwards, Baan, and Lawson, are viable choices but are much more tailored to specific industries, small- to midsize organizations, and particular solutions. SAP, Oracle, and PeopleSoft support all levels of the spectrum, from large, multinational customers to smaller, mid-market clients; thus, they have the major hold on this market space, accounting for almost one-half the revenue dollars of all their competitors combined. While these three leaders are very similar in nature, they are distinctly different in their history and focus. The history of each ERP package is tied to the era for which it was developed and the migration path the vendor has chosen since that era.

SAP

Founded in 1972, SAP served the MRP market during a time when large, complex, mainframe systems ruled. Headquartered in Germany, SAP naturally focused more on global, multinational requirements.

In the early 1990s, when other applications were deployed on the newer, client-server technology, SAP followed with its R/3 client server–based product. Now SAP is the market leader as well as the "safe" choice for large, international enterprises. SAP's strength is in its manufacturing base as well as its back-office applications. The company's main target sectors are chemicals, utilities, aerospace, consumer products, pharmaceuticals, and retail. In the mid-1990s, SAP expanded its HR product suite to the U.S., rounding out its ERP offering and becoming the dominant leader in the global ERP arena. Recently, the company has ventured into the Internet market by delivering mySAP.com, marketplaces, and HTML-deployed, self-service applets.

Oracle

In 1989, Oracle jumped on the ERP bandwagon, offering its first applications to the market. It concentrated first in the financials area, followed soon with manufacturing in 1991, and rounded its solution with the human resources applications in 1994. Its target markets include telecommunications, financial services, consumer products, electronics, and automotive companies.

Called Oracle Applications, the company's solutions were designed to optimize its technology platform and incorporate its database-specific application features into its application solutions. Oracle's application is based on an architecture and technology that most efficiently and effectively integrate the Oracle relational database management system (RDBMS) and the tools that support it. Since the application is focused on one database platform, Oracle can tune and optimize the use of this RDBMS more effectively and efficiently than others. However, Oracle's core business remains its database system, and its staff is very technology focused. As a result, the company has had a somewhat bad reputation for customer service and sales and product support, compared with their competition.

PeopleSoft

PeopleSoft, founded in 1987, developed its initial product in 1989 to support systems that the MRP vendors did not: human resources and payroll. This product was built around the newer client-server technology of the era. Once PeopleSoft mastered that market, for which it is still the recognized market leader, it decided to expand its services. During the 1990s, the company developed its popular Financials package (1992–93) and followed it with Distribution (1994–95) and then Manufacturing (1996).

Figure 1.7 outlines the timeline of the major PeopleSoft package functionality through the past dozen years. Note that the major application releases happened just in time for the major ERP market push in the mid- to late 1990s. PeopleSoft's manufacturing product is aimed at the distribution-oriented discrete manufacturing base. The company's direction from human resources to manufacturing was just the opposite of SAP's and is a major reason why the focus and integration points of the two packages are very different.

Figure 1.7 **PeopleSoft major product release timeline**

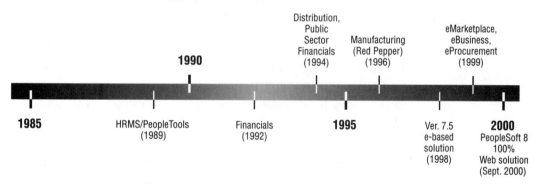

Up until its update to version 7.5, PeopleSoft focused purely on North American–based companies; it provided "local" versions of its software to support other countries (including South American countries and Australia) rather than provide a single "global" solution for multinational companies. Although version 7.5 offered more global capabilities, the package continued to be based on the more liberal rules of the U.S rather than the stricter requirements of Europe. With each subsequent release of PeopleSoft (as with PeopleSoft 8), PeopleSoft is expanding its global capabilities to cover specific business requirements of individual countries.

A great example of this with PeopleSoft 8 is the inclusion of a global payroll engine that supports four initial countries (the U.K., France, Germany, and

Switzerland), in addition to the already available Payroll for North America (which supports the U.S. and Canada). PeopleSoft 8 also provides translated releases in the following languages (in addition to English): French, Canadian French, German, Dutch, Spanish, Portuguese, and Japanese. For its global HRMS applications only, it also provides a translated Italian release. Another key global feature of PeopleSoft 8 is the support for the international standard UniCode multibyte character set. UniCode currently supports over 70 languages, with many more to be added soon. UniCode support enables PeopleSoft applications to store, retrieve, and process data in any one or all of these languages simultaneously.

However, these characteristics are still evolving and have yet to prove themselves in the marketplace. Thus, an organization should really look at how it does business and which model fits better with its organizational makeup.

J.D. Edwards

J.D. Edwards's ERP application had the potential to be dominant in the same way as the other three products and has over the past two years shown a surge in the ERP middle market. Its focus is on the medium-range technology platforms, including the manufacturing-based AS/400 system; thus, it is clearly the dominant player in this market space.

J.D. Edwards's applications are proven to have strong technology components, emerging as a leader in the e-commerce area, and reliable systems. They seem to be a good choice for technologically conservative, midsize companies. They have not proven to perform well for larger, more complex organizations; nor does the company have a large client base to serve as a benchmark.

Baan

Baan was a niche player in the MRP market space, but the lack of a full ERP solution has decreased its market share over the past few years. Its package is known to have the strongest overall functionality for the manufacturing processes, including support of the most complex processes. Strengths are also found in the package's planning and sales force–automation functionality. However, the failure of the vendor to include the more administrative functions within the human resources and financials areas has left Baan behind.

Some organizations have implemented a dual solution (e.g., PeopleSoft integrated with Baan), but this tends to suboptimize the efficiencies, thereby increasing the costs to maintain and support two vendor applications and the interfaces between them.

Lawson

Lawson is very similar to J.D. Edwards, in that the major business focus is on health care and smaller service organizations. Lawson's architecture and approach are cost effective and aimed toward smaller organizations that want a baseline application that has a much smaller technology footprint and tends to support the needs of companies with revenue under $1 billion. Lawson is very strong in the health care industry, where its main competitor is PeopleSoft (each having about 40% of the ERP business). In general, the smaller facilities lean toward a Lawson solution, while the larger organizations tend to choose PeopleSoft.

Final Analysis

Given these very diverse origins, it's important to understand what basic features and functions are core to your business and to the support of your future-state vision. Then you can match them with the vendor profile that best meets your business needs and direction. Figure 1.8 depicts the different functional rollout strategies of the three major systems, PeopleSoft, Oracle, and SAP. As you can see from the diagram, each one's origin was based on a different functional process and application area, although now all systems have functionality in each major ERP area.

All the packages mentioned are highly successful and would not be market leaders today if they didn't support the business needs of the organizations that implement them. What we typically see when an implementation goes sour is that the proper planning and up-front focus on the business drivers were not created initially and managed throughout the project life cycle and going forward—not necessarily that the wrong package was selected.

Another thing to remember is to never lose sight of your key business drivers and to constantly look back and measure yourself against these drivers, matching your goals with that of the package vendor.

Figure 1.8   **Functional evolution of major ERP systems**

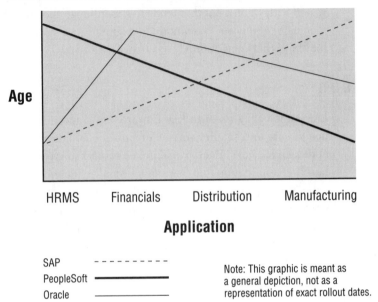

Why Choose PeopleSoft?

PeopleSoft's ERP system was developed in the late 1980s by Dave Duffield, original CEO and founding father of PeopleSoft, and Ken Morris, the technical brains behind the operation, and was based on the new client-server technology. Dave had broken away from a company he had created called Integral (a human resources system leader at the time) because the cultural environment and company direction were getting "too political" for his liking. As the PeopleSoft name indicates, Dave was looking for a company that focused on people—both people within their customer's organization as well as within their own organization. PeopleSoft wanted to be easy to do business with, fun for their clients and employees, focused on people issues, and flexible for the future.

As it quickly became the dominant leader in the HR market space in the early 1990s, PeopleSoft looked at ways to increase its product offerings as well as its market share. It was typically paired with an Oracle, SAP, or Baan solution since those vendors didn't have HR products at the time. As Oracle and SAP were developing HR products, in 1992, PeopleSoft began rolling out its Financials solution to test its hand in other areas and to see if it could compete against those vendors. With the introduction of its Distribution products, the company's system became a viable alternative, especially for service companies that were not manufacturing-based.

PeopleSoft has continued to excel in this market space, leading SAP and Oracle in telecommunications, service, hospitality, and nonmanufacturing-based industries. In 1996, PeopleSoft decided to try its hand in the full ERP solution by targeting discrete manufacturing companies with its first offering of manufacturing products, including integration of the Red Pepper optimization engine. In this area, PeopleSoft has historically not excelled as prevailingly as it envisioned and is now focusing on industry solutions for its major clients. These solutions include special offerings in the financial services, insurance, and services areas.

Recently, several major executive changes were made, including the addition of a new president and chief operations officer, Craig Conway, in May 1999. Al Duffield, long-time PeopleSoft leader and brother of CEO Dave, had retired. Craig joined PeopleSoft from OneTouch Systems, a leader in the field of interactive broadcast networks, where he had been president and chief executive. He had also spent eight years at Oracle working in marketing, sales, and operations. In September 1999, Craig took over Dave's role as CEO. He has assumed all responsibilities for the day-to-day activities at PeopleSoft, including driving the corporate and product strategy into the future. Although Dave continues to work closely with Craig and remains the Chairman of the PeopleSoft Board of Directors, PeopleSoft enters the new millennium with a new leader at the helm— one who is poised to lead a large, established organization into the new "information age." Craig has made several changes to the organization, bringing in more seasoned veterans in the industry and those that understand the new Internet age. His focus is on creating serious competition for Oracle and SAP.

The following types of markets and organizations are ideal for PeopleSoft at this time—markets where the company has had the biggest successes:

> ▶ Fast-growing middle-market and large U.S.-based clients that are focused in the service-based industry, including those in health care, insurance, financial services, telecommunications, and hospitality

► Companies that are not based on the creation of a product but are more focused on the people area

► Companies where flexibility and analysis are keys to success, with the primary focus in the financial and human resources areas

Companies that are large manufacturers with complex process solutions are not good fits for the PeopleSoft application. In addition, the application has not yet proven itself as a solution for large, multinational organizations.

Case Study: Package Selection Example

A large telecommunications company based in the U.S. was determined to create a single vision that would streamline its major back-office systems, including HR/payroll, financials, and distribution—creating a single organization to meet all its diverse market needs. After close analysis of the major packages, the company selected PeopleSoft's application, based on its flexible architecture, ability to work on multiple database platforms, ease and flexibility of reporting, and overall functional fit for its needs. This company was also aware of the large telecommunications community that PeopleSoft provided services to in the U.S. market. It hoped to share knowledge with that community and help to drive the product to more specialized solutions for its industry.

Based on this example, you can see that several key factors drove this decision:

► Overall fit with functionality of system (i.e., focus on people and service-related functionality primarily found in the HR and financials applications)

► Flexibility of architecture (i.e., multiple platforms and hardware configurations available) and reporting capabilities (multiple reporting tools, including batch and real-time reporting)

► Large client base from same industry, with similar needs

In all cases, an organization should analyze the investment direction, customer base, and philosophy of the vendor and then match them with its strategy, direction, and company philosophy of doing business.

Establishing Key Business Drivers

Regardless of your ERP package choice, you should never lose track of why you have decided to implement a solution such as PeopleSoft. For many organizations, these core business values or drivers may not have been realized or benchmarked up front. One key thing to remember is that for your organization to be successful and to drive value, you must understand where you are coming from prior to putting in an ERP system (which we call current-state measurements and benchmarks) and where you are going after implementing your new business strategy (future-state vision). You should continually track progress against these measures and goals throughout the life of your system—well after the initial implementation. You also have to track and monitor key decisions throughout the life of your system regarding trade-offs and future enhancements. If your organization has not done this, it needs to begin immediately. Many organizations are failing to make the most out of their ERP systems, basically because they have failed to stay on the path of their future vision (or maybe never articulated what that vision was), their ambitions overrode their cost figures, they bit off more than they could chew, and their true ability and commitment to change was not strong enough.

Common Business Value Pitfalls with ERP Implementations

Some common reasons why companies fail to receive value from their ERP implementations:

▶ Did not adequately benchmark their current state (i.e., where they started from) and therefore could never articulate a true business case for undertaking the effort

▶ Did not adequately plan for this major transformation with enough resources, both human and financial, resulting in missed deadlines and increased project costs

▶ Did not have the executive sponsorship and business support for this transformation and did not have a solid change-management plan to support it

**Common Business Value Pitfalls with ERP Implementations
(continued)**

▶ Did not adequately map out their goals and objectives for their future state (i.e., no future-state vision) and therefore never knew where they were going

▶ Highly customized their new ERP system to look like their old MRP or departmentalized systems, not leveraging the new technologies, tools, or best practices, as well as increasing support costs for the future

Implementing an ERP system is *not* easy. Most organizations are still very departmentalized and not integrated or willing to integrate across their organization—and their people are incented with individual goals and objectives. So why believe that a computer system can magically make the implementation happen? Strong executive sponsorship at the highest levels is a must.

In Chapter 4, "Building a Basis for Business Development," and Chapter 5, "Planning the Foundation," we take a deeper look into how organizations might approach this change and into understanding the value that this change will bring to the organization. Some areas will benefit much more than others, but it's the premise that the sum of the parts is much more valuable than the individual parts themselves that makes ERP systems so effective. In fact, in order to stay competitive, organizations must be getting the most out of these systems. Their competition is already doing that and then some. Also, with a systems implementation as complex as this, many organizations were not realistic on the cost, time, or resource requirements (and skills) necessary to make this solution happen. These systems take millions of dollars to implement and even more to maintain and support. An organization must be committed both with resources and sponsorship to make this happen. If they don't, they are only delaying benefits, increasing costs, and suboptimizing their solution.

Finally, as mentioned previously, many organizations that have recently implemented these ERP systems did so for very tactical reasons rather than strategic ones, such as Y2K issues with their current systems or the changes in the European market (i.e., the euro). When these factors are the driver and the information technology (IT) group is the direct sponsor—viewing the project as just a system replacement effort—these projects almost certainly fall short of the vision, because the business is generally not involved in promoting and driving this newly integrated solution, and new cross-functional processes are not optimized. It's always important for us all to remember that in order to march ahead to a successful victory, we must all have a battle plan. Your business case or return on investment (ROI) should outline the reasons you are implementing your solution, look at the costs associated with this solution, and clearly articulate the benefits you hope to achieve. This road map or battle plan should always be close at hand, should your strategy change or obstacles arise that were not considered. Always be prepared to modify (and document) your plan, outlining the reasons and the resulting changes to your ending solution.

Trends in ERP

Although we've been looking specifically at today's ERP solutions, the 21st century holds new opportunities and new frontiers in the ERP area. The latest software releases by the ERP vendors include these features more and more. Vendors that don't have work flow, Web enablement, data warehousing, performance measurement, and executive reporting capabilities are falling behind the market leaders. Companies are beginning to look past efficiencies and toward revenue enhancement and acceleration mechanisms. Efficiencies are a must, but innovative business solutions and adding value to the bottom line are becoming primary focuses for succeeding in the 21st century.

Consumers' expectations have increased with the advent of all this new technology and with the reduced barriers in the marketplace, leading to the emergence of a truly global economy. Businesses are competing for the same pool of resources (or percentage of a customer's wallet, or "wallet share") and must focus on the customer and therefore the market even more. Since customer needs and markets are ever-changing, or dynamic, a continuous approach to analyzing customer expectations, rather than a static approach, must be leveraged. Being able to analyze these continuous demands of the market or your customer, whoever that is, has thus become a key business driver. Hence we've seen the emergence of decision support systems and "real-time" data to analyze the shifts in the market or customer and respond to these trends as rapidly as possible. Knowledge becomes king, and the more a business is leveraging this knowledge, the better. Therefore, with any sound solution, you should focus on the next steps and ensure that these considerations are a part of your overall plan. Your base (i.e., the ERP transactional system) must be solid and in place, functioning soundly and efficiently, prior to analyzing your data and reacting to it. The measures you evaluate and observe may differ from user to user. You need to take the time to analyze your user, analyze the user's customer and market, and ensure that the appropriate solution is in place for the user as well as the changing market. The lines between back-office systems (e.g., classic ERP) and front-office systems become blurred, as does your set of "users."

With the expansion of the Internet into everyday business activities and the ability to connect with a company across the globe and with other organizations, flexible, integrated solutions aimed at the user's goals (in most cases, changing from user to customer focus) and objectives are becoming the focus. Most packages are rolling out "my portal"–type solutions that integrate key information that individuals need to maximize their view of the organization (both internally and externally), their roles within the organization, and their ability to service customers—all in a single "desktop" view. These solutions integrate the typical day-to-day transactions and the key information necessary for decision making, including making business reports, news, and basic information available at the individuals' fingertips. These portal packages also integrate all the communities an individual is a part of, including roles as customers, buyers, servicers, employees, and many more.

One of the key trends that this new Internet focus drives is more customized solutions for the customer. The enterprise must look at the key processes that differentiate itself from its competitors and look for the vendor that provides the tools for the enterprise to more quickly and effectively deploy this market-differentiating solution. The other more mundane, "workhorse" functions will also need to be delivered, but at an accelerated pace, to decrease the cost and focus on this area. The vendors will need to provide the core solutions as well as the tools necessary to support these state-of-the-art, company-specific solutions. Rapid development will become the key driver for these solutions. Also, interoperability tools to bring the standard, core solutions together with the market-differentiating ones are important.

As mentioned before, another key element emerging is that of decision support technologies in the form of data warehousing, performance management, and other analytical tool capabilities. Maintaining, reusing, and sharing knowledge to drive decisions is also becoming a player in the market. Therefore, trend analysis and balanced scorecards are just other reporting features that become more important in running and adapting your business. The ERP systems of today contain critical information to support this analysis. This information must be merged with other "real-time" information to form the analysis necessary to react to customer and end-user demands and to continuously improve your business. An open architecture will be key to leveraging this data as well as integrating it with "outside" data from other key internal or external systems.

To provide this data-ready solution, the new language of the connected enterprise or economy is "publish and subscribe," or XML (Extensible Markup Language).

Note   A *publish-and-subscribe* framework is especially powerful because systems are posting (or *publishing*) data along with the data definition or label in a very open-ended architecture, such that other systems can *subscribe* (or pull the data when they need it). A special, unique interface does not have to be developed for each application that wants that data.

With the latest software releases, most ERP vendors are moving toward the XML solution, making their data available to be pulled by any application or process via the Web and allowing for much easier and rapid integration. Another important ingredient that must be considered is performance. Vendors must be able to organize their data for high-volume retrieval through a Web site and dynamically refresh this information for the site's users. The concept of making key data available in real time for high-speed access is known as "commerce data caching."

Finally, linking together multiple enterprises into a single solution, either for outsourced business processes or for linking with suppliers, customers, or traders, is another trend for the 21st century. This has been commonly referred to as an "extended enterprise application" solution. To support this trend, the vendors will have to adapt their products to this new model and can not merely rely on interfaces to link the processes together. This approach will focus on taking a single set of processes and deploying that functionality across a large number of users, both internal and external. To support this, the packages must be easily integrated with external systems and most likely leverage the message broker–oriented technology that is emerging now.

Today, the procurement or purchasing area is a prime example of this "exterprise," or extended enterprise solution. Buyer and supplier data is integrated with your manager's purchase order to provide the best value for your organization and ensure that appropriate payments are made and the product received. This solution is an integration of many systems, including internal ERP data as well as external supplier data.

To adapt to this new frontier, the ERP vendors will need to be flexible, focus on more component-based solutions (unbundling their solutions), look at externally focused integration, and create a new business focus. It's an exciting time ahead for us all in this ever-changing world around us.

Up Next

Now that we've talked about the history of ERP systems, PeopleSoft's main competition, and the reasons you may have chosen PeopleSoft as your solution, including what to be prepared for next, it's time to delve into the major goal of this book: to help you bring value to your organization through a successful implementation. In the next chapter we'll look more deeply into the PeopleSoft application, providing an overview of each of the major components and the functions and features, including some of the enhancements in PeopleSoft 8. We'll also look at the integration points between the modules and processes as well as specific areas you might want to focus some attention on as you implement. More detailed functionality analysis will be provided in Chapters 17 to 20 for those of you who want to understand the specific details of the package configuration and functionality.

CHAPTER 2

A PeopleSoft Overview

FEATURING:

▶ An overview of PeopleSoft's HRMS application, including its history, its key strengths and weaknesses, global trends, and keys to moving ahead

▶ A look at the company's Financials application, including its history, its key strengths and weaknesses, global trends, and key concepts for the future

▶ An overview of the PeopleSoft Supply Chain (distribution and manufacturing) application, including its history, its key strengths and weaknesses, global trends, and keys for the future

▶ A brief analysis of PeopleSoft's market position

A s discussed in Chapter 1, "Enterprise Resource Planning with PeopleSoft," PeopleSoft has come far from its beginnings in the late 1980s, when it introduced the first major client-server, back-office Human Resources Management application. With its recent partnership with CommerceOne for an integrated eProcurement solution, its purchase of Vantive for eCRM (customer relationship management), and its PeopleSoft 8 Internet solution, PeopleSoft is still recognized as a major contender and market leader in the ERP application area.

This chapter will provide an overview of the product and its history and evolution, including its competition and place in the market. We'll look at key strengths and weaknesses in each of the major application areas as well as what the future might hold. Specifically, we'll look at each of the three major areas within the PeopleSoft application (combining the distribution and manufacturing areas into one, Supply Chain Management) in this order:

1. Human Resources Management systems (HRMS)

2. Financial systems

3. Supply Chain Management systems

Figure 2.1 provides a pictorial overview of the modules that make up the PeopleSoft application suite. We will summarize most of the modules in this chapter. The CRM application suite and Portal solutions, new with PeopleSoft 8, will be discussed in Chapter 24, "What's Next on the Horizon."

HRMS Overview and History

PeopleSoft's beginnings were in the human resources (HR) arena. With its release of PeopleSoft version 1 in the late 1980s, the company was the first vendor to have a fully integrated, robust, client-server HRMS application suite. Figure 2.2 shows the modules that are part of the HRMS application suite, including the most recent modules available in PeopleSoft 8. PeopleSoft has continued to be a leader in the HR market; however, competition has gotten more fierce and competitive over the past few years, resulting in a reduced market share and a slip in the market leader position.

Figure 2.1   **PeopleSoft ERP application suite (PeopleSoft 8)**

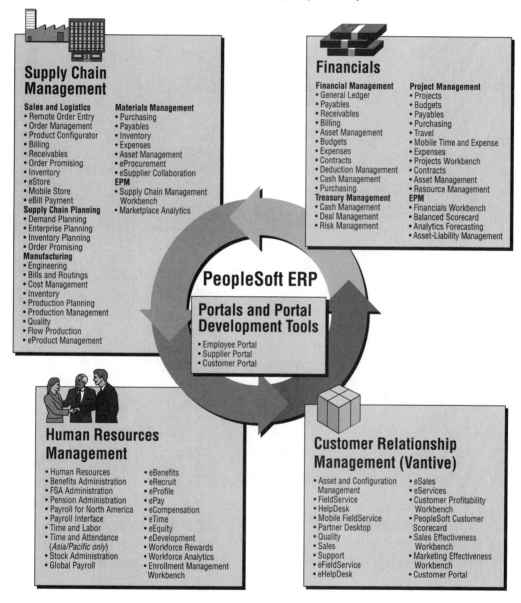

Supply Chain Management

Sales and Logistics
- Remote Order Entry
- Order Management
- Product Configurator
- Billing
- Receivables
- Order Promising
- Inventory
- eStore
- Mobile Store
- eBill Payment

Supply Chain Planning
- Demand Planning
- Enterprise Planning
- Inventory Planning
- Order Promising

Manufacturing
- Engineering
- Bills and Routings
- Cost Management
- Inventory
- Production Planning
- Production Management
- Quality
- Flow Production
- eProduct Management

Materials Management
- Purchasing
- Payables
- Inventory
- Expenses
- Asset Management
- eProcurement
- eSupplier Collaboration

EPM
- Supply Chain Management Workbench
- Marketplace Analytics

Financials

Financial Management
- General Ledger
- Payables
- Receivables
- Billing
- Asset Management
- Budgets
- Expenses
- Contracts
- Deduction Management
- Cash Management
- Purchasing

Treasury Management
- Cash Management
- Deal Management
- Risk Management

Project Management
- Projects
- Budgets
- Payables
- Purchasing
- Travel
- Mobile Time and Expense
- Expenses
- Projects Workbench
- Contracts
- Asset Management
- Resource Management

EPM
- Financials Workbench
- Balanced Scorecard
- Analytics Forecasting
- Asset-Liability Management

PeopleSoft ERP

Portals and Portal Development Tools
- Employee Portal
- Supplier Portal
- Customer Portal

Human Resources Management

- Human Resources
- Benefits Administration
- FSA Administration
- Pension Administration
- Payroll for North America
- Payroll Interface
- Time and Labor
- Time and Attendance (*Asia/Pacific only*)
- Stock Administration
- Global Payroll
- eBenefits
- eRecruit
- eProfile
- ePay
- eCompensation
- eTime
- eEquity
- eDevelopment
- Workforce Rewards
- Workforce Analytics
- Enrollment Management Workbench

Customer Relationship Management (Vantive)

- Asset and Configuration Management
- FieldService
- HelpDesk
- Mobile FieldService
- Partner Desktop
- Quality
- Sales
- Support
- eFieldService
- eHelpDesk
- eSales
- eServices
- Customer Profitability Workbench
- PeopleSoft Customer Scorecard
- Sales Effectiveness Workbench
- Marketing Effectiveness Workbench
- Customer Portal

Figure 2.2   **HRMS applications**

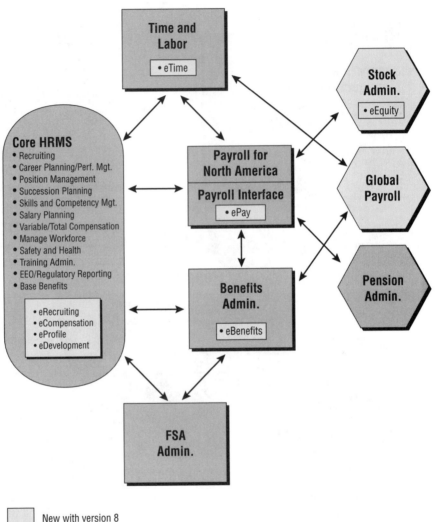

New with version 8

Modules

Following is a quick overview of each of the PeopleSoft HRMS applications or modules available today:

Core HRMS   The core PeopleSoft HRMS application, which includes Manage Workforce, contains the basic functions to hire, transfer, promote, and make job changes for an employee. This portion of the application contains the basic employee information, including history as well as department, location, and job information. Concepts to support basic EEO, affirmative action, labor relations, employment verifications, and basic HR functions are contained in this module. With PeopleSoft 8, an additional module, eProfile, allows employees themselves to update basic employee or profile information.

Career Planning/Performance Management   This functionality is included as part of the core HRMS module. This area supports major career planning processes such as competency planning, career management, employee review processing, and succession planning. With People-Soft 8, a new module, eDevelopment, is also available, providing manager and employee features to help individuals manage their careers more effectively over the Internet.

Recruiting   This functionality is also included as part of the core HRMS module. The recruiting function includes creation of job requisitions and job search or skill search capabilities including applicant tracking, interviewing, and hiring. This application integrates directly with the basic employee information such that applicant data is transferred directly to employee tables once an applicant is hired. A new module in PeopleSoft 8, eRecruit, allows for full external recruiting capabilities enabled through Web technology.

Position Management   The Position Management functions support budgeting and managing job positions within an organization. This functionality, included in the core HRMS application, is typically used for governmental or regulatory establishments that have a predefined budget and a set of job positions that are authorized for employment. Companies that let each manager determine job requirements, which are not tracked on a fixed job basis, don't implement this feature.

Training Administration   The Training Administration module is also included in the core HRMS product. Within this area, training programs can be set up and sessions scheduled to enroll and track employee training. Information on each course and session can be tracked, including instructors and class requirements. Waiting-list features are included.

Pension Administration   Pension Administration is a fairly new application that provides the capability to track and manage pension deductions and allocations, which are then passed to the plan provider. This module is only U.S.-based at this time and doesn't support pension requirements globally. It isn't included as a part of the core HRMS product and must be purchased separately.

Benefits Administration and Base Benefits   As described in Chapters 17, "A Closer Look at HRMS," and 18, "HRMS Specifics," two types of benefits processing are available with PeopleSoft. Base Benefits processing, which is included in the core HRMS application, provides for the basic tracking of benefit plans and links each plan to a payroll deduction. However, any changes to the plan or enrollment processing is done manually. Benefits Administration allows you to automate the benefits enrollment and change process. This module is an add-on to the core package. With PeopleSoft 8, a new module called eBenefits supports key employee self-service features, allowing employees to enroll in their benefit plans and make changes to them. It's available at an additional price.

Salary Planning   This function is included in the core HRMS application. It features the ability to create salary plans, develop salary-increase budgets by department, and process salary changes. Standard salary matrices and review-rating distributions can be accomplished by leveraging this functionality.

Variable/Total Compensation   The features of this capability are part of the core HRMS application. This module allows you to create variable compensation plans and administer them to your staff using eligibility criteria calculation methods, and provides specific payout options for your employees (such as a special bonus check, an incentive payment, or a salary increase). Incentive goals, both group and individual, can be set up as well. A manager's self-service module, eCompensation, is provided with PeopleSoft 8; it allows managers to perform key compensation planning functions, leveraging the Internet.

Payroll for North America   This major application area for the U.S. and Canada includes the processes that support the payroll and pay the employees, including the processing of specific earnings and deductions as well as both on- and off-cycle payrolls. In addition to these features, PeopleSoft 8, with its new ePay module, allows paycheck presentation and electronic stub review via the Internet.

Payroll Interface   This feature includes processing to support the calculations of benefits and deductions, which can be passed to a third-party vendor for payroll purposes. It includes an interface generator that can create specific files that can integrate with payroll outsourcing vendors such as ADP (Automatic Data Processing, Inc.).

Time and Labor   The Time and Labor application has improved over the past few PeopleSoft releases and now supports online (even Web-enabled) time collection, including maintenance of schedules and pay or time rules and retroactive processing. This application interfaces closely with the Payroll module and passes "buckets" of time and expenses by pay period to the pay sheets (found in the Payroll module) used to create the employee paychecks. Another module, Time and Attendance, is also available but only with the Asia/Pacific local version. In addition to this core functionality, PeopleSoft 8 also includes a Web-based, employee self-service module called eTime.

Stock Administration   This is one of PeopleSoft's newest HRMS modules. It supports the tracking of employee stock programs and distributions, including stock purchase plans, restricted stock payments, and stock options.

FSA Administration   This module creates and tracks flexible spending accounts (FSAs) for employees, including tracking deductions, contributions, and reimbursements. Most companies outsource this service and therefore do not need this module. The FSA deduction can be created and tracked within the Payroll module without the use of this additional module.

Global Payroll   This module is new with PeopleSoft 8 and provides a global payroll engine that supports payroll processes for four countries initially: the U.K., France, Germany, and Switzerland. Payroll for North America is still available as well to support the requirements of the U.S. and Canada.

In addition to those modules, there are specific modules that support the student administration functions of an academic institution. This application, called Student Administration, includes functionality that supports academic advising, admissions, student records, advancement, financial aid, and student financials.

Also, with the release of PeopleSoft 8, the Federal/Public Sector HR and Benefits functionality is incorporated into the core HRMS application.

Strengths and Weaknesses

PeopleSoft's HRMS application has been the foundation of the company's product line since inception. The Gartner Group has tracked PeopleSoft as a leader in this area, placing them in Gartner's "best in class" quadrant. However, over the past few years, PeopleSoft has lost ground to its two major competitors, SAP and Oracle, and has felt pressures in the middle-market area as well from Lawson and J.D. Edwards. The latest Gartner Group quadrant rating still places PeopleSoft in the leadership quadrant but behind SAP and just in front of Oracle. Significant investments by these two vendors in employee self-service features, expanded HR functionality, creation of "communities," and key management desktop reporting has helped these vendors compete effectively with PeopleSoft.

Although PeopleSoft has a strong customer base, having obtained a large market share over the past 10 years, the company is clearly losing some of its competitive edge. Why is this happening? Clearly, PeopleSoft's competitors have seized on a few key areas that appeal to the market, specifically globalization of their products and effective self-service and Internet capabilities. PeopleSoft's first self-service features were rolled out in its version 7, with work-flow components featured in version 6. However, having to "pull" its global payroll solution during testing of version 7.5 and being the last of the "big three" to effectively introduce total Web-based self-service have cost PeopleSoft some position in the market. In addition, smaller, niche companies continue to take market share with aggressive Web-based applications and knowledge management. Both J.D. Edwards and Meta4 offer Web strategies for self-service and internal collaboration, which creates some competition for the leaders. Now with PeopleSoft 8, PeopleSoft has invested tremendously in these employee and manager self-service features, providing a 100% Internet solution, and it hopes to propel itself ahead of others. Over the next year, time will tell whether the company has been successful.

Global Trends

PeopleSoft has failed thus far to deliver a truly global HR/payroll solution for its clients. It wasn't able to deliver the global payroll functionality promised in version 7.5; and, as mentioned above, the payroll functionality in PeopleSoft 8 supports only four countries. As a result, the company has fallen a bit behind its competition in the Internet Web-based functionality that could support a global implementation rollout. Certainly, within the service and high-tech areas, PeopleSoft has been able to make inroads on a global basis, but it has failed to create strong competition for SAP, which is still recognized as a leader in this area.

Preserving its strong U.S. base and demonstrating that it can support both global and local requirements will be keys to PeopleSoft's success. With the release in PeopleSoft 8 of its Global Payroll module and its 100% Internet solution, we'll need to watch closely and see how customers react to these new features. PeopleSoft's purchase and integration of the CRM application Vantive, which has a strong footing in Europe, and its creation of a full 360° view of the customer and integration with "people" resources also can help the company capture some additional market share globally.

Version 7.5 supported HR local functionality requirements for the U.S., Canada, Germany, France, the Netherlands, and the U.K. With PeopleSoft 8, this expands to Italy, Spain, and Switzerland. The Global Payroll feature initially supports the U.K., France, Germany, and Switzerland; extensions to additional countries will follow soon. The Global Payroll feature can also be run on the same platform as the North American Payroll (which supports the U.S. and Canada). Support of multiple languages and the European Monetary Unit (the euro) is provided.

Self-Service/Intranet

PeopleSoft's 100% Internet functionality in PeopleSoft 8 will enhance its ability to compete in the self-service market. Early adopters such as J.D. Edwards, Lawson, and Meta4 will be threatened by PeopleSoft's market position and robust functionality as well as its development team. With the PeopleSoft 8 capabilities, PeopleSoft moves from a fairly small footprint (which was available with version 7.5) to a much broader management and employee desktop feature. Self-service features (as mentioned above) cover all areas, including these:

Employee data All personal data, including mailing addresses, phone numbers, emergency contacts, and much more, can be updated. Also, managers can now create reports and pull information via Web-based reporting. They can approve employee changes such as job transfers, salary increases, and pay changes.

Recruiting Job postings, online resume creation, and applicant tracking can all be done via the Web. Managers are also able to view candidate information, schedule interviews, and make hiring recommendations.

Workforce development   Training requirements and information is now delivered via the Web, including the approval processes and competency tracking.

Employee compensation   A suite of self-service applications is available to request salary changes, to award variable compensation, and to make incentive awards. It also contains other total-compensation features.

Benefits   Benefits enrollment and tracking, including viewing current enrollment information, is now available. Savings plan contributions can be changed online.

Payroll   Paycheck information can be viewed online, and changes to basic deductions such as parking, direct deposit, and withholding options can be made online.

Time and labor   Web-based time reporting, including the tracking of clock time, vacations, overtime, etc., is available. Managers can approve time online or modify their subordinates' information.

Stock administration   Viewing ESPP activity and options activity is available online.

In addition to these self-service, managers' desktop features, PeopleSoft now has "communities" available online to support knowledge and information sharing, including a benefits community where merchant content and information is provided as well as self-service transactions—all within one setting.

Keys for the Future

For PeopleSoft to continue its market leadership role in the HRMS arena, it will need to effectively deliver on its 100% Internet solution, provide robust analytical tools for managers' and employees' desktops, and ensure that it delivers on its global capabilities. The company should continue to look at innovative ways to create learning and knowledge communities and to leverage the latest trends in human capital management. With a more mobile workforce that demands a knowledge-sharing environment and flexibility in work schedules and benefits, it will need to continue to evolve its solutions to meet these changing needs and keep up with the rapid changes in technology. The success (or lack thereof) of PeopleSoft 8 will be a key cornerstone in this transition, as will the integration with the company's Vantive (eCRM solution) and other e-commerce capabilities.

Financials Overview and History

In 1992, PeopleSoft released its first set of financial applications, which included only the basic General Ledger, Payables, and Receivables functionalities. In 1994, it added assets and purchasing, and it rounded out the suite in 1995 with the Inventory, Billing, and Projects modules. Since that time, the company has added several innovative solutions, with expense tracking and management (Expenses), Enterprise Performance Management (which includes a balanced scorecard function), and integration with eProcurement. With PeopleSoft 8, several new modules, including Contracts, Deduction Management, Travel, and Resource Management, were added to support professional service organizations, as well as new Internet modules such as Mobile Time and Expense reporting functions (including one for the PalmPilot). Figure 2.3 shows PeopleSoft's diverse product offerings in the Financials area.

Figure 2.3 **Financial applications**

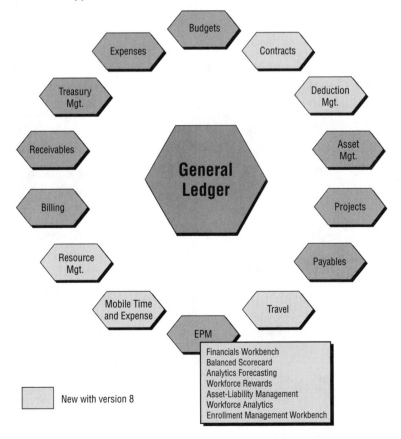

Modules

The specific Financials modules and a brief summary of each follow.

General Ledger   This module was part of the initial release and includes the basic features that support a general ledger financial application, including chart-of-accounts setup and maintenance, basic ledger accounting, allocations, combination edits, consolidations, and equitizations. It also contains financial reporting tools, including the proprietary nVision (an Excel-based drill-down reporting tool).

Accounts Payable   Another original module, Accounts Payable includes the ability to track vendors and process payments for vouchers. It's heavily integrated with other modules, including General Ledger, Purchasing, Asset Management, Projects, and Accounts Receivable. It includes an EDI (electronic data exchange) interface capability.

Asset Management   This function allows companies to track their assets, including contracts and leases, and perform the financial depreciation requirements. It interfaces with Accounts Payable, Projects (costing), and General Ledger.

Accounts Receivable   This module supports customer tracking, core billing, cash processing, payment predicting, adjustments, and bank processing. It includes an EDI interface capability.

Budgets   This module interacts closely with General Ledger and provides the capability for the organization's budget management process.

Projects   The Projects capability includes the ability to track all aspects of a "project," including management of resources, budgeting, and reporting features.

Treasury   The Treasury module supports the areas and functions of cash management, deal management, and risk management. This application is a fairly new set of functions, released in version 7.5.

Expenses   This is also a fairly new module, with initial release in version 7.5, and includes the tracking and management of employee expenses and payments. This module integrates with Accounts Payable and the HRMS/Payroll modules to obtain vendor, employee, and payment information. With PeopleSoft 8, several new modules that together create an integrated travel-and-expense, self-service function called Mobile Travel and Expense are available. Features to support deployment on a PalmPilot are also available. The Travel module provides the ability to make and track travel arrangements and to integrate them with time-and-expense reporting.

Billing   This function integrates specifically with the Accounts Receivable function to provide the billing capabilities necessary for an organization to bill customers. It includes the support for Web-based credit card payments and installment billing. A Web-based electronic billing and presentment/ payment function is also provided.

Contracts   Contracts is the newest of the financial modules, with a controlled release in PeopleSoft 8. (A *controlled release* is provided only to a prequalified set of clients and is not available to the general public.) This module tracks the revenue-generating contractual process for business-to-business transactions. Features of this module include creation and tracking of proposals, capturing contractual terms and conditions, support of billing and revenue-recognition processes, tracking of contractual deliverables, and analysis of earned and unearned revenue.

Deduction Management   This is another new module with a controlled release in PeopleSoft 8. It provides a credit and collections tool that allows companies to analyze their customer deduction trends and activities. This capability is extremely beneficial to the consumer products industry.

Resource Management   This is the last of the three new modules having a controlled release in PeopleSoft 8. It supports the resource-planning needs of professional services companies by tracking project requirements and the skills matching those requirements.

Enterprise Performance Measurement (EPM)   The EPM module is the core data reporting repository supported by a data warehouse. It includes key performance reporting features such as the balanced scorecard; workbenches for contracts, employees, and procurement; and tracking using key performance indicators (KPI).

Strengths and Weaknesses

The PeopleSoft Financials application has enjoyed a quick rise to acceptance in the marketplace and is now recognized as one of the top ERP applications, especially for service-related organizations. With the advent of the Treasury,

Expenses, and Enterprise Performance modules, PeopleSoft has enjoyed increased market share and is recognized as a leader in this area.

The batch processing environment and the interaction among the various financial modules can be a deterrent in situations where the volume of transactions is large. They create a "non-real-time" aspect of the solution, since the processes have to be scheduled and are generally run in the evenings rather than when the changes are made. With PeopleSoft 8, special features to improve the integration of the applications and create real-time processing have been added. Through the publish-and-subscribe technology, information can be integrated much closer to real time than in the past. Some key processes, however, are still done via a batch process.

Nevertheless, key industry templates and solutions in the banking, insurance, and professional services markets make PeopleSoft a major player in the financial and EPM applications area for service industry clients.

Global Trends

PeopleSoft's Financials application supports several key global integration capabilities, including VAT (value-added tax) requirements support, currency conversion to support the euro, and the UniCode multibyte character set, which supports more than 70 languages and allows applications to store, retrieve, and process data in any one or all of these languages simultaneously. Translation releases include English, French, Canadian French, German, Dutch, Spanish, Portuguese, and Japanese. PeopleSoft's global rollout continues to lag about a year behind its major competitors and will depend on the support of several of its largest clients.

Note   The power of UniCode is shown, for example, during multicountry implementations, in which users can access data in their native language (such as Japanese or Spanish). All the translations are stored within the same database.

With the recent acquisition of Vantive, PeopleSoft did garner a large share of global customers, against which they may be able to leverage their product suite. The ability to integrate Vantive's eCRM solution with key financial and distribution applications could help propel the company up the chain on the global front. However, it still has a long way to go in gaining global market share.

Internet Features

Allowing PeopleSoft 8's desktop or Internet reporting capabilities of the EPM module leverages the strength of self-service, "workbench" reporting as well as monitoring of key performance metrics using a balanced scorecard approach. The ability to deliver these tools via the Web to a manager's desktop based on roles is a key feature. Other key Internet features within the Financials application include budgeting via the Web, contract administration, expense tracking and entry, and a travel and expense "community." As with the other applications, PeopleSoft 8 is now 100% Internet capable.

Keys for the Future

To continue building market share in the Financials area and to keep up with its major competitors, SAP and Oracle, PeopleSoft must continue to increase its capabilities in e-commerce and Internet integration and to look for innovative ways to stay ahead of the competition. PeopleSoft's Treasury Management module provides an integrated, comprehensive cash management solution, which can help organizations improve efficiencies, manage capital, and reduce risks. Also, acquisitions such as Vantive and strong alliances such as CommerceOne (with eProcurement) should continue to happen in order to help PeopleSoft accelerate its market position and keep up with the competition. Integration with key Internet exchanges (or what we might understand as key business negotiating markets) and the management of knowledge via the Web are other areas that PeopleSoft might focus on to stay competitive.

Distribution and Manufacturing Overview

Last but certainly not least is PeopleSoft Supply Chain Management, which covers the distribution and manufacturing areas. These functions and features were the last set of applications added to the PeopleSoft system (prior to the Vantive CRM acquisition in late 1999)—the Purchasing module in 1994 and Manufacturing in late 1996. With the acquisition of Red Pepper in 1996, the PeopleSoft product became the first true ERO (enterprise resource optimization) software on the market. Figure 2.4 outlines the basic functionalities found in the Supply Chain Management area, breaking them down into four major groups: Sales and Logistics, Materials Management, Supply Chain Planning, and Manufacturing.

Figure 2.4   **Supply Chain Management applications**

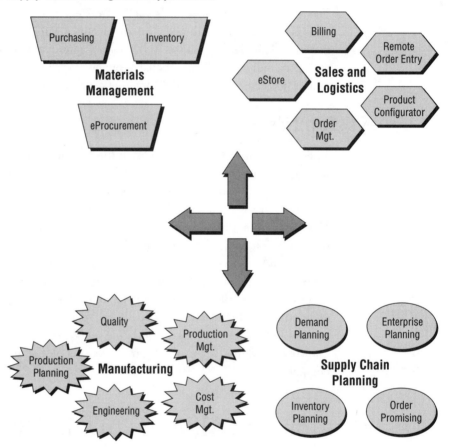

Modules

Following is a brief explanation of each of the components found in the Supply Chain Management application suite.

Sales and Logistics

Order Management   The Order Management function supports product and customer definition, pricing, and ordering. It integrates with self-service Web applications including a Remote Order Entry module.

Product Configurator   This module allows the capability to support configurable products and creates sales orders and manufacturing orders in assemble-to-order and make-to-order environments.

eStore   The first full-featured Web solution from PeopleSoft (initially released in mid-1999) was this out-of-the-box storefront, which is tightly integrated with Order Management and Inventory. Another new module called Mobile Store is also available for ordering via a mobile environment (such as a PalmPilot).

Order Promising   The Order Promising process checks the entire supply chain for available inventory, capacity, constraints, and alternatives. It also supports sourcing capabilities, change orders, ship-from site selection, and automatic updating of orders.

eBill Payment   This module allows for a customer self-service starter kit for electronic bill presentment and bill payment.

In addition to these modules, PeopleSoft Billing and Receivables are included with this suite of products. These modules are described above in the financial applications section.

Materials Management

Purchasing   One of the core modules in the Materials Management area, Purchasing features the tracking of purchases including requisition processing, contracts, purchase orders, and matching (including procurement cards, integration of handheld devices, and electronic procurement). The module is integrated with CommerceOne's market site and an internal Internet "buy" capability to create PeopleSoft's new eProcurement application. Later we'll discuss in a bit more detail the eProcurement capabilities as well as other Internet-enabled processes.

Inventory   This module supports core inventory tracking and processing, including item definition, costing features, put-away, replenishment, and structure inventory to fit organizational needs, as well as integration of bar coding, lot and serial number controls, data collection, and report analysis.

eSupplier Collaborator   This unique function forecasts demand based on order history, economic indicators, and input from employees, suppliers, and customers. It looks at when and where to produce and distribute finished products and how to establish reliable promise dates for customer orders.

This function is new with PeopleSoft 8 and incorporates major features from the Internet.

Also included in the Materials Management suite of products are PeopleSoft Payables, Expenses, and Asset Management, all of which are described within the financial products section above.

Supply Chain Planning

Demand Planning   This Demand Planning function is based on the Red Pepper capabilities and includes collaborative forecasting, product life-cycle planning including promotions, competitive and seasonal analysis, and adjustments. It includes safety stock, levels and exception detection, and correction.

Order Promising   The Order Promising process checks the entire supply chain for available inventory, capacity, constraints, and alternatives. It also supports sourcing capabilities, change orders, ship-from site selection, and automatic updating of orders.

Enterprise Planning (Red Pepper)   The Enterprise Planning module supports the optimization engine provided by the Red Pepper product, creating optimized balance between the production and supply chains. It includes the use of bills of distribution, constraints and performance factors, and real-time asset optimization in advanced planning and scheduling for the global supply chain. It also balances inventory and replenishment, and it plans resources and materials at the correct level of detail using modeling options.

Inventory Planning   The PeopleSoft Inventory Planning module allows you to simulate the effects of various stocking scenarios so that you can select the best strategy possible. You can compare current policy with simulated policies to improve inventory levels—for example, you can compare the cost difference between 90% and 95% service levels. Inventory Planning assists in understanding the interrelationships among forecast demand and inventory investment, inventory turns, customer service levels, frequency of replenishment, and levels of safety stock. You can choose from several different methods for determining order quantity and safety stock, and then see the effect of the variations on time-phased inventory investment, inventory turns, and customer service levels.

Manufacturing

Bills and Routings   This module creates and maintains the bills of material (BOM), resources, work centers, tasks, and routings, and it understands features such as revision control, component yield, and master routings. It tracks production orders and quantities being manufactured.

Engineering   The Engineering module supports the engineering process in managing product introductions and changes, including engineering change requests (ECR), engineering change orders (ECO), version/revision control, and engineering bills and routings. The module helps streamline documentation management, it associates documents with ECOs/ECRs, and it creates an engineering workbench to support engineering without affecting production.

Cost Management   This module supports inventory costing and performance management methods, tracking of costs in production and in the finished goods supply chain, evaluations, and cost simulations. It looks at cost roll-ups, different cost types, and different methods of updating production costs; and it communicates those changes that affect item or production costs, using work flow.

Production Management   The Production Management module supports the planning and scheduling methods within the production environment. It also supports methods of converting planned orders to production orders and schedules and methods of tracking production. It looks at collection methods, closing and re-opening orders, and schedules, and provides visibility of cost variances.

Production Planning   This module supports the planning and optimization of plant-level procurement and production on a real-time basis, and it determines available capacity and load of key resources in order to decide whether or not to accept a proposed customer order. Utilizing modeling options, it also determines the correct level of detail and adjusts constraints and performance factors to produce what-if scenarios.

Quality   The Quality module monitors and collects quality data over the entire supply and manufacturing production chain. Included with this module are the creation and tracking of quality control plans, feedback, process data, analysis of data, and adjustment of production processes based on results.

Flow Production and eProduct Management   These are two new modules found in Manufacturing in PeopleSoft 8. Features of the eProduct Management module allow for self-service scheduling and management for your production process. Flow Production allows for additional functions for managing the production flow across your manufacturing process.

In addition to the modules outlined above, the PeopleSoft Inventory module is included as a part of the Manufacturing product suite. You'll find an overview of this module in the Materials Management section above.

Strengths and Weaknesses

The PeopleSoft Supply Chain Management products continue to fall behind, especially in the manufacturing-based organizations and capabilities. The company's distribution applications continue to grow through acquisitions, development, and partnerships and are a sound solution for most enterprises. However, PeopleSoft's manufacturing products continue to have limited success in penetrating the process-manufacturing base—mostly in the middle to low end of the spectrum. This may be why, with PeopleSoft 8, the company decided to call the product suite Supply Chain Management and to downplay the focus on manufacturing. PeopleSoft will focus on improving the supply chain for any organization.

Global Trends

As with the PeopleSoft Financials and HRMS, the Supply Chain Management area supports multi-currency, including euro currency conversion requirements as well as VAT requirements. The integration of the Vantive eCRM solution with sales, logistics, and order entry can provide a 360° customer viewpoint. Also, the CommerceOne eProcurement solution (which was released in early 2000) provides global Internet capabilities for buy-and-market sites. It also provides the ability to transfer stock between inventory business units using different currencies and supports the new commitment control functionality in PeopleSoft 8.

Internet Features

PeopleSoft's Supply Chain Management applications, which include sales and logistics, materials management, manufacturing, and supply chain planning, incorporate many e-commerce/Internet capabilities—specifically, the eProcurement and eStore capabilities. PeopleSoft first released eProcurement in June 1999 with a PeopleSoft-branded CommerceOne BuySite version 5; in PeopleSoft 8, eProcurement is now fully integrated with BuySite 6. Both eProcurement and eStore are fully integrated with PeopleSoft's Supply Chain Management and Financial applications. Other new features are Web-enabled requisition processing and tracking, receipt management, and inventory control.

Additional Internet integration functions on the manufacturing side include:

- ▶ Web-based catalogs for part location, with desired specifications, to support manufactured products

- ▶ Product management system integration using PeopleSoft's Application Messaging technology to publish messages to PeopleSoft

- ▶ Communications on production orders and schedules

- ▶ Automated data collection systems and devices for quality information, leveraging Web-based messaging for communications across products

This integration can help collect inspection data, assess controls, and return statistical results for use in quality control. In the engineering arena, leveraging the Internet to support inquiries, requests, and approvals can be an added advantage. The ability to view and suggest changes to BOM information by vendors as well as approve and change engineering requests results in a highly collaborative environment.

Finally, PeopleSoft's enhanced EDI/XML (Extensible Markup Language) solutions provide the integration framework to work in an Internet-based business world. Leveraging this XML technology allows new XML-based message formats for invoicing, sales orders, sales order acknowledgments, and advanced shipping notices.

Keys for the Future

PeopleSoft must leverage its current market base and expand its service offerings within those markets. It should focus on providing state-of-the-art solutions to those markets and delivering solutions on time. It should continue to leverage its flexibility, partnering approach, and "go-live-quickly" solutions. It should look at expanding its global reach, focusing on a particular market segment such as Europe.

With the renaming and consolidation of products within PeopleSoft 8 into a supply chain management focus, PeopleSoft has made it clear that it wants to optimize the supply chain yet continue to limit its reach in the manufacturing area. As mentioned above, the company has recategorized its distribution and manufacturing solutions into the following four major areas:

Sales and Logistics   eStore, Order Management, Billing, Product Configurator, and Remote Order Entry

Materials Management   eProcurement, Purchasing, and Inventory

Supply Chain Planning   Demand Planning, Inventory Planning, Enterprise Planning, and Order Promising

Manufacturing   Production Management, Quality, Engineering, Production Planning, and Cost Management

Market Analysis

PeopleSoft continues to be one of the leaders in the ERP market, competing directly with SAP and Oracle. In the middle-tier market, PeopleSoft also has serious competition from J.D. Edwards and Lawson. In addition, new niche players are sprouting up in each area; they are supported by the newer electronics-enabled technology, XML integration, and innovative Internet solutions. It's possible now to offer a single solution with multiple-point solutions without having the customer or user realize the mix.

PeopleSoft has had some stumbling blocks over the past year and a half with major changes in leadership, a lack of global focus, and a slow-to-market Internet solution. Now, with the release of PeopleSoft 8, PeopleSoft has the tools and the large client base that will be necessary to support the company in the future. Key partnerships and acquisitions such as Vantive and Commerce-One have helped position PeopleSoft better in the marketplace. We will have to see if the existing client base and quick transactions will help improve the company's market position beyond 2000. PeopleSoft appears to be ready for the long run but is still looking to prove its global capabilities as well as its ability to support manufacturing-based processes. It should remain strong in the services market, due especially to its recent industry solutions for banking, insurance, and professional services, as well as its solid track record with human resources, financial, and supply chain applications—core functions for these industry groups.

Up Next

You now have a better picture of what functionalities are supported by the PeopleSoft ERP application, where these application products are moving, and what the company's competition in the market is like. In the next chapter, "An Overview of the PeopleSoft Architecture," we'll look specifically at the technical architecture supported by the application and all the underlying features of the product line. PeopleSoft's strong programming tools, open architecture, and various reporting capabilities all support a robust enterprise solution. With the release of PeopleSoft 8, this technology architecture becomes even more important in leveraging the massive capabilities of the Internet, including key integration using XML.

CHAPTER 3

An Overview of the PeopleSoft Architecture

F E A T U R I N G :

- ▶ How PeopleSoft architecture differs from legacy systems
- ▶ Key features of versions 7, 7.5, and 8
- ▶ Key components of the architecture
- ▶ What is two-tier architecture and three-tier architecture?

- ▶ Deciding between two-tier and three-tier—which one is better for you?
- ▶ Third-party technical architecture tools
- ▶ Managing the enterprise architecture

This chapter outlines the basic technical architecture of the PeopleSoft ERP system. It looks at how PeopleSoft is different from other "older" systems, what key features and functions are available, and how to analyze which configuration option is best for your organization. It also gives an overview of the basic third-party tools to consider and discusses all architecture needed across your enterprise. The information contained in this chapter is relevant for all PeopleSoft implementations, as these tools are constant across the human resources, financials, and supply chain management products.

Differences from Legacy Systems

PeopleSoft's application differs from your internally developed, mainframe-type application systems, or legacy systems, in several ways. If you compare PeopleSoft to the traditional definition of the legacy system, the mainframe, these differences become obvious. The mainframe system is, in essence, a super server where all processing and data presentation occurs. Access to information is gained through what is commonly called a *dumb terminal*. This device consists of a monitor and an associated keyboard. The user session takes place on the mainframe, and the monitor is simply a "window" to this situation. These systems are generally based on a formatted sequential file that is scanned for specific records each time a request is made. Although these systems are generally speedy and reliable, they tend to be costly to purchase and maintain. Data is often difficult to access and requires the skills of a programmer to generate meaningful information.

By contrast, PeopleSoft employs a relational database in a two- or three-tier client-server environment. Now, with the use of the Internet and the creation of 100% Web applications, PeopleSoft has transitioned to what many term a "four-tier" application, where the fourth tier is merely a Web-based browser that accesses the three-tier architecture. This configuration distributes processing between the client workstation (PC or Mac) and the server(s). Data is passed to the client workstation, where it is interpreted and displayed to the user. Some computations may take place at this remote end and are then passed back to the server/database for storage. This environment takes advantage of the processing power that exists on the client workstation—power that is generally less expensive and simultaneously used for other applications by the user. The relational database employed for data storage grants information access to all users, not just those who are technically advanced. Figure 3.1 provides a general diagram of the basic PeopleSoft architecture.

Figure 3.1   **Overview of PeopleSoft three-tier architecture**

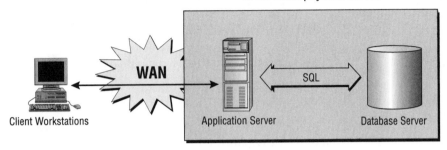

Application/database may be separate
or on same physical server.

WAN

SQL

Client Workstations   Application Server   Database Server

Relational Databases

The relational database is the source of power and flexibility behind the People-Soft system. Storing data in relational database tables offers several advantages over the sequential file format of most legacy systems used in the past. The most important is the ability to directly access desired information, rather than scanning a file in sequential order to locate it. Figure 3.2 demonstrates how easy it can be to retrieve information from a relational database.

Figure 3.2   **Example of relational database retrieval**

·Job Record Fields

Employee ID **30001**	**Job Code** **4005**	**Location Code** **6003**	**Salary Plan** **Mth01**	**Pay Group** **Biweekly**
↓	↓	↓	↓	↓
Linked to **Personal Data table** by Employee ID field, storing info. such as: • Name • Home address • Phone number	Linked to **Job Code table** by Job Code field, storing info. such as: • Job title • Job description • Job grade	Linked to **Location table** by Location Code field, storing info. such as: • Address • Bldg. number • Zip code	Linked to **Salary Admin table** by Salary Plan field, storing info. such as: • Salary grade • Salary amount • Salary frequency	Linked to **Pay Group table** by Pay Group field, storing info. such as: • Pay calendar • Pay cycle

Key field links tables so additional information is not stored over and over again on each table but as a reference to the first table.

Note: This is an example and does not necessarily match directly with PeopleSoft table layouts and field values.

A second advantage of the relational database is that it provides the ability to change the information that is stored without a great impact on the rest of the system. Adding a new field, or column of data, to a table generally will not require that each program in the application be modified to accommodate the change. In a mainframe environment, such modifications are often required. A relational database also permits the addition of new tables—ones that may relate to existing tables or be completely independent.

Another advantage is the ability to create database views. These objects can be thought of as a "window" to a database table. This window may be constructed to limit the amount of information a user sees, alter the format displayed, or combine information from several related tables.

This relational database platform permits PeopleSoft to develop an application that can run on several combinations of hardware, operating systems, and relational database engines, creating platform independence. The definitions for records (tables), panels (pages/screens), and the like are stored in the database itself, enabling the application to migrate from one environment (development) to another (production), even if they reside on different database servers. This feature also permits users to make modifications to a development environment without affecting the production environment. The record and panel (page) definitions may be altered, but the common executable program remains unchanged.

Web Access

With PeopleSoft 8 and the use of the Web, users now have access to the application via a Web-based browser (such as Netscape or Internet Explorer). This capability enables the enterprise to distribute the application over an intranet or, in some instances, the Internet. The advantage of this capability is reduced maintenance and distribution costs. This option reduces maintenance costs because it requires less effort in configuring each client workstation. PeopleSoft application information and database access drivers need not be installed on the client machine. Distribution costs can be lowered because the need for direct access to the server via a wide area network (WAN) may be removed for some users of the system. Prior releases of PeopleSoft's PeopleTools, the technical portion of the application, supported browser access to particular functions; however, release 7.55 of PeopleTools expanded this to the entire application. PeopleSoft 8 supports HTML-enabled panels (a "cleaner" Web interface), as well as XML (Extensible Markup Language) integration tools. Figure 3.3 illustrates the Web access architecture around PeopleSoft.

Figure 3.3   **Web architecture**

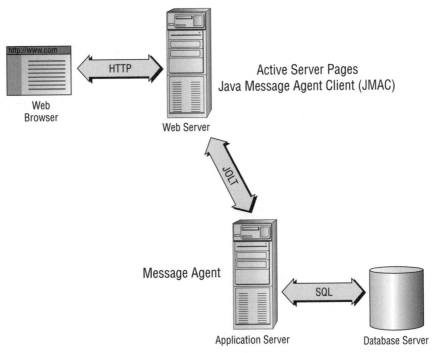

PeopleSoft and Batch Processing

Although the PeopleSoft application was developed to replace the legacy systems of yesterday, it continues to utilize some of the ideas that were developed in the mainframe environment. As a general rule, legacy systems were capable only of performing batch processing. A day's orders were captured in the system during the day and processed at night as a "batch." This processing moves information from the order to the inventory/distribution process (among others) for fulfillment. This type of processing was required by the system because the processing programs needed exclusive access to the file to work properly. Changes to the file during such a process could generate a myriad of issues.

PeopleSoft, in some cases, utilizes batch processing for those functions that require extensive calculation, validation, or migration of data between tables. These batch processes are performed by modules developed in one of the following tools: COBOL, SQR, or Application Engine (a PeopleSoft proprietary scripting language). They are generally executed in batch mode at different times of the day or overnight. The relational database environment doesn't require that modification of data be put on hold; rather, it processes only those records in the appropriate tables that were marked for processing at the inception of the program. The calculation and validation of data is performed online if it's considered critical to do so; however, as a general rule, these functions are executed in batch mode.

Work Flow

Another advantage of the PeopleSoft relational database structure is the ability to configure work-flow processing. This function allows a client to configure the system to assist in streamlining tasks by removing the flow of paper that supports a particular task. For example, a client may choose to route a work-list item (i.e., an item from a list of work to be performed by an individual) to a supervisor if an entry exceeds a pre-established threshold. This function removes the manual labor involved in delivering an approval form to the supervisor for verification and signature. In addition, it improves both the efficiency and the security of the process itself since it happens electronically and the supervisor must review the entry (as opposed to the form that represents the entry).

Figure 3.4 shows an example of a work flow–enabled process. PeopleSoft has several such processes already configured within the application, such as in the purchasing, new hire, and evaluation processes. However, by using the tools provided by the application, a company can set up virtually any work flow–enabled process for its organization. These tools are very powerful in enabling processes based on events (such as hiring a new employee or requesting some supplies) and triggering actions to occur. Work flow also helps to reduce cycle times, facilitate paperless processes, and improve work distribution.

Figure 3.4 **Example of a business process with work flow**

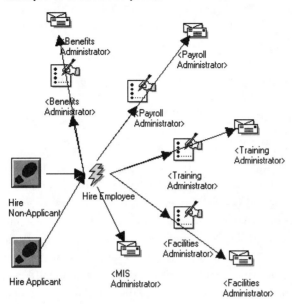

Engines Supported

PeopleSoft supports a number of relational database engines. It certifies that its application will perform on several combinations of operating system software and relational database software. Currently, the most popular combinations are Oracle on a Unix operating system and either Microsoft's SQL Server or Oracle on a Windows NT operating system. (Please don't consider these options as a recommendation of this book, but simply a statement of current trends. Each organization should evaluate its current initiatives and capabilities and make a decision with respect to future strategies.) PeopleSoft also offers the following database platforms:

► DB2/MVS

► DB2 UDB for A/X

► DB2 for OS/390

► Oracle

► Microsoft SQL Server

► Informix

► Sybase

► SQLBase (Single User Only)

PeopleSoft does not specifically certify hardware platforms, although it has performed benchmark testing for some product lines at the request of the manufacturers. In general, the application will run on any server that is capable of running Unix, Novell, or Windows NT operating systems. Please check PeopleSoft's Web site at www.peoplesoft.com for more information on this topic.

Does the Database/Platform Matter?

PeopleSoft is certified for installation on a number of hardware and operating system software platforms, including a DB2 relational database on a mainframe "server," an Oracle database on a Unix server, and an SQL Server database on a Windows NT server, to name a few. The selection of the hardware and operating system is largely one of client preference and does not affect the functionality of the PeopleSoft application. If an organization uses Oracle on a Unix server, for example, to manage its manufacturing and logistics, it would likely choose this same combination for its PeopleSoft implementation, thus taking advantage of the technical skills that the organization already possesses. Another factor to consider is the required response time for the system and the expected workload. The organization might consider a different combination if the PeopleSoft system is expected to handle a workload that is significantly higher or lower than that of the organization's other systems. There are trade-offs to be considered for each platform. Platforms that are capable of supporting a larger workload tend to be easier to maintain and tune than those that support a lower throughput. However, the maintenance and tuning effort depends heavily on your expertise and knowledge of the specific platform and database architecture. Time and effort should be expended in researching and determining the appropriate platform for you.

Key factors that should be considered to help determine the appropriate platform include, but are not limited to:

- ▶ Volume size/number of transactions processed
- ▶ Number of users
- ▶ Amount of history stored
- ▶ Skills available within the organization
- ▶ Skills available in the local support market

- ▶ Number of other PeopleSoft clients with similar needs/industry standards

- ▶ Prior vendor relationships or organization-based contracts

- ▶ Customer support/satisfaction (get list of current PeopleSoft customers for the platforms being considered)

- ▶ Price

Also look at any benchmarks that may have been developed for your desired platform and database configuration. PeopleSoft has a myriad of benchmarking results on its Web site. Also, you can ask each of your vendors to provide benchmarking results to help aid in your decision-making process.

Features of Versions 7 and 7.5

PeopleSoft version 7 introduced the programming tool Application Designer, which permits the developer to view multiple objects (see Architecture Components: PeopleTools) in a single window. Previous versions utilized different tools, or windows, to view different objects. Version 7 also introduced the Data Mover tool, which allows migration of PeopleSoft data from one database to another, independent of the platform.

PeopleSoft version 7.5 represented the company's initial move toward enabling its application via the Web. It utilized a configurable Java applet to permit access to selected functions. This applet could be modified to enable most of the simple functions of PeopleSoft, but it had limitations. Release 7.55 of PeopleTools delivered all panels to the browser and completed the application's initial migration to the Internet.

PeopleSoft 8 Features

PeopleSoft 8 is a step forward for the application with respect to Web enablement. This release delivers PeopleSoft "panels" (now called pages) in HTML format and provides for a true Internet look and feel. It also introduces several new capabilities in application integration. It's capable of exchanging messages with other systems in real time, or almost real time, using XML technology. This improvement should prove valuable to organizations as they look to gain more from their ERP solutions.

Architecture Components

This section covers the basic architecture components that are found in the PeopleSoft application system. Each area is reviewed and discussed to provide you with basic understanding of these components.

PeopleTools

PeopleTools, a term referred to previously in this text, represents several things. The most common application of the term is to reference the toolset with which PeopleSoft applications were developed. This toolset is encompassed in Application Designer (Home ➤ PeopleTools ➤ Application Designer) and permits the user to access and modify most of the PeopleSoft-delivered functions. PeopleTools is also capable of developing new objects that can be considered extensions of the core product. A list of the objects (and related tools) and a subsequent detailed description of each of their related attributes follow.

- ▶ Field definition
- ▶ Record definition
- ▶ PeopleCode
- ▶ Panel definition (or, with PeopleSoft 8, page definition)
- ▶ Panel group definition (or, with PeopleSoft 8, page group definition)
- ▶ Menu definition
- ▶ Business process design (work flow)
- ▶ Project definition

Other PeopleTools functions generally used to support the movement of data for conversions or interfaces are listed below and explained in subsequent sections.

- ▶ Data Mover
- ▶ Import Manager
- ▶ COBOL
- ▶ Application Engine

Additional tools to support reporting, such as SQR, Query, Crystal Report Writer, nVision, Essbase, and Cognos PowerPlay, are also covered in the sections below. Finally, a summary of the new PeopleSoft 8 integration tools is provided, allowing you to leverage the integrative power of the Internet.

Field Definition

The field definition is the base object in PeopleTools and is universal throughout the PeopleSoft system. A field may be defined as a character field, length 30, that permits mixed (alphanumeric, upper- and lowercase) data entry. If the length or description of the field is altered, this change will be reflected on each record definition that contains that particular field. Translate values, the valid code values for a specific field and the descriptive translations of those codes, may be defined at the field level. For example, a status field may possess the following valid codes (with descriptions): N (New), P (Pending), C (Complete), etc. In order for a field to have translate values, it must be defined as a character field and have a length less than 5.

Record Definition

The object of primary importance that can be viewed or modified with Application Designer is the record definition. The record definition is composed of field definitions—objects that determine the characteristics of each column on a table. This object is used for several purposes:

▶ Database table definition

▶ Database view definition

▶ Non-database work record definition

It also acts as a storage mechanism for PeopleSoft's proprietary PeopleCode modules.

A field within a record definition may be designated as a key, alternate search key, duplicate order key, or list box item. The key designation indicates to PeopleSoft, and the underlying relational database, that this field (or combination of fields) indicates a unique row of information. For example, if ID is the only field on a record specified as a key, then each row in the table contains a unique value in the ID field. Key fields will appear in a dialog box as a search parameter if the record is used as a search record. Alternate search keys will also appear in the dialog box and permit users to search for information based on the particular field. It is not used, however, to designate unique rows in the table. List box item fields are those that appear in a second dialog box when a user is searching for a row of information but has not specified the values of the unique key.

Record definitions also hold information regarding field-level validation. The valid values for a particular field may be stored in a different table. For example, valid VENDOR_ID values may be stored in the VENDOR table. An entry that is associated with a vendor should not allow an invalid VENDOR_ID. The record definition permits the field to have a corresponding prompt table (a table from which to chose specific values). In the example, the VENDOR_ID field would have the VENDOR table as its prompt table. This designation, along with the panel (screen or Web page) design, helps to maintain referential integrity in the database. Referential integrity is the concept that related tables contain the required related rows and that they contain valid information to "tie" them together (i.e., both the VENDOR table and the VENDOR_ADDRESS table contain the same VENDOR_ID for a particular vendor's information).

PeopleCode

PeopleCode will also be defined at the record level. It is associated with a particular field and PeopleCode event (which determines when the code is executed) on the record. This code may be used to validate data that has been entered for several fields (field combination validation) or to set a value for a field based on the value entered for another. It may also be used to perform calculations and display values to the user or as a means for setting a default value for a field. Additionally, PeopleCode is the driver behind PeopleSoft's work-flow functionality, which we will discuss in further detail later in this text.

Panel or Page Definition

The Application Designer is also utilized to define the panels, or screens, that users will see when they work with the PeopleSoft application. (With People-Soft 8, a panel is now referred to as a "page.") Fields from specified records are placed on the panel in the desired order, and several attributes may be defined for them (such as enterable or display only). A panel may permit users to add new rows of data to the database, or it may be intended for inquiry only. Another purpose of creating a panel is to capture parameters for a report or process.

When building a new panel or modifying an existing one, several rules must be followed to maintain the integrity of the data that is entered. These rules are the most common ones:

► Fields from only one table may appear within an occurs level unless:

  ► It is a "related-display" field.

  ► It is a translation from the XLATTABLE.

► If a scroll bar exists, the table "inside" the scroll bar must be a child record of the lower occurs table.

Note   With PeopleSoft 8 and its use of pages, scroll bars are not used. Rather, insert push-button keys are on the page to indicate addition of new data.

Panel Group or Page Group Definition

The Application Designer is also used to define *panel groups* (or *page groups* with PeopleSoft 8). This object definition captures the panels that are related to one another or, in some cases, identifies a single panel to be accessed independent of others. This definition also indicates the search record—the record definition that determines the prompt fields—for the panel group. The panel group is also the definition that ties panels to the desired menu option.

Menu Definition

Menu definitions may also be created or modified using the Application Designer. A developer may choose to add a new panel group to an existing menu by creating a new menu item. An entirely new menu may also be created to contain any collection of custom panel groups in a single repository.

Business Process Design

Other objects that may be modified through the Application Designer include business processes and business process maps. These objects are used for two purposes: to define the work-flow process and to define a user process for a particular function (e.g., the steps involved in the new-hire process). This in essence is a visual picture of the steps to go through for a business process, helping you navigate through the PeopleSoft system.

Project Definition

Finally, the Application Designer is used to establish PeopleTools projects (not to be confused with the Financials/Projects module). A *project* is a collection of objects that are related to each other. For example, a developer would create a project to bundle the objects created or changed for a modification to the delivered application. The project is the focal point for migration of PeopleTools objects from one database to another. To duplicate the changes that the developer made in the development database to the test database, the project would be "upgraded" from the source (development) environment to the target (test) environment. Any new objects would be recreated in the target database. Any existing objects would be replaced in the target environment with the modified definition from the source environment. The project, like a subdirectory, is a tool that serves many purposes: It helps in retrieving frequently accessed objects, housekeeping, and preparing for a database migration.

PeopleSoft utilizes the project definition to group together changes that have been made to PeopleTools to resolve a particular issue. These are generally referred to as Application Updates and Fixes and are distributed to clients via the Internet and/or compact disc. They are applied through Data Mover to a PeopleTools-only database (commonly identified by the "AU" that appears in the database name, for example, HRAU and FSAU) to prevent corruption of data that would exist in an "application" database. These changes are then "upgraded" to the application databases that exist through the Application Designer.

Other PeopleSoft Data and Interface Tools

In addition to the powerful PeopleTools, there are other programming tools found within the PeopleSoft application or bundled with the package that can be very helpful to an implementation or upgrade project in building interfaces, converting data, and generating reports. These tools are explained in the following sections.

Data Mover

PeopleSoft's *Data Mover* product is a powerful, stand-alone executable tool that provides PeopleSoft developers with the ability to selectively migrate data between PeopleSoft database environments. For example, a user may export all vendor-related tables for all vendors or for only those vendors that are located in a particular state. This data may then be loaded into a second database, avoiding the need for a full-table duplication. Data Mover may also be used to execute SQL (Structured Query Language) statements against the database—specifically, to insert, update, and delete statements. For this reason, access to the Data Mover tool should be granted only in certain situations.

Import Manager

The *Import Manager* tool is a portion of the PeopleTools toolset. This product permits the import of data from a flat file directly to a PeopleSoft table. The user may insert "default" values into fields as needed to fill the data gaps that may exist between PeopleSoft and a legacy system. Import Manager performs the same edits that would occur during an online transaction entry, preventing the user from loading invalid data. The user may execute this edit process multiple times without loading the data to ensure that all records will load properly. Once the file has passed edits, it can be loaded to the table with a higher level of confidence. The Import Manager tool allows only one table to be loaded at a time; thus, a user must be aware of table-load-sequencing requirements. Some tables are dependent on others for data validation and may be loaded only after those that they depend on.

COBOL

Despite the opinions of some that COBOL is an outdated language, PeopleSoft utilizes the programming language to handle most of the calculation-intensive processing chores. (PeopleSoft 8, however, leverages the use of XML and C++ code much more than the process-intensive COBOL language.) These programs tend to be highly modularized and therefore difficult to read and understand. This is one of the reasons that modification to these programs is discouraged. Another, and perhaps more compelling, reason is the potential for creating support issues. If a COBOL module has been modified, PeopleSoft support analysts may point to that change (one not developed by PeopleSoft) as the reason for the problem a client reports, which may or may not be the case. Understandably, PeopleSoft does not want to use valuable support efforts in debugging developments of others.

One unique aspect of PeopleSoft's COBOL modules is the storage of SQL statements within the database itself (some statements are not stored in this way, but generated by accessing record definitions stored elsewhere in the database). This structure allows the COBOL module to call to a specific table in the database to retrieve the statement required. It also allows PeopleSoft to make changes to processing without necessarily changing the COBOL code itself. In addition, this construct removes the SQL from the COBOL code and simplifies the compile processing required for programs written in this language; this also permits the COBOL code and compiler to be database independent.

Application Engine

Application Engine is a PeopleSoft-developed function that combines COBOL with an SQL-like scripting tool. It uses a standard COBOL program as a "driver" for the script that is defined through specific PeopleSoft panels. This tool is used to perform some of the processes that involve data manipulation and has replaced several COBOL-only modules in previous releases. It can be modified more easily than the delivered COBOL modules and doesn't require clients to perform the compile process to complete the changes. Like COBOL, Application Engine scripts are modularized, but they may be more easily accessed and reviewed. They are fairly difficult to understand if the script is a lengthy one, given the frequent use of variables that may be set throughout the script.

SQR

SQR, *Structured Query Report Writer*, is a third-party language that PeopleSoft utilizes for both processing and reporting. This tool is based on a programming language that is somewhat similar to both Visual Basic and COBOL; however, it's an interpreted language and doesn't require compiling prior to execution. SQR is capable of accessing and updating database tables, and reading and writing flat files for interfacing, as well as printing reports. It's occasionally used by PeopleSoft for processing purposes but is often used for interfacing with other applications and generating more complex, logic-based, reports. Since SQR is used extensively throughout the PeopleSoft application, an understanding of this tool is important for your technical resources.

PeopleSoft Query

PeopleSoft Query is a delivered tool that permits users and developers access to PeopleSoft tables and views. PeopleSoft delivers several standard queries and allows the creation and "publication" of custom queries as well. Access to tables and views may be restricted through security features of the tool, creating a secure online reporting environment and reducing the number of printed reports generated by the system. The Query tool enables nontechnical users in creating their own reports, as it permits the creation of an SQL-based query without the knowledge of SQL syntax. An understanding of the tables, views, and fields desired are all that the user requires to create a query.

The Query tool delivers the ability to "export" results retrieved from the database to either of two third-party applications: Microsoft Excel and Seagate Crystal Reports. Data in Excel may be manipulated through sorting, subtotals, etc., for electronic or printed presentation to others. Crystal Reports may be used to create a formatted report that will be linked to a particular query and executed through an option on an application menu. Vendor checks are produced through a Query/Crystal Report in the PeopleSoft Financials/Accounts Payable module.

Crystal Report Writer

Another report-generating software package that's delivered with the People-Soft applications is Crystal Report Writer. Although this tool can be used with other applications and databases, PeopleSoft has provided several prepackaged reports, thereby leveraging this tool for its users. The tool is effective for basic report writing that doesn't involve a lot of complicated SQL statements or programming-type functions. For basic report writing, it's highly effective and easy to use. Most end users can use this tool to generate very attractive reports.

nVision

PeopleSoft has developed a reporting tool called *nVision* that is integrated with Microsoft Excel. This flexible tool is generally used for reporting that is based on PeopleSoft Trees. *PeopleSoft Trees* are a hierarchical (and graphical) representation of data elements, showing a reporting structure or "roll-up" feature that helps to summarize information. The flexibility of nVision permits the development of a report that remains static. The results of the report generated, however, may be changed by modifying the tree structure with which the report is associated. For example, an income statement may be modified by altering the structure of the account roll-up tree. This functionality also provides clients with the ability to perform "what-if" reporting. They're able to produce two reports that differ only in the way the entities (accounts, departments, etc.) relate to each other. nVision takes advantage of the relational database platform, PeopleSoft's flexible tree manager, and the Microsoft Excel delivered functionality.

Red Pepper

PeopleSoft incorporates *Red Pepper's* manufacturing and logistics package into its manufacturing application. Red Pepper was originally a stand-alone product. PeopleSoft recognized the need for a more robust offering in this area and teamed with Red Pepper to integrate the functionality developed by Red Pepper into the PeopleSoft product.

Essbase

Hyperion's *Essbase* multidimensional database tool is the basis for People-Soft's Budgets module. Budget data is entered and reviewed in this third-party online analytical processing (OLAP) application, then downloaded to the PeopleSoft General Ledger module for comparison reporting. Essbase permits users to view information in a number of ways, allowing them to specify how they would like to view the data. For example, budget information may be viewed simultaneously by account, department, and time period.

PowerPlay

Cognos *PowerPlay* is a second multidimensional database tool that PeopleSoft has incorporated into its product offering for desktop analytical reporting. It isn't currently integrated to the degree that Essbase is; however, future releases will likely take advantage of this OLAP tool.

New Integration Tools with PeopleSoft 8

PeopleSoft 8 provides several new applications that support true Internet-based integration, leveraging the Internet standards such as XML and HTTP. The Internet-based computing platform supports the open flow of information between systems. PeopleSoft's Internet architecture delivers four integration technologies that support the full spectrum of integration, both within and outside the company:

Application Messaging This is the "publish and subscribe," or XML-formatted, technology that supports Internet-based messaging on the Internet. PeopleSoft's application-messaging capability supports integration across multiple systems (PeopleSoft and other third-party systems). Subscribing applications can receive transactions over the

Internet, providing an open-environment framework for internal systems integration as well as EDI and business-to-business integration over the Internet.

Component Interfaces   This integration technology provides real-time, synchronous access to PeopleSoft business rules and to data from external applications in a truly object-oriented manner. This new tool is primarily used within PeopleSoft 8 to integrate PeopleSoft business logic with Internet-based applications using standard Web-authoring tools (i.e., incorporating PeopleSoft transactions into a company's Web site).

Business Interlinks   With the increasingly widespread availability of Internet-enabled application programming interfaces (APIs) for third-party systems to support customer requirements, PeopleSoft's Business Interlinks invokes business logic in third-party applications within PeopleSoft. Business Interlinks, the converse of Component Interfaces, provides a framework that enables customers to extend their PeopleSoft applications to easily invoke third-party systems, using a broad set of technologies such as XML, HTTP, Java, COM (Component Object Model), and CORBA (Common Object Request Broker Architecture).

Application Engine   With PeopleSoft 8, the Application Engine has been completely rewritten to better support more file-based integration, still a very popular means of integration. The newly enhanced Application Engine includes an Application Designer–based development environment and PeopleCode support. Application Engine via PeopleCode enables developers to implement a number of high-volume file-processing options—including sophisticated data mapping, transformation, and validation functionality—prior to committing transactions. Application Engine via PeopleCode can process files that are formatted in either XML or more traditional file formats (e.g., fixed-length and delimited text files) to provide a wealth of options for assisting customers with integrating their legacy applications and trading-partner systems.

Two-Tier Architecture

This section will cover the basic architecture structure for a PeopleSoft two-tier configuration. Both the client and server configurations will be discussed, as well as the basic components.

Client Configuration

The two-tier architecture was the basis for PeopleSoft's initial client-server application. The database was resident on the server, along with COBOL and SQR modules, while the executable and related files were installed and executed on the client workstation. This model evolved, and the executables were moved to the network server and shared by all users with access rights to the specified drive.

Although this approach improved security and simplified maintenance to some degree, it presented the possibility of a negative impact on performance. If the network doesn't have sufficient bandwidth and throughput between the user and the server, the user may experience slower system response times. For example, if a user accesses PeopleSoft via a wide area network, the executable (in particular) tends to perform poorly at start-up. If the executable is copied to a network server that is in close proximity to the user, performance may improve dramatically. Cacheing (copying object information from the server to the client workstation) will not be affected by this "fix" and may continue to create performance issues. This problem may improve over time since the user will cache most of the object definition information to the workstation during the first few days of operation.

In a two-tier architecture, the client workstation stores information about the particular user and their preferences (Configuration Manager), as well as the cached information about the PeopleTools object definitions. The Configuration Manager allows the user to specify the default database and username and the initial menu they prefer. It can be set to allow tracing of SQL and COBOL as well as PeopleCode programs. It also specifies several technical environment variables including, but not limited to, the following: location of COBOL executables, location of SQR programs and reports, location of Crystal Reports, location of database drivers, and addresses of application servers.

Server Configuration

In a two-tier architecture, there may be two servers—one for the relational database engine and one for shared program storage. With a Unix-based relational database, there will most likely be two different machines to handle these functions. With a Windows NT or Novell-based relational database, these functions may be performed by the same physical machine. The executable and related files must be accessible from the client workstation and must be compatible with the client operating system. Other files, such as COBOL and SQR programs, may reside on the same machine as the database engine (in addition to the server that hosts the executables).

Diagram of Components

Figure 3.5 illustrates a typical PeopleSoft two-tier architecture. The database server is usually a machine that is dedicated solely for this purpose and is normally configured to handle a heavy workload. It contains a large amount of hard disk storage and random access memory (RAM). It may also contain multiple processors to increase throughput. The network server is usually one that is already in place within the organization, and a portion of the server's disk space is dedicated to the PeopleSoft application. The client workstation requires a fairly fast processor and an adequate amount of RAM as well.

Figure 3.5   **Two-tier architecture**

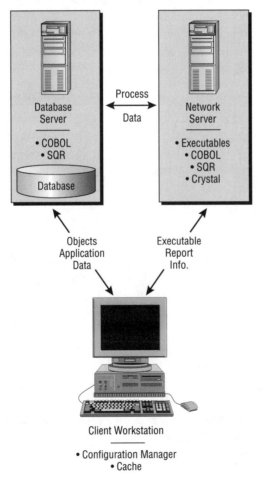

Please review the minimum requirements for both client and database servers on PeopleSoft's Web site. Note that PeopleSoft 8 does not allow users to access the application using a two-tier architecture.

Support and Staffing

Support for the two-tier architecture is fairly minimized. A qualified database administrator (DBA) is required to perform backups, tune the database for the application, and troubleshoot issues with the database. Depending on the size of the organization and consequently the size of the database, this role can range from a part-time exercise for an onsite DBA to one that requires several DBAs for proper maintenance. Network specialists may be utilized if a network problem is discovered; however, they tend to get involved infrequently. A user support staff is needed to answer questions from field personnel—again the size of this group is dependent on the total number of users and the degree to which the application has been customized.

Three-Tier Architecture

The three-tier architecture is another configuration option for the PeopleSoft applications. Introduced with PeopleSoft version 7.0, this option can provide many advantages in performance over the two-tier model. Use of the People-Tools featured in PeopleSoft 8 must be accomplished using the three-tier architecture configuration. Because the user access to PeopleSoft 8 is through a Web browser and is 100% Internet based, the addition of this configuration may be termed a four-tier architecture. The following sections will explain the basic components of this configuration as well as the basic benefits of using it.

Client Configuration

The three-tier architecture is PeopleSoft's recommended structure. The database is resident on the server, while the executable and related files are installed and executed on the network file server. The application server (BEA's Tuxedo) is another piece of software that runs on a separate machine, either physically or logically, and thereby improves system performance. Cacheing of object information is minimized between the server and the client workstation. Rather, this information is stored on the application server for open access to all who log on. This prevents slow response times due to object definitions being downloaded, improving the overall efficiency of the system. Individuals may detect a degradation in performance; however, overall performance for a large audience should improve.

PeopleSoft uses a cacheing scheme in an attempt to minimize network traffic created by sending object definition information to the client workstation. When a user accesses a panel (or page) group for the first time, the related object definitions (records, panels, fields, etc.) are downloaded to the application server's hard drive and stored in the form of cache files. This information remains there until one or more of the objects is modified on the server. When the user accesses this panel group, the application compares the version number on each object on the server with that on the client workstation. If they differ, the new version of the object is downloaded to the workstation to replace the old one. Once object cacheing has occurred, the only information that needs to be transmitted between the two machines is the application data.

Server Configuration

Figure 3.6 illustrates a typical PeopleSoft three-tier architecture. The database server is usually a machine that is dedicated solely for this purpose and is normally configured to handle a heavy workload. It contains a large amount of hard disk storage and RAM. It may also contain multiple processors to increase throughput. The application server is also a machine that is dedicated for its purpose. Even though it doesn't require a large amount of disk storage, multiple processors and a large amount of RAM are recommended. The three-tier architecture is a two-tier architecture with the addition of an applications server, which may reside on either a dedicated machine or an existing file server. The network server is usually one that is already in place within the organization, and a portion of the server's disk space is dedicated to the PeopleSoft application. The client workstation requires a fairly fast processor and an adequate amount of RAM and hard disk space as well. The three-tier architecture reduces the workload placed on the client and minimizes the impact of older client configurations.

Please review the minimum requirements for both client and database servers on PeopleSoft's Web site.

Figure 3.6 **Three-tier architecture**

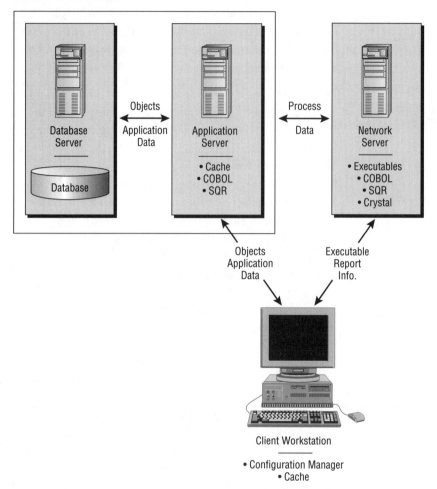

In Figure 3.6, the box encompassing the database server and the application server indicates that the configuration shown, physical three-tier, could be constructed as a logical three-tier environment. In a logical three-tier environment, both the database engine and the Tuxedo application server reside on the same physical server. Although this approach is less costly, it may not offer the performance levels achievable with the physical three-tier model because the same processor that services files must take on additional tasks.

Other Servers

The file server, database server, and application server have already been discussed in conjunction with the two- and three-tier architectures. Another server that may be deployed with the PeopleSoft application is the Web server, which with PeopleSoft 8 is a required configuration. Similar to the application server, this server is an executable and may be implemented on one of the existing physical machines or on a separate piece of hardware. It is used to enable the browser accessibility that PeopleSoft delivers for application deployment over the Internet (or intranet).

Support and Staffing

Use of the Web server doesn't require any additional software (besides the browser software such as Internet Explorer or Netscape) to be resident on a user's workstation. This greatly reduces the amount of support necessary for an end user's workstation. Since the user is basically accessing one page of data at a time, the overhead requirements for the user are minimal. Also, the desktop doesn't have to be a Windows-based system; it can be a Macintosh system. However, it's essential to monitor the load of your Web servers, based on the volume of users and the type of access they have to your application. Most of your workload is processed on your application server, and so it, too, must be monitored closely and sized properly. The use of remote support staff at sites where your users are based is less of an issue with the new Web-based applications. Support may be accomplished from a remote location, leveraging a shared-services environment.

Deciding between Two and Three Tiers

With PeopleSoft 8, there really is no decision to be made between the two- and three-tier architectures—you must have the three-tier configuration (and then the Web four-tier architecture) in place. However, if you are implementing PeopleSoft version 7.5, you have to make this decision. In this section we'll look at how to decide whether the two-tier or three-tier configuration is better for your environment. We'll cover some key decision criteria, discuss some things to look out for, and also address the recent impact of the Web.

Decision Criteria

PeopleSoft recommends that clients deploy the application to users utilizing the three-tier architecture. The primary advantage to this structure is increased performance. In environments where network bandwidth is at a premium, the difference between the two options with respect to response times is noticeable. Some functionalities are available only in the three-tier mode, as are all the Web-based functions.

The three-tier structure adds an additional layer of complexity (compared to a two-tier deployment), and thus the potential for additional maintenance. It also adds some effort to the installation process, since an application server must be configured for each database copy, or instance, that will be accessed in this mode. The three-tier access workstation configuration may be simplified if the user will not be executing SQR or COBOL programs, Crystal Reports, or nVision reports on the client machine. These processes connect to the database directly (similar to two-tier mode) and require the installation and configuration of the database drivers on the workstation. This additional software on the client workstation may generate additional maintenance tasks when new versions of the drivers are released. If the user is not expected to perform these tasks, then the potential for additional maintenance may be avoided by not installing these drivers. Access to the system in three-tier mode does not require these drivers because the communication to the database is being performed by the application server on behalf of the end user.

The two-tier architecture is recommended for use by developers and application support personnel. This mode of access permits a more controlled environment for developing modifications and new functionality in People-Tools, as well as debugging the online application and batch processes. This configuration requires the installation and configuration of the database drivers on the workstation; however, the benefits far outweigh the costs of maintenance.

What to Look Out For

When implementing a PeopleSoft solution, as with most package applications, it is recommended that the delivered functionality be used as much as possible. Although the application provides the capability to make changes with relative ease, modifications to the application to meet a requirement can be costly. These changes require additional effort on the part of the implementation team to design, develop, test, and deploy. They also add to maintenance costs in several ways. If the changes made to the system are significant, the support personnel may experience problems when requesting help from PeopleSoft. If PeopleSoft personnel are unable to duplicate the problem on their support system, it is often difficult or impossible for them to help the client resolve the problem. Modifications to the delivered software also add a layer of complexity to the upgrade process. They must be considered on an individual basis to determine how, or if, they will be applied in the "new" environment. Because PeopleSoft cannot predict the modifications that will be made to the system, allowances for major processing changes are seldom made.

For these reasons, it's imperative that each proposed modification to the system be reviewed to determine the true business need that is served by the change. When an individual who is requesting a system modification is asked to support the desire and provide the argument for incorporation of the modification into the new system, the request will often be withdrawn. Changes to the system should never be made without some review by management. When the initial and long-term costs of a modification are weighed against the functionality that is provided, only those changes that are truly necessary will be approved and completed.

If your organization requires a modification to the system, there are a few guidelines to consider. If possible, do not change a delivered record definition to remove or add fields. Fields should not be added to a record and should never be removed from a record, since this may create issues with batch processing. A field may be effectively removed by providing a default value and setting it as hidden on the appropriate panel (screen or Web page). Rather than add a field to a delivered record, consider creating a new child record to capture this information. The child record will have the same key fields as the original record, plus one additional field, and may be placed on the original panel (screen or Web page) with the other fields from the record by using a hidden scroll bar.

If the addition of a field to a record will not affect batch processing (thorough research should be conducted to confirm this), then the original record should be copied prior to making the modification. Opening the record definition with the Application Designer and performing a save-as process will accomplish this. During this process, it is recommended that the "new" record be saved with a name that identifies it as an original record. Adding a prefix to the original name that will be used to indicate all such record modifications will facilitate the identification of these changes during an upgrade. A similar approach should be applied to panel, panel group, menu, query, and business process definition modifications. For modifications to PeopleCode, SQR, and COBOL modules, comments should be placed in the code that indicate the developer, date, and purpose of the changes. An identifying character combination that remains constant, such as the organization's initials, should be included as well. A search of the appropriate directories for the existence of this character combination will return all modules that have been modified. Saving the original module with a naming convention similar to that described above is also recommended.

Impact of the Web

The Internet has had a profound impact on business and, likewise, on client-server software organizations such as PeopleSoft. As the growth and use of the Internet continue, businesses are demanding more functionalities and capabilities that take advantage of this network.

PeopleSoft has made a commitment to migrate its applications for distribution to users through the Internet. With PeopleSoft 8, the PeopleSoft user-based applications are completely Web based and must be configured using the four-tier architecture explained above (with the three-tier setup and a Web server or servers). PeopleTools are still maintained in the three-tier environment and must be accessed through a Windows desktop computer.

This move to the Web reduces the costs of deployment and maintenance, especially for organizations that are geographically dispersed, since individual desktop support for the applications are no longer necessary; all that resides on the user's desktop is a Web browser. Because almost all of the application and processing is now based on the application server, you must be sure to size and monitor this server adequately. Core support for your applications should be focused as closely as possible to the applications and database servers. Remote user access should be sufficient for supporting your customers with PeopleSoft 8.

Integrating Third-Party Tools with PeopleSoft

Although PeopleSoft has robust functionality and tools, there are several areas that may require integration of third-party tools to meet the needs of your organization. This section will look at the integration capabilities and possible solutions for your PeopleSoft environment.

A variety of third-party tools are integrated with PeopleSoft. These tools include conversion and integration applications, reporting applications, and document scanning and storage applications. Other "bolt-on" applications exist; however, the majority of these on the market fall into one of those three categories. For applications that are not integrated "out of the box," integration with PeopleSoft has been somewhat difficult prior to PeopleSoft 8. Generally, flat files are utilized to interface the system with other applications, although some of these functions may be achieved through database scripts and links. The tools needed to move information into or out of PeopleSoft are delivered for some purposes, but the majority are custom-developed programs. PeopleSoft 8 adds new functionality in this area with the implementation of XML publish-and-subscribe capabilities, which are enabled by the new Component Interfaces, Business Interlinks, and Application Messaging features, as well as the updated Application Engine, as previously described.

PeopleSoft also has a wealth of software "partners" that offer preconfigured integration with the PeopleSoft products out of the box. A list of these products can be found on PeopleSoft's Web page under the software alliance category. Common integration occurs around resume scanning with applications such as WebHire or Resumix and around time-entry devices such as Kronos and TimeCorp. Other common areas of integration include scanning or imaging tools such as Documentum in the accounts payable area, as well as sales tax data leveraging packages such as Vertex. Also, hand-held devices or scanners are commonly integrated for inventory control. Chapter 11, "Converting Data and Developing an Interface," looks at the interface and conversion tools that can be used in conjunction with a PeopleSoft implementation, while Chapter 14, "Testing," covers the automation testing tools that can be considered.

Managing the Enterprise

To ensure that you're effectively managing your PeopleSoft technical environment, you must have the appropriate skilled and trained people as well as the proper tools and techniques to monitor system performance and support.

Staffing for These Models

Support staffing for a PeopleSoft environment is largely dependent on the size of the organization, the number of modules implemented, and the number of users who will access the system. Smaller organizations will generally require a 10:1 ratio of users to support staff, while a larger organization may have a 20:1 ratio. A thorough understanding of the organization's requirements should be acquired prior to making support staffing decisions based on current support models and future needs.

Fitting PeopleSoft into the Other Components of the Enterprise

The PeopleSoft system doesn't necessarily require a dedicated server, but such a structure is recommended for optimal performance. Generally, the applications being run are critical to the enterprise, and a dedicated server makes good business sense. The decision to purchase additional hardware to support the Application Server is one of preference. Smaller organizations tend to implement the system in a logical three-tier structure, while larger organizations—those that require higher levels of performance—tend to implement the physical three-tier option.

Since PeopleSoft is designed to be a platform-independent application, it adapts to most organizations' preferences with respect to hardware, operating system, and relational database configurations. Other applications that don't provide this flexibility may force an organization to acquire new hardware and software that it's unfamiliar with. This may also force the organization to expand its information technology group to support a new environment. At the very least, it would need to retrain existing staff to handle the new technologies.

Overall, PeopleSoft works well with other applications, although it may consume a larger amount of network bandwidth than others. This consideration may cause an enterprise to upgrade its network infrastructure sooner than it might otherwise have done.

Benchmarking Performance

Performance benchmarking information will not be discussed in this book, as the statistics change frequently with the introduction of more powerful processors and increased memory capability. PeopleSoft, as well as some hardware and relational database vendors, can provide this type of information on request. Don't hesitate to ask for such information when making a purchasing decision. Also consider talking to other PeopleSoft clients that are similar in size to your organization (a PeopleSoft representative should be able to provide a list of references). When you do determine which platform to use with your architecture, ensure that you have the proper tools to monitor network, server, and database functions, including space, memory, and access performance. It's critical to constantly and consistently monitor your production environment since the data is constantly changing.

Up Next

Now that we've completed an overview of the basic components around the PeopleSoft architecture and discussed configuration and support, we'll move on to the development of a business case to support your implementation. The next chapter, "Building a Basis for Business Development," will look at potential drivers that might affect your decision to implement this architecture and will discuss the creation of a value proposition that can support your project through implementation. It will cover the basic components of a sound business case and how to leverage that case throughout your implementation efforts.

Building a Basis for Business Development

F E A T U R I N G :

▶ Planning for your business case

▶ Determining what your business drivers are

▶ Identifying the various ERP implementation costs

▶ Defining success for your project

▶ Creating an effective business case to support your project

▶ Communicating your business case

When you are undertaking a major initiative, such as an ERP implementation, you must have a clear picture of why you are undertaking it and must document your business reasons for doing so. Clearly articulating the business reasons behind your decision is the basis of a sound business case. This chapter will look at how to put your thoughts together and develop a sound, clear business case to support your project.

Implementation of an ERP system requires a common alignment of numerous key organizational resources, the dedication of time from these resources, and the investment of large amounts of an organization's working capital plus effort expended to embrace such a change. Each of these resources could have been used to focus on other organizational improvements and agendas; yet over the last several years, the implementation of an ERP system has been a major agenda item on a majority of organizations' key initiatives programs. So why have so many organizations expended efforts to implement ERP systems?

As mentioned in Chapter 1, "Enterprise Resource Planning with PeopleSoft," during the 1990s, organizations implemented ERP systems in pursuit of increases in quality, better information capabilities, higher customer and client satisfaction, and decreases in time to market, product cost, personnel, delivery time, inventory levels, and much more.

All initiatives that require organizations to invest valuable working capital should drive value directly back into the organization, through efficiencies, cost savings, revenue growth, or improved client satisfaction. An ERP implementation should be no different and should drive value into the organization.

In each of the following sections, we'll evaluate the different business drivers that compel companies to implement an ERP solution. We'll also look at the metrics that must be evaluated in order to create a solid value proposition and business case. Finally, we'll explain how each organization must define success and create an environment for promoting alignment across the total organization to ensure that the implementation program will be successful.

Planning Your Business Case

In planning your business case, you'll need to address the following areas:

1. Determining your business drivers and the benefits that surround them

2. Determining the costs of implementing an ERP system

3. Defining success

4. Determining your target audiences to communicate your business case to

With these key ingredients in place, you can have a sound, well-thought-out business case that will show the value your project will have on your organization and the cost associated with that value. This will also help you target your decisions as you move forward, communicate your value, and relate them back to this plan.

Determining Business Drivers for Implementing an ERP Solution

Business drivers that may cause an organization to implement a new ERP system (or improve its existing system) can come in the form of tactical (or, in the shorter term, cost-efficiency-focused) issues or strategic (and, in the longer term, growth-related) issues. Typically based on pressures of the market and the ability of an organization to compete effectively, these drivers when identified can help you create sound strategies for your implementation. Examples of these business drivers include:

► System constraints such as those found during the year 2000 rollover or even with 1999 (in cases where computer systems had hard-coded values to mean one thing but with the coming of that date, really should have meant something else)

► Efficiency issues such as those found in diverse processes that arose from functional silos (that is, staying within one functional area of the business, such as human resources or accounting), multiple mergers or acquisitions, and changes to the business service model, such as shared services operations

► Enabling and driving reengineering to help support streamlined processes and improve business response

► Globalization issues that arose due to a company's expansion around the globe and the company's need to operate as a single entity worldwide

These tactical and strategic business drivers lay a sound path for a solid business case to be developed and supported within your organization. You need to assess your organization and determine which (if not all) of these drivers might apply to your implementation.

System Constraints

The largest driver for implementing ERP systems over the past few years was one that focused on a system constraint—that of Y2K (the year 2000). In the 1900s, organizations developed various custom-made systems to enable their business processes. To save computer space and money, they used a two-digit year notation. The assumption by the system was that these digits would be preceded by "19" to designate the year. With the change of the century, this seemingly minor snafu, which came to be known as the Y2K bug, became a major problem for information systems (IS) departments and company executives to fix.

As organizations evaluated their options for eliminating the Y2K, or millennium, bug, they found that they were facing a problem that was prevalent within each of their legacy systems. Many of these systems were disconnected, nonintegrated, and based on platforms that didn't allow for expansion into many of the new emerging technology areas that were being touted as the next business revolution: the information revolution.

While evaluating the Y2K issues in their systems, many organizations found that they also needed to drive to the next level of reengineering. Faced with huge out-of-pocket expenditures to fix the millennium bug, organizations throughout the world determined that by taking their working capital and applying it to the implementation of an out-of-the-box, vendor-supported ERP system, they could solve many of the business problems not addressed by their legacy systems. Doing this enabled them to achieve the goal of having systems that would be compliant with the Y2K requirements and provide the foundation for emerging technologies.

Like the Y2K bug, there could be other technology reasons for you to choose an ERP system, rather than support your current, antiquated legacy system. The code that you wrote your system in may no longer be supported, or you might not be able to find resources who can still support this code (since all have retired). Or you might find other issues such as the length of a numeric field—for example, a field that represents revenues you were collecting in the past but which you are now surpassing on a regular basis. Any time you are analyzing the cost of updating your old system to support your business needs today and comparing that with implementing a new ERP system, you are looking at technology or system drivers to support you. Though these seem fairly tactical in nature, they might prevent you from a more strategic issue such as growth (i.e., how can you continue to grow your organization if your financial systems or human resources systems can't support you or if their support causes you hundreds of thousands of dollars in extra costs?). Therefore, system constraints or issues may be big drivers for your business case and show that a new, vendor-supported system may be very valuable for your organization now and in the future.

Common Processes

Beyond the specific system issues discussed, organizations began to evaluate the ability of these "best practices" systems (such as ERP) to drive them to the next level of reengineering. Many organizations in the late 1980s and early '90s also added programs to their corporate agendas to reengineer. The goal was to revamp their organizational structures and business processes at all levels, and drive to a standard set of common business practices. These efforts have given many organizations a tremendous boost to their financial and market positions. Since ERP systems support a common process in order to work efficiently and are built on best practices, they became a logical choice for an organization to buy rather than to build and support these new processes.

By driving to a set of common processes, organizations have been able to eliminate waste, resulting in more streamlined business processes. These new processes have enabled organizations to focus on driving down inventories by managing as an enterprise, leverage the total combined strength of the organization, coordinate activities for improved response time, and provide a commonality for all decisions with the management team.

Look carefully at how your organization will benefit by implementing the standard PeopleSoft best practices and a common set of processes. Articulate in your business case the specific benefits a standardized, integrated process will bring and look at the savings you may have with these new processes in place (including time, people, and system resources).

Using ERP for a Shared Services Environment

Once a business has a set of common processes, as outlined above, the next step in this evolution might be to create a central or shared organization to support these processes. Creating and implementing such an organization is known as a shared-service center or shared services. Many companies have realized that there are large savings to be generated by combining areas of processing where the need for localized content and divisional variances are minimal. In this case an ERP system provides a mechanism (or platform) for the move to a centralized/shared environment since it supports a common-process model and centralized input. In order to create a shared-services environment, a new set of practices needs to be created and put in place. By combining resources and establishing a centralized center, you may realize many efficiencies as well as improvements in customer support and capabilities, since you are pooling your resources to support your entire organization.

ERP provides this set of common processes. As companies look at moving HR, Finance, Payables, and Benefits, to name a few, into shared environments, they need an enterprise-wide, integrated system. Though these functions and processes can be centralized in a shared-services model, they would still need to be integrated with the nonshared-services, more operational processes such as distribution- and manufacturing-based functions. Creating these common processes using the legacy departmentalized systems and integrating them with the remaining operational systems would involve a total rewrite of the software; and, in most cases, the technology to support these functions would not support these business requirements. Therefore, these requirements become a driver for a new ERP system that can support these requirements at less cost. Again, remember to not only include the business drivers supporting your business case, but articulate both the tangible and intangible benefits as a part of your case.

Enabling and Driving Reengineering

In many cases, implementing a common integrated system provides a tool for driving change throughout an organization. During the late 1980s, many organizations focused on *white boarding* their businesses.

Note   White boarding is the practice of starting with a clean sheet of paper and creating a new process to support your business function, rather than using an example that has already been used by others and proved effective. ERP systems leverage the "best" from all their customers and have created more of a "best practices" model for the business practices they support.

Breaking paradigms, moving to process-focused organizations, and making radical changes in how work is performed were key tenets of boosting competitive position for companies and were drivers toward these new integrated-process models.

Many organizations, however, found that implementing massive changes throughout an organization was a very humbling task. Old practices are hard to break, and the old adages "We've always done it this way" and "Why fix it if it isn't broken?" became the rallying cries for those whom the changes would target.

By implementing a common/integrated system across an entire organization, it's possible to reengineer the processes and the information reporting across all the entities of the company or organization. Utilizing the software package as the baseline to drive change allows the organization to drive the common processes needed.

In many cases the requirements of the systems can be used to instill the discipline needed on the organization. If the tool (software application) used to complete business transactions, which in turn links into processes used to complete daily activities, is changed, then, by default, the reengineered vision can be transformed into reality.

Many organizations also found that using the "blank sheet of paper," or white boarding, concept of reengineering was very time intensive and costly. When they began to evaluate other organizations, both within and outside their industry, they found that a set of "leading practices" was very apparent. Many of these practices were identified and incorporated directly into the applications of the ERP offerings. Thus, by implementing the ERP application and configuring the system to the company's needs, the organization was reengineering with more speed and with better results.

Mergers and Acquisitions

Mergers and acquisitions proliferated throughout the 1990s. From the megamergers of the automotive and banking industries to the consolidations of suppliers throughout the manufacturing sector, many organizations were searching for additional capital, improved market position, and greater efficiencies through combinations. Many of the true conglomerates that we know were created through acquisitions and mergers. This trend is expected to continue throughout the 21st century.

As mergers and acquisitions continued to drive the consolidation of many markets and businesses, the newly formed organizations struggled with their ability to run these new companies with the required efficiencies. Charts of accounts were different, allocation processes varied, and levels within the organizations were now misaligned with varying levels of compensation. Furthermore, organizations felt that many of the goals and benefits of the mergers and acquisitions were in jeopardy if they could not combine information such as dollars spent with suppliers.

Companies needed to be able to leverage their new combined size in order to gain the benefits of the larger organization. Without the ability to combine information and ensure that each set of reported information was being created in conformance with a common process, the information being reported was highly questionable. As organizations looked for methods to move from many separate companies, divisions, and groups into one efficient entity with a set of common business processes, they looked for their information systems to support and even drive their efforts.

In many cases the effort of "commonizing" the key processes without a common enabler has been viewed as nearly impossible. An ERP solution is perfectly aligned with the needs of an organization facing these issues. The ERP system will help drive this commonality and enable consolidation. ERP systems are designed to be table driven and to support consolidation of processes and entities. This fits right in line with the business driver of efficiency and leveraging your acquisitions more effectively.

Globalization

As the world becomes smaller and the demands of the consumer become larger, organizations are focusing on driving value to the customer or client in numerous ways. In many organizations the ability to drive customer value is tied to the ability to leverage information around the globe. Implementing a solution to issues in a global manner requires a common set of global processes and information, and it must have the ability to manage local, country, and continental issues including taxes, legislation, and regulatory issues, as well as varying languages and cultural differences.

Many companies have selected an ERP solution as the method to create these global processes that continue to support local needs and requirements. This is not an easy undertaking. Coordinating a solution that will allow components of the organization to complete their business while creating a standard for processes and data can be an overwhelming activity. However, the growth of global entities and a global market only make this business driver stronger for those organizations that want to grow their business and their markets. Therefore, the reliance on a true global solution that meets regulatory and local business requirements, yet has a common global process, can be a very big business driver. By contrast, most legacy applications are focused purely on the local needs and then rely on the business to consolidate the information into a global vision. Such a focus can be very time consuming, costly, and inefficient and can stifle growth rather than support it.

Emerging Technologies

One of the largest influences on the growth of ERP systems was the changes in technology and how they supported the business. These newly emerging technologies, which were not present in legacy applications, have driven many organizations to implement an ERP system. Also, the ERP vendor's support allows an organization to leverage all the latest technology with an upgrade, rather than to implement a totally new system or to program the changes themselves. With the move to client-server architecture in the early 1990s, and later the migration to the World Wide Web (or Internet), ERP systems have become increasingly appealing for supporting these emerging technologies at a fraction of the cost an organization might incur in doing it themselves. As discussed in Chapter 3, "An Overview of the PeopleSoft Architecture," client-server architecture allowed organizations to begin focusing on maintaining and developing a distributed system versus maintaining an infrastructure at each location. This move from stand-alone systems to ones that were connected via local area networks (LANs) and then to applications distributed across wide area networks (WANs) was one of the keys to moving to enterprise applications.

In many cases companies evaluated the client-server architecture and realized the increased expense of the design. However, being able to distribute the system throughout the organization provided great benefits to both the functional users and the technical groups supporting the application.

As additional technologies such as the Internet, Web-based applications, and work flow began to be built into the applications, the move to an ERP system had additional value to the organization. If the organization wanted to be positioned to take advantage of the emerging technologies, then implementing the "backbone" became the right choice.

All of these business issues have been used singularly or in combination to justify ERP systems, whether the implementation was within a single business unit or at the topmost level of a global corporation. Although implementing an ERP system can be one of the most difficult challenges that an organization can voluntarily undertake, many organizations have found that it can also be one of the most beneficial in creating value, driving change, and preparing the organization for its future initiatives.

Each implementation and management team must understand the current state of the organization from the beginning in order to clearly define the business case for undertaking this effort and therefore the drivers behind their implementation. Once your organization has a clear understanding of the drivers for implementing an ERP and therefore the benefits the system will have for your business, you must then be able to articulate the costs associated with implementing this great new solution.

ERP Implementation Costs

Implementing an ERP solution may represent one of the largest capital expenditures that your organization undertakes, and it may be one of numerous initiatives that are currently under way. In either case, prior to building the business case, you must understand the costs that will be associated with this activity.

In the planning phase of an implementation, you need to be able to clearly understand and evaluate all costs that will be incurred and how those expenditures will be timed in your project plan. Costs for implementation can be categorized into three main categories: software, hardware, and implementation costs.

Many organizations believe, and begin their business case with, the assumption that once the package has been purchased and the proper hardware has been delivered, the majority of the costs have been accumulated. This is far from the truth. In most cases the implementation costs—such as internal and external resources, communications, training, and post-production support—are the majority of the overall program costs.

To ensure that all costs are being evaluated and properly organized, experts from all areas of the organization should be included when you're putting together your business case. As we work with clients to evaluate options for implementations, we often find a functional team with a business case based on the estimates for hardware and systems costs, or we find the reverse: a technical systems group estimating the costs that will be incurred by the functional organizations.

When evaluating the overall costs, don't forget those costs that will be required to distribute the system to the mass of users and remote locations (i.e., field operations, manufacturing sites, or branch locations). In many larger organizations the cost of the centralized program is incorporated into the overall program; however, the business units or divisions must upgrade their capabilities to be able to use the application or communicate with the servers on a distributed platform.

Software Costs

Many costs fall within the software cost category, including the basic cost you are paying for the application with your initial contract with the vendor. Software costs include not only this application cost but also the costs of additional software needed to support your system, such as other package software (e.g., Microsoft Excel or Word), communications software, your database management software (e.g., DB2, Oracle, or Sybase), any utilities or backup software needed to support your environment, and development software for interfaces, conversions, and reporting or report distribution. All these needs should be considered.

Package Application Costs

The package application costs are those that are directly outlined in your PeopleSoft contract. They should include any projections that you might have on add-on fees for additional software modules (such as purchasing the new Travel and Expense module) or an increase in users (such as those expected through normal growth or acquisitions). Look carefully at any proposed contract you have with a vendor and ensure that you understand how these terms and conditions might affect the application costs.

Ongoing Application Support Costs

This cost area includes the ongoing maintenance costs associated with supporting your application software. In many cases this cost can be upwards of 18% to 20% of the original contract software fees negotiated with the vendor, each year. In addition, any purchases of additional software modules or an expanded agreement (such as those for new users or acquisitions) must be projected into this cost forecast.

System Base Software

In addition to the basic software costs of the application, you have other system base software to consider, such as:

Communication software   Software to support your network, dial-in, or remote users, or your Web clients, should also be considered, as it may not already be in place. Look at any upgrades as well as any contracts or software that you might currently have in place.

Database management software   This software supports the database you'll run your application on, such as DB2, Oracle, or Sybase. Be sure to look at any enterprise license agreement or criteria you might need to support Web-based users.

Backup and system operations software   This software supports the operating systems and infrastructure needs for your overall environment. Look for any software needed to help schedule, run, support, or aid in the operations of your application environment.

In addition to the types of software mentioned above, you might have the need for some automated testing software (as mentioned in Chapter 14, "Testing") or some interface or conversion software (as discussed in Chapter 11, "Converting Data and Developing an Interface"). Also, you may need some software distribution or report distribution software to help support your end users.

Desktop Software Upgrades

When looking at your end users and the distribution software you might need to support them, you should also consider in your costs any upgrades they might need to their current desktop, such as Windows, browser software, and desktop applications like Microsoft Excel and Word, which are commonly used in conjunction with the PeopleSoft application. Ensure that you have sat down with your technical support group and looked at all areas of software costs that might impact your implementation—and therefore the cost of implementation. Even those costs not supported by the project budget but incurred by the individual users or business units should be documented and clearly communicated to those users prior to their approval of the business case. Also, desktop reporting software may be needed if users will be developing or using special OLAP (online analytical processing) reporting tools.

Hardware Costs

Just like software costs, various hardware costs must be considered when implementing an ERP system. These costs include but are not limited to the following:

Servers   Consider both a Web server (for your three-tier architecture) or the application or database servers that are needed. Be sure to clearly diagram your technical architecture (to support all users, including those who will be remote) so that all hardware costs can be determined, as we discussed in Chapter 3. Also look at memory and DASD (direct access storage device) or disk space requirements and ensure that you correctly size your server capacity so that it adequately supports your requirements.

Reoccurring server maintenance   These costs include any upgrade costs or licensing support you have in order to maintain your servers.

Network upgrades   In some cases you may need to upgrade your network to support the additional volume and business requirements of your application. Be sure that a network specialist looks at your proposed solution and how the current network might support your new needs. All consideration of network upgrades or new lines should be evaluated.

Communications upgrades   You should evaluate any additional costs associated with your communications support, including remote users, Web users, and full desktop users (should you support all of these), as well as those who might be receiving information outside the system.

Desktops   Upgrades to existing desktops or new desktops for users should be looked at in conjunction with the overall technical hardware costs.

These costs are examples of the hardware costs you might incur with your solution. You may also need imaging hardware (and software), as well as other types of hardware to support the needs of your business. Ensure that both a business person who understands the future needs of the application and a technical architect sit down together and map out all your hardware and software needs clearly so that you won't have surprises at the end. The vendor as well as consultants with this experience can help you outline your costs in this area. However, don't forget to look at *all* these areas, including requirements that you might not have to fund. You can use this information in the future to ensure that all hardware and software are in place to support you prior to going live.

Implementation Costs

Besides the basic hardware and software costs outlined above, you must also look at all the costs associated with your implementation. These costs include your human resources (both internal and external), end-user support costs, and all the day-to-day administrative costs of supporting your team and project, including training, communications, and support.

Internal Implementation Team

Your internal implementation team should consist of the following individuals:

- ▶ Functional process representatives
- ▶ Technical resources

These resources and the time they will need to allocate to your project must be considered as a part of your overall costs. At the beginning of your project, it is best to get a good idea of the number of hours you will need for each of these two types of resources to support your project. You can then break these hours down by role and specific resource. For example, you might need 10,000 hours for functional support and 15,000 hours for technical support. Based on specific roles, you might then need:

- ▶ 2,000 hours for each application area (e.g., GL, AP, HR, payroll, and purchasing)
- ▶ 1,000 hours for basic application (or DBA) support
- ▶ 1,000 hours for infrastructure support
- ▶ 1,000 hours for system administration support
- ▶ 500 hours per interface (and you have 10 interfaces)
- ▶ 100 hours per custom report (and you have 20 reports)
- ▶ 2,000 hours for conversion of data (1,000 on financials side and 1,000 on HR/payroll side)
- ▶ 2,000 hours for technical configuration
- ▶ 1,000 hours for project management support

By getting a good up-front estimate of your project implementation timeline and hours required by resource type, you can better project (based on these estimates) what your resource requirements and their costs will be. If you are not sure about the hours required and have no planning tools to guide you, you should seek out help from others who have done similar projects or look for consulting advice.

External Implementation Expertise and Assistance

After you've outlined your internal needs, there are some areas where you will want or need external support. Some areas that generally require outside assistance include (but are not limited to):

Software expertise Individuals who know the package and have expertise in implementing it can be invaluable to your team. In general, you should consider having an expert for each module you are implementing.

Implementation and project management expertise Since this is likely your first large enterprise project, you'll want someone who has gone through similar implementations to work with your manager to lead the project.

Technical expertise These individuals have experience with the architecture on which you've decided to roll out your application. In most cases, organizations do not have this expertise in-house since they are not familiar with the application or may not be familiar with the new technical environment.

You may also need expertise and help with your change management efforts, training, and filling roles that you cannot staff within your organization (nor want to hire for a short duration). While you retool your internal resources and they become more familiar with the new systems and processes, you can create a knowledge transfer and roll-off plan for your external project resources. Chapter 5, "Planning the Foundation," provides more details on the roles you'll need to fill within your team. This information can help you determine what resource requirements are necessary to support your implementation, which of those you can fill, and which ones you might need to fill externally. Analyzing and being truthful about which resources you have with the right skills, which resources you can free up from existing work, and which resources you must get externally will help you develop a more sound business case and truer cost model.

Target Audience Costs

Besides the costs of your project team resources (both internal and external), additional costs will be incurred to support your target user base (and audience). These end-user costs come in the form of:

- ► Participation in demos and testing
- ► End-user costs for training time
- ► Lost efficiency due to ramp-up

The time spent by your end users should also be considered in your overall costs, as well as all the project administration costs, change management costs, training costs, communications costs, and additional support costs.

After you have outlined all areas that you believe should be included in your cost evaluation, you'll need to clearly define the benefits and risks associated with the project. Finally, you'll need to determine what criteria you will use to define the success of your project and then communicate these findings to your key stakeholders.

Cost-Benefit-Risk Analysis

Once you've clearly defined your project costs, you'll need to look specifically at the business environment you are currently in and the one you are projected to be in (i.e., your future state) and outline all the costs, benefits, and risks associated with moving from your current-state environment to your future-state environment. Examples of the elements to consider when assessing your business environment include financial position, competitive position, products or services, and markets. Both quantitative (measurable) and qualitative inputs should be looked at.

To help you identify the costs and related benefits, you should follow these basic steps:

1. Identify the categories of costs and revenue (e.g., inventory and labor). Across the enterprise, which categories contain the greatest costs?

2. Identify the drivers for each category. For instance, within inventory, what drives costs up? Having too much inventory on hand would drive costs up.

3. Quantify costs, revenue, and pricing along with profitability. Develop some numbers that clarify what the driver is costing or earning. This can show the enterprise how to reduce costs or increase profitability. For instance, inventory on the shelf costs the company $100 per square foot per day. Each square foot in inventory used rather than sitting on the shelf reduces costs. However, if there is no inventory on the shelf to fulfill an order, obtaining that inventory may cost $200 per order. You want to minimize inventory but maximize order fulfillment.

4. Conduct a sensitivity analysis. Examine how much can be changed by reducing or increasing an inventory (or how sensitive to change the numbers are). For example, if I order 10 more items and put them on the shelf, my cost goes up by 10%. However, if I keep 5 items, my cost per order goes up by 30% since I'm not realizing any volume discounts and I'm also incurring shelf costs to continuously maintain the 5 items. Also, consider whether a particular driver may be off-limits. (Maybe you have a fixed contract under which you're obligated to purchase 100 items per year; therefore you can't influence the level of this inventory below 100 items per year.)

To help assess and find these costs and benefits, look at all the major processes included within your project scope and all business areas related to these processes. Track all costs, benefits, and risks associated with these processes and the related ones. Look at people-oriented areas around these processes, including changes in who might perform the work, how many individuals are needed now and in the future, and what the effects will be on training, support, and other administration tasks such as communications.

Always be sure you have documented all assumptions and that these assumptions are verified by the stakeholders. For example, in the human resources area you might assume that the cost per person for a terminated employee equals one and a half times their salary. When quoting labor costs, the costs are assumed to be fully loaded.

 Note Whenever you get additional information on your assumptions or any item that affects your business case, then immediately understand *how* it affects your business case and communicate this to your sponsors and stakeholders.

Costs

Look at both one-time and recurring costs for all areas. Suppose you have to pay a one-time license fee up front, but a recurring maintenance fee. Be sure that this fee is clearly articulated in your business case document. Also look at categorizing your costs by fixed and variable costs, by direct and indirect costs, and by capitalized and expense items. These categories all affect your analysis.

TIP   Remember to work closely with your finance people. They typically can get you the information you need based on the costs centers you are looking at.

The following list shows an example of some of the cost drivers you might find within an organization. Once you've identified the primary cost drivers, use the data to drive or relate to the processes you're implementing and summarize the costs in one model.

Significant Cost Drivers for ABC Company

- ▶ Raw materials
  - ▶ Inbound transportation
  - ▶ Specification of ingredients
  - ▶ Recovery percentage
  - ▶ Product mix
  - ▶ Extension of growing season
  - ▶ Finished product specification
- ▶ Purchase of finished goods
  - ▶ Sales forecasts
- ▶ Packaging materials
  - ▶ Sales forecasts
  - ▶ Expediting costs
  - ▶ Specification changes/special projects
  - ▶ Repackaging/reconditioning
  - ▶ Number of SKUs

- ▶ Direct labor
  - ▶ Preventive maintenance
  - ▶ Automation
  - ▶ Training
- ▶ Variable manufacturing
  - ▶ Waste
  - ▶ Efficiency of equipment/pretreatment
- ▶ Variable transportation
  - ▶ Warehouse capacity
  - ▶ Percentage of buyer haul
  - ▶ Number of facilities
  - ▶ Lead time premium
  - ▶ Optimization technology
  - ▶ Network configuration
  - ▶ Mode mix
- ▶ Variable warehousing
  - ▶ Sales forecasts
  - ▶ Warehouse automation
  - ▶ Transportation modes
- ▶ Fixed distribution
  - ▶ Casing and labeling equipment space
  - ▶ Sales policy
  - ▶ Number of distribution centers
  - ▶ Network configuration
- ▶ Brokerage and selling
  - ▶ Access to data
  - ▶ Spans of control

▶ Broker training

▶ Broker performance measures/incentives

▶ Marketing

▶ Trade program design

▶ Planning process

▶ Silo management (i.e., getting individuals to think outside their functional area, or "silo")

▶ Skill level/training/effectiveness

▶ Administration

▶ Planning-to-production systems

▶ Order-to-cash systems

▶ Training

▶ Business decision

Benefits

To identify the benefits associated with your initiative, look for changes in the people-, process-, and technology-related aspects of all the major processes that are affected by your implementation. Look to your consultant, subject-matter experts, or outside analysts for best practices that might help drive benefits. Be sure you quantify your benefits in terms of the value drivers identified and according to categories of revenue growth, operating efficiency, and capital avoidance. Use the business drivers mentioned in the previous sections to help identify your major categories.

TIP It takes a lot of effort to detail enough information to quantify the benefits you'll need for establishing a strong business case. Be sure you leverage your time wisely and use the appropriate resources and experts to help you articulate these benefits.

Here are some ways to help you quantify your benefits:

▶ Look for measurable results (e.g., time to deliver, time to market, or percentage of growth).

▶ Try flowcharting the benefit, beginning with what is being changed, and look at who is performing the new activity and how that might change. This could result in an FTE (full-time equivalent) analysis to show reductions in time or resources.

▶ If benefits are tied to access to information, look at prior issues that arose due to lack of information and what those issues cost the company. Maybe in the past, because you didn't have the right termination information, you were sued and had to pay money to resolve the problem. With the right information in your hand, you would have avoided that problem. By compiling a list of these types of activities, you might be able to get to an annual estimate for savings.

▶ Look at your strategic goals and see if your initiative might be a cornerstone in supporting them. This might in turn be quantified and linked to the goals.

▶ Look at areas of expansion or time to implement. For instance, maybe today it takes you two months to set up a new location or office and get its data into your old system. With your new system it will take only two days. Estimate the number of locations or offices you are planning to open per year (or growth rate) to obtain a clear, measurable result.

Risks

Project risks should be assessed up front as well. The project sponsors and managers (as a minimum) should get together and create a joint risk assessment. Be sure to create a plan to manage each risk assessed, which will help you better manage your efforts. Reducing risk in one area may increase risk in another, so look at dependencies.

Types of risks that you should look at include:

Economic and regulatory risks   You might risk being unable to support a certain new government requirement, or there may be risk to your project due to changes in inflation rates, interest rates, taxes, etc.

Product, market, and competitive risks   These are risks associated with the marketplace your organization is working in, including both internal and external factors.

Technological risks   Maybe you have a platform that won't be supported after the end of the year, or you may have risks with using leading-edge technology. Look for hardware failure, lack of vendor support, and communications failures.

People risks   These risks include losing team members or subject-matter experts if a reduction of the workforce is being considered, being unable to train people in new skills, coping with labor strikes, etc.

Assess the probability of each risk you identify. Also ensure that you have a well-thought-out plan for dealing with the risks or minimizing them. Don't underestimate the impact of a risk on your bottom-line results. Once you've clearly defined the potential costs, benefits, and risks associated with your project, don't forget to document the success factors you'll be using.

Defining Success

In building your business case, you must also consider how your organization would define success. How do you know if implementing a new ERP system and enabling the associated business processes have been successful? We've identified eight success factors that have distinguished companies that "won" their transformation projects from companies that failed. Your PeopleSoft ERP implementation is definitely a major transformation project. Here are the eight factors:

1. **Powerful business case**   The trigger or force that drives your change and aligns your organization and strategy.

2. **Vision clarity**   Determines how well your case is understood by your people.

3. **Change leadership and accountability**   A clear picture of your sponsors and their roles in supporting your change.

4. **Change-specific communication**   Your plan and strategy on communication targeted to your stakeholders to support your change.

5. **Increased change capability**   The ability of your team/project to build knowledge and awareness of the change process.

6. **Integrated planning and teams**   Assures that all your teams are considered and brought into one integrated plan and initiative. You should also look at all internal and external events that affect the plan.

7. **Stakeholder commitment**   Shows the support you have within the organization to support the change.

8. **Aligned performance and culture**   Helps to align and sustain your behavior. Be sure to look at this alignment and ensure that appropriate changes are made to reflect your new model. Misalignment of goals can cause serious problems with any change initiative.

Figure 4.1 shows these implementation success factors in a graphic format. Ensure that you have looked at these criteria in detail and have a plan in place for how you will address them. Chapter 5 looks at creating and maintaining your project team and infrastructure to help you keep aligned with these results. Be sure you involve your sponsors and stakeholders throughout the life cycle of your project in helping you maintain and align your factors and in supporting your business case.

Figure 4.1   **Implementation success factors**

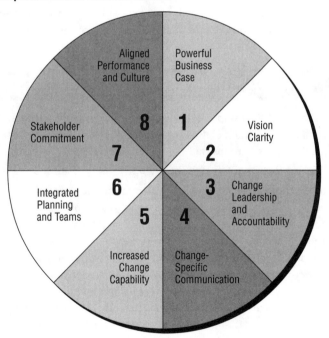

As we mentioned above, many implementation projects are not successful because they are lacking in one or more of these factors. Either the project is such a large undertaking for the organization that the proper resources cannot be brought to bear and the project withers (see Chapter 9, "Preparing Your Organization for Implementation") or the project is completed but the business case that justified the project is not met and the success of the project is limited to the integration of a new system or enabler. Each of these examples relates directly to your success "wheel" as shown in Figure 4.1. You should assess your project throughout its life cycle and ensure that you are gaining the support you need to be successful.

In addition to following and monitoring the success factors above, if you are going to begin building a value proposition or business case for an implementation program, you must first determine how you will define success and claim victory over the forces of inefficiency and lost opportunities that we have outlined.

As an organization embarks on the journey of an ERP implementation, it's very important to define what constitutes success. As we discussed earlier in this chapter, an organization may want to implement an ERP system for varying reasons; none of these reasons, however, will stand without a solid justification or value proposition created with the specifics of the organization in mind.

Example of Describing Elements of Success

Take the Y2K example. Many organizations felt that using an ERP system would be the right solution for their Y2K issues. Each of these companies, institutions, or groups had the option of correcting the code and making their legacy systems capable of handling the required post-1/1/00 dates.

In this example, the implementation of the ERP application may have been determined to be the correct course of action, but not before evaluating the cost variables as well as the tangible and intangible benefits of each option. Therefore, even in those cases where installing the system prior to a Y2K threshold was deemed successful, it must have been completed within the proscribed budget and have delivered the proper functionality and system architecture. If the project was over budget and didn't position the organization to take advantage of new functionality, newly enabled processes, or architecture for future enablers, then the project was not successful. The legacy systems could have been in the same position, potentially with less effort and pain to the organization.

When is our project really complete? In many cases the implementation of an ERP system is the ultimate achievement in a continuous improvement tool. Organizations (groups of humans and group dynamics) can absorb only a certain amount of change at one time. Implementations can be attacked in waves, with each subsequent wave driving additional value into the organization. Clearly articulating and defining your success criteria up front, including time frames for reaching your incremental goals, should be a part of your overall business case. Remember, you should be able to measure these results and determine whether you have reached the goals—if your measures are truly effective.

TIP   Some examples of measurable results include increasing the number of invoices processed each week by 20%, decreasing the cost of inventory by 15%, and decreasing the cost of your purchasing transactions by 40%. Be sure to have input on what your target processes were prior to implementing the system and a clear picture of when you will measure results after implementation (e.g., within six months after implementation).

Creating a Business Case and Value Proposition

Now that you've considered the business drivers, the costs of both the implementation and your business operations, the benefits, and the risks, and have determined what defines success, it's time to dive in and actually create a business case or value proposition.

Note   A *value proposition* details specifically what value will be obtained from a particular project or proposition. This value when laid out in a business case can be the foundation for creating your business case. However, in a business case, you have both value and costs. Your value should outweigh your costs in order for you to be successful.

There are approximately three different steps that you should take when developing your business case:

Step 1: Evaluate the business plan.   Each organization has its own internal process for justifying a major project or program expenditure. With an implementation project, however, it's critical to evaluate your project goals and plans (as outlined in your charter, which we discuss in detail in Chapter 5) to ensure that costs, risks, and benefits are properly aligned and analyzed.

Step 2: Determine your assumptions and document them.   If you're currently planning an implementation, it's essential to document the assumptions for the business case. To properly create the cost-8benefit analysis, you must ensure that the project scope and boundaries are documented and aligned. Each of these boundaries must be documented in the project assumptions.

For example: If part of our project scope is to implement the work-flow and Web-enabled pieces of the ERP functionality, then we must ensure that the costs for additional work-flow and Web servers are included in the cost projections and estimates. Likewise, if we're using the company's total spending on purchases, or "total spend," to calculate the project savings from decreases in purchase order processing, then we must also be sure to create the business case with the assumption of rolling out the application to all users who are responsible for creating purchase orders. If we calculate the benefits based on this total spend, then we must likewise calculate the costs of additional application servers for distributed locations and take into account the risks associated with a divisional rollout.

Step 3: Set clear goals and determine sponsorships.   The lack of clear goals and key sponsorship is one of the primary reasons that programs or projects fail. The business case is not only the justification for the project expenditure but can also be one of the most effective communication and internal sales tools.

Table 4.1 shows an example of a business case outline for an ERP system. As you can see, this business case contains the major components: business drivers or value, tangible and intangible benefits, and all costs, along with assumptions. Defined, measurable goals must be included along with a break-down of all costs. The outline breaks down the major components of the expected deliverable (the business case), including a list of the specific products or sections that should be included in the case (such as the business analysis, communications, approvals, etc.) as well as the major tasks required to develop the plan and the associated products (or sections).

Table 4.1   **Example of Business Case Outline**

Deliverable	Products
Business Case Based on a set of assumptions, the business case provides quantitative and qualitative information regarding the project (e.g., expected project value and implementation risks). The business case also helps manage the project scope by supplying information about the impact of adjustments to the PeopleSoft process and organization. The business case is an effective sales tool to buyers, sponsors, key users, and other stakeholders.	Business Case Analysis PeopleSoft Decision Communication Management Approvals Business Case Executive Summary
Activity and Tasks	**Products**
Conduct Cost-Benefit-Risk Analysis Document cost-benefit assumptions Identify costs/benefits/risks Conduct implementation success factors assessment Construct cost-benefit-risk model	Business Case Analysis
Confirm PeopleSoft Recommendation Plan and prepare for PeopleSoft decision session Conduct PeopleSoft decision session Confirm PeopleSoft recommendation Prepare communication approach for PeopleSoft decision Communicate business case and PeopleSoft decision	PeopleSoft Decision Communication
Review and Approve Business Case Development Stage Develop business case executive summary Obtain management approval of business case	Management Approvals Business Case Executive Summary

Communicating the Business Case

Once you have the business case developed, communicating the value proposition and business case throughout the organization can be as critical as actually developing the business case itself.

The implementation of an ERP system will cause change throughout the organization. Therefore it's critical to the success of any ERP program to create an understanding of the value among all the stakeholders who will be affected.

One tool that you can use, which is utilized by many implementation teams, is called a *stakeholder matrix*. Table 4.2 shows an example of a stakeholder matrix. A stakeholder can be anyone from the executive sponsor who has the complete understanding of the project to the end user who will be affected by the day-to-day changes invoked by the solution, to the shareholder of the company who is assuming that the company is using their working capital to create additional value to them as an owner of the company. As shown in the example, the goal is to outline the major wants or needs of the specific stakeholders, including specific business objectives they will be looking for and any barriers to achieving these objectives.

Table 4.2 **Example of Stakeholder Matrix**

Stakeholder	Needs/Wants	Objectives	Barriers
Supplier	High volume Timely payment	Increase margin	Technology
Maintenance	Sound platform Defect details	Increase performance	Communications
Employee	Timely information Compensation	Increase access to information Performance related	Trust
Manager	Quick response Key performance measures	Increase access to information Allow direct entry	Training/skills Trust

If you are currently implementing an ERP system or are planning to implement one in the near future, be sure to plan activities for revisiting and updating your business case. Since the implementation will be a dynamic project, you will want to maintain your focus. It's easy for an implementation team to lose track of the business value being provided and to focus only on "getting the system turned on."

It's important to keep in mind that what is good for the whole may be negative for one particular portion of the organization. In many cases the solution implemented may cause additional work or significantly change the business disciplines in a department, plant, location, or division. Even a well-prepared business case may not ensure success if the case isn't communicated clearly to the members of the organization that must sustain sponsorship of the program. Likewise, a program cannot be successful if those people in the organization who will be required to support change don't understand the reason for the shift from their current set of tools and practices.

Every organization can be successful implementing an ERP system if it spends the time and effort to clearly lay out, through communication mechanisms, the key success factors—for example:

- ▶ Why are we doing this?
- ▶ What opportunities can we take advantage of by doing this?
- ▶ How will we know if we are successful?
- ▶ How will we know when the project is complete?
- ▶ How will the rest of the organization view this endeavor?

Be prepared through a series of communications, targeted to each specific stakeholder or audience identified, to explain the answers to these questions when they're asked:

- ▶ What's in it for me?
- ▶ How much will this cost me?
- ▶ What will this require of my organization in order to complete the project?

Given a strong business case and value proposition, an organization can utilize its ERP application to drive efficiencies, promote the use and availability of integrated information for decision making, and position the organization with an application that will be the backbone and catalyst for many additional improvement projects in the future.

Up Next

Although creating an effective business case and communicating it to your stakeholders is an important step in getting your ERP project off to a good start, you also need a solid foundation and plan for sustaining it as you move forward. The next chapter, "Planning the Foundation," will provide you with the necessary steps for preparing your project for the future. We'll look at how to create an effective team, create the right plan and support in the form of a project charter, and create all the project infrastructure you must have in place in order to monitor your project effectively. Both an effective business case and a solid plan are important elements in succeeding with your ERP initiatives, and monitoring your plan should be a continuous process by your team.

Part II

Preparing for Implementation

Now that you've read about the ERP market, PeopleSoft's competition, and what PeopleSoft has to offer, it's time to prepare for your implementation (or upgrade) of the PeopleSoft application. Several key areas must be surveyed and planned so that your organization can be successful. Helping to prepare your people and organization for the change you are about to undertake is an extremely large task—a task that many organizations overlook or take for granted. Ensuring that you have the right tools, techniques, and design to be successful is another criterion for success. By taking into consideration your people, your processes and business requirements, and your technological challenges, you're creating that foundation for success.

CHAPTER 5

Planning the Foundation

F E A T U R I N G :

- ▶ A look at what organizational alignment is and how it affects your implementation

- ▶ What to do to better prepare your organization for the changes your project will bring

- ▶ How to get your project started on the right foot

- ▶ What characteristics you should look for in your project manager

- ▶ What a project charter is and how to create one for your project

- ▶ What individuals or roles you'll need for a successful implementation

- ▶ What appropriate project infrastructure you'll need to put in place to be successful

- ▶ How to create the right project plan and budget to ensure that you'll meet your goals and objectives for this initiative

Several areas that are critical to any major change initiative must be considered as you begin your journey in implementing your PeopleSoft application or driving value out of the system you have already implemented.

One of the first steps in planning for your new project is to do a sound assessment of where your organization currently is and where you'd like it to be. You should also analyze the obstacles that may prevent you from getting from your beginning state to the desired end state. Organizational alignment and change management techniques will help you to do just that.

The next step in getting you off and running is to seek out the right project manager who can lead your team to success and keep the project on time and on target. The project manager should be a seasoned person who is familiar with the challenges in implementing a large transformation effort.

After that key project manager is chosen, there are several project infrastructure tasks that are critical to the project start-up, such as creation of a project plan and a budget. Once these items are in place, you'll be ready to kick off your project and to progress toward a successful implementation.

This chapter will discuss each of these areas in detail to aid you in planning your project and laying the foundation for fulfilling your goals for tomorrow.

Assessing the Organization

As mentioned above, a key to successfully getting your project off and running is a sound assessment of how your initiative (whether it's a full-scale implementation or additional changes to existing processes) will affect the current organizational structure—its processes and its people. You must analyze the obstacles that might hinder your progress and ensure that you have an effective plan in place to support these changes. A sound communication plan, appropriate sponsorship, and support for how these changes will affect your organization will help ensure your project's success. By preparing and tackling these issues up front, you will have a smoother ride down the road for your implementation.

Organizational Alignment and Change Management

In order to be successful in managing a large ERP system implementation, your organization must be aligned to support the changes that will occur in moving from the current state to the new future-state vision that is supported by this new implementation.

The art of analyzing the organization to ensure that its goals and objectives are aligned with the project and new system, including the resources and roles necessary to support the new way of doing business, is called *organizational alignment*.

The program that helps manage this change, including the tools and techniques involved, is called *change management*. Change management is a process that helps enable success around all the changes that inevitably occur in a large transformation such as a PeopleSoft implementation or a reengineering effort, shifting the commitment for the current state to a commitment to the new future state. Because people need time and energy to adjust to a new situation, the change management process is a never-ending process and should not be viewed as a point-in-time solution.

To understand the scope that your change management program should cover and how your project affects the organization, the first thing you should do is look at all the individuals who will be affected by this change and map out how they currently are doing their work and how the project will affect that work. Also, you should outline the concerns, questions, and issues they currently have in understanding what their future roles will be with your new system or processes in place. By outlining the current state and future state along with the gaps in understanding that each individual has, you can create a plan of attack to ensure that these gaps are covered as a part of your change management plan. Your change management plan should consist of:

- ▶ A list of individuals affected by your change (also known as *stakeholders*)

- ▶ A list of the changes these individuals will undergo to support the new processes, and any gaps they have in understanding this transformation

> ▶ A plan to target how you will fill these gaps, either through training, communications, sponsorship, or other means

> ▶ Any follow-up activities or assessments that need to be done after you roll out your programs to ensure that they are effective

By creating this change management plan and monitoring it, you will ensure that your organization becomes aligned with your new processes and successfully changes to your desired future state. Remember, though, that you'll need to monitor progress continuously and that this change will not happen overnight—it's a never-ending cycle.

Stakeholder Assessment

To kick off a change management program, at the start of a project, one of the first tasks the team should accomplish is a *stakeholder assessment*. This process involves interviewing each type of stakeholder involved with the project to ensure that issues and concerns are identified and addressed in order to support a successful implementation. Stakeholders include end users, customers, executives, suppliers, employees, and any other individuals who are involved either directly or indirectly in the new processes or system.

By doing a stakeholder assessment prior to starting the project, a company can analyze its current organization as part of its current-state analysis, benchmark the activities that individual roles are accomplishing, and clearly articulate its future-state vision to determine the initial impacts to its organization. These interviews can be one-on-one, questionnaires, surveys, or focus group sessions designed to bring out the issues and concerns of the targeted group.

The team can use the initial assessments to provide a baseline for measuring the impact of the change management initiatives and the overall effectiveness of the entire project. A follow-up assessment should be done a few weeks after the project has "gone live" to gauge the effectiveness of the change management initiatives.

Table 5.1 shows an example of a stakeholder analysis that was performed for a project. Notice that the stakeholders were identified and grouped, and then a communication strategy was identified to target each group. Our next section will discuss the creation of this communication plan, which will help target your stakeholders and prepare them for your changes.

Table 5.1   **Example of a Stakeholder Assessment**

Stakeholder Group	Communication Strategy
Senior Vice President, Human Resources (SVP-HR); corporate-level HR managers	Biweekly summary of status, progress, concerns, and issues, provided by project manager
Executive Committee members	As needed to prepare for presentation, provided by SVP-HR
Business Unit presidents	As needed at a time determined by SVP-HR, provided by SVP-HR
HR supervisors/managers/directors (multiple HR functions)	Biweekly update
HR managers	Biweekly summary of status, progress, concerns, and issues, provided by project manager
Business Unit operational managers (tactical, mid-management level)	Summary of project goals in order to engage group representatives as "customer perspective" for validating vision and requirements
Business Unit operational managers (executive level)	Summary of project goals and progress
Benefits: Flexible/Sec. 125, 401(k)/Pension, and Nonfunded	Biweekly progress update and newsletter; involvement in confirmation sessions will build understanding of project goals and progress
Payroll, Commissions, Staffing/Recruiting, Employee Relations, Regulatory Reporting, OSHA/Worker's Compensation, 401(k)/Pension, Organizational Development, Training, Travel, HR generalists/administrative, Relocation, and Labor Relations	Biweekly update; involvement in confirmation sessions will build understanding of project goals and progress
Accounting: Payroll Interface, Online T&Es, Direct Deposit Reimbursement, Job Costing, and HR IS Functionality and Support (system administration)	Biweekly progress update for specific individuals only; involvement in confirmation sessions and vendor sessions will build understanding of project goals and progress

Table 5.1 (continued)   **Example of a Stakeholder Assessment**

Stakeholder Group	Communication Strategy
General employees	Communicate with specific individuals about specific project goals in order to involve them in the confirmation sessions
Accounting IS, Operations IS, Telecom, Office Automation, LAN (includes network administration), and IS Management	Communicate project goals to individuals for involvement in sessions
Payroll Outsourcers, 401(k) Administrators, Applicant Tracking, Stock Transfer Agents (receive data from process), and Benefit Plan Administrators	Communicate to individuals as necessary

Communications Plan

Once these stakeholder assessments are accomplished, the team can create action plans to address the major issues or concerns that arise. The action plans should include the creation of a detailed *communications plan*. The communications plan can help you alleviate the resistance that various stakeholders might have to your new solution.

Some typical ways that resistance can be reduced on a project include:

Individuals' motivation to change   By identifying pain areas and ways the future state will remedy or alleviate these pains, you can help motivate your audience. Also, by motivating your group early, your stakeholders become your advocates and start to view the future as a success rather than a compliance issue.

Internalizing rather than institutionalizing the change   It is much better for the project to get the stakeholders to internalize the change than to feel as though it is being pushed upon them.

Individuals' feelings of investment   If an individual is fully behind the change, they put their entire "body and soul" into the work rather than just go through the motions.

Price of maintenance   If a group or stakeholder is not behind the project or change, they are more inclined to keep wanting to change the new state back to the old. This generally results in higher maintenance costs.

The communications plan is an integral part of introducing, implementing, and providing ongoing and post-implementation support information to all the key stakeholders of the project. Communications to both end users and sponsors are critical to the success of the project and the continued support of the changed state. The goal of a communications plan is to provide a proactive approach in targeting your identified audience with consistent, persistent information on what's forthcoming. In doing this, the project can:

▶ Foster trust in the project vision (and thus the project team)

▶ Reduce resistance to the new vision, including the processes, technology, and people issues surrounding the change

▶ Enable the stakeholders to continuously focus on the critical elements of their job during the transition

▶ Provide accurate information for the parties involved to make effective decisions

▶ Provide opportunities for everyone to become involved in the implementation (whether directly or indirectly)

A good communications plan is out in front of the project, explaining what each player can expect next and getting the user community and sponsors comfortable with the desired future-state vision. It also helps to keep everyone informed about what's going on, as well as to stay on the "same page" in communicating project status and direction. Without a plan, users and others affected by the change could be left in the dark, thinking the worst and dreading the unknown.

The communications plan involves identifying the different audiences, mechanisms, and necessary modes of communications, as well as the best timing to get the information out to the affected groups so that it is "just in time" and not too far in advance or too late for the message. The plan should be reviewed on an ongoing basis, adapted based on project changes and direction, and modified based on feedback from participants. It should never be created and then shelved for the length of the project.

Figure 5.1 illustrates the communications process during a change project—the process that must be undertaken to promote the change you are undertaking. It's a great example of the types of communications you should look at throughout your project to support your initiative and facilitate the change through to your future state.

Figure 5.1 **Communications process**

Organizational State	CURRENT STATE					TRANSITION STATE	FUTURE STATE
Project Phase	Targeting	Current-State Analysis	Vision-ing	Future-State Design	Transition Planning	Implementation	Monitoring
Commitment Phase	PREPARATION PHASE			ACCEPTANCE PHASE			COMMITMENT PHASE	
Commitment Stage	Establish Contact	Develop Awareness	Build Understanding	Build Positive Perception	Install Change	Adopt Change	Encourage Institutional-ization	Promote Internalization
Communication Channels	Sponsor briefings Memos Newsletters Department meetings	Staff meetings Group e-mail Group voicemail Videos	Presentations Simulations User reviews Group discussions One-on-one dialogue	One-on-one meetings Focus groups Personal e-mail Personal voicemail	Provide feedback on progress* Small group discussions One-on-one dialogue	Obtain feedback* Surveys Focus groups	Deploy consequen-ces*	Behavioral modeling* Reframing* Connect to strategy*
Primary Communicators	Initiating sponsors Advocates	Initiating sponsors Sustaining sponsors Advocates	Initiating sponsors Sustaining sponsors Advocates Change agents	Sponsors Advocates Change agents Targets	Sponsors Advocates Change agents Targets	Sponsors Change agents Targets	Sponsors Change agents Targets	Sponsors Change agents Targets

*Recommended actions

Table 5.2 shows an example of a specific communications plan, outlining all the various project meetings established to support the communications effort. This table outlines all the key sessions used to communicate the project's message, along with the purpose, timing, and audience. Your plan should include a document that outlines all mechanisms used to communicate your project's message and the changes that will be occurring so that everyone becomes comfortable with the pending future state. Once you have identified your target audience (your stakeholders) and created a communications plan aimed to them, you should look for sponsorship to support your efforts and provide credibility to your project.

Table 5.2 **Example of Communications Meeting Plan**

Meeting Description	Meeting Purpose	Information Discussed	Frequency and Duration	Timing	Facilitators	Participants
Executive sponsor update	Update project status	Project status, issues, next steps	Monthly ½ hr.	3:00 Wed.	Steering committee	Executive sponsors and project office
Steering committee update	Update project status	Project status, issues, next steps	Weekly 1 hr.	3:00 Mon.	Project office	Steering committee
MIS steering committee update	Update project status	MIS coordination and estimation, priorities, issues, change requests	Weekly 1 hr.	1:00 Tues.	Project office	Users and MIS
Project kickoff	Initiate project	Demonstrate commitment, define roles, timelines	Project start 2 hrs.	TBD	Steering committee, project office	All Global Corp. Finance (GCF) team
Town hall questions and answers	Inform the company personnel	Open dialogue	Monthly 1 hr.	TBD	Executive sponsor	Company personnel
Major projects review	Major project management	Cross-projects status, issues	Bimonthly 1 hr.	TBD	Global Corp. Finance project office	Other major project office (GCF, National Purchasing Institute [NPI], etc.)
Project office coordination	Project management	Status, issues, plans	Daily ½ hr.	5:00 daily	Project office	Project office
Core team coordination	CTC	Coordinate project activities	Significant daily project information	Daily ½ hr.	8:30 daily	Project office

Table 5.2 **Example of Communications Meeting Plan** *(Continued)*

Meeting Description	Meeting Purpose	Information Discussed	Frequency and Duration	Timing	Facilitators	Participants
Core team project management	CTPM	Report progress, plan next steps	Past week's accomplishments, future tasks	Weekly 1 hr.	8:00 Fri.	Core team leaders
Core team and business experts coordination		Project status and planning	Project status, issues, next steps	Weekly 1 hr.	9:00 Tues.	Core team, consultants
Corp. Finance users and business experts update		Project status, information exchange	Status, information feedback, issues	Ongoing Daily	Ongoing	Business experts
Suppliers update		Notify suppliers	Communicate changes	As required	TBD	Area core team leader

Sponsorship

After assessing your stakeholders and developing both an action plan addressing their concerns and a direct communications plan to support the plan, what needs to happen in order to get the ball rolling and help ensure project success? You should have already written your business case and created support for your change from the appropriate executive sponsors (as we discussed in Chapter 4, "Building a Basis for Business Development"). Now you need to create sponsorship within your organization for the changes you are going to undertake and to directly link this sponsorship to the concerns your people have with these organizational changes. Therefore, by leveraging both your leadership team and business case to support your change and targeting the specific concerns your people have, you are creating sponsorship for the change within your organization. This sponsorship helps gain support within your end-user community and provides a positive influence for your project.

Starting Up the Project

With your organizational support plan now in place, you are ready to get down to business with the actual project and to create your project team.

Note   A key ingredient to starting up your project is defining the project scope. Scope is a key factor in positioning your initiative and determining sponsorship and direction for your project. You should define the scope prior to selecting the ERP package you will be using, through a series of data-gathering methods. To help guide your direction, you must look at your company's current state in order to drive business value propositions to where you want to be in the future. The difference between your current state and future state should be measurable and distinct. We recommend that you benchmark, measure, and track your current-state processes so that you can create your business case for the success of the project. Once you've measured where your organization is today and determined where you want it to be in the future, you should make clear "marks in the sand" as to what specific functions/features are within the scope and direction of this project so that you can tell whether you've been successful or not.

During project start-up, many key activities should occur in order to get your project off on the right foot:

- ▶ Create a project charter

- ▶ Determine and pick your project team

- ▶ Set up the project infrastructure, including project management guidelines and policies necessary to manage this initiative

- ▶ Create a project plan and budget

- ▶ Conduct a formal project kickoff

The following sections describe each of these start-up tasks in more detail.

Creating a Project Charter

The first thing your organization should do is to create a clear document that outlines the project goals, objectives, risks, organizational structure, resource requirements, and scope—both functional and technical. This is called a *project charter*.

The project charter provides a common understanding of the project in one place; the project team can come back to the charter at any time to determine any scope or directional changes or to measure their progress against it. Again, it's critical not only that the project charter be clear and concise but that all key stakeholders have read, understood, and support what is written in it. Many organizations fail to understand the importance of the charter and wonder why the project just doesn't get started immediately on the road toward implementation.

Think of the charter as you would a contract with a builder. Would you let a builder build your dream house without a blueprint and plan along with a formal contract to support your vision? It's the same with the charter: It outlines the blueprint and plan of what you want to accomplish along with the contract of how you plan on delivering the results; and it takes everyone back to the same level of understanding in black and white.

Setting Up a Project Team

Another key ingredient in the project is building the right team so that you'll have the right resources to successfully complete the project. Following the building example again: If you have too many plumbers and not enough roofers on your construction project, your house will not be completed successfully. Each role is critical to the success of the project, all skills are necessary, and without all of them your house will not get built properly. Too many people in one role hinder the success, as well as too few. Also, the timing in resource availability affects the project. The same is true on a PeopleSoft implementation. All roles are critical to the success of the project.

The roles necessary for project success include:

Project management   A core group of individuals must be identified to manage and lead this project. At the top of the list should be the key sponsor(s) of the project along with a steering committee. The steering committee monitors the project and helps the team make key executive decisions in a timely manner. The project manager(s) must be able to manage a project of this size and complexity. Sometimes it's necessary to have more than one project manager—one manager who knows the business side of running the project and another who is familiar with projects of similar size and complexity.

Functional team members   Both functional and technical team members must work together on a project such as this in order for it to be successful. The business must own the project and provide key functional users to ensure that the processes and technology totally support the needs of the business and the business drivers. A project run and operated solely by the IT (information technology) organization and not the business is doomed to fail. Also, it is better to back-fill these key functional team members with temporary employees or others on their current duties in order to free them up to focus on your future-state vision and that of your enterprise. Without this focus, your project is in jeopardy of missing deadlines as well as not realizing all the value you hope to achieve.

Technical team members   The team must have a full complement of technical resources supporting the project. Gone are the days of a few programmers to support a fairly simple mainframe environment. The new technology components dictate strong DBA (database administrator), network, and technical-architecture support, as well as traditional programmer/analyst roles. Members of the team should include package experts as well as company system experts for the various roles of conversions, interface development, and new-package development and integration. Tuning the various system components is also a key task with a client server–based application (whether a two- or three-tier environment), and the DBA is a key contributor to the success of this process.

Change management   A key in driving the organization toward the new future-state vision and realizing the value of the project is gaining the support of your organization and ensuring a smooth transition to the "new way of doing things." Individuals and processes that support this are key to the success of your project. These resources should not be overlooked. In general, we see too often that the organization doesn't invest in these key roles and therefore doesn't realize the benefits and success of the newly integrated system and processes into its business.

Consulting support   Most organizations have not undergone major transformational initiatives, are not familiar with the latest technologies, and do not have expertise in the new package features that are being implemented. Also, they need support to facilitate the strategy and direction of the future-state practices based on best practices collected from a series of client-supporting roles. In this light, it's critical and much more cost effective in the long run to have professional consulting support for your very important business issues. However, here's a word of caution on the extent of consulting support: Your organization must have ownership in the project and provide the key resources who understand the organization, the environment/climate, and the culture, and who really support the initiative. Otherwise, after the consultants pack up and leave, your organization will be left to try to pick up the pieces—and you shouldn't blame the consultants if that's the case.

Table 5.3 outlines some of the major roles that are typically found in an ERP system implementation project or ERP system improvement project. Regardless of whether the project is a new implementation or not, these roles are critical to the project's success. Also, in some cases individuals can fill more than one role, depending on the size and complexity of the implementation and on their skill sets and capabilities.

Table 5.3   **Project Team Roles**

Role	Description
Steering committee	Provides strategic direction to the project Monitors progress of the project against critical milestones Makes decisions regarding changes in scope Manages resource requirements from respective organizations
Project sponsors	Have ultimate authority over and responsibility for the project Approve changes to the scope and provide whatever additional funds those changes require Make the business decisions for the project Make user resources available
Quality advisor	Provides an independent assessment of the engagement processes used by the project or engagement team Recommends corrective actions to deal with identified issues

Table 5.3   **Project Team Roles *(Continued)***

Role	Description
Project management team	Controls the day-to-day aspects of the project
	Participates day to day in one or more projects
	Performs project management processes (structure, plan, control, assess, report, conclude)
	Develops and maintains project charter and project plans
	Reviews and approves major work products
	Executes formal reviews and management reviews
	Tracks and disposes of issues
	Tracks action items and budgets
Subject-matter experts	Supply business knowledge of PeopleSoft, communication industry, and technical architecture
	Supply knowledge of best practices for PeopleSoft
Team leaders	Assist in the day-to-day aspects of the team and project
	Assist with team management processes (structure, plan, control, assess, report, conclude)
	Track and resolve issues
	Track action items and budgets
	Act as decision maker for the team
Business analysts	Responsible for documenting business processes, transactions, and scenarios
	Coordinate and communicate the business requirements for the data conversion and interfaces to the technical teams
	Design procedures
	Design training programs and materials
Package specialists	Provide package expertise on a functional level
	Assess current systems
	Develop and maintain models of business requirements
	Design business transactions
	Design and organize procedures
	Document and analyze business processes

Table 5.3   **Project Team Roles *(Continued)***

Role	Description
Change management analysts	Provide advice on the use of organizational alignment approaches and techniques in an engagement design Analyze people enablers for their alignment with business processes, organizational systems, and the business strategy Assist the enterprise in planning the alignment of people enablers Design people enablers and assist in their implementation
Developers	Develop user interfaces, bolt-ons, extensions, and conversion programs Develop custom reports using PeopleSoft and SQR Reports tools Modify PeopleSoft using PeopleTools Comply with development standards and procedures Implement test scenarios
Technical analysts	Establish project support technology standards Assist team members in the use of project support technology Maintain project support technology Ensure that the technical environment is in place and operational throughout the project Establish and maintain target environment for new applications Maintain and administrate the support environment Support the software packages through implementation Prepare detailed interface design specifications Prepare testing criteria and data conversion strategies
Database administrator	Establishes, coordinates, and maintains databases and the database environment Coordinates access and information on database users
End users	Provide source information to the team Provide expert understanding of their business area Represent the users' area in identifying current or future procedures Participate in testing activities

You should always remember that your staffing requirements are constrained by several factors, including:

- ▶ Budget
- ▶ Resource availability
- ▶ Project timeline and completion date
- ▶ Project roles and skill sets
- ▶ Work to be accomplished

Once the team has clearly defined its game plan (via the project charter) and drafted the right mix of resources, it must have a sound infrastructure supporting it throughout this major initiative. Both the project management and the technical infrastructure must be in place.

Establishing the Project Infrastructure

To ensure that the project stays on track and a structure is in place to monitor progress, the project infrastructure must be established. The main elements behind the project infrastructure include:

Issues management   Uses procedures for monitoring and tracking issues that arise on the project

Scope management   Ensures that the scope of the project is managed and monitored, including analysis of any proposed changes

Knowledge management   Ensures that there is an effective process for team members to transfer their knowledge to each other and to the end users, and captures the knowledge from this project to share with others for future initiatives

Capturing actuals   Ensures that project actuals (actual time and costs spent) are tracked and monitored on a regular basis

Quality management plan   Ensures that quality controls and control points are established throughout the project, including both technical and functional quality controls as well as all deliverable controls

Risk management plan   Helps your team to analyze the risk of the implementation or future state and to target action plans for any risk areas, including people, resources, process, and technical risks

Project equipment   Includes obtaining and installing the hardware, software, and office equipment that is necessary to meet project objectives and support the project as it moves through its various stages

Change management plan   Helps ensure that you have a sound approach to analyzing the change your team is about to undertake across the organization; includes assessing the current environment and the impact the future-state environment will have on your organization

Some of these areas will be discussed in detail below, but *all* must be in place to kick off and start a project successfully. Whether the team is tracking this information electronically or not, the information and plans should be created in order to manage the project effectively and keep it on track.

Project Management

Again, on the project management side, mechanisms to track project status, issues, progress, risks, and changes must be put into place to ensure success, measure results, and track against your vision/value.

The project management effort initially establishes standards and procedures for the individual teams to plan and maintain realistic schedules using a project management application tool like Microsoft Project. Project infrastructure procedures should address the structuring of each new team, development of project charters, development and maintenance of resource-driven work plans, capturing of work-effort estimates and actuals, and consolidation of summarized plans into a project-level schedule. It's important for the project or team leader to monitor progress against goals and to make changes as appropriate based on team performance, team makeup, and ability to meet deadlines.

Issues Management

Project issues must be identified and resolved in a timely manner in order for the project to stay on track, meet deadlines, and reach a successful conclusion. Since unidentified or unresolved issues can slow the project and affect the morale of the individuals involved, sound issues management becomes a critical success factor in the project.

The project team should track all issues in an issues log of some type that's available to all project team members. This log can also serve as a communication vehicle on the status of all issues. The project team should review and update the log weekly if not daily. Anyone involved in the project should be allowed to identify an issue. It should be the responsibility of the project manager to approve, reject, or defer an issue. The project manager should present the issue and proposed resolution to the project sponsor for approval, rejection, or deferral.

Risk Management

Every project carries with it a certain amount of risk. To manage and minimize risk, a formal risk management process should be followed. The risk management plan should be maintained during the project by:

- Maintaining and monitoring open issues to determine how they may affect the overall project risk

- Monitoring project scope and control activities

- Monitoring adjustments to project targets

Project risk factors and a risk management approach should be monitored and updated periodically throughout the project to address new and changing areas of risk.

Scope Management

Should project changes be proposed, they should be documented and analyzed to ensure that those with the highest benefits are implemented, and those with less-immediate benefits are preserved for possible implementation at a later date.

Proposed project scope changes should be submitted and managed through a formal change-management assessment process. The steps in this process should include these:

1. Change requests are submitted by any member of the project team.

2. Once a request is submitted, the project team reviews the suggestion(s), considering the following factors:

   - Effect on the timing of the overall project

   - Resources needed to complete the change

   - Benefits of producing the change

   - Other deliverables that may be delayed by accepting the change

Change Management

Reengineering projects can create a turbulent environment and the need for strong change-management expertise. Implementing change the correct way, the first time, requires a proactive structure and a disciplined approach. By assessing the interdependence of the organization's people, business processes, and technology, organizational-change management can help to:

▶ Prepare the organization's management team for what is necessary to successfully implement the change initiative

▶ Promote involvement in the change process by working with the organization's employees to identify implementation work

▶ Build a detailed transition-management plan to manage implementation risks

▶ Create change-management teams that are charged with the responsibility and who have the capability to manage the transition

▶ Monitor and measure the interim and final results and the effectiveness of the change effort

Technical Infrastructure

On the technical infrastructure side, your team needs the hardware and software necessary to get the project started, including networking resources, project directory structures, and file- and document-naming conventions. The team also needs access to the tools necessary to manage and report the project status, plan, and budget, as well as tools for supporting application development.

It's important to get the application up and running as soon as possible to support your development environment. Once it's in place, key strategies and guidelines must be established to effectively monitor any system changes and the migration effort.

You'll also need to determine your initial configuration and table setup as well as create an initial database instance strategy—i.e., how many environments need to be set up initially and in the future, what the process is for keeping these environments up and running, what data should be loaded in the database tables, etc.

Figure 5.2 shows a diagram of typical PeopleSoft 8 configurations, along with the basic system components. Of course, one of the first decisions you need to make with PeopleSoft is what database structure you are going to implement (such as Oracle, DB2, Sybase, Informix, or SQL Server). Generally, this decision is based on several factors including the size of the organization, current relationships with the vendors, the current skill sets working with any of the database packages, and the ability of PeopleSoft to support your environment. Currently, the database most often used by PeopleSoft customers is Oracle; DB2 is a distant second, and SQL Server is a close third.

Figure 5.2 **PeopleSoft environments**

Internet Architecture

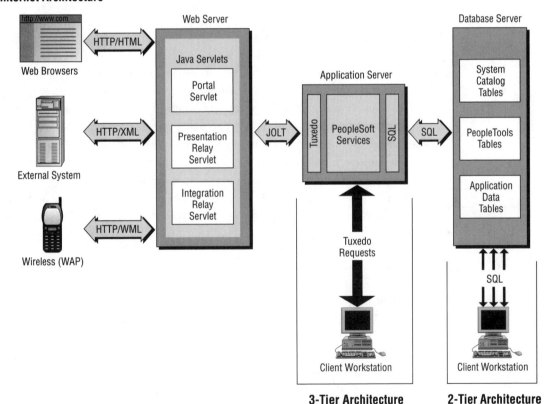

What you also need to do is determine your initial sizing requirements and needs so that you may, in turn, determine what size server you will need and what your memory and DASD or disk space requirements will be. The technology and infrastructure will be discussed in more detail in Chapter 6, "Surveying the Infrastructure."

Creating a Project Plan

The project plan is another key element in getting the project started and off to a great beginning. The plan contains the details on how, when, and who will accomplish the tasks necessary to cross the finish line to a successful implementation. The project plan has two main ingredients:

Project work plan   Describes the detailed estimates, schedule, and resources for the project, including the task list, dependencies, and milestones

Project budget   Documents the costs associated with the project, including labor, travel, living, facilities, hardware, software, support, and solution costs

A detailed project work plan for day-to-day management of the project should be developed. The plan should be task-specific and show dependencies as well as resource assignments and level of efforts. Estimates should be based on experiences such as work done on similar projects or on information from other PeopleSoft implementations (as obtained from your consulting partner or vendor). However, no estimate is perfect, and contingencies should be built into your plan. Your final estimate should allow for overly optimistic estimates and for the unforeseen factors that can put a project behind schedule and over budget. Remember, no project that you or anyone else has worked on has gone exactly as planned, no matter how good your team or project manager was.

TIP   A good guideline is to allow for 10% additional contingency for a project once it has started up and the details of scope and resources are firmly set. For future projects that are not as well set, allow for 20–25% contingency. Adjust the contingency based on risk and uncertainty.

Remember that you should at all times try to balance quality, time, and costs with your originally outlined scope to help set expectations and guidelines for estimating. If you need to make any changes to any of these items, the others will need to be adjusted accordingly. For instance, if you have to accelerate your timeline, you also have to reduce your scope, increase your costs, or decrease your quality. Figure 5.3 helps illustrate this point.

Figure 5.3 **Adjusting the project scope**

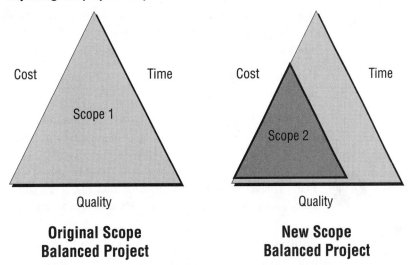

**Original Scope
Balanced Project**

**New Scope
Balanced Project**

Scope must decrease to meet
accelerated time goals.

To increase the reliability of your estimates, you should try multiple estimating approaches (e.g., consult other projects with similar tasks and use special estimating tools that can be provided by the vendor or a consultant). Also, look at the assumptions underlying the estimating guidelines and be sure to articulate what your assumptions were in determining the estimate. Remember the value you are trying to drive when creating your project plan and budget. When estimating according to your three constraints of cost, time, and quality, also consider the value you are trying to deliver. When documenting the internal milestones during the project, be sure to include in your plan the milestones for the value identification and delivery. Also, when looking at the project budget, consider the value to be delivered in relation to the costs you have outlined.

When determining the budget for your project, you need to consider both direct and indirect costs, and fixed and variable costs. You also need to identify the costs that can be capitalized, as well as those that are expensed. Generally, you can break your project costs into six generic cost categories:

Labor To calculate a cost target for labor, you generally take the total hours divided by the average labor rate to get your baseline.

Training In this area you need to understand the training needs of your team and what training each individual would need to complete in order to become a successful project member. Remember to put your training requirements in your project plan in order to track the overall project/cost impact. Look for alternatives to training, including off-the-shelf, self-study modules or information, workshops, and reading material.

Facilities   This is the cost of renting your space or other costs of maintaining your work space.

Travel and living   This cost generally includes transportation such as airfare and rental cars as well as accommodations and meals.

TIP   To help minimize travel and living expenses, create a handbook of expense policy guidelines to share with all project team members.

Solutions   This category of costs includes the people, process, and technology costs around the solution you are designing. These may be costs of new hardware for the end users in order for the PeopleSoft application to work effectively or costs of additional third-party software that's needed for your solution. They also include costs of communications mediums and maintenance fees.

Project support   This area includes your administrative supplies and support, team-building events, informal team gatherings, phone and fax usage, research, mail, etc., that support the project team.

Ensure that the project team is monitoring the plan and associated budget on a continuous basis throughout the life of the project. Project budget and resource variance reports should be produced on a regular basis (usually ranging from weekly to monthly).

TIP   Continuously refine the budget based on changes in sponsorship, direction, organization, resources, and other factors.

The project team should also review and define all key management reporting requirements. Generally these requirements include:

▶ Type of information required by role

▶ Frequency of reporting (e.g., weekly, monthly, etc.)

▶ Medium (e.g., written or oral)

It's very helpful to track key milestones, looking at each of the key areas of your project (such as technical, process, and people), and to set up a "dashboard" that indicates (by a red, yellow, or green status symbol) the current status of the reported area. This helps in analyzing where the major areas of risk or concern are and in drilling down to the cause and actions required to get the team back on track. The green symbol indicates all systems go! Yellow indicates caution and generally signals areas that need attention and additional monitoring or actions to get the project on track. Red signifies major impacts to the project (or a stop to the forward motion of the project) if the issue is not resolved immediately. Generally, for all areas that are not green, we recommend that you indicate resolution dates (just like issues) as well as who is responsible and what the action steps are.

Kicking Off the Project

It is a good idea to officially kick off the project by getting all the team members together to outline the basic project structure, roles and responsibilities, and initial project plan—and to get everyone on the "same page."

In most cases this is also a great opportunity to conduct some basic training (with both the users and the new project members) so that everyone has a basic understanding of the new package (PeopleSoft in this case) as well as the project goals, objectives, and plan of attack.

Generally, the project kickoff meeting includes these components:

▶ Review project history: Why this project has started. What the value proposition is. What activities have occurred to get us here.

▶ Review project charter: Include a discussion of goals and objectives, project scope, team organization, high-level timeline, and major milestones.

▶ Address key upcoming milestones, defining key tasks and deliverables that will be produced. Be sure to outline respective responsibilities by roles.

▶ Provide overview of package: Generally, a PeopleSoft package demonstration is given, outlining the key navigation and structure of the system as well as key functionality. This is just to give all the team a common baseline and is not meant to replace formal training.

▶ Provide any additional training such as methodology training or reviewing terms that members are not familiar with. Include a discussion of how the project will be managed, including issue and scope management.

▶ Provide basic project team information: Names, phone numbers, and key contact information for all team members should be distributed, along with any other common project guidelines.

Once the project is officially kicked off, the team and stakeholders will be prepared to move forward toward their successful implementation—equipped with the information and tools necessary to manage and control the project.

Up Next

Now that we've assessed the organization, created plans to help align it with your goals and objectives, and gotten the entire project infrastructure and team in place, what's next? The next chapter will cover the technical infrastructure and what you'll need to put in place in order to support your project from a technology standpoint. Whether your PeopleSoft system will run as a client-server, two-tiered application or in a three-tiered Web environment, your project must be supported effectively from a technology perspective, with the appropriate procedures and policies in place to ensure success.

Surveying the Infrastructure

F E A T U R I N G :

▶ A look at the key technical infrastructure components

▶ What technical resources are required to support your technical infrastructure

▶ What key policies and procedures you should have in place to support your technical needs

O nce you have your project infrastructure and project team in place and have kicked off the project, what are the key technical infrastructure issues that you need to resolve? This chapter outlines the initial key decisions to be made regarding the infrastructure, and details the key roles and procedures that need to be in place to support your PeopleSoft project and your new or existing system.

We think it's always important to look at the people, processes, and technology involved. If any area is left out of the equation, your implementation might fall short of expectations. By reviewing each of these areas, even though this chapter analyzes only the technical infrastructure components, you'll ensure a very viable and supported environment in the long run.

Technology Components

In this section we'll look at how each of the major technical infrastructure components should be analyzed and the decisions that need to be made in order to obtain a robust infrastructure that will support your project and implementation. The specific components we'll discuss include:

- ▶ Database platform

- ▶ Server

- ▶ Network

- ▶ Client workstation (desktop)

Database Platform

Before you can accomplish almost anything else in the area of technical infrastructure, you need to select the database platform that you'll be supporting. Some ERP packages, such as Oracle, make this decision very easy, while others, such as PeopleSoft, make it a bit more complicated, given the various platforms you may choose from.

With PeopleSoft, the philosophy of the founders was to provide a robust system that could work on virtually any relational database platform. Therefore, the database type would not limit you to just one platform but would allow you to choose the best one to fit your needs. So PeopleSoft is not database dependent and can be changed to support new platforms as they emerge. PeopleSoft's development team realized that the database systems of today just might not be the right ones for tomorrow. Given PeopleSoft's decision, however, the complexity and ability to fine-tune the application is left more in the hands of the project team than in the package itself. Tools are provided to help adapt the application to the platform and to tune appropriately, but the ability to leverage key components of the database architecture (such as what Oracle has done with its application) is just not as plausible.

Which Database Platform Is Best for Me?

Following is a list of your current choices with PeopleSoft.

▶ IBM DB2/MVS

▶ IBM DB2/Unix

▶ Oracle

▶ Informix

▶ Microsoft SQL Server

▶ Sybase

▶ SQL Base

So now that we've established that a database platform is needed, which one is best for you? Here are some key criteria that you should consider:

Volume   PeopleSoft has a detailed sizing questionnaire that can help you assess the volume, based on number of users, types of tasks performed, transactional volume per month (e.g., number of requisitions or invoices per month), number of customers, and number of vendors. Documenting these details can help you narrow down your options. For instance, with lower-volume transactions and smaller companies, the SQL Server and SQL Base platforms are plausible options. For larger and more complex implementations, most clients look to Oracle, DB2, or Informix as their database platform.

Product support   What is the prevalent database of choice by PeopleSoft clients, and thus where are the development dollars being spent? Also, due to the large client base, issues are noticed first with that platform and acted upon more quickly, including extensive testing and/or beta sites.

Note   Currently, Oracle is the #1 platform of choice by PeopleSoft clients, with over 50% of the client base choosing Oracle.

Skill set   With all other factors being equal, does your company have a set of skills in-house that can be leveraged on a particular database platform, as well as a companywide license agreement already in place to support it? If so, that may be your primary driver. For example, if your company has a large IT (information technology) shop with in-house DB2/MVS skills and a companywide contract/relationship with IBM, it might make sense to leverage that and not go with a totally new package such as Informix. In the latter case, another contract and relationship would have to be managed, and a totally new set of IT skills would need to be developed.

Total cost of ownership   Finally, you want to be sure that the overall cost of maintaining your system—your hardware and software as well as your people and processes—is factored into the decision. Also, we recommend that you cost out multiple configurations before making your final decision.

Server

Once you've selected your database platform, the next item to consider is which database server you should buy to support your development and production environments, as well as your testing or training environments. To help with this decision, again you need to look at a few key items:

Current relationships with hardware vendors   Does your company already have an agreement with a particular hardware vendor such as Sun or Hewlett-Packard (HP)? If so, you may already have discount agreements as well as in-house expertise and vendor relationships that you can leverage.

Benchmarks   PeopleSoft has worked with each of its vendors to perform various benchmark studies outlining performance of each configuration to help you identify the platform that might be best for your environment. Work with these studies, PeopleSoft, your consulting partners, and hardware vendors to get the best results for your implementation.

It's up to you to make the final choice since PeopleSoft's philosophy is based on pleasing its customers and giving them choices. Although this won't be your last chance to make these decisions, remember to weigh all components when making your decisions and to call in the experts to help you with these key decisions. Remember, too, that it's best to look at your configuration options and identify any potential problems earlier rather than later. By bringing all parties together early in your process, you might avoid painful surprises in the future. Review options with your package vendor, obtaining feedback about each option; and, during your assessment, identify any potential problems, fixes, or patches. Also, you may find that references from PeopleSoft clients who have already implemented your candidate configurations will be helpful.

Two or Three Tiers

Another key decision you need to make is whether you'll run your PeopleSoft configuration in a two- or three-tiered manner or both. Figure 6.1 outlines these two types of configurations. With PeopleSoft 8, you don't have this decision since you cannot run this version in a two-tiered mode. You need both a database server and an application server, as well as a Web server, to support your configuration.

Figure 6.1   **PeopleSoft tiered architectures**

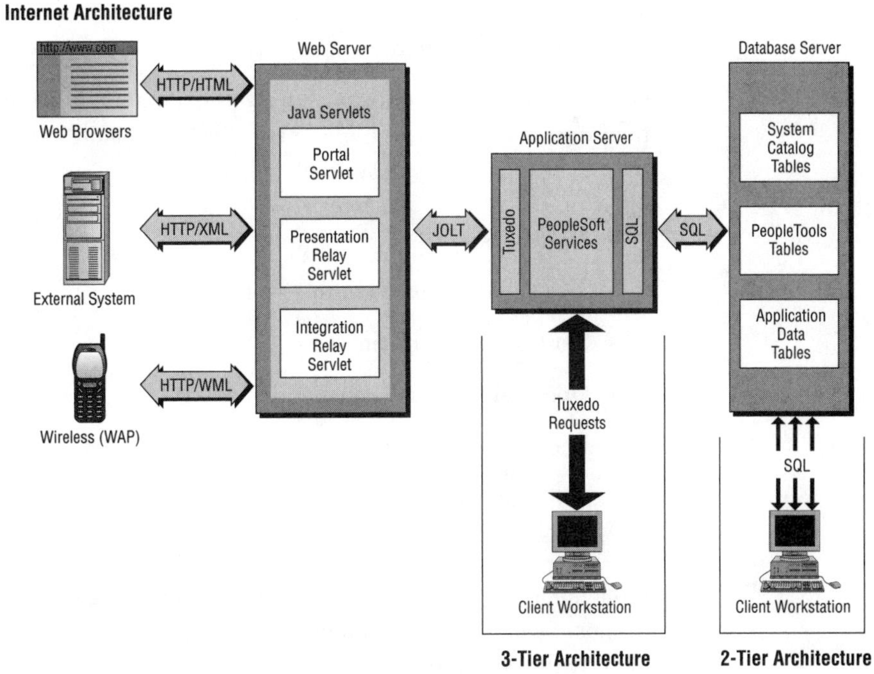

Internet Architecture

For each tier, you need to determine the number of servers required, including whether your application and database server will be on the same physical machine (box) or not. You should produce a high-level diagram outlining your proposed configuration. A key factor in determining size and number is understanding the number of sites that will be accessing your environment. For each site, you should detail the functionality and configuration to be used. For example, will there be one or multiple servers? What will be the physical distribution of the clients? Define any special access requirements, such as specific multisite configurations, data center configurations, remote access by mobile users, and Web access. Be sure to include numbers and frequency of use in your assessment. Define any requirements to interface either with entities outside the company, such as the electronic data interchange (EDI), or through an application programming interface (API) to an "outside" system. All these factors play into your server requirements.

With the new open integration framework (OIF) that's available with People-Soft 8, the application is more flexible in integrating with external systems (both within and outside the company). The OIF allows Internet-enabled APIs, which leverage XML (Extensible Markup Language), thereby making the application much easier to integrate. Take this into account when considering and analyzing your hardware requirements.

Once you have these questions answered, compile a list of your options for platform configurations. Include specifications such as these:

- ▶ Model

- ▶ Memory size

- ▶ Types and number of processors

- ▶ Storage requirements

- ▶ Operating system (name and version)

- ▶ Backup systems

- ▶ Any additional peripherals such as printers and scanners (bar code, image, or document)

Remember to include the *maximum* for each category, such as the maximum memory size, maximum number of processors, etc. For each of your choices, identify the cost and effort involved, including the costs of installation, annual maintenance, and broker commissions.

TIP Plan for growth: Ensure that you are including growth assumptions in your sizing considerations—not only for growth in data but also for growth in your processing and user base.

As mentioned before, in a three-tier environment, you may choose to have two servers (one for your application and the other for your database); but you can physically house this environment on one server if desired, and the system will support your requirements. With PeopleSoft 8, you'll also need to develop a Web server strategy based on the number of self-service users as well as full-time users you have on your application. Many organizations create a load-balancing process to help manage the loads on their Web servers and provide maximum performance support for their end users.

Sizing

To help with sizing your server, including the memory and DASD (direct access storage device) or disk space requirements, you first must outline the number of "instances," or copies, of the database you will need to maintain to support your system, both in the short run (i.e., for the life of your project) and in the long term. To do this, you need to produce a detailed overview of each instance that is required, including:

▶ Purpose of database

▶ Size (data requirements)

▶ Backup requirements

Each additional instance does not necessarily equate to a new server; it's possible to create new instances on an existing platform. Be sure to consult PeopleSoft and experts on the viability of "sharing" your platform with other applications. Disadvantages of sharing include:

▶ Conflicts between maintenance, rapid changes, and availability. For instance, the development environment may need frequent system changes; as a consequence, there may be low availability even though the production, training, and testing environments require much higher availability.

▶ Possible performance loss due to multiple uses of environment components.

▶ Confusion between environments due to inadequate environment separation (sharing table space and other tables).

▶ Reduced ability to obtain isolated environment performance metrics for scaling in the future.

Of course, these considerations must be weighed in conjunction with costs and maintenance ability. In general, it's wise to look at the potential for at least three separate environments, including one for development, one for testing, and the last for production.

Based on our experience, you should consider setting up the following database instances:

Generic PeopleSoft-delivered environment   Sometimes referred to as the "demo" environment, this instance is the generic copy of the PeopleSoft-delivered application, containing no modifications or changes made by you or your team. This environment can be used to test any bugs or potential fixes. When an issue arises in the future, you can also use this environment to determine whether the issue resulted from your modifications or was a problem that existed with the generic application. Generally, this is the instance that PeopleSoft installs at your site during their first visit. PeopleSoft also delivers an instance referred to as "sys," which is essentially a copy of the demo environment but excluding any dummy or test data.

Development environment   This environment is where all your system modifications (from both a coding and a table setup) occur. Since tables can be modified routinely in this environment, we recommend that only a limited amount of data be maintained.

Testing environment   You may need multiple instances for testing your system, including instances for system, integration, and stress testing. You must evaluate your work plan, data needs, and costs to determine whether a single or multiple instances are appropriate. Data sizing for this environment should be based on testing requirements, including the needs for the stress testing.

Conversion environment   This instance may not be needed for all implementations, depending on how much data conversion activity is occurring and within what time span. Some teams use their testing and/or production instances to run conversion. However, the team should assess requirements for this environment and determine whether a separate instance makes sense both logically and economically. Again, you should plan for enough data space based on the amount of data being converted.

Training environment   This environment is used to provide demonstrations and training for the end users and is generally configured with a set of predefined data and sets of exercises. Depending on the number of concurrent classes occurring, there may be a need for additional training instances to support multiple classes. A strategy for maintaining this data and refreshing it after each class should be considered.

Production environment   This is the final "go-live" instance that will be used by the end users once your system is up and running. All converted data and new transactions should be entered into this database. Sizing for this environment should be based on your data history requirements and volume of transactions, including room for growth. The growth strategy should be based on both an expanded user base and an increased volume of transactions as well as changes in organization such as acquisitions and/or divestitures. In some cases customers also set up a "fix" instance, where changes can be applied in the production environment prior to applying them directly to the production instance. Again, you should look at risks, costs, and internal policy to assess whether this is necessary for you.

For each instance, the overall number of users, geographic distribution, and estimates of usage should be considered, in addition to the physical data requirements. Also, the availability of each instance should be looked at in terms of average and peak usage. Remember to look at peak times such as those resulting from coding deadlines and overlaps in work-plan tasks to help derive your requirements. Also consider network capacity and how this may affect your sizing and your interaction with external vendors, suppliers, and customers.

Once you have determined your database requirements, sizing, and usage, your technology team can diagram your requirements and monitor them as the project moves ahead.

TIP   Remember to continuously monitor your technology environment. Don't just diagram requirements and put them on the shelf.

A truly successful implementation project is one that is consistently monitoring its environments and adjusting to changes in your plan, assumptions, and overall technology configuration.

Network

When looking at your network infrastructure, you should focus first on your current configuration, including physical diagrams of the entire network configuration (both LANs and WANs), logical diagrams of each of the network protocols in use, and descriptions of all hubs, routers, and switches, detailing vendor, model, configuration, and capacity. Be sure that you've collected enough detail to make capacity planning decisions. Also, identify the route paths in an effort to identify communication capabilities to other facilities. Often traffic management blocks additional traffic on segments that are close to capacity.

A poor network design can doom a project to failure before it starts and has little to do with your PeopleSoft application. Look for internal or external experts to help evaluate your situation.

To assess your current network, you should:

- ▶ Review the current network in terms of performance, reliability, and expandability. Note any potential trouble areas, such as network traffic bottlenecks or single points of failure for mission-critical segments. This review not only helps to identify potential problems but serves as a communications mechanism for setting expectations.

- ▶ Use readily available software tools to assess performance within a network. Most in-house IT organizations have access or can get access to such "sniffing" devices.

- ▶ Assess all parts of the network, including:
  - ▶ WANs
  - ▶ LANs
  - ▶ Routers
  - ▶ Switches
  - ▶ Internal as well as external components, including Internet connections if necessary

Once you've assessed your current situation, map out your new network, including a high-level design of the new environment that shows the facility backbone and inter-site connectivity as well as the transmission method and speed throughout the network. Be sure to produce a set of designs at the component level, detailing the placement of servers, clients, and network electronics components. Identify any new LAN segments and WAN connections that are necessary, and specify network protocols and transmission speeds throughout the network.

TIP   Remember to consider any global implications for your network, including bandwidth restrictions and compliance with other countries' policies, as these can impact your decisions.

Your proposed network should include:

▶ The placement of new servers, clients, and network electronics (such as hubs, switches, and routers)

▶ Details of communications protocols

▶ An analysis of new elements' impact on existing network performance

▶ Additional hardware and software required by the server and client platforms

▶ The cost and effort involved in implementing the changes (including the cost of training)

▶ The manageability of new network components, with the risks identified

Review the designs from a performance standpoint, looking for potential bottlenecks such as platforms that frequently converse but are not close together. Also review the design for reliability, looking for single points of failure and considering how much redundancy should be built in. Lastly, review the design from an expandability standpoint: Identify the maximum capacity, the amount of expandability, and how the expandability might change the characteristics of the network.

Be sure to test for hardware and software conflicts within the network. This can be overlooked during an implementation and cause great pain in the end.

When looking at performance, benchmark yours against that of organizations with similar configurations to determine where you stand.

TIP   It is a good idea to work with PeopleSoft or your implementation partner to identify similar clients with similar configurations so that you can network and share ideas with them.

Never forget to review designs for any special access methods, including:

▶ Remote/mobile access

▶ Internet/intranet and Web connectivity

▶ Wireless communications

▶ External business partner communications such as an electronic data interchange (EDI)

▶ Firewalls

For these special considerations, focus special attention on security. Also be sure to describe all software that must coexist on the client workstation, including software for network protocol, desktop management, security and passwords, office automation (such as Word or Excel), e-mail, Web browser, virus protection, operating system, and any other locally developed applications.

For Internet access, review the firewall design and, for remote users, the dial-up and authentication procedures. Be sure to assess the customer and vendor satisfaction with regard to response time and technical support. Again, this is a chance to help set expectations and ensure a much smoother implementation. To determine what dial-up requirements are adequate, especially in a three-tier architecture, you must consider the users' roles, the number of users per site, the physical hardware (PCs), the types of transactions, and the reporting requirements.

Note   Always check the release notes for identification of possible hardware and software conflicts or bugs. Also, be sure to check "Customer Connections" at People-Soft's Web site (www.peoplesoft.com) for any issues.

Client Workstation

The final piece of your infrastructure puzzle is your customer's or client's workstation requirements. Workstation information to collect includes vendor, model, memory, CPU type, disk storage (utilized and free), and other peripherals such as modem, browser, and CD drive. PeopleSoft has a recommended list of workstation requirements including printers. When evaluating your choices, you should consider both the cost and the level of effort to install and maintain your equipment.

TIP The minimum requirements are usually not enough. Again, plan for growth and increased responsibilities of the users.

As mentioned before, the client's workstation will usually need additional software, including distributed computing middleware, network protocol stack (such as TCP/IP or IPX drivers), database middleware (e.g., ODBC drivers, SQL*Net, DB-Lib, or Replication stubs), systems management, desktop management, Web browser, and development and testing tools. A full list of required and recommended software applications should be developed (based on project roles) along with their system requirements. Casual users will have substantially fewer requirements (especially with the Web-based PeopleSoft 8) than will your full-time "power" users, who are writing queries, developing reports, and inputting lots of data.

Installing PeopleSoft Software

When installing the PeopleSoft software, it's generally advisable to have People-Soft install the first instance within your environment and perform a set of validation tests to ensure that it's installed properly.

Warning Remember to review your contract to ensure that the vendor is living up to all its responsibilities regarding installation of the software.

Be sure that your end users and technical (IT) staff are reviewing the work the vendor is doing so that when additional copies are made, they can accomplish this task. Recompile all software modules under the current version of the operating system, and catalog all program versions. Also, ensure that all steps are clearly documented, noting any discrepancies or issues identified.

By performing a set of validation tests, you can determine whether the instance is indeed configured appropriately for your environment. Be sure to check all areas of functionality, including communications requirements, peripherals such as printers, and other processes such as reporting. Also remember to check on any special functionality or processing changes regarding global requirements, such as country-specific processes. By incorporating a "day-in-the-life" scenario in your testing, you should be set to move on.

TIP   Remember to check your contract for any limits regarding time to install and test the application after receiving it (e.g., 90 days), including the support you should receive, and for any required payments to the vendor.

Be sure to schedule installation planning meetings prior to the proposed installation date to cover all required tasks and important due dates. Include vendors (both software and hardware), contractors, implementation providers, appropriate users, and your technical (IT) staff in this process as necessary. You should confirm that the following are in place:

▶ Hardware needed to install and run PeopleSoft (what it is and when it will be delivered, so that all is in place prior to software installation)

▶ System software needed to run PeopleSoft (such as the operating system and database [RDBMS])

▶ Communications network requirements

▶ Any other peripherals that will be required

Also, develop contingencies for any alternative sources, should hardware or software not arrive on time. Once you have all this in place, you are ready for the installation.

Technical Resources

In additional to the hardware and software required for this complex implementation, the appropriate technical support personnel must be available to support the project. Table 6.1 shows the primary technical roles that usually are involved in a PeopleSoft or major ERP implementation project.

Table 6.1 **Support Roles in the Technical Environment**

Role	Responsibilities
IT technology team leader	Manage overall team enterprise support Coordinate systems DBA activities Coordinate application DBA activities Coordinate business partners' IT resource requests Interface among business partners/integrators, systems administration, and systems DBA Demos Site visits Software upgrades and maintenance Assist with team enterprise field implementation
IT infrastructure team leader	Manage overall team enterprise field implementation Coordinate desktop software installations Team enterprise Field Determine team enterprise field user configurations
Application database administrator	Application and database [RDBMS] systems support skills transfer Problem determination Testing and facilitation of software changes (maintenance, patches, new releases, etc.)
Systems database administrator	Backup and restore procedures Restart/recovery RDBMS software support Maintenance Patches New releases RDBMS performance tuning

Table 6.1   **Support Roles in the Technical Environment *(Continued)***

Role	Responsibilities
Systems administration	Backup and restore Systems performance tuning DASD administration User administration Operating systems support
Desktop integration	Desktop support
Distributed computing	Server support
Technology integration	Workstation rollout Desktop integration
Communication solutions	Testing communication links and connectivity for e-mail and other communication solutions, including IVR (interactive voice response)
Local site support	Desktop support Local network and printing support

All these roles are key to a successful implementation. Throughout the implementation cycle, you'll need individuals to help manage your large number of database instances, migration of "objects" (such as code, reports, interfaces, and conversion programs), tuning and performance monitoring, security configuration and maintenance, backup and recovery, and installation of system patches at the application (e.g., PeopleSoft), database (e.g., Oracle), and hardware (e.g., HP or Sun) levels. If any role is not covered or managed, it could affect the success of the overall project.

It's important for you to have a few key subject-matter experts associated with the team, either full-time or part-time, who can work with your IT staff to ensure that they are trained and up to speed on the latest PeopleSoft-specific technical issues. It's relatively easy to find a DBA who understands the Oracle database platform, but harder to find one who knows *both* the PeopleSoft application and the Oracle database. Although it's not necessary that your entire IT staff have knowledge of PeopleSoft, it's wise to have a few experts or individuals (either from the vendors or your implementation partner) who, at key times throughout your project, can help transfer knowledge to your staff, based on their expertise.

Policies and Procedures

There are many important policies and procedures around the infrastructure and technology area that should be in place to make your PeopleSoft implementation or current application a success. This section will cover the major areas, which include:

► Development standards

► Migration strategy

► Disaster recovery/backup plan

► Service-level agreement

Table 6.2 outlines some of the major IT processes and procedures that should be in place to support your implementation. Although we're concentrating on the four areas listed above, all are important for a successful implementation.

Table 6.2   **IT Processes and Procedures**

IT Area	IT Process and Procedure

IT administration	IT financial and asset management
	    Financial planning
	    Asset tracking (both hardware and software)
	Sourcing administration
	    Vendor selection
	    Contract administration
	    Vendor performance management
	    Technology life cycle management
	Customer relations
	Application development and support
	Training

Table 6.2 **IT Processes and Procedures *(Continued)***

IT Area	IT Process and Procedure
IT operations	Change management (both hardware and software)
	Risk assessment
	Change planning (including back-out planning)
	Change authorization
	Change tracking
	Change implementation
	Project planning and management
	Hardware change implementation
	Software distribution
	Facilities management
	Computer operations
	Network operations
	Database operations
	Disaster recovery
	Performance and capacity management
IT support	Service management program
	Service-level agreements
	Problem management
	Help desk
	Environment (server, network, etc.)
	Application
	Level 3 support, including:
	Operations support
	Systems support
	Database support
	Integration
	Test mechanism and procedures

Development Standards

As with any IT development project, whether package-specific or custom-developed, a set of development standards should be created and followed by the programming staff to ensure consistency and the ability to maintain your customizations. With a package solution, such as PeopleSoft, this is even more important. Considerations for both upgrades and your ability to easily distinguish your changes from those of the vendors are essential in developing these standards. We recommend that your team develop a developer's handbook that clearly articulates the correct process for modifying any object related to your new PeopleSoft system.

Development standards are important for several reasons. First, they define the conventions used to record modifications to the software programs and related objects, such as interfaces and reports. This eases the task of maintaining the customized code and helps individuals who take over the responsibilities of project members who have moved on to other roles in the organization or another organization. Second, the standards simplify the development and migration process by making it easier to identify changes, including naming and location conventions of programs. Lastly, the identification and naming conventions make it easier to upgrade when a new release of the software comes out.

Most standards documents should include an overview of the development life cycle, including adequate testing and quality control reviews, to ensure that standards are followed and maintained. Also, a detailed design deliverable should be accomplished for every software modification; it basically outlines the business requirements, user interfaces, edits, coding logic, manual procedures, report requirements, and coding changes.

 TIP   No coding changes should begin until the business requirement has been approved and the technical specifications reviewed by project leadership.

All coding changes should be thoroughly reviewed from both a technical and a functional perspective and also for quality control adherence to the development standards. A formal process should be in place to ensure that this happens.

When a vendor, such as PeopleSoft, has standards already in place, these should be followed as closely as possible. In the PeopleTools section of the online PeopleBooks user guide, PeopleSoft has outlined the key development standards that the company follows when developing code. Again, you should ensure that all your developers have access to this information and have reviewed it prior to starting any changes, including reporting and interface development.

In general, it's good to develop a strategy that easily identifies new objects by assigning a special naming convention, such as using the company initials or project initials either before or after the object name.

For example, let's consider a delivered PeopleSoft SQR (Structured Query Report Writer) report, PER021. If we modify this report for our project—let's assume the project is called STAR GAZER, or SG—we might name the modified report PER021SG. Since SQR names are limited to eight characters, we need to take that into consideration in our naming standards. Maybe a brand-new report would be listed as SG001. Again, within our document we should clearly articulate our standards for both new and changed objects.

As shown in that example, an existing object (such as a report) might be modified during the development process, or an entirely new object (such as a report) might be created. Naming conventions for both situations should be developed and put in place so that in the future it will be very easy to identify all new reports (e.g., they all start with SG) as well as all modified existing reports (e.g., they all end in SG). This will help individuals who will maintain the system after the project team departs, as well as those who will assist in the future with major system changes, such as upgrades or major enhancement projects.

Also, in all newly created programs or modified programs, when possible, a standard "source header" should be created to identify *what* was modified, and *why*. In any documentation it's extremely important to include a specific, unique string of characters to identify changes to the "plain vanilla" product. When you upgrade to the next release, this bit of information will come in handy in locating and identifying all changes. Generally, the source header should contain basic information such as the following:

- ▶ Program name and description

- ▶ Inputs (database tables, parameters passed, etc.)

- ▶ Outputs (output files, reports, etc.)

- ▶ Run frequency

- ▶ Special considerations

- ▶ Modification log (which includes date of change, developer, and description of change, and which should be modified every time the program is changed)

In general, it's also advisable to "comment out" any code changes (especially the PeopleSoft-delivered code) and *not* to remove the code. This helps with identification of changes during upgrades, when maybe the PeopleSoft-delivered code is modified but the project team chose to delete that code during their implementation. Since the original code is commented out and thus very easy for your team to identify, impacts to these upgrade changes can be analyzed.

Coding standards for PeopleSoft objects, including SQR, PeopleTools/People-Code, COBOL programs, records, panels, and fields, should all be developed and recorded in your guide. The standards should include not only naming conventions and comment requirements but also storage locations and processes around maintaining the objects.

A checklist that outlines the core development standards can be developed to help ensure that the programmers and staff are indeed following the guidelines. A quality review process should be put in place to help maintain the integrity of the standards as well.

Migration Strategy

Once all the database instances are defined and several are created, a process to migrate both changes and data from one instance to another must be established by the team. This process is defined as a *migration strategy*.

The migration strategy should clearly articulate the flow of objects from one environment to another. For instance, any changes made to an object should first be accomplished in the development database. A development "project" should be created once the changes have been unit-tested and approved for migration. This project should then be migrated to the other instances, based on a predefined strategy. Generally, this strategy is based on moving a coding object from development to testing and then into production. However, with a PeopleSoft system, there are usually many additional environments that may be affected (such as training and data conversion), and the approach to migrating objects to these environments should also be developed. Each environment or database instance should be assigned the following:

An owner   Someone who is responsible for maintaining the integrity of that database instance along with data requirements necessary to maintain it. This person is generally giving their okay to migrate a changed object into their environment.

A tester   Someone who is responsible for testing that the migrated object was appropriately migrated into their database instance.

An approver   Someone who "approves" that the change has been applied and tested in their environment.

All these roles can be assigned to the same person if desired. The key is to have a plan for moving the changes made from one instance to another while ensuring that proper testing and coordination is occurring for all objects, including both those directly related to the database and others, such as reports or interfaces.

In addition to identifying the people responsible for migration, the team should consider putting in place a detailed schedule of when the migrations will occur. Generally, this may be a weekly or sometimes daily activity, depending on the number of changes occurring and the need for the changes to be migrated to the different environments. You can have different requirements for each of your different instances. For example, you may want changes to your training database made only during the weekend (to avoid interrupting classes) or in the evenings. And perhaps only certain changes should be migrated to the training environment, whereas for the testing environment daily changes may not be enough. Also, depending on where you are in the project life cycle, these time frames may change as implementation dates near.

Another key area that relates to the migration plan is change management. You must ensure that a detailed process is in place to record, justify, and approve all these changes to the system, prior to their occurring, and that adequate documentation is in place to support the changes so that for future upgrades or production support, individuals will understand why these changes were accomplished.

Disaster Recovery Plan

Most likely, your organization already has policies and procedures to support requirements for disaster recovery. Also, existing systems may already be categorized and requirements outlined to support pending disasters. The first thing your group should do is leverage that existing work and only modify the requirements based on your new environments and functionality.

A *disaster recovery plan* (DRP) should include reviewing the communications capacity of your new facilities, the power capacity, and the overall risks. It should also consider technical as well as manual and policy changes, based on various disaster scenarios. Depending on the criticality of the functions performed as well as alternative arrangements, your plan should incorporate all aspects of the new processes.

In addition to being prepared for a disaster, you should always have a backup plan for each of your environments. This plan should ensure that adequate backups are in place to restore accidentally damaged data. For instances such as your training database, this may be particularly important since the "generic" set of data is used at the beginning of every class. For testing, the requirements may be very different from those required in your development environment. Again, you should consider resources, time, and costs in making your decisions.

In each backup plan, include a restoration plan that indicates the expected time to restore individual data elements or a complete database. Also, include on-site and off-site storage in your plans as appropriate.

Service-Level Agreement

Although the *service-level agreement* (SLA) is usually one of the last documents your IT staff and project team should develop prior to going live, it's perhaps one of your most important documents. It provides the basic agreement on services between your users and the support group. This document helps to set customer expectations as well as ensure that your support staff is focused on the right services. Your service-level agreement should:

▶ Provide focused attention on customer service, with precise statements of objectives and assumptions. This helps focus on service expectations and ensure that everyone clearly understands them.

▶ Set a standard method for communicating service expectations. Putting these expectations in writing establishes a formal process for communications among the end user, the customer, and the service provider.

▶ Document the IT service process that supports this major application. This gives the end users a clear picture of what is being provided.

- ▶ Clearly define roles and responsibilities from the standpoints of both cost and action.

- ▶ Outline the service objectives, which are mutually agreed on by both the customer (or end user) and the providers.

- ▶ Outline the costs associated with any services or additional requirements that are sought. This enables the end user or customer to make informed business decisions.

- ▶ Provide a basis for continuous improvements in customer service. Data can be collected on the processes and performance based on the objectives outlined in the SLA.

Remember that you might have different SLAs for your environments and that generally your production SLA is much more detailed and stringent than that required for testing or development.

As with the disaster recover plan, you should identify any preexisting SLAs prior to implementing your new system or environment. Leverage the work and requirements of these existing documents to help formulate your new SLAs. However, be sure to make modifications based on changes to the processes and systems.

Examples of service-level measurements that should be considered include:

- ▶ Normal and extended (off-hours) operating hours.

- ▶ System availability during both normal and extended operating hours (e.g., 95% available during normal business hours, which are 8 A.M. ET to 6 P.M. ET).

- ▶ Support availability and responsiveness. This generally is based on priority levels (e.g., high, medium, low—or 1, 2, 3) assigned to the proposed issue or problem and on the time frames for resolution or response to the requestor.

- ▶ System responsiveness, such as the number of transactions processed per day or the average online response time (which might be 10 seconds or less during normal business hours).

- ▶ Report generation, which should include online or on-demand reporting and batch requirements. Also, this might cover times when scheduled reports should be available or how often a report is completed on time.

▶ Administration capabilities, such as time to add a new user to the system (or delete an existing user) and time frames for how quickly software changes will be made.

Remember to include the costs of unanticipated outages and to look at the various durations of these outages in order to assess reaction times. In a critical time period during your payroll processing or close cycle, the times and costs may be much greater, whereas during off weeks of processing or in development environments, the outages might be less costly.

Be sure to identify the inherent or "as-is" capabilities of the environment and what the user or customer will receive based on the normal system expectations. Additional services or options should be clearly articulated, including expected costs and benefits.

Once all this is documented, be sure that all key participants read, understand, and officially sign the agreement.

To summarize: Setting up the technical infrastructure and all the related policies and procedures can be an overwhelming task for most organizations. Many organizations underestimate the time and resources needed for these tasks; or they fail to perform all the tasks, which usually results in difficulties during the implementation, requiring rework and unnecessary anguish. We highly recommend that while planning your project, you ensure adequate support in this area. It's a must, especially when you consider all the different software, hardware, and new technology involved.

Up Next

Now, for many people, the most rewarding and most difficult part of the project is up next: defining your business requirements and your organization's future-state processes, with the new software package in hand. In the next chapter, "Analyzing Company Requirements," we'll look at ways to help you organize and determine what your true business requirements are, how to leverage the best practices and leading-edge processes of the package to drive value into your organization, and what you can do to help support the changes ahead.

Analyzing Company Requirements

F E A T U R I N G :

- ▶ What are business requirements anyway, and who should identify them?
- ▶ Sponsorship—key support for requirements
- ▶ The 80/20 rule
- ▶ Building consensus
- ▶ Impacts on the software

- ▶ Identifying, recording, and prioritizing requirements
- ▶ Performing a gap analysis
- ▶ Finding the right solution
- ▶ Changing your business requirements or processes, not the software
- ▶ Impacts of your decisions and dealing with the change

T his chapter will review the process of defining your business requirements and your future-state processes and how well the software fits those needs. We'll look at ways to address "gaps" or changes to your needs and existing processes, including how to deal with these changes and prepare your organization for them.

Business Requirements: What Do They Comprise?

The character of each business is unique, determined by the business strategies that top management evolves, the way these strategies are executed, and the way the operating decisions are made and implemented. These strategies and implementations are complicated further by the processes and procedures that are already in place. The business environment is dynamic, and to remain competitive, each industry and each company has to mutate itself with increasing frequency and shorter cycle times. As a response, the business processes within the organization also have to be dynamic and evolving.

Note   *Business processes* are the structure through which the organization physically does what is necessary to produce value for its customers. A business process can also be defined as a specific ordering of work activities across time and place, with a beginning, an end, and clearly defined inputs and outputs.

What converts the inputs into a final product or service for an organization is a combination of major processes such as sourcing, vendor (a company supplying a product or service to another individual or organization), production, sales, etc., each broken down into multiple subprocesses. In addition to the core processes, there are support processes such as the knowledge process (which involves capturing, leveraging, and reusing information or knowledge) and the people process (those areas that affect your employees or people). Figure 7.1 shows the supply-chain process and how inputs are processed to produce a specific result for the customer.

Figure 7.1   **Flow/requirements of the supplier process**

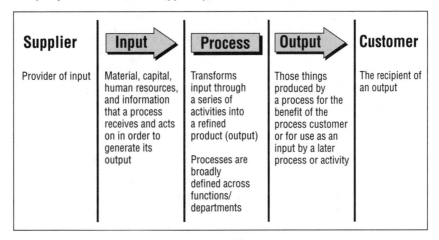

Supplier	**Input**	**Process**	**Output**	**Customer**
Provider of input	Material, capital, human resources, and information that a process receives and acts on in order to generate its output	Transforms input through a series of activities into a refined product (output) Processes are broadly defined across functions/ departments	Those things produced by a process for the benefit of the process customer or for use as an input by a later process or activity	The recipient of an output

Figure 7.2 contains a process grid showing the value-addition chain in a process. The business processes run across organizational units and are measurable in terms of cost, time, output, quality, and customer satisfaction. The same is true for the subprocesses making up the major processes. Hence, an organization can be seen as a combination of well-meshed, efficiently run processes.

Figure 7.2   **Business processes across organizational units**

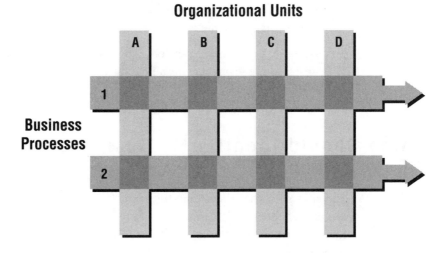

Building from parts to the whole, fulfilling the business requirements of each subprocess, and building up, we can define the requirements for the whole organization; and, as an extension, by designing a set of efficient subprocesses, an efficient and effective organization can be built.

What Should I Do Today about Business Requirements?

What your business looks and feels like today is the response of what the market space needed yesterday. Organizations take time to adapt to changes, and the existing procedures and processes act as restraining harnesses for these changes. For most organizations, this leads to a reactive response to shift in the market space and the consequent loss of leadership position.

The solution lies in analyzing your business with an eye on future requirements while serving today's business processes. The business requirements of tomorrow are contingent on various factors, including:

Environment shifts   How is the Internet affecting your business?

Industry shifts   The packaging industry went through major shifts when plastic was introduced as an alternative to metal, paper, and glass packaging.

Technology shifts   If a satellite-based global phone system such as Iridium had been less costly with lighter handsets, what would have happened to cell phone technology?

Customer preferences shifts   The sports utility vehicle (SUV) is the fastest growing segment of the auto industry. It has forced almost every brand to offer a product in this market segment, which was virtually nonexistent just a few years ago.

Who Should Identify My Business Requirements?

Statistics show that almost one-third of software implementation projects fail because of either underassessment of the scope or exclusion of certain critical functionalities from the scope. These failures represent an alarming amount of resources spent wrongly. One of the key strategies applied by project managers to ensure project success is appropriate assessment of business requirements and, in turn, the scope.

The implementation team for each PeopleSoft module is responsible for the success of that module. This team should have the primary responsibility of critically analyzing the business processes, identifying and documenting the business requirements therein, and getting a buy-in from the end users of the module. To accomplish all these tasks, the team should include people who are at the operational level to chalk the business process, identify how the current process overlaps or conflicts with other processes, identify which areas could possibly lose control, etc.; people who can address the issues and offer alternative solutions; and the people who can make the decisions. You also require some strategic thinkers who are aware of the broad direction in which the business and the company are moving and who can ensure that the solution design is consonant with that direction.

It's a good idea to involve external consultants to help identify your business requirements. Yes, the consultants don't know your business as well as you do, but they can help you through the process in a structured manner and ensure higher success rates and effectiveness. They can also provide insight into best practices and what other companies are doing to address these processes in their organizations.

Once the identification of business requirements is complete, two critical tasks remain: obtaining buy-in from the sponsors and prioritizing the requirements. Each of these tasks is discussed in detail in later sections of this chapter.

Where Is My Business Going?

The meteoric growth and acceptance of the Internet are forcing change in many industries. Every business is working hard to "webify" itself. The telecommunications industry, with a view to providing Internet services, shifted its investing focus from satellite technology to optical fiber and cable technology. Then there are businesses that see cost benefits and incremental productivity gains by serving their customers via the Internet. For example, the cost of processing an airline ticket for a customer buying online is about $1, compared with $8 for a travel agent issuing a ticket using the airline's reservation system. E-commerce is but one external change that is forcing you to rethink, "Where is my business going?"

Along with external factors, there are internal initiatives that force change and hence an impact on your system requirements. You may decide to break your business up into multiple business units, or you may reorganize the business units from, say, a regional focus to a product focus. Such changes affect requirement analysis in many different ways, such as planning for additional features and functionalities. Technically, these changes may result in an altogether different architecture for your solution, or they may require additional fields, chart fields, records, and so forth.

Don't Forget the Technical Requirements (They're Part of Your Business)

The facilitating link in the process of having your business requirements translated into the final solution is technical requirements. The technical requirements serve as the bridge between the functional team and the technical team. Fortunately, the technical requirements document doesn't need to have heavy technical jargon. It can be a summary of technical changes that need to be made to achieve the desired features/functionality in the delivered product. Technical requirements pertaining to modification or customization are to be differentiated from configuration changes or the solutions that can be obtained by tweaking the delivered product.

Most of the time, the technical requirements document is prepared after the delivered package is analyzed in reference to the overall business requirements and a gap document is prepared.

Who Is Sponsoring These Requirements?

Project sponsorship comes from the highest levels in the organization. The broad guidelines of the extent of customization that would be supported in the project should come from the highest levels of sponsors, as these guidelines impact the project cost and implementation schedule. But here you have a dilemma: The sponsors are usually so high up in the organization that they may not be able to appreciate the day-to-day business requirements, while the operating people may not be able to impress the sponsor group about certain issues. Because this is a sensitive issue, the sponsors should develop communication lines to decision makers and pass more authority to the department heads who act as decision makers.

The 80/20 Rule

Software solutions are enablers of your business. Use of an off-the-shelf ERP package is a great way to enable your business and offers the benefits we all know about. Consider two scenarios for deploying an ERP package:

Scenario 1:   Implement the software package without any changes (this is referred to as a *vanilla implementation*). This approach will entail the least amount of time and implementation costs. However, such a solution will require large or significant alteration to your existing business processes, and the shock of implementation will be significant in terms of change management, lost controls, missing functionalities, etc.

Scenario 2:   The other extreme is to completely tailor the package to your existing business processes. This will cause the least shock to your business processes but may require inordinate implementation resources. You will end up spending resources on many noncritical processes that could have run just as efficiently without this change. The return on investment on these processes is far too low.

So where do you draw the line? The answer depends on the complexities of your business processes, relationships with your partners, the age of the organization, the sponsors' appetite for change, etc. A good rule of thumb is the *80/20 rule*. As a guide, look at fulfilling about 80% of your detailed requirements, including all your "critical-to-go-live" requirements, and about one-half of your "nice-to-have" requirements. The remaining requirements, which should not exceed 20% of the total requirements, should be either lived without or changed to match the standard package offering.

Building Consensus

In the sections above, we talked about buy-in for your decisions. The idea here is that for a successful implementation, all the individuals in the project team and the organization should be in consonance. This, if not managed consciously right from the beginning of the project, can grow into big problems down the road. The solution is simple: Involve everybody at all levels within the organization. The suggestion here is not that the project team size should be expanded to an unmanageable size, but rather that there should be a sense of camaraderie in the whole organization, and the feeling of oneness should be consciously cultivated.

There should be formal communications to the organization in a timely manner or based on milestones. And there should be formal communications within the project team, mediated by the project management office. The weekly meetings between various module teams should become more frequent and occur almost daily as the go-live date comes close. Apart from offering a platform for ironing out integration issues, these meetings help build a sense of common objectives and ease the handling of change management.

Shared Services

Shared services are implemented to achieve cost advantages and to have improved access to and quality and consistency of information. From People-Soft's perspective, if you are a multi-product/service, multi-location organization, the preferred route map is a shared-services organization to avoid system duplications and conflicts and to have standard processes, controls, and flexibility in reorganization. Shared services make it very easy to transition an acquisition or a merger onto your existing PeopleSoft platform. If your organization fits the above bill or is looking for these advantages, a shared-services solution should be actively considered.

Single-Image Software

What happens if a company has operations across different countries and different continents? Can you still implement PeopleSoft and have your data residing at one location, to achieve better control and access? Yes, you can implement the PeopleSoft application across all your operations, but instead of having a single-location database, you can artificially partition your single database into subsets of data that are physically placed in different countries. A database managed in this manner is known as a *distributed database* or a *single-image software solution*. *Single-image* implies that despite partitioning the database, it is viewed as a single image and single schema for control and management purposes. Such a solution needs periodic synchronization of the host database with the consolidated database to avoid duplication and conflict of data.

Requirements

Requirement analysis is an exercise fraught with appetite for endless work, as each of the two words imply. *Requirements* have no bounds, and the users want them all. From the users' perspective of building the most user-friendly solution, almost every conceivable feature and functionality should be classified as a "critical-to-go-live" requirement. Then there's the *analysis*. The analysts, who are less concerned about what it takes to deliver those requirements, start pounding on solutions, building extensive models, creating process mappings, etc. Hence, for the success of the analysis exercise, it's critical that boundaries are defined, that there is senior management sponsorship, and that the exercise is time-boxed, structured, and deftly executed. Also, the focus should always be on leveraging the delivered PeopleSoft solution.

Identifying Requirements

Identifying requirements can be rephrased as "What is it that you want, System User?" This approach to the exercise of requirement analysis is extremely open ended and is most likely to be adopted if there are no efforts to micro-manage this process.

Techniques

Techniques and models have been developed to make this exercise effective, focused, and contained. The various techniques can be loosely classified as single-focus, collective-focus, and other.

▶ *Single-focus techniques* such as formal interviewing and questionnaires have been used extensively and continue to be used. Although these techniques are effective in many situations, they have some inherent disadvantages arising from the fact that they consider only one user at a time. The analysts then have to try and build the big picture from multiple responses. The interpreted big picture and the requirements document then require multiple iterations before they can be finalized. This makes the exercise fairly time consuming. On medium-to-large projects, these techniques call for a large team of analysts, resulting in an adverse cost impact on the project. Also, interviewing is a skill that takes time to master.

▶ *Collective-focus techniques* are combinations of various techniques. Certain models within these techniques have achieved a high level of finesse. We'll discuss these techniques in more detail later.

▶ Notable among *other techniques* are observation and sampling. The observation technique produces answers about "soft" aspects of the business; analysts should always be aware of this and apply the technique from both a conscious and an unconscious perspective. The sampling technique is used when the user population is too large to be effectively contacted using either single-focus or collective-focus techniques. In that situation, statistical techniques should be used to ensure the response of a true representation of the population.

More on Collective-Focus Techniques   The first use of the collective-focus technique was by IBM in the 1970s; it was dubbed the Joint Application Development (JAD) method. JAD consisted of two- to four-day sessions in which several key users met with the information systems personnel and formulated the requirements document. An advantage of such an approach was the participatory style, which promoted interaction not only between the users and analysts but also among users, to find solutions and understand linkages and dependencies. This style also gave the participants a feeling of ownership and an early exposure to what the final solution would look like. Over the years, many techniques similar to JAD and complementary to it have been developed by consulting organizations.

A modern variant of JAD is Rapid Application Development (RAD). Strictly speaking, RAD is an extension of JAD and includes a formal software implementation methodology. JAD is used to rapidly identify requirements, and RAD is then used to rapidly implement those requirements. Conference Room Pilot (CRP) is another variation of JAD and is discussed in detail below and in Chapter 10, "Prototyping." Accelerated Solutions Environment (ASE) Design-Shop[SM] is a proprietary technique of Cap Gemini Ernst & Young and can be used for strategy formulation and requirements formulation design for PeopleSoft modules. Micro-, subprocess-level requirement generation should be carried out as a follow-up, within the high-level process architecture and requirements generated in the ASE. See the sidebar for details.

Accelerated Solutions Environment

Overview of ASE

The ASE is a unique adaptive approach to accelerated, collaborative problem solving. The ASE approach utilizes focused problem-solving sessions, called DesignSessions[SM], to focus the decision-making process. It is designed to accelerate solutions to diverse complex, strategic, or tactical business issues. The biggest advantage of the ASE is that it dramatically accelerates the implementation project.

Accelerated Solutions Environment *(Continued)*

ASE DesignSessions

DesignSessions range from one to four days in length. The number and types of participants differ in each session, but all decision makers and content experts for each session must attend to obtain maximum benefit. Each session consists of discrete goals, objectives, and deliverables, but they are customized with the ASE to meet specific client or project team needs. This customization process is accomplished through a close working relationship with the ASE team. ASE DesignSessions are neither facilitated sessions nor team-building sessions. They consist of 10- to 12-hour days that are intense, focused, and extremely productive and are conducted with the aid of ASE facilitators and knowledge workers.

Advantages of Using the ASE Approach

The ASE approach provides multiple benefits to clients and project teams. In addition to providing accelerated solution design and development, the ASE DesignSessions create client ownership and acceptance, increase solution quality, and may reduce overall project costs. By working together and using ASE concepts to define and develop the solution, the client personnel develop ownership, which decreases the amount of time necessary to sell the solution. With the help of experienced knowledge workers and facilitators, the client makes more informed and effective decisions to improve solution quality. Overall, the ASE approach results in increased client buy-in and ownership, more timely and high-quality decisions, and an action plan for moving forward.

Conference Room Pilot   As we mentioned earlier, the focus while implementing a PeopleSoft solution should be on leveraging the delivered solution. Since the client has never interacted with PeopleSoft, it doesn't know what the delivered features and functionalities are. Hence, the client is unable to visualize what the final solution will look and feel like and to identify the missing features and functionalities that are critical to running the business. CRP is a collective-focus technique that involves a detailed review of the application and helps to gain user acceptance of the application and identify final changes. Since a detailed walk-through of the product is included, users get a firsthand feel of the product by overlaying their business processes into the PeopleSoft application and identifying their requirements.

Planning the CRP Session   It's best to approach CRP as a well-articulated workshop. Involve the program management office and sponsors in establishing the session scope, objectives, and broad direction. Draw up the participant list with the sponsors' endorsement; if the participants are not well respected, the remainder of the user organization will be unlikely to eagerly support the session results. Identify a leader from within the participant group, and acquaint the leader with the module, confirm the agenda and methods, etc. The agenda should be structured to include the purpose, duration, methods, and the expected output of the session for each topic. Prepare the session materials, including high-level current- and future-state assessments (if available), the high-level process architecture of the relevant PeopleSoft module, and related documentation.

Depending on the module and the breadth and depth of functionalities, you should be able to assess the duration of CRP. The session should begin with a discussion of the architecture of the module, familiarizing the users with menus and navigation, and an overview of functionalities supported by the product. After the overview session, each function should be walked through and discussed in detail. At this point, the user group can be fine-tuned to include only the users of the functionality or process being discussed.

Conducting the CRP Session   The objective is to walk the users through the PeopleSoft module and verify that the solution elements satisfy the needs of the users and to what extent. The verification of the extent identifies the gaps and the corresponding requirements. Involve participants in discussing and overlaying the business processes over the PeopleSoft solution element. Assess whether a particular requirement is being requested just because it's done that way now. Identify short-term improvement items, generate solution alternatives, and identify process improvement opportunities by using the delivered PeopleSoft solution. As always, don't ignore documentation. After the CRP, review the CRP results with the sponsor team, finalize the list of requirements that would be delivered in the current phase of the solution, and prepare the final requirements document.

Whichever technique or model you use, a few basic principles will always ring true. Figure 7.3 is an attempt to model the requirements identification process and where it fits into the implementation chain. The figure implies that the process requirements are governed by business requirements, which are dynamic, hence the feedback loop. The maintenance process implies that software solutions "age" and that maintenance is an ongoing process whereby you may keep adding a new field here and a new report there. Implementation is the stage where you bring all solution elements together.

Figure 7.3 **Requirements identification process**

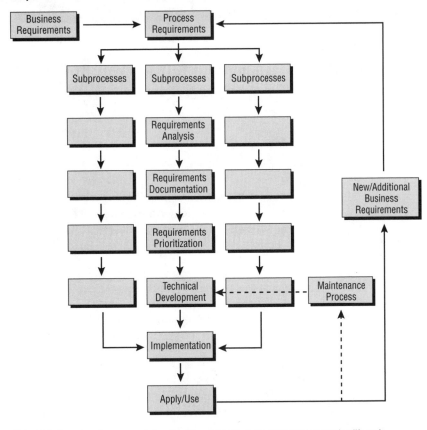

Note: This figure is not a representation of software development or the implementation life cycle.

Case Study: The Cash Sweep

A real estate investment trust (REIT) company has a relatively well-defined stream of rent checks from its properties. The rent checks are deposited in the local accounts of the bank that the property banks with. The cash from these checks usually takes two to five days to get collected and then is used to make mortgage, utility, and other payments. The cash collection pattern is such that about 70% of payments are received during the first five days of the month, and almost 95% of the payments are received by the tenth day. The expenditure pattern is skewed toward the end of the month. The company wants to take advantage of concentrating the funds from all its properties and investing in bulk. The current information system doesn't support that requirement. The company is now moving to the PeopleSoft financial application and wants this functionality to be supported.

Case Study: The Cash Sweep *(Continued)*

What are the questions that the analyst needs to ask to be able to identify the requirements? After spending time with the users, the analyst has developed a requirements outline that reads something like this:

"You need to set up a cash sweep process, wherein every evening the bank transfers the available monies to a central concentration account. The key requirement is that the balance for each of the properties has to be maintained in general ledger (GL) 'by property'; i.e., even if the funds get cumulated in the concentration account, the company should be able to maintain information by individual property accounts. Also, the investment income earned needs to be allocated back to the individual property in proportion to its contribution to the kitty. To complicate the matter further, some of the properties are funded by developmental/promotional institutions like HUD, which will allow investments of these 'HUD properties' to be made only in selected instruments."

The analyst now realizes that the fund concentration process is essentially a combination of three subprocesses: sweeping cash, investing it, and allocating the investment earnings back. The above discussion can be fitted onto the model detailed in Figure 7.3.

Let's drill down further by discussing the cash sweep process, one of the three subprocesses. To set up the cash sweep process, the first question to consider is whether it should be a bank-initiated process or a client-initiated process. A cash sweep is initiated based on a set of business rules and criteria, such as the minimum balance in the local account, the delay in the check-clearing process, the delay in receipt of the amounts processed by ACH (Automated Clearing House), etc. These business rules and hence the swept amount change from time to time. Figure 7.4 shows some of the alternatives that can be generated. (In this figure, PSGL refers to the PeopleSoft General Ledger.)

Choosing one of the options over the others is based on the impact of the chosen process over other business process, the ability of your business partners to support the processes, the organization's resources and inclination to run and maintain the process, and the resources available within the project team to implement the solution. In other words, you should develop a *workable solution* as opposed to building an *ideal solution*.

Figure 7.4   **Examples of the cash sweep process**

Bank-Initiated Sweep
SOLUTION I

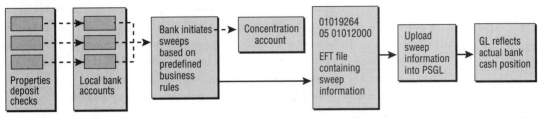

PSGL reflects the cash in bank and not the checks received/deposited. Open-ended system. May take 2–5 days for errors to be identified.

SOLUTION II

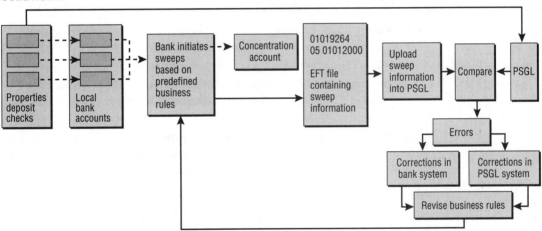

PSGL reflects the actual transactions. Feedback loop helps identification of errors quickly.

 Cash flow   ──────▶ Information flow

Client-Initiated Sweep
SOLUTION III

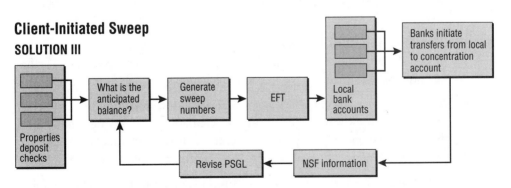

What About Your Current State?

The preceding example of requirement analysis is one of the two situations that you'll find yourself in. That example was the case of a nonexistent functionality that needed to be built fresh. On average, new functionalities account for about 5% to 15% of the functionalities that are implemented. So the question is, do you have to bother about what's been "running perfectly for the last seven years, when we implemented the current system"? Well, the answer is yes. You need to undertake as intensive a requirement analysis for current-state functionalities as that for a new functionality. Why? Read on.

Reengineer Your Process   This exercise gives you an opportunity to analyze your process to fix redundancies and inefficiencies. Try and adopt a toned-down version of the classic reengineering approach of radical redesign and rethinking to take care of the three Cs: customers, cost, and change.

For example, you may come across a conflicting solution in your accounts receivables accounting, where you have traditionally used the balance forward system while PeopleSoft uses open item accounting. This can give rise to a new requirement. But if you drill down into the reasons for using balance forward accounting, you may realize that it was used simply because it was easy to program or the memory requirements were less. Also question whether the accounting system makes sense in today's business world. After such an exercise, you may decide to do away with your current balance forward system in favor of PeopleSoft's open item accounting system.

This exercise is an opportunity to find out not only what's wrong with the current processes but also what's right with them. The team should take cues from these strengths and apply them throughout the exercise.

Understand and Communicate   This exercise gives you the opportunity to take a holistic view of the processes, understand the nuances, and translate them into requirements.

Identify Your Core Processes   Ask yourself what the core processes are in your department around which other processes are built. Which one is the key process that gives you a competitive advantage?

Migration   Migrating to another system is a slow transition to new processes—a new way of doing business. As the new process design unfolds, the documentation will help in understanding the magnitude of the change and in mapping the current processes to the future-state processes.

Benchmark   For each process the current state forms the benchmark for judging the parameters of your future-state process. Once the new process is in place, compare its performance to that of the old one. Once again, extend this exercise to benchmark your processes against the best in the industry, and work to build processes that will be better than the industry standards when your PeopleSoft system goes live.

Documentation   Documentation is the most visible exercise, yet the one that's sometimes emphasized the least! In every single activity discussed above, you should document. Document what your department's processes are, which parts are good, which parts need a fix, what the linkages are between your department and other departments, what new features you would like to add, what is redundant, and so forth.

Recording Requirements

The most important link in ensuring that the delivered solution is what the end users wanted is strong documentation. It's a good idea to have a format identified that will be used for recording requirements. There is no ideal format; the team will have to decide what information they want to capture, at what level of detail, and what method they'll use for classifying the requirements.

A good way of documenting is to have a central requirements repository on a database such as Microsoft Access. Any kind of format can be standardized across the project/program, and all the module teams can upload their requirements on the database. The viewing and editing rights can be managed by the PMO (project management office).

The requirements document can be extended further to include cross-references to other systems, data-element definitions, screens (or pages), menus, report layouts, performance and operations requirements, etc. The key is to have a document that contains manageable information rather than every possible bit of information.

A well-documented requirements database becomes the key resource for the project. It can act as a tracking/monitoring resource for assessing progress on each of the requirements. If it's linked with project management documents (such as Microsoft Project), it can serve as a good control document.

Following is a sample of a requirements document that was created as a deliverable of a CRP session. The first section lists each requirement along with a brief description of a possible solution. The appendix captures the possible solutions in more detail. It also captures briefly the discussion that occurred around each issue, to give a context and the rationale for arriving at the stated decision or solution. Follow-up, discussion, and refinement of each requirement with the end users and decision makers is critical for finalizing the document before it is sent to the technical team.

PeopleSoft Accounts Payable Requirements Document
For Everybody's Restaurant, Inc.

The changes, modifications, and customizations are listed by functionality and are to be provided in PeopleSoft Accounts Payable (PSAP), unless specified otherwise.

The numbering scheme of the requirements identified is a control number for tracking of issues and is not a serial number.

1.00 Accounting

1.02 Accounting entries must be differentiated (and generated) not only by GL accounts but also by restaurant ID.

This would help in matching each accounting entry with a specific restaurant.

1.03 Need to drill into details of journal entries.

PeopleSoft GL standard functionality will enable drill-down capabilities.

1.04 Restaurant number field needs to be included in bank account setup panel group.

Each bank account needs to be associated with a restaurant. This information has to be captured at the bank account setup level.

1.05 Ensure that there are no inter-restaurant accounting settlements.

No accounting entries will be created by debiting one restaurant while crediting another one.

Appendix

Control Number	Discussion Point	Resolution
	Accounting	
1.02	• Accounting entries to be differentiated (and generated) not only by GL accounts but also by restaurant ID.	• Research the modification of accounting templates to accommodate restaurant ID.
1.03	• Need to drill into details of journal entries. *Standard PSTR will enable this.*	• Use delivered PSGL inquiry functionality.

1.04	• Restaurant number field needs to be included in bank account setup panel group. *Each bank account needs to be associated with a restaurant. This information has to be captured at the bank account setup level.*	• Modify bank account setup panel to include restaurant field.
		• Entered restaurant number field must have one of these two options:
		  • Option 1: Required field—Do not save without the information.
		  • Option 2: Warning—Warn about saving without the information, but allow saving of information anyway.
		• Modifications to be reviewed by technical team.

1.05	• Ensure that there are no inter-restaurant accounting settlements. *There should be no accounting entries created by debiting one restaurant while crediting another one.*	• Modify account entry panel to ensure that offsetting entries can happen only against the same restaurant. • Modifications to be reviewed by technical team.

Prioritizing Requirements

After identifying and recording the requirements, the next important step is prioritizing them, which helps in structuring the project scope. There are many ways to classify and prioritize, but the most often used scale is "criticality of solution." The three categories for classifying requirements according to this criterion can be "critical to go live," "nice to have," and "can live without."

You can create a "phased-in" approach, or version, of the implementation to deliver all the critical-to-go-live requirements and some of nice-to-have requirements in first release, and the remaining requirements in subsequent releases. *Versioning,* as this is called, is a great tool for creating a delivery schedule that's achievable. And delivering what is promised per the work plan defines project success.

Identifying critical-to-go-live requirements is relatively easy; the difficult decisions come with classifying what is nice to have versus what you can live without. The second difficulty is identifying which of the nice-to-have requirements should be included in the first release of the solution. In classifying the priorities, it's critical to have buy-in by the stakeholders, including sponsors and end users, to ensure support for the delivered solution.

A second dimension, "complexity of solution," can be added to criticality of solution to convey a more meaningful insight into the prioritization process. Figure 7.5 shows the relationship of these two dimensions.

All the requirements falling in the high-criticality cells are "must-deliver" requirements; similarly, all the requirements in the low-criticality cells can be pushed to subsequent versions/releases. The complexity element enables you to make decisions on the requirements falling in the medium-criticality cells. The sponsors may find it easy to allow low-complexity solutions to be implemented in the current release, while they may consider only a few of the medium- and high-complexity requirements.

Figure 7.5 **Criticality/complexity matrix**

Complexity of Solution ↑ / Criticality of Solution →

	III	II	I
A	Criticality: Low Complexity: **High**	Criticality: *Medium* Complexity: **High**	Criticality: **High** Complexity: **High**
B	Criticality: Low Complexity: *Medium*	Criticality: *Medium* Complexity: *Medium*	Criticality: **High** Complexity: *Medium*
C	Criticality: Low Complexity: Low	Criticality: *Medium* Complexity: Low	Criticality: **High** Complexity: Low

Definitions:

High Criticality: Affects an important core competency of the business. The issue could jeopardize the company's competitive advantage if not resolved. Directly affects a critical function or process.
Medium Criticality: Indirectly relates to a core competency of the business. Could have minor impact on the competitive advantage. Affects a relatively important function or process.
Low Criticality: Not related to a core competency of the business. Would not affect competitive advantage. Issue does not significantly affect any important function or process.

High Complexity: Requires a large bolt-on or an extensive modification to the package/process. High-cost solution.
Medium Complexity: Requires significant modification to the package/process.
Low Complexity: Requires minor modification to the package/process. Low-cost solution.

Reviewing PeopleSoft—Gap Analysis

Gap analysis is another versatile tool that is used extensively, from selecting the package for packaged implementations to confirming the appropriateness of the chosen package, to analyzing requirements. The key advantage of this tool is that it helps in identifying major process gaps in relation to the base package. The exercise can be extended to conducting an investment analysis of each alternative and identifying the costs to close the gaps.

The ERP solutions are optimally designed products, while in business there are rarely any processes that are optimal. The processes lose their optimality when they accommodate an extra step, maybe to provide additional process control, additional data capture, etc. Or a process may not be optimal simply because it was not designed in an optimum manner. Also, the ERP products are generic solutions, while every business is unique; for example, the complexity of the scheduling process is greater for an axle assembly plant than for a hydroelectric power plant. This means that there will always be processes that are not delivered in the product, and there will always be functionalities and features in the product that will not be implemented by the client. This situation is depicted in Figure 7.6. The key lies in maximizing the area of fit.

Figure 7.6 **Gap bar**

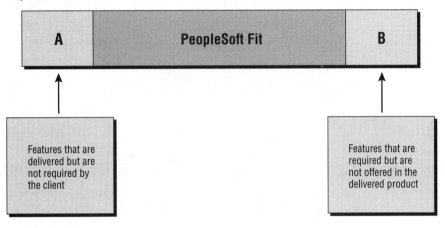

Methodology of Gap Analysis

Gap assessment can be approached from three angles:

▶ Life cycle solution process decomposition

▶ Industry-specific requirements

▶ System demonstration

Life cycle solution process decomposition relates to breaking the process down to its component subprocesses and identifying gaps as the process is synthesized upward to support the equivalent functionality in PeopleSoft. The functionality needs to be mapped to the subprocess's associated business transactions.

A good tool for doing this analysis is PeopleSoft Navigator (or Business Process Maps in PeopleSoft 8). The Navigator details the process steps for all the processes it supports. The drill-down functionality takes the user down to the task level and details the process linkages. On the user's side, once the future-state design has been confirmed, the future-state process flows can be made to support the future-state design. The result of the exercise is a comprehensive analysis of the fit, or the estimated work effort on the identified gap.

Industry-specific requirements are more pertinent in specialized industries such as aviation. The clients follow guidelines set by the industry associations, which the ERP solution should meet. If the market potential is perceived as significant, the ERP vendor itself may consider offering those functionalities in the solution. In line with this, PeopleSoft has vertical industry solutions for health care, banking, insurance, and some other industries.

The system demonstration approach is the Conference Room Pilot approach discussed earlier in this chapter. We'll cover it in more detail in Chapter 10.

Next Steps

Once the base-level package fit has been identified, the exercise boils down to minimizing the requirements side (area B) of the gap bar. Once again, a large part of area B can be reduced by structuring the processes the PeopleSoft way. And this should be the preferred way to leverage the delivered functionality and to minimize customizations.

What about core competencies? We all know that certain processes are more critical than others. For example, the criticality of salary payments being initiated on the 14th and 29th of each month (or an earlier day, if this day falls on a weekend or holiday) is higher than payments to your vendors, which can be delayed by a couple of days in case of need. Similarly, there are certain processes that offer competitive advantage, and they should be assigned the criticality they deserve. Consider two strategies for these processes occurring in area B of the gap bar:

▶ Calculate and report two fit analysis numbers, one to reflect the overall fit of the package and the second to reflect the fit of the package to critical processes.

▶ Where requirement issues exist in core competencies, investigate the ease or difficulty of resolving them with a point solution or a bolt-on.

Consider the following example of gap analysis for Project X.

Example: Gap Analysis for Project X

Table 7.1 contains the initial gap analysis of the Project X requirements. This analysis is meant to be the initial view of the gaps between the future state and PeopleSoft. For each Project X requirement, the team has documented the requirement number, priority, future state, benefits of the future state, current (PeopleSoft) state, degree of gap, impacts if the future state is not realized, and issues, barriers, and risks. A description of each of these follows.

Requirement number The requirement number as found in the Project X requirements document.

Priority The priority assigned to that requirement in the prioritization discussion used for sorting the document.

Identified future state An explanation of the requirement or what you want to accomplish in the future to support your business process area.

Benefits of future state The question "So what?" should be asked: "So what is the benefit of this requirement to Organization Y?" The answer should provide a quick overview of the benefits of the requirement in the future for Organization Y.

PeopleSoft The delivered functionality.

Gap The magnitude of the gap between the future-state requirement and the current-state assessment, represented by one of four notations: significant, large, partial, and none.

Impacts if future state not realized The impacts are defined from the business and customer perspectives. Organization Y attempted to detail the impact to the organization and/or the customer if the specific requirement cannot be delivered.

Issues, barriers, risks The key issues, barriers, dependencies, and risks with this requirement for Organization Y.

Although Table 7.1 is a good example of a gap analysis document, it may not pertain to a specific PeopleSoft module.

Table 7.1   **Gap Analysis Worksheet for Project X**

Req. Num.	Priority	Identified Future State	Benefits of Future State	PeopleSoft	Gap	Impacts If Future State Not Realized	Issues, Barriers, or Risks
B7.1.1	8.5	Provide updated offer information in the ordering system, and information resource tools at all times, to ensure that valid offer information is presented to the customer/ order placer.	All users will be able to see the most current offer info. for Organization Y. The error rate due to invalid offer info. should significantly decrease. Visibility of accurate offer info. at the time a rep places the order with customer will eliminate the need to contact the customer later with a change.	Users have limited capability to the offer info. through PeopleSoft. The info. is available for one customer segment only.	Significant	*Business impacts:* Without the ability to have updated offer info. in the system, available to all end users, the ordering process does not enhance the current process. The fundamental error for Organization Y results from inaccurate/ outdated offer info. As a result, this requirement is critical. *Customer impacts:* Without updated offer info., the customer can be affected significantly. The customer will be expecting a specific offer and may end up with something different. Therefore, the customer is not receiving the high-quality service they expect.	An open issue exists related to the info. resource portion of the tool. The maintenance of the offer info. is still incumbent on the marketing organization. Without this requirement, Organization Y runs the risk of sustaining a high error rate due to invalid offer info.
B8.1.2	6.8	Provide security on who can delete an order request that is in the queue for processing.	Ensure that only authorized reps are deleting orders for legitimate reasons.	Reps have the ability to close requests in PeopleSoft.	Partial	*Business impacts:* As long as Project X continues with a capability to close requests as provided by PeopleSoft, there is no impact. *Customer impacts:* If security is not provided for authorized customers, a potential for loss of a customer's order exists.	This requirement is dependent on Project X incorporating PeopleSoft functionality.

Finding a Solution

Now that the herculean task of identifying and prioritizing the requirements is done, the next big issue of finding a solution begins. Relating this to Figure 7.6, you now need to build the final portion of area B on the gap bar. The standard route maps for finding a solution can be detailed as follows:

Business process change Adapt your business processes to PeopleSoft.

Bolt-on An all-new functionality. Identify the functionality, detailing the panels/pages, reports, logic, records, interfaces, etc.

Extension Identify the items to be extended (e.g., tables, objects, screens/pages, and reports).

Modification Implies changes that need to be made to delivered panels/pages, reports, PeopleCode, and records.

Customization Implies changes or that additional control parameters, user-defined fields, control records, required fields, or default values need to be designed.

Point solutions Implies using other software packages that can be implemented in conjunction with PeopleSoft to meet the requirements.

Evolution Accept the package as is and implement the solution in a future release.

User exit Identify the function that will be given by providing a means to exit the application (i.e., user exit) and the third-party custom module or application that is being proposed to integrate with through this exit.

As we've been stressing in this book, PeopleSoft is an optimally designed package, and your first option in looking for a solution should be pursuing changes in your business process. Also, if there is a requirement that ideally should be automated but can be performed manually and the level of criticality is medium, you should give serious thought to waiting for the application to evolve; the feature you want may become available in subsequent releases of PeopleSoft. Often we come across a situation where a field was added while implementing PeopleSoft 6, but later that field was delivered in the upgrade to release 7.5. Worse still, the client made all the effort to build new records and customize panels, etc., while the delivered fields were distributed across the application. The mapping of those fields and linkages used up valuable resources of the team.

Cost and Benefit of Potential Solutions

It's sometimes said that benefit is a function of cost. That statement holds true for information technology solutions in well-managed projects. Costs and benefits have to be viewed not only from the perspective of the resource requirements in implementing a solution but also from the opportunity cost of *not* implementing the solution.

The cost of implementation is a combination of direct and indirect costs. It's important that a detailed list of cost constituents is built and appropriate costs assigned to each item. Add the costs identified and summarize them for each of the alternatives.

The parameters on which benefits should be measured are monetary value and time. The benefits accrue in both tangible and intangible forms such as reduced cycle times and lower costs. Hence standards or tools should be used to convert the intangible benefits, as well as the perceived tangible benefits, into measurable parameters. The identified benefits should be categorized to help the team recognize the major impacts.

Refer to the "Cost-Benefit Analysis" section of Chapter 8, "Designing a Solution," for detailed constituents of costs and benefits.

After identifying the costs and the benefits of solutions, often there will be two solutions that are workable, each with a unique set of advantages and disadvantages. How do you decide which of the solutions to implement? The organization needs to implement the solution where the economic benefit, measured by the internal rate of return (IRR) or the net present value (NPV) or by any other method, is better than the organization's norm. Hence a solution that has an IRR of 11% may not be a candidate if the organization's norm for IRR is 16%.

Figure 7.7 is an attempt to plot this idea. The solutions that fall below the diagonal line should get implemented, as they offer economic benefits that will act as strategic investments in the software solution and will thereby bolster the overall value to the organization. Conversely, the solutions above the diagonal line will drag the organization's economic value down. The position of point A will be a function of threshold economic value, which each organization defines for itself.

Figure 7.7   **Cost-benefit plot**

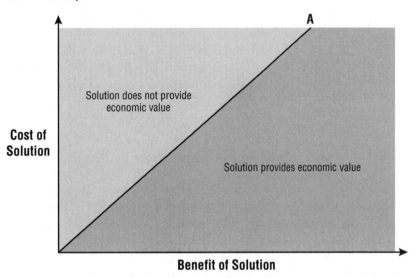

Prototyping Potential Solutions

Prototyping is a technique for applying various software engineering principles to modeling a solution. This model offers the first feel of the solution to the end users. Prototyping as a technique is also used to create models toward the end of the development cycle, where the end users critically analyze and evaluate the solution.

Rapid prototyping is a modular prototyping technique and is currently being used extensively. Rapid prototyping is used mostly in conjunction with RAD and involves developing small working models of the system at different stages. This enables users to continuously evaluate the designed and developed functionality. In PeopleSoft implementations, this technique can be effectively applied and have a two-way dialog between users and developers about the look and feel of the functionality. This also ensures low rejection rates and high buy-in by the users. If the users are dissatisfied with the prototype, the requirements need to be revised and refined, and prototyping undertaken.

Prototyping at the requirements analysis stage is the same as the CRP session discussed earlier in the chapter. As discussed there, the walk-through of PeopleSoft and the discussion during the session give a strong visualization of the solution to the users. During the CRP session itself, the facilitator is able to prototype a solution by configuring or explaining a solution at a high level. However, if there are situations where a plausible solution needs to be tested, extensive prototyping needs to be undertaken and solutions evaluated before the requirements document is prepared. The various solutions are discussed with the end users and decision makers, and the most workable solution is chosen. The requirements document is then prepared for that solution only.

Prototyping as an approach and how it's used to offer PeopleSoft solutions are discussed in detail in Chapter 10.

Changing Business Processes

Any customization or modification that's done in PeopleSoft changes the delivered business process. Again, ideally the existing business process should not be altered, but in practice the business processes do undergo modifications to incorporate additional data elements, additional validations, etc.

Here are some rules of thumb for changing your system:

> ▶ Keep the core business process as it is, changing only a component or two. Making extensive changes will adversely impact the upgrade process.

> ▶ For a specific process, avoid altering the COBOL or the program behind the process. PeopleSoft does not support altered COBOL. If you have to do computation beyond the delivered process, see if you can still build a process outside the delivered program. This will also hedge against the risk of PeopleSoft using a different programming language in future releases.

> ▶ Be sure that the business process is not altered to the extent that upgrades become difficult. Also, while upgrading, see if the modifications and changes made earlier will work with the upgraded version.

- ▶ Preferably, hook your customizations either at the beginning or at the end of the business process. This will avoid altering the delivered process.

- ▶ Provide appropriate documentation of the changes during training sessions, as none of these changes will be covered in the canned training programs.

Impact of Upgrades

In a PeopleSoft upgrade, you use PeopleSoft-delivered functionality to move system changes from one version or release to another, such as moving from PeopleSoft 7.5 to PeopleSoft 8. You have both upgrade changes (e.g., changes with the base or delivered functionality) and custom changes (e.g., changes made by the organization itself and not by the application's vendor).

The story here is simple: The complexity of upgrades increases in direct proportion to the extent of customization that has been done on the base package. An upgrade of customizations/modifications implies that you understand whether the changes you've made are already delivered in the new release of the software and how they interact with the new features/functions of the upgraded software. Prepare a detailed list of customizations/modifications by fields, records, menus, panels/pages, etc., mapped to delivered fields, records, menus, and panels/pages. For modified fields, details such as the field length type, records, and references should be captured. Similarly, a detailed roster should be prepared for panels/pages, menus, records, etc. For each of the modified/customized processes, identify the input and output parameters and study their impact.

Identify any exceptions, especially those that will call for detailed action—for example, a field where the customized field is seven numeric long while the delivered field is only five numeric long. That situation will call for either data truncation or customization of the delivered field in the upgraded version. Bolt-ons don't offer a lot of challenge in upgrades, especially if the input and output parameters are a part of the delivered fields, as the same fields will also be a part of the upgrade process. However, if the input and output parameters were from customized fields, the customization will have to be upgraded first for bolt-ons to work. You also need to ensure that the bolt-on functionality wasn't added to the new release of the system in a manner different from the one you've created.

Hence, at every stage you should be cognizant of upgrades and should build the modifications/customizations with upgrades as a critical consideration. For a detailed discussion on managing changes, refer to Chapter 8.

Impacts of Your Decisions

The decisions you make will have far-reaching impacts on the way your business responds to changes in the market space and the way it responds to your business partners and other stakeholders. Impacts of implementing PeopleSoft are also discussed in Chapter 16, "Post-Production Support," as well as in Chapter 21, "Analyzing Your Support Network."

New Business Processes

New business processes will have the most tangible impact. The impact will be in terms of enhanced business efficiency, seen in improved top-line growth, increased profitability, and faster response times for your customers and vendors. You may also have better control and reporting with the revised business processes.

Staffing the Future State

If your business processes have become efficient, effective, and focused, you should see a favorable impact in terms of enhanced employee satisfaction, employees' ownership of processes, etc. However, the new PeopleSoft system, new business processes, and a new departmental organization will call for training employees to update their job competencies. Training should therefore be a part of implementation planning and will be discussed in detail in Chapter 15, "Go Live—Keys to a Successful Rollout."

Timing/Rollout of Strategy

Changes to your processes and the amount of change to a particular organizational unit or area may affect the planning of your timing or rollout strategy. Look to ensure that you're not pushing out too much change on your users, and create the appropriate rollout strategy to meet these changes. For instance, because of the amount of change to a particular organization, you may want to phase in certain features or functionalities or to roll them out to a pilot group.

Chapter 15, "Go Live—Keys to a Successful Rollout," and Chapter 9, "Preparing Your Organization for Implementation," look at these rollout and phased implementation strategies.

Managing Change Requests

Change requests will most likely occur in every implementation, and worse still, they will happen toward the end of the development phase. Usually prototyping at a later stage of the project (see Chapter 10) helps in identifying any new requirements or changes.

When accepting a change request, be aware of the criticality of the request and the extent of work the change will entail; the change should definitely not be one that could affect the timeline for the module implementation. It's a good idea to establish a standard procedure for making change requests and to set up a simple Microsoft Access or Lotus Notes database to enable the tracking of them. An important aspect of monitoring is identifying and communicating a cutoff date for accepting change requests.

For additional practical suggestions, refer to the "Managing the Change" section of Chapter 8.

Up Next

Now that we've looked at how to determine what a requirement is, what requirements are necessary, how to analyze those requirements against the package, and how to prepare the organization for any needed changes to those requirements, we'll move on to Chapter 8 and look at how to design these solutions. Remember to keep in mind the various techniques that can be used to both document your requirements and analyze them against the package. When designing your solution, you have to keep several things in mind, including upgrades, system performance, security, and more. Chapter 8 will address all these concerns and much more.

Designing a Solution

F E A T U R I N G :

▶ Alternative approaches to designing a solution

▶ How to handle high-impact changes to your application

▶ Managing and tracking the system and design changes

▶ Effects of the changes, both local and global

▶ How to leverage version control to track a change once it's made

P eopleSoft is a full-featured ERP system that has more functionality than any one organization fully deploys. By configuring the as-delivered software, you can activate the functions that are right for your organization. Even so, there are situations in which a business requirement is unique to your organization and the functionality to support it is not in PeopleSoft. In an even fewer number of situations, the business requirement is important enough to consider making a change to the PeopleSoft application.

Question: Now that you've decided to make a change to PeopleSoft, what should you do first?

Answer: Understand the impact that the change could have on your implementation project and beyond.

Other chapters in this book address the technical structure of PeopleSoft, and they will provide benefit to the programmer/analysts in the actual programming of your change. This chapter focuses on five key areas that will help you rough out your design change. Together, they create the framework. Apply the following framework questions to any change that is being considered, and you can better determine what the potential impact of the change will have on your project.

Key Area	Framework Question
Alternative approaches	What are my options in making the change?
High-impact changes	How could this change limit other PeopleSoft flexibility?
Managing the change	How will we manage the creation of the change?
Globalization versus localization	How will this change impact our use of PeopleSoft locally and globally?
Version control	How will we keep track of the change once it's made?

Alternative Approaches

A surprise to many who are new to ERP applications is the bewildering complexity of the programs that make up the application. Like any other ERP application, PeopleSoft is made up of a collection of programs. Assembled together, these programs give the users an interface to the system through panels/pages (screens for data entry and management), perform transaction processing, manage the data, and print reports. The PeopleSoft programs that are delivered to you as the application have been developed in a variety of programming languages and tools:

- ▶ COBOL (programming language)
- ▶ Application Engine (programming language)
- ▶ PeopleCode (programming language)
- ▶ SQR (programming language)
- ▶ Query/Crystal (report-development tool)
- ▶ Application Messaging (XML message programming tool)
- ▶ Business Components (real-time Web authorization tools)
- ▶ Business Interlinks (Internet-enabled API programming tools)

Currently, PeopleBooks (the PeopleSoft manuals) provide some references to which of the programming languages or tools are responsible for specific processes. Each PeopleSoft module (General Ledger, Accounts Payable, Human Resources, etc.) consists of a different mix of the programming languages and tools used. Consequently, a programmer/analyst with experience in your PeopleSoft module and version will be an invaluable source of information in designing and developing a change you require.

You can make your change to the PeopleSoft system by using a variety of tools. If an application change to enhance or add functionality is necessary, consider making your change using PeopleCode, COBOL, Application Engine, Application Messaging, Business Components, Business Interlinks, or SQR. If your change affects output reporting, consider using PeopleSoft Query, Crystal, nVision, or SQR. To help you understand the potential impact on your project, a brief description of each tool follows, along with a description of the skills required to effectively master the tool.

Many projects run into trouble when system or report changes are introduced into the project plan. The following errors are the most common ones:

- ▶ Being overly optimistic in estimating the time to develop, test, and tune the changes

▶ Underestimating the technical skill required to develop an effective and efficient change

▶ Not monitoring the development process closely enough to see the indicators of manageable problems along the way until it's too late

PeopleCode Changes

PeopleSoft provides tools to make changes to its product. Changing PeopleCode allows you to modify the existing functionality, panels/pages, records, and fields delivered by PeopleSoft. All customized PeopleCode programs must be accounted for and reevaluated during the periodic PeopleSoft upgrade process, after the implementation is completed.

Development tools include *Application Designer*, a single, integrated development environment that enables users to view and edit a list of application objects such as records, fields, panels/pages, and menus. It also allows modified objects to be moved into production through PeopleSoft's upgrade process. Application Designer (with PeopleSoft 8) integrates the following tools:

▶ *Application Engine* is a unique, batch-processing tool that PeopleSoft provides as an alternative to SQR or COBOL. With PeopleSoft 8, Application Engine is now incorporated into the Application Designer tool and has a new, more intuitive, graphical tree-type design interface. Because of the integration with Application Designer, PeopleCode functions and the ability to have the system upgrade these processes are now available. Application Engine is explained in more detail in the "Application Engine Changes" section later in this chapter.

▶ *Data Designer* is used to build new table definitions, to add, drop, or modify fields in existing tables, and to facilitate field editing.

▶ *Panel (or Page) Designer* is used to build or modify GUI-based query and data-entry screens or Web pages.

▶ *Menu Designer* is used to build or modify application windows and pull-down screens or menu options.

▶ *Business Process Designer* comprises the tools used to design and build business processes, including work-flow rules and routings.

▶ *Application Upgrader* facilitates customer upgrades to new releases while maintaining application modifications made by the customer.

▶ *SQL Editor* enables you to construct SQL objects and store them in a new SQL repository. This is a new feature in PeopleSoft 8. The SQL Editor is accessible from records based on SQL and Dynamic Views, on Application Engine actions, and from the Application Designer itself.

Required skills   Experienced programmer/analyst(s) trained in People-Tools. The skill will be required to develop a change and periodically to maintain, upgrade, and tune the change after the initial creation.

With PeopleSoft 8, several totally new design tools are also available, including Business Interlinks, Business Components, and Application Messaging. These are explained later in the "Internet Open Integration Changes" section.

COBOL Changes

COBOL programming language can also be used to make changes to the existing PeopleSoft-delivered functionality. Additionally, COBOL's flexibility allows the development of entirely new programs that can be introduced into the PeopleSoft solution. Since COBOL source code can be difficult to follow, be sure that you fully understand the business process being performed before you attempt to work out the solution. All the usual programming disciplines should be applied, such as documenting all program changes, commenting out original code rather than removing it, and logging the date, name, and changes made each time the code is modified.

Required skills   Experienced COBOL programmer/analyst(s) who possesses an understanding of the PeopleSoft data and programming structure. The skill will be required to develop a change and periodically to maintain, upgrade, and tune the change after the initial creation.

Application Engine Changes

Similar to COBOL, Application Engine is a programming language. The code is generally easier to understand than COBOL and has an added benefit: Any programming using Application Engine does not need to be compiled as COBOL does. Therefore, the effect of changes programmed can be seen much more quickly, which increases the speed of development.

Each PeopleSoft module consists mostly of COBOL and Application Engine programs. We've observed that generally there is a greater percentage of

Application Engine programs than COBOL programs in the more recently developed PeopleSoft modules.

As a note to the technical person reading this chapter: Application Engine statements are stored in PeopleSoft tables and are driven by "effective date." A recommended approach to changing Application Engine statements is to never delete original statements, but rather copy the statement, modify the copy, and give the copy an effective date that activates the new statement and deactivates the original statement.

Required skills   Experienced Application Engine programmer/analyst(s) who possesses an understanding of the PeopleSoft data and programming structure. The skill will be necessary to develop a change and periodically to maintain, upgrade, and tune the change after the initial creation.

Internet Open Integration Changes

With PeopleSoft 8 and the new programming tools available, integration using Internet features and functions allows the linking of information or applications over the Web. PeopleSoft 8 delivers three new tools—Application Messaging, Business Components, and Business Interlinks—that leverage the Internet-based technologies such as XML, HTTP, and Java:

▶ *Application Messaging* is a programming-type function that supports the integration of PeopleSoft applications and third-party systems through the publishing of business events as XML-formatted messages. This provides the foundation for internal systems integration as well as EDI and business-to-business integration over the Internet.

▶ *Business Components* is a real-time synchronous programming approach that provides access to PeopleSoft business rules and data from external applications in an object-oriented manner. This is the primary mechanism for integrating PeopleSoft business logic with Internet-based applications using standard Web-authentication tools, such as incorporating PeopleSoft transactions into a company's Web site.

▶ *Business Interlinks* tools are the converse of Business Components; they provide a framework that enables customers to extend their PeopleSoft applications to invoke third-party systems easily using a broad set of technologies such as XML, HTTP, Java, COM, and CORBA.

Required skills   Experienced programmer/analyst(s) trained in Web-based and object-oriented programming such as XML, HTTP, and Java. The skill will be required to develop a change and to periodically maintain, upgrade, and tune the change after the initial creation.

Reporting Changes

Many changes don't require changing the functionality of the PeopleSoft application itself. In the case where the reports delivered with PeopleSoft won't meet your reporting needs, report changes are required.

PeopleSoft query and reporting options enable application users to extract information when and where they need it. Users can also customize output, whether it's importing information from your database into Microsoft Excel, comparing data online, or generating reports.

The following reporting tools are used to access, analyze, and report information:

▶ *PS/nVision* integrates PeopleSoft applications with Microsoft Excel in the production of financial statements, responsibility reports, and other ad hoc financial reports and analyses.

▶ *PeopleSoft Query* builds SQL queries—without having to write SQL statements— that extract and summarize information from an application's database.

▶ *Query Link* provides a PeopleSoft Query interface to Crystal Reports Pro, a versatile report designer and formatter; data can be formatted quickly and easily with a variety of fonts, borders, and other special effects, or imported into a spreadsheet such as Microsoft Excel for further analysis.

▶ *SQR* allows you to custom-develop complex reports that have better system performance. Report development can be from scratch or through using existing PeopleSoft reports as templates.

▶ *Business Intelligence* provides Internet reporting using the Data Warehouse Manager PeopleSoft Workbenches, which are the primary user interface for Enterprise Performance Management (EPM) Web-enabled reporting capabilities.

Choose the right reporting tool for the job. On a continuum, PeopleSoft Query is the least demanding of the reporting tools to master, and SQR and Business Intelligence are the most demanding. Figure 8.1 shows this spectrum.

Figure 8.1 **Reporting tools spectrum**

Least Demanding	Most Demanding
PS/Query - - - Crystal Reports Pro - - - PS/nVision - - - Business Intelligence/SQR	

The continuum can apply to other characteristics of each reporting tool, including the ability to address report complexity and the ability of the tool to process complicated reports efficiently.

Required skills   With training, experienced users can use the least complex tools effectively. Programmer/analysts are best suited to master SQR and the Business Intelligence tools. Any person doing report development should possess an understanding of the PeopleSoft data and programming structure. The skilled individuals will be required periodically to maintain, upgrade, and tune the reports after the initial creation.

Security Considerations

Two types of security should be set up to protect program and report changes: (1) security protecting the approved, production change from further modification and (2) operator security allowing only authorized users to use the added functionality or report that was changed. Activating the security to protect changes should be part of your migration to the production process. Chapter 13, "Security," describes the PeopleSoft security structure in more detail and how to set up security.

Required skills   With training, a dedicated user can administer security effectively. Ongoing security administration is required after the programmed changes are brought into production. Administration is required when individual job responsibilities and authorities change, when new employees require access to the system, and when user access must be removed due to natural employee attrition.

Performance Implications

Changes to the delivered functionality of PeopleSoft will have some impact on performance. Efficiently designed and written changes can enhance system performance for certain routines. In a recent example, changes to the delivered Application Engine code improved the delivered performance of a batch process by over 600%. By contrast, poorly designed and executed changes can bring the system down, literally. We witnessed the results of a rogue query left unattended over a weekend. It consumed so much mainframe processor capacity that the usual weekend batch processes did not finish for the finance users by Monday morning.

In any case, each additional line of code adds overhead to the system and will increase the maintenance overhead of the technical resources in your organization. Effective program code management and disciplined performance testing are essential in managing system performance. Allow a generous amount of time in your project plan to thoroughly test your changes and tune them for system performance before you roll out the changes to the users. This is one case where a good amount of testing and tuning will pay substantial dividends in both technical performance and user acceptance.

Inadequately maintained changes can degrade the system performance over time. Periodically, the call goes out from an organization for a small team of Cap Gemini Ernst & Young performance tuning specialists to look over their system changes. The uncertainty created from inadequate system-change documentation, upgrade maintenance, etc., requires a "stop, drop, and roll" approach to performance tuning.

High-Impact Changes

For our purposes, a high-impact change is one that involves any of these key elements:

- ▶ Structure
- ▶ High-level keys
- ▶ Security
- ▶ Business process design (work flow)

Structural Changes

A *structural change* is one in which the fundamental PeopleSoft program and data structure are being altered. The impact is nearly always very significant due to the complexity involved and the skill, time, and financial commitment necessary for a successful execution. Generally, it's advisable to avoid such changes.

In a real-life situation, a company determined that adding one chart field to the delivered chart field structure in the PeopleSoft General Ledger module would be required. The issue leading to the change was the requirement to capture and report essential statutory information for the company's industry. The solution initially appeared elegant. It took advantage of the technical flexibility of PeopleSoft, met the statutory compliance issue, and left all the delivered chart fields for other management analysis purposes. It was feasible to make the chart field addition without a great deal of fanfare in the table structure and within the SQL Server's 16-key index limitation. However, the reality of the chart field addition was far-reaching within the structure of PeopleSoft. The initial test of the change produced a surprising number of errors. Most errors were rooted in the fact that the PeopleSoft programs also added keys to the table indexes dynamically as routine processes were run. The total combined number of keys then exceeded 16, causing the errors. It was apparent that the cost in time, skill, and dollars would be so significant as to make the solution prohibitive. The conclusion was that although the addition of the chart field was conceptually feasible, it was impractical, and a new approach to the issue was adopted.

High-Level Keys

A number of key setup elements (high-level keys) have a large bearing on the resulting PeopleSoft functionality and ongoing flexibility. A strength of PeopleSoft is the flexibility it has through its Set ID structure elements. Careful planning is required to set up the high-level keys in a streamlined fashion while allowing for future growth. Changing the fundamental setup later is an expensive proposition.

To step through an example, the following high-level keys must be set up for the PeopleSoft financial and HR/benefits modules:

- Set IDs (for all PeopleSoft modules)
- Business Units (for all PeopleSoft modules)
- Employee IDs (for the PeopleSoft HR/benefits modules)

The Set ID identifies a unique collection of functions and business rules that has been configured within PeopleSoft for a particular organization. A Business

Unit is assigned to a Set ID, which grants that Business Unit the corresponding unique collection of functions. The same assignment is made for an Employee ID to the Set ID. Since it's possible to have virtually an unlimited number of Set IDs, Business Units, and Employee IDs, the potential for flexibility is significant. Generally, however, the fewer high-level keys, the better; and structuring to allow for growth and change avoids future problems.

To illustrate the point, let's consider the company that has 10 business units rolling up to a consolidated financial statement. To provide the flexibility for each business unit to adjust the PeopleSoft functionality for its independent needs, a separate Set ID was created and assigned to each Business Unit, i.e., 10 Business Units and 10 Set IDs with a one-to-one relationship. The recommended approach is to have one Set ID with all Business Units assigned to it. This alternative structure better supports the leading practice of standardizing practices across business units where possible.

A series of issues developed for this company. Although all 10 business units were configured the same initially, each business unit made an increasing number of changes, departing from the standard configuration. The results were as follows:

- ▶ Consolidated vendor and customer analysis was lost at the enterprise level.

- ▶ The level of effort to add a new business unit was fairly significant since a new Set ID was required, rather than just assigning the new business unit to the common Set ID.

- ▶ The effort to maintain the system was higher due to the diversity of configurations and the number of Set IDs.

- ▶ The multiple Set ID structure worked in conflict with the organization's desire to standardize practices and move toward a shared-services finance organization.

- ▶ The level of effort required to change from the structure of 10 Business Units and 10 Set IDs to a common Set ID structure was high.

As you can see, a key decision must be made to determine whether or not your organization will standardize (and support this standardized approach). The ability to think through these requirements and ensure that your business units either work together or work differently is crucial to the setup of the application. Before rushing into any decisions on your Set ID and Business

Unit setup, take the time to consider all business rules and the extent to which your organization works toward common processes and goals. After careful consideration, you'll then be prepared to decide how your Set IDs should be configured.

Security Changes

Chapter 13 provides a detailed look at PeopleSoft security. During your initial implementation you'll establish a security tree. Subsequent changes to security are generally modest, such as adding/removing employees or adding/removing departments. High-impact changes occur when a complete overhaul of the security tree is required. Causes of high-impact security changes come from a company restructure or an acquisition. Simple changes to the originally configured security tree are not feasible in these cases.

Business Process Design (Work Flow)

PeopleSoft provides unique tools to help you design your business processes and enable the work to flow from one area to another. Implementing and subsequently changing work flow nearly always involve applications outside PeopleSoft. Consequently, the introduction of work flow to your project increases the complexity and technical skill required.

Integration tools help link third-party products to the work-flow design and build an open network of applications, electronic forms, interactive voice response, and self-service kiosks. Tools used to automate business processes in a paperless environment include Message Agent, EDI Manager, Workflow Processor, PeopleSoft Navigator, Database Agent, Forms API, Worklists, and Workflow Administrator. A brief description of each follows.

> ▶ *Message Agent* processes messages sent to PeopleSoft by external systems, such as interactive voice response (IVR) systems, e-mail, Internet, intranet, extranet, and kiosks; it also provides an application program interface (API) that enables third-party systems to integrate with PeopleSoft in a real-time manner.

> ▶ *EDI Manager* is used to define the data mappings for electronic data interchange (EDI). It can also be used as a general data migration tool between PeopleSoft and files or batches of data.

▶ *Workflow Processor* is a suite of online agents that run and control the work flow in your business processes; once business processes are defined, agents are created to perform the business process tasks.

▶ *PeopleSoft Navigator* or *Activity Designer* (with PeopleSoft 8) is a graphical browser that provides your application users with a graphical map of the business processes they participate in and enables them to navigate, or select, application panels by clicking on icons representing the tasks or activities they need to perform.

▶ *Database Agent* monitors the PeopleSoft database to identify items that need to enter work flow for processing.

▶ *Forms API* enables PeopleSoft applications to route forms to an electronic forms package as part of an integrated work-flow solution.

▶ *Worklists* are ordered lists of work a person or department has to process; the list is sent to the correct person in priority order as defined in the PeopleSoft Business Process.

▶ *Workflow Administrator* provides the capability to access, monitor, analyze, and control work-flow applications.

Cost-Benefit Analysis

For each change that's considered, a cost-benefit analysis should be completed and documented. This is especially important for high-impact changes. Every organization has its criteria for determining what should be included in a reasonable computation (IRR, NPV, etc.). Intangible benefits should also be considered, although they are difficult to quantify. Intangibles include improved employee morale and better access to analytic information.

Following is a list of quantifiable costs and benefits that we recently used in computing a cost-benefit analysis for a company. The benefits were grouped into one-time benefits and recurring benefits. The accumulated benefit was then extrapolated to the company's market capitalization. This allowed the company to determine the shareholder value of its ERP investment. Not all cost-benefit analysis requires such extensive computations, but the simple discipline of a cost-benefit analysis should be applied to the approval process of a contemplated change. Remember that the benefit is realized only if the project is successful, so be sure to allow for enough time and enough suitably skilled people to do the job right.

Costs

▶ Software cost (for additional application, version upgrade, etc.)

▶ Hardware cost (for desktop, server, and connectivity needs)

▶ Consulting or developer fees (to design, develop, test, tune, and implement)

▶ Internal resource time (to design, develop, test, tune, and implement)

▶ Post-implementation cost (for first-year support, tuning, and upgrade)

Benefits

▶ Shorter new customer–acquisition cycle

▶ Decreased new product–commercialization time

▶ Increased plant capacity

▶ Increased plant efficiency

▶ Increased sales efficiency

▶ Reduced inventory handling cost

▶ Reduced cost of stock-outs

▶ Reduction of obsolescence

▶ Decreased unit cost

▶ Increased labor productivity

▶ Decreased overtime

▶ Decreased changeover cost

▶ Reduced cost of system functionality development

▶ Reduced transactional expense

▶ Increased customer profitability

▶ Decrease in the cash-to-cash cycle

▶ Postponed purchases of plant equipment

▶ Decreased receivables balance

▶ Decreased inventory balance

▶ Higher employee retention

▶ Reduced cost of employee benefits administration

Managing the Change

PeopleSoft is a wonderfully flexible application. Additionally, the open architecture allows a nearly unlimited number of imaginative customizations to meet your specific needs. However, there's no such thing as a "simple" change. Be sure to respect the importance of a disciplined approach to change development, testing, tuning, and maintenance.

Making a change is a lot like getting a pet. Once you have it, you must live with it and give it all the care and feeding it deserves. Consider how large it is likely to grow. Keep track of it at all times. Even good ones misbehave at times. Too many of them can overrun the place. Well cared for, it will add benefits and joy to your life. If ignored too long, it will make you stop everything to give it attention. Finally, when its life is over, give it a proper burial.

Programming Changes

Following procedural and coding standards for changes improves the effectiveness of results and the efficiency of the process. Your chosen standards should be universal to all programming changes and not necessarily unique to PeopleSoft. There are books, seminars, classes, and gurus who espouse what specific procedures to follow and what standards to apply. Additionally, your information technology department may have already established procedural and coding standards. So, let's focus on a framework to organize your standards for PeopleSoft.

A lot can be learned from smart people. On a recent project, a team constructed a "development process handbook" specific to their needs that provided a framework that the entire project team could agree on. It consisted of the following elements:

1. Executive Summary

2. Development Process

3. Technical Specification

    a. Description

    b. Roles and Responsibilities

    c. Deliverables

4. Coding

    a. Description

    b. Roles and Responsibilities

    c. Deliverables

5. Unit Testing

    a. Description

    b. Roles and Responsibilities

    c. Deliverables

6. Standards

    a. Description

    b. General Standards

    c. Panels/Pages

    d. Records

    e. Fields

    f. PeopleCode

    g. COBOL

    h. SQR

7. Appendixes

    a. Sample Development Process Work Plan

    b. Sample Source Header

    c. Sample Modification Log

    d. Sample Module Header

     e. Sample Commented Code

     f. QA Checklist

     g. Unit Test Script Template

Additionally, their development processes looked something like this:

1. Approved Change Request

2. Approved Business Requirements

3. Technical Specifications

4. Technical Specification Walk-Through

5. Approved Technical Specifications

6. Development

7. Developed Code Walk-Through

8. Approved Code

9. Unit Testing

With this framework, you'll be ahead of the game. Unfortunately, many projects that include changes don't get this organized. Sooner or later they pay an expensive price.

Scope Creep

Scope creep is the mistake of inadvertently increasing the amount of work on the project without knowing the true impact on timelines and skilled people. It almost always leads to missed due dates. If unmanaged, it can doom a project to failure. Thankfully, managing the scope of a project is a lot like edging the lawn around the garden. Consistent attention and a little effort keeps it in check.

We developed a simple diagram and use it on each of our projects to communicate the effects of scope creep. It's illustrated in Figure 8.2. The equilateral triangle (or pyramid) has three separate elements, each of which is in proper balance relative to the others: Duration, People, and Scope.

▶ *Duration* is the elapsed time it will reasonably take to accomplish the change.

▶ *People* is the number of skilled individuals required to reasonably accomplish the change.

▶ *Scope* is the amount of work to be accomplished within the duration by the people.

Figure 8.2 **Balancing of resources**

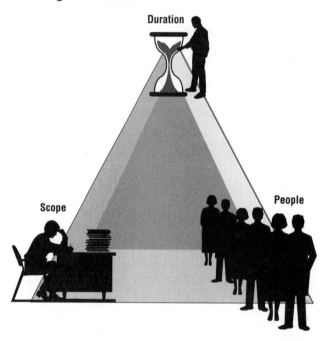

When the project (or any part of it) is properly estimated and structured, the lengths of the three sides of the triangle are equal. When there is a change to any *one* of the individual elements, there must be offsetting changes to the other two to keep the project in balance. (For example, if you increase the scope, you must also increase the duration and/or increase the people). If the adjustments are not made to keep the triangle balanced, the team is headed down the path of missed deadlines, burned-out people, and poor work quality.

An example is the company that properly structures the duration of its project, limits the amount of work to be accomplished to fit within the duration, and properly staffs the project with full-time, skilled individuals to get the job done. During the project a change request is approved. If the team accepts the change request without also considering and adjusting the duration and the people, they will have just made a critical decision. Somewhere, sometime, the project will have to absorb the effect.

This is an easy situation to get into. The rationale goes something like this:

> "The change request is to develop the interface between PeopleSoft payroll and our existing time and billing application. Mary wrote the time and billing system, and she is already part of the PeopleSoft implementation team. She says that the interface won't be too difficult since everything is in COBOL and she can get it done by next Friday. Let's do it."

What is probably going to happen is that Mary will set aside the other things she was working on as part of the PeopleSoft project so that she can pick up the interface development. She completes the interface on time but now is behind on her other PeopleSoft implementation work. So she decides to work evenings and a couple of weekends to catch up. Because she pushed herself so hard, she's not at the top of her game during the next few weeks and doesn't participate in key meetings as much as usual. Consequently, the overall quality begins to suffer, and people are asking her for the other things that are slipping on the work plan that are her responsibility. She's getting fatigued and a little upset that no one else seems to be working as hard as she is.

The problem becomes worse as more, though small, scope changes are being absorbed. After a while, no one can really tell what the accumulated effect to the project is until an important deadline is missed and people are too pooped to suck it up any more. Now you have to "stop, drop, and roll" to recalibrate the entire project timeline without really knowing what caused the situation. It would have been better to be right up front and to adjust the work plan by the amount of time needed to properly develop, test, and tune the interface and assign the right resources.

Upgrade Impacts

PeopleSoft frequently develops and releases patches and new versions of its software. The first consideration should be whether your contemplated program change will be addressed in an upcoming patch or version. If so, it's probably not cost beneficial to go ahead and make a change on your own. Rather, move ahead with the existing functionality and pick up the added functionality later with the patch or upgrade.

You may still decide to make certain program changes. In those circumstances, after the changes have been implemented, you should carefully examine each patch to determine two things:

- ▶ Does the patch affect any of your program changes?

- ▶ Should the patch be applied to your implementation?

The same meticulous analysis of the program changes must be made when evaluating the impact of a version upgrade to your implementation.

PeopleSoft provides a utility to run a "compare report," which will document each modification you have made to your system. Be prepared to spend time sifting through the compare report and the patch or version documentation to determine the level of effort needed to implement the patch or upgrade.

Changes to Documentation

Be sure to adhere to your naming standards and location conventions that are specified in your procedural and coding standards. At a bare minimum, you should document the following for each program change:

- ▶ Catalog the change by module and by date

- ▶ Describe the purpose of the change

- ▶ Record the inputs (parameters passed into the module)

- ▶ Record the outputs (return values)

- ▶ Print out the code

- ▶ Print output reports

Additionally, you can make changes to the online help that's delivered with PeopleSoft. By changing the online help, you can reflect the resulting process changes for the users' benefit. This avoids confusion by the users when the delivered PeopleSoft program has been modified to function differently.

Third-Party Changes

If a third party has made changes to your PeopleSoft system, they should adhere to the same documentation and coding standards that you require of your own developers. Make your expectations clear with the third party, and document the standards as part of the agreement. By having an approval sign-off as part of the development process, you can better manage your risk of paying for effort rather than results.

Web Considerations

In closing this section, we'd like to add a brief but important word about the Internet. ERP vendors, including PeopleSoft, are reconfiguring or Web-enabling their applications to operate over the Internet. The effect is already evident in their products. PeopleSoft has an eProcurement solution using one of the industry-leading solutions, CommerceOne. The benefits of a Web-based application that extends your connections to customers (business-to-customer) and vendors (business-to-business) include quicker customer analysis, quicker cycle time, and lower inventory levels. In other words, the benefits are quantifiable and can enable attaining a competitive edge. In selecting PeopleSoft as your ERP vendor, you should also evaluate its vision of Internet business-to-customer and business-to-business connectivity and consider the vision's compatibility with your company's strategy.

Globalization versus Localization

Global implementations of PeopleSoft are undertaken to increase shareholder value, enhance ability to service customers worldwide, standardize key global business processes, rationalize technology, deploy knowledge cross-culturally, and manage organizational change. The impact of rolling out different functionality by location will be an increase in the time planned for the deployment.

A major agricultural supply and marketing cooperative with operations in 90 countries realized that to improve customer responsiveness, it had to pursue a "single-company" strategy to develop common business processes and information systems. It realized total estimated annual savings of $44 million through the reengineering of its major global processes and the replacement of legacy application systems with an ERP system.

A shared-services center consolidates enterprise-wide functions and eliminates transfer pricing activities and intercompany invoicing, reduces receivables balances with subsidiaries, renews organizational customer focus, reduces cycle time, and improves information access and consistency. Shared-services functions can include:

- ▶ Tax and treasury management

- ▶ Fixed-asset accounting

- ▶ Inventory accounting

- ▶ Accounts payable

- ▶ General ledger accounting

- ▶ Direct billing

- ▶ Data center processing

- ▶ Employee data and record maintenance

- ▶ Payroll and benefits processing

The establishment of shared-services centers reduces the redundant support and infrastructure resources in a global organization. The number and locations of shared-services centers are driven by the organizational head count, key transaction metrics, and countries where present. A leading U.S. multinational white-goods manufacturer with sales of $10 billion and operations in 16 countries implemented a single shared-services center, resulting in a 34% reduction in costs.

Local Changes

Global PeopleSoft implementations are usually designed to standardize core financial, HR, and the back-office processes while providing the flexibility to meet local requirements of currency, language, HR policy, and reporting format. Changes to the local organization occur when global synergy is intended. You'll need to allow longer lead times to address differences among the local sites, which include:

- ▶ Statutory accounts and legal status

- ▶ Cross-border transactions, movements, and invoicing

- ▶ Regulatory restrictions on locations

- ▶ Statutory and fiscal reporting content, frequency, and format

- ▶ Tax treatments

- ▶ Cash or accrual methods

- ▶ Retention of records
- ▶ Technology issues
- ▶ Financial consolidation stages

The global perspective influences change locally when it standardizes technology, HR policies, and knowledge management, and when it introduces shared-services centers.

Desktop Deployment Issues

Issues arise when standardizing technology in global implementations. A common objective is to roll out a standard desktop hardware and load-set configuration. The common load set usually consists of the operating system, desktop productivity tools, communication protocols, and utilities. Local technology or licensing incompatibilities may prevent a single global load set. At best, the organization may accomplish having a single desktop hardware and load set for a region, resulting in multiple load sets globally. The overall impact will be an increase in the time planned for deployment to allow for regional differences.

On a project several years ago, we were to roll out an ERP application to two U.K. offices. We intented to set up the desktop workstations in the U.S. using the full implementation team, then ship the workstations to the U.K. when we flew over to conduct training. We encountered a barrier when it was determined that the workstation power units built into the U.S. computers were incompatible with the U.K. standards. Additionally, at that time there were regulatory restrictions on shipping foreign-built PCs into the country. We resolved the situation by buying the PCs in the U.K., shipping them to the U.S. for configuration, then returning them to the U.K. with the training team. It was an effective and efficient solution, but it added time to the project.

Language Support

PeopleSoft supports multiple languages so that users can interact with the application in their own language through panels, menus, data, and reports. It's possible to have multiple languages set up on a single PeopleSoft system. You'll need to decide up front how many languages and global date formats you want to support. The more languages and date formats you decide on, the more complex your implementation will be—and the more taxing the application will be on the overall system performance.

Local Support

Who will train and support the users for both technical and functional needs when the sun never sets on your company? How will you build an efficient 24/7 support organization? A common way is to view your support in three tiers:

1. The first tier of support comes from the technical and functional "super users" at each site. They can help teach others to self-diagnose their problems and resolve those that are under their control.

2. The second tier is the help desk supported by the more in-depth technicians. Trouble tickets are generated for each call. Delegations of trouble tickets are made to the properly skilled individuals. Resolutions of trouble tickets are also tracked to identify recurring problems, trends, and time to resolve.

3. The final tier is the vendor support departments for both the PeopleSoft application and the other technical components of your system (server vendor, network vendor, router vendor, etc.).

An increasing number of companies are outsourcing their support organization and help-desk functions by entering into service-level agreements with vendors that specialize in their application.

Version Control

Managing the version of PeopleSoft for a single-site implementation is very straightforward. However, in a global implementation where the application resides on multiple servers, the proposition can be complex. The fundamental question is, who controls the application—the corporate organization or the local organization? If the application is controlled by the corporate organization, how will the local needs be addressed and supported in a timely manner to support the business needs? If the application is controlled by the local organization, then changes to the application can be made autonomously, independent of the rest of the company. This inevitably leads to disparate versions of programming languages and utilities, and possibly different versions of PeopleSoft, throughout the organization.

Enterprise-wide application control, version control, and program change standards help curtail the problem. *Change control* is the disciplined approach to migrating the developed change from the development environment to the production environment. PeopleSoft Administration and Upgrade Tools simplify workstation installation, mass updates, the archiving of old information, and the migration to new database platforms. In addition, security tools limit users' access to appropriate applications and data, and developers' access to the objects they can work with. Information systems managers and support staff use these tools to improve the efficiency of implementing and operating PeopleSoft applications.

Several tools are available within PeopleSoft to help with this administration:

▶ *Application Installer* automates the application installation process in various client-server network environments, simplifies workstation maintenance, and facilitates easier navigation through the many hardware, database, and connectivity variables that affect your PeopleSoft applications.

▶ *Data Mover* archives and retrieves data stored in PeopleSoft application databases and helps move data across operating systems and platforms.

▶ *Operator Security* controls the scope and level of data accessibility provided to individuals and classes of users throughout your organization.

▶ *Import Manager* speeds the loading of data generated by other systems into the relational database management system (RDBMS) server for your organization's applications to access.

▶ *Process Scheduler* streamlines the execution of routine tasks and controls time-based events from distributed clients by automatically running, on the client workstation or server, the batch processes or programs—such as journal creation, payroll processing, voucher posting, and other reports—without requiring additional user interaction.

Up Next

Now that you have a clear understanding of how the application supports your business requirements and meets your needs and what type of new solution you'll be implementing, you need to analyze how this new system will affect your organization. In the next chapter, "Preparing Your Organization for Implementation," we'll look at how to prepare your organization for this change and the implementation that lies ahead. Keys to success in that effort include creating a high-performing project team, a good, solid implementation approach and plan, and a sound support organization that will help your users once your system goes live. As always, sponsorship and communication are critical to the success of getting your organization ready for your new applications and processes. Never underestimate the power of a thorough communications plan that is executed effectively.

Preparing Your Organization for Implementation

F E A T U R I N G :

- ▶ Putting together a high-powered implementation team
- ▶ Developing a proper implementation plan and approach
- ▶ Ensuring that your people are ready
- ▶ Looking at the processing-support requirements
- ▶ Putting the proper technology in place to support you
- ▶ Looking at organizational change and getting the right executive sponsorship
- ▶ Determining what communications flow you should have in place

I mplementing an ERP system can be one of the largest or most complex initiatives that your organization will undertake. The implementation of a People-Soft system will provide greater benefit through integration across functions, driving business transactions into a process view and eliminating old practices with a new user application. So how do you prepare an organization for such an undertaking? This chapter should provide you with the necessary insight on how to position your team and your implementation process to ensure that your users are prepared for the change ahead.

Whether you are a Fortune 500 company or an emerging organization, you should prepare carefully for this initiative. A proper approach, an implementation plan, executive sponsorship, and communications are all keys to preparing your end users for the change that's about to happen.

Creating a High-Powered Implementation Team

Let's start by looking at how we can create the implementation team. In many cases individuals have worked in your organization for several years but may have never functioned in a team where members were dependent on one another, as your implementation team will be. Each decision that's made will have an impact on all other decisions. This is true not only because of the integrated nature of the overall application but because of the key elements of rolling out your solution.

In many cases it will take a team a period of time to gel and become a high-performing, results-oriented team. However, achieving this type of model—and achieving it rapidly—should be your goal. As you are implementing your solution, you are moving toward the business case results that you outlined earlier (as described in Chapter 4, "Building a Basis for Business Development"). This business case has bottom-line value to the organization and needs to be achieved as quickly as possible. Also, in many cases we want to begin changing those activities, or processes, that we can change up front without the software up and running. By creating these immediate-term opportunities, we can then utilize the short-term results to fund and promote the longer-term ones.

So what can you do to achieve this quick ramp-up and begin making an impact on the short-term improvements and your overall business case? The biggest challenge that the team faces is becoming *change agents* (as we will describe in detail in Chapter 21, "Analyzing Your Support Network") within your organization.

Note   As described in Chapter 21, a change agent is a champion within your organization who can help the end users of these new processes (and systems) understand the value of your new model and who can encourage support and usage.

Team members have traditionally been in an operational role within the organization. Now they will be given the opportunity to change the way your organization faces its day-to-day activities, the way it takes a process view of completing functional activities, and the way it accepts new processes and tools for completing these activities.

To have a team that will be effective in supporting your implementation, you must have team members that understand each of the business areas that will be affected by the new design and new enablers. It's key to view the team as a collection of the best-skilled individuals from each facet of the organization who can help drive the support you need for your new processes. To create and sustain a high-powered team, you must facilitate the creation process through several steps:

1. Take those individuals from the various operational groups who will bring to the table the mix of skills required.

2. Through training and encouragement, give the new team members new skills that will be required to transform them into your implementation team.

3. Invest in the skills and knowledge that will allow them to implement PeopleSoft, process changes, and support new policies and procedures efficiently but also very effectively.

4. Empower the team to make the right choices and decisions for the organization.

5. Ensure that the team members have individual visions for career-path growth and rewards.

Selecting Team Members

Team members will need to have a varying set of skills and competencies to accomplish this task. Many of the skills, competencies, and knowledge can be promoted on the team through training or knowledge transfer; however, there are certain skills that you'll need to evaluate up front when selecting potential team members.

First and foremost, do they have a deep knowledge of the business operation for the area they will be representing? Implementation team members will be helping their community understand and embrace the future operations supporting your new solution. They will have more respect and credibility if they understand where the users are coming from and have "been there, done that" from the end user's perspective. The team members must also understand all the dependencies and changes that must be in place within the organization for which they're responsible, to ensure that the correct implementation tasks are considered and outlined for a smooth transition.

Once you've nominated several candidates for the team, what are some additional attributes that point toward the individuals who will be most successful in supporting your implementation efforts? Other skills that are key in selecting the right individuals include sound communication and "people" skills, a non-siloed (broader-vision) skill set, and leadership.

Although many organizations initially believe that PeopleSoft implementations are technical in nature, they very quickly realize that the implementation is indeed a transformation project. Each team member must assist the organization through a transformation of its people, process, and technology. During each task, team members will have to draw on their people skills to facilitate completion of activities and ensure results. Thus you should evaluate your pool of candidates on their communication skills, executive presence, ability to empathize with others, and respect by their peers.

Individuals who have both a cross-business and technical-skills perspective can prove to be invaluable to your implementation team. Understanding and embracing the new technology that will support the new processes (or just not being afraid or intimidated by it) can prove to be a key attribute. Technical resources on the team should understand business issues as well, so that they may assist with the overall implementation decisions; they may also be asked to facilitate some key decisions. Technical resources need to understand any local technical contacts and operations and how they might affect or need to be integrated into the overall implementation plan.

Bringing these individuals to the table, in many cases, is very hard on the organization. Most likely, the best candidates from your pool are also very key to the organization in whatever position or capacity they are currently in. At this point, we can only emphasize the importance and scale of the project as a benefit to transforming your organization. Do battle up front and get the best people; it will pay dividends in the long run many times over and help you ensure success.

So you must be able to bring key end users from each of the communities where you're implementing (including technical support) to help you look at all issues and create a solid implementation plan. They should also help communicate and raise the level of awareness with the support areas and end users, who will soon be owners of the new processes and systems.

Your implementation leader should be an individual who has gone through this type of implementation in the past (or supported by someone who has). The leader should also have strong ties to your overall executive sponsor team, should be looked upon by the user community as a leader and someone who understands their business, and should be able to understand the details, react to problems, and calm down concerns during the implementation process. This true leader is key to your successful rollout efforts.

Forming an Implementation Team

Now that you have handpicked your implementation team, how do you get them up to speed on your solutions and ready to run your implementation efforts? You should include an up-front session to get them up-to-date on the project, business case, and overall plan for implementation as quickly as possible.

Many organizations bring a group together and provide project management skills only to the leaders. Though the team leader for your implementation effort will need a strong project management skill set, you shouldn't forget how important it is for your entire team to have a common understanding of the project and how an implementation is accomplished. As we'll discuss later in this chapter, utilizing a strong project management approach is key to the success of the overall initiative; therefore the team members must have a solid understanding of the approach to be used and why this approach is necessary.

Be sure to invest in time during the planning stage of your implementation to have a team-building event. During this event, focus on the time-proven team-building exercises, but also dedicate time to explaining the project management approach you'll be using. Some managers believe that team-building events are soft-sided, costly, and unnecessary; but in most cases these events and activities can help you form a strong-performing team quickly and get through the cycle of "forming, storming, norming, and performing." Table 9.1 and Figure 9.1 show the typical stages a team goes through before it can become high-performing. Having a high-performing team quickly using techniques such as team building can provide a substantial return on investment (ROI) over the up-front costs and time associated with them.

Table 9.1 **Stages of Team Growth**

1. Form	2. Storm	3. Norm	4. Perform	5. Transform
Group is uncertain; group lacks cohesiveness; group will not develop.	Group works through roles; group has a hard time working together.	Group assumes task-related work; group works to involve everyone.	Members work out decisions in a caring way; conflict is accepted, but cooperation is preferred; members prioritize and perform tasks.	Group has now transformed itself into a high-performing team; it continues improving its performance.
Do I want to be in this group?	Who is in control?	We can find ways to work together.	We're working as a team to get the job done.	Now what?

Source: B. W. Tuckman, 1965

Including project management training in this kickoff session will provide everyone on the team with a solid and common understanding of the statuses, communications, and bases for decisions that will be used throughout your implementation. Explain why a detailed plan (or checklist) should be used and why it's critical for all team members to keep the plan updated. Also, during this initial session, outline any key dependencies or milestones in the plan, and stick to them during your rollout.

Figure 9.1 **Team dynamics life cycle**

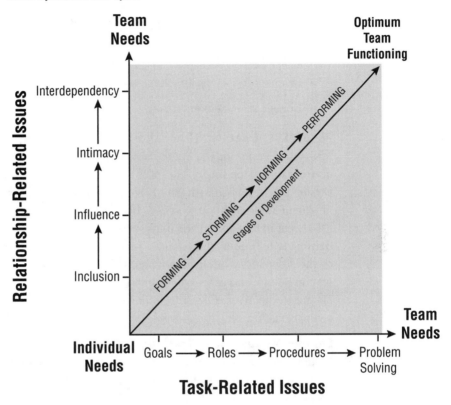

Adapted from Ron Fry and Eric Nielsen

The most successful teams working on implementations are co-located with the entire project team and located in one area. This allows the team members to focus on their implementation tasks and keeps them working with the project team. However, for remote-site support and other business units that might be involved in the implementation rollout activities, you may need to have team members in separate locations. If they're not co-located with the project team, they should be in close contact on a regular basis, especially as implementation nears. Be sure to develop a set of standard update times or an information-gathering approach to keep the checklist up-to-date. (Maybe the members can connect to the same tracking database or network to update the checklist for their items.)

Providing the Skills

So you've selected a team, given them the approach, and kicked off with some team-building sessions. What next? Two types of skills are critical to the team's success:

▶ PeopleSoft-specific (package-specific) training

▶ Change management training

PeopleSoft-Specific (Package-Specific) Training Since the team will be implementing the PeopleSoft application, you should give them a solid, up-front understanding of the software. You can take the current customized version that you have with your project team and use that in getting your implementation team up to speed. If pilot training for end users is available, it's a great idea to have your implementation team members attend this pilot training to help provide insight, direction, and overall, up-to-date information on the delivered solution. Team members should understand all options, integration points, and processes within the new application that support their business objectives. Be sure you have time in your overall schedule for this key package training for your implementation team.

Change Management Training In addition to completing the package training and gaining an understanding of the new processes, the team members will need to act as change agents; to do that, they should take the same training that your change agent network takes (see Chapter 21 for more details on this). Facilitating sessions with the end users, planning for all the issues and nuances around the implementation, and working hand in hand with each site to prepare for implementation require specific skills to help avoid conflicts, create positive reinforcement of the new processes, and generate support for the implementation. Change is a process that's integral to your overall implementation effort. Figure 9.2 shows the change process and how it evolves during a transformation effort.

The baseline goal in almost all implementations will be to drive improvements into the organization. By definition, if we are improving, then we are changing and getting better. Either we are performing our day-to-day transactions differently or we are integrating our transactions differently, or we are being moved from a single, siloed view to a process view.

Figure 9.2   **Change is a process.**

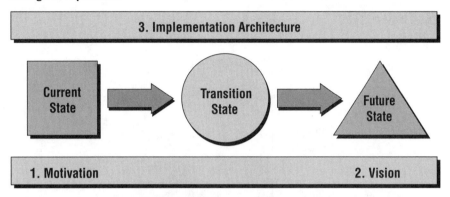

Three Prerequisites for Change

To tackle the challenges of introducing this change, be sure to provide your team with a change management training session and provide key tools they might need, as a toolkit. This does not have to be a week of training—just a day's worth can do it. Focus on the basics of why individuals and organizations fear and fight change, and how to help the team handle this. Team members can be more effective change agents if they have insight into what the different change roles are. Also, to be effective team members, they must understand how the group that's targeted for change will perceive the intended changes. Figures 9.3 and 9.4 show how an individual's emotional response to a *positively* perceived change might differ from the response to a *negatively* perceived change.

Figure 9.3   **Emotional response to a positively perceived change**

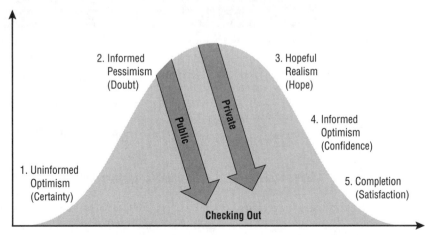

Figure 9.4 **Emotional response to a negatively perceived change**

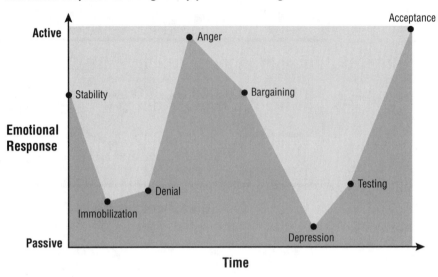

It's also important to understand the phases of acceptance that the change targets might experience (as depicted in Figures 9.3 and 9.4) so that you can tell where in the spectrum your user group might be.

Table 9.2 outlines the key roles in the change process. These roles are instrumental in gaining the acceptance to the change (whether positive or negative) and providing your team the support to help the users in this change process.

Table 9.2 **Key Roles in the Change Process**

Key Role	Description
Initiating sponsor	Individual/group who has the power to initiate and legitimize the change for all the affected targets
Sustaining sponsor	Individual/group who has the political, logistical, and economic proximity to the targets
Change agent	Individual/group who is responsible for implementing the change
Change target	Individual/group who must actually change
Change advocate	Individual/group who wants to achieve a change but lacks sufficient sponsorship

As you work to put in place this new technology and software tool, which will enable your new, refined, or better-integrated processes, it's important to never forget that you are dealing with individual people and their emotions. It's also important to keep in mind that all change, even good change, is viewed as disruptive—and disruption is typically viewed with a sense of foreboding, or at least with a dread of additional effort in a too-busy world.

Empowering and Maintaining Your Team

Once you have a team in place and they are given the skills and knowledge they need to start down the implementation path, everything possible must be done to promote success for the initiative. To have a highly effective team, you must empower them to make decisions. If you've done your job and placed the right team members on the ground, then this team has the best overall skill set possible to make key decisions for implementation. As a sponsor of the initiative or project, you must give the team guidance as to the strategic objectives of the organization, but you must not hinder the potential by maintaining control or approval rights, or protecting sacred cows.

Also, once the implementation is in full gear, you must plan and communicate to the team not only their importance to the organization but the path they will take after completion of their work. Your team members have come from the operations of the organization. Since they've been pulled from their mainstream jobs to assist on this important initiative, you must also show them how much you appreciate their sacrifices by providing them future opportunities to excel. It's vital that team members understand all the new skills they are learning and how valuable that is to the organization. Don't forget that in all likelihood these skills will be very marketable and that you want the members to be positive role models for your end users after you go live—so you don't want them to leave and go to another organization or company.

Key Areas of Focus in the Early Stages

As you bring your implementation team together and care for them during the implementation cycle, you need to ensure that you have the other "right" ingredients necessary to make your implementation a success. These ingredients include:

▶ A solid implementation approach and plan

▶ All aspects of the solution, including people, process, and technology

▶ Initiative management

▶ The complete implementation life cycle, including post-production support

Implementation Approach

Selecting the right implementation approach and guiding principles of the overall project in the beginning can make the difference between a rapid, phased success and a prolonged effort. During the initial planning phases, as discussed in Chapter 5, "Planning the Foundation," it's important to invest in the time and effort of completing a structured plan with a chartering process. Within this overall project plan, you have outlined the basic assumptions, tasks, and risks that will be involved in your implementation.

Now, during implementation planning, it's time to clearly articulate your rollout strategy and give step-by-step details of your plan of attack to ensure successful implementation. Two primary types of implementations are:

▶ Big bang approach

▶ Phased approach

Big Bang Approach

In a *"big bang" approach*, you implement all the new functions and processes together across the entire organization or business. Though this approach involves fewer temporary interfaces, appears less complicated, and may get you to the end result more quickly, it can be too big a bear to manage and support. Three factors—how large your change is to the organization, how ready the organization is for the change, and how much change the organization can take—all play a big part in determining whether this is the right approach. A big bang can cause a "big bust" if there isn't enough support for the change or enough resources to support the new systems and functions that will sustain the change. This can be analogous to "biting off more than you can chew."

However, if after analyzing the change and support requirements, you believe your organization can make it through this large transformation effort in one fell swoop, you can most likely save yourself time and money in the process. You also don't have to worry about keeping two separate processes (the new and the old) in place at the same time (but for different parts of the business) or about keeping old and new systems talking to each other (if you phase in by module or function).

Phased Approach

As we alluded to in the last section, you have two types of phased approaches, generally, when it comes to an ERP implementation:

▶ Phased by module or function (e.g., implement the General Ledger, Payables, Purchasing, and Inventory modules first, and then roll out the HR/ Payroll ones next).

▶ Phased by organization or business unit (or geographic location). This phased approach implements the entire solution but for only a segment of your population, which can be broken down in many ways, such as by organization, business unit, region, or geographic location.

A phased approach allows you to concentrate on a smaller amount of change to maybe a smaller population. You can have hybrids of this phased implementation by mixing modules or functions with certain categories or populations of users. In the phased approach, what you are doing is reducing the scope of the change to a piece that's small enough for your organization to handle, based on limited time or resources. Also, you are changing the process slowly to decrease the overall impact to your organization. However, the overall benefits tend to take longer to develop since the phased approach generally covers a much longer period of time than the big bang approach, and some benefits may not be realized till all the functions or modules and groups are in place.

You must analyze what change your organization can handle and ensure that you are pushing your people hard enough, yet not so hard that they stall, or your implementation may become a nightmare rather than a success—stalled and never on track. The key thing to remember is that you need to stay on track, stay within your budget, and hit your milestones as you've outlined them, so that you can have credibility and add more reliability to the process. This will gain support for your cause rather than cause problems. However, you want to ensure that you are pushing your group forward at the fastest pace they can handle, since you will always have resistance, regardless of the pace. Taking too long can also cause fatigue on the organization and loss of commitment.

As we discussed in Chapter 5, the project charter will provide the "contract between the organization and the implementation team," indicating what constitutes success, what the assumptions are, and what the procedure is for resolving conflicts. During the chartering phase, it's important to document and gain consensus on the approach that the project will use to manage issues, requests for changes, and scope. These areas should not be looked upon lightly. An implementation project will affect all areas of the organization and will definitely present to the team issues regarding process changes, resource constraints, initiative conflicts, and the ever-constant scope creep.

Many organizations and implementation teams begin with a very specific charter and a concise understanding of the scope of their implementation. However, it's not uncommon to find teams who, when moving through their design phase, have changes to this scope, challenges, and many requests for changes to the new processes. In some circumstances, teams experience the need to "sell" their solution to middle management and team leaders in order to justify the new processes, while other teams find themselves working with management to limit the scope, as requested during the first pilot or site rollout.

You as a project manager, sponsor, or team member can best ensure your success by focusing on the scope and maintaining a clear focus on the initial intent of the charter. Implementation projects are not overnight projects, and it's easy to spend valuable time, resources, and dollars if additional scope is added or the original scope is changed in midstream. All scope changes are not bad, and each should be considered appropriately based on the overall business case and the direction of the project. However, in many cases projects that don't maintain a tight hold on their original charter, allowing the initial scope to inch into a much larger scope, fail to hit the implementation mark. Though some additional features may be beneficial, they might be better implemented after your initial rollout. Ensure that your implementation team has a clear understanding of the business case and why the scope and new processes were developed in the first place. With their understanding and support, they can be ambassadors for the project during the implementation phase, putting the changes into the proper context with their support group.

Designing All Aspects of the Solution

One principle to keep in mind as you progress toward your implementation is that an 80% solution that is implemented and providing value to the organization can be refined and is infinitely more valuable than a 100% solution that's still in the design stages and not implemented. Your 80% solution is supporting your business case and adding value to your organization, while your 100% design is not close to being implemented. Also, things learned by a team after implementation can cause some changes as well. Therefore, the quicker to implement, generally the better, given a stable, sound environment and the proper support around the processes.

As implementation begins, keep in mind that you are implementing an overall solution and that that solution should have impacts on your people, process, and technology (not just one of them). It's easy for your team to focus strictly on the technical or package solution and forget how the changes affect your people or how your people might need new skills to support the solution, or forget that the processes must change to support the new technology. Be sure that your team is moving toward a total solution that looks at all areas, including people, process, and technology.

People: The Organization and the Individuals

As mentioned earlier in this chapter, the most difficult area for team members to handle is the organizational change issues that arise from changing the "way it used to be" to the "new way." Many individuals and organizations were just fine and dandy with the old way—thank you very much—and don't understand why they have to change. Two main areas must be planned in the "people" part of your solution:

- ▶ Refocus of individuals from transactions to processes
- ▶ Individuals' need for information about the coming changes

When you are getting ready to start your planning for implementation (or even before that, if possible), begin planning your communications strategy. Every individual within your company, organization, team, or business unit will want to know what is happening, why, how soon, at what cost, with what sacrifice, and for what goal. The earlier you begin providing this information, the sooner you will begin taking advantage of the change management process.

Now, let's consider that I may not want to present all the information to all groups and that I may not have some of the requested information at the present time (i.e., during the initial planning stage). In order to effectively communicate, I must understand which existing groups require communication, what information each group desires, what groups who haven't yet requested information will require it, and what information must be made available to everyone. The easiest way to get your arms around this activity early is to complete a communication matrix, as discussed in more detail in Chapter 21. The matrix should include:

▶ The target communication groups, such as sponsors, team members, ad hoc members, middle managers, change targets, all employees, budget managers, and clerks

▶ Content, including process flows, design information, technical specifications, work plan updates, project expenditures to date, timetables, etc.

▶ Timing of each communication and medium, such as weekly sponsor meetings, monthly status reports, quarterly newsletters, and monthly quality assurance reviews

One other people area to focus on is the move from transactional processing to more of a process flow of the business transaction. In many organizations and especially with non-ERP software, the completion of work is done in incremental, transactional, data entry points or steps and not as an overall process flow. As your organization moves to a PeopleSoft solution, you will not only be asking someone to enter data but also to correct information, resolve issues, and make policy decisions around proper resolutions of the transaction. This is a big change in two ways: First, at the individual level, many persons have not had visibility of the entire decision process; nor have they had training or been empowered to finalize a string of events. Second, at the organizational level, many organizations have created small data entry or transactional groups to keep the data moving. These groups have focused on the efficiency within each segment of the process, and now the focus is switched to the overall process. Consider these potential organizational impacts up front, and plan the time necessary to assist with evaluating them. You may need to create teams with members from several of the old functional groups, or you may want to have teams that focus on the entire process but across a business unit, region, or product line. You may also have to plan for additional training for individuals, to explain the new entire process, not just the new software.

Process: The Way It Gets Done

When looking at implementing any ERP package, begin with the package as the process model. This will give your organization a boost in moving to an implemented solution. In every package, as in PeopleSoft, there will be areas that don't meet your needs or can't complete the overall transaction process in the manner you need. However, keep in mind that ERP packages were built around the input of numerous customers and have many leading practices built into them and their transaction flows. Also keep in mind that PeopleSoft has been running on a 12- to 18-month release schedule, which means that if a feature that's needed to support your process is missing, it might be in the next release cycle; so you should check that out and work with the vendor (and other customers) on that requirement.

When implementing your solution, look at how the package solutions conflict with your current solutions and ensure that there is training, communications, and support for these new ways of running your business. When working on the implementation schedule, ensure that any quarterly, monthly, or annual processes are considered in regard to the impact of shifting to the new processes and new way of doing things. Look at starting at the beginning of a period (month, quarter, or year) to help facilitate this process. Also, consider any interim solutions that must be in place or the impact to them if implemented in mid-cycle. Try to think through all these changes and document them and the actions to be taken, rather than get surprised when you go live. This analysis can help you decide when the best time may be for your implementation-specific activities. Also, by looking at the flow of information, you can better schedule your conversions and data input with an eye toward your new process.

Technology: The Software

PeopleSoft is very flexible in the options and configurations it allows your team to utilize to define the solution that best fits the needs of your organization. PeopleSoft can be configured to address needs of several functional groups and to drive integration among the groups—integration that never existed previously or that had to be achieved manually.

Although PeopleSoft is very flexible, it won't accommodate all requirements for all organizations. Some areas or functional groups within the organization have custom systems and therefore feel that they will be giving up "their solution." Others may want a specific look and feel to the screens (or pages), while some groups may have different accounting or commodity management categories or numbering scenarios that they are used to. Each of these cases and others will be presented to your team as reasons the system doesn't support an individual's or group's needs. Be sure to look at each of these requests or concerns with two perspectives:

Business perspective   Is this required for the overall business? Does it require a trade-off in one area to benefit the whole? Is it truly required, or is it a "nice to have"? Does this difference in business processes provide your organization with a strategic advantage, or is it "just the way we do it now"?

Technical perspective   How significant a change is the technical change? Will it carry forward into an upgrade? Will it hinder the upgrade path? Can the solution be completed inside the PeopleTools capabilities? Can the change be "bolted on"?

Customization of the software may provide your organization with the ability to execute a specific process more efficiently or allow a process or transaction to be completed a certain way as required by your specific industry or corporation. Customizing the software to provide the best possible software solution to enable the overall solution is very important to the acceptance and usability of the overall solution; however, be cautious in not letting the technical solution become the complete answer. Ensure that the overall customizations are limited to what is absolutely needed, and spend your efforts focusing on the people and process areas of your solution.

Another key area to evaluate during the planning phase is the infrastructure upon which the software will be implemented. In many organizations the implementation provides the chance to change platforms, acquire new skills, and switch from the old way of doing things; however, be sure to evaluate closely your needs in the infrastructure area. If you have an in-house expert on a particular platform or network model, evaluate this first. PeopleSoft will also work with you (as will your implementation partner, if you have one) on all infrastructure options. But you should look at what support you have internally to support your needs or look at how easy if may be to hire another resource if you must do that—as well as consider any size or performance issues. Be sure that when creating your implementation checklist or plan, you consider all infrastructure items and when they must be in place to support your rollout, including any upgrades to desktops, networks, or communications.

By integrating an overall approach to your solution and maintaining a solid communications plan for the groups affected, your team will be in a much better position when rolling out your solution and be likely to achieve a much smoother transition when the time comes.

Initiative Management

In addition to planning for your solution and its implementation, you should have a clear picture of what else is going on within your organization that might impact your solution or timetable. Upgrades with certain hardware or software systems, related packages, or processes can all affect your implementation timetable and success. Look at all your touch points in all three areas—people, process, and technology—to ensure that you've outlined all possible situations or initiatives that might affect your implementation.

Outline any action plans or contingencies for initiatives that might have an impact on your schedule or design, and ensure that these activities are noted within your checklist and plan. For instance, if you are counting on the legacy systems you're interfacing with to update their data to your new chart of accounts, but find out just prior to implementation that one or more are not ready, what will you do? You need to have a strategy for determining how this problem will affect your schedule and what you might need to do in the short run to resolve it.

You should also have key checkpoints with these other initiatives so that any delays or changes can be addressed as soon as possible. The more you stay connected with these initiatives, track them, and understand how they might affect your rollout, the better prepared you will be to handle and react to any delays or changes.

Planning for the Complete Implementation Cycle

Be sure that your implementation checklist and plan includes all post-implementation support activities and doesn't end on the day of your go-live event. Also be sure that any follow-on activities or actions that were postponed are included in your post-implementation support activities. Chapter 16, "Post-Production Support," looks at the entire process for supporting your new application well into the future. Your plan should also cover knowledge transfer from the project and implementation teams to the new support group prior to the close of the project.

Preparing the Organization for Implementation

Now that you have a team, an approach, detailed processes, the technology, and all your implementation checklists ready, how do you really prepare your organization for what is about to happen? There are three primary ingredients that will help ensure that your organization is aligned with your implementation and ready to go live:

► Creating a detailed approach to addressing your organizational changes and the impact they will have on your people, including appropriate information and training of your staff

► Developing sound executive sponsorship to support these changes and create an environment of positive thinking for both the new processes and support of the steps for creating change

► Communications to enforce these activities and support and to ensure that all affected parties have the information they need to understand the changes and the business case behind the changes

There's no guarantee that if you accomplish all these steps and activities, all your people will be happy and satisfied, and prepared to embrace and support your new processes and application. However, by doing these things, you can ensure that your organization as a whole will be ready and able to move forward and support these changes—helping you to have a successful implementation.

Organizational Change

As we mentioned before and will discuss in greater detail in Chapter 21, organizational change requires a thoughtful and detailed approach to support it and should never be underestimated. Individuals are always nervous about change and what impact it will have on them. You need to be able to pinpoint what the changes are and who will be affected, and to create a sound plan for preparing the affected individuals for the changes through the appropriate communications and training—along with support, once the changes are in place.

Since everyone reacts a bit differently to change, you need to be sure there is a very personal approach to addressing each employee's (or stakeholder's) questions and needs, to help prepare them for the new processes and application. You need to involve your change agents and managers to help ensure that everyone is "touched" in some way with the information they need in order to understand the change and its impact on them.

We don't think it's possible to spend too much time dealing with organizational changes and the impacts they will have on the success of your implementation. So be sure you have thought through the impacts, approach, and support while helping to prepare your organization for these changes.

Executive Sponsorship

While you might have a great assessment of the changes and the impact they will have on your organization, without the right executive sponsorship you still might fail. Executive sponsorship gives your team and your initiatives the credibility and commitment that you will need to help push the organization to make the changes necessary to support your new processes. Change is never easy, but if your leadership embraces and supports it, generally others will be willing to do the same. If your leadership doesn't support your change, you might as well pack up and go home. It's very difficult to move an organization forward if the leadership is not supportive and behind the change. Executive sponsorship can be visible through specific communications, meetings, and actions.

You should work carefully with your executive sponsors to ensure that they are aware of the changes and the impacts to their organizations and what they need to do to help support the changes. Generally, if your business case has clearly articulated the benefits and costs of your new processes and applications, this is the foundation that you'll use to gain the executive support you need. Once the executive sponsors are committed to this case, they can help you drive change and commitment within their organization.

Communications

As we detail in Chapter 21, communications planning is a big part of preparing your organization for implementation—what your people should expect, when, and why. A clear, well-defined communications plan should support your project throughout its life cycle, but is even more important as you're getting ready to go live. You should look at clearly communicating to each group any expectations you have of them in the move toward a successful implementation. You should also ensure that all your stakeholders and targeted users have been informed clearly about their training, the new processes, the impact to their jobs, and a detailed schedule as it relates to them and their specific piece of the implementation process. All activities outlined in your implementation checklist should be clearly communicated to the group that must take action or perform a role in the implementation process.

Detailed communications or progress reports should be in place to update that group as you move through your checklist, with weekly updates and, as you get nearer, even daily ones. Any issues identified with the items or actions, and any changes, should be clearly discussed as well as resolved. A clear process for documenting, resolving, and communicating this plan should be in place.

In addition to those individuals who are working on the implementation itself and those who have actions on the plan, each user or stakeholder should have a detailed communications plan aimed at them to help prepare them for the implementation. Whether the communications are in the form of weekly news-letters, e-mail, or updates to Web sites, they should be well thought out and provide the appropriate level of information. Also, the different mediums for "getting the word out" should be varied.

Your ultimate goal is to have no one surprised or misinformed about the rollout or about what they need to do to support it. You also want everyone to have a clear picture of what the new processes are, how these processes will affect them, and what the timing is for any actions they need to take.

Up Next

Once you have prepared your organization for the changes, created your approach, pulled together the right implementation team, and put the pro-cesses in place to support your implementation, you are ready to "turn the switch on" and go live. Remember to use your implementation team effec-tively to support these activities and let them be ambassadors to your organi-zation to help you ensure success. In the next chapter, "Prototyping," we'll see how prototyping might help you solve complex issues, gain additional support from your users, and ensure that your business needs are meet. We'll look specifically at two forms of prototyping—conference room piloting and pilot rollout—and discuss how they can be used during your PeopleSoft ERP implementation.

Part III

Implementing PeopleSoft

Now that we've looked at how to get things started, discussed the basics behind the PeopleSoft application, and considered your core design or what you're trying to implement, it's time to get your team in gear, begin setting up the application, and roll it out to your users. This section of the book covers the basic concepts that will help you actually implement the system and move it into production, including configuring your application (or prototyping), converting your data, dealing with all the technical challenges, setting up security, testing, and finally "going live" with your new PeopleSoft application and supporting it in the future. This portion of your journey can be both rewarding and challenging; but remember to always keep your vision, its value, and your future-state design (FSD) at the forefront of your mind so that they can help you make the right decisions along the way.

CHAPTER 10

Prototyping

FEATURING:

- ▶ What is prototyping?
- ▶ Conference Room Pilot—a specific prototyping technique
- ▶ Why should we prototype our solution?
- ▶ Conference Room Pilot tips
- ▶ When is the best time to prototype?
- ▶ What should I include in my prototype?
- ▶ Getting feedback and leveraging it

This chapter will cover the intricacies of prototyping, from defining what it is and how to use it effectively within your project to understanding the best time to use it. We'll look at a specific technique in prototyping, which we call Conference Room Pilot, and how it can be used extensively during your ERP implementation. Finally, because you need to get sound, constructive feedback during your prototyping efforts (otherwise, your time is wasted), we'll concentrate on tips on getting feedback from your participants and leveraging it—which you'll need for a successful project implementation.

What Is Prototyping?

Prototyping is a methodology that assists users in their understanding of what a new system will look like and how it will react. The concept of prototyping is not limited to showing users what the new screens/pages will look like, but rather how the new system will work in the users' specific business environment and, more often than not, how their process will change to work within the framework of the system. Let's not forget that you selected PeopleSoft so that you'll be able to work the way you want to work well into the future and not be constrained by the limitations of your "old" system.

There are several ways to prototype the new PeopleSoft system. They range from demonstrating the functionality of the system to the team that has been assembled (functional and technical) to a full-blown system pilot where a subset of the eventual users will go live with the new software and be the "guinea pigs" for the system prior to its rollout to all users. Far and away the most popular method for prototyping a new system is through a technique we at Cap Gemini Ernst & Young call the Conference Room Pilot.

Conference Room Pilots

The Conference Room Pilot (CRP) method is very much as the name implies: a "pilot" of the system to be delivered, but demonstrated in a conference room with a number of key users. Below we'll describe how to pull off a successful CRP.

CRP Goals and Objectives

The Conference Room Pilot provides the user community with the opportunity to review resolutions to documented gaps between the delivered PeopleSoft functionality and the client's business requirements before the system is put into production. The CRP demonstrates gap resolutions that are applicable to the group assembled in the room.

The overall purpose of the CRP is to come to an agreement on the overall successful resolution of all demonstrated gaps. It's important to have the appropriate decision makers present at the CRP so that they may reach a conclusion about the overall success of the prototype and about any specific changes that may need to be made.

CRP Scope

The scope of your CRP should be decided in advance and should include what you will be demonstrating for that group. Each CRP session will likely cover a subset of all the changes you're likely to make and be targeted at a specific audience.

Any of the completed customizations already in place should be demonstrated for confirmation by the users during the CRP. The scope should focus not only on the functional area changes that will be made, but also on the business areas to be demonstrated. Remember, this is only a representative group; not all the users can or should be present.

 TIP Be sure you identify the decision makers up front and invite them to the session—and be sure they attend! Otherwise, you'll never get beyond the pilot session.

Assumptions and Notes

Wherever possible, use real business-related information to put the processes and changes in context for your audience. Review and provide a list of all assumptions to the group at the beginning of the CRP to level expectations. Remember to include several points of view, from the clerk to the executive, of the functionality and data used in your demonstration. You also should include both inputs and outputs of the information (if possible).

TIP Most users need to see how the system is going to work before they can support the change or believe that the change will actually take place.

Customizations in the CRP

In your CRP, demonstrate any customizations you may have made to date. Try to paint a view of the information the users can relate to. This can include customizing the software, doing software mockups (the screens/pages appear now as they will appear, but functionality is not present), and leading conceptual walk-throughs. Business requirements (that require customizations) that will *not* be demonstrated during the CRP should be clearly annotated and explained during the session.

Note You need visionaries *and* everyday users to attend your CRP so that they will get a good look into how your future system will work, challenge you on your solution, and support the everyday needs of your organization and staff.

Why Prototype?

Many individuals or organizations may ask why you should prototype—why not just go ahead and implement your solution without demonstrating the changes to your users? There are both advantages and disadvantages to prototyping. We'll look at each, and you'll see that in the majority of situations, prototyping can prove effective and outweigh the time and costs associated with it. As we note in Chapter 14, "Testing," it's better and more cost effective to catch any defects early rather than later. Figure 10.1 shows how the cost increases exponentially with error corrections through the life cycle of the project. By finding your defects early, you'll meet the needs of the users earlier and you'll save yourself some money. Also, you won't look as foolish in the process, and you'll gain support with your proposed changes.

Figure 10.1   **Cost escalation in relation to the time the error is discovered**

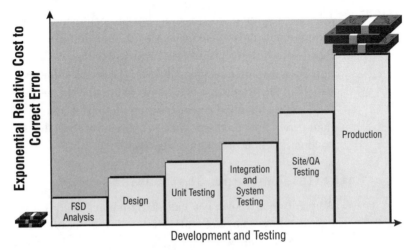

When Error Is Discovered

Advantages

The advantages of prototyping include the following:

▶ The ability to gain user buy-in or acceptance of a change

▶ Ensuring user participation so that your changes support the actual requirements (and there is no miscommunication or misunderstanding of those requirements)

▶ Getting your answer sooner rather than waiting until user-acceptance testing to find out that you are right or, more important, wrong (there could be potential time and cost savings with getting the solution right the first time)

User Buy-In

There is nothing better than getting early user buy-in to your new system and processes. The more involved the users are with your project and the changes you're making, the better off you'll be in helping to alleviate their fears and setting their expectations. You'll also be able to gauge resistance to solutions and to understand whether the business requirement has been fulfilled sooner rather than later.

User Participation

User participation ensures that your project team doesn't misunderstand requirements or become misguided in their interpretation of what the true business requirements are. By involving the users in this activity, you can not only increase their acceptance or buy-in to the solution but also get feedback earlier in the project life cycle and ensure that the needs of the users are being fulfilled. By having the users participate in this activity, you can minimize their direct time on the project, yet maximize the value they bring when you're conducting their prototyping sessions.

Potential Time and Cost Savings

As mentioned above, you can save time and money on your project by not having a large range of end users participating full-time on the project but rather using them wisely through techniques such as these CRPs. Also, by getting your users to view solutions prior to user-acceptance testing or implementation, you can lower your development costs or the cost of fixing problems.

Getting the Answer Right—Sooner

The sooner the key users and stakeholders can see your solution, the sooner you can ensure that you have the right solution. Also, by reviewing the solution with company-specific processes and data, you can ensure that it meets the needs of the business. Again, doing this in a CRP setting rather than waiting for user-acceptance testing or implementation will save you money. Also, by reviewing the solution earlier in the cycle, you will have time to make any changes and ensure adequate results.

Disadvantages

While there are many advantages to prototyping your solution with key end users ahead of time—before you spend a lot of time and effort making the change and affecting other modifications or processes—there are a few disadvantages to this approach as well.

Time and Cost in Relation to Complexity

A key disadvantage of CRP sessions is the time and cost of pulling them all together and demonstrating the solution for modifications or changes that are readily apparent, clear, or easy to implement. You should perform your CRP around complex solutions you are solving or large-scale changes in business processes, and ensure that the business drivers outweigh the cost (in time and resources) of conducting these sessions. By grouping several gaps together and including a rundown of key functions and features, you can optimize the time and effort needed for setting up and conducting these sessions and maximize their value. Be sure that your use of the CRP technique effectively attains the goals of your prototyping: to obtain user support and buy-in and to ensure that user requirements are met. If you don't need one of these things to support your change, then don't conduct a CRP on that area or for that feature.

Getting Sidetracked

Another disadvantage in conducting a CRP session is that due to a lack of understanding of the new system versus the features and functions of the old system, you may end up getting your users confused and sidetracking the actual decisions that need to be made. The best way to combat this problem is to ensure that your users have baseline knowledge of the new system (or to begin the session with a baseline training program) so that they can concentrate on the decisions that have to be made. Also, you can help alleviate this problem by using a strong facilitator who can help manage client expectations and direct discussions toward a focused resolution.

Conference Room Pilot Techniques

When demonstrating your solution in a Conference Room Pilot session, there are several techniques you can use to ensure that you have the right solution. These techniques include:

- ▶ Iterative approach

- ▶ Mock-ups versus full coding

- ▶ Adequate preparation

We'll review each of these techniques in detail. Be sure that you evaluate the applicability of each for your particular situation or resolution.

Iterative Approach

In the iterative approach, you involve your users in several CRP sessions, such as the three-step process outlined below.

1. Define the exact user requirements and how the change might be made.

2. Review a mock-up of the proposed solution; or review a few proposed solutions without making the coding changes or heavy customization to the application, and have the user group choose the solution.

3. Show the final change and how it will be implemented, and get final approval of the change.

With the iterative approach, you should be building on a complex solution or having the end users help you to prioritize the changes as you go forward. This approach involves several checkpoints or steps before you complete the final solution. While this can help ensure that the solution meets the requirements, it generally takes longer and is more costly. You should weigh the complexity of the change against the rewards of having multiple sessions and breaking down the solution into multiple steps.

Mock-Ups versus Full Coding

You can perform effective Conference Room Pilot sessions by "mocking up" your change and not fully coding your solution. This approach allows you to resolve problems up front yet get user input before you make big changes to your system. Before you choose this approach, you need to weigh the effect of the partially shown solution (such as a panel or page mock-up with no processing code) and whether it will adequately demonstrate your solution to the end users. In some cases, it may not be worth the effort unless you can show the full-blown, coded process to the users. Each change or modification will need to be looked at to determine what approach is best. In most cases, it's good to show a mock-up of the solution first to get buy-in of your concept for filling the gap before you spend lots of time programming the change and then have to re-do the whole thing after getting user feedback that you were way off base.

Again, you must weigh the cost, time, and impact of each session to determine what approach is best. You don't have to choose just one solution for all your changes. You can have a mixed set of solutions to target your session reviews with and to determine how your gaps should be filled.

Prep Time: It's a Lot More Than You Thought!

To prepare for any CRP session, you need to think through your approach, decide how to effectively convey your design to your audience, and ensure that you've planned, in detail, the presentation to the group. Handouts and explanations of the identified gap and proposed solutions, as well as alternative solutions that were considered, might also be helpful. Ensure that you have adequate time to prepare for your CRP sessions, that the purpose of each session is clearly defined, and that the appropriate audience is chosen to give you the right results (which meet the business needs yet minimize changes to the application).

This is your chance to get support from your end users and stakeholders and make your project that much more effective. So plan wisely and ensure that you have ample preparation time. Look at logistics, remembering to include break times and arrange system availability, so that all your session time is used effectively.

Can't We Just Wing It? (In Praise of Scripting)

Many folks might ask, "Do we really need to prepare for a session and create a detailed script for our end users?" That would be the wrong approach. You must carefully plan and execute your CRP session to ensure that all your objectives (and those of the end users) are met. Clear expectations and expected results should be included in your preparation, as well as a well-thought-out guide (or script) that uses real business data to show that the solution is the most effective one. Users who can "see" the true solution and how it will work will not only support your solution but feel more comfortable that you've thought through the solution and that they can depend on you to get results and support their needs. For many, this will be their first look at the solution, so now is the time to get them on your side and to obtain their support of your initiative.

What Data Should I Use?

When running your CRP session, you should try to use real, live examples to demonstrate your solution. If possible, set up your scripting so that it uses an example that's applicable to the organization that is reviewing the solution and that demonstrates the appropriate data to support the solution. You don't want to have chosen business unit 38, which might be your marketing department, and to have them process some plant transactions. You want to pick a plant location and have the users process a plant transaction so that they will have confidence that you understand their requirements and that the solution supports their needs. Relating the solution to the users' own environment and using applicable data help to reinforce this notion.

Did I Mention Toys to Play With?

You should make the sessions fun and informative, keeping the audience's attention and ensuring maximum participation. Don't be afraid to get them involved in running the solution and being a part of your script. Also look for creative ways to reward the group and thank them for their participation. When they are involved in the solution and the results, they will have better buy-in to the new processes and systems. For example, you can ask questions, and the individuals who provide feedback or answers can get prizes. Again, this ensures that they are involved and paying attention to your solution.

Don't Forget the Snacks

As with any meeting or session, be sure you have ample food, snacks, and beverages to sustain your audience throughout the CRP activities. Keeping them happy and fed can ensure that they are focused on your solution and on providing you the feedback you need for the session. You can also use treats to reward participation and input as a part of your activities. Again, you want the group to be focused on the results and activities at hand and not be worried about their next meal or their growling stomachs.

When Is the Best Time for a CRP?

The earlier, the better, when it comes to the CRP session. However, you want to ensure that you have collected enough information on the future-state requirements, identified the gaps between that vision and what the package is able to do, and compiled enough information about the current business processes to be effective. Typically, CRPs are ideal after the package has been assessed against the future-state processes and after the gaps, along with proposed solutions, have been defined. Once you've determined what the proposed solutions might be, you can use a CRP to help you determine what the best solution is and whether your ideas really fit the needs of the organization.

You can break down your CRP sessions depending on both the complexity and the scope of your processes. For instance, you might feel comfortable reviewing all the accounts payable processes and how the system supports them, including any proposed modifications, but you might not be prepared at this time to conduct a CRP on your asset management requirements. Therefore, you might do a CRP on accounts payable first and then later do one on asset management. Also, sometimes, based on dependency, you might want to do a particular CRP first, such as one on your chart of accounts design. This design would need to be accomplished first, since all of your other modules depend on this configuration. Once the users have agreed in that CRP to your changes to the chart of accounts, you can follow with your other changes. You also don't need to conduct a CRP for every process. Those processes that don't change, or change minimally, may not need a CRP.

What Should I Pilot?

As mentioned before, you don't have to pilot everything or anything. In some cases, because of radical changes to a business area or process, you might want to pilot your solution prior to rolling it out to an entire group. This "test bed," or pilot, can be effective in ensuring that your new business process supports your needs in a real-time environment. The risks associated with implementing such a radical change across the entire organization are so high that they make you want to test your solutions on a select group of individuals or users.

Piloting a solution can be effective in gaining the support and momentum you need to ensure that your solution will be accepted and used companywide. You might need to prove that this solution will work prior to rolling it out. Also, since the change can be so great, you might not have time for all the change management needed in a large-scale rollout; so by limiting your users and gaining support, you can roll out the solution slowly.

Creating more buy-in, support, and momentum can prove effective for this type of radical change. Also, with this approach, costs may not play as big a role as resolving the change and gaining support for your solution. Besides, a great solution without the right support from your users may never be effective. You really need to look at your organization carefully and determine how willing and supportive they are of the changes that are about to occur. If you chose to pilot, pick a group of individuals who represent all the processes you are supporting (or at least a lot of the complex ones), so that everyone views the pilot as significant enough. Also, a group that is more willing to change and support the initiatives is one that should pilot the solution first (if you can find such a group!).

Now That We Can Do This, Can We Also Do That?

Controlling "scope creep" can be a major challenge when using prototyping techniques. The more times you have the users review your solution, the more time they have for coming up with additional things they need. You need to be sure that all changes relate back to your project objectives and the scope that was outlined in your project charter, as was discussed in Chapter 5, "Planning the Foundation." Also, you need to have a clear focus up front on your original goals and objectives and a mindset for minimizing changes to the application unless there is a very strong business case to support the change.

For each change proposed, you must outline a clear business requirement and align it with your project scope in order to support it moving forward. A clear process for proposing any scope changes must be made and communicated to the users ahead of time so that they'll understand the impact and stay within the prescribed scope of your session. While you want to ensure that you've met the business requirements and goals you set out to accomplish, you also have to be very careful that you don't get off track and create scope creep. Having a clearly defined set of processes, solutions, and scope can help you stay on track with your sessions. Also, by clearly communicating the objectives of each session, you can keep your end users focused on the session and the results. Figure 10.2 shows an example of a sound change-control process that you should follow when requests are made.

Figure 10.2   **Change request process**

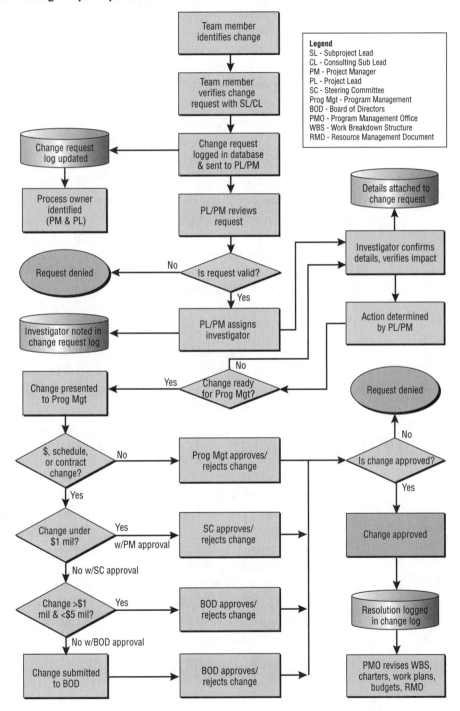

But It's Just a Small Change . . .

No change is so small that you should forgo your defined process. In Chapter 5, we outlined the change-control process in detail and provided you the means to track your scope, changes to that scope, and changes to the system. All changes, no matter how small, have an impact on your solution and take some time, energy, and resources to support. In all projects your people, time, and money must be balanced in order to complete your project on time and within budget. Any changes to the initial scope of your project must be tracked and approved, and any impacts to the timeline and budget must be reviewed and approved.

Small changes, though they may not take time initially, may take a lot of time to maintain due to documentation requirements, training, future upgrades, additional help desk/user support, etc. Every time a change is made, you must make notes so that your support group, your technical team, and your training folks all know about it; and every time you upgrade (which can be almost every year), you have to take time to reassess that change again and again and again. So ensure that you look at the whole picture any time any change is proposed. Initial design and effort may represent only a fraction of the overall time and costs for that change in the long run.

Ensure that all changes relate to a business requirement and that the value of each change is clearly articulated and agreed upon by your decision makers. Look at alternative solutions, and ensure that you've chosen the appropriate avenue to support the necessary change.

Getting Feedback

Finally, once you've decided to do prototyping, CRP sessions, or pilot activities, you need to ensure that you have a mechanism in place to adequately collect and review all the feedback that you receive. One of the key attributes and benefits of prototyping is the feedback that you receive from your end users and support community. Using this feedback effectively to make the change, to put results or reasons in documentation, to clearly articulate the change during training, and to add value to a communications message can all come from these review sessions. Use the feedback to the best of your ability, and think of all the ways you might incorporate it in your project, making it even more successful than before.

Did You Get the Right Feedback?

Be sure that the feedback you receive is attributable, meaning that you know where it came from. Be sure that in your review process you have clear representation from all key stakeholders and that the individuals who actually do the work participate in this review. Clearly, they understand the obstacles and problems that a potential solution might encounter in the day-to-day activities of the process.

This key feedback can also be used to provide better training and documentation to the end user. If during your pilot or prototyping session, a user is confused about a solution, be sure to understand the reasons and look for potential ways to alleviate this issue. The issue may have nothing to do with the actual solution but may affect how you present the solution, what job aids you provide, and what training you put in place prior to rolling out the solution. Your comparative analysis of the old and new ways of doing something might help the user understand the change more effectively.

You can try out these techniques during your CRP sessions and also as a part of your pilot rollout. Always look for ways to incorporate the feedback, regardless of whether it affects a system change.

Did You Get Feedback from Your Supporters?

As we mentioned before, it's essential to have a diverse audience made up of the day-to-day users as well as the key stakeholders and champions of your change. You want to ensure that your champions agree with the proposed way of doing things and that it supports their vision and intended direction. They will continue to be advocates for your change and can help support it during the sessions if they are a part of the sessions. The project team does not have to be the instigators of change—your sponsors and their leadership group can do that for you. That adds more credibility to the situation and helps provide more support for the change. Also, if the sponsors participate in the session, they can communicate directly to the end users why the changes are necessary and how important they are to the business and organization. This support can be very enlightening and uplifting to the group.

It's Curtain Time

There comes a time when prototyping and piloting become a losing battle and you have to go ahead and move your solution into production or roll it out to the masses. Be sure you clearly communicate to your group when this point in the project is and that final decisions must be made. Be confident that you have involved the users and informed them of the new processes, and that you're ready to go into production. Use your time wisely by carefully planning your prototyping sessions, leveraging your resources effectively, and making the decisions necessary for you to go live. These approaches should not prevent or delay your implementation; rather, they should help reinforce and support your new processes.

Remember, Participants Provide Your First Feedback to Everyone Else!

You should always remember that the participants in your prototyping sessions and pilot activities are your first line of feedback and should help you gauge acceptance of and resistance to your new processes and systems. Based on the reactions and results of these activities, you should carefully outline a plan to address any issues, feedback, or reactions to these changes, to support your project. The items identified can result in input to your communications plan, training plan, and implementation rollout plan. Key lessons learned as well as comparisons between old and new processes can be gained from these sessions and passed on in the form of training, procedures development, and communications. Being able to make tough decisions on business requirements and supporting the system into the future can be accomplished based on the feedback from these sessions. Working closely with your user base and sponsorship team, you can ensure a better set of processes and systems to support your future ERP implementation. Learn from these results, use what you learn wisely, and use these sessions to gain momentum and support for your project.

Up Next

As discussed above, prototyping can be a valuable method to ensure that any major system enhancement or modification meets the business needs of the end users. It also gives your project a chance to demonstrate the new system and processes to your users and to gain buy-in for these processes. Another key part of your development cycle is creating interfaces and converting data from your legacy system to your new PeopleSoft application. The next chapter, "Converting Data and Developing an Interface," covers the key steps of data conversion and interface development, including the different types of interfaces that can be developed and how PeopleSoft supports them. Also included is a look at various tools that can support your data conversion and interface development.

CHAPTER 11

Converting Data and Developing an Interface

F E A T U R I N G :

▶ What data you should convert to your new system

▶ How much historical data you should convert

▶ What tools are available to help with the conversion

▶ What steps are involved in a conversion process

▶ What you need to know about interfaces

▶ What types of interfaces are generally encountered during a PeopleSoft implementation

▶ Determining the format for your interface

W hen doing development work on a PeopleSoft implementation, even if you don't make any changes to the basic PeopleSoft system, you'll likely have at least two major areas of development work: data conversions and interfaces. This chapter covers these two major development activities. It looks at the basic concepts in understanding the questions and approach to converting any existing data you have from your old or legacy systems into your new People-Soft application, as well as the different alternatives available for creating and developing interfaces.

Making Key Conversion Decisions

Before you can determine how to convert your existing data, you need to ask yourself some key questions:

- ▶ What data do I really need to convert?

- ▶ How much of my history should I convert?

- ▶ What tools should I use in the conversion process?

What to Convert

In order to determine what data you need to convert, you must first have a good idea of what processes your new system will be supporting and the necessity of the data to be converted. For instance, when dealing with accounts payable, a list of vendors is very important and necessary within the PeopleSoft application. To determine what you need to convert and how you are going to convert it, you need to develop a detailed conversion strategy that outlines your requirements.

The first thing to do in this area is to list all the database tables that you're using in the system based on the functionality you're implementing. Once you've identified the tables, you should identify the owner of each table. The *owner* is the person (or team) that is responsible for determining the content of the table and whether it should contain converted data, is system-delivered, should be blank (i.e., contain no initial data), or configured manually as a part of the initial package setup.

If the table has data requirements (i.e., the table is empty, it's one that you are going to use, and it's not maintained by the vendor), the next step is to identify the source of the data. In some cases, the *source* may be another system, a spreadsheet, or the knowledge in someone's head.

The major types of tables you are bound to encounter when implementing your ERP system are as follows:

Control tables   If the table is more of a control table that is a part of the initial configuration, then no conversion will be necessary since you'll most likely have that already set up and it does not exist in any of your systems today.

Small tables or code tables   For tables that may consist of codes or be small in size (and the number of rows to enter is fairly small—fewer than a thousand), you may determine that the correct approach is converting or inputting the data manually.

Large code tables   In cases where the data is very large (such as a table that contains vendor information for a company that maintains thousands of vendors), an automated conversion process will be necessary.

Transactional tables   For transaction-type tables where the input is based on an event such as employee data, purchasing requests, accounts payable invoices, or journal entries, a decision needs to be made regarding historical requirements as well as how to convert current records. The historical dilemma will be discussed in the next section. Generally, these transaction-type records are the ones that will need an automated approach for conversion. Regardless, you should identify where the data is coming from so that an informed decision can be made on whether the data can be converted programmatically or via another method.

Once you've determined the category of each of your tables, the approximate size of each table, and where the data might be converted from, you must determine how much of the existing data you might want to convert.

How Much to Convert

The decision on how much to convert can be based on various business decisions—you should not always convert all the information you currently have. Again, in the area of accounts payable, for instance, invoices are a great example. You might have a history of invoices for the past five years, but in reality you may choose to convert only "open" invoices or invoices that have been paid out over the past year. The key criteria in this case should be the business driver behind keeping the data and the costs and benefits of doing this.

Another key factor in determining whether the data should be converted or not is how easy it is to access the data another way and how often the data might need to be accessed. Instead of converting your "historical" data to your new system, you may archive it on a file and store it on tape, put copies on fiche, or print the data and/or make hard copies.

With new code values (such as new invoice numbering schemes, new vendor identifications, new chart of account values, or new employee job codes) it may not make sense to convert the data to the new format. In many cases the "history" of code values was not maintained in your legacy system. Since the PeopleSoft application uses effective dates, the ability to "recreate" your history would be very difficult.

TIP   A great example of the difficulties of converting historical data is looking at the evolution of something as simple as an organizational chart or department code. Most companies reorganize many times over the years, thus changing the codes for their departmental structure and the structure itself. Within PeopleSoft, these changes are annotated using effective dating (both on the organizational chart or tree and in the department code table). The codes are then linked to an employees' historical personnel file. However, most legacy systems don't keep a record of such code changes. Therefore, it's very difficult to reconstruct these historical changes of the organization's structure and to link them back to employees' records for the new PeopleSoft system. The result when trying to convert this historical data is invalid-data problems within your new system.

Another question you need to answer in order to help you determine how much to convert is, How clean is the data? You certainly don't want to adhere to the old adage, "Garbage in, garbage out." Therefore, you need to determine the time and cost in "cleaning up the data" or even *whether* the data can be cleaned prior to converting it. The system certainly will not take data that doesn't adhere to the new system business rules that have been set up by your team. Some organizations send out reports and tables to their end users (e.g., vendors, customers, employees, etc.) to verify the data and ensure that they get accurate and high-quality information converted into their system. You need to be sure you are truthful in analyzing how good your data is and the effort required to do data cleanup, and to include this in your plans if you're planning to convert it.

Timing is also a factor in making your decision on how much to convert. This timing relates to when you are implementing your new or improved system and how that implementation affects the business cycle. Companies that implement at the beginning of a new year find it easier to start afresh and convert less data (or in some cases no data). At quarter ends, maybe only balances can be converted rather than detailed records. So timing of your implementation or go-live date is important in this decision and can impact your conversion. Remember also that if you change your go-live date, you most certainly will have to take into consideration any changes to your initial conversion strategy.

Finally, another factor that affects your decision is not only the source but *how many* sources are involved. The more systems you are converting from, the more time consuming and costly your conversion will be.

Again, remember that the decision on what approach to take depends on the magnitude, costs, and how often this data is really accessed (or the business reason for maintaining the data). After weighing the costs and benefits of the requirements, a decision should be made.

Conversion Tools

Once you determine how much, one of the last steps is to determine exactly how the file should be converted if an automated approach is desired. People-Soft offers various tools that can help you with converting your data, and other tools on the market can also help expedite this process. Following is a look at the various tools available:

> ▶ SQR (Structured Query Report Writer) is a programming/reporting tool provided with PeopleSoft that can be used to convert files from one format to another and load them into the PeopleSoft application. This tool should be used for complex requirements that require a lot of data manipulation and large volumes of data. Also, if multiple files are used from various "source" systems or tables, you can use this tool (and other programming tools, some of which are explained below) to merge your files and then convert them to the correct PeopleSoft tables. SQR loads the data directly into the database table and therefore bypasses any online PeopleSoft edits. If you want to activate these edits, they have to be manually coded into your program.

▶ Import Manager is a delivered PeopleSoft tool that can map a small data file to an existing delivered PeopleSoft table and load it into the application as though an individual were keying it into the system. This allows all online edits to be processed without having to rekey them into your program. This approach is very slow and is geared toward small amounts of data from one source table; it's generally targeted for small files under a few thousand rows that can be directly mapped to a PeopleSoft table. It allows you to "default" values but does not allow any complex programming options.

▶ Special conversion/interface development tools such as Convoy/DM and Constellar are also available. These tools are designed to help map data from one system to the other, including creation of translation values using a GUI (graphical user interface) front end, which, once the mapping is accomplished, can generate programming code to perform the conversion or interface. These tools are generally worth obtaining if you have lots of data to convert from many different systems as well as many interfaces to develop. They can generally cut your programming time by at least a third. However, the code is generally not specialized or tuned and may need to be manipulated after it's generated if high volumes are expected. Also, these tools are not included with the package and require a separate contract and costs. You should, however, check with your IT organization because they may have already purchased a tool that can be used for any file conversion.

▶ Other database tools such as leveraging direct SQL code (via scripts) and database load utilities delivered with your database platform (RDBMS) can also be used but generally are for less-complicated data mapping and conversions, since features that you find in programming language tools are not available via this method.

▶ Other programming tools such as COBOL can be used if your people have expertise in this area and either they are not able to learn SQR or they are supporting other systems that use COBOL and are thus more comfortable with that tool.

Again, you need to look at the cost and benefits associated with each option to help you make the appropriate choice. No one tool is right for everything and everybody. Once you have determined the data to be converted, how much of that data to convert, the tools you will use to convert the data, and the means to do all this, you are about ready to begin the process.

Looking at the Overall Conversion Process

The first section of this chapter helped you determine what types of data and how much of your history should be converted, as well as outlined the various conversion tools available for the conversion process.

These questions and knowledge of what tools are available are essential to moving forward in the conversion process. The answers to these two key questions are documented in your conversion strategy.

Once this strategy is determined and approved by your team and sponsors, the next step is to document the detailed requirements and to code the programs necessary to convert your data. This step is generally referred to as the development phase or stage.

The developed programs must be tested and approved prior to using them on the production systems. The last phase (or stage) of the conversion process is the actual implementation, which includes the timing and detailed steps to be accomplished to get all your data into your new system. This section looks at each of these phases of your conversion process, outlining some key areas to consider.

Strategy

During the initial phase of your project, soon after your process design has been completed, you need to detail your conversion strategy. It's important to perform this task *after* your initial process design is complete so that your team can understand the business drivers and requirements needed to support your new system as well as the timing of the implementation and what data (including tables, code values, etc.) will be used. Generally, once you've documented the processes and configuration, it's a good time to start the process of creating the conversion strategy document.

As mentioned above, the first key decisions should be what tables you want to convert and from what sources. How the data is going to be converted (e.g., automated or manual) and how much of the data will be converted are other decisions that must be made. It's good to diagram how you plan to convert the data (see Figure 11.1 for an example) and where the data is coming from.

Figure 11.1 **Example of data conversion process flow**

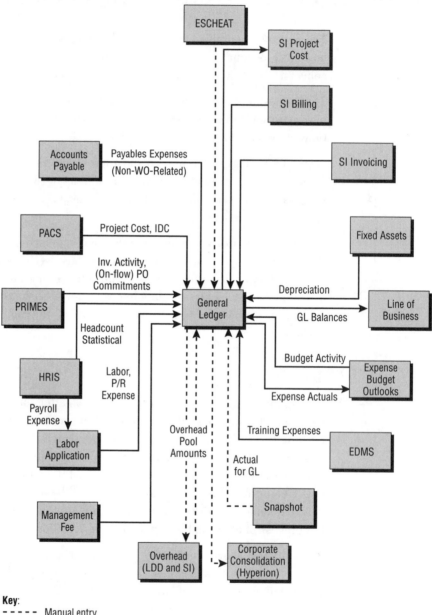

Key:
- - - - - Manual entry
————— Interface

Once these questions are answered and the implementation timeline is in place, you can document all this analysis in your strategy document.

Note   One item to note, which we have not discussed, is the desire to have converted data available for testing. Generally, this is a great idea (if it can be accomplished in time and not slow the project down) and will help not only in testing your system and your conversion programs but also with data cleansing as well, since you have a chance to review and validate data early in your cycle. The sooner you can start converting data and making it available for testing, the better.

Finally, your strategy document should include risk mitigation efforts, including what should be done with "unclean" data, what type of error reporting should be used, and how data validation and sign-off of data by your "customer" should be handled. Timing on when and how data will be converted into the production environment should also be looked at.

Development

Once you have your initial conversion strategy developed and approved by your team and sponsors, you are ready to create detailed program specifications for all the data you'll be converting. The conversion process may include several programming efforts and several programming tools, and all of this should be articulated in your strategy document.

Once all the components are agreed upon and approved, the detailed specifications should be developed for each conversion "routine" or program that you'll be creating. This document should include detailed mapping requirements from the source system into the new PeopleSoft tables.

Figure 11.2 is an example of mapping the prior-year balances for the General Ledger (GL) module. The tasks should be assigned to both functional and technical analysts so that all business rules and requirements, as well as technical considerations, are factored into the specification. Also, error and validation reports should be included in this specification/design process.

Once the specification is approved by all parties, it can be passed to an individual (generally a programmer) for coding. As mentioned before, ideally you would like to get the majority of your conversion programs completed and unit-tested prior to beginning the major testing activities (particularly integration testing). If this goal cannot be met, your team will need to be creative in how the data and conversion routines will be thoroughly tested, as well as how the integration testing data will be provided.

Figure 11.2 **Example of conversion data mapping**

Conversion Data Mapping
This document will provide the conversion data column mapping information from the legacy system.

Conversion Name:	LEDGER
Description:	**PRIOR YEAR ENDING BALANCES(GMP21)**
Parameters:	
Table Name	LEDGER
Template Name	
Map Name	
Data File	
Log File	

File Structure:

Field	Type	Description	Verify	Default	Source Field	Conversion Logic	Comments
BUSINESS_UNIT	Char(5)	Business Unit		'HAM'	<DEFAULT>		LEFT JUSTIFIED
LEDGER	Char(10)	Ledger		'HAMA1'	<DEFAULT>		LEFT JUSTIFIED & MIXED CASE
ACCOUNT	Char(6)	Acco			ACCOUNT-GMP21		
DEPTID	Char(10)	Department			CENTER-GMP21	Insert only if DEPTID is not equal to '99999'	
PRODUCT	Char(6)	Product		' '	<DEFAULT>		SPACES
PROJECT_ID	Char(15)	Project ID		' '	<DEFAULT>		SPACES
AFFILIATE	Char(5)	Affiliate		' '	<DEFAULT>		SPACES
CURRENCY_CD	Char(3)	Currency Code		'USD'	<DEFAULT>		
STATISTICS_CODE	Char(3)	Statistics Code					
FISCAL_YEAR	Nbr(4)	Fiscal Year		'1997'	<DEFAULT>		
ACCOUNTING_PERIOD	Nbr(3)	Accounting Period	Prompt CAL_DETP_TBL				
POSTED_TOTAL_AMT	Sign	Posted Total Amount			PYE_BALANCE 1-12 - GMP21	Occurrences 1 through 12 of the 14 available occurences represent the 12 accounting periods	
POSTED_BASE_AMT	Sign	Posted Base Currency Amount			PYE_BALANCE 1-12 - GMP21	Occurrences 1 through 12 of the 14 available occurrences represent the 12 accounting periods	
BASE_CURRENCY	Char(3)	Base Currency		'USD'	<DEFAULT>		
DTTM_STAMP_SEC	DtTm	Last Update DateTime				Inputted by the user	CURRENT DATE
PROCESS_INSTANCE	Nbr(10)	Process Instance					

Frequency:	
Contact Name:	
Phone:	

Testing

Generally, in addition to unit testing of the actual programs, there should be some type of validation testing performed by the conversion team prior to "releasing" the data for any additional testing efforts, such as in support of integration or stress testing activities. A good rule of thumb is to take a limited amount of (but well-represented) data from the source system, convert it, and create validation reports that can be compared with the legacy (or source) system. These reports should be approved and reviewed by end users who are targeted as "owners" of the data. The validation reports and formats should have been a part of the development specification process and agreed upon prior to the testing effort.

Once the owners have verified that the conversion is working appropriately (sometimes this process may result in agreed changes to the program, and recoding and retesting may occur before final approvals are given), you are ready to move the data to your other environments as appropriate. Allow enough time in the process for changes, modifications, error fixing, etc., to occur. Don't assume that the first functioning program will be perfect. Generally, the team also reruns the conversion process several times to input additional or more timely data into their test systems as testing needs dictate. You may also need to convert data (especially large historical files) prior to implementation and "store" the files so they can be moved into production when the production system is ready. This should be considered in your strategy document.

Implementation

The timing of when to convert your data into production generally is based on these factors:

- ▶ Amount of data to convert
- ▶ System requirements and configuration
- ▶ Timing of when current processes are complete

The amount of data to convert may affect the ability of the program to complete in time to make your implementation timetable and require you to begin conversion much earlier in the process. With historical data that is not changing or can be "frozen" (i.e., no one can be allowed to change it), your conversion can begin as soon as you are satisfied with your testing results and the data quality. The files can be converted and "saved" until you are ready to load them into your production system. For each program you have developed, you should determine appropriate run times as well as analyze whether data can be converted prior to your agreed-upon conversion/implementation window.

In some cases you cannot convert data until you have other data converted first. This is particularly true with control tables and code value tables. In general, you should analyze and ensure that these tables are converted first, so as not to hold up any of your conversion processes. You should have outlined (within your conversion strategy document) any dependencies your conversions have on the availability and conversion of other tables. Also, with relational database tables, you may have "parent" tables that will need to be converted before their "child" can be converted. Be sure all these relationships are analyzed and documented in your conversion process (in both the strategy document and your detailed design documents).

Finally, you must review your processing cycle to determine when it makes sense to begin your conversion process. For instance, in Accounts Payable or Payroll, you generally look at when your current period "closes" for additional input (i.e., the last paycheck run or the last invoice cut for the month) and then convert the data for that cycle. Also, for multiple module conversions (such as with AP and GL), you may be able to convert one piece of data (such as AP) before you complete the other piece of data (such as journal entries for GL), since the close period for AP is generally before the close period for GL. All of this timing should be considered and outlined in your implementation conversion plan.

Your conversion plan should outline *all* steps in the conversion process, including when to copy preloaded or preconfigured tables from your existing databases into the production database, as well as where each of these tables should be copied from. Each program you have to run for conversions should be included in this plan (including all steps and validation requirements), and a detailed plan should be created for this process, which should include estimated times for completion as well as any drop-dead deadlines that you have to meet. Mitigation strategies should be created for any problems that may occur, including impact to the go-live data and operations, should your conversions take longer than expected, and alternative plans for when data may be loaded into the production system. For instance, you may have loaded all your GL data into your system except the most recent period of data and determined that you'll go ahead and let new entries for the new period start processing in your new system prior to verification and conversion of the last period's data. Then you may plan to convert this data a few weeks later so that it's available for your period close.

At all times, your conversion schedule should be tightly managed, and any impacts to the schedule should be assessed as rapidly as possible in order to keep your implementation on track. Don't wait until the inevitable happens and you have a problem to determine how you might handle it. Be sure to plan for the unexpected and think about how you might mitigate any risks. Good, solid testing and estimates on program run times can also help you with this planning.

Note After you have implemented and converted your data, you need to be prepared with the procedures for correcting any data issues or the steps you might take in resolving data problems after you have cut over to your new system. Again, planning will help you be prepared for the unexpected.

Developing an Interface Plan

Within the PeopleSoft application area, besides your data conversion efforts, interfaces are generally a large part of your development effort as well as an area where you might experience problems. Even if you do a completely vanilla implementation, you most likely will still have interface development work to accomplish (as well as the data conversion activities discussed above). A solid interface development approach and strategy can help you alleviate some of these issues.

A big factor in interface development is whether you are going to have interfaced systems change their data prior to providing it to you, or you are going to take their old data files and manipulate them to fit into your new system. In general it's much better for the organization as a whole to go ahead and make the changes needed to your systems to support the new processes. Since ERP systems are far-reaching, this may be tough to do but, if at all possible, should be done.

Generally with a major implementation, there are major changes to your existing business processes, including your main code values and data requirements. Thus, taking an existing file or approach may not even be possible with your new system. You may have to form some type of middle ground in order to get this accomplished.

For instance, in General Ledger, you may have new account codes, business units, and departments, as well as many other new codes. Maybe in your current systems you have an account code field that's 15 characters long, but PeopleSoft's account code field is 10 characters. In this case you may be able to use the new accounts in the old systems (as long as there are not hard-coded business rules based on the old account-naming conventions within the systems). You should review the impact to the systems and determine the best approach. Also, suppose your account field is 8 characters and PeopleSoft's is 10. You might choose to develop new account codes within PeopleSoft but limit them to 8 characters so that you won't have to change the systems that will be remaining.

In many cases a "black box" routine may need to be developed to convert your major code values from the old way to the new way. This routine can be used for conversion as well as for interfaces that stay with the old values. It's generally not ideal to keep this routine in place for long, but rather only until the old systems can be modified, since it requires your users to remember multiple code values for the same entry depending on what system they are entering it in. This generally not only adds confusion and dissatisfaction by the users but results in more errors occurring due to having to remember these codes. Also, your IT organization will have to maintain all of this and keep it going as new codes are added and changes to the system occur. In the long run the routine becomes more costly and inefficient than making the changes initially, although we all know this may not always be possible due to budget or priority constraints.

Determining Your Interface Needs

Once you have determined your overall approach to interface development, you need to identify all your interface needs. With PeopleSoft (as with any ERP system) there could be many interface requirements, including new interfaces. With the new open integration framework (OIF) in PeopleSoft 8 and the new APIs (application programming interfaces) using XML (Extensible Markup Language), the integration of applications, including internal and external, may be easier but should still be evaluated.

The new Application Messaging, Business Components, and Business Interlinks allow for more flexibility and reduce the amount of programming that's required. Application Messaging is an Internet-based messaging architecture that allows PeopleSoft and third-party systems to publish data based on business events via XML and Hypertext Transfer Protocol (HTTP). Then subscribing applications can receive the transactions over the Internet and process them across both public and private networks depending on your security needs. The Business Components and Business Interlinks APIs will enable application developers to easily plug into PeopleSoft's business processes without requiring detailed knowledge of the underlying data structure or embedded business logic. Although all this should help in the integration of systems, the requirements for existing legacy interfaces will still occur. These batch-type interfaces will need to be developed and maintained as well.

Types of Interfaces

As you determine your interface needs, you can classify your interfaces into three basic types:

Real-time   These interface needs link two applications or processes directly together on a "real-time" basis, making updates instantaneously for the end user. Tools such as the message agent, APIs, or XML (including through the new open integration framework with PeopleSoft 8) support this type of interface need.

Batch   These interfaces don't process data directly into the system tables on a real-time basis but occur when a program is run, generally at night or on a scheduled time frame (whether it's every minute, hour, or day). Normal programming tools such as SQR or COBOL can support this process along with the use of a batch-scheduling tool (such as the one provided by PeopleSoft).

Package-provided   These interfaces are already provided by the PeopleSoft application, either between modules or for interfaces that are normally standard for all businesses, and can be in the form of both batch or real-time modes. Examples of these interfaces include delivered third-party benefit interfaces, the standard payroll interface, and standard GL interfaces—both from other package applications and from outside applications as well as an Excel spreadsheet and more. The PeopleSoft documentation for each module outlines the interfaces provided.

You should categorize each of your interfaces into these categories. Look at package-provided interfaces first, prior to creating any totally new interfaces—even if you modify them from their original format. Once you've determined whether an interface is real-time or batch, you should look at the tool in which you'll develop the interface. The timing of the interface is also very crucial in dealing with batch interfaces.

Interface Tools

As mentioned, once you establish the type of interface you have, the time requirements for the interface, and any specific business requirements, you'll decide on the tool you'll use for developing the interface. The possible tools include the normal programming tools such as COBOL and SQR (which we talked about in the conversion section), new tools such as Convoy and others that provide GUI mapping and code generation, and existing PeopleSoft tools such as the Journal Generator (which can upload Excel spreadsheets) and the Import Manager (which can load small data files). Again, as with conversion tools, the right tool to use is based on the volume, complex business rules/ mapping requirements, and the availability of tools at your site. Following is a look at the various tools available:

▶ As we mentioned in our discussion of conversion tools, SQR is a programming/reporting tool that can be used for conversions. It can also be used to create interfaces involving multiple files and complex business rules. It can be used for both inbound and outbound files. This tool is appropriate for complex requirements that require a lot of data manipulation and large volumes of data. Also, if multiple files are used from various source systems or tables, you can use this tool (and other programming tools) to merge your files and then interface them into PeopleSoft. Outbound interfaces can also be created in multiple file formats.

▶ Import Manager can also be used to map a small data file (which must be in fixed-length ASCII format) to an existing delivered PeopleSoft table and load it into the application as though an individual were keying it into the system (as was explained earlier). Remember that although this tool allows all online edits to be processed without having to rekey them into your program, it can be very slow and is geared toward small amounts of data from one source table, generally under a few thousand rows. This tool cannot be used for outbound interface requirements.

▶ Special conversion/interface development tools such as Convoy/DM or Constellar are also available, as explained in the "Conversion Tools" section. Generally, these tools can take data directly from other database tables or from an interface/extract file. They can usually cut your programming time by at least a third. However, the code is generally not specialized or tuned and may need to be manipulated after being generated if high volumes are expected.

▶ As in data conversions, other database tools such as leveraging direct SQL code (via scripts) and database load utilities delivered with your database platform (RDBMS) can also be used for interface development. Generally, these tools are for less-complicated data mapping and interface extracts, since the more complex features that you find in programming language tools are not available via this method.

▶ Other programming tools such as COBOL can be used if your people have expertise in this area and either they are not able to learn SQR or they are supporting other systems that use COBOL and are thus more comfortable with that tool.

▶ PeopleSoft Query can also be used to create data extracts for reporting or small Excel file purposes. It's not recommended for complex data extraction needs.

▶ The functions provided within PeopleSoft's Application Messaging tool can be used to link with other applications such as IVR systems or Internet-based solutions when you want the system to "hook" into the existing database tables, pulling or pushing data directly into those tables. This linkage is generally used for a transactional (one entry at a time) approach and not for large volumes of data that must be loaded at one time into the system.

▶ PeopleSoft Database Agents can be used to "trigger" an update or action within the application. A good example might be that for any overdue bills, a message can be sent to a clerk or customer notifying them to send in their payment. Therefore, this activity may eliminate interfaces or reports.

▶ PeopleSoft's Workflow tool links transactions for use in processes such as approvals, where once an activity is accomplished, the system (or Workflow) triggers the occurrence of another activity. This tool can be used to communicate with outside applications via an electronic form or e-mail. Therefore, in essence, it may replace an existing interface requirement such as sending a list of all new hires to the security department each month. Now you would use Workflow to send an e-mail to the security department when a person is hired, rather than send an interface file.

▶ PeopleSoft's new tools, Business Components and Business Interlinks, can be used to create integration or interfaces between systems, leveraging Internet technology. The Business Components tool provides real-time, synchronous access to PeopleSoft's business rules and data from external applications, leveraging Internet technology. This tool is especially good at integrating with Internet-based applications. Business Interlinks provides the opposite integration, allowing PeopleSoft the ability to easily invoke third-party systems, such as pulling pricing information from a Federal Express Web site into your PeopleSoft application process to determine pricing for mailing materials.

As you can see from the list of tools above, there are many ways that data can be manipulated and sent to and from the PeopleSoft application. In addition to these tools, there are delivered interface programs (such as a standard upload for journal entries, benefits interfaces to third-party providers, an interface to load assets into PeopleSoft, and many more) with the application itself that can be used "as is" or modified. You should review all interfaces (based on the modules you are implementing) that come with the package to determine how they might or might not apply to your organization.

Interface Development Considerations

In addition to selecting the tools and delivered interfaces, there are other considerations to note when programming or creating interfaces between People-Soft and other applications, such as these:

► Platform transfer requirements

► Scheduling requirements

► Special formatting needs

► Interface specifications

► Volume and performance requirements

Platform Transfer Requirements

Many interfaces may need to be transferred from one hardware or operating system platform to another (such as from an HP server to an IBM mainframe). You'll need to look at FTP (File Transfer Protocol) tools to perform these functions (especially if one of the operating system platforms is Unix-based), ensuring that you have the appropriate software needed for the appropriate operating system as well as processes in place to support these needs. Be sure to test each of these processes on all the hardware and operating system platforms you plan to use, just in case any unique combinations of platforms and software cause a problem in formatting or transferring your data.

Scheduling Requirements

Also, many interfaces must be run at a specific time or on a specific schedule—either daily, weekly, or monthly, or even every other Tuesday. Regardless of the schedules, you should create a detailed list of these scheduling needs and ensure that your scheduling application supports these needs. PeopleSoft has a delivered process scheduler that can create the schedules for these interfaces to run on, but many companies use existing job schedulers that are already in place. Be sure to evaluate your current tools with those available with PeopleSoft, taking into consideration your requirements, costs, training, and tool functionality.

Special Formatting Needs

Often when developing interfaces, special formatting must be used. Again, the tools chosen should be based on these requirements as well. In some cases only changed data is required. In those cases you might find benefits in turning on the "audit" feature of PeopleSoft for those fields you are targeting. This will create an "audit table" containing the changed data fields and "old values" when changes are made, as well as who made the changes and when they occurred. This feature can be used to determine what, if any, changes were made to the data you are looking for. You can turn this feature on at the table or field level. Because this feature involves system overhead, increases in response time, and additional DASD requirements (since all of this data is stored in another table), you should be cautious about how you use the feature.

Interface Specifications

As mentioned in the conversion section, it's important to create detailed specifications for all interface requirements (including outlining any functional aspects) as well as to thoroughly test both the interface itself and its integration with the from/to application. An example of an interface mapping table is shown in Figure 11.3. Details on when and how the interface should run in production should also be outlined. A detailed batch schedule should be developed for production, which outlines all processes including interfaces that are run. This schedule should note what processes are run each day, when, and whether there are any constraints in running jobs simultaneously. Resource requirements should be taken into consideration as well as any system conflicts. Also, programming standards should be followed (as outlined in Chapter 6, "Surveying the Infrastructure"), and all programs including interfaces should go through a quality control process. For future upgrades and maintenance, it is imperative to have these processes and programs thoroughly documented, including the business requirements and purposes of each interface.

Volume and Performance Needs

Lastly, it's important to understand the volumes for these interfaces and to arrange adequate performance testing to ensure that your schedules can be met. With large processing requirements and large amounts of data, interface programs can initially run for hours. With some targeted tuning efforts and stress testing, you can create your programs more efficiently so that they use key indexes, temporary tables or arrays, and other techniques to improve your performance. If initial run times are relatively fast and fit your processing windows, it may not be necessary to spend time and energy on this additional step. Be sure to involve your database administrator (DBA) in all tuning efforts.

Figure 11.3 **Example of interface layout mapping**

Interface Flatfile Layout/Table to Table
This document will provide the programmer with a flatfile format for each interface extract table from the legacy system.

Interface Name:	
Description:	**Cash Management Interface File**
Parameters:	
Environment:	Source / Target

Application Name:
Machine Type:
Database:
Language:
Operating System:
Transfer Method:

Flatfile Structure:

Source Field (Description)	Position	Source Type	Target Field	Target Type	Comments
SR-DATA-SOURCE		Char(2)	PS_JRNL_HEADER.SOURCE		CM'
SR-ACCT-NUM		Char(5)	PS_JRNL_LN.ACCOUNT		
SR-DEPT-NUM		Char(5)	PS_JRNL_LN.DEPTID		
SR-EFFECTIVE-DATE		99999	PS_JRNL_HEADER.JOURNAL_DATE		
SR-SOURCE-CODE		Char(10)	PS_JRNL_HEADER.SOURCE		
SR-DR-CR-CODE		Char(2)			VALUE SPACES
SR-AMOUNT	(11)	999999999.99	PS_JRNL_LN.MONETARY_AMOUNT		
SR-DESCRIPTION-1	(5)	Char(30)			VALUE SPACES
SR-DESCRIPTION-2		Char(12)			VALUE SPACES
SR-DESCRIPTION-3		Char(10)			VALUE SPACES
SR-POSTING-DATE		99999			VALUE +0, COMP-3

Frequency:
Contact Name:
Phone:

Up Next

Conversions and interfaces make up a large amount of your development effort during an implementation. How you plan for this effort can make a big impact on the success of your project. Most end users don't care about the time or effort spent in programming these tasks; they are concerned about the results—access to good-quality data when and where they need it. With detailed planning and appropriate focus, this effort will be a nonevent for your users. Done inadequately or without thought, it can be a major thorn in your heel. Ensure that expectations are set and the schedule agreed upon prior to your new system going live.

In the next chapter, "Technical Implementation Issues," we'll look at additional technical implementation issues you might encounter while preparing your system for your go-live event, such as the number of database environments you might need, how to set up these environments, and your migration strategy to support them. The chapter will also look at development and desktop standards, different technical roles, and other technical tools such as reporting, Web access, and work flow. Finally, the chapter will touch on the rollout strategies and technical impacts to consider when you plan this rollout.

Technical Implementation Issues

F E A T U R I N G :

▶ A look at the various technical environments needed to support your project

▶ Deciding between a two-tier and three-tier architecture

▶ What types of standards you should have in place to support your project—development standards, object-naming standards, configuration standards, and more

▶ What technical resources you'll need for supporting your implementation, and what they should do for you

▶ Special needs of the end users that you may need to support technically, such as reporting, Web enabling, and work flow

While implementing the PeopleSoft ERP solution in an organization, one has to give careful consideration to technical implementation issues, as they may change a perfect business solution to a nightmare outing for all the people involved in the implementation. All the technical issues of People-Soft implementations can be addressed and mitigated if a proper technical infrastructure requirements document is defined during the early stages of a project. These requirements are the primary driving force behind making important technology selections/decisions and designing the IT infrastructure for your PeopleSoft solution.

This chapter will address some of the most common technical issues you might face during your implementation and look at how you might handle these situations so that you will be better prepared. The first major decision you might be faced with is how many copies (or environments) of your PeopleSoft system you'll need in order to support an effective rollout.

Number of Environments Required

Installation of new environments and modifications to existing environments through the addition/modification of platforms, software, network components, and information technology (IT) procedures will occur throughout the life of an implementation or upgrade project. Each environment is used for a specific purpose, and therefore security access varies for each environment. Both the application database administrator (DBA) and the PeopleSoft application administrator maintain responsibility for the creation and maintenance of each environment.

We believe that the effective implementation of these IT infrastructure environments is critical to the success of PeopleSoft implementation initiative. The number, types, and uses for the environments listed below are based on our previous experience with similar system deployments. You may have the need for more or fewer environments to support your rollout, but you should consider these examples and ensure that you have adequate support for your development, testing, production, and maintenance of your application.

PeopleSoft System (SYS) Environment

The SYS environment consists of all the PeopleTools tables loaded with supplied data for application objects from PeopleSoft and all applications-related tables without any data. This environment is used for creating the initial environment for any development/production-related activities in the future. This environment is usually created whenever a new PeopleSoft release is installed.

Note   *Users of this environment:* Traditionally, only the DBA has access to this database instance.

PeopleSoft Demonstration (DEMO) Environment

The DEMO environment consists of all the PeopleTools tables loaded with supplied data for application objects from PeopleSoft and all applications-related tables with data supplied by PeopleSoft. This environment is used for demonstration/reference of PeopleSoft functionality and does not contain any customizations. This environment is usually created whenever a new People-Soft release is installed and updated whenever a PeopleSoft patch is needed.

Note   *Users of this environment:* DBA and project team members

PeopleSoft Application Upgrade (AUDB) and PATCH Environments

The AUDB environment consist of four to five tables related to PeopleTools objects and is used only for applying patches supplied by PeopleSoft. This environment is useful for the DBA and not for application development. This environment is usually created whenever a new PeopleSoft release software is installed.

Note   *Users of this environment:* Traditionally, only the DBA has access to this database instance.

In addition to the AUDB and DEMO environments, generally an environment called the PATCH environment is set up to apply the patches using the DEMO environment and to test that the patch works correctly prior to merging the change with any of your system changes. The PATCH environment helps to ensure that valid testing is accomplished prior to overwriting your SYS, DEMO, or DEV (development) database environments. Clients can take backups of these environments and apply patches directly to the DEMO and DEV environments without creating an additional PATCH environment. Those clients who have many customizations or are applying a significant number of patches at one time should consider using the PATCH environment setup.

Conference Room Pilot (CRP) Environment

As mentioned in Chapter 10, "Prototyping," it is essential to have a test bed or prototyping environment (which we call Conference Room Pilot, or CRP) to help determine how the system functions in support of your requirements. The CRP environment will support the PeopleSoft implementation project during the solution definition phase of the project. This environment is usually created by cloning the SYS environment during initial installation of the PeopleSoft software and then made available immediately to all users. This environment is used to demonstrate for the project team the standard People-Soft business processes, along with known business requirements, in order to finalize a future state for the application.

Note   *Users of this environment:* Typically, the DBA and end users involved during the CRP phase and the developers have access to this instance.

Development (DEV) Environment

The development environment supports the PeopleSoft implementation initiatives during the remaining development phases of the project. The source for this environment creation is usually the SYS environment. This environment will support all the significant components for online as well as batch development for the production system. In the initial stage all the unit testing is also done in this environment. Once unit testing has been conducted and approved, this environment serves as a source for the CONV, TST, and PROD environments for all customizations/modifications that are specific to the organization. After the initial configuration of this environment, a snapshot is usually taken for further use in creation of the CONV, TST, and PROD environments.

Note   *Users of this environment:* The DBA, developers, and core team members involved during the development phase

Conversion (CONV) Environment

The conversion environment supports the PeopleSoft project through conversion from the existing PeopleSoft production system/legacy system to the latest upgrade. A snapshot taken after the initial configuration of the development environment is usually used for creation of this environment. This environment contains all components necessary for the development and testing of programs to convert legacy data into the PeopleSoft database.

 Note   *Users of this environment:* The DBA, developers, and core team members involved during the solution development phase

Test (TST) Environment

The test environment supports the PeopleSoft project through all system testing, integration testing, and initial volume and stress testing phases of the project. A snapshot taken after the initial configuration of the development environment is usually used for creation of this environment. For testing, this environment is also used to simulate peak data volumes and throughput to ensure optimal performance tuning of the PeopleSoft system.

 Note   *Users of this environment:* The DBA and a few developers and core team members involved during the testing phase

Training (TRN) Environment

The training environment supports the PeopleSoft training team from the design phase through to production. This environment is used to demonstrate the system to the end-user community, and it serves as a vehicle for communicating the look and feel of the system. The initial source for this environment is usually a snapshot taken from the test environment. The TRN environment will be refreshed frequently from the test/production environment.

Note *Users of this environment:* The DBA, end users, and core team members involved in training

Production (PROD) Environment

The production environment supports the PeopleSoft system beginning with implementation and continuing into production. This environment integrates all the components and services necessary for an integrated PeopleSoft system supporting the client's business processes. A snapshot taken after initial configuration of the development environment is usually used for creation of this environment.

Note *Users of this environment:* End users and core team members involved in supporting the system

User Acceptance/QA (QA) Environment

The QA environment supports the PeopleSoft project during the final QA phase of the project. This environment will be used to conduct system acceptance testing and all the QA-related activities and controlled data entries/ updates for final configuration settings. Transactions are entered to simulate a production environment. This environment is usually created from the snapshot of production just before the system goes live. This environment is also used as the final checkpoint prior to migrating all new modules and converting data into the production environment. The final volume/stress test is also conducted in this environment. Once all test scenarios have been executed successfully, final user approval/sign-off is obtained.

Note *Users of this environment:* End users and core team members involved in the acceptance testing phase

Figure 12.1 shows a diagram of each of the environments discussed above and how they typically interact.

Figure 12.1 **Diagram of typical PeopleSoft environments**

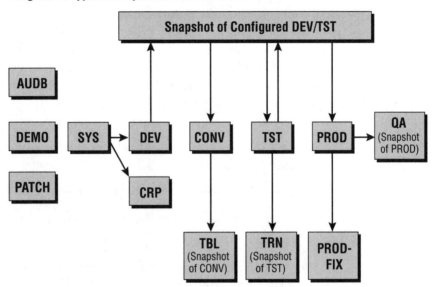

Legend:
AUDB – Application upgrade database
Configured DEV – Configured development environment with static data
CONV – Conversion environment
CRP – Conference Room Pilot environment
DEMO – PeopleSoft demonstration database
DEV – Development environment
PATCH – PeopleSoft patch with demonstration database
PROD – Production environment
PROD-FIX – Production fix environment
QA – User acceptance environment
SYS – PeopleSoft database without application data
TBL – Snapshot of legacy converted data
TRN – Training environment
TST – System test environment

Migration Strategy between Different Environments

Migration strategies are guidelines to be used during the development life cycle and may require modification for use in a production environment. The strategy is intended to be a step-by-step guide outlining the tasks required for migrating objects (new or modified) from one environment to another environment.

The strategy specifically addresses control of the PeopleSoft objects and application-related data. Because of the complexity of the PeopleSoft database and the number of tables involved, it's better to avoid, as much as possible, the migration of application data across different environments. However, there are alternative ways of handling this situation (for example, the configured DEV environment has application-related data loaded, and this environment is used for creating the TST, CONV, and PROD environments). For PeopleSoft objects, there are three types of migrations:

- ▶ PeopleSoft-supplied patches (includes objects other than SQR, Crystal, and PeopleTools software)

- ▶ PeopleSoft-supplied patches for SQR, Crystal, and PeopleTools software

- ▶ Client-specific enhancements, modifications, and customizations

PeopleSoft-supplied patches may be downloaded from the PeopleSoft Customer Connection Web site or acquired directly from PeopleSoft as a "bundled" set. These patches must be applied through the AUDB (or similar) environment. First, these patches are loaded into the AUDB database. Next, they are copied to the PATCH environment for testing and verification. Once they are approved by the application system administrator, they are copied to the SYS, DEMO, DEV, CONV, TST, and PROD environments in sequential order. It's important to have a backup of your environment, as patches cannot be backed out. We recommend applying patches one-by-one rather than combining them (i.e., one patch may override other patch content).

For SQR, Crystal, and PeopleTools software patches, the AUDB environment is not used, as these patches are applied to executables supplied by People-Soft rather than to PeopleSoft-related database objects. Usually these patches replace objects directly into the appropriate directory where they are stored. Directory structures to be used for maintaining different environments should be defined in a document covering naming conventions.

For organization-specific enhancements, modifications, or customizations, all the changes must be made in a DEV environment. After unit testing, changes should be moved to the TST, CONV, and PROD environments in the sequential order. All development is frozen during migration of objects. Some of the changes may not be needed in the CONV environment. The TST environment will test these changes for integration. If there are any problems, they should be corrected in the DEV environment. The same route of migration should then be followed again.

With tools that PeopleSoft has created in its new Compass Methodology (a suite of implementation tools and methodology advice that PeopleSoft is offering in conjunction with PeopleSoft 8) or with an application provided by other software vendors, organizations may track the migration of objects from one environment to another. Figure 12.2 outlines the proposed migration paths in a pictorial view.

Figure 12.2 **Migration paths**

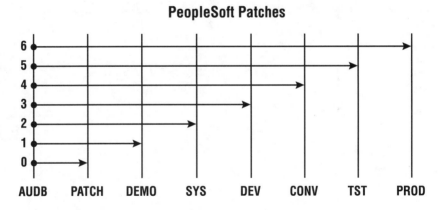

Note: Numbers indicate sequence order for migration.

Recommendations for Modification and Customization Approach

A software vendor may be quick to support modifications or changes to its initial application architecture to meet the client's needs because of the power of the vendor's development tools. But one should be aware of the impacts to upgrades and support of the package in the future, and thus should minimize changes to the package. Whenever possible, we recommend that the People-Soft system not be customized unless the business needs cannot be altered to fit the software functionality. When a modification is identified, it's best to follow a customization development life cycle and ensure that the complete application architecture is approved in a thorough manner.

Figure 12.3 is a graphical representation of the most commonly recommended modification development process life cycle.

Figure 12.3   **Modification development process life cycle**

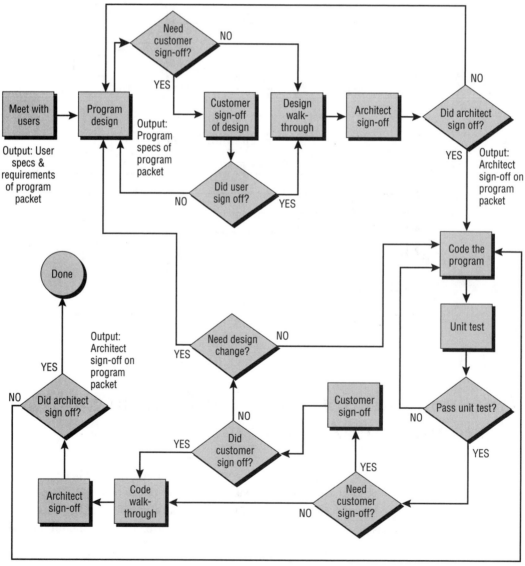

Database Sizing Requirement

The biggest hurdle in database sizing is determining how long you'll need to keep data in your operational system. This issue is often neglected since people are worried about immediate implementation versus the long-term impact on their system. Database sizing issues also play a major role in estimating the size of the disk storage space requirement.

PeopleSoft has made this task simple by providing a sizing calculation worksheet for all their modules. In order to estimate the production database size, the only input needed from an organization is the number of various business transactions per period (e.g., 1,000 purchase orders per month), the growth rate of the transactions, and their retention period in your operational system (e.g., two years). One has to be careful about these estimates, as these sizes may change depending on actual business transactions once you are leveraging your new system. Your DBA has to monitor the database weekly in the production environment and to resize and reorganize the database (tables and indexes). This estimation process is very safe since, in practice, the database size calculated by this worksheet is sometimes about five to ten times larger than the actual database size needed. But in real life it's better to overestimate the size than to underestimate it.

For your production environment, enough space must be allocated for mirroring the database and any future upgrades to your database/PeopleSoft system. Mirroring your database helps in rebuilding the database in case of a database crash. Future upgrades are a reality in the implementation of any packaged solution in an organization.

Another important aspect of sizing the database is to consider the various environments needed for full-life-cycle implementation of your PeopleSoft system. To calculate these environment sizes, one can only estimate based on the production database size (e.g., the development environment will hold a maximum of about 10% of production data, the conversion environment will keep data for at least one year of history, etc.). Based on these guidelines, you can come up with some very good estimates for various environments. A sample estimation that was used in a real-life project is provided for reference purposes in Table 12.1.

Table 12.1 **Development Environments Sizing Sheet**

Environment	Space Requirements
CRP environment	2GB
Development environment	3GB
System test environment	3GB
Conversion environment	3GB
QA environment	6GB
Training environment	2GB
User acceptance environment	4GB
System environment	1GB
Patch environment	2GB
Demo environment	2GB
Application upgrade environment	1GB
Total	**29GB**

After creating your initial estimate for your development environments, you must look at not only your initial size requirements for your production environment but the impact of growth and historical data storage. As an example of sizing this production environment, let's say we have one environment in the production system, with a total of four years of data. We are including a 10% growth factor for each year of data that's being stored. Table 12.2 assumes that we will always maintain four years of history data. This example outlines the steps necessary to properly size your production environment for the future.

Table 12.2   **Production Environment Sizing Example**

System Production Year	Space Requirements
Year 1	21GB
Year 2	24GB
Year 3	26GB
Year 4	29GB

To accommodate the maximum growth year, we should set up our PeopleSoft table with 29GB of disk space. The total requirements for production are shown in Table 12.3.

Table 12.3   **Total Production Sizing Requirements**

Environment	Space Requirements
Production environment	29GB
100% mirroring	29GB
Space for application upgrade	58GB
Total production space	**116GB**

Setting Up Environments

Once you've estimated your space requirements and looked at the number of environments you'll need in order to support your project, you are ready to set up your environments. Along with that setup, basic standards need to be in place to support you.

Development Naming Conventions

In order to make future upgrades to PeopleSoft software easier and more manageable, PeopleSoft recommends minimal changes in objects and functionality of supplied software. But in practice, this is impossible, as each organization works somewhat differently. To accommodate each organization's individual requirements, software needs to be customized. In order to make customization smoother and manageable, organizations should define a standard procedure/process for carrying out these customizations; and for all customized objects, a naming standard should be established. This naming standard really simplifies PeopleSoft system-upgrade projects. Some of the objects that are candidates for naming conventions are tables, views, records, fields, panels, panel groups, menus, new upgrade projects, SQRs, process scheduler jobs, PeopleCode, queries, trees, Crystal reports, nVision reports, etc.

Desktop Configuration Standards

The speed of your PeopleSoft application will be determined, to a large extent, by the speed of your users' workstations. Note that with PeopleSoft 8, the workstation is no longer the key component for end users, since they only need access to a machine with a browser, However, your development staff, key support personnel, and certain key users may still need robust workstations to support the building of reports and other development efforts.

To achieve optimal performance, we recommend that an organization invest in hardware (e.g., standard Pentium machine with faster video cards, hard disks, network interface cards, etc.) that maximizes the performance of its operating system environment. Standard configurations also make maintenance tasks easier and manageable for support groups. If a desktop standard has been set up to automatically retrieve all configuration information from the file server where the client executables are co-located, then even end users can deploy client setups using self-extracting files.

Two-Tier versus Three-Tier Architecture Issues

In a two-tier architecture only two machines are situated between users and the application: the client workstation and the DBMS server. All online application processing logic runs on the client machine, and the client-server network conversation uses SQL to transmit database calls. With this configuration, network traffic increases back and forth quite a lot, and hence it slows down the performance of the PeopleSoft application as well as other applications running in that network. But a two-tier configuration can still provide a facility to process batch and/or big jobs on the DBMS server. One has the option of running these jobs in client workstations as well, but this is not at all recommended in a production environment. This option is really useful if one needs to debug the batch jobs. This configuration also requires DBMS connectivity software to be installed on client machines and hence may require additional licenses for DBMS users.

In a three-tier architecture, three different classes of machines (logical and/or physical) are used: the client workstation, the application server, and the DBMS server. In logical three-tier configurations, the application server and the DBMS server reside on the same machine. Online processing logic is executed on an application server (rather than the client workstation). The benefit of this concept results in very low network traffic and smaller numbers of DBMS connections. This architecture also requires fewer DBMS connectivity licenses (because only application servers—not all end-user machines—need this software). In a three-tier configuration, the client machine no longer has the option to execute batch jobs.

If organizations need Web enablement (which is required with PeopleSoft 8) three-tier architecture is a must, because the Web server and the DBMS server cannot reside on the same machine. This architecture also secures data by adding one more level between users and the data. For big organizations where departments/divisions are situated in multiple physical locations, each location may need an application server (based on the number of end users at each location). This concept is important because of the time required for network traffic to cross LAN boundaries and go further into a WAN. It's good practice to reduce traffic and the number of connections with the WAN as much as possible. For large networks, the key is to minimize hops across routers (network connections or paths) and to get the routers tuned optimally. This is usually out of the hands of the application developers but is something that higher management should be aware of and include in the sizing criteria.

Roles and Responsibilities

This section identifies the technical support roles needed in a typical People-Soft implementation. In addition, it identifies the skills necessary to effectively fulfill those roles. While these roles all have clearly defined responsibilities, some overlap and coordination is required between these roles. It's also important to note that these roles are not necessarily all filled by different people. That is, one person may be able to fulfill the responsibilities of more than one of these roles.

PeopleSoft Application Administrator

This role is responsible for managing the PeopleSoft application system that resides on the file server, administering security, and controlling object migration. They also work as a liaison between end users and developers. They are responsible for coordinating activities with the network administrator and the DBA. They prepare and document workstation configurations necessary to support your PeopleSoft application and identify and document printer configurations necessary to support your application. This person should also review all PeopleSoft Customer Connection issues and identify fixes/updates as necessary for your application software. They develop the PeopleSoft client configuration setup to help in installing the PeopleSoft client for your end users.

In addition, this role should develop workstation backup and recovery procedures, assist the network administrator in receiving the necessary workstation components off the server, developing workstation test plans, developing printer test plans, and helping to execute these plans. This individual should also monitor workstation performance and tune as necessary, develop an application deployment strategy for various releases, and manage the deployment process. They should assist in the development and execution of the volume and stress testing plans with respect to the "workstation impact" and help the DBA and the database server system administrator plan for batch cycle processing and report distribution strategies. Finally, they should coordinate the interfaces between the PeopleSoft application and the other applications within your organization.

Database Administrator (DBA)

This role has many responsibilities, including being responsible for physical database design, implementation, and performance tuning. They assist in the development of the overall production environment design and standards, as well as create, monitor, and maintain profiles of the database users and grant the necessary privileges for various system resources. They should assist the network administrator with installing and configuring the database client software as well as creating and maintaining the various database instances (as discussed in the sections above). They are responsible for developing procedures for backing up and recovering the database and assist in installation of the PeopleSoft software for server as well as client systems. They should manage the migration of software and apply patches to the various components of the PeopleSoft software as directed by the project or support team. They should work with the network, workstation, and server administrators to develop volume/stress tests and monitor them. The DBA should also review the PeopleSoft Customer Connection Web site to identify updates/fixes to be implemented as well as understand the technical architecture and nuances of the database management system being used. Finally, they need to understand the generally accepted principles of underlying database design and as much as possible about the PeopleSoft application that they are supporting.

Database Server System Administrator

This role includes the responsibilities for managing the administration, configuration, and maintenance of the database server as well as working with the network resources to monitor and tune the network connectivity, and with the workstation resources to manage access to the PeopleSoft applications and data.

They are also responsible for the setup and monitoring of the PeopleSoft Process Scheduler program on the database server, and they work with the DBA to install database connectivity software on the database server. They should determine preconfiguration database server requirements (e.g., operating system components, utilities, etc.) and set up batch processing environments for support of COBOL, SQR, and Crystal reporting requirements. They also tune the hardware and software to optimize the application environment and participate in the capacity planning for data storage. Finally, they are responsible for developing procedures for backing up and recovering the server.

Application Server System Administrator

This role is responsible for managing the administration, configuration, and maintenance of the application server, to include these duties:

▶ Work with the network resources to monitor and tune the network connectivity, and work with the workstation resources to manage access to the PeopleSoft applications and data.

▶ Set up and monitor the PeopleSoft Process Scheduler program on the application server.

▶ Determine the preconfiguration application server requirements (e.g., operating system components, utilities, etc.).

▶ Set up the batch processing environment for batch COBOL, SQR, and Crystal reporting environments.

▶ Tune the application environment to optimize it.

▶ Develop the procedures for backing up and recovering the server.

File Server System Administrator

This role is responsible for managing the administration, configuration, and maintenance of the file server. This individual should develop backup and recovery procedures and implement them, create and maintain various logical drives on the file server, and install PeopleSoft software and books/manuals from the CD-ROMs provided. They are also responsible for setting up default workstation configurations on the file servers as well as developing the strategy for monitoring network aspects of the volume and stress testing of applications (i.e., network traffic monitoring and throughput analysis).

Network System Administrator

This very important role should determine and document the overall network readiness assessment checklist, conduct the network readiness assessment, and identify and resolve the issues based on the assessment. They should also develop the network strategy to support various PeopleSoft environments and coordinate the network/workstation approach with the workstation resource team member. In addition, they should install third-party network utilities/ drivers with the workstation resource team member, and they are responsible for managing the file/print services supplied to PeopleSoft developers/users as well as providing network access to the development users. They should work with the DBA and application administrator to develop the strategy and test plans for the volume and stress test events, to execute the volume and stress test, and to monitor the network components and their performance.

Application Security Administrator (PeopleSoft)

This role is responsible for maintaining the security of the PeopleSoft system. This includes the network security, database security, application security, and PeopleSoft application–level security.

Developer/Programmers (PeopleTools)

The online developer is responsible for customization, new development, and implementation of all modifications to the online PeopleSoft system. The batch developer is responsible for customization, development, and implementation of all operational programs, interfaces to legacy systems, conversion of data, and any information access reporting requirements (e.g., Crystal, SQR, nVision, etc.) that are external to the online PeopleSoft system. Developers are responsible for developing program specifications, modifications, unit testing, integration testing, and acceptance testing. Finally, your developers should be responsible for debugging and sorting out all the software-related problems, assisting the functional team in building translation and mapping tables, creating your Conference Room Pilot (CRP) and testing environments, and helping to document training materials.

Application User (PeopleSoft)

The application user is responsible for entering data into the system, creating internal reports, and using the functionality of the PeopleSoft system. They will be responsible for scheduling nightly batch jobs with the help of the application administrator and the DBA.

Tuxedo Administrator

If you are using a three-tier approach, your Tuxedo administrator should be responsible for managing the administration, configuration, and maintenance of the Tuxedo application server. They should also be responsible for balancing the load between different application servers.

Workflow/Worklist Administrator (PeopleSoft and E-Mail)

This role is responsible for managing the administration, configuration, and maintenance of the work-flow/work-list–related tasks. They should understand the flow of business-process approval and work with the organization's e-mail administrator to set up work flow for the PeopleSoft application.

Webmaster (PeopleSoft and Internet/Intranet)

When an element of your implementation includes Web deployment, you will need a Webmaster. This person should be responsible for managing the administration, configuration, and maintenance of the Web application server. They should also be responsible for customizing the Web component of the PeopleSoft application software as well as setting up firewall security across Internet/intranet availability of software. Finally, they need to ensure that your setup has seamless integration into the existing corporate intranet.

Help Desk Representative(s)

The help desk representative is responsible for answering first-hand questions from end users and trying to resolve issues such as invalid or expired passwords, inaccessible databases, and unresponsive servers.

Workstation Administrator

The workstation administrator is responsible for setting up and maintaining end users' and developers' workstations. They also are responsible for first-hand resolution of all issues related to end users' workstations, and they serve as a liaison between the hardware maintenance group and the end users.

EDI Administrator

The EDI administrator is responsible for managing e-commerce transactions with external companies and trading partners. This individual should be responsible for mapping EDI transactions (inbound as well as outbound) between EDI transaction files and staging tables in your PeopleSoft database, as well as running and managing the EDI agent of PeopleSoft software. They should also be responsible for designing, implementing, and managing security related to EDI transactions, as well as monitoring the EDI processing.

Report Distribution Administrator

The report distribution administrator is responsible for managing all the reports generated by the PeopleSoft application. This role is responsible for designing, setting up, and maintaining security for report distribution as well as managing any report distribution server. They work as a liaison between end users and the technical support team and are responsible for setting up print requirements for end users.

Typical Staffing Required for These Technical Roles

Table 12.4 outlines these major technical roles and the typical number of individuals needed to support each role on PeopleSoft projects. These numbers will vary based on the size of the organization, the volume, the number of end users supported, and the particular PeopleSoft configuration.

Table 12.4 **Staffing Requirements for Technical Roles**

Role	Number of Persons Needed during Development Phase[1]	Number of Persons Needed during Maintenance Phase[1]
Unix administrator and Tuxedo administrator (or application server system administrator) (Development: database server and application server. Production: database server, application server, report distribution server, and EDI server)	1 (prefer 2) full-time	1 full-time
Database administrator	2 full-time	1 (prefer 2) full-time
PeopleSoft application administrator (finance and materials management/supply chain track)	2 (prefer 3) full-time	2 (prefer 3) full-time
File server system administrator	1 part-time	1 part-time
Network system administrator—LAN	1 part-time	1 part-time
Network system administrator—WAN	1 part-time	1 part-time

Table 12.4   **Staffing Requirements for Technical Roles** *(Continued)*

Role	Number of Persons Needed during Development Phase[1]	Number of Persons Needed during Maintenance Phase[1]
Workstation administrator—thick client[2]	1 full-time	2 part-time
Workstation administrator—thin client (metaframe)[2]	1 part-time	1 part-time
Developers	6–9 full-time	3–4 full-time
EDI administrator	1 full-time	1 part-time
Application security administrator	1 full-time	1 part-time
Report distribution administrator	1 full-time	1 part-time
Workflow/worklist administrator	At this time, out of scope	At this time, out of scope
Webmaster	At this time, out of scope	At this time, out of scope
Help desk representative	Not needed	1 full-time
Operations support	1 full-time	1 part-time

[1] One full-time person means one full-time person for budgeting purposes. For each role, there needs to be a backup resource.

[2] A *thick client* refers to the client-server configuration, which requires that the software (in this case, PeopleSoft proprietary software) reside on the client workstation. In contrast, the Web configuration is referred to as a *thin client* (or, with PeopleSoft 8, *no client*); in this case, software is minimal or nonexistent on the client workstation, and the software now resides somewhere else, such as on an application server or Web server. With the thin-client configuration of PeopleSoft 8, the only software necessary on the client workstation is a Web browser such as Internet Explorer or Netscape Navigator; no proprietary software is needed.

Major Decisions to Be Made

There are a few major decisions that need to be made in order to determine what technical environment you'll need to support. In the following sections, we'll look at these key areas:

- ▶ Report distribution mechanisms
- ▶ Work flow
- ▶ Security levels
- ▶ Web enablement

Report Distribution Mechanisms

After an end user has access to a set of reports on a given reporting tool, the user may have multiple options for where the output of the report is sent. These options make up the list of possible distribution methods. Some of the criteria used for deciding on report distribution mechanisms are as follows:

- ▶ Number of end users for each report
- ▶ Number of pages for each report
- ▶ Frequency of report generation (i.e., daily, weekly, monthly, etc.)
- ▶ Processing time to generate report
- ▶ Formatting and visual look of the report
- ▶ Security and severity of data in report
- ▶ Output device (i.e., printer, fax, e-mail, HTML browser, etc.) available to end users

The driving factor in developing the distribution component is the use of online methods in order to save the costs associated with printed reports. If you send an electronic version of a report, the recipient is able to use the data in the report in other systems and selectively choose which portions, if any, need to be printed. The tool used is another factor in the development, as certain tools are not compatible with certain distribution options.

More work may be required to ensure that all possible distribution methods have been evaluated, and the methods chosen need to be tested and configured for the PeopleSoft reports.

Following are some of the key features available in various report distribution software:

- ▶ Capability of viewing reports online

- ▶ Distribution of reports through e-mail

- ▶ Publication of reports through the Internet/intranet

- ▶ Build a centralized report warehouse in the organization with security

- ▶ Allows modification of published reports temporarily for viewing and printing

- ▶ Search (simple as well as advanced feature) for specific data in a large report as well as in various generations of a report

- ▶ Allows multiple generations of reports to be published

- ▶ Allows archiving of reports

- ▶ Printing through the network printer as well as the local printer

- ▶ Set up folders in various ways (by department, date, group, module, etc.)

- ▶ Secure reports and report pages through strict security rules

- ▶ Allows viewing various reports side-by-side for comparison

- ▶ Allows "sticky notes" on reports and report pages for future reference as well as for passing them to other users

- ▶ Allows data from reports to be tagged and indexed

- ▶ Allows data from reports to be downloaded

- ▶ Allows data from reports to be copied and pasted to other applications

- ▶ Provides e-mail option with attachments as well as linking (for internal users)

- ▶ Allows multiple view of reports by hiding/adding columns on the fly

- ▶ Supports the report distribution administrator who is responsible for setting up the server, report folders, and their securities. (A report distribution tool that many PeopleSoft customers use is Vista Plus, provided by Quest Software.)

PeopleSoft Workflow

PeopleSoft Workflow provides the capability to get the right work to the right person at the right time for the right action. The concept of work flow in People-Soft has three major elements:

▶ Processes

▶ Technology

▶ People

Each addresses a necessary component of work flow. Each work-flow process/interface is unique in nature and therefore should be constantly evaluated to ensure that all business requirements are being met with effective utilization of work-flow technology. Some of the elements to be considered in the work-flow process are described next.

Work-Flow Types

Following is a list of the types of work flow that should be analyzed:

Tasks that don't require user involvement   Rather than having to remember to query the database for overdue receivables, unprocessed purchase orders, or expired passwords, you can have the system automatically check for work that needs to be done and generate work items when it finds some.

Tasks that involve non-PeopleSoft users   Through the PeopleSoft Message Agent, you can include third-party applications in your automated business processes. Users can exchange information with the PeopleSoft database using the e-mail and forms software they're familiar with.

Tasks that several users work on together   The essence and strength of work-flow software is its ability to link together the activities that make up a business process.

Many of the PeopleSoft applications provide model processes that you can adapt to meet your organization's needs. Here are a couple of examples:

▶ PeopleSoft Payables streamlines voucher approval so that payments are made on time while ensuring proper sign-off authority.

▶ PeopleSoft Human Resources includes model business processes for hiring and terminating employees, requesting and approving job changes, and notifying managers when their employees' reviews are due.

PeopleSoft applications also use work flow to manage work lists to keep users up-to-date on the processes that affect their jobs. For example, PeopleSoft Receivables uses work flow to keep watch for overdue payments and credit balance overruns, and to place these items in credit managers' work lists for timely processing.

Work-Flow Components

Several components make up a work-flow process. Each of these key components is described in the paragraphs that follow.

Rules   In order to design work flow for an organization, three areas for each process must be defined. The first area is *rules*. Organizations have certain business rules that define each process. Rules determine what activities are required to process your business data.

Roles   The second area is *roles*. This obviously deals with the people involved in each specific process. While roles often define who is responsible for each part of a process, we recommend that you set up groups of users in a "class." For example, all department managers would be a class. A class would contain one or many users.

The purpose of setting up classes is to take into consideration possible changes in staffing. If a process were bound to a specific person(s), and that person changed jobs or left the company, the system maintenance would be tremendous. Conversely, if the process were bound to a role, then the person filling the role would be irrelevant to PeopleSoft. If the person changed jobs or left the company, someone else would likely move into the role, thereby causing no system maintenance.

Routings   Once the business rules and user roles are defined, *routings* can be implemented. Routings connect the activities in the work flow. They are the system's means of moving information from one place to another, from one step to the next. Routings specify where the information goes and what form it takes—e-mail message, electronic form, or work-list entry.

Routings also take into consideration the timeline for each process. Certain time parameters can be placed around any process to improve organizational efficiency. For example, PeopleSoft can send reminders (e-mail, etc.) at certain intervals, or it can let the originator know when process times have been exceeded.

PeopleSoft Workflow can interface with external systems in order to aid in the overall efficiency of the work-flow functionality. Among your choices for integration should be the e-mail, database, electronic-form, and work-flow vendors that provide the best features and functions for solving your business problems. The Message Agent API enables these applications—forms packages, interactive voice response systems, electronic kiosks—to communicate with PeopleSoft applications. You can also use the API to build connections between different PeopleSoft systems. The API uses standard Microsoft Windows DLL routines or Dynamic Data Exchange to communicate with the Message Agent.

Levels of Security

Due to the nature of client-server technology, there are several layers of security involved in a PeopleSoft application. These security layers can be categorized as physical location, network resource, database server, database, application server, and PeopleSoft application. When all the layers of security are implemented, users need to pass security authorization at each level.

Physical Location

Physical location requires that the actual access to the server be limited to qualified personnel for maintenance purposes only. This requirement will be met by physically locating the system in the computer center, with security access enforced.

Network Resource

In a networked environment, users share hardware and software resources. Every network has its own security system for controlling user access to its shared resources. Typically, this system includes the following security measures:

▶ Assigned IDs and passwords for user identification and verification

▶ Authorized sign-on times, outlining certain days and times when the end user can sign on to the system

▶ File access rights, such as execute, read-only, read/write, or no access

Database Server

Personnel should have limited access to file services on the database server. This limited access will be administered through the operating system's security system. Typical measures include:

- ▶ Assigned IDs and passwords for user identification and verifications
- ▶ System event audits
- ▶ Insulation of objects assigned to processes

Database

Personnel have limited access to the RDBMS (relational database management system) and any RDBMS tools. Each RDBMS that PeopleSoft supports has its own security system, which works in conjunction with PeopleSoft online security. Although this type of security may vary depending on the database environment, you'll generally rely on RDBMS security to:

- ▶ Control who can log on to a database and what they can do once they log on
- ▶ Control which tables or views operators can access and the commands they can use to manipulate data
- ▶ Control who can perform server system administration activities

RDBMS allows you to customize roles. We take advantage of this feature with two PeopleSoft roles, PSUSER and PSADMIN. The PSUSER role has the privilege to log into the database and perform selects against PSDBOWNER, PSLOCK, and PSOPRDEFN (all required during sign-on). This role should be granted to PeopleSoft operators.

The PSADMIN role is a subset of RDBMS's DBA role. This role should be granted to PeopleSoft database owners.

Application Server

Personnel will have limited access to file services on the application server. This limited access will be administered through the operating system's security system. Typical measures include:

- ▶ Assigned IDs and passwords for user identification and verifications
- ▶ System event audits
- ▶ Insulation of objects assigned to processes

PeopleSoft Application Online Level

PeopleSoft software uses the power of layered security to provide an efficient, effective solution to the organization's security concerns. Security in People-Soft can be set up by User ID, roles, and permission lists. Permission lists and roles are used to group people together with like roles and security permissions. When adding new panels/pages or changes to the system, it's easier to update security and make sure no one is missed if permission lists and roles are used. Within the PeopleSoft system you can establish security that restricts operators to certain Set IDs, business units, departments, etc. The detailed description below defines the different layers of security that are available within the PeopleSoft system.

Sign-On and Time-Out Security   When a user attempts to sign on to People-Soft, they enter an ID and a password. If the ID and password are valid, the user is connected to the database, and the system retrieves their user profile.

If the user is not signing on during a valid sign-on time—as defined in their security profile—they are not allowed to sign on. A *sign-on time* is an interval during which a user is allowed to sign on to PeopleSoft, such as Monday through Friday, from 7 A.M. to 6 P.M. Once a user signs on, they can stay connected as long as their sign-on time allows, and as long as their machine doesn't sit idle for longer than their time-out interval. A *time-out interval* specifies how long the user's machine can remain idle—no keystrokes, no SQL—before the user is automatically logged off. You specify both of these time intervals using Security Administrator.

Menu and Dialog Security   You use the Security Administrator People-Tool to control what parts of the PeopleSoft interface each user can access. You do this by granting or restricting access to the PeopleSoft menu bars (each menu bar represents an application or PeopleTool), menu items (the commands available on the individual menus), and dialog box options.

Process Security   Using Process Scheduler, you can assign your process definitions to various process groups, then grant or restrict user access to those groups using Security Administrator. If a process definition is not assigned to a user's authorized process groups, the user is not allowed to run that process.

 Warning   Running SQRs on the client workstation exposes PeopleSoft access IDs and passwords. As a result, running SQRs on the client workstation is an unsecured method of accessing the PeopleSoft system. If this jeopardizes the security scheme at your site, we recommend that you run all SQRs on your application server.

Object Security   Another security tool, Object Security, governs access to the individual database object definitions—record definitions, field definitions, panel/page definitions, Tree Manager, and so forth—created in the Application Designer and stored in the rows of the PeopleTools tables. Using Object Security, you can protect particular object definitions from being modified by developers.

Application Data Security   Although Object Security is a form of data security (you use it to control access to particular rows of data—object definitions—in the PeopleTools tables), PeopleSoft also provides a number of ways to control the application data that a user is allowed to access in the PeopleSoft system. With Application Data Security you can secure data at the table level (queries only), the row level, and the field level.

Query Security   Query is a PeopleTool that helps you build SQL queries to retrieve information from your application tables. For each Query user, you can specify the records the user is allowed to access when building and running queries. You do this by creating Query access groups, with the Tree Manager, then assigning operators to those groups using Query Security. Query Security is enforced only when using Query; it doesn't control run-time panel access to table data.

Row Security   You can design special types of SQL views—security views—to control access to individual rows of data stored within your application database tables. PeopleSoft applications are delivered with built-in, row-level security functions, tailored to specific applications.

For example, in PeopleSoft Financials you can use security views to determine who has access to which business units and ledgers. You can also use security tables to grant privileges by access group to operators who use PeopleSoft Query to access data from the database.

Field Security   Using PeopleCode, you can restrict access to particular fields or columns within your application tables. For example, if you want a certain class of operator to be able to access certain panels, but not to view a particular field on those panels, such as compensation rate, you can write PeopleCode to hide the field for that operator class.

Web Enablement

PeopleSoft introduced the Java client with PeopleSoft version 7. The Java client behaves very similarly to the Microsoft Windows client, and it has been targeted at the casual user for self-service transactions. Since the Java client resides only in browser cache, it requires that a Java client be downloaded every time the browser is launched, which can take quite a long time. For that reason, it is best suited for use on a corporate network. Another limitation of the Java client is that it cannot execute a subset of Windows-specific People-Code functions (e.g., OLE and WinExec). There are some additional, noticeable challenges associated with Web enabling:

▶ Database licensing may be needed for the broader user base.

▶ Java client runs only in a three-tier environment.

▶ Security and privacy of data are a big concern for the audit and legal departments.

With PeopleTools 7.54, PeopleSoft introduced HTML Access Framework. HTML Access Framework provides a zero-client-footprint alternative that allows customers to deploy PeopleSoft applications through a standard Web browser on any client operating system over low bandwidth (even a dial-up connection). HTML Access Framework generates HTML code, ASP (Active Server Pages) for servers, and PeopleSoft Message Agent definition files for updating the database. The files generated through the HTML Access Framework can then be customized to provide the exact look and feel that end users and developers want. This option requires an organization to maintain Web servers separately, while the publication of pages are maintained by a third-party software vendor. There are a couple of challenges associated with this approach:

▶ Version control for HTML, ASP, and Message Agent is difficult.

▶ A Web developer is needed to maintain HTML pages.

With PeopleSoft 8, the vendor has introduced a pure, 100%-Internet client application. PeopleSoft 8 remains targeted to the casual user over the Internet/intranet. Combining the best traits of HTML Access Framework and the Java client, the Internet client has several attractive features, including these:

▶ It handles complex transactions.

▶ Transactions are designed for a Web user interface, not a Microsoft Windows–based user interface.

▶ The Internet client panel/page includes custom features like hyperlinks, embedded HTML, different scroll and grid metaphors, and custom placement and appearance of toolbar buttons.

Technical Impacts of Rollout Strategies

Many project teams fail to take the time and make the effort to effectively manage and plan for all the technical considerations or issues that may arise as they roll out their technology components to support the implementation. If you don't allocate sufficient time for developing, customizing, testing, and finally migrating your solution into production, a last-moment crisis or rush is likely to occur, causing problems with all your technical components. Conceptually, it appears that once development is planned for and changes are designed, then making the changes and testing them should be a piece of cake. However, because of the integration of your application solution, its technology, and the functions it performs, preserving the integrity of the application can become technically challenging.

Another important component of a solution rollout that causes problems for many organizations is the migration of data, technology, and application software into production. During this phase all the functional users think that the system is working, but the technical team still needs to migrate all system components to the production environment. Even though the technical people take all precautionary measures while migrating the solution from the testing environment into the production environment, errors sometimes occur, such as migrating test data rather than converted data or failing to migrate a report or key system change. Successful teams perform a series of quality assurance tests (from both technical and functional perspectives) in production to ensure that "all systems are go."

The timing of the PeopleSoft rollout with respect to other activities (e.g., changes in networks and rollouts of other applications) in an organization is very critical and should be planned and tested well in advance. These activities sometimes affect the performance of the ERP system, and, as a result, the end users' perceptions of the system can change from good to bad in a very short time.

Up Next

As you can see from this chapter, proper planning, even in the technical area, is paramount; and the more you plan and test, the better off you will be. So remember to give yourself enough time for these two critical elements of your project, and don't spend all your time in the design and development phase. Having the right resources to help you, as well as the right environments to support you, can save you lots of trouble in the long run.

The next chapter, "Security," will look at the various areas of security in greater detail. As we discussed in this chapter, security should be carefully planned and outlined to support your implementation, and PeopleSoft implementations generally involve a number of security components. With People-Soft's move to the Internet, security becomes an even bigger area to manage and support. Therefore, proper planning, integration, and setup are critical.

Security

F E A T U R I N G :

▶ An overview of the security components

▶ What User Security and Permission Lists are and how you should configure these features

▶ What Object Security is and why it should be used

▶ A look at how Query Security is set up

▶ What Process Security is, including the important steps to enable this feature

▶ Use of Field Level Security using PeopleCode

▶ How "trees" are used in PeopleSoft security

▶ Differences in security between PeopleSoft HRMS and Financials/ Distribution

▶ Specific tips and concerns to watch out for when setting up your PeopleSoft security

Whenever you are dealing with company data, whether it is individual employee data or the financial data of your company, security is of paramount concern. Now, take that concern and double it when you are talking about offering the data via the Internet (or intranet). Even if your employees are accessing the data internally using your company's intranet, there are always concerns about whether the data is secure enough, whether it can be accessed by an unauthorized user, and whether authorized users are limited to receiving only the data they need to get their job done.

When dealing with an ERP system, such as PeopleSoft—especially in the three-tier architecture that we discussed in our technology chapters—there are a multitude of security features that must be considered and implemented, including workstation, database, network, Web (firewall), and application security. Below in Figure 13.1, the typical security elements surrounding your ERP (PeopleSoft) application are shown. With all of these security challenges, how can a user keep track of all their passwords as well as the procedures used to access this system, and how can the data be secure while passing through all of these layers?

Figure 13.1 **Components of ERP security**

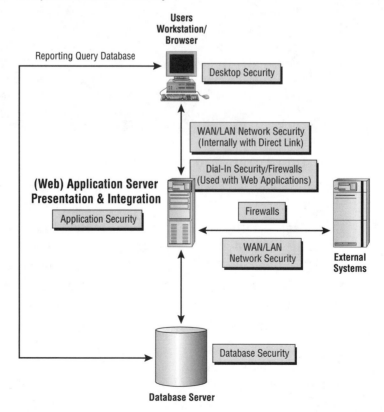

During this chapter, we will look at the various components involved in setting up security around and within your PeopleSoft application. We will look in detail at the PeopleSoft application security setup as mentioned above and look at the issues and questions you must answer in order to properly configure your system to ensure that it is secure, yet still meet the needs of your business.

Overview of Security Components

PeopleSoft's tightly integrated software architecture has both positive and negative effects when dealing with security. For instance, the PeopleSoft modules are compatible and integrated, thus they share tables including the setup and control of security. In addition, the application can be tightly integrated with third-party software such as e-mail (Lotus Notes, Microsoft Exchange, Outlook, etc.), and with other agents such as messaging to third-party software and allowing a single sign-on capability. With all of this integration and information-sharing, security must be tightly controlled and designed. All components should be assessed, including the controls built around each process.

As mentioned and shown in Figure 13.1, there are multiple points of entry to the data within the application, including:

- ▶ Network
- ▶ Database tools (SQL and others)
- ▶ PeopleSoft online pages (screens)
- ▶ SQR and COBOL batch processes
- ▶ PeopleSoft Query

PeopleSoft is built with the intention of "openness," or data availability. It is easy to download data to unsecure environments, and the shared tables concept can be a powerful access mechanism. In general, the security architecture components don't work together and must be managed. Below is a list of the various types of security that an end user typically deals with in relation to their PeopleSoft application.

Client workstation security   Generally, via Windows, individuals have options to put security on their own workstation to prevent others from accessing their tools and system data. This is highly recommended, especially since users can query and pull data from the PeopleSoft application, saving report files and data (e.g., Excel) files on their hard drive. Individuals who have access to another's desktop but not to People-Soft may be able to pull files from the end user's desktop or a shared drive. Security considerations for this data (and where it is stored) should be taken into consideration.

Network and operating security   When a workstation is hooked up to a network or server, the authority to work on that network or server must be established and is another layer of security.

Note   It is recommended that you set up your PeopleSoft file server directories as read-only. However, to run reports (e.g., SQRs), users will need to have read or execute access to the network directories containing the PeopleSoft-delivered SQRs and the SQR program itself. If you don't grant access to these directories to a user, they cannot run reports.

Database security   While the application has security for the functions and features offered, the database itself must also have security so that other tools and processes are controlled through security access.

PeopleSoft security (application security)   Functions and features within the PeopleSoft application must also be controlled through security. This application security is what is found within PeopleSoft.

Web security   Generally, when dealing with an intranet or Web solution, security is required to access the company's internal "secure" sites, and when traveling outside this "secure" environment, a "firewall" security protocol is used.

Server security   Your servers also should have security tied to them for access to the information on the server and the ability to change any server configuration or access data on the server.

Based on all of these layers of security (see Figure 13.2), we suggest that you design and build the "security architecture" around the entire infrastructure rather than just focusing on the delivered PeopleSoft application security. This design should include your operating system, internal network, and remote access options. A formalized business continuity plan should also be created that outlines this strategy.

Figure 13.2 **Layers of security**

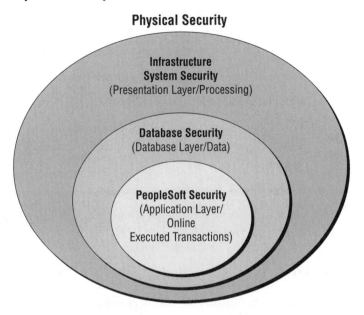

Network/Operating Systems Security Controls

Within the area of Network/Operating Systems security, you should be asking yourself the following questions:

▶ Who has access to servers and directories where data and the application are stored?

▶ Who has access to the application software?

▶ What can operating system users and maintenance personnel do with the files and data once they are in them?

Once you've answered these questions, created strategies to ensure that these areas are secure, and put these strategies into place, you are ready to look at your database security controls.

Database Security Controls

Within the database security area, the specific questions you should be considering when setting up your PeopleSoft application are:

▶ Who can log on directly to the database?

▶ Who has the ability to use/access the PeopleSoft database tables using tools such as SQL (Structured Query Language), and what environments (e.g., development, production, testing) should these individuals be limited to? What tables of data should they have access to?

▶ What can they do using SQL commands (e.g., update, delete, insert)?

▶ What database commands can database users execute?

▶ Who has access to the SYSADM (the all-knowing, full-blown security classification provided by the PeopleSoft application) logon ID and password?

▶ Who performs database administration?

Once you have answered these questions, you should provide database security control based on these needs.

Workstation

As mentioned before, workstation security such as Windows NT or desktop security is not required, but should be reviewed based on the functions and features the user is able to perform and store on their desktop. If important information can be queried and stored to a file that can reside on the desktop, then appropriate security should be in place to minimize unauthorized access to these desktop files. You should assess the functions of your users and how likely it would be for them to download sensitive data to their desktops. By incorporating your security strategy with their training and user support materials—emphasizing how to leverage their desktop security features and how important it is for them to maintain a desktop password—you will help your organization have greater control over your data. You should stress the need to keep the data on the desktop secure and how it is up to each individual employee to ensure that this layer of security is used.

Warning   It is not recommended that you allow your users to run their SQR reports on the client workstation. This exposes the PeopleSoft Access IDs and passwords. Running SQRs on the client desktop may put confidential data at risk and should be considered as an unsecured piece of the PeopleSoft system.

Web Security

When dealing with PeopleSoft in a three-tiered mode, leveraging a Web client, in most cases organizations leverage a sign-on procedure to incorporate a third-party directory service, allowing for a single sign-on process. There are "user exits" (places within the software designed to provide access into or out of the program or application) within PeopleSoft's security application that allow interfaces to utilize this feature. With Web security, this is generally done at crucial times in the authentication sequence between the Web client and the Tuxedo application server (which is the middleware software used in the three-tiered arrangement). Figure 13.3 depicts how this process occurs.

Figure 13.3   **Diagram of the three-tiered (Web) version of a "single sign-on process"**

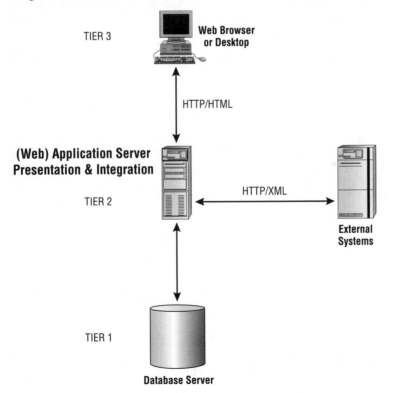

Within the PeopleSoft sign-on process, each new page requested by a user in a single session needs to be authenticated by the Tuxedo server. This is a three-step process, providing first the user's sign-on information while bypassing the

PeopleSoft sign-on dialog box, then supplemental authentication information to the PeopleSoft sign-on information, and finally the callout that validates the user's sign-on and authentication information at the application server. To create the single sign-on process, the HTML code must be modified as noted in the PeopleSoft system documentation. The Web client architecture validates security by the host name (or host address) and port number combination. When a user accesses a new page (or URL), the authentication process occurs. If that page has already been viewed, then the server validates the existing session and continues with no further authorization. If it is a new page that has not been accessed during the session, the server will need authentication to occur again. The Web client will use the LoginInfo cache to get the "best fit," generally based on an entry with the same host and port, or the last entry added to the cache if there is no match with the same host and port. If this proves successful, the information is accessed. If not, then the PeopleSoft sign-on dialog appears and the individual will need to reenter their user authorization information.

With PeopleSoft 8, PeopleSoft's ability to integrate seamlessly has been enhanced with the leading LDAP (Lightweight Directory Access Protocol) directories through the use of the Application Messaging and Business Interlinks technologies that drive creation and maintenance of LDAP user profiles when business events within PeopleSoft require them. This basically allows for a "single sign-on" from the user's viewpoint throughout the entire process. Some key benefits include:

▶ The use of a single, centralized user profile for both PeopleSoft and non-PeopleSoft applications will reduce maintenance costs and errors.

▶ PeopleSoft's business events and data can be used to drive LDAP user profile and group creation and maintenance. For example, when a new employee is hired, this event can trigger creation of a user profile in the LDAP directory, thus setting up security for a user almost instantaneously.

PeopleSoft Application Security

Overall, the PeopleSoft application security centers on its enterprise solution design. The system begins with the individual function-specific modules built in PeopleTools (such as Payables, General Ledger, Budgets, etc.) and then these modules are put together to create business solutions such as materials management (which includes Inventory, Payables, and Purchasing modules). These business solutions are, in turn, put together to create an industry or enterprise solution. With this in mind, the business wants its applications (whether built or bought) to function as a seamless solution that includes its security and control features. The goal is to view your solution and the data as it moves from one system to another (or one application to another) as a single integrated process. Therefore, your internal controls should be looked at from start to finish. Your solution may be very secure in one area, but as you pass information into another area this may no longer be the case. It is important to have advanced planning to enforce enterprise policy and set the stage for pre-approved transactions. By looking at the entire process (from start to finish) and establishing the appropriate control points and approvals enterprise-wide, the data is more secure.

The diagram in Figure 13.4 shows how data can be passed from one area to another and how security should be evaluated through the entire process. This illustrates the control points and issues surrounding security. PeopleSoft's workflow functionality can facilitate this aspect of security through prevention and detection of the controls in an automated fashion. For instance, for purchases more than $10,000, the organization may feel they need to ensure that the appropriate controls are in place so that fraud or abuse does not occur. In this manner, they can create a corporate policy that requires an individual to get director-level approval for any purchase over $10,000. By putting this control in the system and automating it, the control is ensured prior to the purchase, rather than manually and maybe after the fact.

When PeopleSoft set up their security within their application, they looked to fulfill these needs:

- ▶ WHAT information a user can see (by table and rows)

- ▶ WHAT the user can do with this information (by action codes such as "update" and "display")

- ▶ WHOSE information a user can see (by business unit or department— i.e., Row Level Security)

- ▶ WHEN this information can be accessed (through a "time of day" feature)

- ▶ HOW LONG the information can be viewed (with a "time out" feature)

Figure 13.4   **Application security flow**

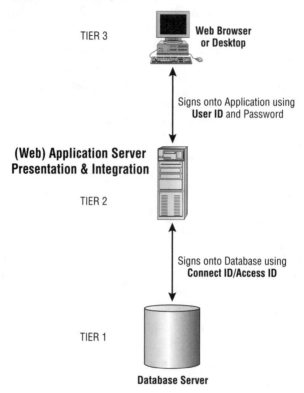

The PeopleSoft system uses various authorization IDs and passwords to control user access. Three IDs and passwords are shared with the database system. Two are assigned using the PeopleSoft PeopleTools ➢ Maintain Security menu while the third is used "behind the scenes." These IDs are:

▶ User ID

▶ Access ID

▶ Owner ID

A PeopleSoft *User ID* is the single ID that is given to each user who will be accessing your PeopleSoft system. Each user will have one unique User ID. The user enters their User ID and password when they log onto the PeopleSoft application. This will grant them the correct online privileges they need to perform their job. In some cases, you will also need to use a *Connect ID*. This ID is used for DB2 and Informix database users who do not want to set up a unique database User ID for every PeopleSoft User ID they create. For other database applications, the Security Administrator feature automatically creates this unique User ID for the database "behind the scenes."

A PeopleSoft *Access ID* and password is the database ID through which the PeopleSoft application(s) are connected once the user's User ID and password have been validated. Figure 13.5 shows the process the system goes through when connecting a user to the database through the online PeopleSoft application. The Access ID usually has the administrator-level access to manipulate data for the entire PeopleSoft application (as deemed necessary by the individual's User ID). Individual users do not know what their Access IDs are and, therefore, cannot use them "behind the scenes" to directly access the database outside the PeopleSoft application. The User and Connect IDs only have access to a few PeopleSoft tables used during sign-on (even if a user was able to somehow determine what the Access ID was) and these only have SELECT access. In addition, the very sensitive data, such as passwords, is encrypted.

Figure 13.5 **The PeopleSoft sign-on process**

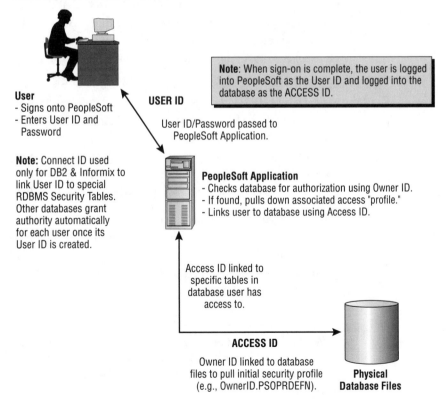

User
- Signs onto PeopleSoft
- Enters User ID and Password

Note: Connect ID used only for DB2 & Informix to link User ID to special RDBMS Security Tables. Other databases grant authority automatically for each user once its User ID is created.

USER ID

User ID/Password passed to PeopleSoft Application.

Note: When sign-on is complete, the user is logged into PeopleSoft as the User ID and logged into the database as the ACCESS ID.

PeopleSoft Application
- Checks database for authorization using Owner ID.
- If found, pulls down associated access "profile."
- Links user to database using Access ID.

Access ID linked to specific tables in database user has access to.

ACCESS ID

Owner ID linked to database files to pull initial security profile (e.g., OwnerID.PSOPRDEFN).

Physical Database Files

Finally, the PeopleSoft *Owner ID* is the database table owner ID. When the PeopleSoft database is created, a single Owner ID is used and this ID must have security administrative authority. This ID is used when referencing PeopleSoft tables from within the application.

When a user has signed onto the PeopleSoft application, they are logged into PeopleSoft as the User ID and logged onto the database as the Access ID. The only three tables the Access ID has authorization to "see" are the PSDBOWNER, PSLOCK, and PSOPRDEFN. As mentioned earlier, the passwords for both the User and Access IDs are stored in the PSOPRDEFN table in either encrypted or nonencrypted form. Passwords are encrypted using the National Security Administrator's DES algorithm. You determine whether you want this data to be encrypted or not when you configure your system.

For each user of the system, a security *profile* that answers the questions above is created and maintained. This profile is associated with the User ID and is generally referred to as the *user profile*. The profile will concentrate on the *pages* or screens that an individual will have access to or "see" when they are signed onto the application; the actions they can perform to that data (such as update or display only); the individuals or departments they have access to; when they can log onto the system; and how long their time-out feature is (when they will be signed off or logged off the system if they are not actively using it).

There are two additional profiles used within the Security Administrator. They are the *class profile* and the *access profile*. The *class profile* has no user password associated with it, but is used to organize a set of users into a group with common security requirements. This ability to create user classes (which within PeopleSoft are referred to as *permission lists*) helps save your administrator time and effort in setting up individuals' rights or access to the system, since generally you can define a few sets of classes and then link the user to them.

Now, every user must be assigned an *access profile*. The access profile provides the necessary "behind the scenes" information to sign onto the physical database and then pull the information necessary to understand the individual's security parameters. Access profiles are very sensitive and must have system administrator privileges.

Warning It is best to limit the control of creating your access profile and associated password to one person. This person can set up the access profiles, and all the other security administrators within your organization can still assign users to predefined access profiles.

Within PeopleSoft there are three main areas that must be configured for the security in the application to work:

▶ Permission lists

▶ Roles

▶ User IDs

The next section will outline what a permission list is and how to set one up within the PeopleSoft application. After covering the setup of permission lists, we will then cover the setup of the role and the User ID (or identification). We will also show how the User ID is assigned to a particular role, and the role is linked to a permission list. Within the application, as mentioned above, there are various types of security. Based on your requirements, you may also need to set up all or some of these types of security features:

▶ Row Level Security

▶ Field Level Security

▶ Object Security

▶ Query Security

▶ Process Security

Each of these areas will be discussed in detail along with the reasons why you might be using these features. After we have reviewed what each type of security is and how it is set up, we will look at an example that will bring all these security features together. Remember, it is best to create a security strategy up front, review each user's or group of users' requirements, and then set up the security that applies to each person or group. Finally, you must have procedures to help you maintain the security effectively throughout the life of your system.

Grouping Users into Roles

Users who perform similar functions can be grouped together into what PeopleSoft calls *roles*. A role is a job or duty the person is performing within the application, such as a Payroll Manager. Each role that is defined within the application can then be granted access to a set of application functions (pages, processes, etc.) by linking to a permission list. The relationship of users to roles, and roles to permission lists, helps decrease security maintenance and upkeep for each security profile. Figure 13.6 shows an example of a list of roles that were assigned to a User ID, PS. These roles are then assigned to the permission lists found in Figure 13.7.

Figure 13.6   **Roles assigned to users**

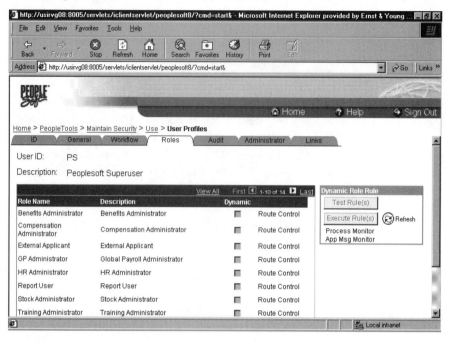

Figure 13.7   **Roles linked to permission lists**

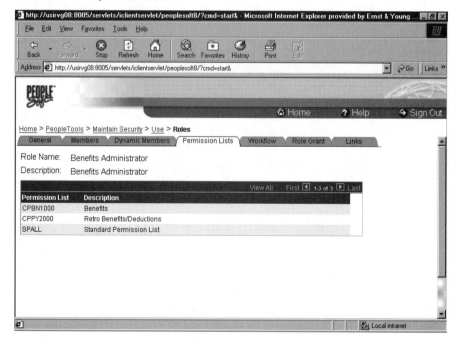

The information a user sees is controlled through granting or denying them access to different menu or page options. Each user or role will be given access only to the pages that are required for them to complete their tasks. For example, an Accounts Payable clerk may have access to view vendor information (therefore, the vendor pages are on the clerk's menu) but not have access to Treasury data or pages (therefore, the Treasury menu items are not visible to the user).

The actions that the user can perform on the information can also be controlled via security features. Following is a list of these action types:

Action Type	View	Change	Insert New Row
No Access	None	None	None
Display Only	Current & Future	None	None
Update/ Display	Current & Future	Future Only	Effective Date greater than or equal to current row
Update/ Display ALL	History, Current & Future	Future Only	Effective Date greater than or equal to current row
Correction	History, Current & Future	All existing rows	Add new rows with no effective date restrictions

As shown in this table, if the user is given No Access, they cannot view or change data. Display Only means that they can view the information but they cannot change it. Update/Display and Update/Display ALL allow the user to view and change the data, but only for future-dated records (not historical data) or entering new rows of data. Correction is the most powerful of all action types and allows users to change history as well as update current and future rows of data. This action is normally reserved for a select few individuals, such as a system administrator for maintenance purposes, and should not be given out to your user base.

The other major area of security is controlling whose data or what data you will see. This is controlled differently depending on your application. In the HRMS application, the data is controlled by the department that an individual is a part of. For instance, if I am a manager of the Accounting Department, I can be given access to view employees who are in the Accounting Department. This type of security is controlled using a "tree" structure or hierarchy. Figure 13.8

is an example of a Departmental Security Tree within the PeopleSoft HRMS application. Within this security tree, or graphical representation of hierarchies of organizational units, the reporting relationship between units can be viewed and updated, and this information can be used to grant or deny user access to the related employees' data. Changes over time can be tracked by creating new trees with different effective dates every time the organizational structure changes. This in turn updates the security.

Figure 13.8   **Departmental Security Tree**

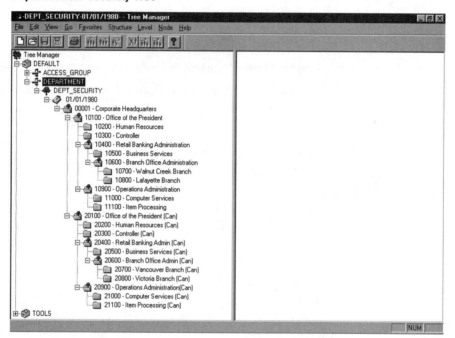

PeopleSoft also controls access to what time of day and which days of the week the system can be accessed. For security purposes, it may be wise to limit online entries from 6 A.M. until 8 P.M. and allow other batch processes to run at night or on the weekends. This can easily be accomplished by not allowing users access to the online application during these batch-processing windows.

The final area of PeopleSoft security is that of protecting against the users who sign onto the application and then leave their desks for extended periods of time, allowing others to have access to the system (and, in essence, to all the security features of the individual who originally signed on). PeopleSoft has a time-out feature that can be used to ensure that this does not happen. This feature automatically logs the user off the PeopleSoft online system after so many minutes of inactivity have occurred. There are no specific time frames that should be set for this security feature. It is up to you to work with your users and security/controls group to determine the best solution possible for processing efficiencies and security concerns. Inactivity in this case is defined as no mouse clicks, keystrokes, import, file print, or SQL activity on the application.

Permission Lists

Within PeopleSoft, the permission list controls which applications and People-Tools (menu bar) each user or user profile can access within the PeopleSoft system. As mentioned above, once you logically group your users together, you are ready to create roles to put them into. The roles will then be linked to permission lists. The permission lists will control which menu items are available to each role defined as representing a group of users. Definitions are stored in the PSAUTHITEM table. Figure 13.9 is an example of a permission list that was created for a group of users and that demonstrates the listing of items a role has access to.

Figure 13.9 **Permission list**

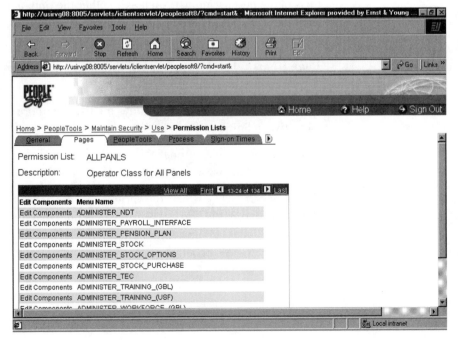

Within the PeopleSoft application, there are already a few permission lists set up. Remember to review who is included in the ALLPANLS permission list, which has access to all PeopleSoft menus. Review who is included in the PSADMIN permission list as well. User access is not validated within the classes, and they should be created within the development environment so that security definitions do not need to be created and re-created often.

An individual can be assigned to only one User ID but a User ID can be assigned to multiple roles. Roles may be linked to multiple permission lists. You must choose which permission list is considered primary for a User ID should there be any conflicts in the definitions.

User IDs need to be assigned before a new user can have access to the system. Each User ID is assigned to existing roles. The User ID, roles, and permission lists are assigned using the same pages, which can be found in the People-Tools ➤ Maintain Security menu item. Whether you are setting up a User ID, role, or permission list, you will still need to access this area. In all cases, there are several areas within this definition profile that must be set up (see Figure 13.10 for an example of the screen and setup). They are:

General   This is the general information used to determine basic settings of the permission list, such as whether the time-out features are used, what page to start (as the home page), and whether passwords can be e-mailed.

Page Items   This area includes the menu items or pages that the definition (or permission list) has access to.

Sign-on Times   This area displays the list of authorized sign-on times for the active definition.

PeopleTools   This outlines the PeopleTools available and allows you to select those that you want this permission list to have access to.

Processes   This view lists the various Process Security groups (which are explained later in the "Process Groups" section) that the permission list has access to. Process groups determine which batch processes the profile can run via the Process Scheduler.

Figure 13.10   **Permission List General page and Tabs page**

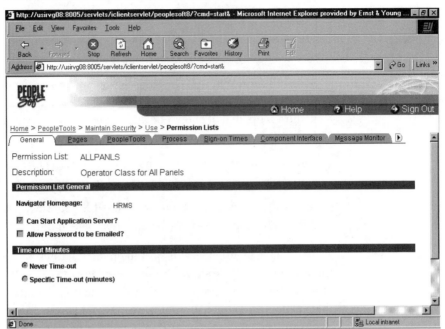

Component Interfaces   This section contains a list of Component Interfaces that this permission list can access. You must add to this list any time a new Component Interface is defined. The Component Interface provides real-time access to a PeopleSoft application from another PeopleSoft or third-party application. Since the Component Interface is really a panel group (now called a component) that is pulled together for use by other programs, it must be secured. The calling program must pass a valid PeopleSoft User ID/password, and, via permission list, that User ID must have access.

Message Monitor   The Message Monitor tab contains a list of Application Message Channels that this permission list has access to through the Application Message Monitor tool. You must add to the list when a new Message Channel is defined or a new Application Message is put into an existing Message Channel. Since the Application Message Monitor provides the user (a real live person in this case) with access to view (and may even change) the actual data contents of Application Messages, it must be secured.

Web Libraries   This tab shows the list of Web libraries that this permission list has access to within the application. If you want a particular permission list to have access to a certain Web library, then you must add the library under this tab.

Queries   The Queries tab links the security required to create and run queries through the PeopleSoft application query function.

Mass Change Security   This section contains a list of the mass change templates that this permission list has access to. If a new mass change feature is created, it should be added to the correct permission lists so it can be used.

Links   This area contains a list of any links to other security settings outside the application that this permission list has access to.

Audits   The Audits tab provides the ability to track changes to this permission list (e.g., last User ID updated, date and time of update).

As previously mentioned, it is best to create the roles and permission lists you think you will need to support your system first and then the User IDs for each of your users. Once you have set up your security definitions, you can print them to help keep track of what you have configured. This can be done through the Print icon on the Security Profile page or using the File ➤ Print command and dialog box. You can select many or all profiles to print using this method.

You need to remember to update your security any time a new process group or page/menu is added to your application. Therefore, your developers or a designated group of individuals will need to have access to the PeopleTools ➤ Maintain Security menu to update the security profiles of those affected by the change(s). It is not recommended that in a development environment only a select few be given this option. However, in production, this process must be highly restricted.

The PSADMIN class is a "super user" definition that allows developers the ability to access new objects as they are created or changed much more quickly than updating their security profile for every change made (which could be several hundred times per day). Anyone who has access to the PSADMIN security class has automatic access to just about any menu item and process definition within the system 24 hours per day. Linking an individual to the PSADMIN security class does not affect their general or User ID attributes such as time-out minutes, background disconnects intervals, password, access profile, and such. It also does not change their process profile dialog settings or access to the Security Administrator Access dialog or Application Designer Access dialog. Access to these dialogs can only be granted by manually adding their corresponding menu bars to a security profile.

When linking a user to multiple permission lists, the following occur:

- ▶ Background disconnect interval is based on the primary permission list.

- ▶ Time-out minutes is based on the primary permission list.

- ▶ Menu items are based on all permission lists. If any permission list grants more access (such as update to a particular page when another only grants read-only), the highest level access (e.g., update) is granted to the User ID.

- ▶ Sign-on times are based on all permission lists. Again, if times overlap, then the earliest start time and latest end time are used.

- ▶ Process groups are based on all permission lists so that the combination of processes a user can run includes all those associated with the multiple permission lists.

- ▶ Process profile is based on the primary permission list.

Administration Group

An *administration group* is a group of users, roles, system privileges, classes, and databases for which an administrator is appointed and given management authority. Before setting up your classes and User IDs, you should first create all the access profiles that you think you might need. Again, remember that only a select few individuals should have the authority to do this. The system comes set up with the access profile of SYSADM. This provides access to the entire PeopleSoft application. You will definitely want to create additional access profiles that are more limited in scope than the SYSADM profile, as well as change the SYSADM password once your initial PeopleSoft database is created (from the default password provided). The default password is contained in your system documentation.

TIP   Remember that the Access ID you set up must be a valid database ID with system administrator privileges.

Row Level Security

Within the PeopleSoft application, you can design special types of SQL views—security views—to control access to individual rows of data stored within your application database tables. PeopleSoft applications are delivered with built-in, row level security functions, tailored to specific applications. For example, a ledger class row level security can be invoked in order to ensure that only authorized users add journals to a budget ledger. The permissions used within row level security is based on the one selected in the security profile, Row Level Security. This feature allows you the ability to get the job done without having to create so many user profile classes.

Classes can be set up based on the information (i.e., pages) accessed and not the rows of data selected. The Row Level features allow you to further segment your classes. For example, in some cases you might want your functional individuals to access one set of menu options and your technical folks to access another (including the PeopleTools features). However, you might not want all individual users in those groups to have access to all the information available; you might want only managers to have such access. By leveraging the Row Level Security option, you do not have to create two operator classes with the same menu access, but you can create two Row Level Security classes (one manager and the other non-manager) where the manager has access to all information in a particular area while the non-manager has a segmented version.

Standard Operator Security in PeopleSoft defines the pages (or screens) that the user may access and the work processes that the user is able to perform within the modules of PeopleSoft, as explained above. The security tree feature in the PeopleSoft HRMS system allows row level security on certain employee-related tables within the HRMS application. The PeopleSoft Financials, Distribution, and Manufacturing (FDM) product has fundamental functionality differences from the HRMS product with regard to security. Both are similar in the way Operator Security functions; however, FDM does not access security trees for row level security but does use the other special security views discussed below.

Following are the steps that should be followed to set up appropriate security:

1. Set up the standard application security for the organization, identifying roles and permission lists on a required job by job function/responsibilities.

2. Identify the data security needs of the organization. Is it necessary to have users with the same job functions but access to completely different

sets of data? If your answer is "yes," identify the keys on which the segregation of data will be based. Chart out which users will perform which functions, then indicate the data that each user will need access to. You may find it very beneficial to put together a user/operator class matrix outlining these characteristics (see Table 13.1 for an example). Then when new features or functions are added to your system, you can analyze your matrix and determine the impacts.

Table 13.1   **Example of User Matrix**

				HR_ALUM	HR_TRAV	HRA	HRAR	HRX	HRNHRIM
Develop Workforce									
	Administer Training								AA
	Use	All							AA
	Setup	All							AA
	Inquire	All							AA
	Report	All							AA
	Competencies								AA
	Tables	Practice Area		x	x	D	D	x	AA
		Competency Categories		x	x	D	D	x	AA
		Competency Rating Scales		x	x	D	D	x	AA
		Competencies		x	x	D	D	x	AA
		Comp Test		x	x	D	D	x	AA
		Keywords		x	x	D	D	x	AA
		Cross-references		x	x	D	D	x	AA

Table 13.1   **Example of User Matrix** *(Continued)*

			HR_ALUM	HR_TRAV	HRA	HRAR	HRX	HRNHRIM
		Engagements	x	x	D	D	x	AA
		Engagement Roles	x	x	D	D	x	AA
		Course Competencies	x	x	D	D	x	AA
	Framework	Framework and Behaviors	x	x	D	D	x	AA
	IndivData	Competency Summary	x	x	D	D	x	AA
		Competency Update	x	x	D	D	x	AA
		Engagement Roles	x	x	D	D	x	AA
		Competency Security Access	x	x	D	D	x	AA
	Manage Competencies		x	x	x	x	x	
	Use	All						AA
	Setup	Competency Table	x	x	D	D	x	AA
		Cluster Table— Competencies	x	x	D	D	x	AA
		Cluster Table— Accomplishments	x	x	D	D	x	AA

Table 13.1 **Example of User Matrix (Continued)**

			HR_ALUM	HR_TRAV	HRA	HRAR	HRX	HRNHRIM
		Competency Type Table	x	x	D	D	x	AA
		Competency Summary	x	x	D	D	x	AA
		Match Evaluation Types	x	x	D	D	x	AA
		Proficiency Descrs	x	x	D	D	x	AA
		Proficiency Rating Table	x	x	D	D	x	AA
		Degree	x	x	D	D	x	AA
		Honor/Award Table	x	x	D	D	x	AA

Key: AA – All Access; D – Display Only; X – Update/Display

3. If it will be necessary to establish multiple User IDs for those who perform the same function on different, exclusive sets of data, it will be necessary to associate each user (or User ID) to more than one permission list linked through the roles assigned.

> ► One permission list (OPRCLASS) will identify the menu items and process groups that the user will have access to, and the user will inherit these attributes. This is set up in the PeopleTools ➢ Maintain Security menu within the PeopleSoft application.

> ► The second permission list (ROWSECCLASS) will identify what data the user will see in the pages based on the business units, analysis groups, projects, ledgers, books, Set IDs, or pay cycles (depending on how your data is segregated and your unique requirements). This class must be created in the PeopleTools ➢ Maintain Security menu, but it is given **No Access** to menu items or process groups. The data restrictions are identified in the Define Business Units—Administer Security pages.

4. In the Maintain Security section, open the Roles section. Under the Roles tab for permission lists, assign the Role to the multiple permission lists. Then, under the User Profile menu within Maintain Security, assign multiple Roles to the User ID established.

Note   The user inherits the maximum level of access for all attributes between the two permission lists, unless the ROWSECCLASS is the primary permission list.

5. Under the Define Business Rules ➢ Administer System ➢ Use ➢ Security Options, the option you select will dictate the type of security you are setting up:

▶ No Security

▶ User Level Security

▶ Permission List Security

The options you select will also dictate which key fields will secure the data:

▶ Unit (Business Unit)

▶ Set ID

▶ Ledger

▶ Book

▶ Project

▶ Analysis Group

▶ Pay Cycle

You will be able to select only one type of security; depending on how the business wants to implement Row Level Security, you may use only one key field to secure the data or you may use several or all of them.

6. Next, you want to go to the following page: Home ➢ Define Business Rules ➢ Administer Security ➢ Use ➢ Security View Names. Figure 13.11 shows the list of all the security views delivered by PeopleSoft. (The contents of this table are listed in the database under PS_SEC_VIEW_NAMES.)

Figure 13.11 **Security views delivered**

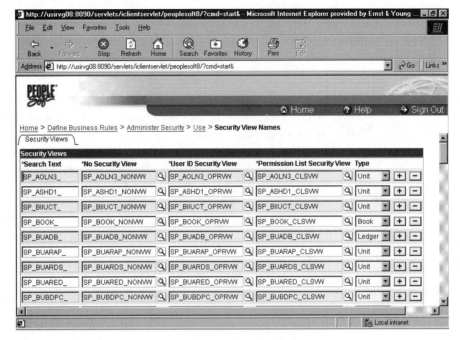

The table contains the following:

▶ The first column is the truncated name of the view.

▶ The second column is the full name of the view for No Security (ending in NONVW).

▶ The third column is the full name of the view for User ID Security (ending in OPRVW).

▶ The fourth column is the full name of the view for Permission List Security (ending in CLSVW).

▶ The fifth column is the type of row security for the view when selected, according to the Secured Field selected.

The values for the Secured Fields are as follows: Unit (Business Unit), SetID, Ledger, Book, Project, Analysis (Analysis Group), and Pay Cycle.

It is possible to identify the purpose of the view by going into the Application Designer. Open the view in question and click Properties to view a description of the view. Alternatively, it is possible to guess the purpose by deciphering the truncated name of the view (e.g., SP_BUN_ would be Business Unit—Inventory).

Note PeopleSoft implements Row Level Security for all of the security views listed on the Security View Names page with the selected Secured Field. So if you want to implement Row Level Security on the business unit level, you select Unit on the Security Options page. The result of this operation is the implementation of this security for all the search views with a Secured Field of B (Business Unit).

7. For the next step in setting up Row Level Security, go into the Application Designer. Open the search view that implements the specific Row Level Security to be applied (e.g., SP_BUN_CLSVW).

8. Insert ROWSECCLASS (field) to the appropriate search view, and include the field as a key on the view. Save the view.

9. Rebuild the view and commit. The system will automatically execute the script to the database and commit if you select Execute And Build Script.

10. Home ➤ Define Business Rules ➤ Administer Security ➤ Use ➤ Maintain Row Level Security (as shown in Figure 13.12). This is where you identify the permission lists that have access to particular SetID/department combinations. Select the permission list, and insert the appropriate SetIDs/departments. Save the permission list. Finally, you need to assign the permission list to the User ID under the User Profile, Row Security List.

11. The final step to implement the Row Level Security process is to run the program that enables the security views. To do so, you need to follow this path: Go ➤ Define Business Rules ➤ Administer Security ➤ Process ➤ Apply Security Setups.

12. Test the functionality to ensure it works.

Figure 13.12 **Row Security page**

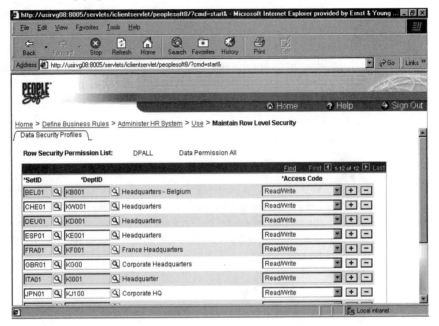

Field Level Security

The concept of Field Level Security is to allow certain fields on the page (or screen) to be visible only to certain security classes or individuals. This is particularly useful with certain key information such as salary and disability information. Within PeopleSoft, the only way to administer this type of security is through a "customization" using PeopleCode, the custom programming language developed by PeopleSoft for its application. You can create code, via PeopleCode commands, that controls the display of data on a page based on the security class the individual belongs to (or the individual's User ID). Using PeopleCode and minor customizations, you can restrict access to particular fields or columns within the application tables. For example, if you want a certain class of user to be able to access certain pages but not view a particular field (such as salary) on those pages, you would write PeopleCode to hide the field for that permission list.

An example of putting PeopleCode into your application is shown below:

If OPRID = 'NONSECCLASS' then hide (job.salary).

This PeopleCode statement is added to the record (Job) using ROWINIT PeopleCode features. Every time User ID NONSECCLASS accesses the Job record, the Salary field is hidden from view.

Another approach to this problem is to create two different pages, one with the field(s) on the page and the other with the field(s) not on the page. You would then associate the correct page with the correct security group (or User ID), associating the page without the fields to those that are not allowed access to them and associating the page with the fields to those that are allowed access. This approach creates additional pages for you to maintain, but allows the modification to be much clearer (since you have to assign the page to the correct group) and does not have a "behind the scenes" connotation, since the PeopleCode is hidden from the casual observer (or from the security administrator in some cases).

Warning   Remember that adding PeopleCode or creating new pages will have an impact on your application. You should carefully document these customizations and the reasons why these changes are being made so that when new security classes or new software (e.g., upgrades) are being implemented, this change is taken into consideration.

Object Security

In some cases, you may want to protect certain data even more closely than others, such as the underlying internal tables of the application. Object Security is a form of data security used to control access to this type of data—object definitions—in the PeopleTools tables. Objects include project definitions, record definitions, page and page group definitions, menu definitions, tree structures, trees, import definitions, translate tables, queries, activities, application engine programs, approval rule sets, business interlinks, business processes, components, component interfaces, file layouts, HTML, images, message channels, messages, message nodes, SQL, and style sheets. Object Security determines who can access the Trees and other tools within the application, whether a user's access will be for display-only purposes or for editing/changing purposes, and whether a user will not have access to that particular object page. Object Security also leverages field level attributes. To change a field on a record, you must have authorization to update all record definitions that contain that field.

Object security consists of two main setup features:

▶ Creation of object groups or Group IDs

▶ Linking of these object groups to permission lists

The object group represents a set of objects that are INCLUDED or EXCLUDED in the security requirements for that group of individuals. To create a new Group ID, go to PeopleTools ➤ Object Security ➤ File ➤ New Group. Select the type of object you wish to review (such as trees or pages). The Object Security page is divided into two sections. The section on the left shows the objects (such as trees or pages) that are going to be INCLUDED in the action assignment (such as Update or Display Only). The right side displays all the objects (such as Trees, Pages, and Records) that are EXCLUDED from the action assignment. The arrow keys on the page are used to move the objects from one area to the other. Once you have moved your objects into the correct areas, click File ➢ Save to save the group under a special name (such as OBJECT_EDIT). Be sure to click the OK button to save the entry; you can then see the name of the Group ID in the title bar at the bottom of the page.

You can create as many Group IDs as you feel are necessary to summarize the objects that might be available for each group of users (such as NO_ACCESS, ALL_ACCESS, BUDGET_INFO_DISPLAY, BUDGET_INFO_UPDATE, etc.). Try to limit the number of Group IDs you create but still maintain enough to ensure a secure environment. Within a production environment, the authority to change objects should be severely limited.

There are check boxes to indicate what PeopleTools permission you are granting. These PeopleTools applications include:

- ▶ Application Designer
- ▶ Data Mover
- ▶ Import Manager
- ▶ Object Security
- ▶ Query

Under the Application Designer option, you have the ability to specify specific types of objects (such as pages, records, etc.) as well.

Once you have established the Group ID(s), you can then assign that group to a permission list. The permission list assignment step of the setup process occurs when the actual action options are chosen (such as Update or Display Only). You can select multiple object groups (Group IDs) for a particular assignment. For each one, you need to determine the appropriate assignment.

To make these assignments, you must go to the File ➢ Open ➢ Permission List page where the Object Security Open dialog box appears. It is within this box that the Group IDs are assigned to the permission list. Once this assignment is saved, you can view your selections under the PeopleTools tab in Home ➢ PeopleTools ➢ Maintain Security ➢ Use ➢ Permission Lists, as shown in Figure 13.13.

Figure 13.13 **PeopleTools security**

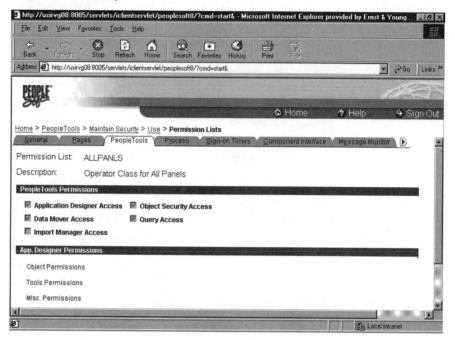

There are a few rules that must be looked at when dealing with Object Security:

1. Any user that has Tree Manager or other PeopleTools features can update any unsecured object.

2. The object must be placed into at least one group for any and all Object Security to occur. If an object is not in any group, no security is placed on the object; therefore, anyone has the ability to change it. This means that if an object was once in a group and is now out of that and all groups, it will not have any security placed on it.

Query Security

Within PeopleSoft, the Query tool can be used to access data. As part of your overall security setup, security must also be granted to use this tool. Within Query Security, access is generally given by groups of tables (or records) down to specific tables based on the job function and user requirements. The People-Soft application gives you the ability to run and/or save queries through the Query tool as well.

For each Query user, you can specify the records that user is allowed to access when building and running queries. This process is done by creating Query access groups. A Query access group is assigned within the Tree Manager and then assigned to an operator class using Query Security. This tool also controls who can use Public queries (queries that an individual user creates and makes available to the general population or "public") as well as places restrictions on joining records during a query and on using unions, subqueries, and other query features.

To set up Query Security Trees, you need to go to PeopleTools ➤ Tree Manager➤ Default ➤ Access Group ➤ *Query Tree* (enter the name of the query tree you have set up) ➤ Business Unit. To provide access to run and/or save queries, you need to go to PeopleTools ➤ Maintain Security ➤ Permission List and then enter Select a Permission List to Use for Query. You should choose the appropriate Query options you wish to give the users who are linked to this permission list. To provide access to the nodes of the Query Security Tree, you should go to the Access Groups Permission link. Choose the options of the Tree (e.g., the nodes) that you want to make accessible or inaccessible to that group. Use the Query Profile link to set up query usage options. Once that is complete, you have the Query security set up. Figures 13.14 and 13.15 show an example of setting up this query profile and assigning it to a permission list.

Figure 13.14   **Query Profile page**

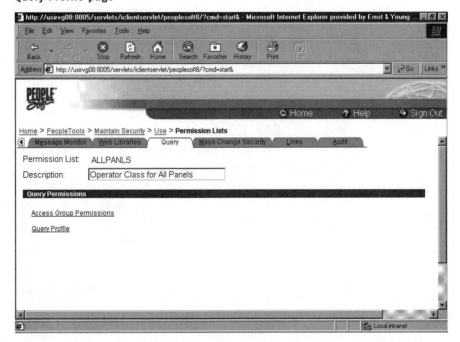

Figure 13.15 **Query Profile page**

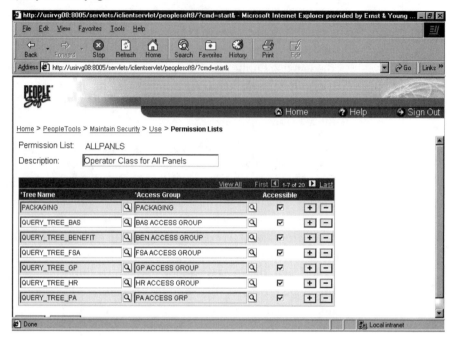

Process Groups

Within PeopleSoft, there are additional levels of security to determine who can run certain processes (such as reports, COBOL jobs, interface files, journal edits, etc.). This concept is known as process groups. Process groups provide the ability to limit access to run these processes. Each report or batch process that is run through the Process Scheduler (which is PeopleSoft's own internal batch scheduler) is assigned to a process group when it is created. Only those users linked to the permission list that provides access to these specific groups can run them, regardless of whether the user has menu access to the report or process. Menu access without process group access will allow the user to open a run control page and complete the parameters on the page, but once the "green light" button is clicked, the Process Scheduler will not access the specific job associated with that run control.

The Process Security groups are named and inserted into the permission lists through the PeopleTools ➤ Maintain Security menu. To access this feature, go to the Process tab of the permission list definition page. From here you can select the process group permissions link. This page and process is shown in Figure 13.16.

Figure 13.16   **Process groups option**

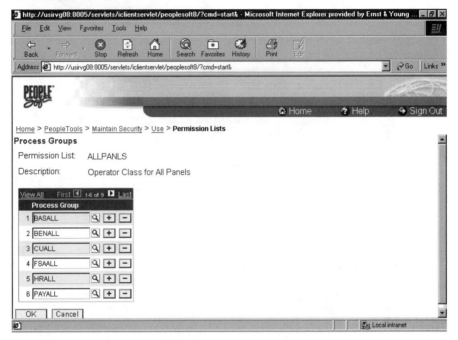

After you assign the processes to the correct permission list, you need to assign the permission list to a role and the role (if not already assigned) to the appropriate User IDs. Figure 13.17 shows the page where the process profile information is assigned to a permission list. This page contains basic information on how processes should be run for this permission list.

Once you have assigned the process groups to your permission lists, you can also set up the process profile options. Only those processes assigned to a particular permission list and granted to a particular User ID can be run by that user.

Figure 13.17 **Assigning processes to permission lists**

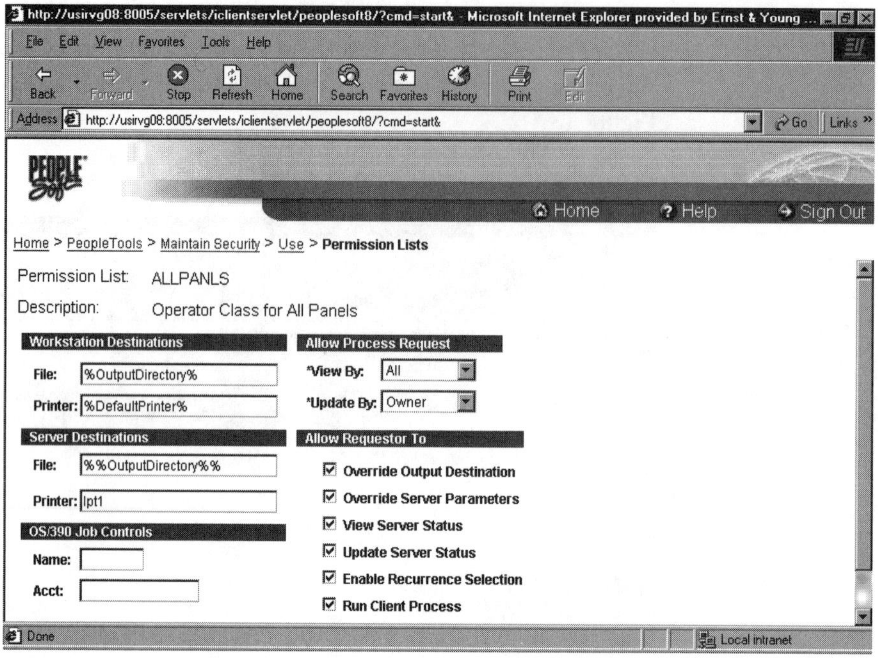

Case Study

Company NewVal was assessing their security requirements during their PeopleSoft implementation. In reviewing their strategy and approach in this area, they decided on some core tenets:

▶ All user workstations accessing PeopleSoft data would need to be secured with desktop security. Desktop security would be a key area covered in their training curriculum and all documentation. The need to control sensitive data, the importance of desktop-level security, and procedures for setting up desktop security would be communicated as essential parts of the company's security strategy. Desktop security strategy should also include looking at how data is extracted and protected when pulled from the system onto the desktop through the use of Excel spreadsheet extracts (how to put passwords on these files) as well as any reports or other information stored to an individual's desktop.

▶ For each major process (such as procure to pay, employee data and payroll process, journal entry, and financial reporting), a security class would be created for three main user types: super/power user (maintains key control tables, develops key reports/queries, and processes data), everyday user/clerk (runs queries and performs processes but does not maintain tables or create new queries), and the occasional user (puts in requisition requests, checks status, runs queries/predefined reports, etc.). The key element to note here is that, based on job function, the user groups are classified as a role, and these roles are given a set of permissions.

▶ Another classification would be created for the developers supporting these user functions (and the objects behind them) that would give them access to all areas within this major functional area along with the ability to update and change objects associated with the functions. However, the Object Security would only apply to development environments, and these developers would have view-only access to the production environment since they were not processing the data. This group would be another class of users, since their requirements are very different from the initial three user groups.

▶ Managers and supervisors of these system users would not require another user group, since they should have the same security as their super users. Row Level Security may grant them greater access to the data itself but not necessarily to the functions performed. Therefore, it would be in NewVal's best interest to have four operator classes for each major functional process defined and to leverage Row Level Security to limit the rows of data they might be accessing for each individual user.

▶ Any additional requirements would be accomplished using Row Level Security (as previously mentioned) to determine the types (or rows) of data the user would be able to access. A minimum number of classifications would be determined based on job function and access, keeping classes down to a manageable number but still fulfilling the necessary security and control requirements.

Once these key tenets had been created and agreed upon, NewVal created a security matrix outlining the requirements of each class and what their major process areas were. This matrix included the overall large process being supported (e.g., procure to pay); a list of pages, functions, queries, and processes that each of the four operator groups had access to within that major process area; and the type of access the operator groups had for each of their features (e.g., update, display, correction). If an individual needed access to multiple areas, when their User ID was created they would be associated with multiple roles and permission lists (which was permitted).

It was also determined that all users would have access to the system from 6 a.m. ET (Eastern Time) until 6 p.m. ET daily so that the other system batch processes could run at night without impacting online response time or the user daily requirements. NewVal also determined that timeout features at the user desktop should be used, and they agreed to place this at 5 minutes. Therefore, when a user did not access the system again within 5 minutes, the system would sign them off and they would have to sign back onto the system if they needed access again later. It was also determined that a user could access any information in the system based on the business unit they were assigned to; therefore, the business unit Row Level Security feature would be used. Object Security would be applied in the development and testing environments, and no objects would be changed (except by one super user classification with access by only a few database administrators) in production.

All of these requirements were clearly articulated in the security strategy documentation that they developed prior to their system testing. Any changes that were necessary or correction of errors found during system testing would be applied to ensure adequate security was in place prior to going live. A user's guide for security was also created, outlining the available security classes, their access requirements, and the procedures for giving new users access to the system. The guide would also outline requirements for changing user security as a result of job changes, transfers, terminations, etc. Each category of employee change, as well as any changes to the database and how that would affect security, would be outlined in this guide. The guide would be tested during the user acceptance testing process so that any modifications or changes could be made prior to going live and to ensure that all security requirements were met by the team. After going live, NewVal was very successful in supporting their user requirements and keeping the system secure, using evaluations derived from internal audits and user feedback.

Security Tips and Concerns

As vividly illustrated by the case study above, this chapter shows that there are several items to keep in mind when dealing with PeopleSoft security. PeopleSoft's application security prevents logon to pages and online-initiated processes if no ID exists. The technology exists to secure various resources and application objects using the security features. The User ID setup is relatively easy . . . so what are the problems to watch out for?

Setting up security requires your administrator to access many different areas within PeopleSoft, including:

- ▶ Security Administrator
- ▶ Business Rules
- ▶ Process Scheduler
- ▶ Application Designer
- ▶ Data Mover
- ▶ Tree Manager

Besides needing to monitor who is given the security administrators password and functions within the application, you need to watch out for and be concerned with a few other key areas within the security setup. These include:

- ▶ Weak password controls. Since the application does not force specific password requirements or "time to change" features, it is up to you to place these requirements on the user base. For instance, you may want your users to create new passwords on a monthly basis. You need to make this happen (or use other software to make this happen), since the system does not do this automatically for you.

- ▶ Lack of transaction audit trails without setting up the "audit trail" features manually within the application. These features must be turned on individually, record by record. If you want specific field-level auditing (rather than by record), you need to also set this up using PeopleTools features. These audit trail features also use more system processing, disk space, and capacity; therefore, the impact must be assessed and agreed upon. This flexibility to audit individual fields or records is useful but must be initially set up and maintained and a strategy developed to handle all the data collected from the auditing features.

- ▶ Correction mode is a feature that can drastically change data without leaving an audit trail, and so must be controlled. Again, the system allows you to control which classes of users have the correction feature, but unless the audit trail flags are set and used, the system does not record the corrections made to the data. You must determine the impact of allowing corrections to be made and whether you need to track these corrections using the audit features based on the risk, resources, and overhead requirements.

▶ Security reports are nonexistent, requiring you to maintain and develop them. Again, the system is flexible and easy to query or report from. However, predefined reports are limited. You must look at your requirements and strategy along with your process and determine the best way to maintain and track this information, which includes user role changes and terminations.

▶ Security logging (violations, changes) features are not provided. The PeopleSoft system does not track the number of times a user tries to sign onto your application and fails. It is up to you to determine needs in this area and whether it is best to leverage additional software to do this or leverage database features to do this (via the Access ID).

▶ In most areas, including batch process, there is a need for direct access to the database. With direct access to the database, unique ID requirements (based on User ID) must be set up and maintained. As mentioned before, it may be beneficial for your DBA to maintain a set of scripts that they can use (based on permission lists) to give the appropriate security to the user who needs direct access to the database. Also, since processes directly access the database, the processes must have a higher level of security in order to operate. This must be closely monitored and managed.

The self-service features now available within PeopleSoft 7.5 and 8 increase security risks, since more individual users are involved in the process, creating the need for additional security setup and lists. Also, data is being passed around at an even greater level (through database extracts and reports). Web-based or self-service applications also increase the risk to data integrity since, again, infrequent users are accessing and updating the system.

When dealing with items outside the PeopleSoft online application, please remember these few items:

▶ When running SQR reports, it is best to run them through a secure server rather than on an individual's workstation.

▶ You can use your PeopleSoft User ID as the authorization ID for running SQR reports, but the ID must have been granted access rights to the tables used by the report. This can be a nightmare for your DBA to set up and maintain if there are many operators and your user turnover is high.

▶ PeopleSoft delivers several views that can be used for ad hoc reporting. Users can access these by giving their User IDs the proper grant privileges. Data can only be looked at (no changes) using these views, and the main tables are not accessible. This can help limit your maintenance as well as your exposure.

▶ With any query tool, users must have the authorized levels of access to the tables to perform their queries, including any updates or deletions. Again, each User ID must be set up individually with the correct access. In most cases, the DBA maintains a set of scripts that generally can be organized by permission lists in order to make this job less arduous.

Always remember to do a complete analysis of your security requirements up front to ensure adequate security. Be sure to test each role and permission list thoroughly to ensure that the appropriate security has been provided. When any new features (pages, records, objects, etc.) are added to the database, ensure that the appropriate security has been updated. It's helpful to create a detailed checklist for development and systems administration to ensure that the proper processes are followed. If a new page is created and not put into any security class, then it will not be accessible to anyone within the application.

It is always good to create an ALLPAGES permission list that has access to the entire system; any time a new feature is added, this permission list should be the first to be updated. Also, generally it is this permission list that your security or systems administrator has access to. Once this is done, evaluate each permission list and determine whether any updates need to be made in all areas of the system including query, process, and object security.

Up Next

Once you have a handle on your security requirements and have created your security classes and User IDs, your next step is to test it all. This doesn't mean just your modifications and your new security classes; it also means your interfaces, your new processes, and all your new features. Testing is an integral part of any solid project. Not only should you test each of your classes and the security around it, you should also be testing your audit features and any documentation you have created to support your security requirements. End-to-end testing of the processes—including adding new users, terminating users, changing passwords, etc.—should all be done during your testing phase. You should also test the effectiveness of your documentation—for instance, by allowing users to contribute to any draft documentation before it is finalized.

In our next chapter, "Testing," we will look at all the types of testing that you will need to accomplish prior to going live with your new system or changed processes/functionality. We will look at the need to create a testing strategy and an approach to how your organization will support the testing effort, including time, resources, and requirements for each testing phase. We will look at the types of testing that is typically supported (or necessary) prior to going live, from unit testing, system testing, conversion testing, stress testing, integration testing through user acceptance, and go-live testing (also called readiness or parallel testing). Each of these types of testing will be defined and looked at in detail. You may call them by different names, but the fact is that they all need to be accomplished prior to a successful implementation. As we mentioned earlier, it is imperative that you not only test your system, but test your processes, procedures, and documentation that is supporting the testing. Use this process as a communication and change enablement device. Get users involved, make change happen, and support your new application—that's the name of the game.

CHAPTER 14

Testing

FEATURING:

▶ A detailed look at what testing involves and what the key components are in a successful testing effort

▶ Creating an effective testing strategy

▶ Tracking results of your testing efforts

▶ A look at each type of testing, including unit or component testing, integration and system testing, performance and stress testing, and user acceptance testing

▶ The resources you will need to support your testing efforts

▶ The environments you might need to support your testing

▶ A look at some of the testing tools that can be used to accelerate your testing

▶ Documenting results and ensuring you have a continuous testing method in place now and in the future

Testing is a key component of any successful project. Prior to going live on a new system and set of new processes, you need to develop a sound testing process to be sure your system is ready to support you. How much testing you need to do depends on several factors, including how much customization you have done to the package software; the number of interfaces, conversions, and reports you have developed; and how new and different the processes are that you are implementing. There is certainly a point of no return where you are spending valuable time, effort, and resources in testing functionality or your processes over and over again and the errors or issues found are minimal. It's always better to find any defects up front in your testing efforts than after you go live, but you can't test forever. At some point, you have to feel comfortable stepping out and into production.

Note *Testing* is the process of examining software components with the intent of verifying required functionality. It should not be viewed merely as debugging your system or as an act of quality assurance.

Testing Objectives

In general, there are three primary objectives you should follow in your testing efforts:

▶ Verify that your solution meets the needs of your business (or the business requirements).

▶ Ensure that your new system and processes are operationally reliable.

▶ Ensure the quality of your new system and processes.

To prove that your system meets the business requirements or needs of your end users, you must outline the key processes and functions your system must support for your own internal environment (not that of the general business population). To support this objective, you need to ensure that you have formally tested the functionality, operations, procedures, performance, usability, and maintainability of the application. All delivered functionality as well as modifications should be tested as part of this process. The final outcome for this objective should be satisfied during the user acceptance testing phase.

To support the second objective, that of operational reliability, you must be sure that you have spent enough effort in uncovering any potential system defects, including but not limited to locating logic errors, coding errors, technical language syntax errors, database integrity errors, and any PeopleSoft bugs related to your business functional needs. Therefore, your testing efforts should carefully consider the input data needed to test out these conditions. The first two objectives may seem in conflict (one to make the system succeed and the other to make it fail); when combined, however, they effectively ensure system success.

The final objective, that of quality, can be met by having stringent testing standards at the start of the development project (e.g., unit testing) to ensure that the development process includes accurate design specifications and coding, and that detailed process manuals are in place to support these new features. Figure 14.1 (where "FSD" refers to future-state design) depicts the escalation of costs in relation to time passed before an error is discovered. The earlier a defect is found in the life cycle of a project, the better off the team will be in relation to the cost of fixing the error. Therefore, your testing should be integrated throughout your project life cycle to maximize discovery of errors early in your cycle and minimize costs.

Figure 14.1   **Escalation of cost in relation to the time the error is discovered**

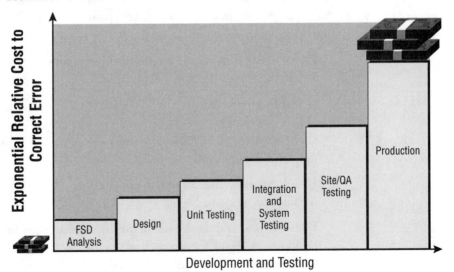

Testing Strategy

When you realize what your testing objectives should be, you need to create a strategy that supports these objectives and ensures your ultimate success. The main components that should be found in a testing strategy include:

- ▶ Testing process
- ▶ Testing design
- ▶ Testing approach

Let's look at each of these components in detail to understand what you have to put in place for a successful testing effort.

Testing Process

The *testing process* defines the different activities that you will need to complete before your software can be moved into production and support your new processes. This process defines the steps necessary to move software from the development environment through testing and ultimately into production. With PeopleSoft implementations, you typically see four types of testing that must be accomplished to move your software from development to production: unit, integration, system, and user acceptance testing. The testing process should focus on the following items:

Early error detection   As depicted in Figure 14.1, the earlier an error is found, the less costly it is to fix.

A stable environment   Who'd want to go live on an unstable platform? More often than not, you see companies that are willing to risk project success with an unstable environment—9 times out of 10, they end up failing in the process.

Quick turnaround on error correction   This should always be a goal in your testing cycle.

User review and approval prior to release into production   Some project teams think they know what the user wants, but find out too late that their design was not what was wanted at all. The earlier you get users involved in the testing process, the better.

A review and approval process to ensure quality   Most developers love to program but hate to document. You need to have a process in place that ensures that your modifications are clearly documented and that any procedures to support them are documented as well. A defined process with checkpoints to help you ensure this is essential. And for future upgrades and package support, this requirement is a must.

Since your system inputs may be combined in a virtually infinite number of ways, it is impossible to run tests that cover every possible set of conditions. Therefore, the leadership or steering committee you have in place must determine an acceptable level of risk. This determination serves as the level of risk when developing your test objectives and should be unambiguous and measurable (via logs and checklists).

Your process that is put in place to support the testing life cycle should focus on four major areas of the application development process. These areas are:

Migration control   A procedure for migrating software through development and testing and into production. This process should be clearly defined and closely followed as well as tested. The worst possible scenario is to have a system that functions well in a system test but when migrated to production falls apart due to poor migration control.

Software control   This includes the process you have for protecting and structuring the software. Failure to have the right version of software or having conflicting releases can prove costly.

Problem reporting and tracking   You must have a clear process in place for reporting and tracking any problems or issues that arise during your testing efforts. This process should track status and results as well as the problems found. We will look at this area in more detail in a future section.

TIP   Testing is specifically for discovering errors. However, it's human nature to want to make a program or process work and thus stop your testing prior to running the appropriate combinations or test cases necessary to find errors based on realistic testing goals. Therefore, clearly document expected results for a tester to verify the process and ensure that you have thought through appropriate test scenarios.

Test tracking and logging   A process to track all of your testing activities and the results of these activities should be in place. You'd hate to waste valuable time retesting a process that has already been tested or to miss an area that you thought was tested by not clearly tracking and logging your results.

Table 14.1 below outlines the major activities and the purpose of each of these activities as it relates to your testing process.

Table 14.1   **List of Activities for Testing Process**

Activity	Purpose
Plan	Define specific types of risks the testing phase will examine. Define the breadth, depth, complexity, and precision required. Define the approach needed to deliver the required level of testing. Define the resources and schedule required.
Design	Define the specific nature of each test. Define the data values to support each test. Define the environment requirements to support testing. Define organization of tests into manageable cycles.
Prepare	Configure the environment for test execution. Load and configure software. Load and validate baseline data. Train team members on procedures.
Execute	Run initial tests. Repeat tests for modified components. Repeat tests for components dependent on modified components.
Validate	Compare expected results to actual results. Document errors and problems along with potential causes.
Report	Capture problems and monitor until resolved. Document potential enhancement for later review. Measure overall performance of the testing team. Measure overall quality of initial and fixed components. Measure overall performance of the problem-resolution effort.
Resolve	Fix problems. Integrate individual fixes back into the solution.

Test Design

Once you have defined and created a detailed process for your testing to follow, you need to create a plan for making this happen. This plan should be broken into business test cases and cycles and makes up your *test design*. The test design outlines the different areas of the system that need to be tested, including:

Technical infrastructure   This testing should include a readiness checklist for all infrastructure requirements, security and audit testing, backup and recovery of your system, user account setup, hardware performance testing, version control setup, environment readiness testing, and operations and systems management procedures.

Business and technical procedures   Without clear and concise written procedures to support your system, your end users and technical support staff may not be able to effectively use your system, no matter how great it is.

Business processes   This testing should include all business processes related to your application and any extensions you might have added, as well as reporting and information needs and any data timing or "day in the life" cycle testing.

Conversions/interfaces   This testing should include inbound and outbound code testing, error logs and batch run logs testing, data retention issues, batch job scheduling (to include daily, nightly, weekly, monthly, quarterly, and annual cycles), and conversion execution and data integrity code testing.

Each of these areas should be tested following the testing process explained above and should include four types of testing: unit, integration, system, and user acceptance. All cycles should look at:

▶ Component testing, which tests changes against specifications

▶ Incremental testing, which builds on other tests and adds additional features to each test run

▶ Value stream testing, which looks at a complete business cycle or function

▶ Regression testing, which identifies which cycles need to be retested based on any modifications made after finding and fixing a defect

TIP Be sure to write test cases for invalid and unexpected input conditions, not just valid ones. It's equally important to see how a program will react to invalid or unexpected input.

The details on each type of testing and what it entails are explained below.

Test Plan

For all phases of testing, you need to create a test plan that outlines the test cases you will perform during that testing as well as the time frames and resource needs to make testing successful. The test plan should also include all assumptions, objectives, and data needs to support your objectives. You should track each test case, outcome, and sign-off in a formal log. Once you have formal sign-off that a particular phase is completed, you can move on to the next phase or step in your plan.

Unit Testing

Unit testing is the most basic level of testing. It is typically done during development for any modifications or changes to the system. You should also do a basic "readiness" testing for each module once it is configured and set up in development—this type of testing also falls under the "unit testing" category. The two major objectives of unit testing are:

▶ To verify that the application software component's code works according to its specification

▶ To validate that the program logic works the way the team configured the applications

Integration Testing

Combining modules or individually unit-tested components together into a complete unit constitutes integration testing. The major objectives of this type of testing are:

▶ To verify that the modules at each level work *together* correctly as one function

▶ To verify that the interfaces between application software components function properly

▸ To verify that the interfaces between the application and its external objects function properly

▸ To verify that the design specifications are developed correctly

Integration testing brings all of your components together and tests the points where they interact. It includes testing the functions that the system is expected to perform, the interfaces between the system's parts, and the interfaces between the system and other outside systems. Regression testing of all existing system functionality should also be included in this testing.

System Testing

Your final level of testing to ensure that the system's functionality, performance, and fit are met is covered in *system testing*. System testing demonstrates that your application meets all original objectives and requirements and that it does so within the time constraints you have defined. Various subtests may be conducted in order to thoroughly test your system; they include:

▸ Usability testing

▸ Final requirements testing

▸ Security and controls testing

▸ Recovery testing to include backup and restoration procedures

▸ Documentation and procedures testing

▸ Production-ready validation

Test cases from previous testing cycles or events can be reorganized and used during this testing phase. Additional testing cases will also be needed to ensure adequate testing of areas such as documentation, security, and procedures. Again, regression testing of all existing system functionality should take place during this testing as well.

User Acceptance Testing

This final testing phase is where you demonstrate to your end users that the system meets their original business needs and satisfies their requirements. This phase includes the necessary service-level agreements and commitments based on operational guidelines to support your end user during production. Once the users have signed off and accepted your system along with your support guidelines, you are ready to move it into production and go live.

Note   In some cases, project teams want to do a parallel test to support their testing efforts. This falls into the "user acceptance" category. A parallel test is a comparison of the old system to the new, using the same input data and being able to account for any data differences between the two systems. This can be hard and very cumbersome to accomplish, since processes, data elements, and even business rules might have changed with your new application.

Testing Approach

The *testing approach* identifies who will be doing the testing (i.e., the roles and responsibilities of the testing team members) along with the procedures to be followed. Testing procedures should outline the tasks for completion and any deliverables that are required to help complete that task. Any exceptions in the testing process should also be noted in your testing procedures, along with expectations of when you will be moving from one test to another and the timing for this.

Your project team should follow a process that looks at investigating, refining, and planning so that they understand all needs for testing and provide detailed plans for each test to include creation of specific test cases and expected results. In Table 14.2, you can see a list of the activities that should be performed during testing.

Table 14.2   **Testing Activities**

Activity	Description
Investigation	
Identify the timeline leading up to implementation.	Gather any information about the timeline for the application development or application implementation effort.
Identify items to be tested.	Review with each group any applications planned for implementation. Define the Cases, Conditions, Cycles, and Subcycles that will provide structure to the area being tested.
Identify those people involved in the project leading up to implementation and those involved after implementation.	Identify the people working on the testing. Also identify those people who will be the users or support people of the application after implementation.

Table 14.2 **Testing Activities *(Continued)***

Activity	Description
Build Design/Case/Scripts	
Build a test design document describing the approach to be used for testing.	Use the information gathered above to build a draft test design. Clarify what will be done during each testing activity.
Publish a draft for review.	Publish a draft for review and make any adjustments to the documentation needed to meet the testing requirements described by the project team. Review and approve test cases design before execution.
Conduct Testing	
Execute business test cases.	Throughout the testing life cycle there are different types of test cases. Unit testing has more detailed module-level testing and site/QA testing offers a higher level proof that the application and users can meet the business objectives after implementation.
Report problems.	As scripts are executed, any problems are logged and reviewed. Problems are submitted to the development team manager/leader for correction. The problem-reporting and fix cycle involves communication between IT and the tester. The issues log is used to document the state of a problem.
Review and approve test completion.	Review and approval documentation and procedures are in place that will allow a test completed without errors to be approved and the application piece(s) that were tested to be moved to the next event of testing or to production.

Warning You should never assume that no errors will be found during your testing process. The primary goal of testing is to find errors, and demonstrating that the program functions as it should is critical but secondary to your effort. See Glenford J. Myers, *The Art of Software Testing* (John Wiley & Sons, 1979).

Testing Resources

Generally, there are four levels of resource needs that are involved in your testing process. They include:

- ► Management
- ► Functional team experts
- ► Technical support
- ► End users

In Table 14.3, you can see a list of the roles, responsibilities, and potential candidates that you might need to support your testing efforts. Each of these roles is critical to the success of your testing process. You should clearly define for each type of test and test scenario who is responsible for what activities. Also, resource commitments outside of the project team—such as with your technical infrastructure support group as well as your end users—should be clearly outlined and provided to these groups well ahead of time so there are no surprises in the end. The success of your testing efforts involves the integration of all these key resources. Without them all, your testing can fail.

Table 14.3   **Testing Roles and Responsibilities**

Phase Roles	Responsibilities	Potential Candidates
Test Director	Responsible for the overall success of a testing phase Ensures that business objectives are met by the testing phase Ensures that the evidence of results is sufficient to gain approval	Project management
Test Coordinator	Coordinates all of the tasks involved in execute, validate, report, and resolve activities Provides direction to the individuals and team involved in these activities Works with BPI (Business Process Improvement) team to schedule use of shared facilities and technical environments Complies with standards and procedures defined by the BPI	Team leads

Table 14.3 **Testing Roles and Responsibilities *(Continued)***

Phase Roles	Responsibilities	Potential Candidates
Test Designer	Plans overall structure of test cycles Creates test design, including test conditions and scripts, and identifies data for testing	Functional team Technical team
Tester	Completes test execution Compares actual results to expected results Identifies issues and problems	Functional team Technical team End users
Correction Team	Creates, revises, and deletes components to fix problems Conducts repeat unit and integration tests for changed components Conducts repeat unit and integration tests for components that are dependent on changed components Documents changes and implications	Functional team Technical team

Your testing team, led by your test coordinator and director, should clearly communicate and coordinate all activities around your testing efforts. The set of procedures developed (as explained in the next section) will be monitored, and a plan to coordinate these activities must be defined.

Testing Procedures

You should create a step-by-step guide that outlines all the components of your testing effort and brings them together into one central repository or *testing procedure.* Each testing procedure should:

▶ Define a particular aspect of the overall testing effort. The scope of the procedure will depend on the needs of the testing effort, resources, and requirements.

▶ Have a clear statement of purpose that will reference any needed test item documentation or test case.

▶ Identify any special requirements that are necessary for execution of this procedure, such as prerequisites, special skills, or special environmental needs.

▶ Contain a detailed explanation of the procedure steps, including those to log, set up, start, conduct, measure, and conclude. Expected results should also be included.

Control procedures should also be defined and cover such areas as:

▶ Data needs (or data conversion)

▶ PeopleSoft system configuration

▶ Extensions or bolt-ons, including interfaces and customizations

▶ Any verification tools

▶ Hardware requirements

Test Cases

Test cases should be developed to support each procedure based on the type of testing conducted and the function being tested.

A test case should contain details on how you will test the process or feature, the data requirements, and the expected results. In many cases, if you use an implementation partner or consulting support, there are test cases from other projects that can be leveraged to create your own unique set. You need to ensure that your test cases cover all the necessary functions or features included in your testing process, as well as involve both positive and negative results. Testing that a feature or function finds an error or problem is just as important as finding out whether the feature supports your requirement. You should ensure that you have tested all your processes and requirements at least once by the end of your testing period. It is difficult to test every combination of data required, but testing the primary functionality and processes is a must.

Table 14.4 gives you an example of a test case created for an accounts receivable process.

Table 14.4 **Test Case (Script) Example**

Script AR-02 External Error Correction – The system does extensive editing and validation during pending item entry for online groups. Test to ensure that the external groups are edited by the Receivable Update program.

Step	Step Description	Test Data	Expected Results	Actual Results	Comments	In Scope?
1	From the External Error Correction page, select the group that was entered in error.		The group in error appears in the drop-down list.		A group from billing was manipulated to force an error. An invalid customer ID was entered. The system accurately reflected this error with a flag of ED1. Once a valid customer ID was entered, the group posted successfully.	Yes
2	From the External Group Action page, delete the group entered in error.		The system deletes the group.			Yes
3	Resubmit the group with correct information.		The group loads into AR successfully.			Yes

More detailed test work plans should be created as part of each testing cycle and phase, and should outline the sequence of the tests as well as expected time to complete. An overall testing sequence and work plan should be included as a part of the testing strategy document as well.

Tracking Results

All test cases should be tracked in a standard test log. Any defects found should be tracked and retested. An example of a test log can be found in Table 14.5. Any defects are assigned a tracking number, and information is collected on that defect.

Table 14.5 **Test Log**

Script ID	Description	Completed by	Date Completed	Pass/Fail	Comments
AM001	Define New Asset Management Business Unit, and Define Asset Book for the Business Unit				
AM002	Define New Location				
AM003	Create a New Asset Category				
AM004	Define Accounting Entry Templates for the New Category				
AM005	Set Up Employee Personal Data				
AM006	Define a New Asset Profile				
AM007	Set Up a New C.A.P.				
AM008	Set Up a New Asset Using ExpressAdd				

Defects should also be tracked in a log and retested once resolved. An example of a problem log can be found in Table 14.6. Again, this log tracks the problem, outcome, assignment, and follow-up results for any defects found.

Table 14.6 **Example of Problem Log**

Problem Number	Retest Counter	Type of Problem	Description	Cycle	Tester	Severity	Date	Status
0001	1	Environment	Appl Server	1.1	Jane Smith	High	2/1/00	Open
0002	1	Inactivate Vendor	Couldn't Inactivate	4.3	Jane Smith	High	3/1/00	Closed
0003	2	Add Customer Address	Couldn't Add Address	4.3	Dan Smith	High	3/4/00	Open

Generally, an overall test report is completed on a regular interval (such as weekly) that outlines the progress made and such statistics as total number of test cases in cycle, number complete (percentage complete), number of defects found, and number of defects resolved. The report should include projections on when this cycle of testing will be complete and comments on overall progress, along with listing any major issues encountered.

Testing Tools

Many times in the testing process, there is a need to simulate results or create a volume of transactions to support a particular test case. With the help of appropriate testing tools, you can target performance issues and volume/stress issues prior to going into production.

Note   Studies show that it is at least 10 times more costly to correct an error after coding than before coding, and 100 times more costly to correct a production error. See William E. Perry, *Effective Methods for Software Testing*, 2nd ed. (John Wiley & Sons, 2000).

A comprehensive stress test can proactively diagnose and eliminate performance problems ahead of time. To adequately support this type of test and ensure you are comprehensively testing the software, it can be very beneficial to use testing tools that are currently available.

Two leading software packages—one of which is included with PeopleSoft—are discussed to provide you with insight into the tools and how they can help your testing efforts. We will look at how these tools provide test management, integration, functionality, and stress-testing capabilities. These automated tools can reduce the time to test and retest the system as well as provide enough "stress" on your system to adequately test performance without using an army of resources. Some things to keep in mind when selecting a testing tool are that it should be easy to use, be easy to support and maintain, and aid in your testing efforts. It should also support multiple platforms (since most companies have systems on all types of hardware from the mainframe down to the Web). This feature helps support your integration-testing efforts as well as the testing of the application itself. Many times you might not have any problems with the application itself, but the integration points become a big issue. Most testing tools should have the capabilities to help perform:

▶ Regression testing

▶ Functional and integration testing

▶ Load/volume stress testing

The types of features these tools might include are:

Test management   This capability or tool would include a central repository for test cases, scripts, and results. Some also include the defect-tracking capability as well as provide standardization in test development, execution, and results recording. This feature can provide requirements traceability, simplify status reporting, and may be able to integrate with capture/replay tools. This feature is most useful during system testing.

Defect tracking   This capability provides a central repository for tracking defects and resolutions for these defects. It helps you avoid duplication of effort and should include an automated notification feature (for instance, sending an e-mail message once a defect is logged and assigned to the person who should fix the defect). Most of these tools provide powerful reporting capabilities.

Capture/replay   This function provides the capability to capture user interactions with the application, which can then be played back at a later time. This is particularly helpful for regression testing or when you have repetitive tasks you want to perform (such as to simulate many users on your system). The tool creates automated scripts that actually generate code and can read data from files to help with data entry or simulation of multiple tasks. Some drawbacks to these tools include inability of most end users to understand how to use them (in most cases, a technically skilled person must create the scripts) and difficulty implementing this function in a changing environment (since most of these packages are based on screens or pages remaining the same as they were when the script was created).

Performance   This tool provides the capability to monitor response times of the application based on a specific action by a specific user. This feature should not be confused with volume or stress testing tools, but should be used to track a particular performance issue with a particular individual or feature.

Volume/stress   These tools are also known as load testing tools; they monitor response time of the application during a large transaction volume test. They are used to simulate an action by multiple users (e.g., show what happens when 300 users simultaneously input a vendor) and can simulate thousands of concurrent users. Generally, this tool can be used in conjunction with the capture/replay tools mentioned above.

Memory leak detection   When an application allocates memory to a task but does not release that memory on completion of the task, this is a *memory leak*. These tools detect such a situation. Memory leaks are extremely difficult to diagnose and locate. Generally, these tools are very easy to use—just guide the tool toward your executable and it automatically locates your memory leak errors. It is available for both Unix and Windows NT environments, but only for certain development languages. This tool is generally most useful during unit or string testing.

Code coverage   This tool can monitor which pieces of code are executed during a particular test. Most code coverage tools provide detailed reports to include the total number of calls an application made, functions missed or not exercised during the test, functions that were used, percentage of functions hit, lines of code not used, lines of code hit or used, and percentage of lines processed. In general, you should expect that your hit rate will decrease during your testing efforts.

You may already have a number of these types of tools available within your organization. You should consult with your Information Technology (IT) department to determine which, if any, are available and could be used to help with your testing efforts. If you decide you need to purchase one of these tools (or more), you should coordinate with your IT group to ensure maximum leverage across your organization, since most of these tools can be used on other development/system projects, not just your PeopleSoft application.

Figure 14.2 shows the breakdown of market share by the leading automated testing tools on the market today. Two vendors, Rational (who has SQA) and Mercury Interactive, are heavily used by PeopleSoft (as well as other ERP) implementations. These two vendors and their respective suites of products will be discussed in more detail below. We will look at these products in conjunction with their capabilities in the following areas:

▶ Test management

▶ Functional/integration testing

▶ Load/volume stress testing

▶ Web testing functionality

Other areas of importance to consider are the product support, company profile, and client base.

Figure 14.2   **Testing tool: market share breakdown**

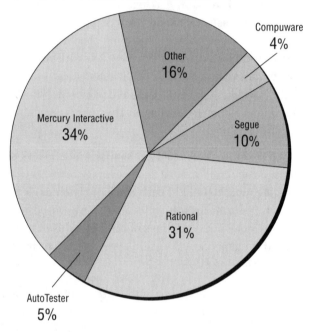

Source: Giga Information Group

Mercury Interactive (www.merc-int.com) provides products to test custom, packaged, and Internet applications. They are a leader in the market in terms of overall revenues ($110 million for 1998) and they have a mature tool suite. This suite of tools includes:

TestDirector   TestDirector provides test planning, execution, and defect-tracking functionality all in one tool. It can organize tests in hierarchical folders to help you plan and track them. The tool can track both manual and automated tests. It allows user-defined fields to be added, and it can be used with a variety of database management systems (Oracle, Sybase, MS SQL Server, MS Access). TestDirector integrates with Mercury's capture/replay tool (WinRunner) and volume/stress tool (LoadRunner). It provides a good set of standardized reports but poor custom reports features. This is a Windows-based tool.

WinRunner   This is Mercury's capture/replay tool for Windows applications, Web applications, and applications accessed through a terminal emulation (e.g., 3270, 5250). It is context sensitive when recording (i.e., objects can move and the tool can still find them—which is a plus!). The tool uses a proprietary scripting language and integrates well with ERP systems such as PeopleSoft. As mentioned above, it integrates with TestDirector as well as the volume/stress tool (LoadRunner). It has many advanced features, such as reading data from a file and excluding regions on a screen.

Xrunner   This is Mercury's capture/replay tool for Unix applications. It is the same basic tool as WinRunner but for a Unix environment only. It integrates with LoadRunner but not TestDirector.

LoadRunner   This tool is a volume/stress testing tool for both Windows and Unix environments. It integrates with WinRunner, TestDirector, and Xrunner (as previously mentioned). This tool can simulate thousands of users and can create scenarios that benchmark performance of different vendors' components, such as servers, databases, and network components. It provides detailed reports that pinpoint locations of system bottlenecks.

Another testing suite of products used on many PeopleSoft implementations is the one supported by Rational Software (`www.rational.com`). Initially, People-Soft used Rational's SQA Robot functional and regression testing tools internally to test their software. Then the two companies formed a deal to bundle a copy of Robot with each of their sales for customers to use in validating the package installation and when customizing its functionality. Recently, Rational developed "Test Foundations," a bundling of its testing tools (including Manager, Robot, and LoadTest) with a library of PeopleSoft-specific test scripts, best practices, and methodology for testing the package.

Rational is a full life cycle tool vendor that supports requirements management, visual modeling, testing, and configuration and change control. They have acquired various vendor products over the years such as SQA, Pure Atria, and Performance Awareness. SQA was the product that has been integrated with PeopleSoft, and their suite of tools includes:

SQA Manager   A test management and defect-tracking tool.

SQA Robot   A capture/replay tool. The scripts created by this product are portable between different Windows versions.

SQA LoadTest   The volume/stress testing tool. LoadTest does not provide support for simulating virtual terminals—a feature necessary for testing large-scale client-server applications (and where LoadRunner has an advantage).

SQA products are limited to Windows and Web testing and can be integrated with Requisite Pro for requirements management that can provide an advantage over their competitors. The suite can be run from within a browser and provides a Web-based component to input defects (which can be great if you have remote sites testing). It provides a choice of two database management systems, Sybase SQL Anywhere and MS Access.

Other tools offered by Rational include:

Performance Studio   This is a performance and volume/stress testing tool that can be used for ERP, client-server, and Web-based applications and offers stress/volume testing with virtual users (which is an advantage over SQA LoadTest). The master user interface for this product runs on Windows NT and not Unix, but Unix machines can be used as playback agents. It uses an MS Access database only.

Rational Visual Test   This tool provides capture/replay for Windows and Web applications (and includes basic test management features). It is tightly integrated with Microsoft Visual Studio 6. Limited support is provided for capturing and verifying objects.

Developer Tools   These are designed to be used by developers and testers during daily unit tests of custom code development.

Pure Coverage/Visual Pure Coverage   Pure Coverage supports C and C++ coding on Sun, HP, and SGI platforms, while Visual Pure supports Visual Basic, Visual C++, and Java code on a Windows NT 4.0 or higher platform. The tools will automatically pinpoint untested code, improve application quality, and help ensure that all code has been executed and, therefore, tested. It provides tight integration with developer productivity tools such as debuggers, run-time error checking, and defect tracking.

Purify/Purify NT   Supports C and C++, with automatic code checking to catch errors early in the development cycle.

Quantify/Visual Quantify   Similar to Pure Coverage/Visual Pure Coverage, these tools support counting of instructions and performance data on executables.

Value delivered by using automated testing tools can come in many forms—for instance, enforcing standardized processes, having a central repository for test cases and data, providing faster and more accurate reporting, reducing time spent on mundane manual test activities, eliminating human inconsistencies in test execution, reducing time spent on diagnosing defects, and reducing the number of human and hardware resources need to perform load testing. For ERP system implementations, performance and load testing can be a key concern, especially for high transactional volumes or users in remote locations. Also, for regression testing and moving code between environments, automating test scripts can be a real benefit. You need to assess your situation and determine whether these tools are beneficial and worth the costs. It's worth your while to ensure that you are leveraging all the tools you might have available via your technical support organization, regardless of whether you decide to purchase one of these tools for your implementation. Most of these tools can be purchased anywhere from a few thousand dollars up to several hundred thousand depending on the number of licenses and the scope of products purchased. Figure 14.3 depicts the trend for testing tools purchased.

Figure 14.3 **Trend for purchases of testing tools**

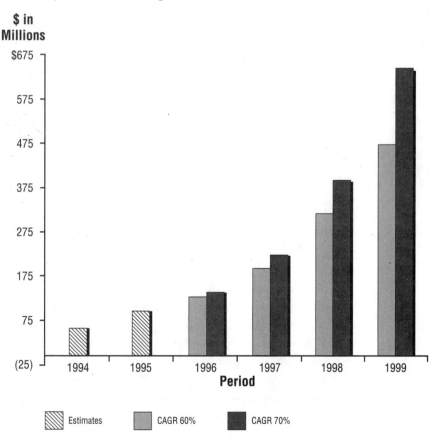

Note: Includes GUI testers, load testers, and test management products only.

Documenting Results and Continuous Testing

As mentioned in earlier sections, it is very important to document your testing results and create an effective reporting mechanism to track your progress. It is even more important to ensure that all of your documents are kept up to date based on retesting problems (regression testing) and making any needed system changes. Your internal audit group, we're sure, would be very interested in what you tested, how you tested it, and what your end results were. Also, should any problems arise during implementation, lessons learned and errors found during testing that relate to that error might shed light on your production issue. When you are in production you want to rapidly respond to any system problems, and the easier it is for you to find this information, the better.

In addition to supporting your initial rollout of your system, saving test cases and data used along with expected results can help you in the future when you need to retest your application due to upgrades, user improvements, or other changes. By reusing your test information, you save yourself and your team time and money.

Finally, since there are always fixes, changes to be made, or future enhancements to your system, you should always ensure that you have a defined test process for moving these changes after go-live from development into production and understand what testing needs to be performed in which environments before making the change to your production system. You don't want to ruin a perfectly good system after you go live by moving untested changes into production. You also don't want to over-test these changes prior to the move into production. Resources might not be as available to test after you go live, but you need to ensure that a smooth process is in place to support testing for any of these changes that need to be made after your system is in production. You also want to ensure that you understand what additional environments you must have in place to support testing after you go live.

Once you have clearly documented this process and have let your support staff know what it is, be sure you enforce it as a part of your change control and software maintenance process. Remember, even new releases of software must be tested prior to going into production because they could have an impact on your system environment. Also, ensure that you have a sound disaster recovery plan (as discussed in Chapter 6, "Surveying the Infrastructure") that is tested and supported for your production environment, and include this review as a part of your testing efforts.

Up Next

Once all test cycles and phases have been completed and meet your outlined objectives, and once you have a defined process for making any additional changes or modification in the future, you are ready to move your system into production and go live. Chapter 15 will cover the key elements you should have in place to help make your rollout or implementation a success. How you roll out your processes or applications and what support you need in place to be successful are all covered in Chapter 15. The key to being successful is being prepared, and this next chapter helps you ensure that you are all checked out and ready to go!

Go Live—Keys to a Successful Rollout

F E A T U R I N G :

▶ A look at the various cutover planning models you might consider when going live

▶ The cutover plan—what it is, and why you should have one

▶ Setting adequate user expectations for your implementation

▶ How to establish your operational processes and ensure that you are ready to go live

▶ A look at how training can help you have a more successful rollout

▶ Post-implementation support planning and its impact on your rollout

The primary key to any successful implementation rollout is your users. If your users feel that the rollout wasn't successful, then overcoming the negative perception and ensuring your project's survival will be an uphill battle. Therefore the scope of the implementation plan needs to consider the number of users, their ability to accept the change in front of them, and the amount of change that will be imposed on them. This chapter will help you choose the right model for rolling out your solution, based on your analysis of the user community and their ability to support and handle the change they are about to undertake. We'll also look at some key areas for you to concentrate on to help you be successful in your go-live activities, including cutover planning, operational support processes, training, and post-implementation support.

Cutover Planning Models

In addition to the implementation strategies discussed earlier in Chapter 9, "Preparing Your Organization for Implementation" (i.e., big bang or phased [vertical, horizontal, or hybrid]), a cutover plan, or strategy, also needs to be developed. (*Cutover* refers to moving from your old system and processes to your new system.) The cutover plan should lay out in detail how the old system and processes will be shut down and the new system brought on line. When you select your organization-specific cutover method (i.e., the exact way in which you'll retire your old system and bring up the new one), you must look at your defined business areas and business processes while considering the various demographic factors that might play into your rollout schedule. The most appropriate method will be determined by reviewing these factors and your implementation objectives. Following is a discussion of some common cutover approaches or methods—parallel, direct, phased, and pilot—and their significance regarding your specific cutover plan.

Parallel Approach

The *parallel approach* is used when the new system and the old system are used simultaneously (i.e., in parallel) for a certain period of time until the new system has proven it can support your operations reliably and correctly. Although this method is very costly, it can be the safest to use when it's critical that you have no interruptions in your operations during cutover. Here are some factors to consider with this approach:

▶ Your staff will expend extra time and effort to support both systems and processes at the same time. Will this additional cost and stress on your staff be worth the effort?

▶ When the processes of your old and new systems are very different (such as in a complete or large-scale transformation), you may not be able to adequately "parallel" your processes and reconcile any differences within your time frame.

▶ How long should you parallel the processes (e.g., through the first cycle, through the first monthly close, through the first quarterly close, etc.)? You might not necessarily be able to parallel all processes within the time frame allotted for cutover, and thus you may still have operational risks down the road.

Remember that while a parallel approach can give you some piece of mind, having a backdrop that you can fall back on may actually cause your change not to take place, or the transformation may not be as rapid as you had hoped. In addition, you might alienate your users by working them too hard, and then they may blame your implementation team or system rather than support the new processes.

Direct Approach

With a *direct approach,* you cleanly and succinctly cut over from your old to your new system, all at the same time. In some circumstances, there are no alternatives to this method. Because your new system and processes are so different from your old ones, you might want to start processing on your new system all at one time during a period break, such as at the start of a new year, new period, or new quarter.

N o t e   For example, when an airline changes its reservation system from a batch system to an online system, creating a parallel environment is not possible. Therefore, a direct cutover approach might be the company's only option.

There are various reasons that many organizations decide to use the direct cutover approach:

▶ They want a "clean cut" from their old system and processes to their new system and processes, thereby forcing and encouraging their users to accept the new way of doing things.

▶ They will be better able to reconcile and track their new processes, since they won't have to convert back and forth between the old and new ways of doing things. Also, reporting and processing for a period will be either all under the old system (before the cutover) or all under the new system (after the cutover), so the organization will be able to more easily compare and track any discrepancies.

▶ It can be less costly (since the organization isn't extending its project team and support organization over a longer period of time).

The direct cutover approach is definitely more risky and should not be used in a very large transformation effort when extensive testing hasn't been completed. Otherwise, you'll spend too much time keeping your head above water, trying to stabilize the system, and, in the process, will alienate your user base.

Remember that if you do select the direct approach, you should have a well-thought-out, detailed cutover plan (as we will discuss later in this chapter), an energized support organization in place, and user support throughout the organization to help you through such a major changeover. Many companies are forced to make this leap into their new system and processes because of drastic changes in their processes, data, or organization, or problems with technology (such as the need to support the changeover to the year 2000, which we just went through). This approach can be highly effective with the right team, right attitude, and right support.

Phased Approach

Cutting over from the old system to the new system in phases, one subsystem or process at a time, is called a *phased approach*. The strategy behind this type of cutover is to stop the old subsystem at a certain time and start the corresponding new subsystem, function, or process for the entire organization. This method reduces risks by isolating problems to a single subsystem or process and allows system support of those systems to be of higher priority than support of general production issues.

With the phased approach, additional resources are spent in designing, constructing, implementing, and removing interim interfaces between the parts of the new application as they are implemented and the parts of the current application that remain. This approach may even involve repeating the entire development and implementation for each subset. Although phased implementation requires more time and resources than implementing the entire system at once, it's usually easier to manage, and your support organizations are better able to adapt to the change since it's being made in smaller increments.

Pilot Approach

Another method of cutting over all at one time from the old system to the new one, yet doing so for a smaller business unit or department, is through a *pilot cutover*. This method incorporates the benefits of a direct cutover, yet manages your risk and overall change issues because your implementation is limited to a "pilot," or select, group. This method is generally used in organizations that are decentralized, such as banks and restaurants; one unit can cut over without affecting the overall current systems it supports.

The strategy for this approach should include a schedule for completion of cutover at each site selected and continuation of the rollout or cutover in the remaining organizational units. Again, the risk is reduced because the possibility of failure is limited to one smaller organization. Problems can be fixed fairly rapidly and the experience of your rollout team increases as you roll out to each site, contributing to the success of your implementation. Also, by framing your initial rollout as a pilot, the expectations are not as high as they are for your final rollout.

Determining Your Cutover Approach

Remember that the cutover methods mentioned above are not mutually exclusive (and thus are similar to your implementation plans), and an implementation strategy can be made up of any combination of these methods. Consider these three underlying factors when determining the strategy that is right for your implementation:

▶ System size

▶ Timing

▶ Target organization size

In general, if you have a large system that's being rolled out to a large target audience, you should consider a phased or pilot cutover approach, since the risk could be large and the changes involved for a large end-user population could be significant. If you have a smaller system size, a smaller target group, and favorable timing, then the direct cutover approach may be your best bet. Be sure to carefully analyze the capabilities of your support organization and your user population, and how drastic a change this will be for them, to help you determine your best approach. Also, in making your decision, consider any major business issues or technology constraints.

The Cutover Plan

Once you have determined which cutover approach is best for your organization, it's time to develop a detailed, time-sensitive cutover plan or checklist. The cutover process is a very time-sensitive event, when your legacy system and processes must be retired and new ones put in place. You need to consider the timing of data conversions, installations of new system software and hardware, interfaces, batch processes, reports, schedules, and more. With all this to keep track of, a detailed plan is a must. No matter which cutover method is used, a detailed cutover or go-live schedule must be created. Table 15.1 shows a sample template of a cutover task list or plan, which was used for tracking all the details during a cutover process.

This cutover schedule should include every task necessary to shut down the old system and bring up the new one (including any changes to the processes and people involved). In our implementations of ERP systems, we call this the "flip the switch" phase—when you put all your new processes and procedures in place instantaneously. In reality, though, your actual cutover plan should span several days and may even span several months. This is the one time during your overall project when tasks should be tracked down to the minute.

Table 15.1 **Sample Template of Cutover Checklist**

Step No.	Parent Step	Task	Who	Criticality	Duration	Max. Time from Start	Action on Error
010	–	**Configuration checks:** Check that required posting periods are open, check parameter table, check batch jobs (reconciliation report suite etc.), check printers, check that all unauthorized user IDs are locked using FSP mass lock/unlock utility, etc.	Juan Cortiz, Mike Johnson, Emily Wong	**Go/No Go:** Inability to print would be fatal; hard copy is essential.	1–2 hrs.	2 hrs.	Fix configuration and batch setup errors directly. Get basis support to fix printer errors.
020	010	**Carry out internal reconciliation before posting begins:** Run Fin technical reconciliation report XXX2000 (Fin summary/item DB reconciliation, including subledgers), Fin reconciliation report XXX500, and proposed Fin reconciliation report. Purpose: Check that PS DBs are consistent.	Lucy Jones, Jack Gomez, Liz Moriarty, with assistance in checking from Finance Dept.	**Go/No Go:** If internal PS differences cannot be fixed, cutover must be aborted.	1–2 hrs.	4 hrs.	Explain and fix any errors.
025	020	**Unix-level backup**	Ken Moore	No problems anticipated.	10 mins. system downtime	4 hrs.	N/A
030	025	**Post unreconciled transactions from DBS:** Run in files from DBS using posting interface program XXX1000.	Charlie Chu, John Lane, Janice Carter	**Go/No Go:** If volume of errors is too high to be fixed, cutover must be aborted.	5–8 hrs. assuming 60,000 items and T11 throughput of 200 items/min. (P11 is one order of magnitude faster), plus allowance for error correction.	12 hrs.	If low level of errors, either post to suspense account or reject each failed document for correction and re-input.

You should have several major objectives for your cutover:

▶ Migrate your PeopleSoft configuration, interfaces, and custom code to your production environment.

▶ Convert your production (or legacy data) from your staging, legacy, or testing area into your new PeopleSoft system (in its appropriate timing and sequence).

▶ Record your closing operations or period in your old system, accounting for any outstanding items or balances.

▶ Validate the converted data in your PeopleSoft system, confirming that it is accurate and was converted in a timely manner (from the legacy system).

▶ Execute contingencies when necessary until all identified problems or issues are solved or rectified.

▶ Have your cutover approved by a group of end users.

▶ Initiate operations on your new system in as smooth a manner as possible.

▶ Complete your cutover with the minimal level of disturbance to your business operations.

By keeping these objectives in mind, you should have a much smoother implementation.

Also, to keep everything on track during your cutover period, you should consider holding regular status meetings to touch base with all parties involved in the plan, since they can be quite numerous and spread throughout your organization. These meetings should occur at least daily—and, in some cases, more than once a day—and after major "events." Be sure to distribute details about when these meetings or calls need to take place so that everyone will be aware and participate. By getting everyone together, any changes, issues, or problems can be discussed as well as updated in the plan. Contingencies may need to be put in place and agreed upon during these meetings. These sessions are crucial to the success of your cutover. All issues or problems should be tracked, and any follow-up actions or communications should be considered.

Setting Expectations for Implementation

With any ERP implementation, the new system and its business processes will need to be rolled out in a very deliberate and organized manner. A smooth transition from your old business processes to the new business processes will require a well-organized communications plan. Critical in executing this communications plan is the need to set the expectations of the executive sponsors, project team members, production support staff, trainers, and end users.

Whenever a new system is installed, expectations and interpretations of the change on the affected personnel must be considered. With the introduction of a system change, reactions may include anxiety, stress, instability, and feelings of inadequacy. These reactions result from a sense of loss of control, which can be minimized by managing expectations of the new system and processes prior to their introduction.

Although each organization can face unique challenges during the cutover, all organizations need to be aware of several critical challenges faced by most implementations and to plan for them. Setting the appropriate expectations up front can only help pave the way for a successful project implementation.

Problems Will Occur

Regardless of how well you plan and prepare your staff prior to the rollout, and how thoroughly you test your new system and processes, chances are good that you'll still encounter a few problems during your implementation. Project teams that have no problems during the initial cutover activities might wonder when the next shoe will drop and will thus panic for no good reason when a small issue is presented to them. Transaction-based systems such as People-Soft contain data that is dynamic. Users will find new and unique ways of entering data, no matter how much training you provide. Also, a very complex layer of diverse software and hardware is underneath the covers, and many organizations aren't as familiar with this layer as they are with their old system and processes.

By preparing your people for these unexpected challenges, by putting a process in place to track the challenges, and by having a calm support staff who will assure your users that all is well, you'll be in a much better position for a successful implementation. Also, if you effectively communicate the types of actions that have been taken to prevent problems, as well as the processes that have been established for solving any problems that do arise, your users will be more confident in you, the system, and themselves as you move forward into production.

The 80/20 Rule

Most organizations utilize the *80/20 rule* when implementing package solutions—that is, they want to ensure that the package meets 80% of their needs, allowing for changes for the remaining, less critical 20%. Due to constraints on time and resources, usually not every user requirement is met. However, after decisions are made and changes are agreed upon by the project team, sponsors, and user representatives, all users need to be made aware of any of these changed or unmet requirements.

During an ERP implementation such as PeopleSoft, an area where the package generally doesn't meet all the users' needs is reporting. Many users, while carrying out their responsibilities, have grown accustomed to the reports provided by the old system, and they didn't have the tools or ability to access the information they needed without help from their technical support staff. With the new PeopleSoft system, users will now have access for updating tables and querying for data or other necessary information, and thus they will need a much smaller set of standard reports than in the past. The package (as delivered) also provides a set of standardized reports, which might look quite different from those the user is familiar with (yet contain the same type of data to meet the business requirement). Upon implementation, some of these reports may have been consolidated, deferred to another wave of implementation (or phase), replaced by query capabilities or access to direct table information, or labeled as noncritical to the mission. Therefore the users need to be made aware of these changes; they need to know which reports will be made available and when, and what alternatives they will have for obtaining the data they wish to continue receiving.

By preparing the users for these changes, not "hiding" the changes, looking at the changes from the users' perspective, and putting together a well-thought-out change management plan to address these changes or concerns, you'll have a much greater chance of success. Chapter 21, "Analyzing Your Support

Network," covers change management techniques in much greater detail; it provides some insights into ensuring that you have the right change management approach in place to support your organization.

User Management

As stated earlier in this chapter, the users' perception of the rollout is critical to the success of your implementation. If the users are prepared for and understand, or are aware of, the changes (as opposed to hidden changes), and if the users understand that the first close cycle may be difficult and involve extra hours of work, they will have a better perspective and attitude about the implementation. As the saying goes, "Prepare your users for the worst (or liverwurst), and they will be quite happy with a few bumps in the road (or pate)." Therefore, user management is a crucial part of your cutover planning and communications. Leverage your change agent network (as described in detail in Chapter 21), create a sound communications plan, and don't hide any of your blemishes.

Users need to receive the proper training and have an adequate support structure in place for the smooth transition from the old system and processes to the new ones. However, during the cutover, a large group will be viewing the new system and processes in an operational sense for the very first time. Be sure to create a quick network to turn around information and get it into the hands of your user base. Any changes to your plan or to the cutover checklist should be disseminated quickly and not hidden. Your project leaders should reiterate reasons that decisions were made and show support of the new system and processes and confidence in the project team. The team must stay focused and on track to deliver the solutions and to help the organization change and accept the "new way of doing things." The more you confront the issues and handle the problems, the more support you will receive.

TIP During implementation, a large group of users will be exposed to your new system and processes for the first time in an operational setting. Be prepared to seek feedback and advice on what was done "wrong" and what needs to change. Provide a mechanism to collect the suggestions and data and use them for targeted communications, including use of a "tip of the day." Be open and honest in your assessment of the suggestions.

Establishing Operational Processes

At the time of your rollout, at least three operational processes will need to be in place to support your implementation:

- ▶ Help-desk services
- ▶ Technical support services
- ▶ Maintenance support services

Regardless of how you provide these services and support, ensure that you have them covered adequately during and after your implementation. Failure to do so can quickly turn a successful implementation sour. Too many project teams get close to the finish line, run out of gas, and miss their chance to cross the finish line victoriously. Be prepared to go the long haul, and then some, to support your users through this major operational change.

Each of these three areas of support is covered in detail in Chapter 16, "Post-Production Support," and Chapter 23, "Next Steps with Integration," which looks at your support organization. However, the cutover planning needs to take into account these three services and how each of these support groups will interact with the users and project team during the cutover period.

Help-Desk Services

There should be few, if any, changes to the help-desk structure from the cutover time frame to the completed implementation time frame. The help-desk group will mainly take calls from the users and channel those calls or issues to the appropriate action party (functional, technical, or otherwise). The help desk(s) should initially contain several members of your project team and core user support group, as these individuals can help facilitate the rapid support and answering of questions as well as help train your help-desk staff. It's a great idea to get your help-desk staff in place supporting the cutover and to let them handle the tracking and monitoring of all issues. This will help them better prepare for the actual go-live event. Many projects even run a "dress rehearsal" for both their support services and their cutover activities to help ensure a smooth transition and help the staff prepare for their new roles. This approach also helps with the knowledge-transfer effort between the project team and the support teams.

Details on frequently asked questions or problems that might occur should be provided to the help-desk team to help them in directing the users appropriately. All support contacts, including security, system, functional, reporting, and otherwise, should be maintained through the help-desk services. As described in detail in our next chapter as well as in Chapter 23, the support organization must be clearly prepared and understand how all issues and problems should be routed, logged, and treated. Clear procedures and processes should be communicated to the staff as well as the user group. Generally, it's best to have a single initial point of contact such as a help desk, which can direct calls to the appropriate party, depending on the issue. Routine questions or issues may be handled by your change-agent network or your key end-user support staff, but your help desk should be prepared to support and direct these questions as well. Again, good planning and communications are key to this support. All questions and issues should be logged and tracked in a common database regardless of whether the help desk solves the issue or it is passed on to another group.

Technical Support Services

Initially during cutover, the primary responsibility for technical support generally falls to the project team. When this group cannot resolve a problem (such as a problem that's outside the system application environment and within the desktop technology or related to the general network environment), they are supported indirectly by your IT support organization (non–team members). After completion of your implementation, your goal should be to have your general IT support staff replace the project team members in all technical support areas and to have a smooth transition in doing so. Involving them sufficiently during cutover and during the implementation process can ensure this transfer of knowledge and can better prepare them for their new roles. The project team should continue to take primary responsibility for the technical, package-specific issues during the cutover, but the more they involve their successors, the better off your organization will be in the long run.

Maintenance Support Services

The maintenance support services are sometimes separated from the technical support services within an organization. This group is usually responsible for the hardware, such as servers and desktop units, and they also provide backup services to your servers. This organizational group usually does not change from cutover support to post-implementation support, since generally their skills are not maintained within the project team organization. However, the service-level agreements usually must change through the life of the project and thus should be re-addressed during your cutover planning efforts. As a part of your cutover, the production hardware should be covered by a production-support service-level agreement rather than by a project-related or testing agreement. However, changes to your backup schedules and normal downtime schedules may be needed in order to support your initial cutover plan and go-live activities. Be sure that all these actions are outlined in detail in your cutover plan and that they will continue to be monitored on a daily basis when any changes occur.

After your cutover is complete, you should have a full-fledged production environment in place to support your users. Any special processes during your "surge" or first month's operations should be worked out with your support staff so that they will understand the parameters and factors that affect the change. You must also determine how long this special processing or surge period might last so that final, full-production support will be in place when and where you need it. Your support services group might need to monitor this closely depending on how your organization supports these processes.

Training

The training surrounding your implementation of PeopleSoft is integral to the success of your project. (We cover this topic in detail in Chapter 22, "Providing End User Training.") A structured approach to the development of this training will help ensure proper use and support of your new system and processes by your end users. The strategy for developing and delivering PeopleSoft training requires a learning system that supports the identified business needs and integrates your cutover plan and timing with your training rollout plan. Your training should focus on the operational business requirements and integrate the learning activities with these requirements. Integrating this training as well as other communications with your cutover planning is crucial to the success of your project.

Any special circumstances or on-the-job learning activities should also be considered and monitored during the cutover process. Additional support in the field may be needed during this transition to help support your help desk and your users. Analyze this requirement and determine what's best for your organization, based on the organizational structure, support structure, change network, and impact of the change.

Post-Implementation Support

No degree of training and preparation can ensure that individuals do not forget a part of their new task or try to revert to the old processes and procedures, since many of them may have become accustomed to the old system over many years. Essentially over a weekend or span of a few days, you are asking your people to move from one way of doing business to a completely different way of doing things. Therefore, to support this transition and ensure adequate support, you need to have a well-thought-out plan and provide a stronger level of post-implementation support (during this surge period).

As we explain in greater detail in Chapters 16 and 23, you must continue to have a strong support group and supporting processes well into the future. When creating your post-implementation support organization, be sure to involve the project team both in providing insights into the new system and processes based on their experience and in getting your support organization up and running effectively. The project team can help you determine:

▶ Whether the new business processes are being performed correctly

▶ Whether a redesigned business process missed an essential component of the old business process—if such an issue is raised

▶ Whether there are any remaining errors in the configuration

These items are among the functions of an implementation support team. As part of the production support, the transition of "ownership" of the system and new processes to the end users and new support organization must occur. The execution of tasks along with the approval of balances, orders, data, etc., are all part of the end users' assumption of ownership of the system. Once operations begin on the new system, project team members should move to more of a support role and take a back seat to the users and support organization. This will help the users and support staff feel more responsible for their actions and take over the responsibilities more rapidly from the project team. Your goal is to make this transition as quick and smooth as possible so that the end users—your customers—will take ownership and embrace the new system and processes.

Up Next

Now that you've outlined the cutover plan in detail, addressed your users' concerns and issues, and put a system, users, and support organization in place, ready to use your new solution, what are the details you need to have in place to ensure that your new system and processes will continue and be strongly supported well into the future? The next chapter will look at these details. You must ensure that you have all the right processes in place to support your organization as it moves forward. As your project team is dismantled, your support organization is established, and the baton is passed, you want to have confidence that you've done all you can to support the transition and that you're ready to move forward, well past the finish line.

CHAPTER 16

Post-Production Support

FEATURING:

- ▶ Creation of new support services
- ▶ Help desk structure and format
- ▶ Shifting from a project to production environment
- ▶ Conducting go-live activities
- ▶ Ensuring knowledge transfer

P ost-implementation or post-production support involves the steps necessary to transition your project from the structure and team that supported the project through implementation to the structure and team necessary to support the system after the go-live events occur.

Planning New Support Services

Once the new system and processes have been rolled out and are in use by the end user and customers of the system, you must transition your support from a project to a production support environment.

To get started creating your new post-implementation support services, you should begin by:

- ▶ Understanding the roles in a production support environment
- ▶ Conducting a review of company resources
- ▶ Determining your own resources/needs by creating an exit checklist

Once these factors have been determined, you can move on to the next steps of actually creating your support environment.

Post-Production Support Roles

A production support environment will most likely include the following roles:

Customer Support   This support generally falls to help-desk-type environments. Whether Web-enabled or phone-enabled, there should be a structure in place to help the end users answer questions and resolve problems. Sometimes "super users" are trained to support large groups of users at a particular site.

Technical Support   The PeopleSoft system, while robust and user friendly, still should be supported by a technical support team once implemented. In general, this team includes support for "patch fixes," upgrades, and day-to-day technical support including database, network, hardware, and software expertise.

Maintenance   In order to keep the system current and operational, there should be a team assigned not only to apply software "patches" from the vendor and upgrade to the latest vendor-supported releases, but also to respond to any bugs identified by the users/customers after testing and going live. Generally, there is a "surge" period right after implementation that lasts the first few business cycles (such as pay cycles, close cycles, etc.) when most of the bugs as well as system issues are identified. After that period, a team should remain in place to support the system and maintain it should new policies, regulations, or enhancements be needed. You may want to look at the possibility of outsourcing your surge period support or your ongoing maintenance as you move forward, depending on your ability to staff and maintain this competency within your organization.

Other Support Services   There may be a need to support future package training for new hires or security setup for new hires or new system users, or to arrange for other services to meet the needs of your business based on the service-level agreements (SLAs) created (as mentioned in Chapter 6, "Surveying the Infrastructure"), as well as to have subject matter experts within the organization to support reporting and other functional requirements. These roles may be new to your organization after roles change to support your new system and processes. More information may be placed in the hands of the end-user and business support personnel rather than in the information technology (IT) department. Table-driven systems generally require additional user support in the departments or organizations that use the systems, while in the past this function fell on the IT group's shoulders.

Conducting a Post-Implementation Review

A review of both the system and support in place, including an analysis of how the implementation activities were performed, should be conducted after the go-live activities (outlined in Chapter 15, "Go Live—Keys to a Successful Rollout") have been completed. This post-implementation review should look at the support services roles outlined previously to ensure that there is adequate support for your new system and processes. It should also look at any ways to improve future go-live activities and document areas that went well during the transition.

Creating an Exit Checklist

We recommend creating an *exit checklist* to determine the major activities that need to be accomplished in order to transition the work effort off of the project team and onto the new support organization. All mandatory transition items should be listed on this plan and monitored to ensure a smooth transition. Responsibilities should be assigned to ensure that any outstanding issues or post-production enhancements are identified and tracked as well as brought to the attention of the new support staff.

Prior to your project team members and consultants rolling off your project, you should ensure that this checklist and associated responsibilities are clearly identified and acted upon. Table 16.1 shows a sample exit checklist.

Table 16.1   **HRMS—Exit Readiness Checklist**

Go-Live Condition	Condition Satisfactory for Go-Live (Yes/No)	Supporting Documentation Reference	Endorsed By (Position)	Endorsed (Signature)	Date
Legacy data converted, cleaned, and verified in PROD	Yes	HRMS Readiness Report	Sue Turner		3 Nov 00
Parallel testing completed	Yes	Parallel Test Report	Sue Turner		3 Nov 00
Acceptance testing completed, documented, and signed off (i.e., all testing completed satisfactorily in terms of functionality, interfaces, integration, accuracy, performance, security, etc.)	Yes	Acceptance Test Report	Sue Turner		3 Nov 00
System and audit controls adequate	Yes	HRMS Readiness Report	Sue Turner		3 Nov 00
System testing conducted, and production environment readiness confirmed	Yes	System Test Report	Sue Turner		3 Nov 00
PeopleSoft security implemented	Yes	HRMS Security Setup	Sue Turner		3 Nov 00

Table 16.1   **HRMS—Exit Readiness Checklist** *(Continued)*

Go-Live Condition	Condition Satisfactory for Go-Live (Yes/No)	Supporting Documentation Reference	Endorsed By (Position)	Endorsed (Signature)	Date
User training conducted and adequate to enable successful operation and support of the new system	Yes	Training Effectiveness Report	Sue Turner		3 Nov 00
PeopleSoft application support in place and adequate for go-live	Yes	PeopleSoft/ ResearchMaster Support Strategy implemented & HRMS Readiness Report	Sue Turner		3 Nov 00
Fallback plan developed	Yes	HRMS Readiness Report	Sue Turner		3 Nov 00

Outstanding Issues

Issue ID	Title	Priority	Show Stopper (Yes/No)	Identified Date	Assigned To	Recommendations	Due Date
53	PeopleSoft patches	Medium	No	10 Jun 00	PeopleSoft	Patches not critical. PS has logged issue.	ASAP
73	Printing of blank pages with HR and Payroll reports including printing running over to subsequent pages	High	No	27 Oct 00	Alex Varnas	Reports cannot be printed from the server, and must be printed from the client. Resolution / Action Plan: Recommend that the standard be reconsidered to accommodate PeopleSoft reporting. Investigate the possibility of duplex printing to save paper resources.	30 Nov 00

Table 16.1   **HRMS—Exit Readiness Checklist** *(Continued)*

Issue ID	Title	Priority	Show Stopper (Yes/No)	Identified Date	Assigned To	Recommendations	Due Date
74	General deductions for a new employee hired did not work	High	No	29 Oct 00	Mariano Llana	The workaround provided by PS is to select deduction codes from the drop-down list instead of typing the deduction code directly. This will be monitored over the next two weeks.	19 Nov 00
75	System performance— panel loading time slow	Medium	No	1 Nov 00	Alex Varnas	System tuning may need to be performed.	30 Nov 00

Project Director: _____   Date: _____

It is also very important to ensure that a formal knowledge transfer process is in place to transfer the knowledge of the current team to the support organization and end users.

At the end of this transitioning process, your project team and your support organization and user base should feel confident that they have made every effort to ensure a successful post-implementation transition to complete the project.

 TIP   Make sure to involve your internal audit group to ensure that proper system controls and a structure for your new supported business processes are in place.

In order to help with the creation of an exit checklist and to support your ability to handle the new processes and system, the project team should review some basic materials:

▶ The SLA and any other support services requirements

▶ Documents on current help desk structure and support including any change documents to support your new system and processes

▶ Staffing plans for end user support requirements

- Lists of any proposed post-implementation enhancements or items that may have been put on hold until after the implementation

- Project team issue log(s), to ensure that any outstanding issues are assigned or addressed adequately

- Any knowledge-transfer documents (if there are none, then create them)

- Any log or plan with post-implementation outstanding activities

Your project management team should work with the new support organization and business owners to ensure that the exit checklist is created and monitored.

Appropriate communications plans should be developed to ensure that the user community understands the support structure and the transition of the project team.

Additionally, the project team should create a summary document that outlines the benefits and value that the project has brought to the organization, along with the associated costs that were actually involved. This document should clearly outline any lessons learned so that future initiatives may benefit from them. The team should ensure that adequate measures are in place to gauge results of the new system and convey these benefits to the appropriate parties, including the end users, customers, sponsors, and executives.

Help Desk Services

In order to be ready to support your new system and organization, you need to ensure that the appropriate help desk services are in place and ready to go prior to the system going live and prior to your project team disbanding. You should review your current help desk structure, including:

- The various levels of the help desk. Typically, there is a local (on-site) IT support organization for those systems that have a large set of users, a general technical support group across the company, and a vendor help desk to consider. Each group is responsible for handling specific types of questions and issues and has the authority to escalate a problem to the next level. The first line of defense is the local IT support organization (if there is one in place); next is the company technical support group; and finally, if the first two groups can't resolve the issue or determine whether it is tied to the hardware or to the software itself, there is the vendor help desk. Each level of help desk should be evaluated.

▸ The performance statistics of the help desk. Are they as expected? Higher or lower? Consider the following: response time, average time to resolution, number of recurring problems, customer complaints, and number of calls handled per person.

▸ Whether there is sufficient staff to handle the calls, and whether they are adequately trained and knowledgeable.

▸ Whether additional training is needed for either end users or technical personnel. Determine this from the types of problems reported to the help desk: analyze end users' questions to identify information that should have been covered during implementation training or orientation. Look for ways to communicate this information to the end users.

Don't forget to include the vendor help desk in your review. PeopleSoft provides a customer support center both via the Web and for immediate problems by phone. Be sure that you are leveraging this capability and that you understand all they can do for you.

Once you have reviewed these components of the help desk, you need to determine how the help desk has transitioned (if any transition was made) to your new system processes and procedures. You should include the following activities:

▸ Document specific major ongoing problems that might occur. Ensure you have a sound tracking mechanism such as Siebel, Vantive, or some other customer relationship management system.

▸ Review the way you are handling calls, including use of additional communications mechanisms such as a daily "did you know" item on your Web site or newsletter to your users.

In addition to reviewing your more functional processes, ensure that you are reviewing all components of your technical support services. Generally, items such as network operations, database management support, and desktop support are maintained within another support services organization (such as your Network Services Group) from your PeopleSoft IT Support Help Desk. Table 16.2 shows how your new help desk might interact with existing help desk features. If this is the case, ensure that the links between the different groups are clearly articulated and processes are in place to coordinate between the different groups. A key to the group abbreviations used in the table appears at the end of the table.

Table 16.2 **Help Desk Integration—Responsibility Matrix**

Architecture Component	Problem or Service	Organization Tier 1--------	Tier 2--------	Tier 3--------	Tier 4------
HP/Unix	System down/crash	OCS	DSNM	SA	
	File system full	OCS	DSNM	SA or DBA	
	Listener down	OCS	DSNM	DBA	
	Cluster failover	OCS	DSNM	SA	
	Disk drive failure	OCS	DSNM	SA	DBA
	Backup failure	OCS	DSNM	SA – Media	
	Restore request	DBA	Media	SA	
	Maestro failure (infrastructure)	OCS	DSNM	SA	
	Network failure (would look like system issue)	DSNM	SA		
	Batch Scheduler failure (PeopleSoft)	OCS	DSNM	SA	
	File system corruption	OCS	DSNM	SA	
	IP failure	OCS	DSNM	SA	
	System failback	OCS	DSNM	SA	
	System failover test	OCS	DSNM	SA	
	Power failure	OCS	DSNM	SA	
	Bug in operating system	OCS or DSNM	SA	Development organizations	
NT/ WinFrame	WinFrame client problem (on local PC)	DSG			
	WinFrame profile issue	OCS	DSNM	SA	LAN Services
	WinFrame policy issue	OCS	DSNM	SA	LAN Services
	WinFrame server unavailable	OCS	DSNM	SA	LAN Services

Table 16.2   **Help Desk Integration—Responsibility Matrix** *(Continued)*

Architecture Component	Problem or Service	Organization Tier 1--------	Tier 2--------	Tier 3--------	Tier 4------
	WinFrame browser problem	OCS	DSNM	SA	LAN Services
	WinFrame printer mapping	OCS	DSNM	SA	LAN Services
	WinFrame local drive mapping	OCS	DSNM	SA	LAN Services
	WinFrame ID/Security-related issue	OCS	DSNM	SA	LAN Services
	Insufficient disk space (WF/NT) errors	OCS	DSNM	SA	LAN Services
	Insufficient memory errors in WinFrame	OCS	DSNM	SA	LAN Services
	NT/WF login script failure	OCS	DSNM	SA	LAN Services
	NT cache server problem	OCS	DSNM	SA	LAN Services
	NT authentication problem	OCS	DSNM	SA	LAN Services
	NT application server problem (loading PS EXEs)	OCS	DSNM	SA	LAN Services
	WAN problem accessing TCP/IP services	OCS	DSNM	Telecomm	
	SQL*Net connection on WinFrame client	OCS	DSNM	SA	LAN Services
Oracle	Process Scheduler restart	OCS	DBA		
	SQL*Net connection problem on Oracle database	DBA			
	Corrupt database	DBA			
	Corrupt index	DBA			
	Missing trigger	DBA			
	Missing index	DBA			
	SQL error	DBA			
	Database instance down	DBA			

Table 16.2 **Help Desk Integration—Responsibility Matrix *(Continued)***

Architecture Component	Problem or Service	Organization Tier 1--------	Tier 2--------	Tier 3---------	Tier 4------
	Runaway query	DBA			
	Poor performance on database	DBA			
	Poor performance for process (SQR, Crystal, etc.)	DBA			
LAN/WAN	Local client cannot access network	DSG	OCS	DSNM	
	Local client cannot access servers	OCS	DSNM	SA	
	WinFrame servers cannot access servers	OCS	DSNM	SA	LAN Services
	Remote site WAN down	Help desk	OCS	DSNM	
	Remote site LAN down	Help desk or OCS	Local Infrastructure		
Desktop	Customer not able to connect to the LAN	DSG/LI			
	Customer not able to access PeopleSoft	DSG/LI			
	SQL*Net connection problem on client	DSG			
	Customer experiencing problems (GPFs/lockups) in other applications after PeopleSoft loaded (incompatibility)	DSG			
	Customer unable to print from within PeopleSoft application	BU	PSHD		
Mainframe	Batch scheduling interface— CA7/Maestro fails	Tech Services			
	MVS/Mainframe down—scheduled	Tech Services			
	MVS/Mainframe down—unscheduled	Tech Services			

Table 16.2 **Help Desk Integration—Responsibility Matrix** *(Continued)*

Architecture Component	Problem or Service	Organization Tier 1 --------	Tier 2 --------	Tier 3 --------	Tier 4 -----
Enterprise Reporting	AP checks not printed/not printed properly	MSS	PSHD	DBA	
	AP checks not distributed properly	MSS	PSHD	DBA	
	Create Check Print File problem	PSHD	DBA	SA	
	Send Print File To Mainframe Print Queue problem	PSHD	DBA	SA	
	Report distribution problem (not received)	MSS	PSHD	DBA	
	Reports not printed	MSS	PSHD	DBA	
	Other report printing	MSS	PSHD	DBA	
Enterprise Scheduling	Maestro fails/application error	SA	DBA		
	Maestro upgrades, patch loads result in problems (Unix)	SA			
	Maestro scheduling error— Job/dependency deleted	MSS			
	Maestro scheduling error—schedule entered incorrectly	MSS			
	Maestro scheduling error—script change not reported by programmer	PSHD			
	Problems with Maestro backup (Unix)	SA			
	Job fails to run in designated time window	SA			
	External data interface fails/data not present	SA	PSHD		
	System resources unavailable (MVS/ Mainframe)	Tech Services			
	Jobs or schedules abend	OCS	SA	PSHD	

Table 16.2 **Help Desk Integration—Responsibility Matrix (Continued)**

Architecture Component	Problem or Service	Organization Tier 1---------	Tier 2--------	Tier 3---------	Tier 4------
	AF operator problems (Messaging software)	Automations Group			
	Process scheduler problems	BU	PSHD	DBA	SA
PeopleSoft	Software defect	PSHD			
	Report or query request	PSHD			
	Batch problem—results in error	PSHD			
	Batch Problem—program aborts	PSHD			
	External interface not working	PSHD	Tech Services		
	PeopleSoft question	PSHD			
	PeopleSoft object baseline change	DBA			
	Change or correct mass Production data	PSHD	DBA		
	Performance poor	PSHD			
	Job schedule change	PSHD	MSS		
	New database instance required	DBA			
	Enterprise-level test required (ETC)	PSHD			
	Database tuning required	DBA			
	Refresh database instance	DBA			
	Operator class: create, modify, delete	PSHD			
	External interface needs to be changed	PSHD			
	Tree/chart of account/translation table maintenance	BU	PSHD		
	Mass change request	BU	PSHD		
	User doesn't have permissions to access PeopleSoft	ISSS	PSHD		

Table 16.2 **Help Desk Integration—Responsibility Matrix *(Continued)***

Architecture Component	Problem or Service	Organization Tier 1········	Tier 2········	Tier 3·········	Tier 4······
	Software Change Request (SCR)	PSHD			
	Process scheduler—problems	PSHD			
Software Distribution	Software incompatibility on installation	DSG	SA	ADDS	
	Space problems on distribution	DSG	SA	ADDS	
	File permissions on distribution	DSG	SA	ADDS	
PVCS	Library management—Cannot access PVCS	PSHD (CM)	ADDS		
	Problems checking in/out files	PSHD (CM)	ADDS		
	Problems creating version labels	PSHD (CM)	ADDS		
	File is locked and person is on vacation/out of office	PSHD (CM)	ADDS		
Unknown PS	Unknown problem, PeopleSoft-related	PSHD			
Unknown IT	Unknown problem, infrastructure-related	Help Desk	Local infrastructure	OCS	
Unknown	Unknown problem, either PeopleSoft or infrastructure	PSHD			

Table Key:		
Group Abbreviation	**Full Group Name**	**Scopus Group Name**
ADDS	Application Development and Deployment Services	Common Case
Automations Group	Automations Group	MCNC Automation Services
BU	Business Unit	PeopleSoft BU#1; PeopleSoft BU#2; PeopleSoft GL

Table 16.2   **Help Desk Integration—Responsibility Matrix *(Continued)***

Group Abbreviation	Full Group Name	Scopus Group Name
DBA	Operational Database Services	DatabaseAdmin
DSG	Desktop Services Group	Desktop Services
DSNM	Distributed Systems and Network Management	XCNC Dist. Sys. & Nwk Mgmt, XCNC DSNM Level 2
Help Desk	Local Help Desk or HQ Help Desk	Local Help Desk, None for HQ Help Desk
ISSS	Information Systems Security Services	Data Security
LAN Services	Local Area Network Services	LAN Services
LI or Local Infra.	Local infrastructure groups	NA
MSS	Management Support Systems	XCNC Batch Scheduling or XCNC Print Services
OCS	Operations and Customer Support	XCNC Ops. & Cust. Support
PSHD	PeopleSoft Services Help Desk	PeopleSoft PSHD
PSHD (CM)	PeopleSoft Services Help Desk— Configuration Manager	None
SA	Systems Administration	XCNC Systems Administration

Be sure to:

▶ Review the multiple levels of technical support for performance and possible improvements in the way they work with each other. Consistently review each class of problem and how rapidly they respond to it. Ensure that there are no delays based on passing the problem off from one group to another.

▶ Review the technical support personnel. Are they trained and knowledgeable regarding the new system and procedures? Is additional package-specific training needed in order for them to do their job faster and more efficiently? Include a look at both internal personnel and any contract services personnel you may have outsourced.

▶ Review your equipment. Is it performing per your specifications? If not, what have you done to ensure that your equipment is working properly and reliably? A lack of confidence in your technology components and hardware can cause the PeopleSoft application to look very bad to your end users. In some cases, it may not be the software that is performing poorly but rather the hardware that is not sized well enough to support your processes and volume. Be sure to constantly re-review the estimates you used to size your hardware, and update any of this information with the actual data collected in production. Many companies are merely guessing how much end users will use their query or reporting tools and make assumptions on this use during implementation, since these are new features that they are unsure of the demand for. In some cases, these assumptions may not be based on what actually happens in production, and you must re-size or re-review your hardware and infrastructure requirements.

Note   Remember to constantly reevaluate the need for additional training or supplemental training for your technical support staff.

Continue to document specific major ongoing problems and review how the help desk is adjusting to meet these demands.

Maintenance Services

As a part of your help desk operations, you should always remember to review all components of your maintenance services, including both hardware and software maintenance requirements. Factor these requirements into your help desk support staff activities. PeopleSoft provides their customers "bug fixes" via their Customer Connection Web site, and it is up to the support organization in most cases to review this site on a daily basis to determine if there are any fixes that might be applicable to your environment. While PeopleSoft is responsible for maintaining their software and providing you upgrades based on new releases, it is up to you to ensure that your production system is current with these patches or fixes and that you maintain your upgrade requirements. In most cases, PeopleSoft requires you to upgrade to the latest release within 18 months of the next release, or you risk losing support or paying for the support above your normal maintenance fees. Therefore, with a major release every 12 to 18 months, you should be planning on upgrading your system about once every two years. Ensure that your budget and support staff are ready (or that you have supplemental resources you can pull in during this time). You also need to ensure that the end users' workstations are up to date, with the appropriate releases to support the PeopleSoft application. With the release of PeopleSoft 8, this requirement will be less of an issue, since many users will be browser-based (but you still will need to have the correct browser).

Ensure that you have properly analyzed your help desk support needs and approach to providing support services. Clearly articulate whether your support is centralized or decentralized. In some cases, some of your services (such as reporting support or workstation support) may be decentralized and some services (such as network and database maintenance support) may be centralized. Be sure to clearly outline how your services are interacting so as to ensure maximum customer support. An example of a common help desk interaction diagram is shown in Figure 16.1. (In this figure, "CMDB" refers to customer management database, and "DB" refers to database.) Review your help desk staffing and ensure that your new processes and procedures are covered by this staffing level. In most cases, your end users will have additional support functions they will have to perform, including maintaining certain user-defined system tables (such as account codes, departments, business units, and trees). This table maintenance may be done centrally or may be decentralized, depending on how often the information is changing, who is able to make these changes, and the sensitivity of the information being maintained.

You also need to decide if you are going to create a unique help desk for your PeopleSoft application or leverage your existing help desk within your IT services group (as one of several applications they are supporting). If you are creating your own unique help desk, you should remember to show how it integrates with your other support services groups. The physical location of the help desk may also be important and the hours of operation based on the demands of the end user and when they are able to work online. With the advent of the Web-based version of PeopleSoft 8, the location of the help services may not be as important as the hours of operation—which in many cases may be 24/7.

Figure 16.1   **Sample help desk interaction diagram**

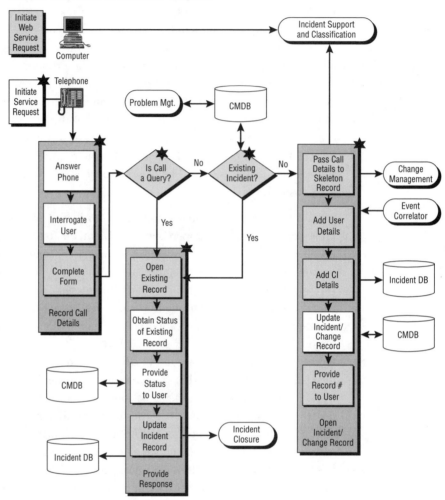

So why are help desks set up, anyway? We all know that no product or technology will work flawlessly for all users at all times, therefore there needs to be a mechanism to support problems for your end users. A company should look at the most efficient way to solve the problems, record the interactions, and report the numbers and types of calls when developing their help desk. By doing this, more proactive measures such as training or communication may be put in place and lead to better productivity and increased business value.

Note   A survey of help desk and customer support practices showed that 72% of support organizations used problem/service management software, while 18% planned to add this in the next 12 months (Help Desk Institute, 1995 Help Desk and Customer Support Practices Report). Also, 26% of the respondents were planning to replace their systems, indicating dissatisfaction with their current systems.

The PeopleSoft application environment is a very complex environment. Three-tiered architecture, Web servers, network traffic, and volume concerns are just a few challenges facing the help desk support. Your help desk support must be able to integrate with all areas of this support network (including your company's browser and Web-based support services—even more so with PeopleSoft 8). This integration must include ties to network and system management software to proactively alert the help desk of situations that may impact their user base. Links to diagnostic and corrective software will allow the help desk technicians to determine the problem and fix it rapidly and remotely. In many cases, organizations believe they do not need these extra diagnostic tools to support their help desk—but they are mistaken. The inability to quickly and accurately find your system problem (with this complex network of software and hardware issues) will most definitely cause you heartache and fail to meet your SLAs. Also, ties to user databases, asset and inventory tracking systems, and other data on the current configuration of your end users' desktops will assist your help desk in diagnosing and correcting any existing problems. Therefore, ensure that your help desk is equipped with the right diagnostic and issue-tracking systems to support your SLA requirements.

Generally, the volume of calls to be managed will often determine the level of satisfaction that the help desk software selected. Therefore, consider your call volume level when selecting the appropriate software to support your center. Use of the Internet can also help in supporting your help desk requirements. Many vendors of help desk management software have responded by adding Web-enabled interfaces to their offerings. Also, many vendors are offering CRM (customer relationship management) solutions that may be leveraged to support your tracking needs. You should consider the use of the intranet to allow users to open new cases and report problems they have (rather than calling your help desk) as well as check on the status of their case or the status of the system (you can post any system problems, outages, etc., to help reduce calls to your help desk).

An example of a report used to track help desk calls for help desk operations is shown in Table 16.3. The help desk should be used to work more efficiently and reduce the time wasted in attempting to solve problems alone or with co-workers. A recent survey of about 1,000 help desks set the mean fully loaded cost per call at $19, but the cost can range anywhere from $5 to over $40 per call. In general, the ratio of cost between a desktop application and a back-office product (such as PeopleSoft) is 10:1. Microsoft's outsourcing services when following this logic could range from $15 for desktop applications to $150 for back-office products. Therefore, with the PeopleSoft application you should plan for this more complex resolution process and costs.

It is important to choose the appropriate software to support your help desk. You should base your choice on the following:

▶ Self-analysis of customer profile

▶ Capacity demands

▶ Integration with other systems

▶ Work flow (answers back to user or to other groups to help resolve problems)

▶ Understanding of business problems to be solved

Managing your problem-resolution process is generally thought of as a reactive process, requiring an outside contact to initiate the process. However, a state-of-the-art help desk may include a group that analyzes your data and looks for ways to avoid future calls and improve productivity through additional training, additional communications, lessons learned, changes to processes, searching PeopleSoft's Customer Connection for problems and best practices, etc. You should be sure that you have identified your high-level criteria for using these services for the post–go live phase of your project.

Table 16.3 **Help Desk Tracking Example**

Error #	Date Found	Person Reporting Error	Contact Info	Type of Discrepancy	Assigned To	Issue	Priority	Date Resolved	Resolution
1	9/22/00	Sue Shelley	444-877-4455	Reporting	John Day	Report #201 ending in error—"compilation not complete"	Medium	9/23/00	Report needed re-compilation with new COBOL compiler.
2	9/22/00	James Hong	444-877-3322	Page	Sally Jensen	Job Data—can't enter job code #2033 on Job Change for Emplid #2356788	Medium	9/22/00	Job Code not added to table. Added new job code, and James was able to input entry.
3	9/22/00	Irene Goldman	222-766-2322	Page	Sally Jensen	Education History page could not be retrieved for Emplid #4456789	Low	9/22/00	Historical Education Data not loaded for BU #202. Checked extract file—not loaded into production. Re-loaded data into production. User able to access data.
4	9/22/00	Jamal Jones	222-766-4321	Interface	John Day	Interface #30-30 ended in error on last night's run	High	9/23/00	Run control data not entered into system. Added run control data to tables and re-ran interface. Interface ran with no errors.

Staffing Your Help Desk

Be sure that you have selected the individuals and trained them thoroughly for your end-user support prior to your going live. Look for individuals who have been on your team or worked with your team who will understand your system, including customizations. Remember that this role is very different from a project role and ensure that your staff is prepared for this change. If new individuals are chosen, involve them up front in the testing and as much in the go-live events as possible. Ensure that your existing team is helping and supporting your new help desk during the transition from project to post-production support.

Post-Implementation Enhancements

Be sure to review all identified post-implementation enhancements to ensure adequate staffing to support any post-implementation development. Review all the solution alternative documentation to help users in the short run prior to any of the desired solutions being in place. Be sure to consider all alternatives, including gaps between bolt-on solutions and third-party applications and ideas for new forms or documents.

Review issues, change requests, and any project or site evaluations to determine if any additional post-implementation activities should occur. Many times project teams decide to delay an enhancement for very good reasons. Your support organization should monitor these decisions to help determine if the modification is needed in the future. For example, in many cases users want to have many "production-ready" reports programmed for them. With PeopleSoft's query tools, these reports may not be necessary in your new environment. By delaying the development of these reports and forcing the users to try the query features, you may save yourself valuable money in programming fees for these reports. This tactic will also force your users to use the new features of the package you paid for. You should monitor this situation and determine, though, if there are reports that may be better off as standard reports, or "public" queries that should be developed to support the organization. As users become familiar with the software and tools, your support staff may be able to relinquish many of the report development tasks. Be sure to have all post-implementation enhancements identified and documented and available to your support staff should they be asked about the status of these items. Keep track of any user issues that may have been resolved with the development of these enhancements as well as the impact these enhancements will have on your organization.

Review all system site-testing issues that arose during project testing to determine if any of these issues may require post-implementation activities or to help resolve these issues. Items that were identified and resolved during testing may provide helpful insight to your support staff in resolving post-production support. Common user errors—such as failing to INSERT a record rather than change an EXISTING record—may help your support staff and end user identify common problems in production and resolve them quickly.

Your support staff should also review all project reports and change requests that can help identify post-production issues or help resolve problems that may arise after implementation. Also determine how popular an enhancement request might be to other companies or users and ensure that PeopleSoft is aware of this proposed enhancement. You may be able to get the vendor to make the enhancement and thus save you time and money. By networking with your SIG (Special Interest Groups) within your industry, you may be able to get PeopleSoft to make many of your enhancements, which affect all companies within a particular user community. Also ensure that you have checked out any pre-release data on PeopleSoft 8 or future PeopleSoft releases to see if this enhancement may well be delivered soon.

As you make the transition from your project team to your support staff, in addition to reviewing all issue logs, communications, documentation, and such, you should meet with the project team leaders to gain agreement on the recommended course of action for each enhancement request. Ensure that you have a process in place for determining how to prioritize these future enhancements, as well as any new items identified once you have gone into production (e.g., production issues or problems). You may have diverse user groups with different goals and objectives. You need to ensure that a defined process is in place to determine how your staff will focus its effort and what items have priority over others.

Be sure to assign post-implementation responsibilities and gain agreement on who will be responsible for the activity and how this will be communicated. Remember that you should continue to have a steering committee that can make final recommendations and approve any shifts in priorities or focus. You may want to create an ongoing system enhancement plan within the company for planning and budgetary needs, as well as add-on, purposes.

Be sure you have developed and reviewed your "exit gate" checklist, as previously mentioned. This is the list created with the project team of all activities that must be accomplished in order to move support from a project environment to a post-implementation support environment. All items listed above including issues, enhancements, documentation review, and transition activities should be on this list. You should use this checklist to ensure a smooth transition from your project team to your new support organization.

Knowledge Transfer

As mentioned above, as a part of your exit strategy, you should have a defined and solid knowledge transfer process from your project team to your new support organization. Many individuals on your team may be consultants or third-party vendors who, once the system is up and running, will disappear and never be seen again. Prior to them leaving, you should have a clearly defined process for them to transfer their knowledge to your remaining staff. Also, individuals on the project team may move to new roles and responsibilities and not have time to answer questions once they leave your project. Therefore, be sure to review the ongoing knowledge management process that was developed in implementation planning. Ensure that your staff has access to all the deliverables accomplished during the project and that someone on your support team has knowledge of what each document is and what it contains. Any missing information should be identified and added to your exit checklist. Consider scheduling lunchtime "share and learn" sessions to transition knowledge regarding the system, unique enhancements, or any special processing activities that may need to be transitioned to your support staff. Remember to identify each key area/role and a specific plan to transfer the knowledge of that role to someone on your support staff. This should include all tips/techniques about reporting, batch processing, tuning, common user errors, table maintenance, and other items. A matrix outlining all areas of responsibility within both the support staff and the user community should be created, and a knowledge transfer effort should be mapped to ensure that a smooth transition occurs.

Be sure to consolidate the support services review, post-implementation enhancements, implementation issues, and the knowledge review into your list of potential post-implementation activities or exit checklist. Review this activity list and prepare a high-level assessment of the effort each activity would take in order to be completed. List any potential business impacts as well. Assign a preliminary priority to complete each item that might roughly equate to the next enhancement project planned. Get an estimate from the vendor on whether any of these items may be included in a future release.

Once you have your support staff in place, the knowledge transferred from your project team to your new support organization(s), and a process in place for monitoring and prioritizing your work effort (including future enhancements), you are ready to say that your project has been transitioned to a fully operational post-implementation support group. Be sure to include the necessary reports, metrics you are monitoring, and communications to your user community to help them realize that you are meeting their expectations and living up to your service-level agreements. Look at establishing formal monthly and quarterly meetings to review your progress, analyze your priorities, and ensure that you are on track in meeting their needs. As with any support organization, this is a continuous process.

Other Support Features

There may be additional features that your support organization must think about that were not implemented during the project phase but are important to supporting an application. These include such items as a detailed backup and recovery program, an archive strategy, and other database maintenance features. Be sure you involve your DBA (database administrator) group in this discussion so that all activities can be monitored or a strategy developed and tracked. For instance, your post-production schedule may need to be tweaked and changed throughout the life cycle of your system. These items should be tracked and a plan put in place to maintain and support these features moving forward.

Backup and recovery plans developed during your initial system setup (as mentioned in Chapters 5, "Planning the Foundation," and 6, "Surveying the Infrastructure") should be reviewed and maintained for production. Any changes to these plans should also be noted, based on changes in your organization or lessons learned throughout the project.

One common area that in many cases goes unnoticed until it is too late is your archive strategy. Each day, as your system is running, new data and transactions are stored in the system. You need to develop a detailed archive strategy on how long to maintain the detailed data on your server, when to store it to tape or fiche or other means, and when, if ever, to delete it. How the data should be archived and when that should be done are questions that you will need to answer based on your business requirements and any legal requirements. Maintaining unnecessary data online can impede performance and slow down your system as well as cost you unnecessary additional money in disk capacity and support. Therefore, do not underestimate the need to develop a sound archive strategy for your system moving forward that should be monitored and changed as necessary. Currently, PeopleSoft does not provide an easy way to do this. However, with the multitude of database tools available, this can be done as a relatively painless process. Your DBA may need to develop scripts or automate processes to ensure that this is accomplished in the best way possible for your environment and organization. Just don't forget to ensure that you have a sound strategy for making it happen. Sound planning and foresight can keep you ahead of the game in this area. Also ensure that you are constantly monitoring your situation and the DASD (direct access storage device), more commonly known as disk space, requirements for your system. Assumptions made during initial project start-up may change when users are actually leveraging your new system to the fullest, and you must have measures in place to track this change.

Up Next

Now that you have the processes, staff, and monitoring in place to track your support services and help desk support functions, you are well on your way to maintaining a successful PeopleSoft application for your users and your organization. Our next few chapters (Chapters 17 through 20) will look in more depth at the features and functions available in the PeopleSoft applications. Finally, in our last few chapters, we will look specifically at some additional key support areas that you will need to have in place to help sustain your organization and its new processes. In Chapter 21, we will look at how to maintain a sound support network during your implementation and beyond. Chapter 22 will cover the end-user training requirements both for your initial go-live events and for post-implementation support. Finally, in Chapters 23 and 24 we will look to the future, including how to integrate new features and functions into your existing implementation, how to plan for upgrades, and what new developments and products might be coming in the future.

Part IV

Configuring the Specifics

The next few chapters, which cover the PeopleSoft 8 package specifics, take a more in-depth look at PeopleSoft applications and modules and the functions that they support. These chapters will also provide you with key tips on configuring the applications for implementation. After reading this section of the book, you should have a solid baseline for understanding the functionality within the HRMS, Financials, and Supply Chain applications.

CHAPTER 17

A Closer Look at HRMS

FEATURING :

- ▶ An overview of the PeopleSoft HRMS application
- ▶ A review of the training administration, recruitment, and position management functionalities supported by the PeopleSoft HRMS application

- ▶ A look at what PeopleSoft's base benefits and Benefits Administration have to offer and why you might consider implementing one over the other
- ▶ An overview of the PeopleSoft North American and Global Payroll applications, including the Payroll Interface option

This chapter outlines the modules available to completely outfit your enterprise with the PeopleSoft HRMS product. As with all leading ERP toolsets, there are several foundation modules that will drive the remaining modules' usability and configuration throughout your enterprise. Those foundation modules are:

- ► Human Resources
- ► Benefits Administration
- ► Payroll

There are numerous key configuration decisions associated with those modules, and those early decisions will drive the organization's ability to utilize and extend the remaining PeopleSoft modules throughout the organization and to attain your program's return on investment (ROI).

This chapter will focus on the core base table configuration and considerations when implementing the PeopleSoft toolset. We will discuss the interaction of the various modules and sequencing of each and discuss lessons learned from other ERP implementations.

Human Resources

PeopleSoft's "core" Human Resources application is made up of several key functions and application areas. We will look at the basic core configuration as well as additional functionality in the areas of training administration, recruitment, position management, and a few other key functions.

Core Configuration

The Human Resources (HR) module is the backbone of your PeopleSoft Human Resources Management system (HRMS) solution. The data and processes encapsulated in this module drive the benefits, payroll, Time and Labor, and other modules. While an organization may choose to implement these other modules without the Human Resources module, the related data will need to be interfaced to these other modules.

When configuring your HR module, there are a number of key tables that will drive your system's usability and overall configuration. Those tables are:

- Business Unit
- Set ID
- Company
- Department
- Job Code
- Location

The core data contained in these tables will be used throughout the HR module and other HRMS modules. For example, the Job Code field may have implications on salary amounts, general ledger coding, payroll processing, training administration and position management modules, and government reporting.

With these implications to consider, there is more than one way to configure your HR module. An integrated team approach to your initial configuration will pay dividends long term, both in terms of rework during the implementation and rework after go live and as you "e"volve your applications for the Internet.

Road Map

Table 17.1 contains a general listing of the HRMS tables and the suggested load sequence. Each installation is unique, and this load sequence should be reviewed, approved, and altered as necessary by your team as well as thoroughly tested in your environment.

Table 17.1 **HRMS Table Load Sequence**

Table Name	Dependent Table—Must Load First
Installation Table	Company Table Currency Code Table
PeopleTools Options	
TableSet ID Table	
Business Unit Table HR	

Table 17.1   **HRMS Table Load Sequence *(Continued)***

Table Name	Dependent Table—Must Load First
Operator Default Table HR (Operator Preferences Table)	HR Business Unit Table Set ID Table Company Table Country Table Currency Code Table
Business Unit Options HR (Business Unit Defaults)	Set ID Table Company Table Country Table Currency Code Table
Business Unit Table HR	
Set Control Table	Set ID Table
Record Group Table	
RT Rate Default Table	Rate Index Table Currency Code Table
Currency Code Table	
RT Rate Table	RT Rate Index Table Currency Code Table RT Type Table
Currency Quote Table	Currency Code Table
Review Scale Table—N/A	Rating Model
Salary Matrix Table	Set ID Table Review Scale Table (as required)
Salary Plan Table	
Salary Grade Table	Set ID Table Salary Plan Table
Location Table	Establishment Table

Table 17.1   **HRMS Table Load Sequence *(Continued)***

Table Name	Dependent Table—Must Load First
Department Table	Set ID Table
Job Code Table	Set ID Table Currency Code Table
Job Code Compensation Rate Table	Set ID Table Job Code Table Compensation Rate Code Table
Compensation Rate Code Table—N/A	
Pay Group Table	Company Table Country Table Earnings Program Table Set ID Table
Company Table	Set ID Table
Compensation Rate Group Table	
Establishment Table	
Company State Tax Table	Company Table State Tax Table
Security Table Department	Company Table State Tax Table

Lessons Learned

There are a few key lessons learned when configuring your core tables for the PeopleSoft HRMS application.

Department configuration   The department configuration is an important first decision point in your configuration efforts. The Department Table is used to define business entities in your organization. If you're using the PeopleSoft Payroll application, you must set up department codes according to the cost centers where you charge wages. Otherwise, you can set up departments using any groupings you like. The departments you create are also the foundation for building security for employee data—granting and denying operator access to rows of data in employee tables, categorized by department.

When setting up departments within your system, you can choose to do it either in the Manage Human Resources area or by using a reporting hierarchy in a security tree in the Tree Manager. In later sections, we will discuss setting up departments in the security tree.

Business Unit Configuration   Business units offer a flexible structuring device through which you can implement PeopleSoft HRMS based on the way your business is organized. In some organizations, the correspondence between existing structures and the business model is quite obvious. In other words, with all this flexibility, a high level of analysis is required to find the optimal balance required to meet your organization's diverse requirements.

To decide where to draw the lines between business units in your organization, you may have to balance a number of different variables. It's a good idea to explore alternative possibilities. First, you might consider the question from one perspective, saying, "If I use these criteria, my business divides into these logical units." Then you'll reconsider from another perspective, asking, "Is this structure going to hold up for other types of business decisions we often make?"

As you work to arrive at the optimal business unit structure for your organization, keep in mind that in some circumstances you must set up multiple business units; if you don't, you'll be restricted from using certain options. On the other hand, there are circumstances in which you may choose to have multiple business units, even though you don't need to; setting up multiple business units in such situations is optional.

When deciding how to establish business units for your PeopleSoft HRMS implementation, keep the following points in mind:

▶ With business unit functionality, you'll have another level for associating an employee to your company's organizational scheme.

▶ Business units are always associated with an employee's job and/or position record.

- ► There is no predetermined definition for a business unit, as there is for Department and Company. You can implement this new organizational level as you determine it is useful to your enterprise.

- ► A business unit is not a legal entity, but rather a way of tracking specific business information for reporting and other roll-up data collection.

While you have the option to build only one blanket business unit for your entire organization and leave it at that, establishing multiple business units for your organization can offer you important reporting and data control options. Multiple business units allow you to:

- ► Maintain a tree structure to facilitate organization-specific roll-up reporting.

- ► Distribute and administer certain control tables such as the Department Table or the Location Table. Large or multinational companies will find this feature of business unit functionality in PeopleSoft HRMS extremely useful for controlling data flow across different parts of the enterprise.

Every organization has different requirements, and it would be impossible to cover all the variables you might encounter as you define your business unit structures.

TableSet Configuration   The terms Set ID and TableSet are sometimes used interchangeably. In many cases this is correct, but it can cause some confusion. A Set ID is the label for a TableSet, and a TableSet is a group of rows identified by the same Set ID. You will always have the same number of Set IDs as you have TableSets.

TableSets enable you to define multiple processing control structures, so that each of your companies or operating entities can work in a way that truly reflects its style of doing business. But the greatest advantage of TableSets is that they enable you to share data among different business units.

To free you from entering redundant information, PeopleSoft HRMS is designed to let you share data among business units, while keeping this data separate and inviolable. Whether you're setting up PeopleSoft HRMS for a single location center or for a multinational corporation, you'll probably find ways to increase flexibility and efficiency by sharing tables among business units. TableSets can also help you ensure consistency across business units.

For most small to medium complex organizations, a single Set ID will be sufficient. While it may present challenges to work through the issues surrounding access to core data throughout your organization, in the long run it is the most efficient and effective method to configure and process.

Training Administration, Succession Planning, and Career Planning

Another key functional area within the PeopleSoft HRMS product includes the functionality supporting Training Administration, Succession Planning, and Career Planning. When you purchase the PeopleSoft HRMS application, all these functions are included with your core system.

Core Configuration

The Training Administration, Succession Planning, and Career Planning functionality are highly visible components of your extended PeopleSoft ERP solution. The data and processes encapsulated in these applications are driven by the core HR-related data, and there is a high degree of integration among the above applications. While this functionality is not usually in the forefront of an initial implementation effort, an organization can achieve a tremendous amount of value from successfully implementing these strategic Human Resource areas. This functionality will enhance the strategic value delivered by the Human Resource organization and is an important step in moving many HR organizations from a tactical compliance organization to a strategic business partner. This functionality may be rolled out as a holistic solution or as individual components, depending on an organization's bandwidth for change and the value added by this functionality.

Road Map

While there is no predefined method for loading the table data associated with the Training Administration, Succession Planning, and Career Planning tables, the following list outlines a suggested approach. A reminder: after your initial configuration load, make sure you take a step back and look at the big picture. Have you defined too many competencies—e.g., are most if not all of the competencies mapped to specific training classes?—and are your career planning tables aligned with both your competencies and your training programs?

Suggested table loading sequence:

- ▶ Manage Competencies—Competency Summary
- ▶ Cluster Table—Cluster Competencies
- ▶ Cluster Table—Cluster Accomplishments
- ▶ Competency Table
- ▶ Competency Type Table
- ▶ Proficiency Rating Table
- ▶ Proficiency Descriptions
- ▶ Match Evaluation Types
- ▶ School Table
- ▶ Major Table
- ▶ Degree Table
- ▶ License/Certification Table
- ▶ Membership Table
- ▶ Language Table
- ▶ Honor/Award Table
- ▶ Test Table
- ▶ Image Table
- ▶ Training Program Table
- ▶ Course Table—Course Profile
- ▶ Course Table—Prereqs/Goals
- ▶ Course Table—Equipment
- ▶ Course Table—Catalog
- ▶ Course Table—Description
- ▶ Non-Course Training Table

- ▶ Job Family Table
- ▶ Job Task Table
- ▶ Plan Careers
- ▶ Career Path Table
- ▶ Job Code Table—Job Code Profile
- ▶ Job Code Table—Evaluation Criteria
- ▶ Job Code Table—Compensation Rates
- ▶ Training Program Table
- ▶ Plan Successions
- ▶ Job Requirements Table
- ▶ Job Requirements Table—Competencies
- ▶ Job Requirements Table—Accomplishments

Lessons Learned

As we implement PeopleSoft Training Administration, Succession Planning, and Career Planning functionality, most often the difficulties are not inherent to the software configuration but rather to the manual or automated processes associated with the functionality and the data required to be collected and maintained.

For the Training Administration functionality, one of the main lessons learned comes from the process of employees dropping a class and letting the training department know to automatically allow any waitlisted employees to attend. The software is easily configured to handle the transaction, but the difficulty is in getting the employee to update the training system in a timely fashion. As with many other employee-initiated activities, this one is usually low on the employee's priority list, and as such it is important to build in reminders as the class approaches to confirm attendance.

Another lesson learned pertains to outside training classes and their impact on training programs and curriculum. While many companies allow employees to be self-directed in their training plans, there has been a steady trend toward companies strongly suggesting training in order to build competencies and in turn reward employees for building and maintaining those desired competencies. As you begin to reward employees for building competencies, they in turn will begin to ask that the companies track all classes taken, potentially in an after-the-fact mode. They will also most likely pressure the company to add more training classes so that they can accumulate competencies, which will require companies to assess the key learnings and track the appropriate information. With PeopleSoft 8, employees can now register and track the status of this registration through the self-service functions on the Web.

When companies formally use PeopleSoft to track their succession planning data, again we have found that the hardest aspect is getting the top executives to articulate and maintain the data. Another key lesson is to look at only the succession plans at the top two or three levels of the organization during your initial implementation. It is important to use a small population to test the process and ingrain the new requirements for maintainability into both your HR organization and your key executives.

From a career-planning perspective, the key area to balance is the proper level of detail in describing various career paths. As many companies are flattening out their organization, they find that career plans are become outdated and the real focus should be on skills and competencies. This is not to say that career planning is not important, but rather that as employees build skills and competencies, they will become more valuable to their companies and ideally will be rewarded both monetarily and non-monetarily to stay at various levels but continue to grow and provide value to their company. PeopleSoft's eDevelopment features in PeopleSoft 8 allow managers and employees to track and manage career plans online.

Recruitment

As with the training and career planning area, the recruitment functionality provided by PeopleSoft is a part of the core PeopleSoft application. Many companies choose to buy a third-party package and bolt it onto the PeopleSoft application to provide resume scanning and extraction of resume information into the PeopleSoft application. However, with PeopleSoft 8, a more robust recruiting application is available through eRecruit. If you choose to use a third-party application, PeopleSoft has a recommended integration partner in this area with WebHire. The WebHire application has a two-way interface that integrates seamlessly with the PeopleSoft application so that, for example, requisitions can be created in PeopleSoft and passed to the WebHire application, and the data for applicants who are hired can flow back into the PeopleSoft application.

This section will cover the basic configuration of the recruitment module (under the Recruit Workforce menu) within the PeopleSoft HRMS application. Key considerations and lessons learned will also be discussed in this overview.

Core Configuration

The Recruit Workforce section is a component of the core HRMS PeopleSoft package. This module can be used by an organization to meet its applicant-tracking needs. The module also will track an organization's applicant flow reporting requirements for the U.S. government.

The recruitment module can be used at varying levels within an organization. At a simple level, the Recruit Workforce module can be used only to track the data required for government reporting such as the applicant's race and gender, the positions for which the applicant has applied, and the overall disposition of the application. At a more complex level, the module can be used to track a wide variety of applicant data, such as education, skills, and other competencies. This additional data can then be searched using specific job criteria to find candidates for a particular job opening.

In order to make use of the applicant pool skill-searching ability, a good amount of applicant data must first be captured into PeopleSoft. To lessen the burden of data capture, some organizations have opted to supplement the Recruit Workforce module with resume-scanning systems that can store an image of the applicant's resume. Unfortunately, this option will not populate PeopleSoft with much data besides the applicant's name and address. In addition to leveraging the application's functionality, many organizations choose to implement a front-end resume-scanning and tracking application (such as WebHire or Resumix) to feed key data into the PeopleSoft database or perform the key recruiting functions. These bolt-on systems have interfaces to import data seamlessly into the PeopleSoft application once an applicant is hired. Figure 17.1 shows a typical integration scenario with a third-party vendor package and the PeopleSoft HRMS system.

Figure 17.1 **Recruiting integration**

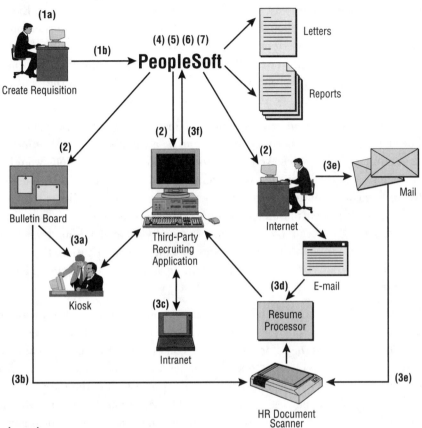

Legend:
(1) Requisition Data Creation
  (1a) Capture requisition data.
  (1b) Create job requisition in PeopleSoft.
(2) Job Posting Creation
(3) Resume and Application Acceptance
  (3a) Posting seen on manual bulletin board; applicant applies for position via kiosk; applicant data automatically captured in Third-Party Recruiting Application.
  (3b) Posting seen on manual bulletin board; applicant forwards resume to HR, who scans the resume; resume processor automatically captures applicant data in Third-Party Recruiting Application.
  (3c) Posting seen via intranet; applicant applies for position via personal computer; applicant data automatically captured in Third-Party Recruiting Application.
  (3d) Posting seen on Internet; applicant forwards resume via e-mail; resume processor automatically captures applicant data in Third-Party Recruiting Application.
  (3e) Posting seen on Internet; applicant forwards resume via regular mail to HR, who scans the resume; resume processor automatically captures applicant data in Third-Party Recruiting Application.
  (3f) All applicant data is extracted from the Third-Party Recruiting Application and then uploaded into PeopleSoft.
(4) Applicant/Requisition Matching
(5) Applicant Evaluation and Decision Recording
(6) Offers and Acceptances
(7) Applicant Hire

Yet another option for data capture is using scannable applications that record applicants' personal information, job preferences, and skills. Even this option is lacking, though, since text-intensive applicant information such as prior work experience is difficult to capture on a scannable form. The ultimate goal would be to allow applicants to data-enter their information directly into PeopleSoft; with the increased use of the Internet and PeopleSoft 8 functionality, this option has become viable.

As more and more organizations perform their recruiting activities via the Internet, the Recruit Workforce module can be a valuable back-office infrastructure for a front-office Web application. The online applications would allow applicants to enter their own information, thus freeing up staff time. Recruiters could continue to perform searches against the applicant data to find the appropriate candidates. This option also opens up an improvement opportunity for applicant communications whereby automated e-mail responses can be sent to applicants to acknowledge receipt of an application. E-mail can be further utilized to maintain contact with the applicant and to set up any interviews.

The decision regarding which data capture option to use depends on various factors. The online application is a likely option for organizations that recruit heavily from the Internet. For organizations that recruit from an applicant pool that does not use the Internet, one of the other options may be more attractive. Another organization may choose to manually process all of their applications and capture only the bare minimum required for government reporting. Regardless of the option that is chosen, it is important to take into account the organization's current business processes and future business goals to select a solution that meets existing requirements while preparing the organization to be competitive in the future.

Road Map

The configuration of the Recruit Workforce module requires the following key tables from the HR module: Business Unit, Set ID, Company, Department, Job Code, and Location. The following are the additional tables used by the Recruit Workforce module:

▶ Accommodation Type Table

▶ Accomplishment Table

▶ Checklist Item Table

▶ Checklist Table

- ▶ Citizen/Passport Tables

- ▶ Contract Clause Table

- ▶ Contract Template Table

- ▶ Contract Type Table

- ▶ Interviewer Availability Table

- ▶ Interview Schedule Table

- ▶ Jobcode Task Table

- ▶ Job Requirements Table

- ▶ Job Requirements Table—Competencies

- ▶ Job Requirements Table—Accomplishments

- ▶ Job Task Table

- ▶ Major Table

- ▶ School Table

- ▶ Standard Letter Table

- ▶ Supporting Documents Table

- ▶ Visa/Permit Tables

Lessons Learned

The Recruit Workforce module can be an attractive option for organizations that do not have an automated method for collecting and storing applicant information; however, the module is often not as robust as many organizations require. There are specific drawbacks concerning internal versus external applicant tracking as well as the standard letter generation.

The delivered PeopleSoft tables and panels used to track external applicants are the same as those used for internal applicants. This design often does not match an organization's needs, since many treat these two applicant populations very differently. Internal applicant processing may require more analysis of company or position seniority data, whereas external applicant processing would not. This processing difference can be significant, particularly in cases where an organization has many unions. To fill the gap for this requirement, some organizations choose to create custom tables and panels specifically for internal applicant processing; others choose to use the Recruit Workforce module solely for external applicant tracking.

The standard letter generation process delivered with PeopleSoft uses an SQR to extract data and a Word macro to combine the extracted data with letter templates. The data that is extracted is minimal and is missing key information such as interview locations for interview invite letters or sign-on bonus amounts for offer letters. Another downside is that the SQR will process all letters and does not include additional criteria for the type of letter or any date requirements. This makes it difficult for organizations that have more than one employment office across the country and who would therefore only want to print letters based on the employment office running the SQR. Improvements have been made with PeopleSoft 8's eRecruit module, including the use of online processing of internal and external applicants and improved messaging, approval, and work-flow options for notifying individuals of their status and progress through the process.

Position Management

The Position Management feature within the PeopleSoft application is one that is optional and does not have to be implemented. However, if your organization requires that you track positions and budget against a set number of them, then you should consider using this feature.

Core Configuration

One of the first and most important decisions your HR organization must make when setting up PeopleSoft is whether or not to use Position Management. Position Management functionality allows you to track each position necessary to run your organization, whether the position is currently occupied or not. The increased functionality provided by Position Management must be weighed against the increased data maintenance that it requires.

Position Management allows functions such as organizational charting and budgeting to be performed at a lower level than department. During initial setup, you must decide whether to drive your organization's HR system by employee, position, or both.

You must choose either None (to drive your system by employee), Full (by position), or Partial (by both employee and position) Position Management in the Installation Table. If you choose None for your Position Management setup, you do not need to read further in this section. When you choose Full Position Management, all employee records in the Job Table must be associated with a position. Choose Partial if you want to use Position Management but don't want to assign a position to every employee and record—for instance, maybe some groups track positions but others don't, or you leave that decision up to the individual department managers.

Information that is input to track positions can be used in several areas of HR, including recruiting, managing competencies, succession planning, budgeting, and career planning. PeopleSoft is designed to reference a position or an employee when using the above functionality.

Several fields within Position Data overlap the employee-level job and employment records. PeopleSoft delivers two fields that users can click on and off to control data flow between the records, one within the Job Data Component, Job Data/Work Location/page (Position Data Override) and another within the Position Data/Specific Information page (Update Incumbents). Users can audit the data within these records for consistency with a delivered SQR. These features help you to reduce the keying of redundant data, but provide flexibility to override data should you have a person filling a position with some exceptional data requirements (such as a higher grade or located in a different office).

Road Map

Core HRMS control tables must be set up in order to use Position Management, including:

- ▶ Company Table
- ▶ Department Table
- ▶ Job Code Table
- ▶ Location Table
- ▶ Pay Group Table
- ▶ Union Table

Refer to the introduction of this chapter for specific information on the table loading sequence and dependencies. Once you have these tables configured and loaded, you are ready to set up the Position Data Table, which stores the information on each position you create. You can have the system automatically assign position numbers as you create your positions, or you can create them yourself.

Lessons Learned

The primary implication to consider when using Full Position Management is that all employees must be associated with a position. This discipline is enforced by a PeopleCode edit in the Position field on the Job Data/Work Location page, which delivers an error message upon a save attempt when the position number is blank. The edit ensures that all employee records added from that point forward will have a position number.

An organization that converts data to PeopleSoft using Full Position Management must be aware that not only the current row but all historic rows must be associated with a position number. You cannot correct or insert historic rows that are not associated with a position, due to the previously described edit. Your organization could elect to remove this edit, but you may as well use Partial Position Management at that point. Without the edit, there is nothing to keep records from being entered without a position for the future. One technique used is to create a "history" position that can be used to populate history records but will not require that you recreate the entire position history information. In essence, you are creating a "dummy" position that is valid in the past but cannot be used in the future so that your data integrity is maintained.

If you are converting from a system that does not use Position Management, you will need to create positions and assign them to your employees. You will want to avoid manual entry when you perform this task. Consider an approach that first converts legacy data to job and employment records, then uses the existing job and employment data to create positions with a script.

Drawbacks of using Position Management include increased data maintenance. Not only will you maintain fields unique to position data, but you must be cognizant of necessary similarities and differences between the position and employee-level records. Many organizations do not need to maintain data at the position level. Those who do not need to report, budget, or build organizational charts at the position level may want to think twice before jumping into Position Management.

Finally, process inconsistencies can wreak havoc on your Position Data. Your organization must develop set procedures for the maintenance of positions during specified HR transactions. For example, if a position and an incumbent employee change departments, the transaction could be treated as a transfer. However, typically this would be referred to as a reorganization. How your organization handles this situation is not as important as the consistency with which your rules are applied. For PeopleSoft guidelines regarding which record to update for a particular transaction, see the PeopleBooks section entitled "Incumbent and Position Data—Which Is Which?"

Benefits

Within the benefits area, there are two options that an organization can choose in their purchase of benefits applications. These are:

▶ Base benefits

▶ Benefits Administration

We will look at each option as well as any core configuration issues and lessons learned in the benefits area. The base benefits application is provided as a part of the core PeopleSoft HRMS application. The Benefits Administration option is an additional module that must be purchased. With PeopleSoft 8, a new self-service feature to maintain changes to benefits and collect employee options at the start of each benefits enrollment period is available. This new feature is called eBenefits. You can also purchase and use the Benefits Community B2B (business to business functionality), which can link all your various benefits vendors together in one environment on the Web so that your employees can see all benefits information in one place.

Core Configuration

The base benefits process is the foundation of your PeopleSoft HRMS solution. The data and functions encapsulated in this area drive the benefits and payroll process. While an organization faces a choice whether to implement the base benefits or the full Benefits Administration functionality, many of the initial decisions are similar, and an organization may choose to design their system as if they were implementing full benefits administration functionality, while using only the base benefits functionality.

To reduce the complexity of the benefits areas, the PeopleSoft base benefits process is designed so that it can be reduced to four main phases of operation: setting up benefit plans, associating benefit plans with a benefit program, enrolling employees in benefits, and calculating deductions. A quick look at these four phases will provide a better understanding of the big picture of the PeopleSoft base benefits process.

Phase One   In the first phase, you set up your benefit plans and supporting tables. You identify benefit plans and plan providers, define available coverages, and establish rate schedules, calculation rules, and payroll deductions.

Phase Two   In the second phase, you associate your benefit plans with one or more benefit programs. A benefit program is a collection of benefit plans that your company offers to a group of employees.

Phase Three   In the third phase, you assign your employees to benefit programs—and enroll them in benefit plans. The benefit program that an employee is enrolled in determines the selection of benefit plans that the employee is eligible to participate in.

Phase Four   In the fourth phase, you calculate rates and benefit deductions for payroll. If you pay employees using a payroll system other than PeopleSoft Payroll, you will use PeopleSoft Payroll Interface to link the PeopleSoft benefits information to that system.

Road Map

Before you can define benefit programs and plans, you must establish deductions. Deductions are amounts taken from employee pay during regular payroll processing. There are two types of deductions: benefit-related and general. An example of a benefit-related deduction is medical insurance—an employee pays an amount, usually each pay period, toward the cost of medical insurance. An example of a general deduction is union dues or parking. You will use the Deduction Table to define each deduction your organization processes, both benefit-related and general. You link a deduction to an employee by entering a deduction code for each appropriate benefit plan, using the Benefit/ Deduction Program Table. After you enroll an employee, during the next payroll cycle Payroll processes the deduction. Below is a general listing of tables and the suggested load sequence.

Benefit Program   A collection of benefit plans your company offers to a group of employees. For example, you might have one benefit program for hourly employees, another for salaried employees, and a third for executives.

You can build as many programs as you need to support your business rules and operational policies.

Benefit Plan Type   Any type of benefit category, such as health, life, or savings. A benefit plan is a specific benefit offering within a plan type. For example, for a life plan type you might set up three benefit plans—one times salary, two times salary, and three times salary. Benefit plans are associated with benefit programs.

To define a benefit plan, you identify the benefit plan type and name the benefit plan. You can link any benefit plan to any number of benefit programs, so you will not need to enter the same benefit plan information more than once, no matter how many benefit programs include the plan.

Rates   Set up as age-graded, flat, percentage-of-salary, or service-related, depending on your requirements. And you can associate each set of rates with any number of benefit program and benefit plan combinations.

Calculation Rules   Include as-of dates for age, service, premium, and coverage calculations, rounding rules, and minimum/maximum coverage amounts. As with rates, you associate each set of calculation rules with all appropriate program and plan combinations.

Lessons Learned

You will need to make some basic decisions about your strategy before you set up deduction rules, and these decisions depend in part on how you want to report deductions to employees.

From an accounting viewpoint, you can use a deduction for more than one benefit plan if both plans are the same. For example, if you are processing characteristics for all medical plans, such as GL expense and liability accounts and tax implications, you might consider using the same deduction rules in order to reduce data entry.

However, besides accounting considerations, you will want to consider how benefit deduction amounts and descriptions appear on employee paycheck stubs. Do you want pay stubs to show the amount deducted for each benefit plan, such as the amount for medical insurance and the amount for dental insurance? Or do you want pay stubs to show the total deduction for a plan type, such as the total of all health plan deductions? Or do you want stubs to show the total for more than one plan type?

Table 17.2 is a chart that will help you understand the steps that you need to take depending on the way you want your deductions to show up.

Table 17.2   **Deductions Set-Up for Benefits Plan**

If You Want...	Do This...	For This Result on Pay Stubs:
To report the amount for each benefit plan	Define a deduction code for each benefit plan, such as one for each medical, dental, and savings plan.	Itemized descriptions and deduction amounts appear for each chosen plan type.
To report one total for a plan type	Define a deduction code for a specific plan type, such as a single deduction code for all medical plans.	The total of all deductions for the chosen plan type appears, along with the plan type's generic description.
To report one total for all deductions	Customize your paycheck print program to print the total deduction for several plan type series. For example, you might print the total deductions for all health and life plan type series, while still showing a separate deduction for a savings plan, like 401(k). You must customize your system because you can't automatically "roll up" to a higher level than plan type.	The total deduction of all plan types you customize appears.

In addition, to simplify your process, you may decide to establish most of your base benefit deductions as general deductions. The only deductions you may need to set up as benefit plans are your group term life insurance and your 401(k) deductions. This will simplify your configuration and testing efforts while for payroll purposes still correctly calculating the deduction amounts.

Benefits Administration provides a completely automated approach to processing your benefits requirements, including annual enrollment sign-up, family status benefit changes, and plan eligibility requirements. If you outsource your benefits processing or have only one set of benefit plans or options, you will most likely need only the base benefits module. Chapter 18, "HRMS Specifics," provides greater detail on how to analyze which module is right for your organization.

Payroll

As with benefits, the payroll area has two basic options you can choose from depending on how your payroll is supported. If you outsource your payroll to a third-party vendor such as ADP, PeopleSoft provides a payroll interface that can extract the necessary data it needs from the HR and benefits tables and pass it to your vendor. If you run payroll in-house, you will need to purchase the full Payroll module (either the North American or Global Payroll version depending on your needs). Additionally, with PeopleSoft 8, there is a new ePay feature that allows employees to view their paycheck and pay history online via the Internet.

Core Configuration

The Payroll module is the caboose of your HRMS train. Changing almost any one piece of data within the basic HR and benefits functions will probably influence some data element within the payroll cycle. The data and processes encapsulated in the Payroll module are primarily driven by the Human Resources and benefits (either basic or Benefits Administration) modules with interaction from the Time and Labor module. While an organization may choose to implement these other modules without the Payroll module, the related pay data will need to be interfaced to the other third-party systems to calculate payroll.

Road Map

Table 17.3 gives a general listing of tables and a typical load sequence for the Payroll application. Each installation is unique, and this load sequence should be reviewed, approved, and modified as necessary by your team and thoroughly tested in your environment.

Table 17.3   **Payroll Table Sequence**

Table Name	Dependent Table—Must Load First
Action Reason Table	
Action Code Table	
Balance ID Table	

Table 17.3 **Payroll Table Sequence** *(Continued)*

Table Name	Dependent Table—Must Load First
Balance ID Definition	Balance ID Table
Balance ID Quarter	Company Table
Deduction Subset Table	
Holiday Table	
Holiday Date	Holiday Table
Deduction Table	
Deduction Subset Code	
Deduction Class	
Deduction Frequency	
General Deduction Table	
General Deduction Frequency	
Special Accumulator Table	
Earnings Table	
Earnings Accrual	
Earnings Special Accumulator	
Earnings Program Table	
Earnings Program Definition	
Benefit Plan Table	
Benefit Definition Program	
Benefit Definition Option	
Limit Table	Benefit Definition Program Special Earnings Table

Table 17.3   **Payroll Table Sequence** *(Continued)*

Table Name	Dependent Table—Must Load First
Limit Exclude Table	Benefit Definition Program
Limit Impin Table	Benefit Definition Program
Limit Included Table	Benefit Definition Program
Bank Table	
Pay Form Table	
Pay Run Table	
Pay Calendar Table	
Pay Online Print Control Table	Company Table Pay Group Table
Pay Message Table	
Retropay Program Table	
Retropay Program Definition Table	
Mass Retro Request	
Mass Retro Definition	
Bond Table	
CSB Series Table	
CSB Frequency Table	Company Table Pay Group Table
CSB Denomination Table	
Garnishment Rule Table	
Garnishment Exempt Table	Garnishment Rule Table
Garnishment Payee Table	

Table 17.3   **Payroll Table Sequence** *(Continued)*

Table Name	Dependent Table—Must Load First
Garnishment DE Definition Table	
Garnishment DE Deduction Table	Garnishment DE Definition Deduction Table
Garnishment Prorate Definition	
Garnishment Prorate Rule	
State Tax Table	
State Tax Rate Table	
State Other Tax Table	
State Tax Reciprocity Table	State Tax Table
SWT Marital Status Table	State Tax Table
Tax Location Table 1	
Tax Location Table 2	State Names Table
Local Tax Table	
Local Tax Table 2	
Local Reciprocity Table	State Tax Table
Local Work Tax Reciprocity Table	
Taxable Gross Definition Table	State Tax Table
Taxable Gross Base Table	State Tax Table
Taxable Gross Component Table	
Company State Tax Table	Company Table State Tax Table

Table 17.3 **Payroll Table Sequence *(Continued)***

Table Name	Dependent Table—Must Load First
Company Local Tax Table	Company Table Company State Tax Table Local Tax Table
Company UI Report Code Table	
WageLS Plan Table	
US SOC Table	
Shift Table	Company Table Location Table
W2 Company Table	State Names Table Country Table Company Table
Tax Form Table	
Tax Form Box	
Tax Form Deduction	Deduction Table Deduction Class
Tax Form Earnings	Earnings Table
Tax Form Tax	State Names Table
Tax Form Form	
Tax Form Print	
Termination Action Reason Table	

Lessons Learned

From a Payroll perspective, the sheer amount of data can overwhelm a seasoned team of payroll specialists. Many implementations have suffered from the premise that how we do payroll now is how we need to configure PeopleSoft to process payroll for our future. This assumption couldn't be farther from the truth. We have seen numerous companies make the PeopleSoft HRMS package into a batch-oriented, monolithic processing machine. We have also seen companies completely restrict access to correction mode, prohibit future-dated HR or payroll transactions from being input, and even require everyone to get off the system while off-cycle checks are being processed. We are sure that at the time these decisions were made and software configured they seemed appropriate, but our experience implementing at both small and very, very large companies is that the team didn't challenge the requirement that forced the payroll process into a batch-operating environment. With the proper training and coaching, the individuals who utilize the PeopleSoft system can ensure that it is as flexible as the business requires, giving you the ability to process when, what, and where you want to.

Additional lessons learned are mostly focused on the nuisances of garnishment processing, state and local tax processing, and group term life insurance configuration.

From a garnishment perspective, PeopleSoft offers more functionality than the average organization requires to successfully process a garnishment. The most difficult aspect of the garnishment configuration is the mapping from your existing legacy processing system to PeopleSoft. In many legacy systems, an organization would have to trick the system to process the correct amount, or—even worse—the system could not calculate the correct amount and each pay period an individual would have to manually calculate both the garnishment amount and the remaining paycheck amount. With PeopleSoft, your challenge will be to find the original garnishment letter and correctly interpret the letter into the proper PeopleSoft rule. In many cases, when you begin to test your garnishment process, you'll discover that your old system really didn't correctly calculate the garnishment deduction amounts; for many teams, it takes time to accept that PeopleSoft is actually correct in its calculation.

The same can be said for local and state tax calculations. PeopleSoft provides a quarterly tax update file with the latest and greatest tax information. Generally, legacy systems did not do this. Changes had to be tracked and made by the payroll specialist using a systems programmer to input the changes, or an agency was relied on to provide you the data, which the programmer then input into the system. In addition, since PeopleSoft is a table-driven system, the integration of several local taxing options must be thought through to correctly configure individuals' tax liability.

In the group term life insurance configuration, you must ensure that you have the appropriate configuration for including setting up the deduction as a taxable benefit and also ensure that you have identified the proper Taxable Gross Component ID. This code tells the system to use a defined taxable gross base different from the federal one, and you will then need to select an option of GTI (gross taxable income).

As with any application, but especially with payroll (since generally everyone at the company is affected directly and monetarily), you should ensure that you have thoroughly tested your configuration and setup before going live. As was mentioned, though, in many cases, you find out that your legacy system was not correct and you need to have a plan to address any changes identified to help alleviate employee concerns. Any change that impacts the amount or even the appearance of an employee's paycheck is likely to upset them, and you must plan ahead and communicate to them to minimize any disturbance.

Up Next

Now that we have a basic understanding of the core PeopleSoft HRMS modules—HR, benefits, and payroll—along with key configuration and lessons learned, we will move on to more detailed topics in our next chapter. Chapter 18, "HRMS Specifics," covers additional modules such as Time and Labor, Flexible Spending Accounts (FSA) Administration, and Pension Administration, as well as other key decision points and functionalities that should be considered, such as COBRA processing and Benefits Billing. As with any implementation, you should look at your company's business needs and the best approach supporting those needs, whether it be leveraging an additional third-party tool, outsourcing of key functionalities, or implementing the features within your new ERP application. In determining which functionality to roll out when, you also need to consider the level of integration and change that your organization can support. Chapter 9, "Preparing Your Organization for Implementation," looked at ways to prepare your organization for change and analyze how much change they may be ready for. Chapter 15, "Go Live—Keys to a Successful Rollout," also looked at various rollout strategies. Whatever decisions you make, we hope these discussions will help you understand the options available.

CHAPTER 18

HRMS Specifics

FEATURING :

▶ Key decision points including whether to buy Benefits Administration or use the base benefits functionality provided

▶ Whether to use payroll (Global or American Payroll) or whether the Time and Labor module is also needed

▶ Whether to consider outsourcing key functions or leverage the PeopleSoft functionality

▶ Using the Flexible Spending Account module

▶ What Benefits Billing does and how to integrate it with other modules

▶ Whether Pension Administration should be part of your implementation

▶ The features and benefits of COBRA processing

▶ Key points about tax processing

P eopleSoft's structured, rule-driven, integrated design can sometimes seem like a mixed blessing. The opportunities for leveraging information across modules and for automation are exciting, but the actual implementation can be daunting. The system requires discipline across the applications on use of data and how the processes are implemented, standardization, and adherence to set table rules as defined by your organization. The decision to implement certain modules may involve reviewing policies and procedures to determine whether a process or policy change, system customization, or, perhaps, outsourcing is the best solution. Considerations for this type of review include business process integration, processing capacity to accommodate an organization's volume and complexity, maintainability of software modifications, product direction, and suite direction of all PeopleSoft products (HRMS, Financials, and Supply Chain Management).

This chapter delves deeper into the HRMS application suite and the integration between the application modules that most often raise such questions.

Base Benefits versus Benefits Administration

A key decision point that many organizations discuss is whether they need to purchase the additional Benefits Administration module or just use the base benefits functionality provided with the PeopleSoft HRMS application. This section looks at some key questions you need to ask yourself to help you make the right choice.

Decision Points

As mentioned in Chapter 17, "A Closer Look at HRMS," the PeopleSoft base benefits are delivered as part of the PeopleSoft Human Resources system. Base benefits functionality provides the capability to set up and assign benefit plans and to process enrollments. It automatically passes the deduction information to the PeopleSoft payroll system whether you are using the Global Payroll module or the North American version (if installed) for all benefit plan types. However, the maintenance of employee elections is completely manual. PeopleSoft's Benefits Administration module, on the other hand, provides the setup of rules that enable automation of open enrollment, event maintenance, and eligibility determination.

Table 18.1 summarizes some of the key differences between base benefits and the Benefits Administration module.

Table 18.1   **Base Benefits versus Benefits Administration**

Process	Using HR/ Base Benefits	Using Benefits Administration
Identifying and acting on events that affect benefits (e.g., family status change or new hire)	Manual processing or setup of process scheduler is required.	Event Rules Table automatically handles any event that is defined in the system. Action/Reason Table defines various rules that Benefits Administration follows.
Determining benefits eligibility	Eligibility is limited to the Benefit Program code, which is associated with the Pay Group.	Eligibility Rules Tables define the fields used to determine benefits eligibility. Users can define additional criteria.
Calculating waiting periods	This is a manual process.	The Event Rules Table defines waiting period dates, termination dates, and the begin and end dates for payroll deductions.
Open Enrollment	This is a manual process.	Open Enrollment Rule Tables schedule different groups or all employees, monitor the enrollment process, report errors, allow dependent/beneficiary enrollments, and allow overrides.
Event Maintenance	This is a manual process.	Event Maintenance schedules produce enrollment forms for all events defined in the system outside of open enrollment. This includes COBRA and direct billing.
Generating COBRA notification letters	No automation is provided. Process scheduler must be set up to trigger notification letter.	Action/Reason Table and Event Maintenance rules set up to automate letter generation.
COBRA Enrollment	This is a manual process.	Automated through the Event Maintenance process.

Given the obvious difference in the level of automation, why wouldn't a company opt for the Benefits Administration route? The key is that the automation is rule driven. This means that company policies that allow for multiple exceptions or that use unique criteria will be difficult or impossible to fit in the delivered framework without customization or manual workarounds.

An organization can determine its ability to implement Benefits Administration by conducting a fit-gap analysis. The analysis should consider the benefits processes to be supported and lay out the different employee populations, benefit plans, eligibility criteria (for each employee population and relevant plans), triggering events, and rules for responding to multiple events. Walking through the analysis will help you identify current policies and procedures that may not fit easily within the provided, rule-based framework of PeopleSoft's Benefits Administration. As an example, the types of situations that may be more difficult to handle are rates or eligibility requirements that differ by project, as for temporary employees, or contracts, as for union employees.

The following are some key questions to consider in your analysis:

▶ Are the eligibility criteria based on standard fields such as employee class, full- or part-time status, etc.? If not, you may be able to use eligibility configuration fields to fit your requirements. However, you will have to consider how you establish defaults and how you will ensure the integrity of these fields.

▶ Are there multiple "exception" situations? The Benefits Administration processes work best with minimal manual intervention, which ensures greater data integrity.

▶ Are events to be triggered from the job record, or will there be external interfaces or batch processes that affect benefits eligibility? The delivered processes are primarily triggered by job record entries, although this is changing somewhat with the newer release (see "Evolution" section below).

▶ Will there be many retroactive or future-dated events? Event coordination can be complex, and manual review or spot checks are recommended for actions affecting benefits. If these scenarios are numerous, you will want to carefully consider their impact.

▶ What is the basis of your service calculations? You may require customization if it is not based on the event date or a specific date in this or the previous calendar year.

Configuration Challenges

The implementation of Benefits Administration, as with any other module, requires careful thought and planning. The following are some challenges, selected based on past implementation experience, that may be helpful to you in thinking through your implementation.

Providing automatic coverage   It is not uncommon for an organization to have the requirement to provide automatic coverage starting on the event date and lasting until the actual employee election is made. Furthermore, this default coverage may vary based on the level the employee is enrolled in at the time the event occurs. To handle this, you may want to set up two separate events or to look into methods of reprocessing the event after it has been finalized with default coverage.

Coordinating events   Event coordination can be a challenge. Some can be handled automatically through effective dating, standard setup of event rules, and event class priorities. However, others will require manual review. The implementation team should think through these scenarios and define the appropriate review processes and roles. For example, consider the handling of retroactive events, future-dated events, events that will require reprocessing after being assigned an enrolled status, and multiple events that occur on the same day.

Maintaining leave accrual balances   Time can be accrued for different leave plan types based on rules that you set up. You can accrue time based on either the number of hours worked or length of service. However, more involved criteria such as basing accruals on hours worked under a particular project or contract may require modification. Also, keep in mind the integration with the Payroll module. When a confirm process is run in Payroll, the system will automatically track hours taken and update the employee's accrual. If you have not implemented Payroll, a process will need to be created to reduce hours taken.

Communicating across functions (HR, Benefits, Payroll)   A common challenge related but not limited to the configuration of the system is the fact that HR will typically be entering the data that determines the employees' initial eligibility as well as subsequent changes. Depending on existing cross-functional communications and work flows, this may be a significant process change. Therefore, when setting up event rules and criteria, ensure through selection of fields and training that the different functions understand the benefits implications of entering and processing certain data in a timely manner. Also, if eligibility configuration fields are used, be sure to consider defaults and update rules for these fields.

Evolution

The Benefits Administration module capabilities have been enhanced and streamlined with each release. Some key changes with PeopleSoft 8 include:

► Expanded features in the Savings Plan area, including support for 403 (b) and enhanced limit testing to handle regulatory limits

► Increased support for multiple jobs to automate your benefits, allowing you to specify which job (or groups of jobs) controls benefits eligibility and how multiple jobs should combine to satisfy eligibility criteria

► New eBenefits features to provide for online updates and viewing of benefits and beneficiaries

These changes are aligned with PeopleSoft's move toward global functionality and enabling of self-service capabilities.

Payroll versus Payroll with Time and Labor

Another question that your company may face is whether to use PeopleSoft's Payroll and Time and Labor modules in concert. Alternatives to using PeopleSoft's Time and Labor could include using a third-party timekeeping application (such as Kronos or TimeCorp), custom-building a bolt-on application, or importing relevant time information directly into the Paysheets (which are PeopleSoft's employee pay period records).

Decision Points

The decision on which approach to take should be based on careful analysis of fit with business requirements, cost, maintainability, process integration, and vendor stability and support. Keep in mind that different organizations have successfully implemented the various alternatives. The key is understanding what your organization's requirements are.

Let's take a step back for a moment and consider the pieces of the puzzle at their simplest. The Payroll module can be viewed as a processing engine.

PeopleSoft's Time and Labor module, in itself, may be viewed as a time repository. The ability to integrate the Time and Labor module with the Payroll, Projects, and Project Management modules enables labor distribution and analysis. The Time and Labor module also comes with rules, edits, processes, and reports that enable some validation, security, and analysis.

Your analysis should focus on what functionality is truly important to your organization, how well your organization's time and labor requirements are supported by the delivered fields and edits, and how well you can fit within the delivered, rule-based framework. Given current functionality, Time and Labor appears to be most suited for an environment with fairly consistent shifts and scheduling, and an employee population that can be effectively grouped into logical segments for processing and validation. The following sections, which describe some of the configuration challenges and the products' intended evolution, may help you organize your analysis.

Configuration Challenges

PeopleSoft's Time and Labor can be integrated with the Payroll and Projects modules, or used as a time repository on more of a stand-alone basis. How Time and Labor is implemented and its level of integration with other People-Soft modules or external applications will depend on the function you expect this module to perform. Are you looking for a central repository of time data from multiple sources? Do you have complex labor distribution rules? What kind of data-entry model are you going to support with your applications? Again, the analysis must be driven by your business requirements.

Once you've defined your requirements, their fit with delivered functionality will help you decide how to best configure your solution. The following paragraphs outline some challenges that have been faced in past implementations, which may be helpful in your endeavor.

To start, you will need to set up the basics such as Task Groups, Work Groups, and associated processing rules. The key to success is being able to effectively segment your employees into logical groupings that are subject to the same processing rules. Being able to find patterns and commonality is important. Common, consistent schedules across groups of people are best suited for the delivered functionality. If your rules are not generic enough or are subject to frequent change, you may end up with an overwhelming number of Task Groups. Maintenance with a large number of groups will be more challenging.

When you think about actual time reporting, think about how different segments of your employee population will be required to report their time. Are they using a Web-enabled application, a clock device, the phone, paper forms, etc.? This will help you understand your interface requirements and needs for data entry screens (or pages). As you think about the data flow and data entry, issues such as data validation, speed, and security may arise. For example, delivered functionality provides some capability to limit data entry at an individual level, but has fewer controls for mass data entry screens. Process changes or customizations may be required.

Labor distribution is another important topic. PeopleSoft's Time and Labor integrates with Payroll and Projects and supports labor distribution. However, there are some limitations because not all of the information that is tracked within Time and Labor is passed to Payroll. When time is passed for processing, it more or less gets lumped together. The delivered options for distribution are by hours, by percentage, by equal distribution, or by using a prompt. Depending on the complexity and consistency of how labor is distributed, these options may or may not be sufficient. The prompt option is helpful, but may not be viable for large volumes.

Lastly, a couple of additional notes. First, the delivered integration with Payroll is definitely an advantage of using PeopleSoft's Time and Labor. However, it is important to note that reversal adjustments and check cancellations that are processed in Payroll will not get communicated back to the Time and Labor module. Clients have dealt with this by establishing manual processes to keep the two synchronized. Second, Time and Labor is delivered with a number of standard processes that must be run. These processes ensure that the proper indicators are set and updated as the data is processed. Even if you do not use all of the delivered rule validations, etc., these processes must be run and may seem a bit labor intensive. With PeopleSoft 8, these processes have been combined into a single batch process to prepare reported time for Payroll and streamline the process.

Evolution

The Time and Labor module was new in version 6. It has been evolving since then to provide more global functionality and greater Web enablement. It is also moving to an open integration architecture to better enable sharing of data across modules and greater freedom of sharing data with multiple systems.

PeopleSoft is also working to expand its capabilities so that it is better able to support a greater variety of industries. Some improvements that have been added with PeopleSoft 8 include flexibility for configuring the data entry screens and streamlining the required processing steps for Time and Labor, as well as allowing all forms of "clock time" (which is the reporting of hours and minutes regardless of the technology used).

Other PeopleSoft Modules versus Outsource Options

Many organizations consider outsourcing as one alternative solution. Typical process candidates for outsourcing are:

- ▶ Discrimination testing for benefits administration
- ▶ Pension administration
- ▶ Savings and investment [401(k)]
- ▶ Payroll
- ▶ Employment
- ▶ Training

Major drivers for such discussions include cost, quality of service, accuracy, and customer service. According to the Gartner Group, a nationally recognized research group, the major benefits and risks of outsourcing are:

Benefits	**Risks**
Potential cost savings	Loss of control
Removes capital outlays from the books	Cost may be greater than anticipated
Frees existing staff to focus on strategic tasks	
Capacity on demand	Poor customer service
Variable versus fixed pricing	Vendor may not survive
Value-added services	Unanticipated change

Additional risks and benefits may surface depending on the process(es) and vendor(s) that you select.

If you do want to pursue an outsourcing alternative, there are some general points to consider:

▶ What is the strategic value of each service, and how will the information be used?

▶ What are the total costs of in-house processing versus the cost and value of an outside vendor?

▶ Which tasks will the vendor perform, and which tasks will the organization retain?

▶ What are the system specifications for initial loading of data as well as creating tapes or transmitting electronically?

▶ What is the flow of information from the system—how will data be accessed and reports produced?

▶ Are our goals for outsourcing clear?

▶ Will the outsourcing be over the short or long term?

▶ Who will control the outsourcing decision and why?

▶ Will the organization's culture support an outsourcing decision?

▶ Is it better for our operation to be centralized or decentralized before outsourcing?

▶ How difficult is it to measure and predict the present and future price, quantity, and quality of service?

▶ How difficult is it to agree on the meaning of quality standards, shared information, and future policies and procedures?

▶ How much does the service provider have to invest to provide unique (customized) services to our organization?

▶ How easy is it to find competing service providers for comparing cost and quality?

▶ How important is our relationship with the service provider? Is quality highly dependent on the identity of the person providing the service?

▶ How tangible are the goods and services provided? Is it difficult to identify concretely when they have been provided or when they have not?

The additional applications and functions from the modules described in the sections below may also be candidates for outsourcing. We have had experience both with clients that choose to outsource select functions and with those that choose to process in-house. The descriptions of the modules, their links to base HR and Payroll functionality, and where the functionality of the module is heading should help in the overall analysis outlined above.

Spending Accounts

PeopleSoft's FSA (Flexible Spending Account) Administration module is aimed at managing employee health care and dependent care flexible spending accounts. This module is dependent on data and tables in the HR and base benefits modules and is linked to Payroll for payment processing. The basic functionality provided with the FSA Administration module is:

- ▶ Setting up of base information
- ▶ Paying claims
- ▶ Tracking claims and payments
- ▶ Reviewing information online

The key tables for configuring the module are:

- ▶ Installation Table
- ▶ Forms Table
- ▶ FSA Run Table
- ▶ Benefit Program Table

When configuring the FSA Administration module, some things to consider include the layout of your forms, the layout and security requirements for your online inquiry screens, the layout and security requirements for your data entry screens, the process for handling claim or check reversals, and the process for handling mid-year changes or exception situations. These are key aspects to determining the fit of the software with your requirements.

When testing, make sure to focus on integration points with Payroll and with Benefits Administration (if being used). For example, you may want to note that deduction balances are based on paycheck date, while the Payroll FSA calculation is based on pay period end date. This means that when you look at your setup for the year, the way you build your deduction balances will be different from the way deductions are taken. It's important to understand and carefully test the various calculations of deductions and balances, particularly in situations when enrollments may be changing mid-year or in situations when an employee is receiving partial pays.

With PeopleSoft 8, an additional module that can be used to help with online benefits enrollment and changes to benefits plan information by employees is the eBenefits module. The ability to have a community of information and processes with your third-party benefits providers is available through the Benefits Community feature. Additionally, updates to your dependents and beneficiaries for plans can be accomplished online through eBenefits.

Benefits Billing

Another key component offered within the benefits application area is People-Soft's Benefits Billing. This area is closely integrated with the COBRA Administration, HR, and base benefits modules. The provided functionality includes:

▶ Generating billing charge records

▶ Generating billing statements

▶ Data entry for payments, charges, and adjustments

▶ Online inquiry screens for summary information by individuals

To make this work, the key tables for setting up the Benefits Billing module include:

▶ Installation Table

▶ Parameters Table

▶ Calendar Table

Questions to consider in making implementation decisions for Benefits Billing include:

▶ What are the interface requirements from the benefits carriers?

▶ What are the interface requirements to your Accounts Receivables system?

▶ Do the layout and data printed on reports and forms meet your business requirements?

▶ Are there additional reporting needs based on how you manage your billing process?

▶ How do you handle late payments and adjustments?

▶ What are your conversion requirements?

Pension Administration

PeopleSoft's Pension Administration is integrated with the HR, benefits, and Payroll modules. It is meant to help you manage defined benefit pensions and is targeted at U.S. defined benefit plans. Functionality includes data entry and data maintenance, benefit calculations, processing payments, administering retirees, and summary inquiry screens and reports. An assumption is made that a trustee will handle tax withholding calculations and generation of final pension checks. The system is therefore set up to generate the necessary information for an interface to your trustee system.

Stock Administration

PeopleSoft's Stock Administration is also integrated with the HR, benefits, and Payroll modules and provides the tools for an organization to administer and maintain stock option and employee stock purchase plans. Key features include:

▶ Ability to administer a variety of stock option types, such as incentive stock options, non-qualifying stock options, and tandem stock appreciation rights

▶ Ability to award stock options or grants to groups of identified individuals

▶ Support for many stock exercise types online and interfaced with Payroll, including cashless same-day sale, cashless sale-to-cover, cash, cash on margin, swap, and tandem SAR

▶ Standard reports to comply with stock regulatory requirements

▶ Online tracking of employee stock payment program (ESPP) activities to include contributions, stock plans, offering period begin and end dates, and purchase prices and sales

With eEquity in PeopleSoft 8, ESPP participants are able to review their activities, enter sales and transfer transactions, and enter issuance instructions. Option participants can also review their activities, enter sales and transfers, and model exercises and releases.

COBRA

PeopleSoft's COBRA Administration is meant to work with base benefits, Benefits Administration, and Benefits Billing. It can be used without implementation of Benefits Administration; however, the process becomes much more manual and may seem more cumbersome than it's worth. It can also be implemented without Benefits Billing. Some clients use the COBRA Administration module primarily to identify qualifying events and generate the necessary letters. Managing the billing and tracking of payments may be outsourced or handled with another application.

In general, COBRA Administration provides you with functionality to:

▶ Set up eligibility criteria

▶ Manage multiple qualifying events

▶ Generate notification letters

▶ Validate elections, process enrollments

▶ Terminate COBRA coverage

▶ Initiate Benefits Billing enrollments

Standard qualifying events recognized by the system are:

▶ Termination

▶ Retirement

▶ Military leave

▶ Death

▶ Reduction in hours

▶ Divorce

▶ Married dependents

▶ Over-age dependents

▶ Reaching Medicare entitlement

These events are identified based on employee data changes in the HR and benefits modules. A batch process updates an employee's status and enables the generation of letters as well as election of benefits. Key tables for setting up the COBRA Administration module include:

▶ Installation Table

▶ COBRA Administrator Table

▶ COBRA Event Rule Table

▶ Benefit Program Table

▶ Action/Reason Table

In deciding whether and how to use this module, consider the following questions:

▶ What are your data entry and security requirements for the enrollment process? For example, the delivered screens or pages may contain data that you are not accustomed to sharing with employees who process COBRA. This may require a change in expectations or some system modification. Also, you may have requirements for viewing additional information that were not included in the delivered screen (or page layout). Again, you may choose to establish a process for pulling up multiple screens, change your requirement, or customize the system.

▶ Based on the way you track/record job status and family status changes, will the process for identifying qualifying events fit your needs? If you have made any changes in the way you utilize action/reason codes, it may affect your ability to identify qualifying events through the delivered process.

▶ What are your requirements for communicating to employees and to benefits carriers? For example, are the fields included in the notification letter sufficient to meet your needs?

▶ What are your conversion requirements? Remember that for anyone who is not an employee with the organization, you will need to set up some basic data first.

Payroll Tax Processing

PeopleSoft tax processing functionality is a part of the Payroll module and is integrated with the HR and Benefits modules. A number of tables are delivered and maintained by PeopleSoft; however, you will be responsible for setting up state and locality information by company (Federal EIN) in each state and locality where you do business. Because tax rules are standard and based on government regulations, PeopleSoft maintains more control over this functionality than others. It is therefore an area where you want to be even more cautious of making any changes. This may seem fairly straightforward. However, key areas to consider are conversion, any changes to payroll processing, and timing of tax updates.

Let's begin with a few words regarding conversion. The structure of People-Soft is somewhat different from that of many legacy systems. It offers greater flexibility and greater accuracy in the way that you tie and process tax location information for employees. Many legacy systems maintain tax information at the employee level. With PeopleSoft, tax processing is driven by tax location, which is tied to certain tax localities as determined by your setup. The employee is tied to tax localities through location and tax location assignment at the employee level. This provides you with the ability to have multiple locations (e.g., buildings, floors) that are tied to the same tax location and tax localities. It avoids redundant data at the employee level, but this difference may add to the data cleanup work that you would normally encounter in data conversion efforts.

Be careful with any changes to the pay process. We have seen clients make changes to the pay process without carefully considering implications to tax functionality. Again, because this is an area where PeopleSoft maintains more control, you may be limiting yourself in the short term and setting yourself up for more difficulty in maintenance and upgrades in the long term.

Lastly, consider the impact of regular tax updates on your configuration and testing work plans. Tax updates are sent on a scheduled basis and impact your calculations. You should be aware of them and include the time to incorporate these updates into your testing and environment maintenance plans.

Up Next

Now that you have a basic understanding of the features and functions covered in the PeopleSoft HRMS area, including a look at how you might analyze which functions might be candidates for outsourcing, we will move on to our next major functional area, PeopleSoft Financials. Chapter 19 will look at the basic features and modules associated with the PeopleSoft Financials application suite, from financial reporting features in General Ledger to payables and receivables processing. Other key areas found within PeopleSoft Financials include the newer Expense module/asset management, projects, and budgets.

A Closer Look at Financials

FEATURING:

- ▶ Interaction with other key applications (HRMS, Supply Chain Management, CRM, and EPM)
- ▶ Version 8 update: What's different
- ▶ Why choose PeopleSoft Financials over others: A look at the key concepts within the application
- ▶ An overview of PeopleSoft General Ledger and integration with Budgets
- ▶ A review of the procure-to-pay process: key processes and concepts within Procurement, Accounts Payable, and Asset Management

- ▶ A look at PeopleSoft Projects and the Expenses module
- ▶ A review of the collections process: Billing and Receivables
- ▶ Update on new Professional Services Automation (PSA) offering
- ▶ What the new Enterprise Performance Management (EPM) module and Treasury module are all about, including key concepts and configuration tips

The PeopleSoft Financials application is a wealth of functionality rolled up into several key processes that are tightly integrated through various real-time and batch processes. This chapter will provide a summary of these key processes, look at key concepts, and provide insight into the new features of PeopleSoft 8, as well as offer some tips and considerations for dealing with global issues.

Integration with Other Applications

PeopleSoft Financials is at the center of the Enterprise Resource Planning (ERP) system, and the center of this application suite is the General Ledger module, which brings all the financial data together to provide the key financial information to run a business. Figure 19.1 shows the key integration points across these major applications. As you can see from this diagram, several major processes cross from other PeopleSoft application suites into the PeopleSoft Financials modules. Specifically, the following major process areas flow to and from the PeopleSoft Financials product:

Expense tracking/management   This Financials Application is integrated with the Human Resources suite of products, pulling key employee data from the HR repository and updating payroll information at the individual level with the expense reimbursements.

Labor distribution/general ledger interface   The payroll system provides a general ledger interface that provides key information on labor distribution and expenses, which are used in financial reporting.

Distribution update   The Inventory and Billing applications generate journal entries that are sent to the General Ledger for posting financial results. Within Purchasing, purchase orders are created and used by the Payables module to match against vendor invoices, and vendor information is shared across the products. Information on receipts of products and inventory also can be used to update project information as well as assets. Sales orders that are closed in the Billing module create accounts receivables for the Receivables module.

Figure 19.1   **Financials integration with other applications**

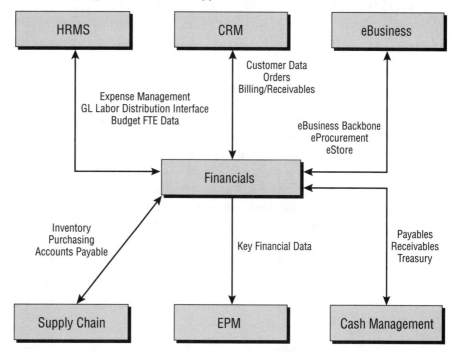

Financials History Overview

As mentioned in Chapter 1, "Enterprise Resource Planning with People-Soft," the PeopleSoft Financials application was first introduced in 1993. This set of modules was introduced as the second line of products within the PeopleSoft ERP solution after the Human Resources module. Original applications include the General Ledger, Receivables, and Payables modules. Quickly following this initial release were the Budgets, Asset Management, and Projects modules. Over the past few years, Expenses, Treasury Management, and EPM have joined the set of modules making up the Financials application suite.

PeopleSoft 8 and Beyond

The latest release of PeopleSoft includes more robust and enhanced features leveraging the latest Internet technology and solutions. Within the Financials suite, PeopleSoft has focused on new reporting features and functions around its Enterprise Performance Management (EPM) module as well as the recent eProcurement release 2, which integrates CommerceOne's BuySite (an online Web-based market site to purchase goods for your company) into the People-Soft Supply Chain and Financials applications (specifically the purchasing and accounts payable areas). In fact, with PeopleSoft 8, PeopleSoft has combined all its distribution, manufacturing, and supply chain planning products into a combined suite of products called PeopleSoft's Supply Chain Management solution. Chapter 20, "A Closer Look at Supply Chain Management," provides a more in-depth look at this solution set. We will review each product offering, including looking at key concepts and terms as well as new People-Soft 8 functionality.

In general, a few key functional enhancements provided with PeopleSoft 8 Financials include:

- ▶ Integration of eProcurement with Payables functionality.

- ▶ New Internet-capable reporting features leveraged from the enhanced EPM features.

- ▶ New modules to include Contracts, Deduction Management, and Resource Management—all of which are controlled releases and used with the new Professional Services Automation (PSA) application.

- ▶ Support of document sequencing to meet global requirements for recurring and spread standard journals.

- ▶ A new chart field (we will review what the chart fields are and how they are used in the "PeopleSoft Financials—Key Concepts" section) for tracking operating units. The Operating Unit field can be used to track plant, office, branch, clinic, store, or other detailed segmentation necessary to produce financial statements for your organization.

- ▶ Giro processing (Giro is a common payment method used in many countries such as Italy and Singapore to perform direct debits and credits).

- ▶ Letter of Credit feature to support international trade requirements.

▶ Enhancements in the revaluation process for PeopleSoft Payables and Receivables, including:

  ▶ Improved value-added tax (VAT) requirements and capabilities to support global implementations

  ▶ New Commitment Control capabilities

  ▶ A new generic currency conversion utility to better support European Monetary Union (EMU) requirements

Integration of customer information, sales information, and other financial data with the new PeopleSoft CRM—Vantive—solution will be an area that PeopleSoft focuses on in upcoming service pack releases.

Why Choose PeopleSoft Financials?

PeopleSoft's new 100% Internet solution provides enhanced features that allow for greater integration between its modules as well as integration with external applications and tools. These features allow greater flexibility to integrate data to and from other applications and Web sites. Within the Financials application, these core features translate to management reporting capabilities and the ability of PeopleSoft to provide easy-to-use tools to aid in obtaining valuable management and financial information.

Using a combination of key features (which will be discussed in greater detail in the "PeopleSoft Financials—Key Concepts" section) such as trees, ledgers, chart fields, and reporting tools, users can design and produce a variety of reports on their own without all the programming support of the Information Systems group. In the past, most companies (very likely including yours) relied heavily on their IT (Information Technology) department to support these requirements through custom reporting and modification of existing delivered reports. With the flexible tools available through PeopleSoft, users can do their own reporting and also make future changes leveraging the table-driven, effective dating features within PeopleSoft. In addition, the user-friendly and easy-to-use "pages" or screens are consistent throughout the application. Other user-friendly features include extensive options to create allocations and provide multiple ledgers to track a variety of financial information (or books), including forecasts, budgets, actuals, etc.

PeopleSoft Financials—Key Concepts

Within the PeopleSoft Financials application, there are several key concepts that should be reviewed to understand the structure of the system and how to configure the application. As mentioned earlier, one of the key attributes that appeals to most customers is PeopleSoft's flexibility and ease of use for reporting purposes. To fulfill your financial reporting needs, setting up these key attributes and understanding these key concepts are the foundation for a successful implementation. The major concepts are explained in the following sections.

Business Units

PeopleSoft is based on key reporting relationships that can be scaled down to a few basic concepts. At the top level of this relationship lies the concept of business units. A *business unit* within PeopleSoft is an organization or subset of an organization that is independent with regard to one or more accounting or operational functions. Business units represent key categories of business that are used for reporting financial information or tracking key accounting or operational information. They do not have to be legal entities and can consist of various departments or subunits under them. A business unit is basically a mechanism to group or categorize departments into a single unit. Many companies use the business unit to represent regions, product lines, or key businesses under their corporate umbrella.

 TIP   With the new chart field of Operating Unit in PeopleSoft 8, you have another level of detail within your organization structure that you can distinguish and report against in addition to business unit.

Within the PeopleSoft General Ledger, business units generally comprise individual entities for financial and tax reporting purposes.

In order to determine how many business units you need to create for your organization, you need to consider your financial reporting needs and how you group information other than cost centers (or, as PeopleSoft refers to them, departments). When financial data needs to be rolled up and reported within a group of cost centers or departments, you have a business unit.

In release 7.5, PeopleSoft only supported creation of up to 500 business units; therefore, a strategy on how to use them had to be considered. However, with

PeopleSoft 8 this field has been expanded and the operating unit has been added as an additional chart field to help segment the financials data. The operating unit is designed to capture detail-level information to produce a financial statement (thus providing another level, which can be used below the business unit yet above the department). Organizations that have a large number of groupings—for example, a large retail organization that owns drug stores, grocery chains, and maybe department stores—may benefit from this new structure. You may want to report financial information all the way down to the store level. Based on this demand, if you have more than 500 combinations of stores, PeopleSoft 7.5 would limit you to the use of the business unit field. However, for most organizations this was not a hindrance, and with PeopleSoft 8 it becomes much more of a non-issue. With this large retailer example, to report and group information easily for financial reporting purposes by store, you would need to set up a business unit code for each store. (Note: With the new Operating Unit chart field, you could have each store be an Operating Unit and could group the stores by regions or business area using the Business Unit chart field.) Then each department or cost center that was under that store would be rolled up (or consolidated and summarized) under that business unit.

Several key areas or processes are used in conjunction with business units besides the need to consolidate or summarize information (as well as see the detail) for reporting requirements. These include:

Creation of security   You may have a need to create security by business unit depending on how you roll out your PeopleSoft solution and what features or functions you employ.

Currency requirements   You may want to create multiple business units based on currency requirements to track and maintain financial information based on currency.

Segmentation of accounts   In order to segment data to support interunit accounting, the business unit field allows for this feature.

Creation of an eliminations entity   Creating separate business units can support eliminations within the consolidations process.

Definition of business rules   You can define various business rules based on business units, including controlling the edits on your chart of accounts (combination rules), summarization structures, roll-ups, ledger definitions, calendars, and closing rules.

Configuration of approval options You can set up different approval requirements by business unit (e.g., a specific approval rule is used prior to posting a transaction, or assume the journal entry can be processed without approval based on the business unit).

TableSets (SetIDs)

Another unique concept within the PeopleSoft application is the TableSet, also called the SetID. Based on the groups of business rules you need to set up and associate with your business unit, PeopleSoft provides a mechanism to categorize these requirements or rules using what they label as Table SetIDs. These SetIDs control the sharing of information by business unit. This feature helps you to minimize redundant data and system maintenance tasks when various business units share the same rules in one area but not in another. The SetID feature allows you to create multiple accounting structures, which can then be "shared" based on the particular business situation.

For instance, maybe several of your business units share the same group of accounts but use different timespans (such as two different meanings for year-to-date because of differences in the start of their fiscal year). By setting up unique SetIDs for each of these different timespans, you can create the right combination of rules without having to type them in for each entity or business unit every time. One set of IDs can be set up for each timespan used by your organization (or business units) if, for instance, one uses a YTD (year-to-date) timespan starting January 1st and ending on December 31st while another uses a YTD starting October 1st and ending on September 30th. You can set up two separate IDs and associate them appropriately to each business unit (and therefore don't have to create a timespan for each business unit). Figure 19.2 shows how one TimeSpan record control can be assigned to a SetID—SHARE in this example—and then assigned to an overall Set Control Value (or TableSet Control), US001.

When business units are created within the application, you associate the tables that contain the core financial rules to the business unit using the SetID (or Table SetID) feature. Figure 19.3 shows the table within PeopleSoft that associates the SetIDs to the business unit. These TableSets form the basis for the financial rules used by the particular business unit. You should tailor your business requirements for each business unit using this TableSet concept.

Figure 19.2   **TimeSpan SetIDs example**

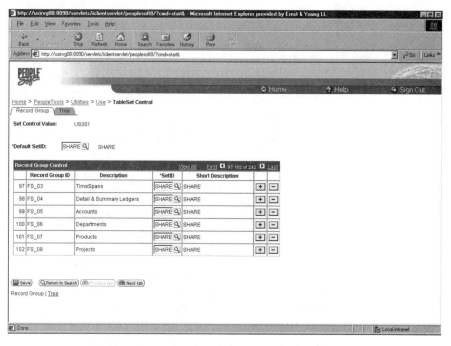

Figure 19.3   **Linking SetIDs to business unit**

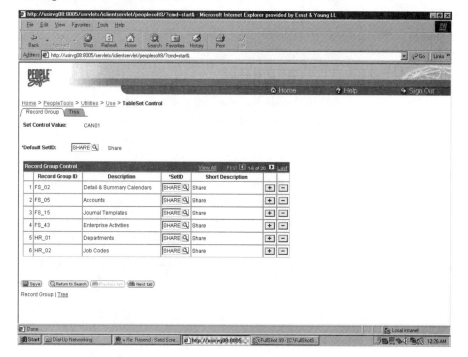

TIP   Remember: When looking at how to name your Table SetIDs, consider global implications as well as regional needs. The TableSet field is 5 digits long, so one approach may be to use a two-digit entity identifier with a three-character geographic identifier, since the TableSet sharing might be driven by certain local requirements such as statutory requirements by country or region. You might consider using the supplied PeopleSoft three-character country field (such as USA and GER) as your basis.

Suspense versus Recycle

Another important concept to grasp, especially within the posting of general ledger transactions, is whether a journal entry that is considered in error should be posted to a suspense account or recycled and corrected before being posted. Recycling your journal entries is preferable to posting to a suspense account, because this forces your staff to research and fix errors more quickly. When you correct errors prior to closing your books, you get a truer picture of your financial situation because the source of the transaction is held accountable to input the right value up front prior to accepting the transaction. This is a "front-end" mechanism rather than a "back end" one. If you wait and put the errored transaction into a suspense account and correct it later (on the back end), you might find it harder to resolve because time has passed. Additionally, it is preferable to have the entry source be the person responsible for fixing or resolving the error rather than someone who is not as aware of where the transaction should be posted.

Chart of Accounts

Within PeopleSoft, the entire set of codes used to book a financial transaction within the General Ledger is referred to as the *chart of accounts*. The chart of accounts is much more than the account codes used by the organization. It includes the following set of chart fields:

Business Unit   As already discussed above, a business unit represents an independent unit with regard to accounting functions. The meaning and use of business units can be different for the various applications such as Payables, General Ledger, Asset Management, and Receivables.

Account   This is the field that specifies the account code used to track/segment financial data. It is used to designate financial classifications (including subcodes usually associated with greater detail levels of the natural account classifications). Typically, the types of accounts include asset, liability, equity, revenue, and expense. PeopleSoft General Ledger uses accounts in combination with other chart fields to create journal entries. This is a required field that must be set up before you can create journals and post to the general ledger. You can inactivate accounts for historical purposes and reactivate them if necessary. In addition, you need to create accounts for any statistical requirements you may have. Statistical accounts (such as head count and square footage) are used to capture statistical amounts and not monetary amounts. Within PeopleSoft, statistical and monetary accounts are stored in the same table and are mutually exclusive. Statistical accounts use units of measure rather than currency types. With PeopleSoft 8, the account code field has been expanded from 6 to 10 characters in length. This allows for greater flexibility in creating account code values.

TIP   You might want to create a defined set of account types for each SetID to avoid potential problems with loading of data if you plan on using the Import Manager (a table-loading tool within PeopleSoft).

Department ID   Within the financials organization, this is commonly the cost center or lowest level of financial reporting within the organization. This field is used in conjunction with reporting departmental budgets and information at a manager level. This is not a required chart field within PeopleSoft.

Product   This field is used to track or segment financial data by the use of a product code, which an organization may utilize, for instance, to track financial data against. Examples could include an organization using product codes to track its different lines of products or markets. For instance, the large retailer in our earlier example might want to set up product codes for grocery, drug, and department stores, such as codes for dairy products, vitamins, shoes, etc. You determine how low within your organizational structure you want to track financial data (for instance, you may only want to track financial data down to the grocery store and not down to the dairy products). Trees (a concept we will address later in this chapter) can be used to link the various levels of products together to consolidate them into groups (such as rolling up all the dairy products within a store or group of stores). This field is not a required chart field within PeopleSoft.

Project   This field is tied to the PeopleSoft Projects module and is used in conjunction with project accounting. If you are tracking various projects, you can use this field to track financial information by a project code. This is also not a required chart field within PeopleSoft.

Operating Unit   This new chart field delivered with PeopleSoft 8 allows organizations another option to capture detail-level information to produce financial statements between the existing business unit and department ID levels. You can use this field to identify information for such things as plant, office, physical location, branch, building, store, hospital, clinic, or geographic area. This field can be used to facilitate responsibility reporting or group information by profit centers (revenue and expense flow) and can be used to assist in reporting for tax purposes. It can be used at the city, county, or state levels for both the P&L statement and Balance Sheet. Basically, this allows you the detailed reporting you might need at a lower level than was previously provided by the Business Unit field.

Trees

Within PeopleSoft, a very flexible system called *trees* is used to provide hierarchical relationship information, mainly for reporting purposes. These trees generally depict relationships between the various accounting units such as business units, operating units, and departments as well as various other roll-up or reporting structures. You can create various trees to roll up sets of accounts under a common hierarchy or relationship as well as any of the other chart fields provided. The trees are then used in reporting to help group information together and provide for a much easier method to maintain these hierarchical structures. You can also create multiple trees to signify multiple hierarchical structures, depending on how you want the information shown on a particular report. Trees are effective dated, and a historical representation of the various structures can be maintained so you can analyze data on both historical and current structures. Figure 19.4 shows an example of a tree within the PeopleSoft application.

Figure 19.4 **Tree structure example**

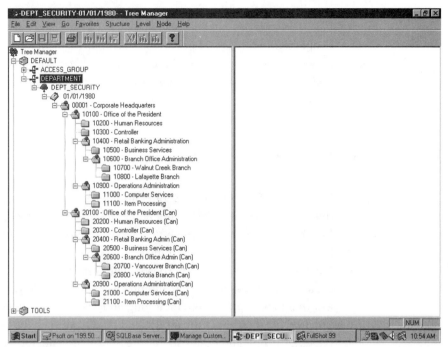

Workflow

Another term that you may hear a lot about when looking at an ERP or People-Soft application is the term *workflow*. Within PeopleSoft, the workflow feature is a background process that creates a list of administrative actions based on your selection criteria and specifies the procedure associated with each action. In essence, workflow moves tasks and data to various individuals, depending on the process you set up. A common use of workflow within the applications is to seek approvals for transactions such as purchase orders, invoice payment, journal entries, etc. PeopleSoft's workflow is embedded within the application and a part of its internal tools set. There are other workflow products on the market that could be used "on top" of the PeopleSoft applications if an organization desires this option. However, the workflow product is included with the PeopleSoft application and is not an additional cost to the organization.

TimeSpan

Last, but certainly not least, is another key term that is used throughout the PeopleSoft Financials application: *TimeSpan*. TimeSpan represents relative periods in time such as year to date, current period, quarter to date, etc. Many Ledger functions use TimeSpan rather than a specific date when a rolling time frame is required.

General Ledger Overview

PeopleSoft's General Ledger application can be considered the core piece of the PeopleSoft Financials application and was one of the first modules that PeopleSoft released under the PeopleSoft Financials umbrella. Most of the Financials modules provide transaction data into the General Ledger application for financial reporting purposes. The General Ledger application provides a standard process of posting and processing transactions both internal and external to the application, including an Excel upload process. Figure 19.5 provides an overview of the integration points between the General Ledger and the other PeopleSoft applications and shows the integration points with outside/external systems.

There are several key considerations to look at when reviewing the capabilities of the PeopleSoft General Ledger. Specifically, we will look at the following core process areas within the General Ledger application:

- ▶ Ledger
- ▶ Allocations
- ▶ Combination Error Checking
- ▶ Journal Processing
- ▶ Consolidations
- ▶ Currency Issues

Figure 19.5 **Financials points of integration**

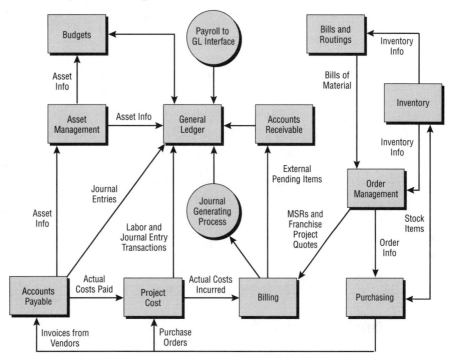

Ledgers

Within the PeopleSoft General Ledger application, the core structure and key component is the ledger itself. Within PeopleSoft, you can create and maintain many ledgers to track your financial information. A *ledger* is defined as a set of posted balances that represent a set of books for a particular business unit within the PeopleSoft application. A ledger supports a single chart of accounts, and the PeopleSoft General Ledger system supports detail, multiple, and summary ledgers.

A summary ledger is used primarily in allocations, inquiries, and nVision (PeopleSoft's drill-down reporting tool). The summary ledger stores combined account balances from detail ledgers. This allows for increased speed and efficiency in reporting by eliminating the need to summarize data from the detail ledger balances each time a report is run. Therefore, you should analyze your reporting requirements and determine what information you may need to have a summary ledger for. Rules for the rolling up of data into a summary ledger are created and processed in order to create a summary ledger.

Types of ledgers that may be created by an organization include actuals, budgets, business unit, forecast, corporate summary, and many more. Closing rules define how the General Ledger system will calculate retained earnings and carry forward balances into the new year. The system provides great flexibility in how the retained earnings can be calculated, including options to:

▶ Close all profit and loss accounts to a single retained earnings account in total

▶ Close all profit and loss accounts to a single retained earnings account but break this amount down by department, project, or any other chart field

▶ Close selected profit and loss accounts and chart fields to multiple retained earnings accounts

▶ Organize and structure rules with contingencies

Combination Error Checking

Within the PeopleSoft application, you may want to leverage certain business rules that prevent you from using a particular set of chart field values together or in combination with each other. This ability is known as *combination error checking*. You must set up the valid chart field combinations you wish to implement, and the system will leverage these rules when processing your journal entries. A great example of combination error checking is the use of certain accounts by departments. You may want the account codes to be used only by a particular set of departments. Therefore, you would set up a combination definition or rule to cover this requirement. You can group sets of these rules into combination groups and apply them to a particular set of journal entries to be processed.

 TIP Remember to keep your rules effective, but simple. A great deal of overhead can be added to your processing and maintenance time based on becoming overly restrictive on combination rules. Also, when exceptions occur, it's virtually impossible to process that entry. You should limit your error checking to covering specific incorrect entries, not to providing excessive control.

Allocations

Within PeopleSoft, an automated allocation process can be created. Many companies enter allocations manually, and therefore this feature is a great benefit to their monthly close process, eliminating steps that they had to accomplish manually in the past. An example of an allocation might be the process of "spreading" or sharing the cost of a building (rent, maintenance, etc.) with the tenants or departments using the building. With PeopleSoft you can allocate the expense of maintaining that building to each department based on a certain calculation or proportion, such as head count, square footage taken, or a fixed percentage.

You need to determine your desired end result, and then you can set up the allocation you wish the system to process. The pool source used in the allocation includes the amounts to be allocated. This amount can come from a ledger or any table or be a fixed amount. A basis is then applied that includes how and in what proportion the pool amounts are distributed to the various targets. The target or destination is where the amounts defined by the pool and basis are allocated (in our example, this would be the departments within the building). Offset includes the entries that balance the targets. These entries usually reflect the clearing of pool amounts as they are transferred to the targets. The mapping of these fields (from the pool and basis amounts) are allocated to the target and offset. The target and offset ledgers contain the results of an allocation. Ultimately, they are updated ledgers, but the output of the allocation can be to journals that you choose to post in these allocations or can be used in a separate process that is then used later to update the ledgers.

The various allocation types within PeopleSoft include:

Copy   Copies pool amounts to the target/offset with some percentage changes.

Spread Evenly   Divides pool amounts equally among the specified basis field.

Fixed Basis   Allocates on a fixed basis and percentage of pro rata allocation.

Pro Rata with Record Basis   Divides the pool amount among the targets based on amounts stored in the basis record.

Arithmetic Operation   Defines the allocation calculation as a mathematical operation between the pool and basis (add, subtract, multiply, or divide).

You can define multiple allocation steps for step-down allocations across chart fields using the PeopleSoft application. Each step's target can become the next step's pool or basis. Leveraging these characteristics allows an organization to be able to set up about every type of allocation processing needed to support their requirements.

Journal Processing

Journal entries can be processed within PeopleSoft manually, directly into a journal, or from other modules or external systems of both non-PeopleSoft and PeopleSoft applications. Through use of a "journal generator," PeopleSoft is able to create journal entries for posting to your general ledger. There are only two types of standard journal entries within PeopleSoft General Ledger, recurring and template:

Recurring   Contains the same accounting information and same amounts on each entry (for each cycle or process). Examples include rent, lease payments, or amortization expense.

Template   Contains the same accounting information, but the periodic amounts vary. Examples include payroll, utility, and telephone expenses.

You can create specific templates (called journal templates) that help you create the proper entries based on the system the entry is coming from and rules about how that system provides information to the journal. An example may be to create accounts payable entries where certain chart fields are pre-populated with information based on the accounts payable entry.

A Journal Source field is used to help track from which area a journal transaction originated, should you have errors or problems with the transaction and need to track down the owner. You can also summarize information based on the type of transaction (or source) you are using. For instance, a Payables template may summarize all detailed entries by department so that you don't have a journal entry for each accounts payable invoice or transaction processed for a department during the period, but instead have only one. This prevents your ledger from becoming too detailed and overloaded with too much data. Since the systems are integrated, if you have a question about why a particular department is paying out so much money on invoices, you can link back to the Payables module and obtain the detail on that transaction rather than having to post all that detail to the ledger.

Consolidations

PeopleSoft provides the capability to combine your financial data into one consolidated ledger and provide a consolidated "set of books" for your organization. Since this process is based on the ledger concept and summarizes information from various applications, it is a fairly simple process to support. Reporting tools such as Essbase's Hyperion product are no longer necessary to support a picture of a single set of consolidated information for a multi-conglomerate business. PeopleSoft's flexible trees, nVision reporting, and ledgers all support this process.

Enhancements with PeopleSoft 8 include the ability to perform consolidations across ledgers that may have different chart field values. For example, if you choose to have different charts of accounts for each of your entities that in turn need to be consolidated, you can now use the consolidation process to support this feature. The consolidation process can also support entities that are maintained in non-PeopleSoft general ledgers but must be consolidated at the parent company level within PeopleSoft General Ledger.

Currency Handling

When considering how to store your financial information within the PeopleSoft application, you have several options. You can balance by base currency or by all currencies. Each journal can contain lines in multiple foreign currencies, one additional foreign currency (in addition to the base currency), or no foreign currencies (i.e., only the base currency is accepted). This flexibility within the system allows you to keep your financial information in almost any format. Which option to choose should also be considered in relation to your business units, since the business unit drives this selection.

Currency rates also allow you to use different exchange rates between two currencies. For instance, you might set up rates based on official, current, historical, or average exchange rates—these are known as *currency rate types*. By associating several different exchange rates with a combination of currencies, you can have several associated currency rate types. PeopleSoft 8 supports an eight-decimal exchange rate ability (7.8 format), providing even more precision on currency conversions.

PeopleSoft General Ledger will generate journal entries whose amounts represent the periods of time indicated by the TimeSpan for the translation rules being processed. TimeSpans normally used include a balance (BAL) for balance sheet accounts and a Profit & Loss (ITD, income to date) for profit and loss accounts. With these TimeSpans, the system would total the account balances in periods 1 through n for P&L accounts and periods 0 through n for balance sheet accounts. TimeSpans can be used to retrieve specific data for use in allocations, inquiries, or reporting using a set of timeframes or number of periods. Typical TimeSpans provided with PeopleSoft General Ledger include:

- ▶ PER, which pulls activity from period selected

- ▶ YTD, which includes year-to-date amounts for items selected

- ▶ BAL, which retrieves life-to-date amounts (balance forward amounts) for balance sheet accounts

You can set up as many TimeSpans as you feel are necessary to support your needs.

Budgets

The PeopleSoft Budgets module integrates very closely with the PeopleSoft General Ledger to track and maintain budget-to-actual information. The Budgets module creates and maintains the annual process of collecting budgeting information and distributing key reports or information to the end user (or manager) on their budgeting budget, including updates of the budget and tracking of budget changes. Workflow is a key component integrated with the process. The foundation of the Budgets application is the use of the Essbase data warehouse reporting "cube" to consolidate and slice and dice information by each budget entity for use in the budgeting process.

When setting up your Budgets module, you need to consider whether you will be importing key Human Resources data into your financial database to track such information as salary expense and position statistics. The module provides the capability to import this information from the HRMS database fairly seamlessly.

You also need to determine what statistical information you wish to track related to budgets, including overall head count and breakdown of FTE (full-time equivalent), part-time, full-time, regular, temporary, new, and existing (i.e., already within your HR database) employees. A key feature within the Budgets module is the budget cubes that you will create using the Essbase reporting tool. This tool creates cubes of data that can be used to distribute budget information more effectively to your users. Various types of cubes you may want to create include actual, budget initial, budget revision 1, etc. Various cubes can be restricted (as in read-only) or be allowed update privileges by the user. You can also set up various budget phases to track your budgeting process to include initial, revised, approved, etc. A budget phase provides a way for you to organize your budget cycle sequentially by date. This budget phase or cycle includes a specific start and end time for the budget collection cycle and assigns a specific coordinator to monitor and control the process for this particular cycle.

TIP   It is important that you enter and save data in your budget cube only at the detail level. This is so data can be imported back and forth into PeopleSoft ledgers.

With PeopleSoft 8, the budget process includes Commitment Control functionality. The use of this functionality impacts not only the Budgets and other Financials modules but also the HRMS and Supply Chain Management e-business products. Commitment Control will use a centralized approach to address budget control and encumbrance accounting consistently throughout the organization or enterprise. It is based on a flexible definition-based design to accommodate new products that may be added to the system. It also includes application programming interfaces (APIs) that support the integration of the new budget formulation products and new products that require budget control.

There are two types of budget control offered with PeopleSoft 8 Commitment Control—System Enforced Budget Control and Early Warning System:

System Enforced Budget Control   Using the Business Process Flow Control, you can enforce budget control at the system level. For example, if an account or department is over budget, you'll be able to set the system to hold purchase orders from being dispatched or withhold a voucher for payment for that account or department.

Early Warning System   You'll be able to specify a budget tolerance setting such that you automatically receive advance notice of a budget nearing an overage state.

Commitment Control will support departmental, project, and organizational budgets, individually or in combination. Individual transactions against budget data can be verified in real-time or background batch mode. If you choose to use real-time mode, you'll immediately provide feedback on each transaction on whether it is within the budget's available fund limit. Budgets can be set up either in the Budgets module (as is delivered in version 7.5), Projects module, or Human Resources system and be incorporated into the Commitment Control system.

The new Commitment Control module includes comprehensive budget inquiries that will allow you to drill down on budget, expense, encumbrance, preencumbrance, or revenue data to view supporting details and source system transactions. The OLAP (online analytical processing) tools can be used to analyze your budget data as well.

New Features

Additional enhancements to the Budgets module with PeopleSoft 8 include features that make PeopleSoft Budget chart fields available on the same journal entry as the actual ledger and, via your Web browser, give you the ability to update your budgets worklist items, perform limited data entry, and view budget data.

Integration with the Treasury Management module to provide and capture the impact on Cash when budgeting your capital acquisitions is also provided with PeopleSoft 8. Additionally, there is now a tighter integration with PeopleSoft HRMS for position budgeting. Salary budgeting and salary-related expense tracking can also be done via new features in the PeopleSoft 8 Budgets module, as can planned salary adjustments and a spread for a position's salary and related expenses across multiple chart field combinations. The Asset Management feature of capital planning is now shared with the Budgets module to help view current and planned assets and assign assets to existing capital acquisition plans.

Benefits

Leveraging the Budgets module of PeopleSoft can bring an organization several benefits, including:

- ▶ Online update of budget information, empowering your users to develop and maintain the budget information directly

- ▶ A mechanism to help standardize processes for security and control of your budget's data, thus ensuring consistency

- ▶ Flexible reporting view for "what if" analysis and other automated tools to facilitate budget information updates to accelerate the budget development process

- ▶ Online review to reduce time for decision support

- ▶ Automation of budget approvals through the use of workflow, accelerating the time necessary to approve and maintain budgets

- ▶ Full integration with the Projects module for detailed capital budgeting

The Procure-to-Pay Process

Within the PeopleSoft application, there are two main streams of data that make up the Financials set of modules. These are the procure-to-pay process and the order-to-cash process. In between there are several modules that interact or make up these two main streams of work within an organization.

While the General Ledger module is one of the core areas within PeopleSoft Financials, receiving transactions from most applications, another key process is the procure-to-pay cycle. It centers on the purchasing of items to support the enterprise or organization and flows through how these items are purchased, received, tracked, and administered, and how their impact to the company's financial position is recorded. This process includes the Purchasing and Inventory applications (which are reviewed in Chapter 20) as well as the Accounts Payable (or Payables), Projects, Expenses, and Asset Management modules, and is finally posted (or tracked) to the General Ledger module. We will take a look at these Financials modules and how they support the overall procure-to-pay process. Figure 19.6 is a flow diagram which depicts the procure-to-pay process, integrating the Purchasing and Inventory modules with Accounts Payable.

Figure 19.6   **Procure-to-pay process**

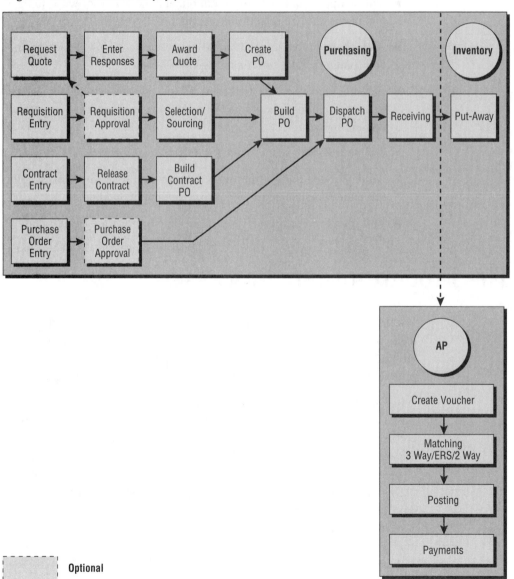

Accounts Payable

PeopleSoft Payables is one of the cornerstone modules that supports the procure-to-pay process. Once an item is selected and a purchase order is approved and sent to the vendor, this process takes over after the item is received and the payment for the item is due. The Accounts Payable (AP) module tracks the payment of the item back to the vendor and provides the means to ensure that proper payments are made at the right time for the organization. Two key features found in the Payables module that integrate closely with the purchasing process include:

Vendors   The ability to maintain key vendor information including payment terms and conditions, contract information, and other key data necessary to support payment of an invoice to a vendor. PeopleSoft shares the vendor information so that duplicate tables and information do not have to be maintained for each module. The vendor table should be a joint process that is created and maintained as a part of the overall procurement process.

Matching   A company's ability to track and ensure that adequate payments are made for items that actually are requested and for which work or products are received involves a process commonly known as "matching." The following items are looked at:

- ► Purchase order or request
- ► Order of receipt
- ► Invoice/voucher request

The process of comparing these items to each other to ensure that they are all created and reviewed prior to payment is defined as the matching process. An organization may require two- or three-way matching.

Within the Payables process, another set of Accounts Payable business units can be defined (which can be different than the General Ledger business units already set up). A separate business unit should be set up for each set of control process information that governs the payables processing. Where possible, the companies participating in a Payables implementation should be urged to "share" (maintain one set of terms and rates rather than maintaining separate tables). These controls may be overridden at the lower level (e.g., voucher origin, vendor, or voucher levels); you should consider defaulting your control information from the AP business unit level. Benefits of this approach include:

▶ Reduced time to enter vouchers, since the system automatically defaults voucher terms, etc., from the pre-entered values at the higher levels

▶ Increased control of predetermined default values by permitting only AP managers to maintain control of predetermined default values

▶ Elimination of most voucher entry errors and subsequent "recycled" (saved with error) vouchers by the immediate rejection of erroneous vouchers at the time of entry

You should try to maintain a common layout of your chart fields across your various companies or entities as well as your user classifications, currency tables, tax structures, payment processing rules, vendor pay groups, and vendor classifications. Some items that are generally different by company or entity include the accounting ledgers themselves (which are at a business unit level), chart fields, locations, business calendars, journal generator, payables accounting entries, high-dollar checks or limits, bank account information, contract and vendor controls, payment formats, and pay cycles.

Unlike the general ledger, the AP business unit is used to *control* transactions. These business units should *not* be thought of as a separate legal entity. Your method of controlling and processing your vouchers is the key to configuring your AP business unit. Configuration differences may be based on special controls for banks, a type of transaction, a company, division, or department. AP business units *do not* summarize, consolidate, or split AP transactions across GL business units. They do not have to match the GL business units, either. Additionally, you may want to create AP business units to help control different types of transactions, such as refunds, or for different currencies. An AP business unit cannot be split into multiple GL business units, but several AP business units can be consolidated into one GL business unit.

As mentioned in the "General Ledger Overview" section, several AP transactions can be summarized into a single GL entry. The detailed transactions are stored and maintained as historical information within the Accounts Payable module, but the summarized data (generally summarizing at the department level) is posted to the ledger.

Funds Transfer

A best practice that many companies follow and leverage with the PeopleSoft Payables module is the use of electronic funds transfer (EFT) or electronic data interchange (EDI), which provides funds to the vendor for payment of services electronically via the bank. PeopleSoft makes these capabilities fairly easy to implement, providing an EDI Manager that sets up the electronic payment process.

The use of a positive pay method to help prevent abuse or fraudulent activities by vendors should also be considered. By turning on a flag within the system, you can create a file that can be sent to your bank each payment cycle for the bank to use to reconcile and pay the checks it receives from vendors. Transactions can be automatically matched and reconciled (or you can manually match and force them to reconcile) using the delivered bank account reconciliation process. If your bank can provide you with account transaction information in an electronic format, then you should be using the automatic reconciliation process. Otherwise, if you receive only printed format, you can manual reconcile yourself or you can use an online panel entry method to record the bank statement information yourself and then use the automatic reconciliation process.

PeopleSoft provides for payment via a system check, wire transfer, manual payment, EFT, draft, or Giro. As with any payables process, you should ensure that adequate controls are in place within your process when creating payments.

Taxes

Within the Payables application, processing the correct tax information is key to creating and paying your vendors. Many PeopleSoft customers use a third-party vendor to provide sales tax calculations within the PeopleSoft application (rather than having to maintain the information in the tables provided by PeopleSoft). Several well-known vendors in this area are Vertex, Inc., and TaxWare International, Inc. Both vendors are PeopleSoft software partners and provide seamless interfaces (at a price) to customers of PeopleSoft. If you desire this level of support for your system, contact the vendors directly for detailed information on their products and pricing alternatives.

Another common tax area that many companies, especially global organizations, need to handle is VAT (value-added tax) requirements. Within Payables, you can create various VAT transaction types that can then create the appropriate VAT tax amounts based on the transaction taking place. So in essence, you would set up a VAT tax code for each tax authority your organization uses, and when you enter a voucher, you determine which VAT you should use. You can combine multiple tax authorities into one code if you choose. PeopleSoft 8 provides additional VAT functionality to support the calculation of VAT on advance payments as well as to specify VAT on Freight and Miscellaneous Charges. Finally, when goods are brought into a country, importers must pay VAT directly to the customs authorities before they can take possession of the goods. In PeopleSoft Payables, you can enter vouchers containing VAT-only information, so you can properly track and report the VAT paid to customs. This feature also allows for entry of any VAT adjustments. The system allows you to create reports to facilitate creation of VAT returns, sales list reports, and other supporting documentation needed for VAT reporting.

Other Features

The PeopleSoft system supports the annual 1099 process required for your vendors as well as the ability for you to maintain and track your recurring voucher contracts. The system can maintain contract information and generate appropriate payments based on this information. As you can see, the flexibility and diversity of the payables system allow it to be one of the most used financial modules by PeopleSoft Financials customers.

Some of the most difficult parts of implementing the Payables module include:

▶ Determining the historical information to support refunds processing, open voucher payments, open contracts, etc., that must be converted

▶ Converting your vendor master file, including cleaning up and possibly merging various vendor files (which may have lots of old, historical data in them) and creating a vendor hierarchy in the format that the system supports (which is basically parent-child related, placing all vendor data from one company into a single vendor ID, including parent organizations and subsidiaries at multiple locations)

▶ Setting up all the payment terms, banking information, and tax tables correctly to support your payment processes

▶ Testing your electronic files to and from your banks and vendors

▶ Ensuring that if you have large volumes, your processes are adequately stress tested and performance "tuned"

▶ Creating the most effective method for tax calculations (which in some cases means using a third-party vendor, as mentioned earlier)

Other common features that may help streamline your processes and leverage the system capabilities include:

▶ Use of workflow for voucher payment approvals, contract approvals, worklists for work distribution with your AP clerks, etc.

▶ Imaging of invoices to ensure adequate payment and record keeping. PeopleSoft provides the capability to store attachments; however, many organizations use third-party imaging systems that interface with People-Soft (such as Documentum) to store images of their invoices.

▶ Automating payment of recurring transactions.

▶ Eliminating paper checks through leverage of the EFT process.

▶ Replacing intercompany invoicing with automated journal entries.

▶ Using common numbering for your AR/AP vendor records.

A big benefit that is not necessarily tied to the system but should be looked at concerns the handling of your vendor contracts. Negotiating vendor contracts across business entities and leveraging the buying power of your entire organization can greatly improve your item costs. Having a single integrated system that tracks the amount your organization spends on each of your vendors (or *vendor spend*) and provides key vendor information to monitor and track its performance helps provide greater insights when renegotiating vendor contracts.

Asset Management

Once an item is purchased and received, as a part of the procure-to-pay process you need to record the item as an asset. Since the PeopleSoft Purchasing, Inventory, and Payables modules are all integrated with Asset Management, this is very easy to do. Information from the purchase order and receipt documents can be used to populate information and record that item into the Asset Management module as received. Any additional details that should be tracked (such as the identification number) can then be entered and set up upon receipt.

Key processes supported within Asset Management include:

▶ Asset additions

▶ Asset transfers

▶ Asset retirements

PeopleSoft allows you to set up and define multiple books. Asset books are used to store financial information on assets such as costs and depreciation rules. The number of books you might need to set up depends on a number of factors, including reporting needs, tax processing requirements, regulatory requirements, and locations.

Within the Asset Management module, the Asset Management business units are defined by PeopleSoft as a subset of your organization that maintains its own set of books. You should evaluate your existing accounting structure, such as how your organization assigns depreciation and allocates shares of asset amounts across multiple locations, and other factors, prior to deciding on your business unit structure for assets. The relationship between Asset and General Ledger business units is flexible enough to provide you with the ability to manage multiple asset organizations independently while sending journal entries to a central ledger business unit if you so desire.

Each business unit can use three different books for calculating taxes on assets: federal, alternative minimum tax, and adjusted current earnings reporting requirements. You'll need at least one financial book per business unit. You can also have other federal, state, and foreign tax or financial books as well.

Note PeopleSoft has the capability to specify the book type for each asset book. This feature acts as a filter for your tax and financial options when setting up depreciation and tax information for asset transactions. If you want a single book for both financial and tax information, you must select the "financial with tax information" option and *not* the "financial book" option.

Transaction codes identify special asset transactions and are used in combination with transaction types to create accounting entries. Examples of transaction codes for a disposal code transaction type might include sale, trade-in, abandoned, inventory, salvage, donation, etc.

Cost types represent different components of the cost of an asset such as materials, labor, and overhead. A great example is when you want to differentiate between the cost of building an asset and its market value. In this case, you would set up the cost of production to one cost type and the margin of profit to another cost type. Cost type, in combination with asset category and transaction code, determines into which accounts the costs are entered in the General Ledger. If you wish to record only the cost details without affecting your general ledger, you can use the Acquisition Details panel to categorize these costs as non-capitalizable.

Additions

When an asset is added (if you have the Purchasing and Payables modules implemented, most if not all asset information would already be set up), the following information is collected on an asset:

▶ Description of the asset

▶ Where the asset is physically located

▶ Details of the acquisition

▶ Capitalization information

The basic types of assets or categories of assets (such as artwork, construction in progress, telephones and switches, computer equipment, etc.) should be created and maintained within the system. You can also set up asset classes (such as Furniture and Fixtures) to help categorize your assets for reporting purposes.

Classifying assets by type for accounting purposes allows you to reflect how the assets are reported on the balance sheet (e.g., Land, Building, Equipment). The combination of asset category and transaction code determines the accounts that an asset transaction debits and credits to. You also reflect depreciation status for asset categories. For example, land may be non-depreciable while equipment is depreciable.

The system also allows you to store and retrieve images of your assets for a visual effect, if you so desire. A wide variety of image file formats can be used to insert a picture or drawing of an asset. Detailed attributes can also be maintained. Asset locations can be used not only to track the asset but also to help populate appropriate data (such a region or state) for posting of ledger transactions. The location attribution affects the tax reporting requirements as well. Custodian information, which includes project ID and departments, can be used to tie information together for reporting purposes. Any license or registration requirements for the asset can be stored in the system. Manufacturing data (which can be populated upon receipt or via the purchase order) can be maintained.

Types of assets that you may want to consider when creating an asset include:

Composite asset   This is used within the utilities industry to group many assets together so that their total costs are carried and depreciated as one asset. The one asset is called a composite asset, and the various parts or associates are called composite members. All transaction detail is rolled up to the one composite asset level rather than done individually.

Parent/child asset   Some assets stand alone, while others are grouped together for ease of processing and reporting. PeopleSoft allows you the capability to group these together using a parent/child relationship. An example of this might be a computer that includes a keyboard, monitor, and CPU. You can create a parent/child asset that groups these together but still keeps detailed information separate. You can create an asset ID that is not really an asset but is used to group a bunch of "children" together under a single reporting umbrella. PeopleSoft refers to this as a Parent-Only ID.

The details of the asset acquisition include keeping track of the separate costs and acquisition details of components that make up the asset for your internal use. Once this information is entered and approved, you can then capitalize the costs; the total capitalizable costs entered in this section are defaulted into the Capitalization panel. If your system is integrated with the PeopleSoft Payables, Purchasing, or Projects modules, these source systems can enter the acquisition detail automatically. Both capitalized and non-capitalized costs can be stored and maintained on a book level.

Asset profiles can be set up that can default key depreciation criteria on an asset when it is added based on the asset type and its corresponding asset books.

Note   Asset profiles should be defined for all major asset categories within your organization.

Financing codes can be set up to help you analyze your debit/equity relationships for capital intensive and government projects. For example, you can identify bonds, such as IRBs (industrial revenue bonds), IDBs (industrial development bonds), and TEBs (tax exempt bonds)

The system also allows you to distribute ownership of an asset based on leveraging the joint venture processing capabilities. In this case, you define the percentage of asset ownership allocated to each joint venture participant, and the system will do the rest.

If leased assets are tracked within your system, you must have at least one payment schedule defined. This information will integrate back to the payables system for ensuring payments are made.

If you decide to retire an asset using its original cost basis adjusted by all non-excluded transactions, you can set up a retirement basis reduction code. With this approach, you can exclude any indexed revaluation adjustments.

Cost Adjustments/Transfer

Periodically, you may need to make changes to your asset records because of error or new information you've received. Therefore, PeopleSoft provides the ability to change cost, quantity, depreciation rules, location, and physical attributes. Some of these changes may affect your financial or tax impact. This same feature supports the adjustments of cost and transfer of assets. Making these changes will also update your ledger appropriately.

Retiring an Asset

Within PeopleSoft, the assets are retired when they are either disposed of or no longer in use. When you retire an asset within the system, it will create all the necessary journal entries to support this transaction. An example of this is when you sell an asset. The system will calculate depreciation through the date of the sale, as well as any gains or loss. In addition, journal entries corresponding to each of these events are created. Gains and losses are booked to separate accounts, allowing for flexibility in updating general ledger journals and balances. An asset is retired by book within the system, so an asset can be retired in one book and still depreciate in others. Retired assets can be reinstated at any time. Once reinstated, depreciation will start again for assets that aren't fully depreciated. The system allows you to record information on the disposal method (e.g., abandoned, casualty loss, missing asset, retirement by sale).

Depreciation Calculation

One of the key processes within PeopleSoft Asset Management is the depreciation calculation process, which must be run every time an asset transaction is done that affects depreciation. Such transactions include adds, adjusts, transfers, changes to depreciation attributes or amounts, or retires. The system allows you to view cost, salvage value, accumulated depreciation, and net book value for your assets for any fiscal year and accounting period.

The system provides a range of depreciation conventions up to the year 2025. You may need to add additional periods and date information for assets with longer lives. The system includes the majority of U.S. depreciation methods. PeopleSoft provides you with depreciation schedules that are based on the percentage tables found in IRS Publication 534. If you require different depreciation schedules, there is a table provided for you to create your own schedule. If you have limits on the amount of depreciation for certain assets, depreciation limit tables are provided to assist in limiting the expense amounts on assets for each year of their life. Certain limit tables are already pre-loaded, but you can add additional limit tables as required for your organization.

The system also tracks assets that are considered qualified investments. A qualified investment table is used to determine the portion of the asset's basis qualified for tax credit. Certain standard qualified investment codes corresponding to a specific tax system and life are delivered with the system. However, if additional codes are needed, you can input the information into the table.

Tax classes are used to specify the period over which tax depreciation is expensed. The PeopleSoft system provides a tax table with values that match the guidelines for class lives of property. If you want to set up additional ones for your organization, a table is provided. The Asset Management module is delivered with the following tax credits:

- ▶ Energy Tax Credit
- ▶ Regular Investment Tax Credit
- ▶ Rehabilitation Tax Credit

Additional tax credits can be added to the system along with the rules that must be followed for each case.

Journal Entries

Asset Management is integrated with the General Ledger application and will automatically create journal entries that can be posted to both the general ledger and budgets system. You define how the transactions are posted. You set up defaults and summarization options that determine how entries are summarized into accounting entries and create journals. You can summarize entries at the account or chart field level. In most cases, you want to set up Journal Generator templates for each application system source distributing to the general ledger, as well as each type of transaction. For example, you might set up a template for depreciation expense for PeopleSoft Asset Management. Non-PeopleSoft systems can use a Generic Journal Generator template or create their own customized Journal Generator template. Typically, the Journal Generator templates will be established by your project's General Ledger team.

The Accounting Entry template is used to create the appropriate accounting entries (the basis for GL journals) and defines entry types based on the asset category, cost type, transaction type, and transaction code. For each entry, you specify the accounts used during accounting entry, the Journal template used for recording actual transactions, and the Budget Journal template used for recording budget transactions. Each asset event has an associated set of accounting entry types. For each possible category/cost type/transaction code combination, you must set up an accounting entry template for each of the following transaction types:

ADD	Additions
ADJ	Adjustments
TRF	Transfers
RCT	Recategorizations
DPR	Depreciation Expense
PPD	Prior Period Depreciation
RET	Retirements (also used for processing reinstatements)
LPY	Lease Payments

If you enter a transaction for a combination value where no accounting entry template has been set up, your accounting entry process will fail when you run it.

Other Areas to Note

With the Asset Management module, a few additional items you should focus on during your implementation include the conversion of existing assets into your new application and obtaining the necessary and accurate information you need for the future. Also, the module provides the capability to load assets that are stored in other systems for the use of tracking the financial impact in one place. Therefore, if you have a system that tracks all of your office equipment, you don't necessarily have to retire that system (though it might be the right thing to do)—you can import the necessary information for financial reporting purposes into the application. Finally, if you have many assets with complicated depreciation schedules, you should look at tuning the depreciation calculation process to ensure the best performance possible. The depreciation process can be a source of pain if you don't pay careful attention to this up front during your testing phase.

PeopleSoft 8 provides additional features including:

▶ Improvements with the global asset management features, such as support for asset revaluations by percentage used in multiple countries

▶ Broader ranges of Japanese depreciation methods

▶ French derogatory depreciation method

▶ Capital cost allowance calculations used in Canada

▶ Annual depreciation limits based on percentage of net book value commonly used in Germany

▶ Support of VAT requirements related to asset retirements

▶ Support of the like-kind exchange regulations under the U.S. Federal Tax code that provides the ability to forgo the recognition of a gain or loss that results from exchanging similar property types

Projects

Another important module in the chain of procure-to-pay—which in some cases and for some business might actually be the center of financial processing—is the Projects module. This module brings together all financial information that is associated with a defined project ID. The system creates an integrated picture of all financial activity associated with the project. Therefore, for companies that operate their business on a projects basis, such as service companies, this is a very important module indeed. People-Soft's PSA module is specifically designed to handle a project-centric organization. This special industry solution will be discussed in a later section of this chapter.

As with all other Financials modules, the Projects module also has a Business Unit field. This field is used to create groupings of projects where the rules and business model are shared. The following items should be considered when determining how your project business units should be set up:

- Each project tree is associated with a single business unit. Therefore, if you want to have a group of projects in one tree, be sure to place all of these projects within the same Projects business unit.

- A single Projects business unit can post to as many General Ledger business units as necessary.

- Each project tree has its own security. Using this security, you can keep users from seeing specific nodes or entire trees.

Projects can be grouped into project types for reporting purposes as well as to associate specific accounting entries for each group. Therefore, you can set up project types such as construction projects, maintenance projects, and capital projects.

Analysis Groups

One of the most flexible tools within Projects for analyzing projects is what PeopleSoft calls *analysis groups*. With analysis groups, you can group analysis types and define relationships among them in order to analyze the costs of the project.

A multiplier determines how the amounts and quantities for a specific analysis type are to be factored into the analysis. The total quantities and amounts in all transactions identified by a specific analysis type are multiplied by the number you enter. For example, if you want to add the amounts to the analysis, enter a 1; if you want to subtract the costs from the analysis, enter a –1; if you only want to add half of the amounts to the analysis, enter 0.5.

The easiest way to create analysis groups for analyzing projects is to start by writing out the equation you want to use. This often makes it easier to determine which multipliers you should assign to which analysis types. For instance, if you want to create an analysis group to determine whether or not you are over budget, you might write out the following equation: Budgets – Actuals = Budget to Actual Variance.

You would then assign a multiplier of –1 to the Actuals analysis type and a multiple of 1 to the Budgets analysis type. When you use this analysis group for online analysis or reporting, all of the actual costs from the project you are analyzing are subtracted from the budget costs. If the result is a negative number, you reverse the multipliers so that the budgeted costs are subtracted from the actual costs. Multipliers can be applied to quantities for each analysis type that you include in an analysis group. For those analysis groups that you create for the purpose of analyzing your project costs, you will probably want the multipliers to be the same for both the amount and the quantity. Tolerance levels can be applied to a defined cost analysis group and certain threshold actions taken at the project or activity level. Threshold warning messages include Reject and Warning.

All projects created will contain activities. Activity types are labels to identify and group projects in PeopleSoft Projects. Therefore, if you consistently use these activity types, you can report across the projects on those activities (such as design, build, or test).

Resources are the center of the Projects system. They allow you to track, analyze, and report on all costs, both actual and planned, in your projects. Resource types along with resource categories and subcategories can be used to identify your resources in groupings at a very granular level. For instance, you can create a resource type of Labor, with categories of overtime and standard and then a subcategory of overtime for weekend or business day. The system also allows you to create resource groups, which allow you to combine multiple resource types together for project analysis and billing purposes. The system requires you to have at least three resource groups:

▶ Items—Inventory Items

▶ Labor—Total Labor

▶ Mater—Total Materials

If you choose to not use these resource types, you will have to customize these resource groups or create new ones to be used with these features.

Before you can begin to track your projects and the costs associated with them, you must first define your integration templates. *Integration templates* are high-level templates that define the integration between PeopleSoft Projects and your other financial applications. A new project should be assigned an integration template when created. The integration templates also are used to restrict access to ledger business units. If you want to prevent users from adding resource transactions to your project, select an integration template that has no general ledger business units defined for it. You can also identify the default business units for your Purchasing and Asset Management applications should you integrate your projects with those modules.

 Note   Each project must be assigned an integration template.

Project status codes are used to track the status of your project and activities changes. The system also allows you to use status types for defining project events, which are the actual changes in status that require approval. In using this feature, you have the capability to use workflow to obtain appropriate approval prior to moving to the next stage of your project. The system also has the capabilities to track and define various project phases, such as clean-up, testing, etc. These phases can be given a begin date and an end date for tracking purposes. Time can also then be tracked against a phase.

Each transaction line that you create must have a distribution type. Distribution types are defined within the system and are used to determine what type of account is being used for the transaction.

Employee Project Time

If you choose to track your employee time and labor directly using the Projects module, you must set up project job codes, which will be used to track time as well as labor distribution against that project. Projects has the ability to store personal data about employees you have working on projects, data that can be loaded from your human resources system. Name, address, status, phone number, and such information can be stored.

Accounting Entries

As with the other Financials modules, the Projects module contains the ability to create accounting entry templates, which are then used to process your resource transactions correctly into entries that are then ready to be sent through to your general ledger. You link your generic transaction types to an appropriate accounting entry template so that it is processed correctly. You use your accounting entry template to apply the transaction to a specific general ledger account. This capability saves time in keying and reduces errors when processing your transactions. In most cases, you would want to set up accounting entry templates for each functional combination of project elements, as listed below (* is for optional elements):

Templates

Analysis Type

Resource Type

Transaction Type

Integration Template

Project Elements

GL Business Unit (from/to)

Resource Category*

Resource SubCategory*

Project Type*

Transaction Code*

Warning If you have not created an accounting entry template for a specific resource transaction, distribution lines will not be generated. PeopleSoft Projects is delivered with a query that can help you find all of these resource transactions.

Key Items to Note

The Projects module is used to bring together all resources related to a project and track them in a single location. How you set up the information to track your projects using transaction codes, resource categories and subcategories, and project phases and types all play an important role in how effectively you can report this information. Ensure that you carefully think through your requirements before setting up all the tables within the application. For capital projects, such as those heavily supported by telecommunications companies, Projects provides the mechanism to accumulate all costs including goods and labor from Payables and Time and Labor and then pass the costs of completed projects to Assets so depreciation can be initiated. The Budgets module is then used to compare budgeted costs versus actual costs for these projects.

PeopleSoft 8 provides a Projects workbench that uses the new Web-based browser application PeopleSoft Decision Master to provide key content designated for executives, project managers, and project team members. This fully customizable workbench tool can allow you to see the results of whatever specific alerts or key indicators you wish to monitor, such as projects nearing their budget limit (let's say within 5% of estimate), those over their budget limit, or those with resource shortages. However, in order to leverage this new Projects workbench tool, you must purchase it separately from the Projects application.

In addition to this new workbench tool, PeopleSoft 8 provides enhancements with project billing and revenue recognition leveraging the new Contracts module (see section to follow for an overview of this new module). Some of these new billing and revenue recognitions include using milestones to trigger events, define schedules, and trigger the percentage complete. There is also additional integration with the PeopleSoft Billing module to send any adjustments made directly in Billing back to Projects. On the Receivables side, PeopleSoft Receivables will feed Projects receivable items and revenue related to any adjustments. This will allow project managers the ability to visualize the progress of the project in terms of outstanding revenue, ensuring complete financial control of the project. There is also further integration with tables shared with Time and Labor for time entry.

Expenses

A fairly new product that PeopleSoft released with PeopleSoft 7.5 is the Expenses module. This module allows an organization to provide a mechanism for employees who are travelers, on the road for many days at a time, to manage their expense reporting. Organizations that have individuals such as consultants and sales representatives may have the need for a flexible system that tracks and manages individual expenses. While this module is not directly linked to the procure-to-pay process, it does integrate directly with Accounts Payable for payment (to employees or third parties), and with Budgets to look at actuals versus budget; it also tracks expenses related to the project (in the Projects module), integrating total costs to an initiative. Expenses can also be used in conjunction with the Payroll application through the Time and Labor module, making expense payments directly to employees through their paychecks.

The system allows you to set up tracking of expense-related items, including limits and approval processing for types of expenses such as hotel/lodging, air, meals, and other out-of-pocket expenses. With PeopleSoft 8, a "hotel wizard" feature is also included to track charges on an itemized hotel bill.

The system also allows your organization to import information from your corporate cardholder that can prepopulate your expense sheet. Individuals have both a mobile (or Internet) and a desktop option for expense reporting. With PeopleSoft 8, all expense entry and approval functionality is available on the Web, including travel authorizations and cash advances. Various reporting tools and reports are also provided to help track various expense thresholds, perform analysis, and such.

Information that is captured in the expense system can then be consolidated and paid through either the Payroll (via an employee's paycheck) or Accounts Payable (as a separate check) module. Payment to any third-party vendors can also be tracked and integrated with the Payables module.

With PeopleSoft 8, PeopleSoft gives travel and expense departments the ability to maintain compliance with corporate travel policies. You can define preferred vendors (merchants) and link them to expense types, which will allow you to limit the choice of merchants available for selection on an expense line for a given expense type. Reporting of where these preferred vendors are not being used can also be accomplished. Auditing features are also provided to help expedite expense sheet processing, and to generate cash advances if necessary. Per diem rates that might be dictated by the federal government can also be imported into the system, which can automatically calculate per diem reimbursements based on the days or hours traveled by an individual. Another control feature includes the ability to import purchased airline flight segment data to control your air travel costs, and you can prepopulate the employee's expense sheet with that data or via credit card transaction data. Unused tickets can also be reconciled and submitted against purchased tickets. The process of verifying receipts during audits can also be done online to avoid additional paper processing. Travel authorization approval processes are supported by the system, as are cash advances including providing a cash advance withdrawal via an ATM.

Expense Workflow Overview

Prior to actually entering expenses, several tables within PeopleSoft must be configured in order for the expense process to function properly. These tables include employee and expense information. The employee information (as mentioned above) can be imported from the HRMS application. The system comes with a set of expense types pre-loaded; however, you must ensure that you have an expense type set up for every type of expense that might be incurred by your employees. Each of these expense types can have limits and various required field information. For example, you might want to require that the ticket number be entered whenever airline ticket information is put into the system. Once these base tables are configured, you are ready to process expenses within PeopleSoft.

Figure 19.7 shows the approval/auditing workflow process used when submitting an expense within PeopleSoft. After a user enters and submits their expense sheet, the sheet can be automatically routed to the department manager for approval. An e-mail notification is also sent. The department manager, once notified, would then approve or deny the expense sheet submitted. If further dollar approval capability is required, the expense sheet could be routed for further approval.

Note   The functionality of multiple dollar-level approval routing is not delivered in the "vanilla" PeopleSoft system. However, this functionality can be set up using the workflow routing tool and alternating the PeopleSoft business process. Remember that a workflow process for approval is static and must always be routed to the same person.

Once the expense sheet is approved, it would be available for accrual posting. In addition, the expense can be routed to an auditor for further review. This person would likely compare the expense sheets and actual receipts to policy and approve the sheets for payment, depending on the specific process within your organization. The auditor must audit the relevant expenses in order for them to be paid.

Note Within PeopleSoft, you set up a range of expenses to be audited, which can be based on certain expense type(s) that are over a certain dollar amount. For instance, you may choose to audit all airfares over $500 or all meals over $50.

Once released, these expenses are then submitted for payment either through the Accounts Payable system (for an expense-related check, which is produced based on your company's schedule) or through the Payroll system, which would then be paid through the employee's paycheck.

Figure 19.7 **Expense workflow**

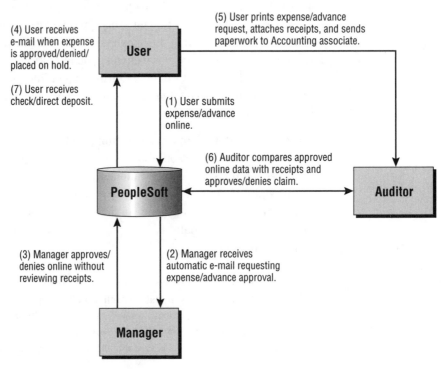

The above process pertains to claims entered both online and remotely.

Whenever a claim is approved/denied/placed on hold, the user receives an automated e-mail. Whenever a claim is submitted for approval, the manager receives an automated e-mail. The automated e-mails requesting approvals from managers will contain a breakdown of the expenses by expense type and amount.

If expense/cash advance request requires modification by the user before it can be accepted, then the expense is denied and returned to the user online. The user must resubmit the expense for approval after making the required modifications. Remotely entered expenses that require modification must be resubmitted on a new expense sheet if denied.

Benefits

Some of the key benefits an organization might gain from using the Expenses module include:

- ▶ Online and offline Web-enabled expense entry by end users for direct input in and out of the office

- ▶ Online approval by managers for reduced cycle time

- ▶ Online auditing of expense forms for reduction in cost of compliance via strategic review

- ▶ Central database for expense tracking and analysis over time

- ▶ Defaulted account coding

- ▶ Removal of all expense data entry by Accounts Payable, thus reducing duplicate keying

- ▶ Direct deposit of expense payments for personnel

As we will discuss in our section that looks at the new Professional Services Administration application, Expenses is a key component of that solution. It includes the introduction of the PeopleSoft Professional Traveler, which integrates both time and expense reporting features.

The Order-to-Cash Process

As with the procure to pay, another key financials process that the PeopleSoft application supports is the entire cash collections process, which is integrated with the larger order-to-cash flow. As shown in Figure 19.8, this process integrates several key PeopleSoft Financials modules including Billing, Receivables, and Treasury Management with the Order Management system. We will look at each of these applications to understand how these are integrated and posted through to the General Ledger application.

Figure 19.8 **Order to cash**

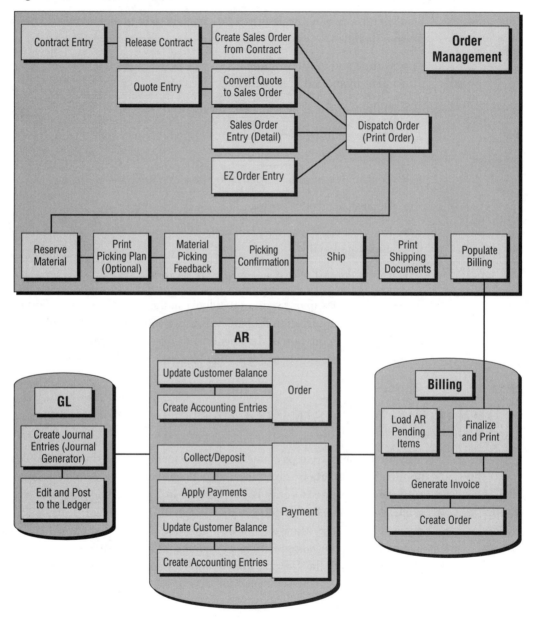

Billing

PeopleSoft provides the basic support of your billing processes using a centralized customer file. Therefore, you can maintain and update a single record entry on a customer, and all system users will have access to this information. This allows you to streamline your customer maintenance process. The customer's historical information is also maintained via the use of effective dating. As with vendor data, the customer file can provide a hierarchical structure to support relationships between a group of customers. PeopleSoft's flexible tree format also provides the ability to group customer data multiple ways.

With the new Contracts module, the PeopleSoft Billing application can now receive and bill the customer based on information set up in the Contracts module. This integration provides efficiency and effectiveness in the billing cycle and ensures that contract terms are followed automatically.

You can define various billing types that control the processing of that billing arrangement. You also have the ability to produce pro forma invoices for review to reduce the number of voids prior to creating a final invoice. The system supports the ability to credit and rebill for invoices as necessary to support your billing process. Standard note codes can be set up for invoices to remind you or to support reporting requirements based on the code created. A consistent invoice format and laser printing are provided with the product as well as support for production of remittance advices. International addressing is also supported by the application.

PeopleSoft provides for online adjustments to your bill and lets you monitor totals and accumulating balances as necessary to support your billing processes.

Receivables

The PeopleSoft Receivables module integrates closely with the Billing and General Ledger application as well as provides information to the Projects module, as we have already discussed. This application supports the major processes of automating the cash application process by matching cash to billed invoices (from the billing system, whether PeopleSoft or external) through what PeopleSoft calls the payment predictor. An automated lockbox file from your bank can be loaded into PeopleSoft and used in this cash process. The system has the capability to generate customer statements and reports to help you manage your cash collections process. Different dunning letters can be generated based on the aged days of specific invoices/bills, and various reporting features to monitor your aged inventory are available.

The PeopleSoft Receivables module supports the ability to enter manual items and to bring over billed items from your billing system. It tracks the cash collections against these receivables via in-house, lockbox, and regular deposits (direct journals or other internal methods). The system provides the ability to process write-offs and collection items, generate correspondence, and track returned checks. You have the ability to set up multiple collection status codes to track the progress of your collections, including identifying when a collection is turned over to a particular collection agency. Customers can be placed on credit hold until a certain action is taken.

In addition, you have the ability to set up payment terms timing if you want the system to handle the payment terms automatically, automatically calculated payment due dates, discount amounts, and discount due dates. You can set up direct debit profiles to automatically collect payments electronically. Finance charges can be applied based on the information you set up within the system.

 Note The Payment terms timing table is owned by the Payables module; thus your Receivables group will have to work with your Accounts Payable team during setup to ensure that the terms meet all needs and are consistent (for instance, that NET30 means the same for both groups).

Should there be disputes over a particular customer, contract, or other area, you can create various dispute status codes to track and report this information within the system.

Finally, the module supports the creation of the appropriate journal entries based on the transactions within the system, including posting and aging of outstanding inventory. A cash reconciliation process is also provided.

Currency

Foreign currency conversion features include the ability to produce aging reports in various currencies, the ability to book foreign currency as manual items, the ability to apply foreign currencies against items, and the provision of information in virtually any currency.

Additional Features

The Receivables module also provides the capabilities to maintain a tickler file to record all conversations with clients or individuals during the collections process and to provide reminders to follow up with customers based on days outstanding or a date defined in the future. As with payables, billing information and invoices can also be stored as images.

Areas to Consider

PeopleSoft Receivables provides a solid framework to support the overall order-to-cash process. By integrating the order entry and billing process with the Receivables module and linking to funds management (using the functions of the Treasury Management module), you can support all forms of electronic funds transfer, thereby streamlining your process and improving your cash basis.

Treasury Management

The PeopleSoft Treasury Management application serves an important function of managing corporate cash flows related to receipts, disbursements, debt, and investments. As Figure 19.9 indicates, corporations have to constantly balance cash inflows and outflows from different sources.

Figure 19.9 **Company's cash flow diagram**

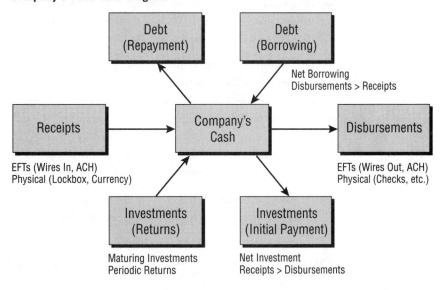

The PeopleSoft Treasury Management module, first incorporated into the 7.5 release, is based on three major submodules or subprocesses:

▶ Cash Management

▶ Deal Management

▶ Risk Management

Each of these major areas will be reviewed below, and information will be provided to help you decide whether or not Treasury is beneficial to your organization.

Cash Management

The Cash Management module provides the ability to perform bank reconciliations. Bank reconciliation functionality allows you to reconcile receipts, disbursements, and banking fees via three options: automatic, semi-manual, or manual. With an automatic process, bank statements are electronically downloaded and reconciled against the system entries. With a manual process, physical bank statements are matched against the system transactions.

The Cash Management module provides the ability to understand your true cash position. The cash position worksheet (CPW) provided by the system allows you to maintain and monitor your company's cash position—and with PeopleSoft 8 includes the capability to provide this information via the Internet. By utilizing PeopleTools Tree Manager functionality, you have the flexibility to set up and connect your CPW to a variety of internal sources, such as AP and AR, and external sources, such as banks.

Bank/counterparty control data is also provided by the application, as well as bank account analysis to track and analyze your bank fees. The system supports a wide variety of treasury-generated banking fees and charges. In-house banking capabilities are also supported, including the calculation and storing of internal account balances, interest accruals for internal banks (in PeopleSoft 8), inbound and outbound confirmations for in-house banking transactions, settlement activities, and creation of bank statements.

Bank account transfer functionality allows you to move money between different bank accounts with appropriate accounting.

EFT management and electronic banking are also supported, leveraging the Payment Manager, a new PeopleSoft 8 feature for creating flat files for treasury settlements and wire requests directly out of the Treasury Management module, rather than using the AP Pay Cycle Manager.

Cash Management reports include current cash position and a forecast by specified time horizon. Additional reports include a bank reconciliation report, a processed payments report, a processed advancements report, a cash flow status report, and a pending payments report.

Deal Management

The Deal Management module allows you to capture, track, and account for financial deals and trades.

Before you can capture and administer deals and trades, you must first define your financial instruments. PeopleSoft Treasury Management provides a medium that enables you to define base instruments using core building blocks. You provide a low-level definition of a simple vanilla instrument, and PeopleSoft's flexible definition capabilities enable you to create complex ones combining attributes from your core building blocks. PeopleSoft provides four fundamental instrument base types from which you can build simple and complex instruments. These base types include:

▶ Interest rate physicals: The purchase or sale of interest rate instruments such as bonds and commercial paper

▶ Interest rate swaps: The exchange of fixed and floating rate instruments

▶ Foreign exchange (FX) deal physicals: The purchase or sale of a foreign exchange instrument on a spot or cash basis

▶ Option: A right to purchase or sell a financial contract

The Capture Deal functionality allows treasury professionals the ability to record "deal header" information, which includes instrument type (e.g., T-bills), investment bank involved, and accounting treatment. The Deal Detail panel or page, which follows, allows you to enter deal-specific information such as amounts, interest rate, and maturity date. Settlement instructions allow you to define with whom and through what account your trades will be settled.

With the Administer Deal functionality within the Deal Management module, you can automatically receive deal confirmations and generate treasury accounting based on transacted trades.

Real-time quotes enable treasury professionals to download market rates (interest rates, FX rates, etc.) directly from the Reuters or Bloomberg terminal.

Risk Management

The PeopleSoft Risk Management module empowers you to manage any kind of financial risk exposure. Specifically, the risk exposures that can be managed through PeopleSoft can be described in the following terms:

Currency exposure   Risk associated with volatility of the foreign currency cash flows

Interest rate exposure   Risk associated with exposure to variable interest rate fluctuations

Counterparty exposure   Risk associated with creditworthiness of banks that the organization deals with

Country exposure   Risk associated with funds invested in foreign countries

Individual dealer positions   Risk associated with trade positions undertaken by individual dealers

Specific financial instrument limits   Risks associated with exposure to particular investment and debt financial instruments

Using the Tree Manager, you define hierarchical structures that describe the specific exposure that is important for your organization to manage. With the Tree Manager, you are able to depict the hierarchy for a position via tree nodes, specify the data sources to include, and define which fields to sum together to provide the total for a given position.

Evaluating the risks associated with financial exposures requires the use of complex analytic models to value these deals, obtaining analytic sensitivities used to analyze the deals. PeopleSoft allows you to connect to external analytics software, such as FEA (finite element analysis, a method for simulating how an object will perform in service), to revalue the financial portfolio. This revaluation allows you to mark-to-market your portfolio.

The JP Morgan FourFifteen connector enables you to run value at risk (VAR) calculations, a snapshot of the corporation's global exposures to interest rate, foreign exchange, commodity, and equity risks across the enterprise.

Other Considerations

The PeopleSoft Treasury Management module should not be viewed as a solution exclusively geared toward corporate treasury departments. The

Cash Management module's bank reconciliation functionality, for example, enables organizations to improve efficiencies and attain timely access to payment and receipt information. However, because bank reconciliation processes usually reside within the accounting function in organizations, the reconciliation features are often neglected by departments outside finance.

Although the PeopleSoft Treasury Management module comes with some delivered reports, users generally require more information and in different forms than what these canned reports provide. Be prepared to utilize People-Soft Query and Crystal Report Writer to write additional customized reports with your implementation.

Electronic Payments and Receipts

This section gives an overview of the electronic payments and receipts processes found within PeopleSoft and found within both the procure-to-pay and order-to-cash processes.

Payments

The following types of electronic payment files can be generated from either the Treasury Management module or the Accounts Payable module using the pay cycle process in the Accounts Payable module:

- ▶ Treasury wires
- ▶ Treasury ACHs (Automated Clearing Houses)
- ▶ Treasury federal tax payments
- ▶ Treasury state tax payments
- ▶ Treasury direct debits
- ▶ AP wires
- ▶ AP ACHs
- ▶ AP federal tax payments
- ▶ AP state tax payments
- ▶ AP positive pay file
- ▶ EFTs in Europe and other countries

The AP pay cycle and the relevant bank accounts can be configured within PeopleSoft to output flat files for the types of payments mentioned above. Customized panels have to be added for processing tax payments. EDI Manager can be used to output the files in the required formats. Other options include:

▶ Modifying the delivered SQCs (subprograms or components of SQR report programs) to directly output the files in the required formats for the banks

▶ Using middleware products like integration brokers for converting the formats once flat files are produced by the PeopleSoft system

The files are transmitted to the banks using the available communication software packages.

In release 8, PeopleSoft introduces the EFT Manager, which has the same functionality as the Pay Cycle Manager. All the treasury payments are now handled by the EFT manager.

Please refer to Figure 19.10, the electronic banking interface process flow for AP, AR, and Treasury Management.

The following types of transactions can be downloaded from the banks and input into either the Treasury Management or the Accounts Receivable module:

▶ Bank balances

▶ Bank statements

▶ Lockbox receipts

In addition to the above, a direct debit file can also be generated from the Accounts Receivable module and transmitted to the banks.

Bank balance and bank statement files can be downloaded from the banks using a communications software package. EDI Manager can be configured to translate the files and load the PeopleSoft staging tables. Internal PeopleSoft processes can be executed to load the relevant application tables from the staging tables. The other options include:

▶ Developing an SQR program to parse the bank files and load the application tables directly

▶ Using integration brokers with PeopleSoft adapters to read bank files and directly load PeopleSoft application tables

Figure 19.10 **Electronic banking interface flow receipts**

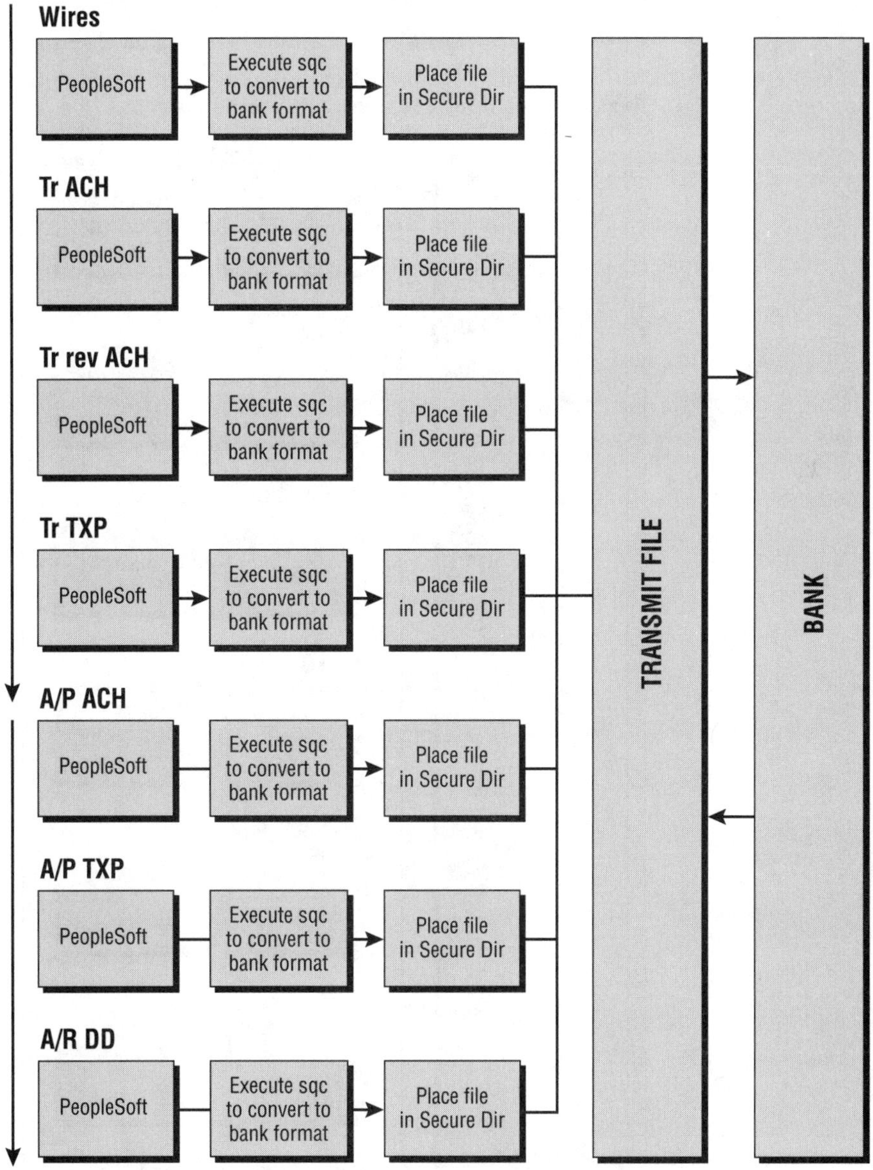

Lockbox receipts files can be downloaded using a communication software package. If the bank provides the file in PeopleSoft business document format, this file can be directly loaded into PeopleSoft tables using a delivered process. If the bank does not provide the file in the required format, then the file has to be reformatted into PeopleSoft business document format to use the People-Soft delivered process for loading the application tables. Please refer to Figure 19.11 for bank balance interface and cash position process flow.

Figure 19.11   **Bank balance interface and cash position process flow**

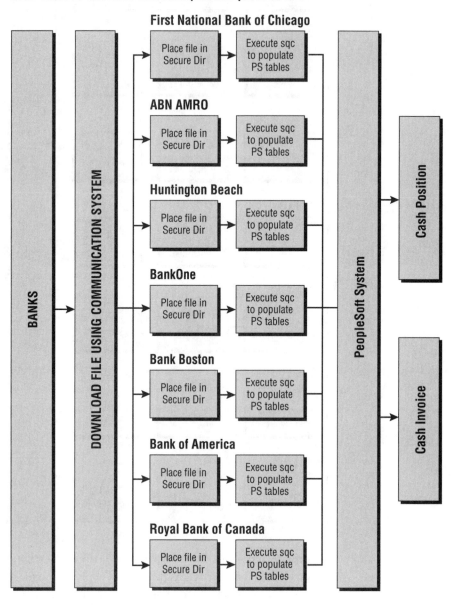

A direct debit file can be generated from the Accounts Receivable module using the delivered processes. This file has to be reformatted to suit the bank's requirements before transmission to the bank. Please refer to Figure 19.12 for the AR Direct Debit process flow.

Figure 19.12 **AR Direct Debit process flow**

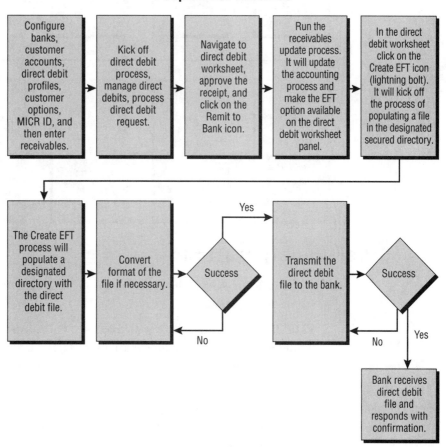

In Europe and other countries, the lockbox process is not used for processing the receivables. Bank statements are used for getting all the receipts. Bank statement files have to be processed for extracting all the receipts. These can be input into the PeopleSoft staging tables using the EDI manager. A different PeopleSoft process (not the lockbox process) is then used to load the Accounts Receivables application tables. Please refer to Figure 19.13 for the European AR Electronic Banking Interface process flow.

Figure 19.13   **European AR Electronic Banking Interface**

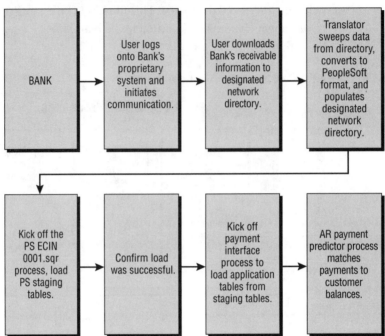

Other Considerations

The following are some of the areas to consider while implementing electronic payments and receipts:

Establishing relationship with banks   This is an important step in implementing the electronic banking interfaces, as it is time-consuming. Working closely with the banks' representatives during all the phases of the project is essential for an accelerated implementation.

Finalizing file formats   All file formats for different payments and receipts files have to be finalized with the banks during the design phase of the project. The development time can be considerably reduced if the banks can convert the formats at their end. In some cases the formats can be simplified by eliminating optional data.

Approval procedures   Make sure that all the required approvals for payments are completed within the PeopleSoft system. In cases where the banking software packages have their approval procedures, make sure that the approval processes are not duplicated.

Connecting to banking software packages on the premises of clients
In cases where the clients already have banking software packages on their premises, explore the possibility of importing the payment files from People-Soft into these packages and make use of these packages' communication features to transmit the files to the banks. Similarly, for the receipts, explore the possibility of using the available bank software to download receipts from the banks.

Transaction volumes   Make sure that the transaction volumes are not very high per transmission. Lower volumes will facilitate recovery of data if transmission fails. A single batch of payments can be split up and transmitted as several packets.

Communication packages and encryption requirements   Depending on the transmission and security requirements, appropriate communication packages with high degrees of encryption should be selected in consultation with the banks involved.

Error recovery and crash recovery procedures   Appropriate error recovery and crash recovery procedures have to be developed to enable the recovery of data at various points of failure in the generation and end-to-end transmission of the files.

Backup and archiving procedures   All the files have to be backed up and archived using appropriate naming conventions for a specified period of time for satisfying audit requirements.

Automation   Depending on the degree of automation required by the client, solutions can be developed to fully automate the end-to end payments and receipts processes.

Enterprise Performance Management

The center around supporting enterprise-wide performance measurement or metrics is provided by PeopleSoft's Enterprise Performance Management (EPM) module. This suite of products includes workbenches, data warehousing features, and balanced scorecard features to support all of your enterprise performance management needs.

The basic components of the EPM product from a functionality perspective include:

▶ Forward perspective: planning and simulation

▶ Customer and instrument level profitability

▶ Integrated profitability

▶ Multidimensional profitability

▶ Activity-based costing

▶ Funds transfer pricing

▶ Risk-weighted capital

▶ Asset/liability management (includes liquidity analysis)

▶ Balanced scorecard

▶ Workforce Analytics, including compensation and retention analytics

▶ Various workbenches to provide Web-enabled reporting templates for role-based information including financial analysis, human resources, customer analysis, merchandising, supply chain, projects, and academics

The open architecture of this solution centers on the Essbase Data Warehousing solution and provides a mechanism to support the multidimensional views and key analytics necessary to support the solutions. This architecture is highly scaleable and flexible, supporting most any environment.

PeopleSoft Professional Services Automation

The new PeopleSoft Professional Services Automation (PSA) suite of products is designed to support service companies, specifically targeting companies with:

▶ Consulting/systems integration

▶ Software

▶ Accounting

▶ Internal service organizations

The application suite is focused on four key areas along with the following functions they support:

▶ People: recruit, retain, deploy, resource management

▶ Pipeline: opportunity management, customer relationship management

▶ Performance: Workforce Analytics, Project Analytics, Financial Analytics, CRM Workbench

▶ Project: customer management, engagement management, invoice management, time and expense capture, revenue management

Figure 19.14 provides an overview of the core processes that support this new suite of products and PeopleSoft's schedule in supporting these processes. The new modules associated with these processes include:

▶ Professional Traveler

▶ Contracts

▶ Resource Management

Figure 19.14 **Professional Services Automation processes**

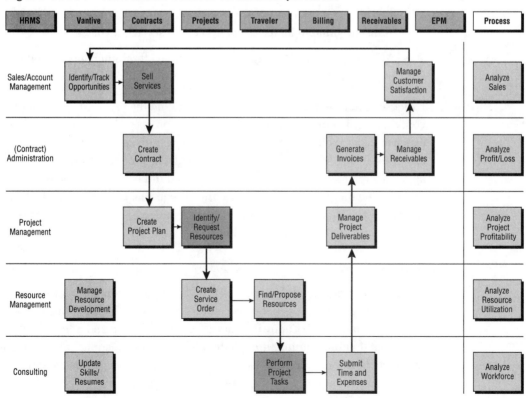

These new applications are covered in a bit more detail in the following sections.

PeopleSoft Professional Traveler

A key module in this new product line is the PeopleSoft Professional Traveler. This core application fills an important role by helping employees manage time and expense reporting while they travel on business. The Professional Traveler provides the ability to record billable and nonbillable time, expenses, and schedules in a mobile environment without having to be in the office. Your employees can create travel authorizations and cash advance requests as well as track time and expense information on the go, then upload their documents for processing while continuing to work on a project.

The Professional Traveler will allow individuals to submit time cards used for project billing and payroll purposes, and the submission of time cards is integrated with the expense reporting process. Professional Traveler's billing features will:

► Allow employees the ability to record the number of hours worked on a specific project

► Translate billable hours from a project to service invoices

► Allow employers to calculate accrued time off or other specialized compensation plans

Expenses can be entered and submitted daily, and the report functions include verifying credit card transactions to expenses processed; recording detailed expense items such as merchant, expense type, mileage, and costs; allocating expenses among several projects, departments, or products; and obtaining approvals remotely. Control data will be stored in PeopleSoft Expenses and include data on processing advances, travel requests, time cards, and expense reporting. The Professional Traveler module integrates with the Expenses, Projects, and Time and Labor applications.

Contracts

The new Contracts module supports the PSA application and focuses on facilitating the revenue-generating contractual process found in business-to-business transactions. Capturing contractual information and administrating the flow of that information through the PSA suite, this module enables organizations to better manage the way they engage with their prospects and customers. Target audiences for this feature include:

► Large business systems integrator companies or consulting services organizations (or entities within an organization)

▶ Suppliers of technology components (printers, fax machines, copiers, personal computers, etc.)

▶ Security firms or other entities that contract for services, including legal and administrative staffing organizations

The Contracts module supports the process of generating and capturing a proposal, including the status and tracking of that process along with resources, time, and cost committed. Other features include the ability to capture contractual terms and conditions associated with a contract, and the ability to support multiple billing arrangements and multiple revenue-recognition scenarios. The bundling of products and services is also included, as is the capability to track contract deliverables, acceptance criteria, and change orders. Integration with a document management system to manage the physical contract is also provided.

Resource Management

Another new controlled release product with PeopleSoft 8 includes the Resource Management module, which, again, is a key component of the PSA offering. This application is designed to meet the resource planning needs of professional service organizations. It integrates human resource project planning, competency management, and resource scheduling with the needs of project contracts, expenses, time tracking, revenue recognition, and billing.

The module is intended to help identify and track project resource requirements, manage both information requests for services and service orders, track external use of resources, link resources to required openings, have the capability to maintain information on the preferences of the resources on staffing as well as a profile on the individual, look at and analyze a resource's skills and competency assessments, review project assignments and schedules, and produce reports and status on resource availability as well as manage any conflicts with resources. The application also provides the ability to analyze workforce utilization and turnaround to help manage the resource pool.

The center of this application is a *request for service*, which contains a profile of the requested resource need. The other, equally important portion is the *worker profile*, which helps to match a resource with a service need. Since this product is Internet ready, all parties can access information regardless of location.

Up Next

As you can see, the PeopleSoft Financials suite of products is indeed a robust set of applications that support not only the basic back-office financial requirements, but also the more complex performance reporting, treasury management, and in some cases industry-specific solutions. PeopleSoft's new Internet product suite found in release 8 is a robust product that can support most organizations' requirements into the future. The focus on service organizations with banking, insurance, and professional service offerings makes this an excellent choice for these industries, and the popularity of this solution is almost as strong as their Human Resources suite of offerings.

Our next chapter, "A Closer Look at Supply Chain Management," will focus on the offerings found around the manufacturing-based solutions that contain some innovative approaches to supply chain management and optimization. While these suites of modules are not as popular or as well known as the Financials and HRMS suites, they provide some unique features that fit many organizations' requirements. You will get a look at the solutions PeopleSoft provides to the Distribution and Manufacturing product areas along with some insights into these solutions.

CHAPTER 20

A Closer Look at Supply Chain Management

FEATURING:

► An overview of the PeopleSoft Materials Management applications, including the Inventory and Purchasing modules

► A look at the Sales and Logistics area, including the Remote Order Entry feature, Order Management, Product Configurator, Billing, and new features of PeopleSoft 8 including eStore, Mobile Store, and eBill Payment

► Leverage of special tools, Enterprise Planning Tools, to optimize the supply chain network found in the Supply Chain Planning area

► An overview of the PeopleSoft Manufacturing application, including Bills and Routings, Production Management, and Cost Management modules

► How PeopleSoft Engineering provides basic document management and engineering support for a typical engineering environment

► What ERO (enterprise resource optimization) is and why PeopleSoft is the first to deliver this fully integrated feature

Beyond the Enterprise Resource Planning (ERP) concept, PeopleSoft uses the concept of *enterprise resource optimization* (ERO) in its client-server distribution and manufacturing systems across the enterprise. This innovative approach allows the enterprise to be very competitive in a complex and challenging distribution/manufacturing industry on a global basis. As buyers demand quality products with minimal lead time and maximum flexibility and innovativeness in products, suppliers face the daunting task of meeting the customer demands in a timely manner while maintaining the desired profitability of their business. The manufacturing and distribution organizations today face the challenges of:

- ▶ Introducing innovative products faster with minimal engineering lead time and reduced product life cycles

- ▶ Faster customer order processing with short delivery schedules and accurate promised dates

- ▶ Global product demand and local customization to suit specific market needs

- ▶ Reduced lead times in procurement, distribution, and manufacturing

This chapter provides a closer look at the components that make up People-Soft's Supply Chain Management application. This application is broken down into four major areas:

- ▶ Materials Management

- ▶ Sales and Logistics

- ▶ Supply Chain Planning

- ▶ Manufacturing

Also within the Supply Chain application, two additional tools from the EPM (Enterprise Performance Management) application are available:

- ▶ Supply Chain Management Workbench

- ▶ Marketplace Analytics

These major application areas will be discussed along with the distinctive solutions or approach the vendor uses to support these critical areas of business.

Materials Management

PeopleSoft's Materials Management (or what is also known as Distribution) application is designed to meet the changing business demands of global enterprises. The main objective here is to conduct seamless business globally in different languages using multiple currencies. The Materials Management modules' global capabilities include:

▶ Multi-language features

▶ Multi-currency functionality

▶ VAT/GST (value-added tax/goods and services tax) processing and movement tracking between European Community member states

▶ Support for the European Monetary Union and the use of the euro currency

In the next sections, we will look at the major modules that make up the PeopleSoft Materials Management system and how they interact together to deliver the solutions and supplies necessary to support a global enterprise. (Note that the Payables, Expenses, and Asset Management modules are also part of the Materials Management system. Since they were discussed in the preceding chapter, "A Closer Look at Financials," they will not be covered in this chapter.)

Inventory

PeopleSoft Inventory is an extremely flexible application for warehouse and inventory materials management. At the heart of any materials management system lie the following five core functions:

▶ Receiving and put-away

▶ Order interface and fulfillment

▶ Inventory replenishment

▶ Inventory costing

▶ Physical counting

Each of the five core functions is analyzed in the following sections.

Put-Away

Let's begin with the process of putting away inventory. Put-away normally occurs when materials are shipped against a purchase order created by some type of procurement system. For the purpose of this discussion, we will assume that the PeopleSoft Purchasing module (which is reviewed in our next section) is installed and that we are receiving against a PeopleSoft-created purchase order. In this case, the Receiving—Receipt Lines page would be used with the Select Purchase Order and Putaway Information options. This page is displayed in Figure 20.1. If the PeopleSoft Purchasing module was not being utilized, the same page would be used with the Insert NonPO line option for Inventory receipts. For the most basic receipt, this is the only page in which receipt information must be input.

Figure 20.1   **Receiving—Receipt Lines page**

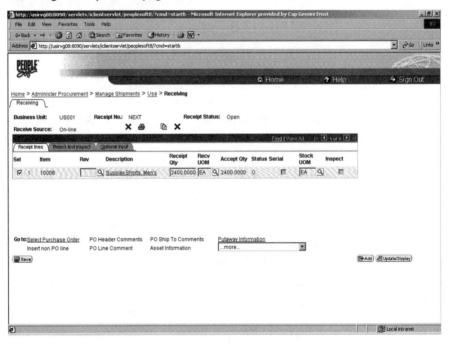

Several data elements of configuration control must be entered as a part of the put-away processing after the receipt information is input. These pieces of configuration include the Inventory business unit's put-away setup, the item's default put-away location, the receiver's operator preferences, and the put-away processes that are run. Depending on the way these configuration items are set up, a company can have the following put-away models:

▶ The item can be automatically put away into a predefined storage location without any other end-user interaction after the receipt is performed.

▶ For high-volume receipt environments, the items can be put away into a staging area temporarily until warehouse personnel have time to transfer the items into a desired storage location.

▶ For warehouses that stock items in multiple storage locations (examples would be bulk, WIP (work in progress), or high-moving locations), a multistep put-away process can be used. In this process, a report is produced that suggests multiple storage locations for put-away. The person doing put-away would make a decision as to which location items should be placed in. When the location is selected, the person performing the put-away would check the location information on the put-away plan. After all items are placed in appropriate locations, the actual put-away locations are input into PeopleSoft using the Stockroom feedback page and the information is written down on the hard copy report. After feedback is entered, the put-away process is run in order to update Inventory balances.

Order Fulfillment

PeopleSoft Inventory provides extremely robust demand fulfillment capabilities. Demand to inventory can be processed from a wide variety of sources within PeopleSoft or third-party applications. Some of these sources include PeopleSoft Inventory, Order Management, Enterprise Planning, Production Planning, or third-party planning applications.

Within the Inventory module, PeopleSoft provides two main mechanisms to create demand for inventory. The first mechanism is intended for use in a walk-up demand environment, similar to a person walking up to a concession stand. In this environment, the demand is created and fulfilled immediately. Inventory relief in this environment should be immediate, and the intervention of inventory personnel should be as limited as possible. For this application, PeopleSoft provides the Express Issue page. An example of Express Issue is shown in Figure 20.2. When doing an Express Issue, Inventory is picked and shipped in one transaction.

Figure 20.2 **Express Issue page**

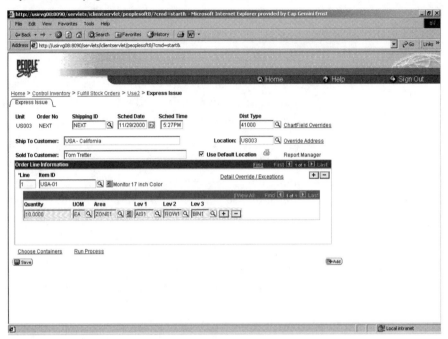

The second method of creating demand in inventory is through the use of material stock requests (MSRs). This function is used in cases where orders are being placed remotely from the storeroom and items are being delivered to the requester from the storeroom. Using MSR functionality enables a multi-step fulfillment process to be utilized. This multistep process is used to fulfill all sources of demand outside of PeopleSoft Inventory as well.

The full set of steps to fulfill a demand usually include reserving available inventory, printing a picking plan, physically picking the items demanded, inputting picking feedback, confirming feedback, and shipping the order. Businesses can vary the control of this fulfillment process by utilizing the AutoPick and AutoShip functionality, which enables the picking confirmation and shipping steps in this process to be skipped. It is important to remember that both Express Issue and MSRs can be utilized to enter orders internal to a corporation or external to a customer, or to initiate transfers between inventory business units or return items to a vendor.

Inventory Replenishment

PeopleSoft Inventory gives customers great flexibility when it comes to replenishing inventory items. Replenishment is set at the business unit level to enable various replenishment models to be used at different warehouse facilities. There are two options for replenishment: standard reorder point replenishment and a fixed bin replenishment, which suggests the replenishment of bins based on available bin quantities and predefined stocking levels. Three standard reorder point models are provided as options: EOQ (economic order quantity, where quantity for reorder is based on predetermined variables with the objective of optimizing the reorder quantities), Min/Max (which allows for automatic reordering when a minimum quantity level is reached and allows the inventory to reach the prespecified maximum inventory level for the item), and static reorder quantity (which allows for the ordering of a fixed quantity based on preestablished reorder points for inventory items). Functionality is also provided to calculate the appropriate replenishment variables for each item based on the replenishment model selected.

Inventory Accounting and Costing

The Cost Management module is used to handle the accounting for all inventory transactions. The Cost Management module functionality gives companies the ability to create high-level default accounting controls that can be overridden at several levels down to the individual transaction in Inventory. In addition, there is the ability to drive the costing method at the item level. The following four costing methods are provided:

► Average Cost: Calculates a weighted cost average by item.

► Standard Cost: Represents a predetermined cost by product element.

► Actual Cost: Represents the true cost to procure an item.

► Non Cost: Used to track quantities transacted without any financial accounting impact.

Physical Accounting

Two physical counting processes are delivered within PeopleSoft. The first counting process consists of functionality to close an inventory facility for a count of all items within the facility. Transactions are halted by setting the Prohibit Materials Movement flag on the business unit. Once transactions are stopped, a counting event can be established and completed. This process involves the following steps:

1. Create a counting event for all storage locations.

2. Run a counting sheet for the created counting event.

3. Perform a physical count and record item counts.

4. Input count quantities into PeopleSoft.

5. Run a reconciliation report.

6. Recount appropriate items identified on the reconciliation report.

7. Re-input counts.

8. Run the inventory update process for the counting event.

The second delivered counting process is cycle counts. Many different processing options are provided for cycle counts. In addition to these options, items can be included and excluded from cycle counts by a Utilization Type that is assigned at the item level. This Utilization Type can be calculated for each item automatically based on various predefined parameters.

PeopleSoft Purchasing

Another key module within the Materials Management application is the Purchasing module. This module is made up of several key functions, including:

▶ Creation and management of an item catalog

▶ Creation and processing of item requisitions and purchase orders

▶ Requests for quotes and contracts

▶ Integration to support the overall procure-to-pay process with the Financials suite

Each of these areas is explained in greater detail in the sections that follow.

Catalog Management

At the heart of any procurement system is the item catalog or item master. A good procurement system must have consistent and timely catalog information. PeopleSoft has extremely deep catalog segmenting abilities and flexible item-processing controls. These abilities make PeopleSoft's catalog management capabilities a very powerful tool. There are more than 20 different ways to classify an item in PeopleSoft. Multiple item vendor relationships can also be set up with different pricing structures based on the quantities placed on orders. PeopleSoft uses its Tree Manager tool to create multiple catalogs based on the item category field. These catalogs can be assigned to requesters in order to facilitate item searches during the requisitioning or ad hoc purchase order process. All catalogs are updated as new items are added into the system. A final option delivered is the ability to turn Item Approvals "on" for each business unit.

Requisition-to-PO-Dispatch Life Cycle

The core procurement process lies within the requisition-to-PO-dispatch life cycle. Requisitions can be entered with ease online in PeopleSoft Purchasing through the Purchase Requisition page application. An example of the delivered Requisition page is shown in Figure 20.3.

Figure 20.3   **Requisition Form page**

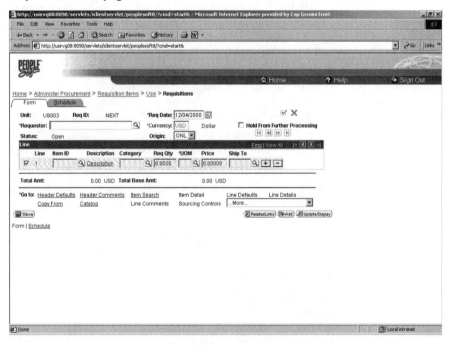

Items can be searched for and added to requisitions through a number of methods. Each method has its own advantages. Overall, PeopleSoft delivers just the right amount of tools to make searching for items and creating requisitions an easy process for any person accessing the system. Five of these tools for item searches are outlined below.

Description-only requisition line item   This is the simplest functionality for a requester. It can be used when an item is not established or the item cannot be found. A purchasing specialist will source the description-only requisition line to a supplier before a PO is created.

Catalog functionality   A requester can use this to search for items using any predefined catalog that consists of a category-based tree structure.

Requester favorite items functionality   A requester can search a list of items that the individual has previously ordered on requisitions. This list of favorite items is dynamically updated by PeopleSoft each time a new item is ordered on a requisition.

Kitting functionality   This lets a requester order a predefined basket of items that is set up by procurement specialists within an organization.

Requisition template functionality   A requester can mark requisitions as templates as they are being entered online and use that template any time in the future to reorder the same items.

Outside the Purchasing module, requisitions can be pulled in through Requisition Loader from Production Planning, Manufacturing, Order Management (drop shipments), Inventory (replenishment and backorder ad hoc requisitions), Project Costing requisitions, and third-party sources. After a requisition is created, the requisition lines can go through an automatic sourcing process if the item is marked as Auto Select. The sourcing process will pick a vendor and pricing, if established for the given item. The requisitions can also go through approval workflow if requisition approvals are turned on for the business unit. If the items are marked for Inventory on the item master and the requisition line is selected to source from Inventory, the Build Inventory demand process can check inventory availability before creating a PO for a supplier.

If an item on a requisition is not marked for automatic sourcing, it will have to go through an online sourcing process where a purchasing specialist will determine the appropriate vendor and price for the item. If necessary, a quote can be performed for the item. After the lines are sourced to suppliers, they are eligible for the PO Build process that creates a purchase order. PeopleSoft also provides the ability to skip the requisition process completely and add a PO manually online (ad hoc PO). If this method is used frequently, PO approval workflow can be turned on and set up for the business unit. After POs are created and approved, they are eligible for dispatch to suppliers via EDI, fax, phone, or manual printing.

Request for Quotes and Contracts

Two additional tools that PeopleSoft provides for the procurement of goods are Requests for Quotes (RFQs) and Contracts. RFQs are used to track the communication between a business's procurement personnel and vendors and the establishment of pricing for goods and services. Quotes for items can be dispatched to one vendor or a group of vendors. Vendors do not have to be approved to receive an RFQ. After responses are received, they can be recorded in the system using the Enter Responses—RFQ Response page displayed in Figure 20.4 below. When the procurement specialist analyzes the responses and chooses the appropriate vendor (awards the quote), a PO or contract can be created from the quote.

Figure 20.4   **Enter RFQ Responses—Line page**

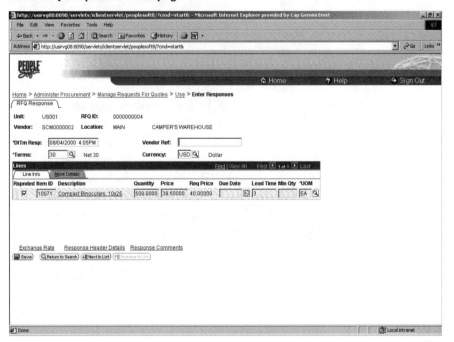

Contracts are a binding agreement between two parties. PeopleSoft Purchasing contracts are usually based on pricing agreements between a buying company and an individual vendor. Contracts that are related in form or function can be linked through a Master Contract. The two contract types used in PeopleSoft purchasing are fixed and open item contracts. *Fixed contracts* relate to specified items purchased by the buying organization from the vendor, while *open contracts* are used to apply some discount percentage to all items purchased from a given vendor. Contract releases may also be used to plan purchases in advance of creating the actual PO. The Build Contract PO process can be used to automatically create POs based on predetermined release schedules.

Financials Integration

There are several items of Financials integration functionality that should be extensively considered when implementing PeopleSoft Purchasing. The three main pieces are listed below.

- ▶ Matching (Accounts Payable)
- ▶ Receipt accruals (Accounts Payable)
- ▶ Commitment tracking (Project Costing)

Automated matching is an area that can have a large return on investment (ROI) for any organization depending on its legacy system and matching policies. Many companies' accounts payable departments perform matching using paper-based documents and a filing system. This process is an extremely time-consuming administrative task. Since PeopleSoft is an integrated computer-based system, the information required for matching is stored online and the matching process can be performed automatically using customizable rules and delivered matching processes. PeopleSoft delivers two-way (invoice to PO), three-way (invoice to PO and receipt), four-way (invoice to PO, receipt, and inspection), and Evaluated Receipt Settlement (ERS) matching processes. ERS has additional ROI considerations because a voucher is automatically generated when the receipt is matched to the PO. An invoice is not required for payment. ERS eliminates the administrative task performed in Accounts Payable when personnel are required to create a voucher.

The next Financials consideration is receipt accruals. *Receipt accruals* is a method of accruing uninvoiced receipts for non-inventory items. The accrual process is run at the end of each accounting period. It is a function that allows a company to record the payable and expense in the proper accounting period based on when the vendor sends the invoice and the voucher is recorded. Receipt accruals are configured at the Purchasing business unit level.

The final Financials consideration is the functionality provided in PeopleSoft Project Costing to track committed dollar amounts. The term *commitment* refers to the fact that a company is, in effect, promising or committing to the extended dollar amount on a PO to a supplier. A commitment is recorded in Project Costing at the time a PO is dispatched to a supplier. This commitment does not get relieved until the PO is vouchered in Accounts Payable and an actual dollar amount is recorded. Commitments are tracked through delivered Project Costing application engines, which pull data into Projects from both the Purchasing and Accounts Payable modules. The main purpose for tracking commitments is to gain a better view of the available budget for a project. Most companies analyze only budget-to-actual variances. If you introduce commitments to the variance calculation, the calculation of available budget becomes:

Available Budget = Original Budget – Actuals – Commitments

This calculation gives a much clearer picture of available budget.

Blanket Orders

A key configuration point discussed in this section is blanket orders and how they are handled in PeopleSoft.

Blanket Orders Not Handled in PeopleSoft

An often confused concept by many people within purchasing organizations is a *blanket order*. The term *blanket order* or *blanket purchase order* can be used in a wide variety of contexts when it comes to procuring goods and services. Some people view them as a way of obtaining an open line of credit with their suppliers, while others use them as a simple means to procure goods without going through an organization's formal purchasing system.

Note APICS (Association for Purchasing and Inventory Control Specialists) defines a blanket purchase order as "a long-term commitment to a supplier for material against which short-term releases will be generated to satisfy requirements. Often blanket orders cover only one item with predetermined delivery dates." (APICS Dictionary, 9th ed., APICS—The Educational Society for Resource Management, 1998.)

Blanket orders are not specifically addressed in PeopleSoft; however, People-Soft does provide several features that can be utilized to handle blanket order–type purchases. The key pieces of functionality in PeopleSoft to handle blankets are contracts and standard purchase orders. Table 20.1 lists a number of situations that come up in day-to-day operations. Next to each scenario in the table is an example of how each specific case can be handled within People-Soft. This table will not handle all possible scenarios that will come up in operations; however, it will give you an idea of how the system can be used to handle certain situations.

Table 20.1   **Blanket Order Scenarios and Viable PeopleSoft Solutions**

Scenario	How Blanket Order Should Be Entered into PeopleSoft
Blanket order is for material with no other specific requirements.	Create PeopleSoft Item and set up item-supplier relationship with appropriate pricing and expiration date. No other configuration or setup should be necessary.
Blanket order is for material and has a maximum dollar amount associated with total material purchases.	Create PeopleSoft Item and enter a fixed item contract with a maximum dollar amount.
Blanket order is for material and requires scheduled releases with defined delivery schedule and quantities.	Create PeopleSoft Item and enter a fixed item contract. Enter release defaults and release schedule. Explode releases to be picked up by Purchase Order (PO) Build according to release date.
Blanket order is for fixed payment to a supplier for goods or services. (Example: Lease payments)	No setup in the Purchasing module should be required. Using Accounts Payable functionality, enter a recurring voucher contract. The recurring voucher contract will handle the fixed payment schedule.
Blanket order is for material and service combined with known quantities of each or for service only with releases that can be scheduled.	Enter a fixed item contract with description-only line item(s) and enter release defaults and release schedule. Explode releases to be picked up by PO Build according to release date.

Other Materials Management Modules

With PeopleSoft 8, an eSupplier Collaboration feature is also available within the Materials Management suite of products. This feature provides collaboration between your employees, customers, and suppliers. This capability allows you to forecast demand based on order history, economic indicators, and input from these three constituents. Then the collaborator looks at when and where to produce and distribute finished products and how to establish reliable promise dates for your customer orders.

Also within the purchasing area, customers can choose the eProcurement module, which provides for tight integration with CommerceOne's BuySite for buying materials through an online marketplace and allows for better collaboration with suppliers, better tracking and transfer of orders to suppliers, and ability to create better pricing for goods based on shared contracts with other organizations or better tracking of your own internal spending trends. More information on the eProcurement process and trends are outlined in Chapter 24, "What's Next on the Horizon."

As previously mentioned, the Asset Management module (in tracking materials purchased), Payables module (to pay vendors), and Expenses module (to pay employee expense) are also considered a part of the Materials Management suite of products.

Sales and Logistics

The Sales and Logistics suite of products includes the processes from entry of a sales order through order fulfillment. One of PeopleSoft's first true Internet modules, the eStore, is where the sale begins. Through an online storefront, customers can order items and obtain key information on the status of their orders. The eStore module is tightly integrated with the Order Management module. Another feature very similar to the eStore, the Mobile Store, is the capability to take orders via a mobile environment such as a cell phone or PalmPilot. These modules allow for greater flexibility in customer orders and allow information to be in the hands of the customer from almost anywhere.

The sections that follow outline some other key areas within the Sales and Logistics suite:

► Order Management and Remote Order Entry

► Product Configurator

► Order Promising

Also included in this suite of products are the Billing and Receivables modules. These modules allow for the customer billing and collections for the sales cycle process. (These modules are also available with the Financials suite of products and were explained in Chapter 19.) With PeopleSoft 8, eBill Payment is also provided, enabling online bill presentation to customers via the Web. Additionally, the Inventory module is key to the Materials Management cycle by providing direct information to the customer on the availability of an order or in keeping your supply chain up to speed with your orders.

Order Management

The Order Management module primarily handles transactions related to the sales orders and sales contracts of a business. When planning the setup of the Order Management module, it is very important to consider the level of integration to other key modules such as Inventory, General Ledger, and Accounts Receivable. It is critical to establish the relationship between the business units across these modules, as it impacts the movement of data from one module to another. From a sales and marketing point of view, Order Management can be the heart of the enterprise, with tight integration with related distribution and manufacturing modules.

It is easy to put the power of PeopleSoft Order Management and PeopleSoft Product Configurator at the fingertips of the enterprises sales force by using PeopleSoft Remote Order Entry (PROE). When the sales force is on the road with customers, this tool can be used to create regular and configured orders and quotes, and manage customer information.

PROE is designed to provide a subset of the PeopleSoft enterprise data by selectively setting up datasets of the catalogs, customers, and Order Management and Inventory business units. Salespeople will receive only the information they need—only the data the enterprise authorizes them to see—thus accelerating data transfer.

In addition to order-taking and quote creation, PROE includes complete customer and order inquiry functionality. Salespeople can easily access customer information, pricing, product availability, and shipping information from PeopleSoft Order Management.

PROE pages have a slightly different look from those of standard PeopleSoft Order Management. This is done to facilitate efficient data retrieval and transfer between the laptops of the salespeople and enterprise servers. Figure 20.5 shows the vital order information as captured in the sales order page, Order Entry Form—Order Header.

Figure 20.5 **Maintain Sales Orders—Order Entry Header page**

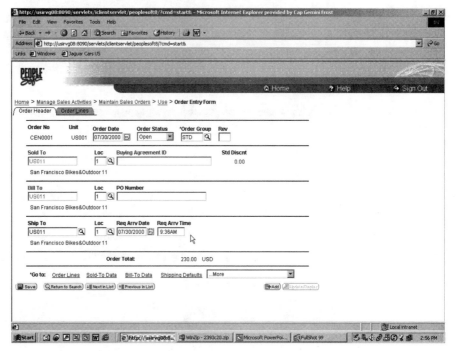

Configured Orders and Quotes

One can capitalize on the sophisticated and powerful rules-based functionality of PeopleSoft Product Configurator to enter and validate configured products remotely. It is easy to put the knowledge of the enterprise's various departments at the fingertips of the sales force. Product Configurator can be used to take orders for configured products that are stocked, as well as for products that are make-to-order. In situations where "buy" parts constitute the final products to sell, Product Configurator can automatically create purchase requisitions. When "make" parts are involved, Product Configurator can automatically send a production order with manufacturing details (e.g., bill of material). In addition, Product Configurator can also price and cost the enterprise's products based on the unique configuration.

The page in Figure 20.6 depicts the PeopleSoft sales order line (details) prompting a new product entry.

Figure 20.6 **Maintain Sales Orders—Order Entry Line page**

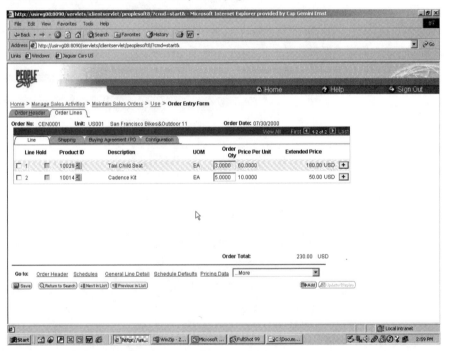

Flexible Order Tracking System

PeopleSoft's Remote Order Entry system helps salespeople to improve customer service by using exception information. This exception information captures all the changes to the original orders. Salespeople can use exception information that is downloaded from the corporate server to keep customers informed about any of their order changes. Examples of exception information include any changes to the order based on customer credit problems, delivery dates (when the original delivery date changes), inventory shortages (such that your order may not be met or is delayed based on these shortages), and price. By tracking these changes on an "exception" basis, the salesperson easily sees any changes to the original order and is able to notify the customer and answer any questions they might have based on these changes.

Product Configurator

The Product Configurator is part of the PeopleSoft Sales and Logistics software. It is a rules-based system that allows users to capture customer requirements and dynamically generate corresponding production requirements. Users can define order entry pages for entering and validating configuration information. The configuration information that users enter determines the specific components and operations used in the production process. It can also support complex pricing based on the specific configuration options chosen. Configured order information then can support production order generation, dynamic kit assembly, and configured purchase orders.

By the time the Product Configurator is installed, you should have already begun setting up the PeopleSoft Inventory, Order Management, and Manufacturing applications. This includes setting up tables, business units, Set IDs, and so forth. Figure 20.7 outlines the key integration and process flow of information with the Product Configuration and the other PeopleSoft modules.

The Product Configurator has two primary functions:

▶ It enables users to create a valid configuration for a product and determine pricing and shipping based on the options chosen, at order entry time. This is done through pages from which users can select options for configurable items. Users control the pages to display, the default values to use, and the option combinations that are valid.

▶ It generates production orders. Users can use either traditional bills of material and routings or rules defined in the configuration process to generate component requirements and operations requirements for production orders.

Figure 20.7 **Product Configurator—Integration with other PeopleSoft Modules and Process Flow**

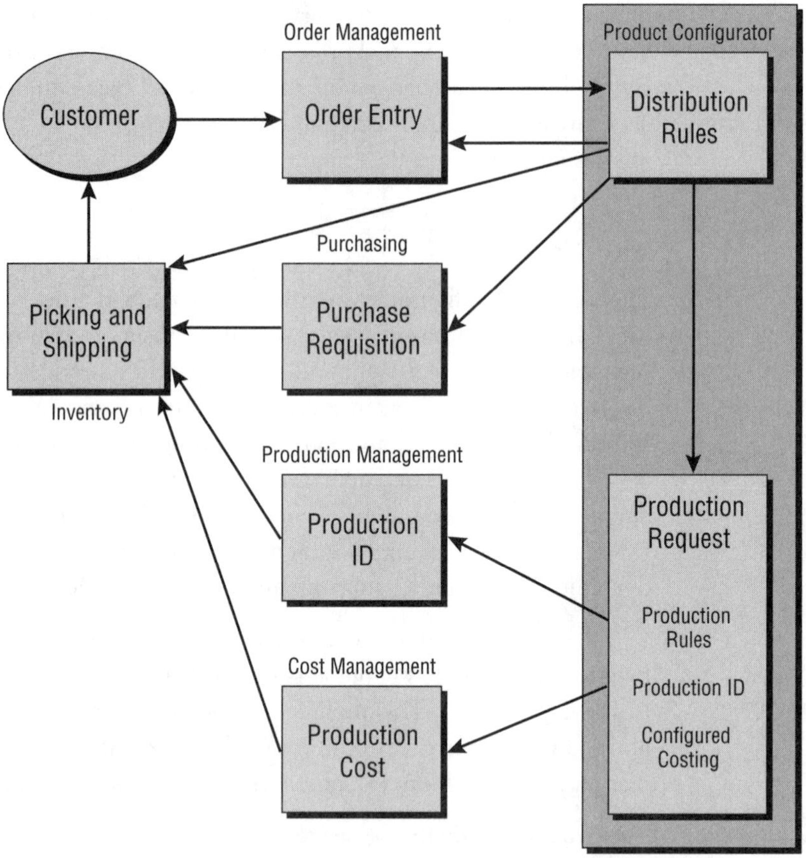

The Product Configurator module supports multilevel and multiple business unit configurations. Users can configure components of a configured item and generate a custom work order for any business unit defined in the system. Users can also generate a purchase order for any component, configured or otherwise.

The exception to the usual order of rules processing occurs when users take advantage of the Product Configurator's multilevel processing. Each configured component within a configured item uses its own rule tree situated within the larger one. When the rule tree releases a configured component rule, the overall rule tree is suspended until the component rule tree has completed processing. This processing order is similar to the usual one, which pursues the rule structure down before continuing across levels. However, it differs in that the system treats the Component rule tree as an independent entity, beginning again with the virtual rule. This modular approach enables users to initiate the configured component from any number of parent items without affecting the way that the component's rule tree is processed.

Since any configured component can include other configured components as child items, the execution of rules may pass down more than one level, suspending the processing for each parent rule tree.

For example, suppose that you are setting up rules to configure a PC that has a configurable monitor and CPU. The monitor in turn has a configurable part—the tube. The diagram below outlines this rules-based logic tree that would be set up and followed.

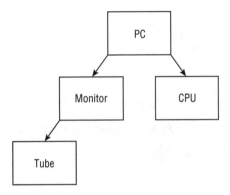

The PeopleSoft Product Configurator owes much of its adaptability to the powerful grammar of the rules that define the process. PeopleSoft ships the tools to create the system, and leaves the steps of any particular product configuration up to users. This means that optimizing the configurations depends on having a sound grasp of rule syntax and how to put the rules together into a working logic tree. Having many choices and capabilities, though, doesn't mean that users are entirely on their own. The Product Configurator offers a limited number of rule actions, operands, and variable types that are easy to master at the same time that they give users maximum flexibility.

The Product Configurator performs these functions through user-defined rules, tables, matrices, and variables. Each configured product is associated with:

▶ One or two sets of rules, one for sales order entry (distribution rules) and possibly distribution (kits), and one for production. All of these rules reside in the same database.

▶ A set of permanent tables and matrices where the rules can access a variety of information. Matrices allow users to specify up to five dimensions of valid data combinations to retrieve a specific value. In a matrix, users can define unlimited numbers of values for given options, variations, or variables.

The screen in Figure 20.8 shows the PeopleSoft Product Configurator at work after the Save Order button is hit. Custom road bike options, matrices, and rules are launched in this example.

Figure 20.8   **Product Configurator**

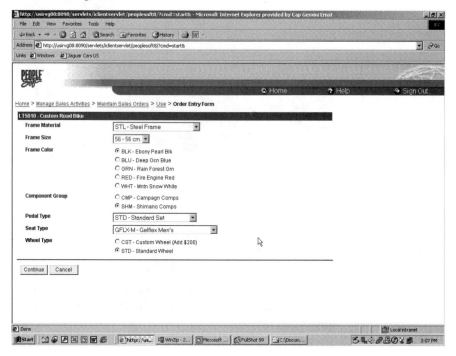

Figure 20.9 shows an example of how the custom road bike configuration rules and matrices were executed after the road bike options were saved.

Figure 20.9   **Maintain Sales Orders—Order Entry Line page for configured bicycle**

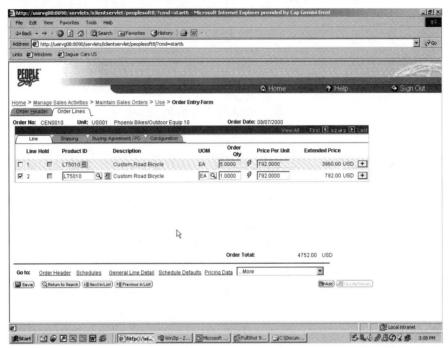

Order Promising

Order Promising searches the entire supply chain to determine the best way for a customer to receive the quantity they want, when they want it. People-Soft's goal here is to achieve optimal promised dates along with a reduced order-to-cash cycle. The software attempts to achieve the above goals by providing visibility into all components starting from vendor contact and raw material procurement to order fulfillment and outbound shipments. The software strives to offer the capable-to-promise capability as opposed to the traditional available-to-promise offerings of most ERP packages. Even though the capable-to-promise functionality can be further enhanced, it allows the manufacturer to accept new unplanned orders by adjusting the manufacturing plans and reallocating its resources, materials, and capacity. This flexibility of adjusting to varying market demands—as opposed to the traditional model of accepting orders based on existing inventory, capacity, and production plans—is an extremely attractive option for dynamic, growth-oriented enterprises today.

When considering options for order fulfillment, Order Promising takes advantage of the data in the Planning modules, looking at both the enterprise capabilities (what may be in inventory around the enterprise) and production (what may be in production) to determine the most feasible options for sourcing the order across the entire supply chain, including the warehousing and production options. Key features of Order Promising include:

▶ Ability to review capable-to-promise options with the assistance of the enterprise and production planning data

▶ Visibility into the enterprise to locate the requested products and related data on the products

▶ Ability to identify other material sourcing options to allow the enterprise to fulfill its customer demands

▶ Capacity evaluation across the enterprise

Order Promising can be used in conjunction with the Product Configurator or the Order Management module. When invoking Order Promising via Order Management, the various order fulfillment options can be reviewed at the time of entering the sales orders at the line item level. Two main evaluation options used are:

▶ Product cost

▶ Delivery date

Order Promising can also use the Product Configurator to define the rules for availability for configured items and calculate the expected availability dates. In addition, the Configurator can define rules based on product, quantity, and business unit.

Supply Chain Planning

The Supply Chain Planning application suite includes key elements to help plan for your demands, enabling you to fulfill your supply chain needs. Key modules within this suite include:

▶ Demand Planning

▶ Order Promising

      ▶ Enterprise Planning

      ▶ Inventory Planning

The Order Promising module was discussed earlier in the Sales and Logistics section. Following is a look at the other modules that make up the Supply Chain Planning functions.

Demand Planning

Demand planning is an integral part of the supply chain model that links the customers, enterprise operations, and suppliers. PeopleSoft has a fairly robust, customer-centric Supply Chain Management (SCM) package covering advanced planning, optimization, collaboration, and transaction management. Most manufacturers and distributors face the challenge of fulfilling constantly changing customer orders. The changes in the customer requests can impact the quantities, size, product/service configurations, delivery schedule, and perhaps a series of other variables. Factors contributing to these change requests can range anywhere from varying user demands to changes in the buyer's financial status to changes in services/product requirements.

As an example, the high-tech industry is faced with the challenges of changing demand patterns almost on a daily basis. Component prices can change every day, resulting in huge shifts in demand patterns. All in all, the need for quality forecasts are essential to the success of most enterprises today and can contribute heavily to the success or failure of the business. The order forecasts created by demand planning are shown in the example in Figure 20.10.

PeopleSoft generates demand forecasts by conducting the statistical analysis of a series of variables. Some key components include sales order historical data, economic factors, special promotions and discounts, seasonal variations, and feedback from the supplier-customer network. The integration between the Demand Planning and Inventory Planning modules allows for a very effective supply chain management tool. Key features of the Demand Planning module are further discussed in the next few paragraphs.

The Demand Planning module offers detailed audit trails for data as well as functional input at field value or user array levels. The graphical representation for forecasting is helpful, as it provides a visual representation of data for expedient review.

Figure 20.10 **Order Forecasts**

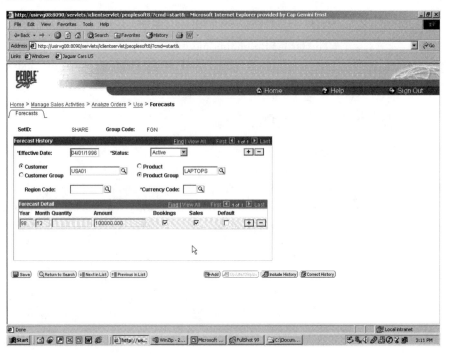

The flexible forecast master table in the module allows you to store user-defined arrays to support both historical and future data. The user-defined array can be linked to a forecast item with the flexibility of copying the array to new items. Other features include unlimited user-defined unit of measure conversions and key future demand data such as current actual demand, adjusted demand, adjustment reasons, and monetary demand value. The system also allows for automatic updates on the inventory planning side as the demand planning gets updated.

The software computes the MAPE values for all available forecasts. MAPE (mean absolute percentage error) measures the accuracy of forecasts. A MAPE value of zero implies a perfectly accurate forecast.

The overall integration between PeopleSoft Demand Planning and other PeopleSoft distribution modules is robust, which allows for efficient data imports into the Demand Planning module.

Enterprise Planning

In today's economy, most large enterprises operate globally with production and distribution centers located all over the world. Companies today often resemble life-sized Lego™ sets. A CEO of an enterprise may constantly shuffle business components, like Lego pieces, from one location to another to improve business efficiencies. Major drivers forcing this change are:

▶ Improve customer responsiveness

▶ Reduce lead time

▶ Reduce logistical costs

▶ Improve supplier relationships

▶ Reduce inventory

▶ Maintain overall low-cost position and market dominance

Effective enterprise planning can be achieved in the PeopleSoft implementation by using the production and distribution planning tools across the supply chain network. Using the Red Pepper engine (a product acquired by PeopleSoft in the mid-1990s that provides an "engine" to calculate resource optimization) planners can prioritize deliveries and minimize shortages. Variables that can be considered in the planning process include:

▶ Customer-requested delivery dates

▶ Raw material availability

▶ Inventory (finished goods)

▶ Available capacity

▶ Sales order details

▶ Demand forecasts

The end result of the enterprise planning process is a globally balanced enterprise with clear understanding of how to maximize the balance between capacity and resources on a global basis. In Figure 20.11, an example of setting up an Enterprise Plan DataLink for demand and supply options is shown.

Figure 20.11 **Enterprise DataLink—Demand/Supply**

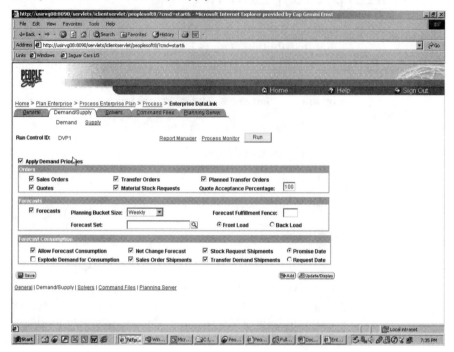

Inventory Planning

Within the PeopleSoft Inventory Planning module, you can simulate various inventory stocking scenarios so that you can select the best strategy for your situation. Current policies and procedures can be compared with proposed strategies to improve your ability to maintain your inventory, attempting to maintain the lowest amount of inventory possible to meet the demands you have. This simulation allows you to better understand the relationships between your forecasted demand, inventory investment, inventory turnover, customer service levels and ability to meet customer demands, frequency of replenishment, and levels necessary to ensure a safe stock level. Several methods can be used in this simulation process to determine order quantity and safety stock while seeing the effects on time-phased inventory investments, inventory turns, and customer service levels. These features allow you to optimize your inventory levels and look at potential trends or changes to these levels based on potential policy or process changes.

By properly balancing your demand, inventory, enterprise planning, and order promising, you will improve customer service and the management of your supply chain, both internally and externally for your organization. These are key features within the Supply Chain product.

Now that we have looked at the key modules that form the Supply Chain Planning channel for the PeopleSoft application, we will take a closer look at the newest line of products, PeopleSoft Manufacturing.

Manufacturing

PeopleSoft Manufacturing is built to provide optimization around production and related processes. The software is most suitable for the high-technology businesses handling global requirements with a large number of components in a dynamic product-demand/supply environment. The PeopleSoft Manufacturing application is designed to support integrated engineering, demand planning, production, quality, and production cost requirements. This is a relatively new product with limited implementations, compared to market leaders such as SAP.

Bills and Routings

The Bills and Routings module is designed to support the material and resource requirements for the production processes, allowing the planners to specify how the products need to be built. This module allows the production department to achieve higher efficiencies in the engineering and production functions. Some of the key components tracked include:

- Bills of material (BOMs)
- Product configurations
- Resource requirements
- Job locations
- Details on tasks to be performed
- Routing information
- Revision control
- Component yield
- Master routings

Accurate bills of material and routing data also help in other production support functions, such as material planning, material allocations, forecasting, and cost roll-ups. Bills and Routings is integrated with related Supply Chain Management modules such as:

► Engineering

► Production Management

► Quality

► Cost Management

► Inventory

► Purchasing

► Asset Management

► Production Planning (Red Pepper)

► Enterprise Planning

Figure 20.12 shows the page in PeopleSoft where routing data is captured.

Figure 20.12   **Routing Definition—Operations**

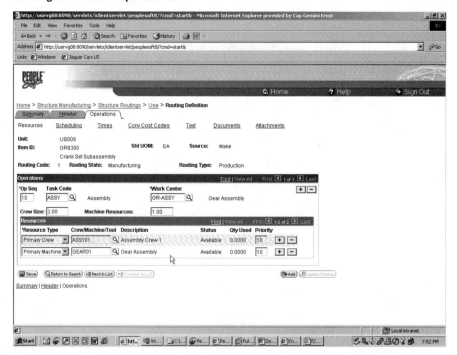

Key features of the Bills and Routings module include:

► Flexible BOM maintenance, including summaries and components

► Ability to make mass BOM changes

► Ability to maintain BOMs by revision or effective dates

► Flexibility in maintaining revisions

► Ability to attach multimedia revision documents for reference

► Support for subcontracting/non-subcontracting scenarios

► Maintaining and displaying assembly documents, including components and attachments

► Detailed and summarized BOM cost calculation and tracking

► Resource management by crew, by machine, and by tools

► Changeover and associated penalty and time

Production Management

Production Management is designed to maintain diverse production areas, covering details by each item on production planning recommendations. It offers the capability to review production plans online and make near real-time adjustments to the plan to accommodate last-minute customer change orders. Production orders can be set up for discrete orders, batches, or production runs with shop floor production progress and cost-tracking capabilities. Main production-planning activities covered by Production Management are:

► Component lists maintenance

► Operations list maintenance

► Part substitution

► Subcontracted production to vendor

► Production and process scheduling

► Release production and production document generation

► Issuance of component material to the shop floor

► Operation completion and movement out of production

► Scrap maintenance

Production Management also works very closely with the Production Planning real-time planning engine. After the planning engine optimizes the production plan, the current plan data as well as the revised plan data can be fed to Production Management for review.

The planning tool can be used for what-if analysis, and by using varying input parameters, several optimized plans can be developed and recommended to the planners. Planners can then review the recommendations. This integration provides the capability to transfer production plan information back and forth between Production Planning and Production Management.

For production planning purposes, the maintenance utility tools provide key production data on a daily, weekly, and monthly basis. These tools are vital to the production planning process, as they provide total visibility into the current shop floor production activities as well as the proposed plans. Key features of the production maintenance utility include:

- Selectively view production information on an as-needed basis
- Maintain and adjust production quantities
- Add new production IDs
- Adjust production schedule quantities

Several variables can impact the production schedule, including these:

- Item ID
- Status
- Production quantity
- Production type
- Actual start date/time
- Actual due date/time
- Production start date/shift
- Production due date/shift
- Routing code
- Revision

The Component List Summary, which is tracked as part of the production management process, is shown in Figure 20.13.

Figure 20.13   **Component List Maintenance—Summary**

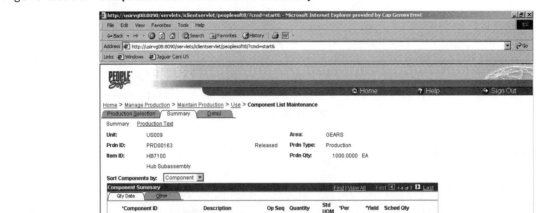

Cost Management

PeopleSoft Manufacturing is based on standard costing, hence Cost Management primarily uses the standard costing method, though other cost methods are available. Using the standard costing method, one can calculate the cost of manufactured items based on the cost of purchased components, the manufactured items' product structure, routing or operations list, and applicable rates for the manufacturing business unit.

When making cost revisions, Cost Management changes the costs for the available inventory, raw material, work in process, and finished goods storage areas at the revised standard cost and can post an adjustment entry to the general ledger to reflect the revised inventory balances.

For standard manufactured items, the cost calculation is relatively straightforward. The cost is basically the cost roll-up per the item's manufacturing bill of material (MBOM) and its routing. The manufactured item could consist of multiple component levels, both purchased and manufactured.

For configured items, the cost is computed based on the components selected and their characteristics. The actual product configuration occurs in the Order Management module during the quote or sales order generation. Once the product is configured, the Cost Management module can compute the standard costs in two different ways:

- ▶ Configured cost
- ▶ Nonconfigured cost

For the configured cost, the cost roll-up is based on the item's components and operations list. The components can be manufactured, purchased, or configured. The cost roll-up process can be performed at the time of the product configuration. This has the advantage of providing the cost immediately at the time of configuration. Even the cost changes due to either routing or component changes can be computed immediately by using the cost roll-up process.

For configured products that are nonconfigured costed, the standard bill of material and routing is used to determine the standard cost. The cost roll-up process does not automatically calculate the costs unless flagged to do so.

Key points to note about the Cost Management module are:

- ▶ Cost calculations factor in the bill of material yield or component yield loss to account for the loss of material during the manufacturing process.
- ▶ Subcontractor-supplied and non-owned items are not considered in the item's standard cost.
- ▶ For purchased items, the cost can be either the current actual purchase price or the forecasted purchase price.
- ▶ Additional costs such as freight, duty, inspection, and warehouse costs can be included in the total cost.
- ▶ Cost groups can be used to define a set of items and perform cost roll-ups, cost comparisons, or inventory valuation.
- ▶ Table-based design for the item costing allows maximum flexibility in the cost management.
- ▶ Many options are available to support transfer prices.

- ▶ User-friendly inquiry pages exist to allow for easy review of cost information online.

- ▶ Costs can be computed for engineering BOM, manufacturing BOM, or component BOM.

Engineering

PeopleSoft Engineering is designed to provide the basic engineering and document management–related capabilities that are needed in a typical engineering environment. Main components of the Engineering module include:

- ▶ Engineering change requests (ECRs)

- ▶ Engineering change orders (ECOs)

- ▶ Engineering bills of material (EBOMs)

- ▶ Engineering routings (ERTGs)

- ▶ Item revisions

- ▶ Document management with version tracking

- ▶ Cost management of engineering items

The integration of the Engineering module with Manufacturing allows for improved workflow and increased efficiency, which was generally not available in the traditional MRP applications of the past.

In today's dynamic and challenging business environment, an enterprise desperately needs the ability to effectively coordinate tasks of all the participants in the design and approval process. The timeliness of this coordination is critical, as it has a tremendous impact on the product's quality, costs, and time to market. Some instances of this integration include:

- ▶ Need for outside vendors to actively participate in the engineering design process by providing quotes

- ▶ Need for the purchasing department to have access to the vendor quotes for tracking purposes as well as for tracking the lead times

- ▶ Review of financial impacts of the engineering design, such as profitability and ROI for products

- ▶ Visibility for production and other planners to forecast capacity and raw material requirements

► Manufacturing's involvement in the engineering design process to provide early feedback on the manufacturing options and design feasibility

► Input for sales and marketing to get the customers' perspectives

PeopleSoft is integrated with the Documentum Enterprise Document Management System (EDMS) to provide a comprehensive document management solution for the enterprise. The main components of the EDMS include:

► Documentum Server for the document database

► Documentum client such as WorkSpace or SmartSpace

Other Manufacturing Modules

Two new modules within the Manufacturing suite found in PeopleSoft 8 are the Flow Production and eProduct Management modules. The Flow Production module provides additional features to manage your production flow across the manufacturing process. The eProduct Management module allows you to schedule and manage your production process through self-service components on the Web. This allows you to gain greater flexibility in your production cycle.

The Quality module is used to monitor and track data related to the quality of your entire supply and manufacturing production chain. You can create quality control plans and track these plans against your production process. The module allows you to input feedback as well as analyze your data to make adjustments to your production process based on your analysis. This is a key component to ensure strong quality control of your processes.

The Inventory module is also key to this overall process to ensure that you have the right materials to support your manufacturing production process. Available inventory needs to be in place to ensure that you produce goods on schedule and meet the demands of your customers.

Enabling Full Integration

PeopleSoft considers itself to be the first ERP application vendor to offer the full integration solution in the form of enterprise resource optimization (ERO). This was achieved by adding the advanced planning and optimization technology to their existing ERP capabilities.

Enterprises today are looking for an end-to-end solution covering the entire spectrum from initial customer contact to service and product delivery, resulting in a fully satisfied customer—ideally, one with timely cash receipts.

The fully integrated solution needs the solution components identified in Figure 20.14.

Figure 20.14 **Fully integrated solution**

Currently no tier 1 vendor is offering all of the capabilities outlined in the diagram. With a strong demand for a fully integrated solution, most vendors are rushing to form alliances with vendors offering complementary product offerings. For example, PeopleSoft acquired Vantive in December 1999 in a bid to offer the CRM and customer service integration, and continues to offer integration via application programming interfaces to other leading CRM packages such as Siebel.

With a strong demand for e-commerce, PeopleSoft has taken an equity position with a leading e-procurement vendor, CommerceOne, to offer an integrated e-commerce environment within PeopleSoft. As we discuss in Chapter 24, both of these areas are key expansion points that the ERP vendors are looking to capitalize on in the future.

Overall, PeopleSoft, along with other ERP vendors, will continue to strengthen its integration in its quest for an end-to-end solution.

Up Next

After looking more closely at each of the major application areas within People-Soft (HRMS, Financials, and Supply Chain Management) and providing you with an overview of the key features and functions of each, it's time to move on to a new area, setting up the support you need to be successful in your implementation. Chapter 21 will look at the critical area of change management and how you can create an effective change-agent network to help support your project as it moves into production.

Part V

Setting Up Support

Once you have your new system configured, tested, and ready for production, you
still need to ensure that the appropriate support network is in place to maintain
it all. The next chapters look in detail at this support network, helping you
ensure that you have sound production support and post-production support in
place prior to closing down your project, and that you have specific plans for
evolving this system to support future requirements and future needs. This support network is critical to the ongoing maintenance of your application, and it
will help ensure that the maximum business value is derived from your new
system throughout its life.

<caption>CHAPTER 21</caption>

Analyzing Your Support Network

F E A T U R I N G :

▶ How to identify and create "change agents"

▶ How to analyze changes to your organization

▶ What your communications plan should look like

▶ How to track your progress

O ver the course of this chapter, you will begin to understand how many individuals affect your project and how you can make them "change agents" for your initiative rather than roadblocks to your success. When major systems such as PeopleSoft are implemented, many people's roles, responsibilities, and jobs—even the company structure—may be affected. We will look at ways to help support these system changes through creation of a network and an overall communications plan. This approach should make everyone aware of what changes are being made, understand how the change impacts them, and help them facilitate this change for you. People are much more cooperative when they feel they are being included in the planning for a new system and set of processes rather than excluded from decisions that include these changes. This overall approach will help leverage the support of the user community as an advantage and help create a smooth path for your project's success.

Before looking at creating and understanding a change network, let's cover a few basic points about change and why it is important to involve users and sponsors in your project to help facilitate this change.

Note Change is a process—not an event. Therefore, you can't just communicate on one occasion or demonstrate one activity and expect your end users to follow you throughout your entire change process or implementation. You need to keep them informed about each change and involved in the entire process.

Individuals do not resist change, they resist a disruption in their expectations or daily activities. If you help them understand why this disruption is occurring and why it's of value to them, they will be more supportive of the change. Organizations as well as individuals can only handle so much change at one time—so don't try to inundate them with too much information or too much change at any one time. Finally, the perceived degree of change is very different for each individual, so the "one size fits all" mentality is not necessarily a sound solution. Individuals are different. This is why change networks and the use of various communication mediums is important within your plan. Always keep in mind that more communication is better than less and that there really is no such thing as overcommunicating. Visibility and repetitive communication of the reason for the change and the value it will bring to the organization or individual is critical.

Change Networks

In order to get the support your team needs to make your project successful, you need to have a group focused on the effects of the changes your implementation will have on a very important company asset—your people. Generally, an ERP system has dramatic effects on the organizational structure of the business areas in which you are implementing it and on the roles and responsibilities of those personnel. Since major changes to your process are generally involved, this translates to major changes for your people. Major change generally translates to major fears. To help alleviate these fears and generate support for this new way of doing things, establishing a network of individuals to help support the proposed project changes and inform your organization of these changes is a big step forward.

John Kotter, a leading Harvard Business School professor and renowned business leader, believes that there are phases that an organization goes through in a successful change effort. Kotter's "Eight Steps to Transform Your Organization" include the steps we paraphrase here:

1. Establishing a sense of urgency

2. Creating a guiding coalition

3. Developing a vision and strategy

4. Communicating the change vision

5. Empowering broad-based action

The change network and communications plan that we are discussing in this chapter directly support this successful change model, providing the drivers and support mechanisms to make your change a success.

By creating a network to help you enable this change successfully, you can help empower your users and generate a clear vision throughout your organization. The group or network that is established to do this is what we refer to as a *change network*, and individuals who are involved in this network are referred to as *change agents*.

Change agents are supporters within your organization who can help the end users of these new processes (and systems) understand the value and encourage usage. They are responsible for implementing your action plan to help in your change effort and form a critical link between your end users, your change leaders and sponsors, and your teams. You might have excellent processes and an excellent system to support them, but if users resist this new system, your project will have failed. The change network and change agents help promote your new system and foster a successful organizational change initiative. Think of them as your marketing team, geared to support your new product. You should also have a change manager on your team who coordinates with your network and ensures that the network has the materials, training, and support they need to be successful. This change manager should also help coordinate activities between your teams, your sponsors, and your network.

Change Agent Selection

To select your change agents and support your change network, you should ask yourself a few key questions regarding the individuals you choose:

- ▶ Do they have time to dedicate and support the network? Generally, about 20% to 30% of their time is needed to support the network, with higher percentages during user training and implementation.

- ▶ Are they good communicators? They should be comfortable giving project overviews and PowerPoint presentations to their co-workers and business organization, whether it be in a large or a smaller group.

- ▶ Are they well thought of within the organization? Their span of control may be small, but they need to be known and have credibility within the business community they are representing. If they are new to the organization or have been poor performers, they would generally not make good choices for your change agents.

In addition to the characteristics of the individuals you might choose to be change agents, another typical question asked is "How many change agents do I need?" That answer depends on several factors, including:

- ▶ How many physical locations are you rolling out your solution to? Generally, you should have at least one person per geographic (or physical) location to serve as your change agent. If you have several very small physical locations—sites where there are only a few end users—you might consider one person for a particular group of sites (or regions) who can travel between these sites fairly easily. The goal is to have a person who can communicate one-on-one with your users on a regular (i.e., at least once a month) basis.

▶ How diverse is your user group? Generally, you want individuals who can relate to the specific groups that are affected by your change, such as individuals from your finance group, your controllers out in the field, your sales representatives, your payroll clerks, and others.

▶ How much of a change are you creating? The more fundamental the change in the organization and the greater the effect on the processes that each individual will perform, the more change agents you are likely to need to help ensure that training and communications are adequate throughout the organization. There will also be more to communicate, since the changes are more encompassing.

In general, you should count on one person being able to handle between 10 and 100 individuals. We would not recommend that a single change agent be responsible for more than 100 individuals, no matter how small the change. On average, you are most likely looking at having a change agent handle approximately 20 to 30 users.

So, now that you've determined how many change agents you might need and the types of skills a change agent should have, what are the duties of the change agent in addition to just communicating?

Change Agent Roles

The change agent should be asked to do several things, including:

▶ Provide input into the types of communications that work for their organization.

▶ Provide input into the scope of the change and the specific items that are changing for their targeted population. This helps the change agent better focus the communication and training for their group.

▶ Ensure that their user base is enrolled in the appropriate training classes and are prepared for the new system and processes. This might include additional training with Windows, Microsoft Word, or other tools in addition to the PeopleSoft-related training classes.

▶ Monitor enrollment and training scheduling, including providing input into the training schedule. In some cases, certain groups have commitments that need to be considered when scheduling their training, such as month-end-close cycle and pay cycles. The change agent should provide that input to the project team.

▶ Attend initial change agent training. Every change agent should be trained in their new roles and responsibilities. A training program should be developed that includes information on communications, team building, project goals/scope, the business case, the value of the solution to their organization, and tips and techniques that can be used to manage change and resistance.

▶ Help provide and support training of their user base in conjunction with the project team, including attending and evaluating training programs. Generally, your change agents should be included in any pilot or initial training prior to it being rolled out to your end users. They should be your first source of feedback regarding the training.

▶ Provide feedback to the project team on morale and perceptions of the project prior to the new system being implemented, and serve as your eyes and ears once the system is implemented. Your change network should be a mechanism to monitor your user community prior to any major issues arising. They also can serve as feedback loops when a problem does occur and communicate action plans and steps back to their user group to give them confidence that the problem is solved and will not happen again.

As you can see, your change agents should be your main line of communication into your user community. They are critical to the success of your implementation and can help you have a good, solid perspective of the project's successes and failures so you can remedy the failures and accentuate the successes.

Changes in Organizational Structure

As mentioned in the change agent section, your project may effect many changes, including the more dramatic organizational structure changes within a company or smaller subset. New systems and processes of the magnitude of PeopleSoft are likely to bring changes to an organization and to the roles that individuals have within the organization. What is important is that these changes are clearly communicated, an action plan is put in place to facilitate the change, and any needed training is available. Users must be informed both as a group and individually regarding changes. Overall, they must understand the scope of the project and how much the organization will need to change to support the new processes. Once this is clearly outlined and communicated, the first question that follows is usually "How does this change affect me?" or "Which role am I going to play in this new organization?" The quicker the project team can answer these questions, the better. Whether you have all the answers or not, you need to communicate sooner rather than later, and remember to be honest if you don't know the answer yet. For example, you may realize that you need five financial advisors within your new organizational structure, and you know what types of skills are needed to fill this new role. However, you have not yet determined which individuals would most likely be able to fill the new role. Be honest and say this during your initial meetings with the affected users.

Once you have the organizational structure and the roles/responsibilities identified and communicated to the affected user community, you should be prepared to explain how these roles will be filled and what happens to individuals who might choose to go on to other roles within the company—or whether there will be individuals who will be asked to leave the company. You should have a clear idea of what your game plan is for this scenario and the steps you are prepared to take as an organization to support this transition. Be sure that your Human Resources representatives are involved in this process.

Communications

Communications is the lifeline between your project and your user community. It is a way that individuals can become aware of, have opportunities to question, understand, become involved in, begin to support, and finally show positive acceptance of a change. Figure 21.1 shows a diagram of this "change acceptance curve." As you can see, there are six stages outlined in moving an individual from total confusion and nonacceptance to ownership and a very high acceptance level. These stages are:

Awareness   This is the first point at which an individual becomes aware of a change and that it might affect them. At this stage, a person can be very confused about what is going on.

General Understanding   At this point, an individual understands—or believes they understand—the general issues or change that is going to take place. However, they could have some negative perceptions or misunderstanding of the information presented to them at this time.

Personal Understanding   This is the point at which an individual actually understands how the change is going to affect them and their job or tasks, which in many cases causes a person to be reluctant to learn the new tasks or processes.

Willingness to Accept This stage is when an individual comes to a realization that they will either accept or not support the change.

Buy-in At this point, an individual either subverts the change and tries to dodge it or buys into why the change is occurring and accepts that they must adapt to the change and move on (which takes them to the ownership level).

Ownership This is the final stage of acceptance, when an individual takes true ownership of the change and feels "empowered," as Kotter says. They no longer are interested in the change since they have accepted it and are moving on to other items or concerns.

In order to accept a change, a person must move through each of these stages. As mentioned above, at any point they might resist moving forward (as indicated by the downward arrows) or they will advance to the next stage. Your goal is to get all of your end users (or as many as possible) to the Ownership level.

Figure 21.1 **Change acceptance curve**

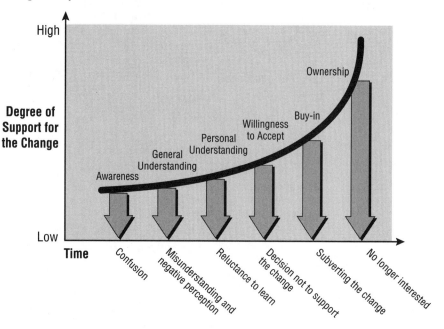

Your communications are a means of promoting the acceptance of change with your end users and stakeholders. By understanding your audience and their needs, you can give them the information they need to increase their degree of support and move upward on the acceptance curve. If your communications are not effective, there is a danger that the end users or a part of your organization might reject the change and cause your project to not be as successful as planned. When creating your communications, be sure you use the communications adequately to ensure project success and a smooth transition to your new future state. The more effort and time you spend communicating with your user group(s), the better off your project will be. In order to be highly successful, your team needs to have a *communications plan*. A communications plan should be clear and concise, outlining your target audience and the mediums your team will be using to communicate with. The frequency and timing of the communications are also key to your success. Prior to major events or milestones during the project, or when these milestones are completed, there should be a clearly thought out communications approach, message, and strategy. You want to ensure that your overall goals aim at:

▶ Avoiding misinformation, which can lead to confusion or frustration

▶ Supporting your project sponsors and encouraging trust and respect for your management team

▶ Helping alleviate fear and resistance to the changes that are about to occur

▶ Increasing morale and productivity as your project moves ahead

Communications Plan

A communications plan consists of:

An overall communication strategy   What are you trying to accomplish?

A budget   No one has an unlimited supply of time, resources, or money, so what budget constraints do you have?

Mediums you can use to communicate   These mediums may be your organization's internal Web site, newspapers, bulletins, various scheduled meetings, or other avenues.

Timing of communications   You should look at all major events within the project and create a communications timeline showing what should be communicated when, to whom, and by whom. This timeline should be further narrowed down to exact timings, scripts, presentations, and material. Each "event" should include target audiences, approach, timing, and delivery.

A mechanism to track results   You should always be looking at ways to measure whether your communications are effective. Follow-up surveys, targeted calls, responses back from your change agents, or feedback mail are examples of how to track your results. You might be looking at different mechanisms based on the type of communications used.

Clear definition of who your intended audience is for the communication You may have various target audiences such as your executive team, core project team, end user management team, or other categories of end users. Your plan should ensure that all of your target audiences are communicated to.

Types of Communications

As mentioned above, there is a wide variety of mediums that you can use to communicate your message with. In most cases, these mediums can be broken down to these categories:

Face-to-face meetings Whether you have regularly scheduled meetings where you can introduce the information or you schedule special meetings to announce your information, these are all methods of communication.

Paper-based This medium includes newsletters, articles in your company's or organization's newsletters, company bulletins, direct mailings, posters, etc.

Intranet site You can post information, communications, etc., on your internal organization's Web site, including user guides, tips of the day, code translations, and more.

Other forms There are many other ways within your organization that you can communicate, such as via e-mail, bulletin boards, voicemail messages, or videoconferencing.

You should consider all avenues or methods of communications (including combining these methods) during each targeted event on your timeline. Creating a communication campaign can help your audience identify with the change and recognize communications regarding this change. Your project may already have a team name or logo. Use it with all your communications and consider creating a "tag line" or slogan to help your target audience identify with the change and logo.

Risks you might want to watch out for when delivering and monitoring your communications plan are:

▶ Raising expectations higher than reality can satisfy. Don't sugar-coat your communications—be honest! If your expected response time for a particular transaction will be 30 seconds or a minute, let your end users know this ahead of time. Don't let them expect to have sub-second response times. If there are issues with any tools or processes, let them know.

▶ Creating unnecessary concern in the early stages of your project about what is unknown by the users or "unexpected." Be sure to time your communications far enough in advance to a project phase or milestone.

▶ Encouraging a wait-and-see approach. Try at all times to give as much information as possible to your users, rather than asking them to wait and see what the outcome is.

▶ Losing touch with your audience. You don't want to communicate some information up front and then not talk to a particular audience for months afterward. This can cause anxiety or misunderstandings.

You can create plans for each of your target audiences. Remember to focus on the relevant audiences, those who need to know about or be involved with the change, including any immediate peer groups. Don't create too broad an audience group, since it may be hard to communicate with them on a regular basis and many of the members may not be interested in your information when they are not directly affected by any change.

Ensure that you have a disciplined approach to bringing the appropriate people into your communications loop, and look at leveraging established links between these groups through current activities (such as any regular communications, meetings, or other venues where it might be appropriate to communicate your changes within). Your communications plan should include:

▶ The communication item or change you are focusing on, such as a change in policy for approving an employee's vacation schedule

▶ Appropriate mediums for delivery, which might be articles in organization newsletters, individual letters to managers and employees affected by this change, etc.

▶ Frequency of or schedule for the communication, which in this example might be three focused communications done once a month prior to implementation

▶ Any issues that might need to be resolved prior to completing that item or plan, such as what level of manager must approve vacation changes

▶ Who is responsible for the communication, such as the benefits office in this case

Table 21.1 contains an example of a template that can be used to create your communications plan. Remember to think it through and ensure that all appropriate audiences are targeted adequately based on your project life cycle and that all key events or activities are associated with key communications.

Table 21.1 **Communications Plan Template**

Group	Required Level of Commitment		Message	Channel	Initiator	Frequency
<Group 1>	<e.g., awareness>	<Ref #>	<e.g., status>	<e.g., e-mail>	<Corporate Communications>	<e.g., weekly>
Payroll Executives	Awareness	1.1	Project status and budget	Report	Proj Mgr	Monthly
		1.2	Basic understanding of project goals, value to be achieved, and how project affects the payroll organization	Presentation	Proj Mgr & Key Proj Team Members	After each phase of project
<Group 2>						
Payroll Clerks	Buy-in	2.1	Understand key changes that new processes and system will bring to them	Town Hall Meetings	Change Agent	Monthly
				Newsletters	Proj Change Mgt Team	Monthly
		2.2	Understand how their jobs will be affected	One-on-One Mgt Meetings	Change Agent & Sponsor	Month prior to training
<Group 3>						
<Group 4>						

Measuring Results

When creating your change agent network and developing your targeted communications plan, you must always ensure that you have ways to measure your results so that you can learn from them as well as leverage successes on future initiatives. You should also be tracking the costs associated with each communication and how effective that communication was. While it may be nice to post on an electronic bulletin board the messages to your targeted audience, they may not read the messages—and even if they do, this method may not be as cost-effective as sending them the information via targeted messages.

In general, you might want to take a survey at the beginning of your communications planning, to determine how much individuals know about your project and what mediums they generally review and use. This survey can help you pinpoint your strategy as well as understand the types of communications you might need to be effective within each user community. When the project is completed and after post-implementation activities, you should also take a survey to determine how effective (in general) you were with your communications plan and note which communications were well received by your users. This is great feedback that can be used for follow-up activities or other projects within that user group.

Up Next

Creating your change agent network, implementing an effective communications plan, and measuring the results of these key support efforts should be a focus for any major change initiative. It is vital to keep your employees and end users informed about what is going on within their organization. The time and effort it takes to create and maintain this support plan should not be overlooked. In surveys we have done with our clients, they identify the major reasons why a project fails within their organization as resistance by key end users and not gaining the appropriate executive support of the organization.

The change techniques covered in this chapter, along with solid training (which will be discussed in the next chapter), are keys to ensuring that your project is a success. Don't underestimate the importance of this or the effort that must go into making your change network a success.

As mentioned, another vital means of gaining end-user support and commitment is through a very sound training program. Chapter 22, "Providing End User Training," covers this critical topic and provides you the guidelines to put together and implement a successful training program. This chapter will include how to develop a sound training strategy, what types of training are available and appropriate, and how to cost out your training requirements, look at the technical requirements, and develop the appropriate training material for your class. It will also look at measuring results of your training and monitoring training needs for the future.

Providing End User Training

F E A T U R I N G :

▶ How to develop a training strategy

▶ How to analyze your target audience

▶ A look at the different types of training mediums and options

▶ What costs are involved in training

▶ What components are involved in training

▶ Measuring results of your training both during and after training

▶ Considerations for future training needs

I n this chapter, we will cover the topics listed above so that your organization can be better positioned and prepared to leverage your new solution. Without adequate training and planning for your new solution, all of your team's hard work and dedication might go to waste. Many times an implementation's success is based on the ability of the end user to understand and use the solution. Training should be targeted to help your end users become comfortable with and understand the new solution adequately to support your new process and system. Training is a critical component in your implementation and should be thoroughly thought out and planned according to the specific needs of your audience—the end user. The size, location, and user roles all play a part in what type of training is necessary and when it should be delivered.

Training Strategy

Strategy: . . A careful plan or method . . . the art of devising or employing plans or stratagems toward a goal. (*Webster's Collegiate Dictionary*, 10th ed.)

As with any strategy, your training strategy should be a detailed plan of action—in this case, to support training of your end users. A key to your organization successfully using and leveraging your new system and the processes it supports is the end user's ability to adopt and embrace the new technology and business process changes. Training is critical to this objective. Your training strategy should be developed based on input from key stakeholders, review and analysis of project documentation (including your project charter and the goals and objectives of your project), discussions with key project members and internal leaders within the end-user organizations, and a look at both internal and external benchmarking in determining success of your training efforts.

Your training strategy should address the key issues of:

▶ Who needs to be trained?

▶ How much training will be required for each individual or role?

▶ What training-delivery approach best meets the trainees' needs?

Target Audience

When looking at the training needs for your project, you must first be able to articulate (or chart out) who your end users are, what their primary characteristics and roles are, and where they are located geographically. This analysis is called *role-based training*. Role-based training is the most effective approach to meeting the end user's specific learning needs. By creating a suggested curriculum path by role, this approach enables a "customized" program from the end user's perspective. In general, the roles that you'll find in a PeopleSoft implementation are likely to fall into these major categories:

Executives   Senior managers across business units or divisions who will request and review reports from your system, either frequently or on an ad hoc basis. This category includes your executive team, who are key sponsors and play formal roles in the planning and execution of your project.

Management   Management of your various business areas, such as the finance management team or human resources management team, who will request information from other users as well as access the system to perform various analysis or reporting functions or require some type of approvals.

Clerks, Accountants, Payroll Administrators, etc.   Your core staff members who use the system on a daily basis to perform their job functions. You can break them down by process or by general business area/role.

Power Reporters   Individuals within each organization who will create and run reports on a frequent basis and provide in-depth analysis and ad hoc reporting capabilities.

Corporate Control   Generally, a group of individuals who maintain your core tables across the company and who will need to create new table entries for your code values, such as new earnings codes, deduction codes, account codes, department codes, etc. Again, this category may be divided up by major business area or function.

Inquirers   Individuals who typically report on information within the system or query the system for information but do not perform major functions on the system. You may also have "approvers" in this category— individuals who approve invoice payments, salary changes, or other actions but typically do not perform major functions on the system.

Technical Support   Individuals who support your system and will provide technical support and assistance with user help desk calls or fix technical system problems for your new PeopleSoft system.

For example, within the NewVal Company, your population consists of 2,000 individuals who perform Human Resources, Payroll, and Financial functions throughout your enterprise. Each of these functional areas could be broken down into categories of end users that you would need to train for your new ERP system. Maybe within that number you have various individual roles such as manager, clerk, or self-service customer. You need to create a chart that outlines each major role and shows the number of individuals who fill or perform that role along with their location. These are all key components in identifying your end users. See Table 22.1 for an example of this classification within the Accounts Payable area.

Table 22.1 **End User Identification Table (Accounts Payable)**

Roles	Competencies	No. of End Users	Location
AP Inquiry	Maintain Vendors Enter Voucher Information Create Payments	40	Hdqtrs (New York)
		5	St. Louis
		15	Chicago
		10	Orlando
AP Clerk 1	Enter Voucher Information Maintain Vendors Create Payments	60	Hdqtrs (New York)
		10	St. Louis
		25	Chicago
		15	Orlando
AP Manager	Enter Voucher Information Maintain Vendors Create Payments	4	Hdqtrs (New York)
		1	Midwest (St. Louis/Chicago)
		1	Orlando

After documenting who your end users are and where they are located, it is important to analyze their existing competencies, levels, business units, and skills as well as what their future roles and needs should be. You will need to develop a plan for each individual (an individualized training plan) to identify how they move from their current set of competencies and skills to their future set of competencies and skills. But first, you must understand the major key roles that you will need in your new organization. Then you can develop the necessary core training you will need to get your current population at the correct learning level to support your future state. In the example above, this may be several roles.

Let's just take one area of finance—Accounts Payable (AP)—and look at that area. You might have a local AP clerk who will process invoices for a particular business location or unit, an approving manager who approves the payment amounts based on a certain monetary level of the invoice, a supervisor who is responsible for managing the group of AP clerks (maybe by region), and an overall executive in charge of this organization (the Director of AP). Therefore, your AP users may be broken down into the following key roles:

- ▶ AP Approver: Generally, a manager within the organization who approves certain invoices up to a predefined amount of money.

- ▶ AP Clerk: The person who inputs the invoice into the system once the approval has been received and ensures that the check is sent to the payee. The AP clerk may also be responsible for following up on any invoice issues, running manual checks, ensuring that electronic payments are made, setting up new vendors, etc.

- ▶ AP Supervisor: Manages a group of AP Clerks.

- ▶ AP Executive: Responsible for the overall AP function and generally would not have any direct hands-on link to the new system or process but must support the new processes and serve as sponsor.

Once you have outlined all your key roles, based on the business processes that your new system supports, you may combine roles or functions into one group (or role). Approvers, for instance, might be able to do more than just approve AP invoices; they might also track purchasing requests. Then these two roles could be merged into one for training purposes. However, it is best to outline all roles at first and then, after analyzing the training requirements and the specific individuals who fill each role, determine if any target roles for training purposes should be combined.

As mentioned earlier, once you have analyzed all roles and noted their locations, you can look at what specific training goals must be accomplished, as well as what special needs accompany each profile. For example, if your AP clerks are dispersed geographically, you might need to deliver training in a central location that they can all travel to, or you might look at other options or training mediums for delivery to their specific locations. If you have a central shared service center where all your AP clerks are located, then it may be very easy for you to deliver classroom training on site at this central location.

Training Mediums

Once you have identified the types or categories of end users and what their basic training needs are, you should then consider the appropriate *medium* to use for delivering the training. A training medium is the medium through which learning will take place. This may include classroom size and supporting environments, computer-based training (CBT) or Web-based training, interactive distance learning (IDL), or other environments that can maximize the training/learning experience yet minimize productivity loss and logistical costs.

When assessing the appropriate training medium, another key consideration (besides location) should be the time frame you have to present the training in—or, more simply, how long you have to train your individuals. Short training times might dictate options such as one IDL offering or a CBT option that can deliver training to a lot of individuals in a very short time.

The various mediums or training delivery mechanisms that we will look at specifically will be:

- ▶ Instructor-led classroom training
- ▶ Interactive distance learning
- ▶ Computer-based or Web-based training
- ▶ Simulated production learning labs

Some key factors that can affect your decision of which delivery method is appropriate are:

- ► End user learning experience
- ► Logistical complexity and costs
- ► Development complexity and costs
- ► Long-term reuse

Instructor-Led Classroom Training

In general, with all other factors being equal, the end user learning experience is maximized with instructor-led classroom training. Each student has a "live" instructor who is focused on their needs, can answer their questions, and can monitor the progress of the class directly. However, this training can be the most costly and time-consuming, as we will discuss later. You should consider this option when you are making major changes in an individual's job processes or in the systems they use to support their job, or when you are instituting major skill enhancements. It is also a desirable alternative when all your end users are in a central location and can be taught together in one area. Time is also a factor—in general, instructor-led classes take more time to administer and monitor than the other mediums.

Computer-Based Training (CBT)

CBT is more of a self-study-paced training. The maximum "fit" for this choice of training is when the learning content is the key factor and individual interaction with an instructor is not a big part of the process. Typically, training involving navigation courses, overviews, or understanding of new key terms is good use of the CBT method. PeopleSoft also provides a few CBT training classes that can be leveraged with your program. These cover the basics on security, navigation, and key terms and should be evaluated as a part of your training strategy process.

Interactive Distance Learning (IDL)

With IDL training, the optimum interaction with the trainee is maintained via a video linkup with an instructor as well as access to the training system using computer interactive devices over the Web. This method can prove effective for individuals who are dispersed geographically and who have access to these IDL capabilities. However, cost can have an influence, depending on how easily accessible facilities and technology are within each of the locations and on the cost for the equipment and environment supporting this interaction. This method of training is becoming more popular with the increase in technology performance and decrease in costs of the technology necessary to support the effort.

Simulated Training Environment

In a simulated training environment, a student has access to the application and can perform exercises in a "safe" environment; therefore, the hands-on nature of the tasks is what maximizes this learning option. Generally, this technique is not the only method used but rather is paired with the other options to provide a post-training method that allows students to increase their capabilities. Personalized assistance from a lab coach can help make this option more viable, but increases the costs. Another benefit of having an environment like this in place is that individuals who are hired after the initial training or who go on extended leaves can retool their skills on an independent basis.

There are other avenues for providing learning experiences, such as through focused communications, on-the-job-training (OJT), or other techniques not discussed above. However, the four options discussed encompass the primary types of learning that might be chosen to deliver training with a PeopleSoft or other major change initiative.

Factors to Consider

When considering what type of training is best for a particular topic, many considerations can come into play. Some of the primary ones—such as logistical complexity, costs, development of materials, and long-term reuse—are discussed below.

Logistical Complexity and Costs

In general, the most costly and logistically challenging method of training (though the most popular) is instructor-led classroom training. The logistics of planning the training location, arranging student enrollments, and obtaining instructors are generally the most complex, and travel costs generally the highest, with this option. The least challenging in logistical complexity and costs, assuming a technical environment is readily accessible by end users, is the CBT self-study method. Since schedules do not have to be planned or maintained, instructors supported, or travel costs considered, this is the cheapest and least complex method available for training. Both interactive distance learning and simulated production learning labs are moderate in terms of logistical complexity and costs. Travel to IDL centers and catering costs for meals may be required, but these costs are generally much lower than for instructor-led training; IDL costs may be minimal if facilities are within your regional locations. With a lab environment, there are costs for the coaches and technology to support the lab, but again, costs are generally much lower than in an instructor-led environment.

Training Materials Development

In the development of the actual training materials, IDL training is generally considered the most costly training method to develop materials for (though travel costs are reduced), followed by CBT and instructor-led classroom training. The least costly to develop is the simulated environment, since you are dealing mainly with exercises and case study–type activities. The technical environment, case studies, and resources to support the lab are your basic requirements.

Long-Term Reuse

Long-term reuse of the material or environment should also be considered when analyzing which medium is best for your particular course. Generally, in the case of long-term reuse, the best option is CBT or IDL–type training, since it is maintained electronically and with minimal instructor support. CBT materials can generally be accessed any time by anyone, even after your implementation, so that new hires who come to your organization after your initial training rollout can still benefit from the CBT training based on just-in-time (JIT) needs. On the IDL side, broadcasts and most of the courseware can be reusable, and an agreement could be set up with your vendor to provide service as necessary after your initial go-live events. The information could also be deployed via your intranet as video clips and be coupled with the material, rather than using a "live" instructor for future use. Learning labs provide minimal long-term reuse since case studies and the lab environment may not be maintained for the long term or be beneficial to maintain. However, the material could be packaged via screen camera shots or converted to a CBT for reuse in a JIT format. Instructor-led classroom training generally falls in the moderate reuse category, since manuals and paper-based products can be maintained and reused but instructors and a full class size are hard to maintain. In Table 22.2, you can see how these factors might affect your training decisions.

Table 22.2 **Training Factors Matrix**

Key Factors	Delivery Approach			
	Trainer-Led, Classroom	Computer-Based, Self-Study	Interactive Distance Learning	Simulated Production Learning Labs, Supplemental
End User Learning Experience	Most favorable	Most favorable	Most favorable	Most favorable
Logistical Complexity and Costs	Least favorable	Most favorable	Moderately favorable	Moderately favorable
Development Complexity and Costs	Moderately favorable Most favorable	Moderately favorable	Moderately favorable	Moderately favorable Most favorable
Long-Term Reuse	Moderately favorable Least favorable	Most favorable	Moderately favorable Most favorable	Least favorable

As mentioned previously, you may analyze all these areas and, based on your particular circumstance or audience, choose a set of these mediums to use. For instance, for course pre-work or basic foundation requirements on key terms, navigation, product overview, and such, the CBT environment might be your best bet. For more complicated scenarios and super user requirements, an IDL or classroom instructor-led training environment might be the right answer depending on how widespread your user base is, the timeline available for training delivery, and your budget. For follow-up and reinforcement exercises and training (or during upgrades or minor changes to your system), the lab environment might be best suited to your needs. Again, your budget, resource skills, training material needs, location of end users, and timeline to deliver training all play a part in deciding your best approach, and this approach must be balanced for each scenario, as the diagram in Figure 22.1 depicts.

Figure 22.1 **Balancing of training factors**

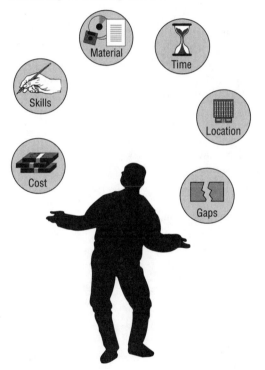

During this analysis, you need to clearly articulate your end user's starting point or baseline of knowledge, their training requirements, the analysis you undertook to determine which solution was best for them and why, as well as your recommended solution. All of this is part of a well-documented training strategy. Table 22.3 is an example of the table of contents for a typical training strategy document showing the basic elements that should be contained within your strategy document.

Table 22.3 **Training Strategy Table of Contents**

	TRAINING STRATEGY Table of Contents	
Section	**Subject**	**Page**
1	INTRODUCTION	1
1.1	Purpose of This Report	1
1.2	Background	1
1.3	Audience	1
1.4	Action Required by You	1
2	TRAINING STRATEGY	2
2.1	Strategic Principles	2
2.2	Training Objectives	2
2.3	Development of Training Implementation Plan	3
3	SCOPE OF TRAINING	4
3.1	Introduction	4
3.2	Audience	4
3.3	Training Developed	4
3.3.1	Key User	5
3.3.2	End User	6
4	RESPONSIBILITIES	7
5	COMMON PROJECT TRAINING SUPPORT AVAILABLE	7

In addition to what we have mentioned above, PeopleSoft provides a set of training materials and tools that can be purchased as a part of your software contract or as additional services. These tools are called End User Training

(EUT) Tools. This option provides you with the basic training materials around a vanilla and generic PeopleSoft application environment, but also provides the software tools to customize and maintain the materials for your specific situation and business objectives. This toolset also allows you to easily make modifications to the core set of PeopleSoft training materials and maintain your materials for use after your implementation, or to update them for any future upgrades or changes to your processes or systems. These materials were designed to be used in an instructor-led or IDL training situation and are not CBT-type materials.

CBT self-paced classes generally require little to no involvement from the project team except for the distribution of the materials and time spent developing the CBT. During the individual end user's learning experience and after your system moves into production, CBT training is very self-sufficient. It is advisable, however, to have a troubleshooting call-in number for anyone who has problems with their CBT or questions on any of the material presented.

Critical Success Factors

Some critical success factors that should be considered when developing a successful end user training program and strategy are:

Timely training   Ensure that your schedule allows for training as close as possible to the actual time an individual will be using the system or new processes for the first time. You don't want the training to occur months ahead of time, nor on the day of implementation. Generally, two weeks prior is considered to be ideal.

Appropriate training   As mentioned before, the medium and content are key in delivering successful training. You should ensure that your audience is analyzed and the correct training is targeted toward the correct audience. Your project team can get caught up in the training development and can target the same training for all audiences, which is generally not the appropriate thing to do.

Sponsorship   Sponsorship must be in place to get the support needed for your end users to attend training and take the training seriously. You should look at the impact the training commitments have on your end users' current jobs and ensure that the end user are away from their normal daily tasks when performing their training so they can focus on this training effort. This is especially critical for CBT or IDL training, which can be delivered to an end user's desktop.

Communication   Again, communication is always key to a successful program. You should ensure that you have adequately communicated to all end users about what training is available and when, which training options best support their needs, and when training needs to be completed. Any necessary scheduling approvals or deadlines also should be clearly communicated.

Evaluation and measurement   We will discuss this in greater detail later in the chapter, but for now suffice it to say that all training should be evaluated and improved upon and results measured to ensure adequate support and improve overall quality.

Implementation support/Long-term user support   You should clearly articulate your approach to supporting the users after their initial training, during implementation and well into production. This long-term approach should also be a part of your training process so that all users understand how to get support or help and who to call when necessary.

Ongoing training   As mentioned above, you should have a plan for how you will support your users after initial training, with follow-up training during implementation and beyond and with new-hire training.

Costs

There are many factors that must be analyzed when outlining the cost components of each training class and medium. When doing your cost analysis, you should generally be looking at the following areas:

▶ Travel and other related expenses such as food, catering, lodging, airfare, transportation fees, etc.

▶ Administrative material costs, such as copying, graphics support, any administrative materials (paper, pencils, poster board, etc.), and certificates of course completion. Charges for any support materials—such as PeopleSoft's EUT material, existing CBT material, or material used during the registration process including communications material to advertise the training—should be considered.

▶ Personnel, both internal and external, to support the training development and delivery (including any enrollment process and follow-up or measurement support). Any related expenses for travel for instructors or course developers also should be included.

▶ Technical environment. Creation and support of the training environment(s) to support your courses, including hardware and software and technical support, should be included. When looking at technical costs, consider any special network connections or high-speed network connectivity lines (or upgrades to existing lines) that might be necessary as well as monthly charges, including DASD, special training servers, and other additional infrastructure charges.

▶ Equipment to support the training, such as overheads, slides, projection screen, computer rentals, LCD unit rentals, printer rentals, and such.

▶ Facility costs for the training rooms, including room rental charges, charges for any local taxes or charges, any room setup requirements, etc.

Specific drivers that have an impact on your overall training costs include the total number of classrooms needed to deliver the training in the time frame committed, the number of weeks during which the training will be delivered, the number of instructors needed to support the training schedule, the number of facilitators (per classroom), and the number of students per class.

Remember to assess your existing training materials and internal capabilities to leverage them as much as possible, especially with any pre-work activities such as browser or Internet basic training, Microsoft Windows, Excel, or Word training, etc. that might not be specific to the application and may already be available within your organization.

Curriculum Plan

Once you have decided your basic strategy in supporting your training needs and the type of training that will be necessary to support your implementation, you need to develop a detailed curriculum plan that outlines all the key components of the courses you will be developing. A curriculum plan brings all of your course information together in an easy-to-follow document. The plan should include:

▶ Identification of what audience the course is designed for

▶ A description of the course and its contents

▶ The learning path of the program: a depiction of the logical order and grouping of courses that are offered by role

▶ Performance objectives for each course

▶ The medium and delivery mechanism to be used for each course

▶ The suggested training schedule with definitive dates and locations

Training Needs Assessment

Typically during the design phase, a training needs assessment should be conducted of your end users and technical support staff. This assessment will determine gaps between their knowledge of the current system and their knowledge of the future system and processes. Generally, an instructional analysis should be performed to determine the required competencies necessary to perform the new job tasks.

Note Knowledge, skills, and attitudes make up what is called a *competency*. *Knowledge* can be defined as the element of the competency that indicates whether the person has the information or strategies concerning the competency that allow it to be carried out. *Skills* are what enable the performer to execute the competency, and *attitudes* are the element that motivates the individual to perform the competency.

An example of a competency within the PeopleSoft area might be the ability to generate vendor invoices. The knowledge an individual would need for this activity might be to understand the data requirements to create an invoice within the new application, such as the new codes to signify the vendor and any key information to record the invoice in the new system. The skills needed would be the ability to enter this information into the new system (i.e., knowing how to navigate to the correct panel/screen/page). Finally, the attitude might be an appreciation of how easy and helpful the new system is in recording and paying this invoice, tracking the payments, and analyzing the invoice data.

The curriculum plan should contain the suggested learning paths for each job profile that is developed. The best medium to deliver the training is then determined based on the analysis of the trainees who will be using the course and on the topics to be taught.

 TIP Courseware standards and guidelines should be used to ensure that the material is all being developed consistently, should different developers or authors be used.

Once the gap between the new competencies and existing competencies of each job role is determined, the medium for delivery of each course, the size of the target audience, and the software and hardware requirements should also be detailed out. Don't hesitate to interview your employees and their supervisors to gain insight into how these new processes and technology will really affect them or the groups they supervise. It's generally helpful to create a matrix of job profiles on one side (or axis) and key knowledge, skills, and attitudes or competencies on the other. Completing this matrix can help you identify the appropriate areas to target with your training. Table 22.4 shows an example of how this matrix might look. Ideally, you should collect this data on all individuals affected; however, that may not be practical or may be too time-consuming and costly. Therefore, be sure you get a good mix of employees and supervisors across the various organizations and roles affected. Also, ensure that the security profile is considered—e.g., by reviewing the security profiles you have set up, you can verify whether all roles have been considered and visa versa. Be sure to incorporate into your training any associated forms, user procedures, or other knowledge objects that might aid the training experience (such as internal Web sites or help desk information).

Table 22.4 **Training Needs Matrix (for Accounts Payable)**

Application	Competencies	Hours by Competencies	Total Hours
Accounts Payable	Maintain Vendors Enter Voucher Information Create Payments Process Bank Statement	0.5 hours 3 hours 2 hours 2 hours	7.5

When doing your analysis, you should also be identifying the training demographics you will be faced with. By looking at the company's existing organizational charts, job titles/codes, and interview information, and working with your company's Human Resources (HR) department personnel, you should be able to determine the following information for each job profile:

▶ Total number of trainees for that job role

▶ Number of trainees at each geographic location

▶ Number of trainees by organizational unit

▶ Range of job experiences and education

▶ Training media preferences and dislikes

▶ Language choice (if this is an issue)

It may be easier to identify your knowledge gaps by creating a tree where the topmost gap might be the package itself (since we generally know this is a new concept to most individuals), the next level the execution of the transactions that make up the package, the next level being the various subtasks to execute the transaction, and so on down to the lowest level of skills needed. Figure 22.2 shows an example of this knowledge tree concept. Gaps may include new manual processes as well as the automated ones, so don't forget that in your analysis—for example, operating system functions, typing, or mouse operations may be unfamiliar to some individuals in their current job role.

Figure 22.2   **Knowledge tree**

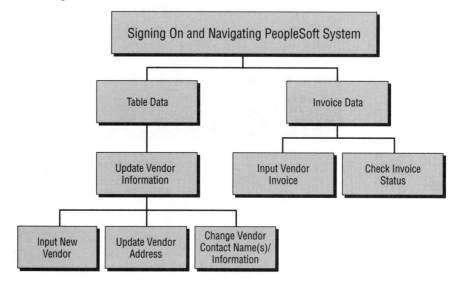

Learning Objectives

The next thing you should do is to take the gaps you have identified and create learning objectives from them.

Note   A *learning objective* is the foundation on which your training is based and describes what the trainee must accomplish prior to completing this course or learning experience.

These learning objectives should always be used to help you stay on track when developing your training. They should provide a precise statement of the expected results of the training so that the trainees, trainees' managers, and training developers can all have a single idea of what changes in behavior are expected to result from completing this course. The three parts of a learning objective are:

▶ What the trainees must accomplish (the action)

▶ The level of performance that must be displayed to indicate competence (the standard)

▶ The conditions under which the trainees must accomplish the desired actions (the condition)

TIP   The most important part of the objective is the action (which must be a verb to describe the competence). Don't use words like "know" or "understand," since they are too imprecise. Use words like "recognize," "execute," or "state."

Generally, the standards are set at 80% or greater for the ability to perform the act, and the condition is in the office (or simulated in the classroom).

If the gap is too great, you may want to hire individuals rather than retrain existing employees to fill the new roles. Management and your Human Resources department should help make that decision. Some competencies are difficult to teach, as well, or take a long time to learn, and these should be targets for hiring or selecting new individuals for those areas. Other competencies are ideal to teach and should be what you concentrate on in your training development. The available labor pool can also play a big part in your decision whether to hire or retrain because some competencies may not be easily hired or fit your current compensation profile.

Training can also be affected by "wave rollout." Generally, a waved implementation is one of two types: geographic or modular. Geographic waves are where the entire new process (or software) is rolled out in one geographic area at a time, and module-based waves are where a portion of the software (module) is rolled out to an entire organization. In either case, training will be affected. Be sure you are in close contact with your technical staff and project team to determine the appropriate time and location for training based on any rollout effects.

Course Development

After your training needs assessment and curriculum plan are developed, the next area to cover is courseware development. Materials that should be collected to aid with courseware development include any user procedures (both old system and new), package user guides, vendor training material, forms, and other materials used to document job processes. The courseware development process should always keep the learning or training objectives in mind as well as use the standards developed initially by the team. To develop the courseware, these steps should be followed:

1. Create detailed content outlines. These should include outlines of the instructional approach, the course objectives, related scripts, and any exercises or activities for each course, including timings for each element. You should have a course outline and synopsis following the creation of these detailed content outlines.

2. Develop approved course prototype and templates. This prototype can be used as a development model and to test any targeted design elements. It should provide the basic framework to develop your course, including the medium of delivery.

3. Draw up a work plan. A work plan provides the labor and material resources required for completing the development of your course and determines the sequence and timeline for the development activities.

4. Validate content. Be sure to review all course content and ensure that the content matches your objectives and audience. You might consider

having other individuals outside your project team (maybe those you interviewed to review the content or subject-matter experts [SMEs] in your organization) validate the content as well. You should also be looking at and validating the organizational chart (to ensure that all appropriate job roles have been taken into account), job descriptions, process flow diagrams, solution objects (such as existing manuals), and any reusable course material (like the PeopleSoft End User Training Tools).

5. Draft courseware. You should have a draft of your courseware developed and ready for a "pilot" training class along with any electronic (or other) job aids. This material should include both manual and automated business procedures and work process overviews. Be sure that all exercises and examples are focused on the end user (or trainee) with their culture and job roles in mind (as well as making the material company or business unit specific). Ensure that your SMEs review all materials thoroughly. Have selected individuals (not associated with the project team or developers) test the case studies and exercises to ensure that instructions are clear and that they achieve their purpose, that the time allotted for each exercise is adequate, and that the transitions between content and exercises are smooth. This can also be done during the pilot class.

6. Review courseware as necessary. Based on feedback from your initial pilot class as well as after each session, take another look at any issues or items that may require updates to course material or the data used. Also monitor user acceptance testing, learning from the mistakes or input of the end users performing the test to help provide insight into training needs or focus. Don't assume that all training will be conducted in English. Courseware should be translated by native speakers of the languages used to ensure it is done accurately. The translator should work closely with a member of the project team to ensure that literal translations are made and to eliminate any jargon. Also ensure that the targeted instructor has a command of the language being used.

Remember that when you make any changes to a process, you will usually be making changes to both the people and the technology. All gaps you identify will not be filled by training alone. You can use other mechanisms such as "town hall" meetings, PowerPoint presentations, information notes or newsletters, company intranet pages, or help information. Therefore, during your training strategy be sure to analyze which gaps will benefit the most from a defined training program and which may require other avenues. In general, you will almost always experience a learning curve or loss of productivity initially with any new process; however, the speed with which an individual or organization overcomes this experience depends on the strength of their training as well as the support of the end users.

Training Environment

For most training courses, a "live" working and breathing training environment that can be used by class participants in performing exercises and providing hands-on experience with the application is generally needed. When looking at your training environment needs, a few items need to be considered:

▶ Location of class participants. Connectivity to your application server and access to your database (generally a training-specific database) must be considered. The worst possible scenario would be to work hard on the materials and then have a poorly tuned system for your trainees to access. This will be their first experience with the new application (for the most part), and you don't want it to be a negative one. You want a positive, supportive team!

▶ Number of concurrent users. With multiple classes, you might need to consider creating multiple copies of your training database or be very clear about how you are going to minimize any conflicts with sharing data across classes. Reviewing your course content and exercises should help you determine any areas of potential conflict or additional stress to the system with concurrent users.

▶ Specific data requirements. Creation of specific training exercises or data to support your learning must be populated within the database and is generally better received the more company or business unit specific it is. You should also develop a strategy not only to input the basic data but also to refresh the data after each training session is over so that it is ready for the next class. Therefore, ensure that before training begins you have met with your database administrator (DBA) and created a refresh strategy and approach.

The training environment includes all hardware, software, other supporting equipment (like copiers, printers, or overhead projectors), and supplies. Test all equipment at each training location and create contingency plans as necessary should printers or local area networks fail. Ensure that appropriate security and access have been provided for your class situation and that all software and data can be accessed. Be sure to test the classroom environment, including acoustics, temperature, and security.

There are two ptions for your training database environment:

▶ Ideally, a new and separate database environment should be dedicated to training. This approach ensures that remaining testing and implementation activities are not affected by the training schedule.

▶ Another, lower cost alternative is to have a separate company or business unit within the existing test environment be dedicated and used for training. However, this would still impact performance, timing, and the factors listed above.

When creating your training database, ensure that all table values, records, and information necessary to support the course have been designated and are input into your database. Ensure that there is a "reset" procedure to refresh your data prior to each new class, and ensure that the information is tested thoroughly after each refresh to avoid problems during your class.

Course Enrollment

A sound communications plan targeted at your training audience should be developed and followed as a part of your training strategy. This plan should include (but is not limited to) information on course content, when classes will be offered, who should enroll and what the enrollment process is, whom to contact with questions, and when the enrollment period is over. Be sure to have a mechanism to track training enrollment, whether manually or electronically. You don't want to have one class with 5 participants and another with 75. Classes, in general, should be limited to fewer than 20 students. Also, provide confirmation notices back to the enrollees giving them the details on the class, including:

▶ Any prerequisites required

▶ Any material that trainees should bring to class themselves (such as existing forms or manuals, or pen and paper)

▶ Any cost for the training (generally can be a per-day cost or per-class cost) that their organization would expect to incur

- Dates and times of the training

- Location and any logistical information such as directions to the facility, the room number, hotels in the local area, transportation from and to the airport, etc.

- Cancellation policy requirements in case they have to reschedule or cancel a class

- Person to contact with questions, concerns, or changes

Each trainee should be given a document that outlines the recommended training path their job role or function should take, along with a list of individuals they should contact with questions. It is also helpful to have a frequently asked questions section (including answers to these questions) in your material, and a course description for each course developed that includes the suggested target audience. Communications can be accomplished through many channels, including written (in the form of flyers, company announcements, direct mailing within the organization, newsletters, etc.) or electronic (via the intranet, e-mail, video, or other means). Also, monitor the enrollment process to determine if the appropriate audience is being notified and responding, and look at follow-up actions should a group not be responding.

Pilot Training Class

It's very important to test-drive your training program prior to delivery, whether it's instructor-led or electronically based. Generally, it's a great idea to use your change agents, super users, or project team members to help provide feedback and attend your pilot training.

Note You should not have your entire pilot class come from your existing project team members. Be sure to include true end users who were not so closely involved in the project to help adequately "test" your course.

Be sure that during the pilot course you are testing all of your training materials including handouts and job aids, exercises, data set-up, security, and the overall training environment. Ensure that there is extra time on the schedule to take "time-outs" to critique the material and course progress as you go along. Ensure that there are enough old-to-new analogies and information to gain insight into the changes that are to be undertaken and to improve the delivery of the course. Obtain feedback from course attendees on whether there is enough information on the old versus new approach.

You should check to ensure that the training environment is stable enough to support the training requirements and should adequately test it prior to rolling out full-blown training. Also, any problems or errors with the system should be documented and provided to all instructors. The documentation should include any suggested workarounds or alternatives if an error is encountered. Instructors should also have a mechanism to provide feedback to the technical support team or debrief problems as they occur and share with others who might be experiencing the same problems. It might be helpful the first few times a course is taught to have conference calls or debriefing sessions with the instructors and the support staff after each training day. It can be very helpful to have a "help desk" number that the instructors can call, linking them with the appropriate project team or technical support personnel, should they encounter problems that might hinder the progress of their class.

Training should be delivered just in time (JIT) and, if possible, no more than two weeks before the individual is required to use the information learned during the course. If the class is delivered too early, the information may be forgotten; if it is too late, there will not be enough time to react to feedback or absorb all the information and changes. Ensuring that the trainees have an environment in which they can practice the skills they learned during training can greatly help this situation and support training that might have to be delivered earlier based on rollout schedules and plans. While the extra "practice" environment might be costly, it may not be as costly as having to retrain users or absorb greater losses in productivity. Also, existing databases such as the production copy or user acceptance testing copy could be a potential environment to use as your practice area. You could limit the access of your trained users to a special test business unit or company set of data and specific actions (such as view and update only) within this environment.

Ensure that your students are communicated with both before and after the training course. This communication technique results in a more supportive user group with a more positive approach to change and helps make the end user, more comfortable. A lack of communication can cause anxiety and unnecessary hostility with the new system or process based solely on the fear of the unknown.

"Train the Trainer" Approach

Another approach to delivering instructor-based training and leveraging off of the piloting concept is to do a "train the trainer." When you take a person at a particular site or from a particular group of individuals and train them on the new processes and system and how to *instruct* others on this new competency, you are using a train-the-trainer approach. In general, it is wise to identify key super users who have the knowledge, capability, and credibility to perform the training to other end users. These individuals are then put through an intensive training program aimed at gearing them up to teach the particular curriculum. When you leverage this approach, you can use the pilot training to test out the material and have additional training to prepare the individuals to train others. Therefore, another pilot class may not be necessary.

Measuring Results

With any great course come not only the training manuals (or student guides) but also a detailed instructor guide, practice exercises, student competency evaluation, course evaluation, and more. The course evaluation generally should obtain feedback on the quality of the materials presented and how well the audience understood and could relate to the materials, the instructor's performance, the training site (e.g., comfort, problems with room temperature, ability to see slides), as well as the exercises and how well they reinforced the information presented. An example of a course evaluation form can be found in Table 22.5. This example allows students to evaluate the course (at the completion of their training) and provide input into course content, format, instructor, overall satisfaction, and what can be done following training to better prepare end users. There should always be a section for additional comments and feedback, should that not be covered in a specific question. This information can then be used to improve the course and monitor instructor performance and progress.

Table 22.5 **Course Evaluation**

Course:					
Instructor(s):					
Date:					
Evaluation Questions	**Strongly Disagree**	**Disagree**	**Agree**	**Strongly Agree**	**Not Applicable**	**Total**
The course content and format:						
Focused on information that will be useful in my job.						
Included the appropriate distribution of lecture and in-class exercises.						
Contained the appropriate amount of information and was the right length of time for the information covered.						
Were well organized and easy to follow.						
The instructor that led the course:						
Had sound knowledge of the material presented.						
Was easy to understand.						
Understood the audience and held my attention.						
Encouraged participation throughout the course.						
Stayed focused on the course objectives/goals.						
Encouraged course participants to ask questions.						
Was skilled in listening and questioning.						

Table 22.5 **Course Evaluation** *(Continued)*

Evaluation Questions	Strongly Disagree	Disagree	Agree	Strongly Agree	Not Applicable	Total
Overall, I am satisfied with:						
The course I just completed.						
The instructor of this course.						
The time spent on this course, in terms of the information imparted.						
After this course, I will:						
Apply the information gained/ skills taught in class.						
Use/refer to the course materials on the job.						
Additional Comments:						

Students' feedback after their competency evaluations—especially if a large percentage of the class fails this evaluation—could indicate increasing the amount of practice opportunities (maybe having a "safe" practice environment to help reinforce classroom activities), decreasing course time to spend more time on topics, or increasing student comfort if distractions are a factor. Always look for ways to increase student participation in a class and ways to increase the value of the experience they will have yet keep costs down. Ensure that there is enough time to demonstrate competencies (or a lack thereof) prior to completing an evaluation of the student and determining whether they meet the prescribed requirements.

After you have obtained feedback on the course itself through a course evaluation process and looked at competency assessments, you should not forget to have a mechanism in place to follow up after your implementation and go-live date to see how effective the training really was. Remember to conduct this evaluation a few weeks or maybe even months after you have gone live to give the end users time to adjust to the new system, assess their skills, and get over any go-live issues. An example of such an evaluation can be found in Table 22.6. Notice that this evaluation looks at how prepared the individual was for their new role, how effective the exercises and material were to their job tasks, how much they have used the training material to get their jobs accomplished, and what other mechanisms they used (such as help desk, users guides, templates, job aids, etc.), and also looks for ways to improve the learning experience.

Table 22.6   **Post-Implementation Evaluation**

Role:						
Today's date:						
Length of time (days, weeks, months) on new system:						
Follow-Up Evaluation Questions— Post-Implementation	**Strongly Disagree**	**Disagree**	**Agree**	**Strongly Agree**	**Not Applicable**	**Total**
The course content and format:						
Focused on information that has been useful in my job.						
Included the appropriate distribution of lecture and in-class exercises.						
Contained the appropriate amount of information and was the right length of time for the information covered.						
Have allowed me to perform my new tasks and duties effectively.						

Table 22.6 **Post-Implementation Evaluation** *(Continued)*

Follow-Up Evaluation Questions— Post-Implementation	Strongly Disagree	Disagree	Agree	Strongly Agree	Not Applicable	Total
I've found the following to be useful:						
My designated support staff						
My course materials						
Job aids given to me during class						
Web page tips & techniques						
Newsletters & articles						
Communications packet						
Other: PLEASE LIST						
Additional Comments:						

Training materials should be updated with any system changes, vendor patches, upgrades, fixes, or input from the help desk or in response to user questions. A plan for how often these updates should occur and who will be responsible for making them should be established prior to project completion and shutdown.

Future Training Needs

You may want to consider outsourcing the maintenance and delivery of training in the future after the project is over. Whatever your decision, ensure that there is a detailed plan for how to transition the material and support of the material to the "new group" or owners of the training material before your existing staff rolls off the project. Communicate closely with this group, documenting all delivery policies, procedures, and leading practices for the new group as well as lessons learned during the initial training process and all required infrastructure needs to deliver future training.

Also ensure that communications to end users about how training will be supported in the future is accomplished. Everyone should understand what training will be offered and when after the initial training has been completed, and whom to go to with any future training needs. Ideally, through use of an intranet site or newsletter, you can provide additional information or learning opportunities after going live via tips or techniques and helpful hints from the field. This proves very valuable for specific issues or problems that arise during a certain special process. Remember, keeping the flow of information open always benefits your end users.

Up Next

Finally, as always, any activities or interactions you have with your end users should be positive and an informed process. Success of your project depends on that. Training is much more than putting together a few examples and having an individual stand up in front of your end users and preach to them about the new process or system. It involves a well-thought-out strategy, an action plan, and a series of never-ending activities to monitor and reinforce the learning. You should never underestimate or skimp in this area. You want highly productive and enthusiastic users.

In our final chapters of this book, we will discuss what the future might hold for you and your new system, including what areas you might want to focus on in supporting your organization in the future and the changes and trends that are under way. Chapter 23 will look at the next steps you might need to consider in further integrating your new system and its processes both internally and externally to your organization. Chapter 24 will look at other opportunities that are on the horizon that you might want to consider, if you haven't already done so, to help keep your organization competitive and ahead of the game.

Part VI

Looking to the Future

Now that you've completed your PeopleSoft implementation or upgrade project, how should you support your new application in the future, and where is the ERP marketplace going? We hope that our final two chapters will answer those key questions for you. First, we'll look at how your organization can properly integrate your new solutions into an everyday operational model that's prepared to support changes within your business, changes within your industry, and changes in the vendor product that you've implemented (through upgrades and service-pack enhancements). Next, we'll also try to look into the future—the crystal ball—for ERP solutions and others to see what trends are emerging in this ever-changing environment. Where is the next generation of the ERP (ERP II) market taking us?

CHAPTER 23

Next Steps with Integration

FEATURING:

▶ A look at various governance models and how to choose the right one for the long run

▶ How to cover your long-term support costs and what your options are

▶ The change control process—what it should be and how to maintain, manage, and track these changes

▶ What you should do to ensure continuous learning within your team

▶ How to ensure that you're evolving your ERP system to keep up with your competition

▶ The impacts of functional enhancements, new modules, or even a new organization

▶ How often you should make upgrades and what you should expect

N ow that this new system of yours is in place and operational, what should you be doing in order to maintain it and integrate it with new initiatives and activities that are happening throughout your organization? This chapter looks at the various issues or problems you might face after your PeopleSoft ERP system is in place and what you might consider doing about each of them. Having a proper plan to support these changes is crucial to the continued success and effectiveness of your new system and processes. Nothing ever stands still; things are always changing, and you need to be prepared to handle the changes as you move forward.

Governance

You have gone live and have a support organization in place (as discussed in Chapter 16, "Post-Production Support"). What's next? You need to have a process for managing any changes that are requested by your end users and vendors while balancing the concerns of the many stakeholders you have to support. Generally with an ERP system such as PeopleSoft, many different groups are involved in the decision-making process. During your project, you most likely had a steering committee in place to resolve any issues and to make final decisions on what to do and when. Now that your project is finished, you need to ensure that there is a defined process, or *governance*, in place to support any decisions that must be made, especially those that are not covered by your day-to-day operational budget.

 Note A governance should establish an operable framework to align your resources (money, people, and technology), balance the business initiatives (maximize return), and facilitate execution.

There are various types of governance models that you might consider putting in place for the long term, ranging from the strict hands-on models to the "call us only when you have a major problem" variety.

In general, there are three sets of processes that a governance body or board should enforce:

Legislative   These are the processes that set out "rules" that your team must follow. They create the parameters for your support team to operate in and provide the procedure for you to follow when changes are considered.

Executive   These processes monitor and enforce the rules. Your governance body should be able to determine if your support team is following the correct procedure, and any complaints by end users would be addressed through these executive processes.

Judicial   Finally, you have judicial processes, which deal with challenges to the board's decisions and look at any exceptions to the rules established.

A sound, supportive governance board should follow and enforce all these processes; however, the board should not be overbearing, nor the processes too burdensome.

TIP   Thomas Jefferson said it best: "He who governs least governs best."

When determining what your governance process should look like, consider that governance is needed in proportion to the potential conflict. Therefore, if you're going to support many different business areas with varying views of what is important to the organization and your new system and processes, you might need a rather formal governance process. However, if you have a key set of stakeholders and a central business function to support, you might not need such a formal process.

A few examples of some unsuccessful governance board models are depicted below:

Seagull board   These board members fly in, make a lot of noise, dump on management (or the support organization), and fly out, failing to resolve any problems or reach any decisions.

Gaggle of geese   They stick together, have shared leadership, are looking for the golden egg, and cheer each other on, but do they accomplish anything? All they do is honk, honk, honk!

Martin Luther King   "I have a dream." This board has a vision or dream but no backing or understanding of what needs to be done to get there.

Keys to a successful governance structure include:

► Stating a clear *mission*, which includes answers to the following questions:

  ▸ Who are we?

  ▸ Who are our customers?

> ▸ Who is our constituency?

> ▸ What is our role in the new process/system environment?

▸ Establishing a set of *core values,* to include outlines of the following:

> ▸ What the board or organization stands for

> ▸ How the organization will ensure that the core values expressed are deeply imbedded throughout the organization

▸ Articulating a *vision* that is not just a bunch of ideas, a task force, or a feasibility study

Governance boards should have *kaleidoscope thinking* (adopted from *Rosabeth Moss Kanter on the Frontiers of Management,* Harvard Business School Press, 1997): "It's not *reality* that's fixed, it's our *perception.*" Kaleidoscope thinking involves a process that:

▸ Fosters change

▸ Tunes into the environment and what is happening (e.g., with the competition and the market)

▸ Has a clear vision and a compelling business case

▸ Includes stakeholders and coalitions that will support the governance board

▸ Fosters collaboration

By adapting these principles to our model, we would have a fully supportive organization that's in touch with our constituents and ready to make a decision, with clear reasons why the decision should be made. You should have these same goals for your PeopleSoft governance process.

Some possible governance structures include (but are not limited to) these examples:

▸ A central governance committee made up of key executives and sponsors of the various business groups that the new system and processes support. This structure is very similar to the project steering committee and may be made up of managers rather than executives from the groups. This type of committee meets on a regular basis and makes decisions on the priorities of any changes; it also helps to create business cases or resolves conflicts for proposed changes.

▶ A "shadow" committee that "votes" on the changes proposed and is not a physical body of individuals.

▶ A process that is used to make decisions. However, the IT leadership enforces that process and does not have a committee of customers supporting these decisions.

▶ An organization-wide board that determines what changes the organization will make (linked to the budget process) and is not the sole support organization for the new process or system.

As mentioned before, you should consider the types of conflict that might arise and establish the model that would best help you and the support team resolve these problems and help make the appropriate decisions for your organization in the fastest, most expedient, and most cost-conscious way possible. You do not want an overburdening process for changes; yet you want to make sure that the changes are justified and worth the time and effort to make. You also want to ensure that there are processes in place to help prioritize the many change requests you will undoubtedly receive and resolve any conflicts between different customers.

If you do create a formal governance board, you should evaluate its effectiveness continuously and ensure that you are providing the kind of support that your customers need. Cap Gemini Ernst & Young has created a model that can assess any board, including a governance body to support your ERP system, called the *governance spider*. This evaluation process looks at key attributes that your board should have to be effective and rates each of them on a scale of one to five. Ideally, you want the process to be evenly distributed across all measures. Although you can determine the key attributes, or metrics, used, we offer some suggestions:

Board structure   Evaluate the governance roles, responsibilities, and processes to ensure that they are flexible enough to take advantage of strategic opportunities.

Communication and information   Look at the materials presented and ensure that your information contains more than one view or option (when a change is considered), identifies the stakeholders' concerns, forecasts results, and is clearly articulated.

Measurement and evaluation   Do you have specific measurements or guidelines for evaluating your proposed solutions or options for the change requested?

Membership and selection Does your governance body have diverse membership with a wide range of perspectives, and do the members represent your customers adequately?

Leadership effectiveness Does your governance body work collaboratively with your management team and IT organization?

Staff alignment Is there involvement and communication with your end users through the governance process?

Education and development To stay current with new offerings and what other organizations or your competitors are doing in this area, what type of training or educational development do you have in place for your board members to help them understand the issues and trends within this market?

Figure 23.1 shows an example of this governance spider evaluation model and how an organization might be evaluated against it.

Figure 23.1 **Example of a governance spider model**

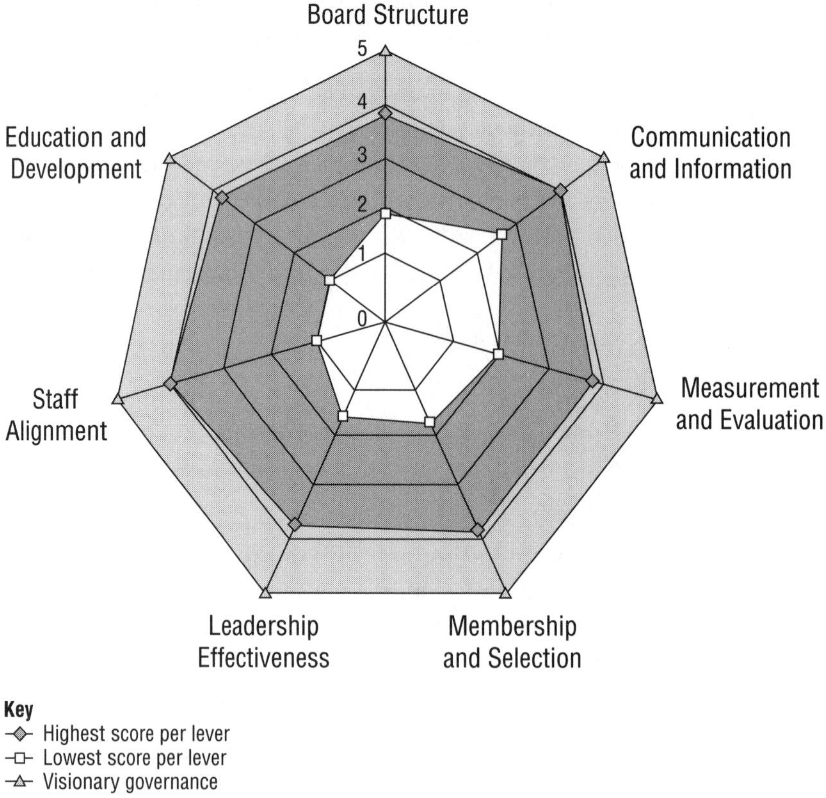

Key
- ◆ Highest score per lever
- ☐ Lowest score per lever
- △ Visionary governance

Source: AHA/EY 1997 Governance Survey; System Board Chari Responses

Remember, your governance process should follow these basic guidelines for you to be successful:

▶ Govern by exception.

▶ Manage critical risks, such as financial, legal, and ethical concerns, with appropriate due diligence.

▶ Have simple, clear checks and balances.

▶ Ensure that a governance review and improvement process (like the spider model) is in place.

▶ Adopt best governance practices, which help provide speed and flexibility to your model.

▶ Focus on long-term growth (don't be shortsighted).

▶ Understand your organization and the environment in which it operates.

▶ Be willing to speak out and take action in a crisis, but refrain from managing the business (on a day-to-day basis).

▶ Maintain strong, two-way communication between your board and management.

▶ Have a responsive, effective, engaging governance board.

Change Control

Once you have a governance model selected and in place, you'll need a change-control process to determine which changes you will support and when. You'll also need to establish the key metrics you'll use in making a decision on each proposed change. With respect to a PeopleSoft system, you can generally break down changes into the following categories:

Minor system changes   These are package-delivered fixes or minor programming changes to support everyday use of the current processes and system.

Major system enhancement   This type of change may be the result of a new regulatory requirement or business need that must be met, but the package does not yet support this change.

Major upgrades   These are major system changes driven by a new vendor release that impacts the existing processes and system. The organization is not requesting this change; rather, the vendor is requesting that you make it.

New module implementation   A new set of functionality has been requested and can be supported through implementation of existing modules supported by the vendor; or the vendor has introduced a new module that your customer is interested in implementing (for a business reason).

When dealing with system changes, your team should attempt to preserve the integrity of your new system and processes, yet be able to support future business needs. You should provide a process for tracking, prioritizing, and monitoring these changes. That process is often referred to as a *change request process*. There should be adequate investigation into the proposed change, along with documentation on the potential impact of that change (both making the change and not making it) as well as alternative solutions. A formal review and approval process should be used (no matter what your governance structure is), and a standard reporting process on the status of the change should also be followed.

A change request should provide complete information about a proposed change and the impact it will have on the current system and processes. That information should include the following:

▶ Description of the proposed change

▶ Reason for the change (including a business case and costs)

▶ Implication of not making the change (as well as alternative solutions)

▶ Areas or businesses that will be affected

▶ Priorities, such as high (1), medium (2), or low (3)

▶ Any related change requests that might be in the system already

▶ Responsibilities or assignments

▶ Tracking number and status (approve, reject, defer/on hold, or investigate)

▶ Any additional attachments, related information, or supplemental documentation

▶ Dates, including date submitted and dates of any status changes or any required completion dates

An example of a change request form is shown in Figure 23.2.

Figure 23.2 **A change request form**

CHANGE REQUEST		
Client/project name:		**Change request ID:**
Change request name:	**Priority:** (circle one)	
	High Medium Low	
Identified by:	**Assigned to:**	**Date submitted:**
Teams affected:		
Description of proposed change: (attach documentation as necessary)		
Reason for change (benefits):		
Implications of not making this change:		
Related change requests:	**Attachments/references:**	
Approved for investigation: (Y/N) _____		
Approved by: _____ **Date approved:** _____		
Investigation budget: _____ hours	**Investigation start date:** _____	
	Investigation due date: _____	
Comments:		
Approval signature:		

Status: (circle)	Investigation				Change		
	Identified	Approved	Rejected	Deferred	Approved	Rejected	Deferred

Anyone should be able to request a change, although it is typically the support team or end users who make change requests. However, other groups might also request changes, such as interface or informational changes.

You should have a process in place to track, categorize, and approve or disapprove these changes. You may need to assign someone to further investigate a change request before you can make your decision, or you may decide to put the change on hold (that is, deferring the change to a later time). The investigation process should determine three things:

▶ Work effort

▶ Schedule

▶ Costs and benefits

Generally, the manager of your support group or the leader of your governance board would determine whether an investigation is necessary in order to determine the priority or the acceptance of the change.

Figure 23.3 shows an example of a typical change request process and how a change might be tracked within the organization.

Figure 23.3 **A change request process**

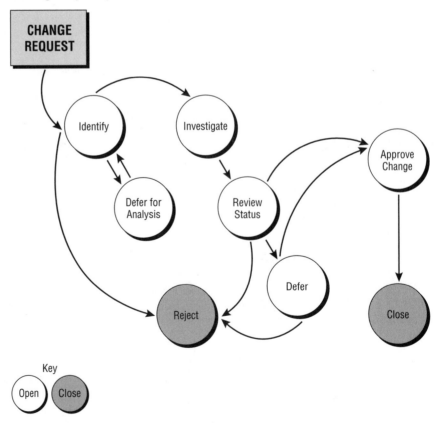

You should always provide a mechanism or log to track your change requests and provide the status of them to your end users or customers and to the originators of the requests. Historical information on change requests might provide valuable insight into future requests. You can also summarize the number of changes that have been requested per period along with documentation on what changes have been made or supported.

Costs

To support your changes, there should be a budget and costs associated with the proposed changes to your organization. Generally these costs can be broken down into two categories:

Operational costs   Costs that fall within the normal budget and constraints of the existing support organization

New project/funding   A new project or new funding that's required to support a major change

Costs should include not only out-of-pocket expenses but internal resources, any required schedule commitments, facilities, hardware, software, and loss of business.

The following sections will look at each of these cost types in more detail and help you determine your support needs.

Operations

Everyday support for your new system, including "fixes" and minor system changes to support current processes and system requirements, should be considered within the normal operating budget of your organization.

A baseline service agreement must be created prior to going live with your user community in order to outline what support staff you need to support your overall implementation (as was discussed in Chapter 15, "Go Live—Keys to a Successful Rollout"). How quickly you respond to help-desk calls and resolve problems, and how stable the system is, help determine what your operational support costs might be.

In your overall operational budget, you should plan for support of PeopleSoft patches, quarterly updates, and upgrades. Operational costs should also include any phone support, query support, training support, issue resolution and research time, help-desk support, batch-process support, and any other basic system support you'll need to keep up with your service-level agreements and keep the application current (and thus supported by the vendor).

In addition to these normal operational costs, if you have too many requests for minor changes, you may still need to categorize the changes and prioritize them based on your existing budget and resource constraints. Examples of such changes might be additional reports to support your end-user community, small panel/page changes that will make the users' jobs easier but are not based on any major process changes, changes to existing interfaces to support current business requirements, and implementations of PeopleSoft-delivered patches to keep your system current and up-to-date (including the latest tax information). All these changes are considered a part of normal operations and support of your ERP system. For these changes, you still need a process in place to prioritize them using a governance model and to determine whether a new budget is needed.

New Funding

Changes that are not covered by the normal operating and support agreement would need funding in order to be supported. These changes might be turned over to the governance committee or board for a decision on whether the item is a legitimate business requirement. Based on that need, the board would assign a priority to the request, which would dictate whether the change would be approved and when. In some cases—including requests for major changes such as new module implementations, major system enhancements, major upgrades, and creation of new organizations—a "project" or change budget would be developed and approved to support the initiative. Based on the availability of resources and the number of these initiatives to support, the board would determine how many of these major changes should be supported each period (which is usually one year). Figure 23.4 shows an example of how this process might work and what might be included in an existing operational budget (and then prioritized within that budget) or require creation of an entirely new project and budget.

Figure 23.4 **Analysis process[**

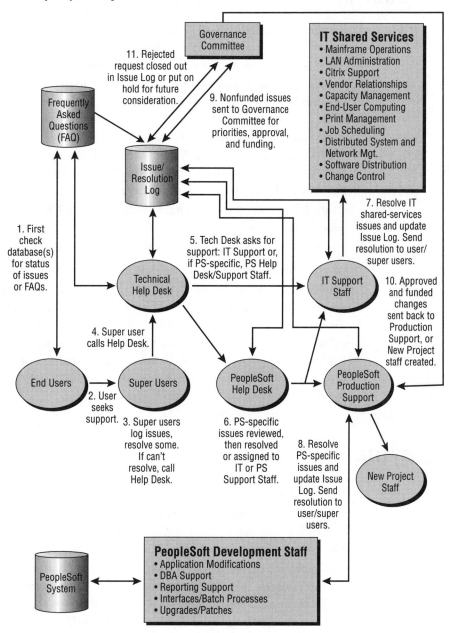

Continuous Learning

Another key operating cost is the cost of continuous learning. You should ensure that your support organization and end users are aware of what People-Soft is doing in the market and what changes they are making to their software. You should also be aware of your competitive situation—what your competitors are doing and what new technology is on the horizon—so that you're prepared for the future. In general, it's a good idea for your organization to be involved in both special interest groups (SIGs) and regional user groups (RUGs) for PeopleSoft. You should also stay in close contact with what People-Soft is doing, through your customer support services (the help desk as well as PeopleSoft's Customer Connection Web page) and the annual user conferences. It's important that you are aware of any changes to your support, any major upgrade releases, and the trends in the market so that you can be better prepared to support your organization now and in the future.

Besides PeopleSoft, it is important to stay current through articles, analyst reports (such as those from DataPro and Gartner Group), and industry publications. You should put in place a continuous learning plan for your organization and its staff so that all of you will stay current with your vendor, its software, and the market. This not only helps you better support your stakeholders but also provides insight into future budget requirements and planning. Your governance model should also include a tie to the latest information about the vendor and the market.

Staying Current

Besides fostering a continuous learning environment, how do you ensure that your new ERP system stays current with your competition? You should understand what your competition is doing and consider creating a process to benchmark or analyze your results against your competition. By monitoring your progress, customer satisfaction, and market trends, you are better positioning yourself and your organization for the future. Chapter 24, "What's Next on the Horizon," helps outline some of the current trends in the ERP market that you should be considering. (It also looks at the question of when is the right time for your organization to handle these issues.) You should continuously stay up-to-date on the changes in this market, which is changing very rapidly. By doing so, you won't be surprised when your CFO comes to you and suggests that performance in support of operational reporting is out of line with your competition and causing your company to fall behind competitively. You should consider establishing an operational scorecard, which can help you track performance against a set of measures and thus guide you toward the appropriate decisions.

Using an operational scorecard, which targets key metrics of customer satisfaction, response time, and any other attributes you believe will help you assess how well your system is supporting your customers (the end users), is a key characteristic of a first-rate organization that is concerned and listening to its customers as well as measuring results. This automated means of tracking key metrics can help you keep in touch with system performance and be prepared should issues arise. Always be sure you are monitoring key performance metrics for your system well after you go live. Buildup of data in your database tables, for instance, can drastically change response time. It may be a gradual trend that, if not monitored, will surprise you in a not-so-nice way.

Organizational Changes

In addition to staying current and monitoring your environment and competition, there are many organizational stimuli that will force you to change or integrate your application differently, such as the creation of new entities or a pending merger or acquisition. These organizational changes may force you to make system or process changes to your existing application. You should be prepared for these changes and have a plan in place to support them, especially if the climate of your organization or industry is to acquire or divest businesses. It's very useful to create a detailed plan or strategy regarding how new organizations will be supported using your new set of applications or processes.

When setting up a new organization or entity, it might be important to outline the key steps you need to go through in order to support it, such as (but not limited to):

▶ Setting up new control tables and updating your organizational structure within the system (including trees and reporting relationships). Consider creating a list of key tables and objects affected by adding a new department, new business unit, etc.

- ▶ Updating security appropriately, adding new organizational entities, reporting requirements, and query or individual user profiles.

- ▶ Considering any additional learning or training needs for new users.

- ▶ Making available new reports or changes to existing reports or queries, based on changes to the organization.

- ▶ Looking at the impact on support and the budget, including your licensing agreements with your vendors.

All these changes should be looked at carefully, and any impacts to the organization assessed. Having an up-front plan in place to support potential changes will most certainly ensure a much smoother transition.

Upgrades

One major change that will occur, even if your organization stays stagnant for years, is that of upgrades. On average, PeopleSoft applications have a major upgrade about once every 18 months. It's wise to plan within your budget on needing to support a major upgrade at least once every two years. To continue support for the application, most PeopleSoft contracts require that the organization be no more than one release behind the current major release. Therefore, since PeopleSoft 8 is now available, you must be using version 7 or higher in order to continue getting package support from the vendor. If you are not on a supported release (that is, you're using a "retired release"), you run the risk of either not getting product support should you have system problems or having to pay extra money for that support. If you are unsure whether or not you are on a supported release, you can find out easily by looking at the PeopleSoft Web site, which contains an up-to-date list of the releases that are currently supported, or by contacting the company's Global Support Center.

When PeopleSoft retires a release, it withdraws several key services, including:

- ▶ Tax updates and regulatory changes

- ▶ Updates and bug fixes

- ▶ Support for bundled third-party products (such as Cognos and SQR)

- ▶ Global Support Center management of cases (i.e., your help-desk support)

- ▶ Training availability from PeopleSoft Educational Services

However, customers using retired releases *and still paying for their annual support services (software maintenance)* still have access to the following services:

- ▶ Customer Care Business Center
- ▶ PeopleSoft Advisor (in North America) and Account Management (in international areas)
- ▶ PeopleSoft Consulting Services (for a fee)
- ▶ PeopleSoft Customer Connection (the Web-based support center)
- ▶ PeopleSoft Ask Professional Services and Technology Lab programs (for a fee)

PeopleSoft also has a group, the Release Retirement Team, that works with customers that (according to PeopleSoft's data) don't plan to upgrade to a currently supported release. This group is designed to help you, the customer, get back into support or establish an alternative means of support (although most likely this will be for a monetary fee). Therefore, staying current on releases is very important indeed.

Another reason to stay current, and probably one of the reasons you chose a package to begin with, is to ensure compliance with and support for the latest leading business processes and technology. By staying on an older version of the application, you run the risk of failing to support new legal or regulatory requirements as well as not getting the latest and greatest technology tools and functionality to support your requirements. All of this has already been paid for with your contract fees and maintenance agreement. These costs are wasted if you don't stay on the proper release schedule.

Of course, it's much easier to upgrade with a "vanilla" implementation. Keep that in mind as well, since you'll be upgrading constantly, and any customizations will have to be incorporated each time (not just the first time), should the customizations not be integrated into the application. It's better to get the vendor to make the changes and wait till they are released (if possible) than to make the changes yourself.

Many organizations fail to fully appreciate the costs and implications of upgrading on such a continuous basis, since they haven't had to deal with these issues in the past or don't understand how fast technology can change. It's best to be prepared and to understand these costs up front rather than be surprised after you have gone live.

Up Next

As you can see, there are many reasons why you might have to make changes to your processes or application once you've gone live, and you can also see the importance of understanding these changes and the effects they will have on your budget. You need to have a process in place to support these changes and spend your money wisely. A sound governance and change-request process is paramount to your success.

Conflicting priorities and business drivers make this a challenging task. Since most organizations don't stand still, you have to ensure that you have a flexible process and system to support future changes. The better prepared you are for these changes, the better off you'll be. And you'll be less surprised by the costs and the continuous changes that will still need to occur after you go live.

The next and final chapter will look into the future and help you see some of the challenges ERP systems (and thus you) will be facing. How will your system need to evolve to support these changes, and what will you need to know? We hope that chapter will provide you with additional insight to better prepare for the future. However, remember that this is a never-ending cycle of change and that in order to be successful, you'll have to adapt. Good luck!

CHAPTER 24

What's Next on the Horizon

FEATURING:

▶ How to get the most "E" out of your ERP

▶ Trends in the convergence of front-office and back-office systems

▶ Verticalization—what it is and how it's affecting your ERP

▶ E-commerce and the Internet

▶ Data warehousing and trends in executive reporting

▶ The move from national to multinational to global

▶ Mega-modules—where they are going

▶ Procure-to-pay and eProcurement

▶ The order-to-cash cycle

▶ Predictions for the 21st century

Technology is constantly changing, faster and faster than ever before. These changes directly affect your PeopleSoft application, so the more you know about these changes and the impact they can have on your system, the better prepared you'll be. Your decision to purchase an Enterprise Resource Planning system has guaranteed that these changes will be available to you should you choose to implement them. It also guarantees that your existing processes and organization will have to change to adapt to these new paradigms. This chapter will take a look at the major trends we currently find ourselves in and how they impact the ERP offerings, specifically the PeopleSoft application that you currently have. We'll also dare to look into our crystal ball and take a journey into the unknown future to see what our new century might have in store for us.

Getting the "E" from Your ERP

To get the most from your existing ERP system, you should ensure that you've looked at all the ways to integrate your back-office systems and are leveraging your existing application for all these business needs. For various reasons, you may have decided not to implement your system in one particular area. You should always be looking back and re-evaluating that decision based on changes to the application or changes to your business. There might have been good reasons why you chose to keep an existing asset-tracking system, for example, but you might want to create an evolution plan that outlines if and when you plan to "retire" existing systems that are supported by your new ERP system. This plan should be reviewed annually and updated based on changes to the software and to your business. You might also look again at key functionality that you decided not to implement based on certain business drivers and re-evaluate on an annual basis whether now is the time to implement. Again, drivers behind a single, integrated, and supported back-office system are generally reasons why this is practical.

As with any application, after going live, you should never view your ERP evolution as being finished. Systems, functionality, business, and people all change, and you need to adapt your system to these changes. Some new trends in the market might force you to make these changes, but generally the competition or your existing environment, which may stifle your ability to grow in the market, will be key drivers.

Always challenge yourself and your organization to assess whether you're getting the most value out of your ERP system. Remember why you implemented the system in the first place, and ensure that you're measuring your results. It's always a good idea to do a post-implementation assessment and evaluate where you are against your vision—and where you need to be in the future to continue supporting this vision. Don't pack your bags and leave once your system is operational. Doing that is the kiss of death in this market and in the e-speed environment that we find ourselves in today.

To support your e-business needs for the future, you need to ensure that you have a stable back-office system to support and integrate with your e-business solution. If you don't have a solid foundation, you may never have a house that's stable and in order.

Convergence of Back-Office and Front-Office Systems

Clearly in today's ever-changing and flexible environment, there is a convergence of what was typically known as ERP functions—the back-office support functions—and the front-office functions that other systems supported—that is, the customer-facing functions such as customer relationship management (CRM), sales, and order entry. The major ERP vendors today are integrating more with these front-office systems to provide a seamless process for the business, either through alliances and partnerships or through new development or acquisitions. These single, integrated processes from customer to supplier are driving changes in the ERP market today, and the vendors are taking notice.

PeopleSoft has responded to this trend, and in December 1999, it completed a major merger with Vantive Corporation, developer of a leading CRM system. With this merger, PeopleSoft became the only business software company that offers a completely integrated front- and back-office enterprise-wide solution. With this solution, since customer information is now linked through the entire process, from front office to back, organizations are better able to respond to customer inquiries and needs, which can lead to profitability and increased sales. Oracle is also rolling out its own CRM offering, and currently SAP has a tight alliance with Siebel to deliver this solution. PeopleSoft is continuing to integrate its Vantive product more tightly with its core ERP system beyond PeopleSoft 8 and is planning service-pack and release updates for the coming year.

In addition, PeopleSoft has extended its procurement functionality and partnered with the market sites of CommerceOne, a leader in the electronic-procurement arena, to provide the integrated eProcurement marketplace solution that connects businesses with their suppliers throughout the order-to-pay process cycle. Linking the business to its suppliers can help to drastically reduce internal buying and selling costs as well as improve customer service and streamline the overall buying process. Seamless integration is the key to customer satisfaction, and it helps in monitoring buying trends, compliance, and control. With eProcurement, purchasing departments no longer need to ensure that buying guidelines are followed and to track the progress of goods. Customers can do this themselves.

PeopleSoft also is offering an end-to-end e-commerce selling solution with its recent rollout of PeopleSoft eStore. This solution links customers to inventory, billing, and order fulfillment, creating another front- to back-office integration point. All these factors point to a clear blending or convergence of back-office and front-office solutions into a single, integrated process. Not only does this save you the cost of ownership, but it also can improve customer service, affect speed to market, and ultimately increase your profitability. This convergence makes your ERP solution even more important to your overall business, and your solution becomes the foundation that supports your e-commerce strategy.

If you fail in delivering what your customer is requesting, you lose. In this competitive market, speed and dependability are key. With a tightly integrated, stable solution from front to back, you can improve your chances of being successful in satisfying your customer.

You should evaluate these new offerings as well as how your e-commerce strategy fits with your ERP offerings, and should understand your integration costs and impacts. By clearly outlining the impacts and any trouble points, you can determine when and what to implement as a part of your ERP system and what to continue supporting outside this application. However, the choices are only going to increase, and the line between front-office and back-office systems is surely blurring.

As we noted in Chapter 1, "Enterprise Resource Planning with PeopleSoft," ERP applications have evolved over the years. Recently, the Gartner Group (Research Note SPA 12-0420, Oct. 4, 2000) named the newest ERP phenomenon *ERP II*. Gartner defines ERP II as "a business strategy and a set of industry-domain-specific applications that build customer and shareholder value by enabling and optimizing enterprise and interenterprise, collaborative operational and financial processes." (Note that "financial processes" as defined by Gartner are accounting, purchasing, order entry, and costing.) Table 24.1 shows this shift from ERP to ERP II, as described by Gartner. We'll have to see how this ERP II market evolves and to what extent the extended enterprise reaches.

Table 24.1 **Gartner Group's ERP II Definition Framework**

	ERP		ERP II
Role	Enterprise optimization	➤	Value-chain participation and collaborative-commerce enablement
Domain	Manufacturing and distribution	➤	All sectors/segments
Process	Internal, hidden	➤	Externally connected
Function	Manufacturing, sales and distribution, and financial processes	➤	Cross-industry, industry-sector, and specific industry processes
Architecture	Web-aware, closed, monolithic	➤	Web-based, open, componentized
Data	Internally generated and consumed	➤	Internally and externally published and subscribed

Verticalization

Another area that the ERP vendors are really taking hold of and supporting is the *verticalization* of their products. Industry solutions that go deep within a particular market or market segment (e.g., retail, utilities, and telecommunications) are considered *vertical solutions*. The ERP vendors, especially SAP, have begun to offer their solutions not as general solutions that should fit all markets but as specific industry solutions that are rich in content and support the needs of a particular market. These vertical solutions have become prevalent based on market needs and the convergence of back- and front-office systems, as we discussed in the preceding section. While core back-office systems may have similar requirements across industries, manufacturing and front-office applications are very different by industry and thus drive the ERP vendors to a more industry-specific solution. To gain new clients and market share, the ERP vendors are branching out their solutions to these vertical offerings.

SAP was really the first vendor to go down the verticalization path. PeopleSoft is trailing its competitors in delivering true vertical solutions. One of People-Soft's first vertical solutions was in the student administration and government areas with its public sector and student administration offerings back in the mid-1990s. Now the company is rolling the public sector functionality into its core package and offering various combinations of modules to a market. Figure 24.1 illustrates PeopleSoft's vertical market strategy. Notice that the company is "componentizing" its solutions; and by combining them, it is creating specific offerings, whether by major process such as procure-to-pay or by industry such as education or retail.

Figure 24.1 **PeopleSoft's modular approach**

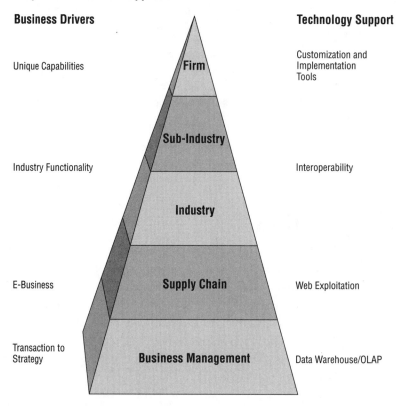

Business Drivers

Unique Capabilities

Industry Functionality

E-Business

Transaction to Strategy

Technology Support

Customization and Implementation Tools

Interoperability

Web Exploitation

Data Warehouse/OLAP

Firm

Sub-Industry

Industry

Supply Chain

Business Management

PeopleSoft has also developed additional industry solutions for the financial services and telecommunications sectors and other service-focused organizations. With its acquisition of TriMark (a provider of policy administration software for the insurance sector) along with Intrepid (a retail/merchandise management solution), PeopleSoft has been looking to expand its offerings to more traditional industries and other vertical markets through partnerships, acquisitions, and alliances. It has also partnered with several vendors, such as SPL WorldGroup and Indus in the utilities sector, to offer industry solutions. Recently with PeopleSoft 8, PeopleSoft announced its new suite of products aimed at the professional services market. This suite is called the PSA, or Professional Services Automation, solution.

Will vendors of ERP systems succeed in delivering true end-to-end solutions by industry, and will customers buy those solutions instead of others? According to a study by Forrester Research, Inc. ("Industry Apps Aren't Read" by Bobby Cameron, February 1998), keys to success in this area include:

- ▶ Being able to target an industry to serve, based on the level of spending and commitment the industry might have to the vendor's package.

- ▶ Identifying the right mix of solutions or products to sell to that industry in order to be successful. To do this, the vendor needs industry expertise to understand the industry's requirements and demands so that it can concentrate on the areas that will bring the most value to that industry.

PeopleSoft will have to commit to hiring industry expertise, continue acquiring or partnering with vendors on industry-specific solutions, and creating a compelling business case to their customers to support these solutions. PeopleSoft is well positioned to do this in the services market but has been behind the curve in the manufacturing and product-based industries. Their strong client base within the services market suggests that they should continue investing in these vertical solutions as well as continue supporting the government and education markets, which they dominate.

One key question you have to answer is how integrated and dependent you want to be on your ERP solution. Having a single system to support can be great (as was mentioned before) for skills and training development of your support staff, as well as for speed, integration, and data integrity. However, the other side of the coin suggests more-complex solutions and in some cases a decrease in functionality (based on best-in-breed solutions). As the ERP vendors offer more verticalized solutions, we are seeing these gaps in functionality decrease. It will be up to you to analyze these tradeoffs on a continuous basis and determine whether it's time to get rid of your old industry solution and pick up PeopleSoft's version, or whether you'll continue supporting a mix of products.

Regardless, you need to continuously be aware of what PeopleSoft is doing in your industry. SIGs (special interest groups) by industry are among the customer support groups that PeopleSoft offers. You should be involved with your SIG to help you stay current with what the vendor is doing in your industry. SIGs are a great place to network with others who have similar needs and concerns as well as to understand what PeopleSoft is doing in your market. With things changing so rapidly, this connection can help you stay current.

Exterprise Solutions

The next, and more challenging, step in integration is linking not only internal processes but external ones as well to create a *virtual extended enterprise* (or *exterprise*) solution. This will require the vendors to take another look at their licensing agreements, customer targets, and product offerings/requirements. With a more virtual set of customers or end users, the current cost structures become prohibitive. However, with a focus on this new virtual market, ERP vendors will undoubtedly come up with another opportunity.

PeopleSoft 8 is well positioned to leverage a virtual enterprise with the application's open integration framework using XML (Extensible Markup Language) formatting, Application Messaging, Business Components, and Business Interlinks. Business Components is a new feature within PeopleSoft 8 that allows the application's business rules and data to integrate in real time with external applications. This is the primary tool that PeopleSoft is using to integrate its business logic with Internet-based applications using standard Web-authorization tools. Business Interlinks, on the other hand, provides the capability for PeopleSoft to easily invoke third-party systems using a wide set of technologies including XML, HTTP, Java, COM, and CORBA. PeopleSoft will continue to offer its application engine as a means to do file-based integration.

As you can see by the actions that PeopleSoft is taking, it's even more important now for your ERP vendor and product to have an open architecture that can support these changes and integrate your solutions not only within your organization or enterprise but by linking outside organizations together. Although this area is very new and exciting, failing to seamlessly integrate with your customers, employees, partners, or suppliers can hurt your competitiveness in this new market. Therefore, interaction points should continue to be a big focus, and the realm is growing (to include outside organizations, not just inside systems). You need to be prepared to take your solution to that next level to support your company in the future.

E-Commerce and the Internet

With the advent of the World Wide Web and the creation of the Internet, impacts to ERP applications have been great. All the vendors are now offering Internet solutions that include the creation of communities and portals from which information can be viewed.

PeopleSoft 8 is based on a 100% Internet solution. PeopleSoft's direction is for every enterprise application such as sales, order management, billing, shipping, distribution, customer support, and employee management, to be leveraging Internet technology. The company is creating a three-pronged approach (similar to its competitors), which includes these initiatives:

▶ Development of new e-business applications such as the eStore and eProcurement offerings, which we discussed above.

▶ Creation of communities or marketplaces, which are new applications that support the activities and information needs of a specific group within an organization. They allow you to converge content from a transaction with knowledge, analytics, and collaboration between the parties involved. PeopleSoft's initial offerings in this area include Marketplaces for Benefits as well as Travel and eProcurement—and these are just the beginning.

▶ Use of an enterprise-wide portal that ties all services and employee information together on an individual's desktop, including portals for not only employees but suppliers and customers outside the organization. SAP is making a similar initiative with its "mySAP.com" offering.

These new offerings drastically change the platform, hardware, and support requirements an organization will need to be successful in the future. So you need to look carefully at the impact of moving your organization from where it is today to this new 100% Internet solution of the future. Also, the reporting requirements, via the Web and a portal, change as well. The use of a scorecard and key metrics that are delivered and updated via the portal are key to managing your business successfully in the future. PeopleSoft's solution in that area is its Enterprise Performance Management (EPM) software, which provides a Web-enabled reporting tool that can extract information by role and deliver it to the individual's desktop. EPM can also create a balanced scorecard, which converts an organization's vision and strategy into performance and action measures that provide a basis for a strategic management system. Again, managers can get an at-a-glance view of key indicators, delivered to their desktop, and they can drill down into these indicators for more specifics.

Another important element of an Internet solution is the ability of the application to integrate with other applications seamlessly and easily. PeopleSoft has created its solution using various tools: Application Messaging, Business Components, and Business Interlinks. As explained above, these solutions leverage the latest technology to address these issues.

With the more tactical issues behind them, businesses are focusing now on the more "strategic" issues of today, such as leveraging the World Wide Web, cost control, revenue enhancements, and creating the virtual business models discussed above. The use of communities, portals, and key integration tools supports this direction, as does the incorporation of more growth-oriented applications (or more customer-facing, front-office applications) and the more concentrated vertical offerings. To succeed in the 21st century, your organization must adapt your ERP offerings to these changes, ensuring that you keep up with the latest technology and functionality to support these solutions. To do so, you need to ensure that you have a well-thought-out plan that ties your ERP system with your e-commerce strategy, leveraging all its capability in this connected enterprise model. You should have an evolutionary or migration plan to link you from where you are today and to where you need to be to support these future business needs. To be successful and ensure maximum speed, growth, and flexibility, you must integrate this strategy tightly with your e-commerce strategy from beginning to end—and even extend it outside your organization. Your competitiveness will be greatly impaired if you don't look at these newer business requirements.

Data Warehousing

As mentioned in the preceding section, reporting is a key component in the world of Internet business. Managers must be able to obtain key indicators and performance measures at their desktops in order to monitor and improve their business. A key element in delivering these services is a data warehouse. A *data warehouse* is where information for all types of applications can come together and create these reporting solutions in an efficient, accurate manner. Real-time updates and integration are key in how useful this information will be to your end users (customers).

Note   According to a study by Forrester Research ("The Forrester Report: Data Warehouse Strategies" by Ted Schadler et al., September 1997), the use of data warehousing has exploded. The two benefits cited most often by respondents were better data for guiding decisions (42%) and ability to resolve issues more quickly (42%). See Figure 24.2 for the results. (This study was based on interviews at 50 Fortune 1,000 companies.)

Figure 24.2   **Business benefits from data warehousing**

PeopleSoft provides business-reporting and data-warehousing capabilities through its EPM module. Its Data Warehouse Manager, new in PeopleSoft 8, is a tools-based, Web-enabled reporting capability that, in the form of work-benches, provides the capability to extract data by job role (e.g., financial manager, department manager, or sales representative) from the EPM system and deliver it to an end user's Web browser. The Data Warehouse Manager allows users to build multidimensional star schemas and generate the work-bench and analysis templates used for this reporting. Figure 24.3 outlines the key technical components that make up PeopleSoft's EPM offering. Notice that the data-repository, or data-warehousing, feature is at the core of this diagram. However, key to supporting your end users is the availability of the reporting tools—such as OLAP (online analytical processing), desktop reporting, and ad hoc querying with drill-down features—that they need to be able to analyze the data. All these features are provided through PeopleSoft's new solutions.

Figure 24.3 **Technical components of EPM**

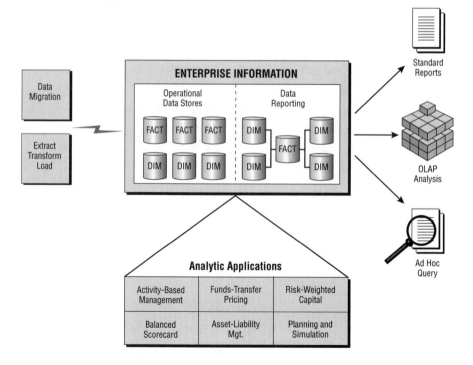

Key markets that PeopleSoft is targeting with its EPM templates include health (patient cost profile), managed care, insurance, services market with banking (profitability management), consumer packaged goods, utilities, transportation, and higher education.

With PeopleSoft 8, EPM includes new products and enhanced integration with its suite and external systems. This solution now includes these products:

PeopleSoft Balanced Scorecard   The Balanced Scorecard delivers an at-a-glance view of the key organizational performance indicators to the manager's desktop and directs discovery of performance improvement opportunities.

Workforce Analytics   This product enables organizations to analyze their current workforce situation and simulate future scenarios in such areas as compensation and employee retention. It also provides a closed-loop capability to send compensation and retention data back to the HR system.

PeopleSoft Workbenches   As mentioned before, this product provides a Web-enabled reporting capability that extracts information from the warehouse (EPM) and delivers it to the desktop.

Figure 24.4 shows a more functional view of the EPM offering that's provided with PeopleSoft 8; it illustrates the key financial reporting features, including profitability analysis, planning and simulation, activity-based management, risk-weighted capital, funds-transfer pricing, and more.

Figure 24.4   **Financial components of EPM**

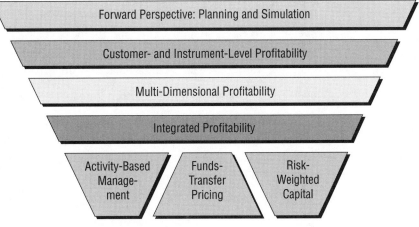

From National to Multinational to Global

With the trends in Internet-supported technology and ability to seamlessly deploy globally from anywhere, the business world is converging from a national or even multinational approach to a truly global one. ERP applications are also supporting this trend by incorporating individual local copies of their software into one global application. As companies are expanding globally and running their business as a single entity rather than a group of multinational organizations, the applications are following this demand. The introduction of the euro to support a single monetary system for Europe highlights the importance of a more global focus on software so that it will support these changing business needs.

Some obstacles in moving from a national or multinational organization to a truly global one include:

▶ Internal obstacles and politics

▶ Balance of global versus local needs

▶ Coordination of regions

▶ Cultural differences

▶ Complicated product to deliver

According to Forrester Research ("The Forrester Report: ERP Portfolios for Europe" by Greco Steenmetz, September 1999), in order to make a global organizational structure pay off over the long term, organizations need to focus on building global customer intimacy. With this comes software that can support the global customer and the need for ERP systems or, for that matter, all customer-facing systems to adapt. If your organization is a global one, integrating globally should be a key concern.

Some of the global capabilities within PeopleSoft 8 are listed below.

Commitment control   This centralized approach addresses budget control and encumbrance accounting in a consistent manner throughout the enterprise. It allows organizations to maintain budgets, track commitments against those budgets, and stop new transactions when the budget is depleted.

Currency (euro) conversion tool   PeopleSoft supported euro mainten-ance and conversion with its version 7.5. In PeopleSoft 8, the vendor delivered a generic conversion tool to enable customers to perform mass conversions of their data to facilitate the move to the euro, as required by 2002.

UniCode support   With version 8, PeopleSoft fully supports UniCode, which allows multilingual options—including Japanese, Greek, and other complex language requirements—in a single database structure.

Global Payroll engine   In the past, there were country-specific payroll applications as well as a global HRMS version of PeopleSoft, which interfaced with local payroll outsourcers or vendors. With version 8, PeopleSoft delivered its first global payroll solution, in which the local business functionality by country is built into the core package in key markets.

Additional features for financial management   These global features include Giro processing, accounting entries by draft type, letters of credit, and bank holiday processing, to name a few.

To support the euro requirements and multi-currency needs of a global organi-zation, PeopleSoft offers the triangulation method to convert from one currency to another, where the euro is the intermediate currency. By 2002, when all countries will be using euro-denominated bills and coins and the use of their current currency will cease, this method of triangulation will no longer be needed; but until then, it will be.

PeopleSoft allows you to use one of three methods to generate exchange rates:

Triangulation   Used for currencies associated with the euro currency.

Cross Rates   Used for currencies not associated with the euro. Uses a "common currency" such as the U.S. dollar (USD) to convert between currencies.

Manual Input   Used when the exchange rates are manually keyed into the application or done so programmatically.

Example of the Cross Rates Method

8.88 Swedish krona (SEK) = 1 U.S. dollar (USD)

122.32 Japanese yen (JPY) = 1 U.S. dollar (USD)

USD is the common currency used to convert from SEK to JPY:
122.32 ÷ 8.88 = 13.7748. So 1 SEK = 13.7748 JPY.

In addition to currency requirements, there are many statutory requirements that must be supported. These include specialized reporting by country such as alternate requirements for the chart of accounts or for document sequencing. In general, one global chart of accounts is created, but there may be additional requirements by country and therefore the need to have alternate charts of accounts. Document sequencing provides a detailed audit trail of business documents such as journal entries, vouchers, and cash receipts, which certain countries may require.

Some countries require you to carry a set of your financials (or books) in their local currency while the reporting books are in the parent company's currency. Within PeopleSoft, this multi-book capability is allowed and captured based on the consolidations process. The multi-ledger feature of PeopleSoft allows you to book your transactions to one ledger, some ledgers, or all ledgers (e.g., corporate and local) based on given business requirements.

In addition to currency and monetary reporting, with a global implementation there is also the desire to view information in the native language (or produce reports in the local language). Multi-language capabilities need to be met in your global solution to support this need. Currently, PeopleSoft provides delivered multi-language capabilities for English, German, Dutch, French, Spanish, Portuguese, Japanese, Canadian French, and International English.

Another key global issue in a multi-country implementation is VAT (value-added tax). VAT is a tax on all final-consumption expenditures for goods and services and is a percentage tax that varies depending on the country that is charging it. It utilizes a system of tax credits to place the ultimate burden on the final consumer, and the European Union has exerted efforts to harmonize the VAT systems of its member countries. The left column of Table 24.2 shows the countries that report VAT. The countries in the GST column have a goods-and-services tax structure but are not covered under VAT rules. For companies based in GST countries, any tax charged in the VAT countries can be reclaimed.

Since VAT deals with the purchase of goods and services, the functionality to support it is found in the Payables module within PeopleSoft.

Table 24.2   **Countries That Report VAT**

VAT Countries	GST Countries
EMEA (Europe, Middle East, and Africa): U.K., France, Germany, Ireland, Italy, Netherlands, Spain, Norway, Denmark, South Africa, etc.	**North America:** Canada
Latin America: Mexico, Venezuela, Chile, etc.	**Asia:** Australia, New Zealand, and Singapore
Asia: Thailand, Taiwan, China, Korea, Indonesia, Philippines, etc.	

On the cash collections side of a global implementation, the tracking of realized or unrealized gains and losses due to cash receipts must be tracked. Realized gains and losses are tracked at the actual time of payment, while unrealized ones are tracked during revaluation of customer accounts. These rate differences are caused by the exchange-rate fluctuations found in the market. You must look at how you will account for these differences.

With the vendors incorporating global capabilities within their applications (and not just offering local solutions) and with the widespread use of the Internet, more organizations will be moving from a single-site installation and focus to a truly global view of their organization. With these new technologies and support, to stay competitive, an organization will need to connect their organization and business partners into a global network, reacting to changes in price, market, and needs in order to stay ahead of the game. An organization's challenge is to be ready both culturally and emotionally to handle this shift, as well as to be able to provide round-the-clock technical support of this environment. You must carefully analyze your strategy in this area to position yourself for success in the future.

A key critical success factor to help you with a global implementation would be to ensure "buy-in" and responsiveness from each country that's required to supply information on the configuration ahead of time. Start your process early; the more countries that are looked at for statutory requirements ahead of time, the better. Consider employing a tool or scorecard to track responses and to assess global configuration requirements for each location that is a part of your implementation.

A critical challenge that ERP vendors, including PeopleSoft, will face in the future is managing consistent execution across the breadth of verticals, functionality, markets, and technological initiatives that are under way today. Right now, the vendors have no intention of slowing down their aggressive expansion into these areas.

Mega-Modules: Where Do You Go from Here?

As mentioned, the capabilities of ERP packages are expanding both horizontally and vertically to support the changing needs of the organization. Looking at a process horizontally requires integrating several functional areas into one solution—for example, merging the procure-to-pay process with Order Management, Purchasing, Inventory, and Payables to create one "mega-process" or module. PeopleSoft's solution, as mentioned above, is to offer products that can be very easily integrated and built upon (like the pyramid in Figure 24.1) and to support these processes as desired by the particular organization. In the next two sections, we'll look at two of these areas and see how they are evolving toward more of a seamless "mega-solution":

▶ Procure to pay

▶ Order to cash

Procure to Pay and E-Procurement

As mentioned before, with the trends in integration of applications and the leverage of Internet technology, the procure-to-pay cycle requires even tighter integration with external and internal features. Figure 24.5 provides a picture of the typical e-procurement (or procure-to-pay) process. As shown, this mega-process includes all the processes from ordering to payment. What this does is extend the enterprise to customers and business partners as well as internal employees. In many cases, implementing this solution reduces operating costs by shortening the cycle time and streamlining operations, and it can also open up new markets and revenue channels for the organization.

Figure 24.5 **The e-procurement process**

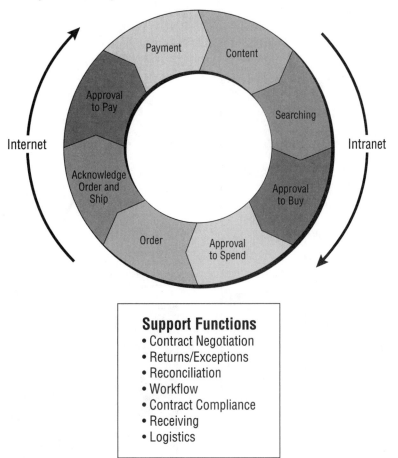

Gartner Group believes that the emergence of virtual organizations and exterprise applications will change the buying choices for end-user organizations. Electronic marketplaces (such as those with CommerceOne) are now becoming available, where suppliers' products and services are displayed for sale and the buying power of a group can be pooled together. These marketplaces allow companies more choice at cheaper rates while giving the supplier access to a larger customer pool. Figure 24.6 shows how, for a typical organization, costs can be drastically decreased with an integrated e-procurement solution.

Figure 24.6   **E-procurement value proposition**

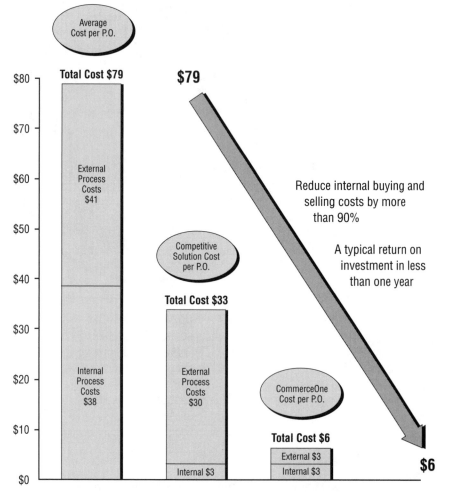

Source: R. B. Webber & Associates. Derived from sources including CAPS, NAPM, and Stanford University.

PeopleSoft's eProcurement solution and the integration of the buying capabilities with the ERP system's tracking and financial requirements allow organizations to increase integration, reduce costs, and support their customers even more effectively. eProcurement is designed for organizations that want a Web-based solution to decentralize, automate, and control the purchase of goods and services for the organization. PeopleSoft allows organizations to control these processes internally as well as externally to the enterprise, streamline vendor relationships (allowing vendors to track and update their own information), dramatically reduce both processing and materials costs, effectively track supplier performance, leverage spending to negotiate better contracts with suppliers, and reduce inventory levels. Figure 24.7 shows how the PeopleSoft eProcurement process and the CommerceOne solution are integrated to achieve an end-to-end solution.

Figure 24.7   **The CommerceOne eProcurement solution**

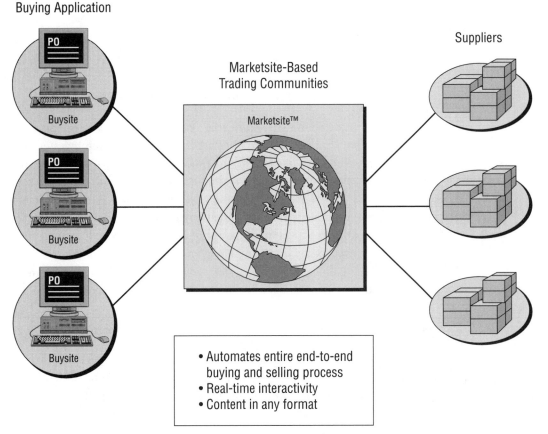

Buying Application

PO

Buysite

PO

Buysite

PO

Buysite

Marketsite-Based
Trading Communities

Marketsite™

Suppliers

- Automates entire end-to-end buying and selling process
- Real-time interactivity
- Content in any format

Some key features that support this solution include:

Integrated supplier access   Customers (or buyers) use self-service and procure items in real time, including viewing an item's availability and pricing from an approved supplier group without having to involve a buying department (or purchasing department).

Catalog content maintenance   Via electronic catalogs that are maintained by the supplier, the buyer can view options online, and the internal purchasing department does not have to maintain a database or catalog internally.

Integrated decision support   Options, both internal and external, will be presented to the customer at one time.

Desktop receiving   Recording receipts of goods can be done by customers from their desktops.

Procurement cards   These cards can be used online to purchase catalog items, thus eliminating the need to create many vendor invoices.

The goals of cutting your costs, improving your customers' choices, and maintaining control of your expenditures are all considered in this integrated solution. From the customers' viewpoint, the process is easy to use and they don't have to understand which parts are maintained internally with the application and which are handled externally by the vendor. The purchasing department can still create business rules and procedures to ensure proper compliance as well as track the total spending power of its organization. Having a seamless process from needing and purchasing an item to paying for and receiving the item is the goal of this solution. It is now well within the reach of an organization.

Order to Cash

On the billing and receivables side, the integration of customers and cash receipts also should be viewed from an integrated and streamlined process. In addition, you should consider how you might improve the management of cash flow across your organization and through your bank accounts.

With the Vantive solution, eStore, and the PeopleSoft Inventory, Billing, and Receivables modules, this process can now be viewed as a single megaprocess. When a customer enters their request, you can immediately tell them whether the requested item is in stock, when it will be available, and where it is at any point between ordering and delivery. You can also determine whether a customer is delinquent with any previous payments and, if so, prevent them from making other orders. You can also understand their buying habits or preferences.

The Twenty-First Century: What's Next?

A key challenge that vendors will need to overcome in this new century is how to price these new Internet-delivered and externally integrated solutions. Since the user base is expanded to include global organizations, outside entities, and businesses from partners to suppliers to customers, the current number-of-users or size-of-company pricing methods cannot be used. Vendors will have to look at this to be competitive in the marketplace. However, we believe they will do just that, and the more flexible a system is, the more in line it will be with these new trends. One key is to make integration seamless and painless. If a vendor can accomplish this, it will most certainly help the vendor to lead during the coming years.

While moving forward, you as a customer and user of an ERP system must be able to integrate your processes with both external and internal systems to succeed, whether you choose the vendor-offered solution or the best-of-breed approach. You'll also need to leverage the strengths of your networks (both internally and externally) as well as to consider sharing knowledge across these networks. Thus, the creation of communities and knowledge-sharing mechanisms that are integrated with your ERP system becomes an even more important component. As you connect all these pieces together—all the way from your customers or employees through your business and to your suppliers—stability and ability to leverage the latest solutions will be important. Therefore, as always, the ability to take the packages as they are and leverage their strengths is a major key to success. Also, adapting your current process or situation to what is delivered rather than changing what is delivered is a big plus (since the delivered product may include many modules, packages, or applications woven together to form a single, seamless solution). You should focus your energy on what you believe are your key differentiators rather than reinvent a common wheel.

Technology also plays an even bigger role in this picture, and if you don't feel your organization can support these changes, you might consider outsourcing your support to an organization that is dedicated to staying current with the latest technologies. This approach lowers your risk, creates a faster implementation (or upgrade), and most likely lowers the cost of ownership. Through a "time-sharing" or ASP (application service provider) offering, you can improve your solution, reduce your costs, and still support your end users effectively. This approach also frees you up to concentrate on developing true market differentiators rather than focusing your time and efforts on common delivered solutions.

A key point of change in this new century is that an ERP system will have to change its focus of integration from an internal view to an external one, and be able to link the system's solutions to external markets, customers, software, and communities. As organizations assess their needs in a vertical market, the need to integrate with multiple applications will be essential, since external integration involves higher degrees of complexity and risk.

The 21st century will bring the world closer together, creating networks and new markets that were never dreamed of in the past. To leverage these changes, you must be flexible, fast, and nimble. Ensure that your ERP system or approach is the same! Best of luck.

Index

Note to Reader: In this index, **boldfaced** page numbers refer to primary discussions of the topic; *italics* page numbers refer to figures.